CW00765821

Slavery, Family, and Gentry
British Atlantic

From the mid-seventeenth century to the 1830s, successful gentry capitalists created an extensive business empire centred on slavery in the West Indies, but interlinked with North America, Africa, and Europe. S. D. Smith examines the formation of this British Atlantic world from the perspective of Yorkshire aristocratic families who invested in the West Indies. At the heart of the book lies a case study of the plantation-owning Lascelles and the commercial and cultural network they created with their associates. The Lascelles exhibited high levels of business innovation and were accomplished risk-takers, overcoming daunting obstacles to make fortunes out of the New World. Dr Smith shows how the family raised themselves first to super-merchant status and then to aristocratic pre-eminence. He also explores the tragic consequences for enslaved Africans with chapters devoted to the slave populations and interracial relations. This widely researched book sheds new light on the networks and the culture of imperialism.

S. D. SMITH is Senior Lecturer in History at the University of York. He has previously edited 'An Exact and Industrious Tradesman': The Letter Book of Joseph Symson of Kendal (2002).

Cambridge Studies in Economic History

Editorial Board

Cambridge Studies in Economic History comprises stimulating and accessible economic history which actively builds bridges to other disciplines. Books in the series will illuminate why the issues they address are important and interesting, place their findings in a comparative context, and relate their research to wider debates and controversies. The series will combine innovative and exciting new research by younger researchers with new approaches to major issues by senior scholars. It will publish distinguished work regardless of chronological period or geographical location.

Titles in the series include:

Slavery, Family, and Gentry Capitalism in the British Atlantic

The World of the Lascelles, 1648–1834

S. D. Smith

CAMBRIDGE
UNIVERSITY PRESS

CAMBRIDGE UNIVERSITY PRESS
Cambridge, New York, Melbourne, Madrid, Cape Town, Singapore,
São Paulo, Delhi, Dubai, Tokyo

Cambridge University Press
The Edinburgh Building, Cambridge CB2 8RU, UK

Published in the United States of America by Cambridge University Press, New York

www.cambridge.org
Information on this title: www.cambridge.org/9780521143004

First published 2006
This digitally printed version 2010

A catalogue record for this publication is available from the British Library

Library of Congress Cataloguing in Publication data
Smith, S. D. (Simon David), 1964–
  Slavery, family, and gentry capitalism in the British Atlantic : the world of the
  Lascelles, 1648–1834 / S. D. Smith.
    p. cm. – (Cambridge studies in economic history. Second Series)
  Includes bibliographical references.
ISBN-13: 978-0-521-86338-4 (hardback)
ISBN-10: 0-521-86338-4 (hardback)
1. West Indies, British – Economic conditions – 17th century. 2. West Indies,
British – Economic conditions – 18th century. 3. West Indies, British –
Economic conditions – 19th century. 4. West Indies, British – Race relations.
5. Slavery – West Indies, British – History. 6. Lascelles family. 7. Lascelles,
E. (Edward), 1740–1820. 8. Lascelles, Edward Lascelles, Viscount, 1764–1814.
9. Lascelles, Henry, 1690–1753. 10. Sugar trade – West Indies, British – History.
I. Title. II. Series.
HC155.5.S64 2006
331.11′7340972909171241–dc22
2005037572

ISBN 978-0-521-86338-4 Hardback
ISBN 978-0-521-14300-4 Paperback

For he that hath, to him shall be given:
and he that hath not, from him shall be taken even
that which he hath.

***

For AS, DS, and AJS

Contents

List of Figures   *viii*
List of Maps   *ix*
List of Tables   *x*
Preface   *xiii*
List of Abbreviations   *xv*

1   Introduction: Remembering and Forgetting   1

2   Halls and Vassalls   11

3   Rise of the Lascelles   43

4   Lascelles and Maxwell   54

5   The Gedney Clarkes   91

6   Merchants and Planters   139

7   A Labyrinth of Debt   177

8   Managing a West India Interest   226

9   The Enslaved Population   260

10   Between Black and White   317

11   Epilogue   351

Archival Sources   *359*
Index   *367*

List of Figures

4.1 Simplified pedigree of the Lascelles family   57
5.1 Simplified pedigree of the Clarke family   92
8.1 Data envelopment analysis: the efficiency frontier   245
8.2 Sugar output on two Jamaican estates, 1775–1838   246
8.3 Sugar output on three Barbadian estates, 1791–1839   247
8.4 Sugar output on two Tobagonian estates, 1794–1820   248
8.5 Monthly allowances of fish and pork on Belle and Mount estates, 1837   257
9.1 Population totals on four Barbadian estates, 1772–1835   264
9.2 Population totals on three Jamaican estates, 1767–1836   265
9.3 Probability of death (q_x) by age group on six estates, 1817–34 and two model life tables   284
9.4 Probability of death (q_x) by age group: males and females on six estates, 1817–34   288
9.5 Kaplan-Meier cumulative survival plot for six estates, 1817–34   290
9.6 Kaplan-Meier cumulative survival curves by age group, 1817–34   292
9.7 Kaplan-Meier cumulative survival plots by origin, 1817–34   294
9.8 Proportion of children on Williamsfield and Nightingale Grove matched with 'mothers', 1817   297
9.9 Cross-plot of 'mother's' age and matched child's mean age on Williamsfield and Nightingale Grove, 1817   298
9.10 Child participation rates on ten estates, 1787–1834   299
9.11 LRC generated population pyramid for six estates, 1817–34   310
10.1 Population pyramid for slaves of colour on six estates, 1817   333
10.2 *Un Anglais de la Barbade vend sa maîtresse* (1770)   346

List of Maps

1 Major trade routes of the British Atlantic xvi
2 Barbadian estates owned or managed by the Lascelles 180
3 Jamaican estates owned or managed by the Lascelles 187
4 Tobagonian estates owned or managed by the Lascelles 188

List of Tables

3.1	Business correspondents of Hugh Hall Jr	14
3.2	Stated destinations of persons applying for tickets to depart Barbados, 26 February–4 November 1679	20
3.3	Legislation passed by the Barbados Assembly to promote inventive activity, 1669–1737	37
3.1	St Michael's Parish levy assessments for Edward Lascelles, 1687–1706	47
5.1	Debts owed by Gedney Clarke Sr (deceased) and Jr, c. 1774	94
5.2	Real estate holdings of Gedney Clarke Sr and Jr	104
5.3	Estimated gross asset value of real estate owned by Gedney Clarke Sr and Jr c. 1755 and c. 1776	106
6.1	Chronological distribution of Henry Lascelles' lending (£ sterling)	144
6.2	Henry Lascelles' English loans by type of security	147
6.3	Short-term trade credit supplied by Lascelles & Maxwell on account current	150
6.4	Analysis of interest arrears on loans in 1753	151
6.5	Comparative rates of return earned by Henry Lascelles on loans and securities, 1732–53	153
6.6	Summary of stock market positions taken by Henry Lascelles	154
6.7	New lending compared with holdings of securities and real estate, 1735–53	154
6.8	Sugar exports and the colonial terms of trade, 1701–70	170
6.9	Alphabetical listing of the West Indian loans of Henry Lascelles, 1723–53	174
7.1	Acquisition of West Indian estates, 1773–1818	178
7.2	Capital out on loan in the West Indies, 1769–77	184
7.3	West Indian assets and liabilities of the Harvies, 1765 and 1777	200
7.4	Analysis of debts owed to Alexander Harvie (all colonies), 1765	202

7.5	West Indian assets and liabilities of the Blenmans, c. 1784	212
7.6	Indebtedness of four major loan clients at foreclosure	221
7.7	Alphabetical listing of loan clients, 1777–1820	222
8.1	Revenue and performance of twelve estates, 1791–6	230
8.2	The evolution of 'Lascelles & Maxwell', 1732–1886	240
8.3	Disinvestment of West Indian real estate, 1791–1975	241
8.4	Revenue and performance of eight estates, 1805–20	243
8.5	Production data for eight estates, 1805–20	244
8.6	Relative efficiency levels on twelve estates, 1791–1839	246
8.7	Estimated value and income of the Harewood estate and Edward Lascelles' personal estate, c. 1799–1805	250
8.8	Comparative estimate of Henry and Edward Lascelles' gross wealth, c. 1753	251
8.9	Compensation payments to the Earl of Harewood, 1835–6	252
8.10	Annual output and gross revenue of six Barbadian and Jamaican estates, 1829–48	256
9.1	Characteristics of ten estates included in the Enslaved Database	262
9.2	Population totals on ten estates, 1767–1835	263
9.3	Gender and origin of the populations of four Barbadian estates	266
9.4	Gender and origin of the populations of three Jamaican estates	269
9.5	Summary occupational classifications for nine estates	272
9.6	Name changing among mothers listed on Nightingale Grove and Williamsfield estates, 1817–32	280
9.7	LRC generated life table for six estates, 1817–34	283
9.8	Hazard ratios for six estates (univariate analysis)	291
9.9	Hazard ratios for six estates (multivariate analysis)	293
9.10	Hazard ratios for children aged three and under	294
9.11	Family groupings recorded on Nightingale Grove estate, 1777	300
9.12	Net-reproduction rates on six estates, 1817–34	301
9.13	CWR and FMR on six estates, 1787–1834	302
9.14	Consistency of age reporting: Thicket and Fortescue estates, 1787–1834	307
9.15	Survivorship on Thicket and Fortescue estates, 1787–1817	309
10.1	Chi-square analysis of births and deaths of coloured slaves for six Barbadian and Jamaican estates, 1817–32	334
10.2	Female births on six Barbadian and Jamaican properties, distinguishing coloured children, 1817–32	335
11.1	Performance of Barbadian properties, 1937–8 and 1951–2	354

Preface

Fire, fire – grand copper, grand copper.
Michael Scott, *Tom Cringle's Log* (originally published 1820–33;
New York: Dodd, Mead & Co., 1927), 374

The fieldwork for this book was undertaken at intervals over a period of seven years. It is a pleasure to acknowledge the generous assistance received from individuals located across the globe during this time. Indeed, so many people submitted information or suggestions, in response to queries, that it is quite possible a few names have been omitted inadvertently from the subsequent list. Sadly, some of the contributors did not live to see the project completed, among them Professor Richard B. Sheridan and Mr Tom Wilkinson – both of whom, in their own ways, contributed greatly to the history and cultural heritage of Barbados. Special thanks are also due to Professor James Walvin, whose constructive criticism, friendship, and deep knowledge of Caribbean history were much appreciated throughout the investigation.

I wish to thank Adrian Almond, Henrice Altink, Oswald Ames, Tim and Una Anderson, Roger Avery, Bernard Bailyn, Robert B. Barker, Paul Bassett, Edmund Berkeley, Adrian Bodkin, Eleanor Brackbill, Trevor Burnard, Ann M. Carlos, Dave Clarke, Dominik Collet, Bill Connor, Marion Diamond, Harry Duggan, David Eltis, Jane Fairfax, Sue Fitzgerald, Margaret Gardner, Eleanor Gawne, Robert Griffiths, Charles Kearney Hall III, Lord Harewood, Anstice Hughes, Ronnie Hughes, Phyllis Hunter, Lisa Jenkins, Michael Jessamy, Mary Lib Joyce, Paul Knights, David Lascelles, Karen Lynch, John J. McCusker, Rod and Michelle McDonald, Emily Mechner, John Meriton, Mary Mill, Sheila Millar, Kirstynn Monrose, Elizabeth Odell, Bill Overton, Bob Paquette, Susan Pares, Christer Petley, William Pettigrew, David Pott, Jacob M. Price, Neon Reynolds, David Richardson, Dan Richter, James Robertson, Henry Robinson, Winifred B. Rothenberg, George Russell, Carolyn Smith-Pelletier, Terry Suthers, Clare Taylor, Thomas Truxes,

Johan van Langen, Roderic Vassie, Michael Watson, Ernest M. Wiltshire, Pat Wood, Sheila Yeo, and Nuala Zahedieh.

Almost all of the project's funding was donated by independent charitable trusts. The two principal sponsors remained supportive of research from its inception to completion; to them is owing a particular debt of gratitude. The Harewood Trust provided access to manuscript materials and contributed financially to the initial stages of research. Without two timely grants from Leverhulme Trust (in 2000 and 2004) it is doubtful whether this work would ever have been completed. The first of these awards (F/00224A) enabled Dr Douglas Hamilton to be employed as a research assistant for two years. Douglas' collegiality and patience (when following leads, or extracting material from the national archives of Britain and Jamaica), are gratefully acknowledged. A second Leverhulme grant (RRFG/10734) provided respite from teaching and administration duties for two terms, thus enabling most of the book to be written.

The editors of *Economic History Review*, *The New England Quarterly* and Microform Ltd kindly granted permission to publish material (in Chapters 4, 5, and 6) that originally appeared elsewhere. Significant revisions and additions, however, have been made to these earlier published versions. Also deeply appreciated are the efforts of the staffs of all the archives and libraries cited in the book, especially those who found the time (out of increasingly busy schedules) to answer the more detailed written enquiries, submitted in advance of visits.

In February and March of 2005, The John Carter Brown Library awarded the author a Paul W. McQuillen Memorial Fellowship. The stimulating environment at Brown University, coupled with the sociability of the JCB fellows and Professor Roger Avery's (almost) boundless enthusiasm for the study of demography, provided an inspirational setting in which to complete the work. Two shorter visits to the McNeil Center at the University of Pennsylvania also reaped rich dividends. Mr Michael Watson, Ms Isabelle Dambricourt and Ms Monica Kendall expertly guided the book through the final stages of publication at Cambridge University Press, and Ms Chantal Hamill compiled the excellent index. Professor Trevor Burnard kindly read an earlier draft with a critical eye and offered some very useful advice. Thanks are also due to two anonymous referees and to Professor Gavin Wright (the series editor) for their valuable comments on the manuscript. Lastly, Jonathan, Sarah Beth, Rondo, and Brio helped immeasurably in conquering the many trials and tribulations confronting the travelling historian.

List of Abbreviations

BA	Barbados Archives, Cave Hill, Barbados
BL	British Library, London
BPL	Boston Public Library, Boston, Massachusetts
CKS	Centre for Kentish Studies, Maidstone, Kent
CSPC (A&WI)	*Calendar of State Papers Colonial, America and West Indies* (1860–)
CLRO	Corporation of London Records Office
CRO	Carlisle Record Office, Cumbria
HH:WIP	Harewood House, West Yorkshire, West India Papers
HSP	Historical Society of Pennsylvania, Philadelphia
IGI	International Genealogical Index
JA	Jamaica Archives, Spanish Town Jamaica
JBMHS	*Journal of the Barbados Museum and Historical Society*
LBMH	Library of the Barbados Museum & Historical Society, Bridgetown, Barbados
LMLB	S. D. Smith ed., *The Lascelles and Maxwell Letter Books, 1739–1769* (Wakefield, 2002)
MCD	Corporation of London Records Office, Mayor's Court Depositions
MHS	Massachusetts Historical Society, Boston
NA:PRO	National Archives: Public Record Office, London
NAS	National Archives of Scotland, Edinburgh
NEHGR	*New England Historical and Genealogical Register*
NMM	National Maritime Museum, Greenwich, London
ODNB	*Oxford Dictionary of National Biography* (Oxford, 2004)
PEM	Peabody Essex Museum, Salem, Massachusetts
PRONI	Public Record Office of Northern Ireland, Belfast
WRA	West Riding of Yorkshire Archives (WRA), Sheepscar Branch, Leeds

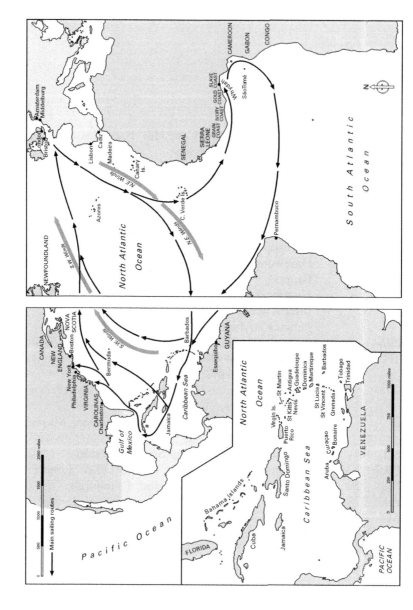

Map 1. Major trade routes of the British Atlantic.

1 Introduction: Remembering and Forgetting

During the eighteenth century, spectacular fortunes were gained and lost in the West Indian colonial trades. European powers, chiefly Britain and France, competed for control of Caribbean islands and shipping routes in a series of naval conflicts. And more than six million Africans were forcibly transported across the Atlantic to be sold into plantation slavery. This book examines commercial success and failure in the British transatlantic nexus by analysing the activities of the Yorkshire-based Lascelles family and their associates over three centuries. It is thus a micro-history, in which Henry Lascelles emerges as a paragon of success, while his business partner Gedney Clarke exemplifies a certain type of failure. The rationale underpinning this volume is that detailed analysis of these and other case studies enriches understanding of the processes shaping the course of history.

In the pages that follow, hypotheses or conjectures regarding these historical processes are advanced based on surviving sources documenting the activities of the Lascelles. Some of these conjectures are related to previous research; others are more original in the sense that they emphasise aspects of the past that feature less prominently in existing accounts. The first of the hypotheses argues that a new framework for business association was established by mercantile communities based in London, Barbados, and North America between the later seventeenth and early eighteenth centuries. The second thesis argues that a key element of this framework lay in control of complex credit networks, crucial for the success (or failure) of Atlantic commercial ventures. Merchants' strategies were shaped by the working of the credit market, ultimately obliging the Lascelles to become large-scale plantation owners. The third hypothesis argues that by the mid-eighteenth century Caribbean colonies and transatlantic trade were subject to fiscal-military control through the medium of naval power and metropolitan credit. However, it locates the instruments of control in gentry capitalist networks of kinship and regional affiliation, matrimonial alliance, mercantile expertise, and public service. In consequence, the concept of a centralising authority and a dependent periphery is inadequate when applied to an imperial relationship that was poorly regulated in many aspects, and which possessed fluid trading boundaries.

The Lascelles are interesting and worthy of study not only for what their records reveal about the course of development in the eighteenth-century Caribbean and Atlantic economy. Events that took place centuries ago are also linked to present-day concerns. The research for this book was sparked in 1998 by an approach from the Harewood House Trust of West Yorkshire.[1] During an inventory of one of the 'treasure houses of England', a black metal deed box was found to contain West India papers, including details of several plantations. More manuscripts were subsequently discovered in a locked bureau during the recataloguing of artefacts at Harewood. Lacking information about the Lascelles family's past connections with slavery, the trustees sought guidance from historians working at the University of York, in order to place these finds in context. Around the time of its initial approach, the Harewood Trust received designated museum status.[2] As a result of this award, a number of initiatives were launched to stimulate research into Harewood House and its collections. Among the projects sponsored by the trustees was a preliminary study of the involvement of the Lascelles in Caribbean trade and slavery. Shortly afterwards (in 1999), the University of York established its Yorkshire Country House Partnership, with the aim of fostering links between seven country houses (including Harewood) and the academic community.[3]

---

[1] In 1986, ownership of Harewood House was transferred from the Lascelles to a charitable trust, charged with the preservation of the estate and also the promotion of educational activities. Under the terms of the trust, the Lascelles family continue to reside at Harewood.

[2] Harewood House was the first stately home to receive designated museums status: originally, a classification awarded by the Museums and Galleries Commission (MGC) to non-national registered museums with collections judged to be of national and international importance. In 2000, the MGC was replaced by the Museums, Libraries and Archives Council (renamed Resource: The Council for Museums, Archives and Libraries): a national development agency responsible for providing strategic leadership for the museums sector and advising the British Government on policy issues.

[3] C. L. Ridgway and Allen Warren, 'Collaborative Opportunities for the Study of the Country House: The Yorkshire Country House Partnership', *Historical Research*, 78 (2005), 162–3, 167. Between 1996 and 1999 (later extended to 2000), the York History Department hosted the HEFCE funded project, 'Heritage Studies as Applied History', directed by Dr Simon Ditchfield. As a result of this initiative, twenty courses were established at twelve higher education institutions in the United Kingdom, along with eight conferences and teaching workshops. See John Arnold, Kate Davies, and Simon Ditchfield eds., *History and Heritage: Consuming the Past in Contemporary Culture* (Shaftesbury, Dorset, 1998).

Localised factors clearly played an important role in establishing contacts between Harewood House and academics.[4] Indeed, initially the invitation to research the Lascelles' West Indian interests appeared as an intriguing, yet self-contained project. With the benefit of hindsight, however, the investigation can also be seen as part of an ongoing re-evaluation of slavery's legacy. The historiography of the African Diaspora stretches back over several centuries and the accumulated bibliography of slavery reflects the repeated iteration of written history and social memory.[5] It would be misleading, therefore, to claim that the 1990s witnessed the inauguration of an entirely different form of scholarship. Nevertheless, in retrospect the decade does seem to mark the emergence of a new phase in the relationship between history, heritage, and the public understanding of slavery. Consciously or subconsciously, social and political events in Britain and the wider world influenced the trust's decision to adopt a policy of openness about Harewood's past links with slavery.

During the 1980s, a breakdown in British race relations contributed to rioting in Brixton (1981) and Broadwater Farm (1985). This decade also saw the formation in 1982 of the British National Party (BNP). The anti-immigration policies of the BNP gained limited electoral support in areas of high unemployment possessing ethnic minority populations, such as east London. Indeed, in 1993 the BNP shocked many observers by winning a local council seat in the Millwall ward of Tower Hamlets. While the electoral gains of the BNP were extremely limited, the organisation's enhanced public profile stimulated the relaunch of the Anti Nazi League, which sought to assemble a popular coalition against racism by staging protest marches, concerts, and festivals.[6] Also in 1993, a widely publicised media campaign was launched by the Commission for Racial Equality (with support from the Professional Footballers' Association and the Football Trust). The campaign's slogan – 'Let's Kick Racism Out of Football' – resonated beyond a sport widely regarded as the English 'national game'.[7]

---

[4] Formal links between Harewood and York date from 1963 (the year the university was established) when the 7th Earl of Harewood was invited to become the first chancellor.

[5] Ralph A. Austen, 'The Slave Trade as History and Memory: Confrontations of Slaving Voyage Documents and Communal Traditions', *William and Mary Quarterly*, 58 (2001), 229–44; Celeste-Marie Bernier, review of 'Transatlantic Slavery: Against Human Dignity', 'A Respectable Trade?', and 'Pero and Pinney Exhibit', *Journal of American History*, 88 (2001), 1,006–12; Michael L. Blakey, 'History and Comparison of Bioarchaeological Studies in the African Diaspora', in *African Burial Ground Final History and Final Skeletal Biology Reports Prepared by Howard University* (Howard University and General Services Administration: 3 vols., New York, 2004), vol. I, 38–96.

[6] The latter events were organised in association with Rock Against Racism (established in 1976).

[7] James Walvin, *The People's Game: A History of Football Revisited* (Edinburgh, 2000).

A growing awareness of race issues received added impetus after failings in the police and criminal justice system were exposed. In May 1997, a Labour Government was elected. The following July, the new Home Secretary, Jack Straw, announced that a public inquiry chaired by Sir William Macpherson would investigate 'the matters arising from the death of Stephen Lawrence': a young man of Afro-Caribbean descent, murdered in 1993 in south London. Macpherson's terms of reference included the identification of 'lessons to be learned for the investigation and prosecution of racially motivated crimes'. The Macpherson report was duly published in February 1999. Among other findings, the inquiry concluded that the Metropolitan Police Service had exhibited 'institutional racism', which manifested itself in 'processes, attitudes and behaviour' that disadvantaged minority ethnic people, 'through unwitting prejudice, ignorance, thoughtlessness, and racist stereotyping'.[8] By introducing the concept of institutional racism into mainstream political debate, Macpherson encouraged both public and private sector organisations to examine their inclusiveness and accessibility.

As a consequence of this shift in public opinion, the museums and heritage sector joined with other public organisations in devoting greater consideration to racial issues. During the 1990s, the custodians of heritage sites and special collections were urged to do more to acknowledge slavery's legacy and Britain's past involvement in the transatlantic slave trade. In 1993, for example, the Labour MP for Tottenham, Bernie Grant (1944–2000), founded the United Kingdom branch of the Africa Reparations Movement (ARM).[9] ARM called on the British and other Western governments to issue an apology for the enslavement and colonisation of Africans, for the return of cultural artefacts, and for a more accurate portrayal of African history in order to restore dignity and self-respect to African people. One of the most widely reported events co-organised by ARM occurred in 1997, when Grant led a ceremony of remembrance on the Devon beach of Rapparee Cove, Ilfracombe, following the discovery of manacled human remains (presumed to be slaves) from the 1796 shipwreck of *The London*.[10]

Remembrance of slavery has continued to gather momentum in Britain as the 200-year anniversary of Britain's abolition of the slave trade in 1807 approaches. There is insufficient space here to list all of the

---

[8] *The Stephen Lawrence Inquiry: Report of an Inquiry by Sir William Macpherson of Cluny* (London, 1999).

[9] 'Reparations or Bust', speech given by Bernie Grant MP 12 November 1993 at Birmingham Town Hall: Middlesex University, London, Bernie Grant Archive, BG/ARM/16/4/4.

[10] *The Times*, Monday 24 February 1997.

activities taking place, but museums, archives, and heritage centres in London and the provinces have launched events to mark the bicentenary. Parallel developments in the United States have influenced greatly the re-examination of slavery within Britain. By the end of the 1990s, reparations had emerged as one of the most racially divisive issues in American politics and established itself as an extension of the Civil Rights agenda.[11] A growing number of North American museums and heritage centres, dedicated to presenting the colonial past, have accepted that the public's implicit trust in museums as a repository of historical truth requires that slavery's significance be disclosed.

By no means all institutions, towns, or cities have chosen to confront the role slavery has played in their histories. Nevertheless, the events of the 1990s made a difference and the extent of public acknowledgements of slavery, on both sides of the Atlantic, appears unprecedented.[12] As Ira Berlin declared in his presidential address to the Organization of American Historians: 'Slavery has a greater presence in American life now than at any time since the Civil War ended.'[13] In terms of public memory, it is tempting to claim that slavery similarly enjoys a higher profile in Britain's national consciousness than at any time since Emancipation.

The Lascelles' three-centuries-long association with Barbados ensured that their West Indian connections were never forgotten entirely by the family. Much uncertainty, however, existed in 1998 concerning the precise nature of Harewood House's past associations with slavery, notwithstanding that the Lascelles had owned Caribbean sugar planta-tions as recently as 1975. The absence of a written history of the family was one important consideration responsible for collective amnesia. A second factor lies in the disorganised state of surviving documents at the house itself, coupled with a devastating bombing raid in 1940, which destroyed a large amount of manuscript material relating to the

---

[11] Four articles that comment on a large and growing literature are: Richard F. America, 'Reparations and Public Policy', *Review of Black Political Economy*, 26 (1999), 77–83; Tuneen E. Chisolm, 'Sweep Around Your Own Front Door: Examining the Argument for Legislative African American Reparations', *University of Pennsylvania Law Review*, 147 (1999), 677–727; John Topley, '"Making Whole What Has been Smashed": Reflections on Reparations', *Journal of Modern History*, 73 (2001), 333–61; Alfred L. Brophy, 'Some Conceptual and Legal Problems in Reparations for Slavery', *NYU Annual Survey of American Law*, 58 (2003), 497–556.

[12] The 1990s also witnessed increased interest in comparative slave regimes, including Islamic participation in the slave trade, John Hunwick, 'The Same but Different: Approaches to Slavery and the African Diaspora in the Lands of Islam', *Saharan Studies Association Newsletter*, 7 (1999), 9–14.

[13] Ira Berlin, 'American Slavery in History and Memory and the Search for Social Justice', *Journal of American History*, 90 (2004), 1,251–68.

Lascelles and the West Indies kept in the London offices of the firm of Wilkinson and Gaviller.[14] While it is not possible to analyse the process of memory loss with precision, events occurring in the early twentieth century probably exerted a significant influence. In 1918, the Barbadian estates of Thicket and Fortescue were sold and the 6th Earl of Harewood devised the two remaining plantations, Belle and Mount, to his younger son.[15] Four years after these West Indian properties were severed from the main branch of the Harewood estate, the Lascelles were connected dynastically with the British royal family through the marriage of Princess Mary, the Princess Royal, to Henry, Viscount Lascelles.[16] A sense of deference may have contributed to the drawing of a discreet veil over links with slavery during the first half of the twentieth century. Pevsner's history of the buildings of England, for example, comments judiciously that, 'the Harewood estate, with Gawthorpe as the house on it, was bought by Henry Lascelles, a wealthy man whose money came from the ribbon trade and the collecting of customs in Barbados'.[17]

Since forging links with the University of York, the Harewood Trust has sought to raise awareness of the Lascelles' past involvement in slavery in a variety of ways. The BBC's *House Detectives* programme (broadcast in March 2002) featured Harewood House and included a segment investigating the Barbados slavery connection. An exhibition entitled 'Sugar Table Decorations at Harewood' was prepared in 2003 under the direction of David Stockdale. This presentation included, for the first time, a panel devoted to the family's West Indian plantations. In the same year, a 'New Freedoms' conference was organised in association with the Interculture organisation.[18] Recently, the Trust formulated a Learning and Access agenda, which includes plans for a Festival of West Indian Culture and the production of education packs for use in British secondary schools. Existing outreach activities include liaison with Afro-Caribbean community leaders in Leeds, and the Yorkshire Museums, Libraries and Archives Council. Members of the

---

[14] Richard Pares, 'A London West-India Merchant House, 1740–1769', in Richard Pares and A. J. P. Taylor eds., *Essays Presented to Sir Lewis Namier* (London, 1956), 75–107. Limited space prevents discussion of the history of the Lascelles' archive in this volume, but see S. D. Smith, 'An Introduction to the Records of Lascelles and Maxwell', in LMLB.

[15] See Chapter Eight.

[16] In 1922; Viscount Lascelles was heir to the 5th Earl of Harewood.

[17] Nikolaus Pevsner, *Yorkshire: The West Riding* (Harmondsworth, Middlesex, 1959), 245.

[18] 'Estates for Profit and Estates for Pleasure: Unlocking the Links Between the West Indian Sugar Plantations, Slavery and the English Country House', Discussion Document by Terry Suthers (Director and CEO of the Harewood Trust), March 2005.

Trust have also established contacts with overseas organisations facing similar challenges, including the Barbados Museum of History, Monticello House, and the Colonial Williamsburg Foundation.[19] In August 2005, Diverse Productions broadcast the documentary-drama, *How to Make a Million from Slavery*, based loosely on aspects of the career of Henry Lascelles. This programme, though strongly critical of Henry Lascelles, was made with the cooperation of the Trust.

Yorkshire provides the starting point for this book. However, the web woven by the Lascelles transcends the county. Their business network extended upwards into Scotland, passing through the East Lothian region and reaching as far north as the Orkney islands. To the south, English associates of the Lascelles can be found in East Anglia and the West Country. To the west, the family firm injected credit into the slaving port of Liverpool; across the Irish Sea, their early ventures also touched Dromore, Lisburn, and Belfast. While Barbados formed the Lascelles' most significant and longstanding colonial connection in the Americas, their Atlantic interests were never confined to this island. Antigua, Jamaica, Grenada, Tobago, Demerara, and Essequibo all feature in the colonial portfolios of the family's circle. Along the eastern seaboard, from Nova Scotia to South Carolina, commercial attachments were formed with leading merchants of North America. The Guinea coast of Africa attracted both direct and indirect investment by syndicates of London merchants and Liverpool mariners, either headed or underwritten by the Lascelles. During the later seventeenth and eighteenth centuries, their vessels traversed the Atlantic ocean, carrying slaves, dry goods, sugar and rum, and victuals. Family members also sought business opportunities in South-East Asia, sending ships out to trade across the seas and investing in the East Indian Company.

In Chapter Two, the origins of the London–Boston–Bridgetown trading network are traced by examining the careers of the Vassall and Hall families, whose business interests intersected with those of the Lascelles at various points. Chapters Three and Four examine the Lascelles' own commercial origins and analyses the complex business networks they constructed, linking associates based in Britain, the Caribbean, and North America. By the death of Henry Lascelles in 1753, one of the greatest of all fortunes earned from West Indian commerce had been accumulated by combining the pursuit of private profit with patronage of colonial and naval offices. Chapter Five analyses the remarkable career of Gedney Clarke, one of the Lascelles' most important associates. Clarke's activities emphasise the role of London

---

[19] Ibid.

financiers in underwriting the expansion of sugar and slavery in the English-speaking West Indies; his business operations also reveal how commercial networks were capable of cutting across formal national boundaries in the Caribbean. The themes of capital and credit are developed further in Chapters Six and Seven, which examine the Lascelles' financial dealings with slave traders and planters, stressing the extent to which metropolitan lending contributed to expansion in the sugar trade.

During their first twelve decades of participation in Atlantic commerce the Lascelles owned surprisingly little real estate in the West Indies. This situation changed abruptly after the American Revolution. Within the space of fourteen years, the family acquired an immense property portfolio as its business empire was restructured. The remaining chapters provide three different perspectives on the management of West Indian estates. Chapter Eight examines the profitability of slavery to the Lascelles as absentee proprietors. In Chapter Nine, the human cost of involuntary servitude borne by the enslaved population is assessed. A quantitative analysis of plantation demography conveys something of the indescribable tragedy that was Caribbean slavery. Finally, Chapter Ten investigates intercultural relations between the enslaved and white communities – a difficult subject that is only partially documented in surviving archives.

Reconstructing the world of the Lascelles reveals much about the operation of the Atlantic trades during the eighteenth century. Strand by strand, historians have been slowly unravelling the complex business partnerships that enterprising merchants and their financiers fashioned to develop transatlantic commerce.[20] Communities of 'outsiders' or 'strangers within the realm' have attracted particular attention, including ethnic groups of Scots, Irish, and German migrants, and religious minorities, such as Puritans, Quakers, and Jews.[21] This book examines the Lascelles' Yorkshire-based circle and argues that English provincial

---

[20] See e.g. David Hancock, '"A World of Business to Do": William Freeman and the Foundations of England's Commercial Empire, 1645–1707', *William and Mary Quarterly*, 57 (2000), 6–8; Nuala Zahedieh, 'Making Mercantilism Work: London Merchants and Atlantic Trade in the Seventeenth Century', *Transactions of the Royal Historical Society*, 9 (1999), 152–8; Peter Mathias, 'Risk, Credit, and Kinship in Early Modern Enterprise', in Kenneth Morgan and John J. McCusker eds., *The Early Modern Atlantic Economy* (Cambridge, 2000), 15–35.

[21] See e.g. Bernard Bailyn and Philip D. Morgan eds., *Strangers Within the Realm: Cultural Margins of the First British Empire* (Chapel Hill, 1991); Alan L. Karras, *Sojourners in the Sun: Scottish Migrants in Jamaica and the Chesapeake, 1740–1800* (Ithaca, NY, 1992); Marianne S. Wokeck, *Trade in Strangers: The Beginnings of Mass Migration to North America* (Philadelphia, 1999); David Hancock, *Citizens of the World: London Merchants and the Integration of the British Atlantic Community, 1735–1785* (New York, 1995);

groupings proved capable of operating in similar ways. Its members possessed a strongly defined regional identity, centred on Anglicanism, kinship, and shared cultural pursuits. Two important strengths enjoyed by the Lascelles lay in their access to political patronage and also their ability to integrate with other networks, particularly through Scottish mercantile associates.

The term 'gentry capitalism' is used to describe the institutional structures of trade and finance underpinning the growth of Atlantic trade during the eighteenth century. Gentry capitalism should not be confused with 'gentlemanly capitalism'. The latter term is applied to non-landed mercantile families who sought to acquire wealth and social respectability through participation in imperial trade.[22] In contrast, gentry capitalism refers to families who were already landed and respectable yet which attempted to increase their wealth and influence through colonial trade. The social and political context in which Atlantic trade was conducted resulted in the emergence of a particular type of super-merchant personified by Henry Lascelles and his leading associates. These well-connected and advantageously situated individuals reaped extraordinary profits in the expanding but poorly integrated and loosely regulated colonial economy. In so doing, families like the Lascelles and their associates also helped forge a political consensus that empire was worth creating and defending.[23]

Confining business to kinsmen or to well-connected groups of individuals helped reduce the enormous risks of long-distance commerce And insofar as that strategy succeeded, it had the effect of integrating, and of expanding, the Atlantic economy. But the Lascelles network did not exert a wholly positive influence. The associates sought to deny trading opportunities to outsiders, and they manipulated naval resources and colonial government to protect their own interests. In the long term, the trading system created by the Lascelles proved unsustainable in the face of credit instability, tighter imperial regulation, and colonial bids for greater autonomy. After coming close to bankruptcy in the 1760s and 1770s, the Lascelles adopted new business strategies as a different type of Atlantic economic community came into being.

Douglas Hamilton, *Scotland, the Caribbean and the Atlantic World, 1750–1820* (Manchester, 2005).

[22] P. J. Cain and A. G. Hopkins, 'Gentlemanly Capitalism and British Expansion Overseas. I: The Old Colonial System, 1688–1850', *Economic History Review*, 39 (1986), 501–25.

[23] Patrick K. O'Brien, 'Central Government and the Economy, 1688–1815', in Roderick Floud and Donald McCloskey eds., *The Economic History of Britain Since 1700* (2nd edn, 3 vols., Cambridge, 1994), vol. I, 205–41.

The Lascelles' association with the Caribbean is striking for its longevity. No fewer than 327 years span the earliest appearance of a Lascelles on Barbados (1648) to the sale of the family's last plantation in 1975. Involvement in the sugar trade can be documented from 1680 and the family remained tied to the same London commission house from 1732 until 1954. Continuous ownership of plantations in the West Indies lasted 202 years; on Barbados alone, estates were managed without interruption for 194 years. The continuity of the Lascelles' West Indian interests provides a valuable opportunity to survey the long-term development of the British Atlantic economy and to understand how merchants and planters responded to the challenges of warfare, political upheaval, revolution, and ultimately emancipation.

2　Halls and Vassalls

'Strangely ... Metamorphosed from a Student to a Merchant'

In early June 1717, a twenty-four-year-old colonial visitor walked nervously on to the floor of London's Royal Exchange, anxious to make a good impression on the traders assembled there. Hugh Hall Jr felt 'strangely Metamorphosed from a Student to a Merchant'. Less than a year earlier, the bookish Harvard graduate, with 'Inclinations ... to a Pastoral Function', had been recalled to Barbados by his father, Hugh Hall Sr.[1] After being admitted into co-partnership, Hall Jr was promptly despatched to London on what he described as 'a Very Probable Scheme for my Advancement'.[2]

The man young Hugh set out to meet on the Exchange also doubted whether trade was the new arrival's natural vocation. Edward Lascelles, a prominent West India merchant, was vastly experienced in trade; after spending nearly two decades on Barbados, he had returned to England in 1701 and established himself as a leading sugar merchant. While on Barbados, Edward married Hugh's aunt, Mary Hall; his household also included Hugh's twelve-year-old brother Charles, sent to England to better his education. The meeting between the two men was brief. Lascelles scanned the letter of introduction Hall's father had written, issued a cool summons for his young kinsman to wait on him, and then turned abruptly on his heel.[3]

---

[1] Houghton Library, Harvard, Massachusetts, MS Am 1,042, Hugh Hall Letterbook, Hall to John Leverett, 28 February 1716[17]; Hall to Lydia Colman, 6 March 1716[17]. Hugh Hall graduated from Harvard in 1713 but remained in residence until 1716, Samuel E. Morison, 'The Letter-Book of Hugh Hall, Merchant of Barbados, 1716–1720', *Transactions, Colonial Society of Massachusetts*, 32 (1937), 515. Notes on fourteen sermons heard by Hall Jr in Boston from 3 February 1708[9] to 13 March 1708[9] are preserved in MHS, Hugh Hall Papers, Sermon Notes, 1709.

[2] Hugh Hall Letterbook, Hall to Hugh Hall Sr, 6 September 1717. Note the following vital dates: Hugh Hall Sr (1675–1732) and Hugh Hall Jr (1693–1773).

[3] Ibid., 20 June 1717.

Matters scarcely improved once Hugh accepted his kinsman's offer of hospitality. Away from the Exchange, Lascelles conducted business from Tokenhouse Yard, Lothbury. His counting house formed part of an elegant two-storey building, presenting to the street no less than fifteen crown-glass sash windows, and overlooking a paved courtyard. Within walls, reception rooms were decorously wainscotted with bead-work; fireplaces of marble and Portland stone afforded a warm welcome to visitors accustomed to warmer climes.[4] To escape city life, Lascelles retreated to a country estate at nearby Stoke Newington: a favoured resort of affluent London merchants, and still a predominantly rural community during the early eighteenth century. And it was to the fine Georgian house situated along the London road that Hugh Hall Jr found himself invited.[5]

At Stoke Newington, Hall's ears were soon dinned by his hosts' 'Harangue upon the Old-Threads-bare Tautology of ye Discourage-ment of Trade by ye Vast loss in Remittances'. While Edward Sr lam-basted the commercial reputations of Barbadian merchants, his son, Edward Lascelles Jr, sought to demolish his colonial cousin's cultural pretensions. In the course of a single day, the younger Lascelles (whose head Hall likened in shape to a bass viol), put no fewer than twenty volumes before him, 'which from their *late* publication, he Supposed new to me, & particularly Recommended Dr Sacheverells trial, a book he thought I had never seen'. Hall was heartily glad when finally able to take his leave, and pitied his aunt Mary and his younger brother Charles for having to suffer such boorish company.[6]

The most notable business opportunities Hugh solicited in London related to slaving. On his return to Barbados at the end of 1717, Hall Jr and Sr acted as agents for the city firm of Samuel Betteress and William Allen. On behalf of these two London merchants, father and son han-dled the importation of at least 642 Africans between 1716 and 1719. Many of these slaves were sold to planters within the island, but Virginia also formed a promising market. Numbered among the Chesapeake clients were Henry and Nathaniel Harrison (the latter a member of the Virginia Council), Henry Jenkins of Southmark, and Robert Blight of

---

[4] Guildhall Library, London, Add. MSS 754, Counterpart of a lease, [Edward] Lascelles to [Samuel] Vanderplank, 1719. Lascelles owned five other properties in Tokenhouse Yard and Whitechapel, NA:PRO, PROB11/614, Will of Edward Lascelles, 1727; C11/837/11, 'A True Rental of the Real Estate of Edward Lascelles Esqr. Deceased' (1745).
[5] Victoria K. Bolton ed., *Victoria County History: A History of the County of Middlesex, vol. VIII* (London, 1985), 168. The house still stands at 187 Stoke Newington High Street, a contemporary stone inscription states that the year of construction was 1712.
[6] Hugh Hall Letterbook, Hall to Hugh Hall Sr, 20 June 1717; NA:PRO, C11/838/11; see also MHS, Hugh Hall Papers, 1709–73, [Mary] Lascelles to Hugh Hall, 25 August 1731.

Prince George County.[7] Blight's will of 1720 indicates that the Halls' business connections extended along the eastern seaboard, since he bequeathed to his son-in-law, James Jones, 'all money I have in hands of Hugh Hall, Esq., in Barbados', and charged Hall Sr with remitting 'what money I have in New England'.[8]

Competition for the Betteress' account was fierce and rivals in both London and Barbados attempted to steal the Halls' business. Edward Lascelles' support would have been useful in defending the reputation and credit of the house. In addition to trading in sugar, the well-connected Lascelles engaged in slaving in his own right and also extended loans to planters.[9] Nevertheless, even without the help of their kinsman, the Halls proved able to consolidate their position in the slave trade, overcoming in the process 'Ungentlemanlike & Ungenerous Supplanters'.[10]

An indication of the scope of the Halls' business affairs is provided by Table 2.1, which lists the location of Hugh Jr's correspondents for eighteen months following his return from Boston in January 1719.[11]

---

[7] David Eltis, Stephen D. Behrendt, David Richardson, and Herbert S. Klein eds., *The Trans-Atlantic Slave Trade: A Database on CD-ROM* (Cambridge, 1999), #76,133 (this consignment of slaves was possibly sent to New England rather than Barbados), #76,490, #76,500, #76,524; Hugh Hall Letterbook, Hall to Samuel Betteress and Company, [24 February?] 1717[18]; 25 February 1717[18]; 13 March 1717[18]; 2 September 1718; 2 October 1718; 22 June 1719; Hall to Henry and Nathaniel Harrison, 6 February 1718[19]; 25 February 1718[19]. In May 1720, the Halls were expecting shipment of 200 slaves from the Guinea coast and received news that the Harrisons had sold fourteen of their slaves in Virginia at around £30 per head, Hall to Messrs Harrisons, 3 May 1720. Nathaniel Harrison (1677–1727), of Wakefield in Surrey County, was elected to the Virginia Council in 1713.

[8] Library of Virginia, Richmond, Virginia, Deeds and Wills, Bond of Captain Henry Jenkins (Southmark Township, Virginia) to Hugh Hall of Barbados, Surrey County Court (1710); Prince George County Court, Will of Robert Blight, 13 February 1710[11]. James Jones held 1,908 acres of patented land in Wyanoke and Westow parishes, suggesting he was a wealthy man.

[9] See Chapter Three.

[10] Hugh Hall Letterbook, Hall to Thomas Cocke, 30 May 1720.

[11] The following is a summary of the known movements of Hugh Hall Jr between 1716 and 1719. Hall was in Boston and delivered an oration at Commencement, Harvard, (June?) 1716. He was then in Barbados from 26 November 1716 (opening of the letter book) until 6 April 1717 (date of his departure for England). He stayed in London from 25 May 1717 (first London letter) until 25 October 1717 (last London letter), except for a brief visit to Cambridge. He was in Barbados again from 20 January 1718 (first Barbados letter) until 29 March 1718 (last Barbados letter); in Boston from 29 April 1718 (date of arrival) until 20 October 1718 (last Boston letter); then back in Barbados by 10 January 1719 (first Barbados letter). The last entry in the letter book is dated 18 July 1720. By 31 October 1722, the date of his marriage to Elizabeth Pitts (1703–49), Hall had returned permanently to Boston, Morison, 'Letter-Book of Hugh Hall'; Hugh Hall Letterbook; Clifford K. Shipton, *Biographical Sketches of Those who Attended Harvard College in the Classes 1713–1721 with Biographical and Other Notes* (MHS: Boston, 1942), 15.

Table 2.1. *Business correspondents of Hugh Hall Jr*

	Correspondents (number)	Letters (number)
London	18	67
New England and northern colonies	24	74
Chesapeake	10	38
Not stated	16	28
All regions	*68*	*207*

Note: Letters written from Barbados, 10 January 1719–18 July 1720.
Source: Houghton Library, Harvard, MS Am 1,042, Hugh Hall Letterbook.

Twenty-three of these letters are singletons and take the form of spec-ulative enquiries for business, but the remainder form part of established trading relationships.[12] The London merchants Samuel Betteress and William Allen received nine letters; Philip Nisbett a further eighteen. Henry and Nathaniel Harrison of Virginia also received eighteen letters, while John Binning (or Benning) of Boston was sent fifteen. The cor-respondence reveals that the Halls combined slaving with an import–export trade, handling sugar and European manufactures.

By January 1723, Hugh Jr had returned to Boston, yet he continued trading with Barbados. In an almanac compiled for this year, entries and clearances of nineteen ships in which he was interested are recorded. Ten vessels sailed between Boston and Barbados, seven to London and back, and one each to Virginia and St Kitts.[13] Newspaper advertise-ments provide information about the merchandise Hugh consigned in these and similar vessels. In 1727, he advertised the sale of imported sugar and rum, along with dry goods. Alongside these items, Hall Jr and Sr continued to traffic in slaves. Three ships brought fifty-seven enslaved Africans into Barbados on Hugh Sr's account, for example, between October 1723 and April 1724.[14] On the mainland, six adverts placed by Hugh Jr in the *Boston Newsletter* and *Boston Gazette* between July 1727 and September 1728 publicise the arrival of cargoes of enslaved persons for local sale. Additional details of their slaving

---

[12] Eight of the singletons were addressed to New England, six to London, and nine to correspondents whose residence is not stated.

[13] New England Historic Genealogical Society, Boston, MS C1093, Hugh Hall Diary (Almanac), 1723.

[14] NA:PRO, CO28/18/320–30 and CO33/15, 'A List of Negroes imported into this island from the 25 March 1708 to the 25 March 1726'. The three ships were the *Providence* (John Hutchings) 22 October 1723 carrying eight slaves for Hall, the *Schooner Squirrel* (John Stephenson) December 1723 carrying forty-eight slaves, and the *Brig Sidney* (Richard Moseley) which brought just a single slave.

interests are preserved in a volume of accounts spanning the years from 1728 until 1731.[15] This source documents, firstly, the names of Hall Jr's suppliers and the net proceeds owing to them arising from the sale of Africans for the years 1728 to 1730. Secondly, the volume records the names of eighty slaves imported in the single year 1729, along with their shippers and purchasers. Thirdly, the account balances of customers who purchased slaves and other merchandise from Hall between 1728 and 1731 are stated.

A total of forty-seven suppliers are listed in the manuscript, at least twenty-seven of whom can be linked with Barbados.[16] The data reveal that in 1729 the largest single supplier of slaves were the Halls themselves, who shipped twenty-seven Africans to Boston (more than a third of the total) on their own accounts.[17] The partners supplemented returns from direct trading, however, by selling fifty-three slaves on commission received from twenty-eight suppliers.[18] Newspaper advertisements and the account book suggest that Hall's sales were confined to Boston and the port's immediate hinterland.[19] Of the sixty named clients, who purchased a total of seventy-three Africans, all but eight bought only a single slave. While clients included such known dealers as Daniel Gosse, Nathaniel Cunningham, and Jacob Royall, sales to final customers were probably the norm, since even the largest two purchasers took only four slaves each.[20]

[15] Elizabeth Donnan ed., *Documents Illustrative of the History of the Slave Trade to America* (4 vols., Washington DC, 1930–5), vol. III, 31–2; Robert E. Desrochers, Jr, 'Slave-For-Sale Advertisements and Slavery in Massachusetts, 1704–1781', *William and Mary Quarterly*, 59 (2002); MHS, Account Book of Hugh Hall, 1728–33 (but few details after 1731). The present study is based on an examination of a numbered photocopy of this item kindly supplied by the Society. Extracts from the account book are published in Donnan ed., *Documents*, vol. III, 31–5.

[16] Based on an analysis of subscribers to William Mayo's 1721 map of Barbados and internal evidence within the accounts, 'The Mayo Map, 1721', in Richard B. Goddard ed., *George Washington's Visit to Barbados, 1751* (Barbados, 1997), 97–109. Since only one individual (William Gibbons of Jamaica) can be linked with another West India colony, it is likely that Barbados' importance was greater than the figure of twenty-seven matches suggests.

[17] There is evidence that the Halls were attempting to run a well-integrated family operation since Benjamin Hall (a brother of Hugh) received slave cargoes on Barbados in 1732 and 1734, Donnan ed., *Documents*, vol. II, 427–31.

[18] A feature of the accounts is a lack of concentration among suppliers: of the merchants listed, only five dealers sent more than two slaves to Hall, and only three despatched more than four.

[19] Hall sought a permit to ship just ten of the enslaved out of New England, Account Book of Hugh Hall, 'Memo to get Certificates for ye following Negroes Ship'd out of ye Province' 15 February 1728[9] (p. 5 of the library's photocopy of the original) and 'Negro's Receiv'd from Barbados in the year 729' (p. 16 of the photocopy) reproduced in Donnan ed., *Documents*, vol. III, 31–5.

[20] For details of Gosse, Cunningham, and Royall see Desrochers, 'Slave-For-Sale'.

The account book emphasises the credit relations underpinning the business of enslavement. No fewer than thirty-nine of the buyers (accounting for forty-six slaves) were customers to whom Hall extended finance. The total amount of credit granted between 1728 and 1731 was approximately £3,021, of which £2,110 was secured by penal bond.[21] On the reverse side of the ledger, Hall recorded in January 1730 that he still owed £1,071 in 'Ballances due to my Employers': a sum consisting of the net proceeds arising from the sale of forty of the slaves imported in 1729. If these accounts are representative of the cargo as a whole, the seventy-seven enslaved persons who survived the journey from Barbados to auction were sold for approximately £5,050.[22]

In return for shipping slaves to Boston, suppliers received the gross sale proceeds minus expenses, an import duty of £4 per head, and Hall's 5 per cent commission. About two-thirds of Hall Jr's obligations to suppliers were discharged immediately after sales were completed. Credit extended to purchasers unable to pay cash down was almost certainly generated from Hugh's own resources. The account book records that annual balances owing from buyers of slaves (and other merchandise) ranged from £9,774 to £12,991 during the years 1728 to 1731.[23] Marriage to Elizabeth Pitts in 1722 conferred significant business advantages on Hall Jr. The bride's father, John Pitts, was a Boston merchant and provided his new son-in-law with warehouse facilities. The match was also an important source of capital. In addition to the marriage settlement itself, Elizabeth received legacies of £1,000 from her father in 1731 and a life interest in the dwelling she and Hugh occupied. A further windfall came the way of the Halls in 1732, when Elizabeth inherited £800 and a house in Boston from her grandmother, Susannah Jacobs.[24]

Balances owing to Barbadian suppliers were discharged primarily by consigning cargoes of New England produce. In the course of 1728, a total of £1,982 was remitted to twenty-one creditors in this way; the

---

[21] All sums in this section are Boston currency unless otherwise stated.

[22] This figure suggests that 60 per cent of Hall's total sales were made on credit.

[23] Account Book of Hugh Hall, 'A List of Debts' taken 1 November 1728, 1 March 1728[9], 1 January 1729[30], and 1 January 1730[31], (pp. 7–10, 11–14, 22–5, and 25–8 of the photocopy). It is interesting to note that Hall's account with his father Hugh Hall Sr stood at £970.11s.2d., suggesting that the twenty-seven Africans imported on the Halls' account and sold on credit were either charged as a debit against the Barbados account, or that account balance remained in favour of the son, even after receipt of the slaves.

[24] [Elizabeth H. Payne], *Portraits of Eight Generations of the Pitts Family From the Seventeenth to the Twentieth Century* (Detroit, 1959), 8; Daniel Goodwin Jr, *Memorial of the Lives and Services of James Pitts and his Sons, John, Samuel, and Lendall, during the American Revolution, 1760–1780* (Chicago, 1882), 2, 35, 50.

following year, Hall Jr sent shipments valued at a further £580, leaving £1,071 still to pay. The most frequently mentioned items shipped to Barbados are candles, fish, turpentine, and foodstuffs.[25]

It has been suggested that the late 1720s and early 1730s constituted 'the busiest period of slave importing in the history of Massachusetts', and that slaves supplied from Barbados accounted for most of the trade.[26] This remarkable episode in Boston's maritime history represents a departure from the pattern of trade described by Hall Jr during the years 1717 to 1720, when Virginia and Barbados itself formed the primary markets for slaves handled by the partners. Hugh's correspondence does note, however, that Boston's merchants had begun to settle their accounts with London correspondents by remitting sugar and bills of exchange from Barbados, rather than by direct bilateral payments. The advantages of this method of exchange were explained in detail to the London merchant Philip Nisbett:

Atho it's Circular & by Consequence you are kept longer out of Your Effects, yet I think it has as much more Plausible Aspect of Proffit, considering the Trifling Amount of a New-England Cargo, & ye Low Rate the Bills of Credit there have sunk to: & since they are falling to a greater Ebb, & Bills of Exchange prodigiously Advancing I fear it will be in a little time as Chimerical a Trade as that of Carolina.

Around the same time, Hall Jr also commented that New England had become a mart for the disposal of surplus manufactured goods imported into the island, including German and Dutch linens.[27]

Slave imports into Boston between the late 1720s and early 1730s coincided with a fall in their price that helped render involuntary servitude more affordable to Massachusetts purchasers.[28] However, Hall Jr's correspondence suggests that the state of New England's balance

[25] The account book provides details of what Hall calls his 'Directions for Remittances to My Employers' in forty-three cases for the years 1728 and 1729. In these accounts the frequency with which commodities are mentioned is as follows: candles or tallow (26), fish (23), foodstuffs (15: cereals 8 and meat 7), turpentine or oil (13), furniture (6), other items (13).

[26] Desrochers, 'Slave-For-Sale'. Desrochers concludes (on the basis of a survey of newspaper advertisements) that slaves sent from the West Indies outnumbered African importations by about 3.5 to 1 and that '80 per cent of all slaves identified as "West Indian" appeared for sale in the 1725–1739 period'.

[27] Hugh Hall Letterbook, Hall (Barbados) to Nisbett (London), 15 January 1718[19]; Hall to Nisbett, 25 March 1719; Hall to Andrew Fanueil (Boston), 3 April 1719. The Boston account book may confirm this trend, since it lists sale details of 'Garletts' and 'Bagg Hollands' (two species of linen) that in 1733 amounted to £4,173. Hall sold linen to fifty-two customers. The distribution of linen differed greatly from his sales of slaves. Two clients, Edward Bromfield and Hannah Demming, accounted for nearly 48 per cent of total sales. Only nine individuals buying linen also purchased slaves.

[28] Desrochers, 'Slave-For-Sale'. According to data collected by Richardson, the average price of slaves exported from Africa during the decade 1721–30 was about 81 per cent of the average during the seven decades from 1701 until 1770, David Richardson, 'Prices of

of payments was an additional factor in the trade's expansion, particularly the operation of a multilateral clearing system that linked Boston with Barbados and London, generating the means of paying for slaves. If his accounts are representative, the enslaved arriving in New England were obtained primarily from merchants in Bridgetown: a port city similar in size to Boston and one of the largest centres of urban slavery in the Americas.[29] Analysis of the names of the Africans sold by Hall, coupled with the reported ages of slaves advertised for sale in Boston's newspapers, suggest that slaves brought to New England via Barbados were young and recently taken from Africa. Nevertheless, dissemination of practical knowledge regarding the uses to which enslaved labour could be put outside of plantation agriculture may have encouraged a market for slaves to develop in Boston.

'Memorandums for times to be looked over by myself and by my family when I am no more'

In the midst of economic depression, John Winthrop Jr wrote in 1642 that the Massachusetts Puritan community had begun to 'look to the West Indies for a trade', and to Barbados in particular, as a market for their cargoes of fish and lumber. Two years later, Winthrop himself sent a slaving vessel to the colony (via the Cape Verde Islands and Senegambia), while in 1645 his cousin, George Downing, commented that slaves shipped to the island arrived at a flourishing market.[30] In crude economic terms, the trade Winthrop described was probably of greater importance in assisting sugar's growth on Barbados than in providing the Massachusetts Bay colony with an escape from its commercial difficulties.[31] Fortunes generated by the West Indian trade, however, were concentrated into the hands of a relatively small number of individuals; such overseas earnings underpinned the creation of New England's first

---

Slaves in West and West-Central Africa: Toward an Annual Series', *Bulletin of Historical Research*, 43 (1991), appendix.

[29] Pedro Welch, *Slave Society in the City: Bridgetown, Barbados, 1680–1834* (Kingston, Jamaica, 2003), 53.

[30] James E. McWilliams, 'New England's First Depression: Beyond an Export-Led Interpretation', *Journal of Interdisciplinary History*, 33 (2002), 2; Donnan ed., *Documents*, vol. III, 6; Bernard Bailyn, *The New England Merchants in the Seventeenth Century* (Cambridge, MA, 1955), 83–5. Richard Vines (who emigrated to Barbados from New England in 1645) noted the potential purchasing power of planters in 1647: 'provisions for the belly [are] very scarce … men are so intent upon planting sugar that they had rather buy food at very deare rates than produce it by their labour', R. B. Sheridan, *Sugar and Slavery: An Economic History of the British West Indies* (London, 1974), 315.

[31] McWilliams, 'New England's First Depression', 1–20; Barry Higman, 'The Sugar Revolution', *Economic History Review*, 53 (2000), 213–36.

mercantile elite. Regardless of the scale of this sector of the economy, it is clear that relations between the merchants and the Puritan leadership influenced the political and social direction taken by the colony during the second half of the seventeenth century.[32]

Commercial exchange between the northern colonies and the Caribbean is a recurrent theme in the historiography of New England.[33] Exports of provisions and lumber to Barbados grew markedly during the 1660s and from this decade until the end of the century between thirty-five and sixty-five vessels entered Bridgetown annually carrying these products shipped from Boston, Salem, or Newport. The importance of the trade led to the public wharf being renamed 'New England Row' during the early 1670s, and the street in Bridgetown adjacent of the landing place 'New England Street'.[34] The strength of the region's ties with Barbados are revealed by the itineraries of nearly six hundred persons who applied for a ticket to leave the island in 1679. While London was the most popular destination, New England ranked second. Indeed, the number of colonists journeying to the northern colonies was double that of Virginia, triple that of New York, and 2.7 times the total for the Carolinas (Table 2.2). Barbadian wills provide a further indication of the continuing importance of New England connections. The testamentary papers of the islanders do not routinely list kinsfolk or business partners on the mainland; indeed, only 2 per cent of a sample of 542 wills recorded between 1680 and 1725 mention New England directly. Nevertheless, it is significant that the wills replicate almost exactly the geographical distribution of the earlier travellers. These documents contain twice as many references to the northern colonies as to the Middle Colonies or the Chesapeake, and three times as many as the Carolinas: a region whose early settlement is thought to have featured significant Barbadian involvement.[35]

---

[32] Bailyn, *New England Merchants*. See also Phyllis Whitman Hunter, *Purchasing Identity in the Atlantic World: Massachusetts Merchants, 1670–1780* (Ithaca/London, 2001), 14–32.

[33] The distilleries, shipyards, and fisheries spawned by the West Indies trade along the north-east seaboard are investigated by Richard Pares, *Yankees and Creoles: The Trade between North America and the West Indies before the American Revolution* (London, 1956), and Lorenzo J. Greene, *The Negro in Colonial New England, 1620–1776* (New York, 1942).

[34] Martyn J. Bowden, 'The Three Centuries of Bridgetown: An Historical Geography', *JBMHS*, 49 (2003), 38–9.

[35] Joanne McRee Sanders ed., *Barbados Records: Wills and Administrations* (3 vols., Houston, 1979). See also Barbara Ritter Dailey, 'The Early Quaker Mission and Settlement Meetings in Barbados, 1655–1700', *JBMHS*, 39 (1991). For a revisionist account of the role played by Barbadians in the early settlement of Carolina, see P. F. Campbell, 'Barbadians in South Carolina', in *Some Early Barbadian History* (Barbados, 1993).

Table 2.2. *Stated destinations of persons applying for tickets to depart Barbados, 26 February–4 November 1679*

Destination	Number	Percentage
London	152	25.4
Bristol & Liverpool	50	8.4
Total England	*202*	*33.8*
New England	113	18.9
New York	35	5.8
Virginia	61	10.2
Carolinas	40	6.7
Total North America	*249*	*41.6*
Antigua	66	11.0
Jamaica	34	5.7
Other West Indies	28	4.7
Total Caribbean	*128*	*21.4*
Others	20	3.3
All destinations	*599*	*100.1*

Source: John Camden Hotten ed., *The Original Lists of Persons of Quality ... and Others who Went from Great Britain to the American Plantations, 1600–1700* (New York, 1874).

At the beginning of the eighteenth century, Boston and Barbados occupied dominant positions within the British Atlantic as the primary general entrepôts and the leading shipping points for sugar – the most important colonial export. More than one hundred ships carried cargoes of timber and provisions from New England to Bridgetown (seventy from Boston alone) in most years between 1711 and 1720.[36] A number of prominent mercantile families of Boston and Salem were among those moving between Barbados and New England during the later seventeenth or early eighteenth century. In addition to the Hugh Halls, notable examples include Conrad Adams, Gedney Clarke, George Plaxton, Andrew and John Trent, and Dudley Woodbridge.[37] This period marked the zenith of the commercial relationship; subsequently, Philadelphia and

[36] Bowden, 'Three Centuries of Bridgetown', 39.
[37] For details of Clarke and Plaxton, see S. D. Smith, 'Gedney Clarke of Salem and Barbados: Transatlantic Super-merchant', *New England Quarterly*, 76 (2003), 499–51; for Conrad Adams, see I. K. Steele ed., *Atlantic Merchant-Apothecary: Letters of Joseph Cruttenden, 1710–1717* (Toronto, 1977), 6–7, 19–20, 34–5, 48–9, 60–1, 71–2, 76–7, 91–2, 115, 119; for the Trents, see Donnan ed., *Documents*, vol. III, 30; for Woodbridge, MHS, Benjamin Colman Papers, 1641–1763, Dudley Woodbridge (Barbados) to Benjamin Colman (Boston), 10 July 1711.

New York began wresting leadership of the trade from Boston, while shipping links with Virginia and the Carolinas also developed. Although by the 1740s New England's relative share of the provisions trade had declined, the contribution of the region during the period when sugar on Barbados developed most rapidly had been critical. The region's influence also persisted in other areas of the economy. Merchants such as Gedney Clarke, for instance, redeployed their capital and connections and moved away into privateering, victualling, planting, and slaving.

The role of slave-related commerce on the development of Massachusetts and Rhode Island has been debated extensively. While care must be taken to ensure that the importance of the West India trades is not exaggerated, the sector is widely regarded as 'the cornerstone', 'pivot', or 'most vibrant' sector of New England's overseas commerce, and a vital source of foreign exchange earnings.[38] In view of this, the region's subsequent association with the campaign for abolition and the underground northern railroad ought not to obscure the extent to which New England was itself affected by slavery (and slaveholder values) during the eighteenth century.[39]

The impact of slavery on New England has to a considerable degree been treated indirectly. Nearly all attention has been placed upon the provisioning of the plantations, the traffic in sugar, the processing of molasses into rum, and the supply of shipping services such as freight and insurance. By this reckoning, New Englanders were 'the Dutch of England's empire'.[40] Such an approach presents slavery as an exogenous influence on the colony; it portrays North America's merchants as service providers, skilled principally in the art of fetching and carrying. Notice must also be taken, however, of the dynamic role New Englanders played in creating and maintaining the plantation system in the Caribbean.[41]

Contrary to the impression conveyed by Winthrop, the creation of links between the northern colonies and Caribbean was not a sudden development brought about in the early 1640s through dire economic

[38] David Richardson, 'Slavery, Trade, and Economic Growth in New England', in B. L. Solow ed., *Slavery and the Rise of the Atlantic System* (Cambridge, 1991), 250, 256, 263. An important corrective is John J. McCusker, *Rum and the American Revolution: The Rum Trade and the Balance of Payments of the Thirteen Continental Colonies* (2 vols., New York, 1989).

[39] Richardson, 'Slavery, Trade', 262–3; Desrochers, 'Slave-For-Sale', 623–64.

[40] John J. McCusker and Russell R. Menard, *The Economy of British America, 1607–1789* (Chapel Hill, 1985), 91–2, cited in Richardson, 'Slavery, Trade', 237.

[41] An example of the 'acted upon' approach is Winthrop D. Jordan, 'The Influence of the West Indies on the Origins of New England Slavery', *William and Mary Quarterly*, 18 (1961), 243–50.

necessity. The interests and networks of leading promoters of New England made highly probable that such linkages would be formed.[42] Among these individuals, the Vassall family are of particular interest. The brothers Samuel (1586–1667) and William (1593–c. 1655–7) were founder members of the Massachusetts Bay Company in 1629; collectively, the brothers held a stake of 18.3 per cent in this venture. William Vassall resided in New England during the years 1628–30 and 1635–43, whereas Samuel spent most of his career as a London merchant (though he too is thought to have settled in Massachusetts towards the end of his life).[43]

The Vassalls were active in nearly all aspects of English Atlantic colonisation during the first half of the seventeenth century. Samuel Vassall (a London alderman and one of the City's four members of parliament in 1640 and 1641) launched his career as a Levant Company merchant. Yet by the later 1620s he had formed partnerships to supply provisions to Virginia and Barbados, becoming in the process one of the leading London importers of Chesapeake tobacco.[44] In addition to promoting the Massachusetts Bay Company, Samuel worked to secure political and financial support for the settlement of Rhode Island, and was also involved in an abortive effort to colonise South Carolina in 1630. The Vassalls, however, were not the sort to be easily discouraged and the family persisted in their efforts to develop this region. In 1664, brother William's son John (1625–88) formed a Barbados-based consortium and made a second attempt to settle the area around Cape Fear, this time in partnership with his cousin Henry Vassall.[45]

---

[42] Larry Gragg documents upwards of twenty ships plying trade between New England and the English Caribbean islands during the 1630s, 'An Ambiguous Response to the Market: The Early New England–Barbados Trade', *Historical Journal of Massachusetts*, 17 (1989), 177.

[43] BL, Add. MS 62,898, 'Memorandums for times to be looked over by myself (Florentius Vassall) and by my family when I am no more', f. 1a, 1b; Robert Brenner, *Merchants and Revolution: Commercial Change, Political Conflict, and London's Overseas Traders, 1550–1653* (Cambridge, 1993), 417; John C. Appleby, 'Vassall, Samuel (*bap.* 1586, *d.* 1667)', in *ODNB*.

[44] Brenner, *Merchants and Revolution*, 185–90. Samuel Vassall's European trade included commercial intercourse with Spain and this line of business probably provided him with experience of colonial trade since England's Spanish trade was intimately connected with Atlantic exchange.

[45] Charles M. Calder, 'Alderman John Vassall and his Descendants', *NEHGR*, 109 (1955), 91–102; Brenner, *Merchants and Revolution*, 417; Daniel W. Fagg, Jr, 'Sleeping Not with the King's Grant: A Re-reading of Some Proprietary Documents, 1663–1667', *North Carolina Historical Review*, 46 (1969), 171–85; William S. Powell, 'Carolina and the Incomparable Roanoke: Explorations and Attempted Settlements, 1620–1663', *North Carolina Historical Review*, 51 (1974), 1–21.

Slavery formed an integral part of the Vassalls' colonial operations. The DuBois transatlantic slave trade database contains a very large sample of slaving voyages; indeed, it has been suggested that it includes around nine-tenths of all British ventures.[46] Unfortunately, the dataset is far from comprehensive in the details it contains of the ownership of slaving vessels. Only two entries, for example, list Samuel Vassall as an owner and both are dated 1652. It is clear, however, that the Vassalls' involvement in the slave trade was more extensive than this. For example, between 1642 and 1645, and again in 1647, Samuel joined syndicates owning ships trading between the Guinea coast and the Caribbean, supplying Barbados with slaves.[47]

Under the tutelage of Samuel Vassall, family members (and their business associates) exploited commercial opportunities generated during the Civil War and Commonwealth periods.[48] The Irish rebellion of 1641, for example, was followed by participation in the 1642 Additional Sea Venture to Ireland. This parliamentary scheme treated Ireland as a colony, inviting private subscribers to 'pacify' the island in exchange for land grants. Involvement of the Vassall family in Barbadian affairs dates from around 1648, when William is known to have settled on the island.[49] By 1652, Vassall was commissioner of the highways and three years later he was appointed a commissioner for implementing the Navigation Acts. At the time of his death (c. 1655–7), William was owner of a plantation in St Michael, as well as substantial New England property.[50]

---

[46] For a discussion on the database's capabilities, see Philip D. Morgan and David Eltis eds., 'New Perspectives on the Transatlantic Slave Trade', *William and Mary Quarterly*, 58 (2001).

[47] Eltis, Behrendt, Richardson, and Klein eds., *Trans-Atlantic Slave Trade*, #99,023 and #99,024; Brenner, *Merchants and Revolution*, 164, 192; Larry Gragg, *Englishmen Transplanted: The English Colonisation of Barbados, 1627–1660* (Oxford, 2003), 122–3.

[48] For interesting comments on the impetus given by the English Civil War to commerce between North America and Barbados, see Richard B. Sheridan, *The Development of the Plantations to 1750 and An Era of West Indian Prosperity, 1750–1775* (Kingston, Jamaica/ Bridgetown, Barbados, 1970), 18, and P. F. Campbell, 'The Merchants and Traders of Barbados: I', *JBMHS*, 34 (1974), 86.

[49] Surviving recopied deeds indicate that approximately seventy-five English merchants invested in Barbadian plantations during the decade 1640 to 1650, John J. McCusker and Russell R. Menard, 'The Sugar Industry in the Seventeenth Century: A New Perspective on the Barbadian "Sugar Revolution"', in Stuart B. Schwartz ed., *Tropical Babylons: Sugar and the Making of the Atlantic World, 1450–1680* (North Carolina, 2004), 295–6; Gragg, *Englishmen Transplanted*, 132.

[50] Brenner, *Merchants and Revolution*, 401–3, 594–5 (Samuel Vassall in 1643 had been appointed to parliament's commission for plantations, headed by the Earl of Warwick); NA:PRO, PROB11/265, Will of William Vassall; John C. Appleby, 'Vassall, John (d. 1625) [incorporating William Vassall]', in *ODNB*.

The capture of Jamaica from the Spanish in 1655–6 by Common-wealth forces generated a further Caribbean opening for the family. William's son, John Vassall, acquired large tracts of land shortly after the colony had been secured. By the eighteenth century, his descendants ranked among leading planters on Jamaica. Florentius Vassall (1689–1778) owned three plantations during the 1770s; his brother Leonard Vassall (1678–1737) was proprietor of a fourth estate, which he bequeathed to his son William.[51]

Reviewing the Vassalls' involvement in colonial trade, a number of themes can be noted. Firstly, their success was not built on the foun-dations of a long-established English mercantile or landed lineage. Rather, the dynasty was established in England by John Vassall (1544–1625), a Huguenot mariner and refugee from Normandy.[52] Gentry pretensions arose early, however, in the family's English history. John Vassall was granted a coat of arms by Elizabeth I for his role in the defeat of the Armada; by the early eighteenth century, the family were claiming descent from the Plantagenets, no less.[53] Religion is a second binding element in the Vassall story. Huguenot John Vassall fitted out and commanded two ships against the Spanish invasion fleet in 1588. From the late 1620s onwards, the colonising ventures of his sons, Samuel and William, aligned them with John Pym and other Independents.[54] Yet despite their involvement with militant Puritans, the Vassalls were not religious radicals. In New England, William Vassall opposed strict Calvinism and was among the merchants of the colony to petition for a widening of church membership and the civil franchise during the early 1640s.[55] Successive generations of Vassalls, however, retained a

---

[51] BL, Add. MS 62,898, f. 5b–6a; JA, Inventories, IB/11/18/26, Administration of Florentius Vassall, 17 April 1779; *William Vassall Letter Books, 1769–1800* (Wakefield, 1963), introd. by Walter E. Minchinton. Florentius Vassall's 'Memorandums' state that John Vassall moved his family to Jamaica after the ceding of Surinam (where it is claimed he also owned land) to the Dutch in 1667. This is supported by the IGI which records John Vassall's marriage to Anna Lewis in 1670 (though it should be noted that this information is based on family pedigree material submitted by a member of the Church of Jesus Christ of Latter-day Saints and is not an extracted entry from a parish register). Notice can also be made of the inventoried wealth of Lewis Vassall and John Vassall of St Elizabeth's Parish, amounting to £20,560 and £21,630 currency respectively, Jamaica Archives, Inventories, IB/11/3/60 (1778) and IB/11/3/61 (1780).

[52] It is also worth noting that Samuel Vassall, prior to his departure for New England, purchased property in Yorkshire at Bedale and that Florentius Vassall also chose to move his family from Jamaica to Huby in Yorkshire during the 1730s, BL, Add. MS 62,898, f. 2a–2b.

[53] Ibid. f. 8.   [54] Brenner, *Merchants and Revolution*, 242–6.

[55] Bailyn, *New England Merchants*, 107.

commitment to Protestant orthodoxy and later supported the Anglican establishment in Boston.

Leonard Vassall of Jamaica granted land for the construction of Boston's Trinity Church in 1730. His son William (1715–1800) studied at Harvard, where he graduated in 1733 and received an MA in 1743.[56] William's brother Florentius later arranged for a marble memorial from London to be erected in the King's Chapel in Boston, commemorating Samuel Vassall's stance against Charles I's extra-parliamentary taxation, and also the action of John Vassall in fighting the Armada.[57] The timing of this gesture, executed during the Stamp Act controversy, is significant. Once war broke out in 1776, however, the Vassalls elected to remain loyal to Britain, whatever sympathies they may earlier have harboured for colonial grievances. The family's private business affairs were too closely aligned with the apparatus of colonial administration and regulation for detachment to be a feasible option. Because of his Loyalist stance, William Vassall was forced to return to England in 1775; subsequently, he suffered confiscation of his American property.[58]

Other New England merchants followed the paths taken by the Vassalls by moving beyond the shipping and provision trades and repositioning themselves as plantation owners and slave traders. A noted example is Gedney Clarke (1711–64) of Salem and Barbados. Clarke's personal details replicate many aspects of the Vassall blueprint for success. These include non-establishment origins and provincial connections; gentry pretensions and aristocratic marriage alliances; an allegiance to orthodox Protestantism and the Anglican establishment (including New England churches); a willingness to finance and prosecute private military action when opportunities dictated; and the combination of public office with private business interests. Like the Vassalls, successive generations of Clarkes displayed a capacity for mobility within the Atlantic world in response to favourable business opportunities. Underscoring all of these activities was an investment in plantations and participation in the slave trade. The networks of the Clarkes and Vassalls intersected at several points. Florentius Vassall was a correspondent of Henry Lascelles, Clarke's principal business partner,

---

[56] Bettina Norton ed., *Trinity Church: The Story of an Episcopal Parish in the City of Boston* (Boston, 1978); *William Vassall Letter Books*. In the same year Leonard Vassall also gave a silver paten (communion plate) to Boston's Old North Church.

[57] This extraordinary monument features a bust of Samuel Vassall (executed by W. Tyler of London) above a ship medallion, and a collection of books and manuscripts including Magna Carta, the memoirs of John Thurloe (Cromwell's Secretary of State), and Civil War chronicler John Rushworth's *Historical Collections*.

[58] BL, Add. MS 62,898, f. 4a–4b; *William Vassall Letter Books*.

during the 1740s.[59] Henry's sister, Elizabeth Lascelles, in 1741 married into the Batson family of Wiltshire: another family of West India merchants who were business partners of Samuel Vassall and his closest associate Maurice Thomson. The Batson's estate was subsequently inherited by the nephew and heir of George Maxwell (Henry Lascelles' co-partner in his London commission house).[60]

'Ye shaking of a Tree in the Orchard'

In 1686, Hugh Hall the elder added his name to those of sixty-eight other Barbadian Quakers at the foot of a testimonial written on behalf of Roger Longworth, an itinerant minister about to depart for Philadelphia after spending three months on the island.[61] The elder Hall was a prosperous merchant of Bridgetown; he owned property on Cheapside and Palmetto Street – thoroughfares where the richest merchants congregated. In addition to his Barbadian property, Hall possessed land tracts in Pennsylvania, purchased from John Edmondson, an immensely wealthy Quaker, who owned 67,000 acres in Maryland and Delaware.[62]

Quakerism was still a new religious movement when missionaries Ann Austin and Mary Fisher arrived on Barbados in 1655.[63] Initially, responses to the Quakers appear to have been relatively mild, owing to Governor Daniel Searle's promotion of religious toleration. Within a short time, however, the Friends had become targets for persecution, in part because of Quakerism's confrontational style at this stage of its

[59] *LMLB*, Pares Transcripts, H595, Lascelles and Maxwell to F[lorentius] Vassall, 8 September 1744; National Library of Jamaica, Kingston, MS 1,142, indenture between Daniel Lascelles, George Maxwell, Florentius Vassall, and others, 24 July 1760.

[60] Brenner, *Merchants and Revolution*, 135–6, 160, 162–3; NA:PRO, PROB11/324, Will of Richard Batson, 1667; PROB11/329, Will of Henry Batson, 1669; S. D. Smith, 'Introduction to the Records of Lascelles and Maxwell', in *LMLB*, 24; Bodleian Library, Oxford, MS Eng. hist. b. 122, exports of Henry Batson and Thomas Batson from Barbados, 1664.

[61] HSP, Etting Papers, vol. XXXVII, 73, Certificate Respecting Roger Longworth, 1687.

[62] BA, RB3/20/230–1; RB3/21/345–6; St Michael's Levy Books, vol. I (1686–1712), ff.1, 15, 47, 121. The rateable value of Hall's Cheapside property (where he also resided) as a per centage of the street average was 97.5% in 1686, 156.5% in 1690, and 98.7% in 1695. Hall's Pennsylvania lands consisted of two plots at Duck Creek: a parcel of 1,200 acres called Greenfield and a parcel of 1,000 acres called Wappin. Edmondson was one of the greatest landowners in North America, with holdings of 40,000 acres in Maryland and 27,000 acres in Delaware. To raise funds, however, he mortgaged the Duck Creek tracts to Hall in 1688–9. The Hall family took possession of the properties after Edmondson's executors sold land to pay legacies specified in Edmondson's will, BA, RB6/1/1–4; HSP, Logan Papers, vol. XVII, 1; Frank B. Edmundson and Robert E. Emerson, 'John Edmundson: Large Merchant of Tred Haven Creek', *Maryland Historical Magazine*, 50 (1955), 223, 229.

[63] Barbara Ritter Dailey, 'The Early Quaker Mission and Settlement Meetings in Barbados, 1655–1700', *JBMHS*, 39 (1991), 24; Gragg, *Englishmen Transplanted*, 75.

history. Opposition intensified during the 1660s and 1670s as the Quaker commitment to pacifism increasingly conflicted with concerns for the island's security.[64] The number of able-bodied whites available to serve in the Barbadian militia dwindled at the same time as the majority black population increased; in consequence, the Friends' refusal to bear arms threatened the social order.[65]

George Fox addressed West Indian slave owners on the subject of slavery in a tract published in 1657, which argued that all races possessed the right to hear the good news of Christ's salvation. The message of equality of opportunity and humane treatment of slaves was reinforced between 1671 and 1677 by Richard Baxter, Alice Curwen, William Edmundsen, and Fox himself.[66] Quaker opposition to the institution of slavery, however, was not yet as ideologically rooted as it was to become during the later eighteenth century.[67] The community of Barbados Friends included such substantial plantation owners as the Rous family, while John Grove ranked among the island's most prominent slave importers. Military command and a willingness to bear arms, however, were prerequisites of slave trading and plantation ownership. On Barbados, the owners of large sugar estates usually held the title of major: a reflection of their role as militia organisers. Slaving vessels similarly carried weapons as a matter of course and liaison with naval commanders occurred frequently.[68] In England, the adoption of the 'Peace Testimony' of 1659 assisted Quakers in countering accusations of subversion. On Barbados, however, it became problematic to practise pacifism in a society where the population of enslaved blacks outnumbered white enslavers.[69] After the discovery of a planned slave rebellion, the Barbados Assembly

---

[64] Gragg, *Englishmen Transplanted*, 163.

[65] Ibid., 77; Gary Puckrein, *Little England: Plantation Society and Anglo-Barbadian Politics, 1627–1700* (New York, 1984), 98.

[66] Herbert Aptheker, 'The Quakers and Negro Slavery', *The Journal of Negro History*, 25 (1940), 333, 341; Larry Gragg, 'The Pious and the Profane: The Religious Life of Early Barbados Planters', *The Historian*, 62 (2000), 4; Richard Baxter, *A Christian Directory; or, A Summ of Practical Theologie and Cases of Conscience* (London, 1673), 558; Moira Ferguson, 'Seventeenth-Century Quaker Women: Displacement, Colonialism, and Anti-Slavery Discourse', in Gerald M. MacLeon ed., *Culture and Society in the Stuart Restoration* (Cambridge, 1995), 228–9.

[67] For example, Quaker John Farmer's plea for Barbadian and Maryland masters to free their slaves (made during a visit to the Americas between 1711 and 1712) was denounced by sections of the Society of Friends, Aptheker, 'Quakers and Negro Slavery', 340.

[68] Smith, 'Gedney Clarke', 516–21.

[69] By 1680, African slaves comprised c. 95 per cent of the island's labour force and outnumbered whites by a ratio of two to one, Richard S. Dunn, 'The Barbados Census of 1680: Profile of the Richest Colony in English America', *William and Mary Quarterly*, 26 (1969), 8.

passed an Act for the Settlement of the Militia in 1675. The new legislation required all freemen to appear in arms at specified times and obliged landowners to supply horses and foot soldiers. Quakers failing to comply with these provisions faced increased persecution.[70]

By the time of the 1680 census, at least six Quaker congregations were meeting on the island; approximately 1,000 colonists (out of a total white population of 20,000) were Friends. From the later seventeenth century onwards, however, Quakerism declined on Barbados and in other colonies of the Lesser Antilles.[71] The Barbadian community of Friends diminished in size because it proved unable to recruit enough new members to replace those succumbing to disease or electing to emigrate to other colonial regions, particularly Pennsylvania. Falling numbers accompanied a restructuring of Barbados' external trade, resulting in a contraction in the number of agents and small-scale shopkeepers. The island's middlemen were undermined partly by the rise of commission trading: a system enabling planters to establish direct correspondences with merchants in London and the English outports.[72]

---

[70] In 1669, 29 Friends were fined a total of 111,125 lb of sugar, whereas 80 Friends were fined 209,496 lb in 1674, 110 Friends fined 358,601 lb in 1685, and 90 Friends paid 494,435 lb in fines in 1689, Joseph Besse, *A Collection of the Sufferings of the People Call'd Quakers* (2 vols., London, 1753), vol. II, 287, 290, 318. The militia issue flared up again after 1693 and also in 1702–3 when enforcement of the 1675 Act was prosecuted more vigorously after a period of relative laxity, Harriet F. Durham, *Caribbean Quakers* (Florida, 1972), 31; Library of the Society of Friends, Minutes of the London Yearly Meeting, vol. II, epistles received from Barbados, ff. 74–5; Dailey, 'Early Quaker Mission', 31. Despite the levying of fines and periodic attempts by unsympathetic governors to suppress Quaker meetings (e.g. Governor Sir Richard Dutton's objection to the Bridgetown meeting in 1682), there is evidence that had it not been for the militia question Friends would have been tolerated on the island. In July 1703, for example, at the same time as fines for non-participation in the militia were extracted, the Council passed an Act permitting Friends to affirm rather than swear oaths in response to a petition from Quaker representatives, Larry Gragg, 'A Heavenly Visitation', *History Today* (February 2002), 46–51; John Rylands University Library, Manchester, Eng. MS 900, Minutes of the Barbados Council, 1703–4, ff. 49b–50a, 92b–93a.

[71] The estimate of c. 1,000 Friends on Barbados is based on an analysis of the 1679–80 census and listings of Friends (in Besse, *Collection of the Sufferings*; LBMH, Quaker Files; and Henry J. Cadbury, 'Barbados Quakers 1683 to 1701' and '186 Barbados Quakeresses in 1677', *JBMHS*, 9 (1941–2). The 1707 Quarterly Meeting noted that 'as to our present condition we are a remnant left as a few after ye shaking of a Tree in the Orchard'. By 1717, only two of the six monthly meetings on the island still existed; by 1764 the congregation of the Bridgetown meeting was reduced to half a dozen or fewer; by 1785 John Cresson (sent over from London to survey what remained of Quaker property on Barbados) noted that 'things in this island [are] at a very low ebb', Durham, *Caribbean Quakers*, 31. See also George Vaux, 'The Decline of Friends in Barbados', *The Friend*, 71 (1898), 265–5, 75 (1902), 245–6, 79 (1906), 205–6.

[72] Welsh, *Slave Society*, 119–26; K. G. Davies, 'The Origins of the Commission System in the West India Trade', *Transactions of the Royal Historical Society*, 5th series, 2 (1952), 89–107.

In consequence, it became increasingly difficult to turn a profit as a merchant on the island outside of participation in plantation slavery and the slave trade.

The experience of the Halls illustrates the contradictions that slavery increasingly posed to Quakers seeking to reconcile acceptance of enslavement itself with opposition to violence and commitment to a universal Christian mission. As one of Bridgetown's leading merchants, Hugh Hall the elder was expected to form part of the Governor's life guard. His refusal to participate resulted in the imposition of a fine in 1689. Hall's stance combined opposition to the established Church (the life guard accompanied the Governor to St Michael's Cathedral each Sunday) with the pacifist objection to bearing arms.[73] Hall's trade consisted of handling sugar exports and selling return cargoes of provisions and manufactures from a shop that defiantly opened on the Sabbath. In this way, Hall avoided plantation ownership, thereby evading additional militia commitments.[74] He was not able, however, to distance himself from slavery entirely. The 1680 census records eight slaves living in Hall's household (double the average for Bridgetown); in his will of 1698, Hugh bequeathed a total of eighteen enslaved men and women to his children.[75] Moreover, the Quaker merchant John Grove was the master of Hall's son Joseph. Grove was one of Barbados' largest slave importers, handling 1,362 enslaved Africans during the years 1700 and 1704 alone.[76]

---

[73] The collections of the Barbados Museum of History include an unsigned and undated (but probably early eighteenth-century) canvas depicting the governor's procession to church. Hall was also fined in 1674 (2,340 lb of sugar) for refusing to bear arms and in 1678 (1,562 lb) for the same offence and for trading on holy days. In 1689, he was one of four Friends who petitioned the Lieutenant Governor for relief, but Hall was fined a further £12.10s. between 1690 and 1693, Besse, *Collection of the Sufferings*, vol. II, 288, 316, 339, 342.

[74] In 1686, for example, Hall obtained 4 acres of land from a debtor named John Harper in St Andrew's Parish by marshal's sale, but immediately transferred the property to a third party, BA, RB3/16/43–5 (1686).

[75] David L. Kent, *Barbados and America* (Arlington, 1980); BA, RB6/1/1–4. The will does not contain any explicit manumission clauses, though two house slaves named Betty and Nanney were each given 7s.6d. over and above what Hall called 'their usual allowance', as an acknowledgement and reward for 'their honesty and care of my children'.

[76] Donnan ed., *Documents*, vol. II, 27. John Grove transacted business with his brothers Silvanus and Joseph Grove of London, MCD, 27 March 1703[4] and 3 March 1707[8]. George Fox visited Barbados in 1671 and preached inclusive worship between slaves and masters and a form of benevolent paternalism but not a message of outright opposition to slavery. The prospect of slaves moving around the island to attend Quaker meetings was viewed negatively by Barbados' authorities and in 1676 the Assembly

Despite suffering a number of financial penalties on account of his religious convictions, Hall the elder remained a committed Friend to the end and was buried 'according to the Planne and manner of the People of God called Quakers'.[77] In contrast, his son, Hugh Hall Sr, swiftly detached himself from Quakerism. By the time of Hall Sr's second marriage to Mary Buckworth (in 1705), all links with the community of Friends had been severed. Hugh Sr's new bride was an heiress of a gentry family of Barbados and London with establishment connections.[78] After Mary's death in 1711, Hugh sent a trunk to his son and namesake at Harvard, containing her 'Furbelowed Gold gauze scarf, one silk Handkerchief with gold edging and one black flowered Gauze hood'. These garments, he noted, were merely 'trifles with short ordinary wear': the bulk of her wardrobe being 'richer than are commonly worn'. While such fashionable attire was frowned on by Barbados' Quakers, it had been acceptable to the congregation of St Michael's. Hall hoped the clothing might now find a ready sale in Boston.[79]

Following his reversion to Anglicanism, Hugh Sr worked his way up the scale of parish administration. After baptising a son (Charles) in St Michael's in 1706, he was selected as a member of the parish vestry in 1708, junior church warden in 1709, and senior church warden in 1711.

---

prohibited interracial worship by Friends in order to counter a situation 'whereby the Safety of this Island may be much hazarded', Dailey, 'Early Quaker Mission', 11–19; Gragg, 'Heavenly Visitation', 46–51; William Frost, 'George Fox's Ambiguous Anti-Slavery Legacy', in Michael Mullet ed., *New Light on George Fox* (York, 1991).

[77] BA, RB6/1/1–4, Will of Hugh Hall, entered 24 November 1698.

[78] Hall's first marriage was to Lydia Gibbs (daughter of Benjamin Gibbs), who was born in Boston 1669/70 and died in Philadelphia in 1699. It is not clear if Lydia Gibbs was a Quaker. She was descended from the Gibbs and Scottow families of Boston who were members of the Puritan establishment (her maternal grandfather Joshua Scottow, author of *A Narrative of the Plantation of the Massachusetts Colony*, circulated at least one anti-Quaker tract). Hugh Hall Jr notes his grandmother was born Lydia Gibbs (1645–1727) and that his mother Lydia Hall, though she emigrated to Philadelphia, was buried 'at the church Door', IGI; James Savage, *A Genealogical Dictionary of the First Settlers of New England* ... (4 vols., Boston, 1860–2), vol. IV; New York Public Library, NYPW03-A201, Weather Almanac of Hugh Hall Jr, 1714–17. The head of the Buckworth family was Sir John Buckworth of West Sheen in Richmond. Buckworth's offices included deputy governorship of the Royal African Company, 1672–3, and he was also a commissioner of the Royal Mint, 1680–4. At the time of the marriage in 1705, Mary's father Charles Buckworth contributed a marriage portion of £1,000. Yet by his death (in 1715), Charles Buckworth was indebted to Hugh Hall, BA, RB6/35/367, Will of Charles Buckworth.

[79] LBMH, Family Files: Hall, Hall to Hugh Hall Jr, 28 May 1712. In 1699, the epistle sent from Barbados Friends to the London yearly meeting complained of 'freinds Children yt were modestly adorned, by the Example they had at London, are grown too high and Extravagant in their apparrell', Library of the Society of Friends, Minutes of the London Yearly Meeting, vol. II, 345. See also Richard S. Dunn, *Sugar and Slaves: The Rise of the Planter Class in the English West Indies, 1624–1713* (Chapel Hill, 1972), 103–4.

Hall's responsibilities included collecting and administering the local taxes levied on property within Bridgetown. He also played an active part in beautifying the cathedral, taking the lead among vestrymen responsible for installing a new clock, a set of bells, and a copper figure of St Michael. Reintegration into the established Church was confirmed by his enlargement of the gallery in 1710 to create a family pew. Thus Hugh Hall Sr took his place alongside leading families of the island, looking down on the assembled congregation.[80]

Commercially, Hugh Sr continued his father's trade as a Bridgetown merchant, but the range of his business interests was extended. During the 1720s, he acquired additional warehouses and property in the town; at the same time, he affirmed his readmission to Barbados' governing elite by acquiring plantations and slaves.[81] His third marriage (in 1722), to the Barbadian heiress Anne Swan, enabled him to gain control of a 90-acre plantation with twenty-nine slaves in St Andrew's Parish that had been the property of his new wife's father.[82] A tax levy of 1729 assessed Hall at the rate of the daily labour of six slaves, indicating ownership of 60 acres of land within the parish of St Michael alone. Further land was acquired in Christ Church sometime during the 1720s. As Hugh Sr increased his stake as a property holder, he made further progress up the ladder of preferment. In 1719, he became judge of the Barbados Admiralty Court. Material success at last won over the recalcitrant Edward Lascelles. Guided by his wife Mary, Lascelles worked the appointments system in favour of his kinsman and in 1732 Hall Sr was nominated one of the colony's twelve members of Council.[83] By the time the royal mandamus arrived elevating him to the Council, however, Hall Sr was in the last stages of a fatal illness.[84]

---

[80] LBMH, Family Files: Hall; Goddard ed., *George Washington's Visit*, 48–9. Other leading merchants of Bridgetown occupied family pews in the gallery of St Michael's Cathedral; see Smith, 'Gedney Clarke', 530.

[81] BA, RB3/28/196–7 (1720) 312 sq. ft land in Bridgetown (but resold immediately); RB3/30/364–5 (1720) 1,000 sq. ft land in Bridgetown; RB3/32/286–7 (1722) house and 2,246 sq. ft of land in Bridgetown; RB3/36/518–21 (1727) storehouse and 379 sq. ft land in Bridgetown.

[82] In 1730, 45 acres and twelve slaves were added to this estate.

[83] According to the Revd William Gordon, the admiralty commission was held up by Governor Robert Lowther, who attempted to install another candidate in Hall's place, [Anon.], *The Barbados Packet* (London, 1733), 52.

[84] BA, RB3/31/143–4 (1722), 31/145–51 (1722), 34/555–6 (1730), 34/557–63 (1730); St Michael's Levy Books, vol. III (1722–9), 150; Hughes-Queree Collection, Names, File 3 (N–Y), Swan; Hugh Hall Letterbook, Hall to Hugh Hall Sr (Barbados), 25 September 1717; Hall to Lydia Colman (Boston), 10 July 1719; Hall to William Allen (London), 23 July 1719; Goddard, *George Washington's Visit*, 49. Hall also owned land in Christ Church Parish, where he purchased 10 acres in 1722, BA, RB3/32/100 (1722), 32/102 (1722).

By the early eighteenth century, three generations of Halls had lived on Barbados. From their island base, the family formed connections with the North American mainland. Hall Sr owned land in Virginia and Maryland, along with business interests in Boston.[85] Yet despite their longstanding colonial presence, the family maintained gentry pretensions arising out of their English ancestry. Hugh Hall Jr's armorial, three Talbot heads erased between eight or nine crosses, is identical to Gyles Hall's (c. 1603–87) of St Peter's Parish. The common source for the arms appears to be the English Halls of High Meadow, Gloucester.[86]

Although the precise nature of the connections between the Halls is unclear, Gyles Hall's career is worthy of comment in its own right. Gyles was established on Barbados by 1656 and during the following six years he bought up $58\frac{1}{2}$ acres in St Peter's Parish; by the 1679–80 census, his estate had grown to a substantial 195 acres.[87] From 1663, Gyles was a member of a Barbadian syndicate seeking to develop the Carolinas; in 1671 he duly received lot twelve of the Charleston plots granted by Lord Shaftesbury.[88] His business strategy in the Americas shares common ground with the Vassalls' own plans for advancement. Gyles joined the syndicate headed by William and Henry Vassall to develop the Carolinas

[85] MHS, Hugh Hall Papers, Mary Hall (Stoke Newington) to Hugh Hall (Boston), 25 August 1731; Richard Hall (Barbados) to Hugh Hall (Boston), 25 August 1731; Richard Hall (Barbados) to Hugh Hall (Boston), 4 September 1733.

[86] Vere Langford Oliver, *The Monumental Inscriptions in the Churches and Churchyards of the Island of Barbados, British West Indies* (London, 1915), 153, no. 1,054; LBMH, Major Henry Albert Thorne, 'Monumental Inscriptions of Barbados', 46; Morison, 'Letter-Book of Hugh Hall', between pp. 514 and 515; BA, RB6/17/562–4, Will of Hugh Benjamin Hall, 1766, 'In witness whereof I have hereunto set my Hand and the arms of the family'. Gyles Hall was born in Whitminster, Gloucestershire, and the coat of arms is recorded in the 1623 herald's visitation of the county, LBMH, Family Files: Hall. Prosopography suggests that of fifty-eight leading London merchants engaged in colonial trade in 1686, one-half were born in the provinces and one-sixth originated from abroad; only one-third were members of established London families (qualification: export of more than £1,000 of merchandise or imports of more than £5,000), Nuala Zahedieh 'Making Mercantilism Work: London Merchants and Atlantic Trade in the Seventeenth Century', *Transactions of the Royal Historical Society*, 9 (1999), 148. Zahedieh emphasises Quakerism and Jewish mercantile networks at the expense of Anglicanism. In the case of Barbados, however, Quaker members declined from the highpoint reached c. 1686, while the direct participation of the Jews in slave-related business on both sides of the Atlantic appears to have been more limited than this dataset implies, Eli Faber, *Jews, Slaves, and the Slave Trade: Setting the Record Straight* (New York, 1998), 11–56.

[87] BA, RB3/5/131 (1656), 5/384–5 (1659), 5/851–2 (1660), 3/304–5 (1661), 15/154–7 (1688); Kent, *Barbados and America*.

[88] Agnes Leland Baldwin, *First Settlers of Carolina, 1670–80* (South Carolina, 1969); 'Proposals of Several Gentlemen of Barbados' dated 12 August 1663, reprinted in *Collections of the South Carolina Historical Society* (5 vols., South Carolina, 1857–97), vol. V, 10–12. Gyles Hall Jr departed for Boston on 31 July 1679, possibly to improve his education, Hotten ed., *Original Lists*, 377.

and shared their commitment to Anglicanism, becoming a member of St Peter's Parish vestry. After their deaths, Gyles and his wife Maudlin were buried within All Saints in a tomb decorated with the family coat of arms. A set of silver salvers, engraved with both the couples' names and their trademark gentry armorial, were also bequeathed to the church.[89]

'Men of bright Characters and good figure'

After Hugh Hall Jr answered his father's summons in 1716 and returned to Barbados, he was initially impressed with the quality of the society he found on the island.[90] 'I was by my Father introduced an Acquaintance not only with men of ye highest Distinction', he informed the Revd Elisha Calendar, 'but of ye best Character'. Individuals could be found on Barbados, he maintained, who were 'not only of Strict Morality, but of true Devotion'. A rebuff was offered to those 'who think that here a Christian & a Gentleman are Inconsistent Appellations in ye same Person'. Those holding negative opinions of the island were simply 'out in their Augury'. Far from being 'a Mighty Colossus of Vice', Barbados was portrayed as a place where even 'great Professors in Religion may find many Worthy of their Imitation & Converse'.[91]

During his subsequent visit to London, Hugh Hall Jr's ears burned with indignation as he encountered prejudice inveighed against Barbados' business community. Ill-informed criticism was voiced by persons whose status Hugh considered grossly inferior to that of Barbadians themselves. On the Royal Exchange, he complained of 'Petty Traders' who freely impugned the characters of reputable merchants whose shoes they were no more worthy to wipe 'than ye meanest Subject the Pope has to Kiss his Toes'. And while Hall Jr gratefully acknowledged Harvard President John Leverett's introductions to members of the Royal Society (intended as a consolation to his former pupil), he gained access to 'men of bright Characters and good figure' in London through the recommendations of Barbados' own social elite.[92]

[89] Thorne, 'Monumental Inscriptions', 46; BA, RB6/43/238, Will of Maudlin Hall, 1700; LBMH, Eustace Shilstone Notebooks, vol. XIV, 18.

[90] During the years from 1714 through 1717, Hall Jr maintained a daily almanac of weather observations in Barbados and Boston. An interesting feature of the document is the author's use of symbols and abbreviations to introduce consistency into the daily record, subordinating personal responses to the physical environment, Hugh Hall Diary (Almanac).

[91] Hugh Hall Letterbook, Hall to Calender (Boston), 26 February 1717[17].

[92] Ibid. Hall to Parsons, 26 November 1716; Hall to John Leverett, 26 February 1716[17]; Hall to J. Horagan (Sierra Leone), 16 July 1717; Hall to Samuel Betteress & Co. (London), 2 September 1718; Hall to Leverett, 2 August 1717. Hall's self-pronouncements of virtue and gentility are a feature of his letters. It is also noteworthy that outside of his staple

Historians are reassessing the reputation of Barbados during the seventeenth and early eighteenth centuries. Contemporary pamphleteers, including a number of Quakers, portrayed the colony as an irreligious society, inhabited by thrusting, avaricious planters and dishonest tradesmen who were always late with their remittances. Profanity, drunken excess, sexual licentiousness, and cruelty towards the enslaved were among the literary devices employed to depict Barbadians during the middle of the seventeenth century.[93] Among other failings, the island's whites were accused of adopting the linguistic conventions and mannerisms of African slaves, rendering them the natural subjects of parody and ridicule. Religious groups, particularly Quaker missionaries, seized upon these traits in order to emphasise the godlessness of Barbados society.[94] Despite a more positive portrayal of the colony's achievements during the later decades of the seventeenth century, in the works of Dalby Thomas and John Oldmixon among others, criticism was far from silenced – as Hall implies.[95] For example, the letters of Thomas Walduck to his London correspondent James Petiver (written just a few years prior to Hugh Hall Jr's arrival at Bridgetown) similarly contain a collection of negative images and stereotypes. Walduck alleged that natural succession had been corrupted by the decay of primogeniture and the mortgaging of estates to the hilt. According to Walduck, the few legitimate heirs who succeeded in retaining possession of property did so only by cheating his siblings of their rightful inheritance. Walduck's Barbados was overrun with greedy widows, dishonest estate managers, and crooked merchants, all of whom he portrayed as dismantling core elements that bound society together.[96]

Yet the social fabric of Barbados was far more robust than many contemporary commentators allowed. Studies, by Campbell, Greene, and Gragg, have argued that the cultural identity created by white colonists on

business interests, Hall dealt in books and watches, offering an extensive Barbados library for sale to a Boston correspondent, Hall to Samuel Gerrish (Boston), 26 August 1719. John Leverett had been elected a Fellow of the Royal Society in March 1713[14], Raymond Phineas Stearns, *Science in the British Colonies of America* (Chicago, 1970), 710.

[93] Jack P. Greene, 'Changing Identity in the British Caribbean: Barbados as a Case Study', in Nicholas Canny and Anthony Pagden eds., *Colonial Identity in the Atlantic World, 1500–1800* (Princeton, 1987), 225–6.

[94] Gragg, *Englishmen Transplanted*, 8, 188–9. Examples of critical pamphlets are John Rous, *A Warning to the Inhabitants of Barbados* (London, 1656) and Richard Pinder, *A Loving Invitation (to Repentance and Amendment to Life) Unto All the Inhabitants of the Island of Barbados* (London, 1660).

[95] Greene, 'Changing Identity in the British Caribbean', 226–30, 234–6.

[96] BL, Sloane MS 2,302, Letters of Thomas Walduck (Barbados) to James Petiver (London), 1710–12, letter dated 12 November 1710. For discussion of this source, see Stearns, *Science in the British Colonies*, 351–6. See also Greene, 'Changing Identity in the British Caribbean', 236–47 for additional examples.

the island compared well with other regions of the Americas. Far from meriting the title of a godless isle, a strong Anglican Church was established early on Barbados, while Anglicanism responded strongly to the challenge posed by Quakerism and other forms of sectarianism.[97] Indeed, criticism of religious practice on Barbados can be interpreted as expressions of frustration at the strength of the emerging Anglican oligarchy and the level of control the wealthiest planters exerted over the island's parish vestries.[98] Allegations of irreligion, for example, accompanied Quaker persecution during the 1660s and 1670s, and the obstruction of the missionary work among slaves of the Society for the Propagation of the Gospel (SPG) during the early eighteenth century.[99]

As for the remittance problems complained of by London merchants encountered by Hall Jr, these appear less a symptom of Barbadian dishonesty than a short-term phenomenon, generated partly by the dislocations of the War of the Spanish Succession (1702–13). Payment difficulties partly reflected the restructuring of trading relations between England and the colony, resulting in the exodus of smaller-scale island merchants and growth in commission trading.[100] Fundamentally, the island of Barbados was an affluent society with per capita income probably between one-third and two-thirds higher than in England. In terms of wealth and creditworthiness, the owners of Barbadian plantations had few rivals.[101]

Hugh Hall Jr's letters describe a colonial society that was populated by individuals of high intellectual distinction. In 1731, Samuel Keimer (Benjamin Franklin's former business associate in Philadelphia) succeeded in establishing the *Barbados Gazette* in the colony. One of the earliest editions of the newspaper announced the arrival of 'an ingenious Person' who publicised a course on anatomy in Bridgetown; the editor commented, 'tis said, that some of the most Learned of our Gentry will

[97] Jack P. Greene, 'Society and Economy in the British Caribbean during the Seventeenth and Eighteenth Centuries', *American Historical Review*, 79 (1974), 1,499–517; Gragg, *Englishmen Transplanted*, 8–9, 84–6; P.F. Campbell, *The Church in Barbados in the Seventeenth Century* (Barbados, 1987), 71–80, 85, 95–7, 111–17; Philip Morgan, *The Early Caribbean, ca. 1500 to 1800* (Providence, RI, 2003), 172.

[98] Keith D. Hunte, 'Church and Society in Barbados in the Eighteenth Century', paper presented to the 15th ACH conference, Puerto Rico 1974, cited in Stephen J. Hornsby, *British Atlantic, American Frontier: Spaces of Power in Early Modern British America* (Hanover/London, 2005), 61.

[99] John A. Schutz and Maud O'Neil, 'Arthur Holt, Reports on Barbados, 1725-33', *Journal of Negro History*, 31 (1946), Arthur Holt (Barbados) to the Bishop of London (Edmund Gibson), 30 April 1725, 448, 3 April 1732, 466–7. See also Chapter Four.

[100] David Hancock ed., *The Letters of William Freeman, London Merchant, 1678–1685* (London Record Society: London, 2002).

[101] Dunn, 'Barbados Census of 1680', 3–30; David Eltis, *The Rise of African Slavery in the Americas* (Cambridge, 2000), 211–12.

subscribe thereto'.[102] The potential audience for the anatomy lectures included Dr James Brown, a physician, with degrees from Edinburgh and Rheims, who had been on two European tours and for a time worked as a doctor for the Turkey Company in Constantinople. Another possible subscriber was William Rawlin, elder statesman of the island, compiler of an edition of the island's legal code, and the host of music concerts at his plantation house. There was also a slave trader, Captain John Gordon, who regularly composed 'smart Pieces' for Keimer on his return from the Guinea coast. Planter Christopher Moe similarly published details of experiments in new techniques of rum distilling in the *Gazette*, while Griffin Hughes' study of the island's natural history is revealing of slave owners' interests in botany and the cultivation of rare plant species on the island.[103]

Patent grants provide further evidence that the early decades of the eighteenth century were accompanied by innovation. The Barbados Assembly is known to have passed only two Acts during the second half of the seventeenth century, in 1669 and 1670[71], designed specifically to promote inventive activity.[104] In contrast, a clutch of fourteen Acts were passed between 1709 and 1737 seeking to reward and encourage inventors (Table 2.3). This period also witnessed Barbadian experiments in crop cultivation, including the first documented transplanting of coffee seedlings to the British West Indies and the shipment of coffee seeds grown on the island early in the 1720s to botanical gardens in Britain for further examination.[105]

---

[102] [Samuel Keimer], *Caribbeana* (2 vols., London, 1741), vol. I, 22.

[103] Ibid., 250–1, 316, 403–4; vol. II, 242–5; Griffin Hughes, *The Natural History of Barbados* (London, 1750). Hughes' book was criticised by members of the Royal Society for inaccurate scholarship, Stearns, *Science in the British Colonies*, 358–61. Nevertheless, the negative reaction to the book ought not to detract from the links it reveals between plantation agriculture and applied natural science. The list of nearly 500 subscribers (including many Barbadians) signifies that the book was more than 'a masterpiece of salesmanship' (358). Griffiths' book was successful because of the level of interest in applied science by individuals with investments in colonial agriculture, who operated outside the libraries and laboratories of the Royal Society.

[104] There is evidence that non-patented inventive activity continued during the earlier period. Eltis notes, for example, that Barbadian producers succeeded in adding value to their exports between the 1660s and 1700 by substituting refined or clayed sugars for muscovados and also by marketing molasses and rum. He also indicates that per capita income on the island remained high, with little evidence of poverty relief, Eltis, *Rise of African Slavery*, 197–8, 200–3, 211.

[105] S. D. Smith, 'Sugar's Poor Relation: Coffee Planting in the British West Indies, 1720–1833', *Slavery and Abolition*, 19 (1998), 69. Coffee never became a significant export commodity on Barbados, but it was grown for domestic use by planters, Joshua Steele (Barbados, Kendall plantation) to the Royal Society of Arts, 10 September 1786, cited in D. G. C. Allen, 'Joshua Steele and the Royal Society of Arts', *JBMHS*, 22 (1954–5), 84–104.

Table 2.3. *Legislation passed by the Barbados Assembly to promote inventive activity, 1669–1737*

An Act for the more advantageous Hanging of Coppers and Stills [c. 1669]

An Act for the Encouragement of the Manufacture of this Island [c. 1670/71]

An Act for the Encouragement of Robert McCurdey, in his new Projection of raising Water with an Engline Forty Foot High in this Island [c. 1709–13]

An Act for the Encouragement of a new Projection (by Samuel Cox) for Grinding of Sugar-Canes, and Drawing of Water, &c. by means of an Horizontal Wind-mill [1714]

An Act for the Encouragement of John Perrat Gent. In his new Improvement of Wind Mills for grinding Sugar Canes [c. 1715–17]

An Act for the Encouragement of Thomas Sainthill Gentleman, in his Projection of a Mill for the grinding of Sugar-canes [1718]

An Act for the Encouragement of William Massett in his new Projection of making Worms, and altering Still-heads, for the better Improvement of Distillation [1719]

An Act allowing a Sum of Money to Constant Kelley Esquire … for every Cart or Vehicle which shall be made in this Island in the same Manner and Form with a Model of a Cart or Vehicle contrived by him the said Kelley [1722]

An Act for the Encouragement of William Ramsden Gentleman, in his new Improvement of Cattle Mills, for grinding Sugar Canes [1728]

An Act for the Encouragement of Thomas Stevenson Gentleman, in his new Projection of Windmills for grinding Sugar Canes [1730]

An Act for the Encouragement of Thomas Sainthill Esquire, in his new Projections of hanging of Coppers for making Sugar, making Cattle-mills, Horse-mills, and Horizontal-mills for grinding Sugar Canes, Lime Kilns for burning Lime, and Engines for raising Water, and of cleaning Cane Liquor without Fire [1732]

An Act for encouraging Thomas Sainthill Esquire, in his new Projection of cultivating the Soil, and preventing the Blast in Canes in this Island [1732]

An Act for the Encouragement of Major Thomas Spencer Esquire, in a new Project or Method he has invented in the place and stead of Lead on Coppers, being less expensive, more durable and convenient than what hath heretofore been used [1735]

An Act for the Encouragement of Thomas Spencer Esquire, in a new Project or Method he has invented for the more easy and expeditious straining of Liquors for making Sugar and Rum [1735]

An Act for the Encouragement of Thomas Sainthill Esquire, in his new Projection of a Machine, for the more expeditiously taking off the outward red skin, and the inward white Parchment Skin from Coffee [c. 1735–6]

An Act for the Encouragement of Simon Scantlebury* and Philip Jackman, Esquires, in a new Project or Method they have invented for recovering and making blasted Canes in this Island [1737]

Note:
*The Scantleburys were kinsmen of the Halls, LBMH, Family Files: Hall, transcript of will of Gyles Hall, 16 January 1687.

Source: [Barbados], *Acts of Assembly* (2 vols., London, 1732 & 1739).

Where did resources come from to finance attempted improvements in Barbados' plantation agriculture? The ending of the War of the Spanish Succession (1702–13) is thought to have marked an upsurge in capital exports to the slave colonies of the Caribbean, supplementing funds available to planters from ploughing back plantation profits and local lending.[106] Commission trading probably also increased its share of the sugar trade during the early eighteenth century, thereby extending short-term credit facilities to planters shipping their sugars to British merchant houses in London and provincial outports such as Bristol.[107] At the same time, the legal interest rate on domestic loans in Britain was reduced in 1714 from 6 to 5 per cent. A study of Hoare's Bank's lending policy confirmed that nearly all loans made by this City institution were at the usury maximum rate; in consequence, credit rationing (rather than a variable interest rate) was used to allocate funds. After 1714, fewer loans were made by the bank, but the amount of each loan increased. Successful borrowers were characterised by an ability to offer collateral (in the form of mortgages of land or securities), and possession of aristocratic titles or minor nobility.[108] The widening of the interest rate 'gap' between Britain and Barbados after 1714, combined with the restriction of banking overdrafts to gentry borrowers, may help explain the attractiveness of West Indian investments.[109]

Although Hugh Hall Jr criticised negative views of Barbadian society, his own appraisal of the colony contained equivocal elements. Slavery lay at the heart of his unease. Unsuccessful attempts were made between 1663 and 1695 to legislate for the Christian baptism of Africans on Barbados. The island's Assembly rejected these measures and in 1676 an Act was passed prohibiting Quakers from bringing slaves to their meetings.[110] The issue of religion and slavery in the colony revived after

---

[106] Jacob M. Price, 'Credit in the Slave Trade and Plantation Economies', in Solow ed., *Slavery and the Rise of the Atlantic System*, 293–339.

[107] Davies, 'Origins of the Commission System'.

[108] Peter Temin and Hans-Joachim Voth, 'Financial Repression in a Natural Experiment: Loan Allocation and the Change in the Usury Laws in 1714' (working paper), http://www.econ.upf.edu/~voth/usury.pdf.

[109] Balance of payments calculations are imprecise for the later seventeenth and early eighteenth centuries and are accompanied with large margins of error. In consequence, the relative importance of domestic (island) investment and lending from Britain remains unclear during this period, R. C. Nash, 'The Balance of Payments and Foreign Capital Flows in Eighteenth-Century England: A Comment', *Economic History Review*, 2nd series, 50 (1997), 110–28; Eltis, *Rise of African Slavery*, 215–19. Nevertheless, an interest rate differential, coupled with the effect of usury laws, would provide encouragement to reinvest surpluses within Barbados as well as an incentive for British-based lenders to invest in the colony.

[110] [Barbados], *Acts of Assembly, Passed in the Island of Barbadoes, Part I from 1648 to 1718, Part II from 1717[18] to 1738* (2 vols., London, 1732, 1739), 94–5; Nicholas Trott, *The*

1701, following the creation of the Society for the Propagation of the Gospel in Foreign Parts and Christopher Codrington's bequest to found a missionary college on Barbados to instruct ministers and promote acceptance of the slave baptism. In March 1720, Hugh Jr remarked with disgust that the enslaved were widely regarded on Barbados as having 'no more Souls than Brutes'. Ministers, he added, 'Slight & Ridicule all Attempts of their Conversion to Christianity even in Private Family's'. Hall expressed concern that 'the Pious Legacy of General Codrington's for the Propagation of the Gospell among our Poor Negroes here will be Imprudently Thrown away'.[111] Controversy over the issue during the early 1720s resulted in the emergence of a form of Anglicanism that excluded slave baptism; at the same time, nonconformity on the island entered into a period of decline.[112]

Confronted by this climate of opinion, Hugh Hall Sr opted to send his sons and daughters away to Boston for their education, partly for family reasons but also out of sympathy for the form of religious observance practised at Harvard.[113] It is interesting that Hall Sr himself authored a tract sent in 1718 to Edward Cordwent for publication in London, though it is not known whether its subject-matter was religious in nature.[114] Despite harbouring criticisms of the colony's social order, the Halls remained committed to Barbados and occupied administrative positions on the island. Hugh Jr's brother Richard Hall was a lawyer who served as a justice of the peace, a magistrate, and an Assembly

Laws of the British Plantations in America, Relating to the Church and the Clergy, Religion and Learning (London, 1721). Parish registers for four parishes (Christ Church, St Michael, St Philip, and St James) record the baptism of 135 black inhabitants during the second half of the seventeenth century; Gragg comments that slave baptism was occasional and only rarely was accompanied by freedom, Gragg, *Englishmen Transplanted*, 163–4.

[111] MHS, Benjamin Colman Papers, Hugh Hall Jr to Benjamin Colman, 30 March 1720.

[112] Campbell, *Church in Barbados*, 80, 155; John Oldmixon, *The British Empire in America* (2nd edn, 2 vols., London, 1741; 1st published 1708), vol. II, 143.

[113] Hall Sr's will states that his son Hugh Hall Jr and daughter Sarah were residing in Boston. The will instructed that his youngest sons John and Charles should be educated at Harvard 'as soon as their years will admit of', and that his blind daughter Eliza, living on Barbados, should be instructed in the Christian religion 'according to the church of England' as far as her condition was capable of, BA, RB6/35/72–7, Will of Hugh Hall, 1732. Earlier, two more of Hall Sr's children, Sally and Richard, had been sent to Boston for their education, Hall Sr Letterbook, Hall to John Binning, 22 October 1719; Hall to Lydia Colman, 22 October 1719.

[114] Hugh Hall Letterbook, Hall (Boston) to Edward Cordwent (London), 15 July 1718. Cordwent was a merchant mariner who had been based in Barbados during the years 1704 to 1706, when Edward Lascelles had acted as his attorney. He was also a slave trader and imported 695 Africans between 1699 and 1702, valued at £16,716 (currency), NA:PRO, C11/676/15, *Vickery vs Cordwent* (1739); Donnan ed., *Documents*, vol. II, 26.

member on Barbados. Richard was responsible for producing an edition of the laws of Barbados, a work continued and expanded by his own son Richard Hall Jr.[115] This exercise in legal codification was Hall's most substantial achievement, but he also completed an interesting manuscript account of Barbados. The short treatise of sixty pages, written around 1755, includes a narrative of the island's early settlement. Hall's principal concern, however, lay in compiling an account of the island's population, trade, and civil administration. The finished work gives an impression of an ordered, well-regulated society characterised by institutions modelled on their English equivalents, including an effective system of parochial administration.[116]

The Deeds of the Mansion

Hugh Hall Jr returned to Boston permanently in 1722[3]. There he built a prominent mansion house, donated books to Harvard College, and commissioned emerging artists, such as John Singleton Copley (whom the Vassalls also favoured), to paint family portraits.[117] In religious affairs, Hall Jr promoted the building of the West Church, subscribed towards the purchase of a peal of bells for Christ Church, and contributed to the organ fund at King's Chapel.[118] Gentrification is underlined by some of the material possessions listed by Hall Jr in a diurnal compiled in 1750. At this time, he was owner of no fewer than sixty-one oil paintings and mezzotints, nineteen sets of arms and

---

[115] The reasons for the Halls' production of a revised legal code are not stated. Elsewhere in the Atlantic world, publication of laws was related to the emergence of a legal culture that sought to reconcile colonial adaptation of English law with the requirement that such laws remain consistent with the common law tradition of the mother country. For examples and a discussion of transatlantic legal culture, see Mary Sarah Bilder, *The Transatlantic Constitution: Colonial Legal Culture and the Empire* (Cambridge, MA, 2004).

[116] Richard Hall, 'A General Account of the First Settlement and of the Trade and Constitution of the Island of Barbados' [c. 1755], in *Goddard, George Washington's Visit*, 54–92, 162–3; Richard Hall, *Acts Passed in the Island of Barbados from 1643 to 1762* (London, 1764). Hall's eldest son, Richard Hall Jr, continued his father's legal studies and completed the publication of this compilation. Like his father before him, Richard Sr was also selected as a parish vestry officer; his responsibilities including the management of Harrison's Free School. For details of educational establishments on Barbados, see Gragg, *Englishmen Transplanted*, 171–2.

[117] Josiah Quincy, *History of Harvard University* (Boston, 1860), 530; *Portrait of Hugh Hall* (1758), pastel on paper, 40.5×33.5 cm, Metropolitan Museum, New York; *Portrait of William Vassall and his Son Leonard* (1771), oil on canvas, 126.7×103.8 cm, De Young Museum, San Francisco, accession number 1979.7.30. The letter book records an earlier gift of Bishop Beveridge's *Thesaurus Theologicus* (4 vols., London, 1710–11), Morison, 'Letter-Book of Hugh Hall', 516.

[118] Shipton, *Biographical Sketches*, 16.

scutcheons, and a large collection of silver plate.[119] Marriage into the Pitts family aligned him with leading families of Boston. Brother-in-law James Pitts (1710–76) became Governor of Massachusetts and a kinsman of the wealthy Bowdoin family. Hugh entered into business with the Pitts, Bowdoins, and their associates during the 1730s and 1740s.[120] In local politics, Hall Jr's connections and reputation as a respectable merchant and church supporter made him a natural selection as a Suffolk Justice of the Peace in 1739.[121]

From Boston, the Halls continued to carry on trade with the West Indies, maintaining their involvement in slavery. Sarah Hall (sent from Barbados as a child by her father to learn dancing and to finish her education) married into the well-connected Wentworth family of Portsmouth, New Hampshire.[122] Her son, Hugh Hall Wentworth, possessed extensive commercial interests; he was involved in the southern European grain trade, traded with his Barbadian uncle Charles Hall, and invested in West Indian real estate. By 1771, Hall Wentworth was owner of a plantation on Grenada (of 479 acres and 172 slaves) valued at £65,708 currency. Other members of the family acquired slave-related interests in Dominica, another of the Ceded Islands.[123]

Yet despite these outward signs of success, not all boded well for the Boston Halls. In 1747, Hugh Jr was investigated by a committee of the Massachusetts Assembly for his wrongful arrest and imprisonment of an alleged army deserter, and for maladministration. The committee found against him and in 1748 Hall was dismissed as a Justice.[124] Financially, Hugh may also have suffered financial reverses during the mid-1750s. In January 1754, he was obliged to advertise 'a great part of

---

[119] Hugh Hall Diary (Almanac).
[120] [Payne], *Portraits of Eight*, 8; Goodwin Jr, *Memorial of the Lives*, 2, 35, 55–6; Shipton, *Biographical Sketches*, 15; *Journals of the House of Representatives of Massachusetts* (55 vols., MHS: Boston, 1919–90), vol. XVI (1738–9), 36, 92.
[121] *Journals of the House of Representatives*, vol. XVI (1738–9), 189.
[122] Sarah Hall (c. 1711–90) married John Wentworth (1703–73), son of Lieutenant Governor and a wealthy merchant mariner John Wentworth (1671(2)–1730).
[123] *LMLB*, Pares Transcripts, W&G VI, Lascelles & Maxwell to Charles Hall (Barbados), 7 September 1754; Hamilton College, New York, Beinecke Collection, M173, Devonshire and Reeve (Bristol) to Hugh Hall Wentworth, 24 October 1765; M176, Henry Lloyd (Boston) to Hugh Hall Wentworth, 17 February 1766; M185b, Charles Hall (Barbados), to Hugh Hall Wentworth, 25 September 1767; M206e and M212, list of slaves and valuation of Mount Nesbitt estate, Grenada, 24 June 1771; BA, RB6/17/562–4, Will of Hugh Benjamin Hall, 1766, refers to brother James Ashley Hall 'late of this island but now of the Colony of Dominica'.
[124] *Journals of the House of Representatives*, vol. XXIV (1747–8), 66, 71–2, 74, 82, 131, 150, 232, 255, 319, 327–8, 330, 340, 351.

his Boston property' for sale; protracted lawsuits relating to business affairs followed in 1760–1.[125]

In 1748, the old Vassall mansion was acquired by James Pitts from Henry Vassall. This house subsequently became a meeting place for colonial leaders seeking greater political autonomy for New England. Patriot clubs, including the Sons of Liberty, met here as members of the Pitts-Bowdoin families took the initiative in opposing British imperial policy during the 1760s and 1770s. The Vassalls and Halls found it difficult to follow the lead of their colonial relations. An over-commitment to business networks based on slavery aggravated the adjustment problems faced by the Halls. Family members, investing heavily in the Ceded Islands, suffered losses when the value of plantations plummeted following the 1772–3 credit crisis.[126]

Merchants such as the Hugh Halls were not lackeys who fetched and carried plantation stores and produce. Like their Vassall counterparts, they aspired to be masters of the Atlantic slave economy, rather than its mercantile servants. Others held similar aspirations, among them the Lascelles and Clarkes, whose careers form the principal subject of this book.[127] During the eighteenth century, the exploits of such gentry capitalists brought into being a business empire of great complexity, built on slavery and patronage, linking together groups of merchants in Britain, North America, and the West Indies. As will be seen, their energy drove the engines of the Atlantic trades, stretching the system of imperial commerce to its limits and beyond.

[125] Shipton, *Biographical Sketches*, 16; *Journals of the House of Representatives*, vol. XXXVI (1759–60), 168, 230; vol. XXXVI (1761, part 1), 84.
[126] Beinecke Collection, M217, Hugh Hall Wentworth to [?] (incomplete letter).
[127] The connection between the Halls and Lascelles was recalled as late as 1780, when descendants of Edward Lascelles visited a daughter of Hugh Hall (1673–1732) who had married Captain Robert Manley and was living in London, WRA, Harewood Estates, Antiquarian, Extract of a letter from John Prettyjohn and Thomas Graeme to Mr Daling, 10 September 1790.

3   Rise of the Lascelles

ARRIVALS: 16 April 1718 *Edward & Mary* (Benjamin Mackey) 250 tons, from London.[1]

A Solo Entry and a Brotherly Quartet

Two transactions document the beginnings of a connection that was to last a further 327 years. In 1648, Robert Oswicke conveyed a Barbadian sugar estate called Frames to a syndicate of three merchants that included Edward Lascelles. The following year, the same Edward Lascelles purchased a further 100 acres in St Andrew's Parish to augment his holding.[2] These twin acquisitions formed part of a wave of inward investment that saw 10 per cent of Barbados' total acreage change hands in just two years, as more than £140,000 of capital (much of it originating from London) was sunk into the island's real estate.[3]

Little is known about Frames' owner, except that he was a Bridgetown merchant with shipping assets.[4] In October 1655, the St Michael's Parish vestry awarded Edward the contract to replace the Bridgetown's 'Indian Bridge': an enterprise that appears to have involved him in financial difficulties. He was sued by the vestry in 1657 for failing to

---

[1] NA:PRO, CO33/15, Barbados Naval Officers' Lists, 1708–26. The *Edward and Mary* was built in Deptford in 1709 and registered to the Port of London. Her owners were Benjamin Mackey, Edward Lascelles, and George Strode. The inward cargo was 110 tons of manufactures and 10 chaldron of coal; she cleared out 1 July 1718 with 422 hhd, 115 tierces, and 35 barrels of sugar, supplemented with 9 bags of cotton and 40 goads of aloes.

[2] BA, RB3/3/453, Indenture between Robert Oswicke Jr and Edward Lascelles, Walter Bluiston, and Richard Grove (1648); RB3/3/572, Indenture between Thomas Goodwicke and John Morse, and Edward Lascelles (1649).

[3] John J. McCusker and Russell R. Menard, 'The Sugar Industry in the Seventeenth Century: A New Perspective on the Barbadian "Sugar Revolution"', in Stuart B. Schwartz ed., *Tropical Babylons: Sugar and the Making of the Atlantic World, 1450–1680* (North Carolina, 2004), 295–6.

[4] In June 1655, for example, he purchased a ship named the *Return of Dover* for 11,000 lb of sugar, BA, RB3/3/839.

complete the promised work; two years later, the new structure was badly damaged by a serious fire.[5] Lascelles himself may have suffered losses in the conflagration of February 1659, since he owned warehouses situated close to the bridge. Deeds dated May 1660 and June 1661 record him raising money by mortgaging a house and five slaves, perhaps to raise capital needed to rebuild his business.[6]

After this point, Edward disappears from the Barbados archives. His name is absent, for example, in the list of merchants and planters exporting sugar and other produce from the island between 1664 and 1666.[7] Lascelles may have quit Barbados after a financial reverse; equally he could have joined in a general exodus from direct plantation ownership as the initial boom in the sugar industry subsided. By the 1660s, many merchants had sold up their plantations and repositioned themselves as the suppliers of commercial and financial services to planters, leaving others to bear the risks and shoulder the effort required to manage sugar estates.[8]

Twenty years later, the name of Lascelles reappears in Barbadian history as four brothers – Edward, Philip, Robert, and William – broke into the Atlantic trades together.[9] The London anchor role was occupied by Philip (assisted initially by Edward), while William went out to Barbados and began shipping home cargoes of sugar and cotton.[10]

[5] Warren Alleyne, *Historic Bridgetown* (Barbados National Trust: Barbados, 1978), 58; Bobby Morris, 'Transfer of Wealth from Barbados to England – From Lascelles Plantation, Barbados to Harewood House, Yorkshire', *JBMHS*, 50 (2004), 91.

[6] BA, RB3/3/937; RB3/5/255; RB3/5/799.

[7] Bodleian Library, Oxford, MS Eng. hist. b. 122, 'A Coppie Journall of Entries Made in the Custom House of Barbados Beginning August the 10th 1664 and ending August the 10th, 1665'; Hispanic Society of America, New York, M. 1480, 'A Coppie Journall Entries made in the Custom House of Barbados 1665–1667'. The author is grateful to David Eltis for making these sources available in the form of a searchable database; see also David Eltis, 'New Estimates of Exports from Barbados and Jamaica, 1665–1701', *William and Mary Quarterly*, 3rd series, 52 (1995), 631–48.

[8] McCusker and Menard, 'Sugar Industry', 302.

[9] Cooperation between brothers and treatment of the Atlantic trades as a family project forms a consistent feature of the merchants studied in this book. The Vassalls, Lascelles, Halls, Clarkes, Freres, Harvies, Blenmans, Franklands, and Douglases all shared this trait. The existing historical literature on younger sons remains limited, but there is increasing recognition that younger sons occupied important positions within aristocratic and gentry families. See Joan Thirsk, 'Younger Sons in the Seventeenth Century', *History*, 54 (1969), 358–63; D. R. Hainsworth, 'The Lowther Younger Sons: A Seventeenth-Century Case Study', *Transactions of the Cumberland and Westmorland Antiquarian and Archaeological Society*, 88 (1988), 149–63; Linda Pollock, 'Younger Sons in Tudor and Stuart England', *History Today*, 39 (June 1989), 23–9; Susan E. Whyman, 'Land and Trade Revisited: The Case of John Verney, London Merchant and Baronet, 1660–1720', *London Journal*, 22 (1997), 16–32. See also fn. 17

[10] William Lascelles' name is absent from the 1678–9 Barbados census, signifying that he arrived shortly before sending this consignment to Philip. In 1681, William and his wife

A first consignment was sent in October 1680; by July 1683, annual turnover exceeded £923.[11] Philip Lascelles remained a London merchant until his death in 1713. His name appears in the 1695 enumeration of the city's inhabitants and also in a petition of Barbados merchants dated 1702.[12]

Brother William's career on Barbados proved of much shorter duration, despite a promising start. In either 1686 or 1687, William was trading as a commission merchant on Bridgetown's High Street, receiving merchandise from London for sale and sending back hogsheads of sugar.[13] Between 1684 and 1685, William purchased Townes estate in St George's Parish, demonstrating he had sufficient credit to combine mercantile activities with sugar planting.[14] Within three years of his arrival he had been selected as a parish vestry officer for St Michael's; in 1685, he also acted as an overseer for the poor.[15] And then his career was cut short. Sometime after 1686, like many other white settlers, William died suddenly – probably a victim of the unhealthy disease environment.[16]

In the meantime, Robert Lascelles acted as ship's master, commanding vessels that sailed across the Atlantic to Britain, laden with sugar and other produce consigned by his brothers, other merchants, and planters.[17] Much of his life was spent traversing the Atlantic, a legal

---

Frances baptised a son. The couple may have gone out to the island together since there are references in surviving accounts to Frances' mother residing in England during the early 1680s, MCD 40, Deposition of Philip Lascelles, 24 December 1686; Joanne McRee Sanders ed., *Barbados Records: Baptisms, 1637–1800* (2 vols., Baltimore, 1984), vol. I, 21. In 1681, William Lascelles acted as witness to a will, Joanne McRee Sanders ed., *Barbados Records: Wills and Administrations* (3 vols., Houston, 1979), vol. I, 26.

[11] MCD 40, Deposition of Philip Lascelles, 24 December 1686.

[12] *CSPC (A&WI)*, vol. XX (London, 1912), 507–8; D. V. Glass ed., *London Inhabitants Within the Walls, 1695* (London Record Society: London, 1966), vol. II, 179–80 (Philip Lascelles' tax rating in 1695 was £600); NA:PRO, PROB11/529 sig. 213, Will of Philip Lassells, 'citizen and weaver', 13 March 1712[13]. The will leaves the residue of Lassells' estate to a daughter named Elizabeth (a daughter of this name is also listed in the 1695 enumeration). Traders within the city walls joined companies to gain the civic freedom; the designation 'weaver' in consequence does not indicate the nature of the trade followed.

[13] BA, St Michale's Levy Books, vol. I (1686–1712), ff. 7, 20; MCD 40, Deposition of Benjamin Suzan, 2 August 1686; MCD 41, Deposition of Richard Curtis, 22 April 1684.

[14] BA, RB 3/13/513–14, Indenture between John Young and William Lascelles, 2 June 1684; RB3/4/33–5, Indenture between James Townes and William Lascelles, 2 June 1685.

[15] St Michael Vestry Minutes', *JBMHS*, 16 (1949), 196, 199–201, 204.

[16] MCD 40, Deposition of John Meane, 28 October 1686.

[17] That Edward, Robert, and Philip were brothers is confirmed by Edward Lascelles' will, NA:PRO, PROB11/614 (proved 1727). See also MCD 40, Deposition of Hugh Grainger, 1 November 1686. William Lascelles is assumed also to have been a brother, on the basis of his substantial trading connections with the other three. A Jamaican sugar planter, James Lascelles, is documented between 1674 and 1684, but no

case of 1716 recording that 'Robert Lascelles hath been a master &
Commander of Ships for about 25 years last past'.[18] His vessel, the
Lascelles Frigate (a splendid sailing ship of 220 tons burthen), was a
regular sight in Carlisle Bay.[19] When in 1707 Robert, Edward, and
Philip invested in an even larger ship of 300 tons, the brothers retained
the family name: *Lascelles*.[20] While Robert specialised in the shuttle
route linking Barbados with London, he may also have developed a
sideline in New England trade, since a 'Robert Laseels' of Boston sold a
quarter share of a ship to William Harte of Barbados in 1710.[21]

The most successful of the quartet proved to be Edward. In 1687, his
name is listed in the Bridgetown levy book under the heading 'New
Comers Traders'. By 1689, Edward had set up in trade on the High
Street, doubtless taking over deceased brother William's premises. An
indication of the rate at which his business grew is given in Table 3.1,
which records the parish levy (a combination of the rateable value of
property and a head tax) paid between 1687 and 1706.[22] Two features of
the data can be noted. Firstly, Edward consistently paid more than the
average rate levied on inhabitants of the commercial districts of the High
Street (250 lb sugar) and Cheapside (500 to 600 lb). Secondly, his
change of address during the later 1690s was followed by a significant
increase in his tax liability. Taken together, these findings suggest that
Edward's wealth increased faster than that of most of his mercantile
neighbours prior to his return to England in 1701.[23]

connections are known linking him with the Barbados Lascelles, Carl Bridenbaugh and
Roberta Bridenbaugh, *No Peace Beyond the Line: The English in the Caribbean, 1624–1690*
(New York, 1972), 202–3, 293; *CSPC (A&WI)*, vol. VII (London, 1889), 563–4.

[18] NA:PRO, DEL/1/352, *Lascelles vs Bovell and others* (1716).

[19] NA:PRO, CO33/13; MCD 44, Deposition of Theophilas Hastings, bookkeeper to Philip
Lascelles of London, merchant, 6 March 1706[7]; NA:PRO, T70/1198, 'Sworn value of
cargoes and amounts levied (Inwards)' [n.p.] 1 August 1701, 27 November 1708–1
January 1709; CRO, Lonsdale Archive, Barbados Plantation Records, Box 1,033,
Barbados Council Minute Book (1718–19), 61–2.

[20] NA:PRO, CO33/15. In 1718 this vessel was commanded by Alexander Glass; she was
built and registered in London in 1707.

[21] BA, RB3/25/346–7. The name of this vessel was *William & Edward*, possibly after his
two brothers.

[22] According to the Acts of the Assembly, the levy was raised on the 'houses Trade &
personall estates' of Bridgetown inhabitants, John Carter Brown Library, Providence,
Rhode Island, Codex=Eng 9, 'Acts of [the Barbados] assembly passed from 4 June 1705
to 4 September 1706', 3–4, 31–2, 55–6. The levy lists themselves, however, distinguish
between taxes on houses by street and taxes on inhabitants residing in each street.

[23] By the 1690s, Edward had developed commercial links with other colonies as well as
trading with Britain, Vere Langford Oliver, *The History of Antigua* (3 vols., London,
1896), vol. III, 140, 'Will of John Langford of Bristol, late of Antigua', proved 11
October 1692.

Table 3.1. *St Michael's Parish levy assessments for Edward Lascelles, 1687–1706 (lb of sugar)*

Year of levy	High Street	Cheapside
1686[a]	300	–
1687[b]	100	–
1689	200	–
1691	300	–
1692	450	–
1693	400	–
1694	600	–
1695	300	–
1696	300	427
1697	500	800
1698	500	900
1699	–	2,735
1700	–	2,600
1701	–	1,770
1702[c]	–	1,495
1703	–	1,872
1704	–	2,170
1705	–	2,425
1706[d]	–	600

Notes:
[a] William Lascelles' levy assessment; [b] listed among 'New Comers Traders'; [c] listed as 'going for London'; [d] not listed after 1706.
Source: BA, St Michael's Levy Books, vol. I, 1686–1712.

On Barbados, Edward married Mary Hall, daughter of the merchant Hugh Hall Sr.[24] High rates of infant and child mortality in the tropics frustrated the couple's attempts at raising a family. By May 1701, the Lascelles had buried no fewer than three children, aged between four months and three years seven months. Yet a daughter, named after her mother, defied the odds and survived.[25] A desire for male heirs and a marriage partner for his daughter helps explain Edward's relocation to London at the turn of the century. Business calculation, however, must also have prompted the move, for Edward Lascelles was an ambitious man with good prospects of succeeding (or supplanting) his brother Philip as London agent.

On his return, Edward joined the Grocers' Company in July 1701, thereby gaining the legal freedom to trade within London's city walls.

---

[24] See Chapter Two.
[25] Vere Langford Oliver, *The Monumental Inscriptions in the Churches and Churchyards of the Island of Barbados, British West Indies* (London, 1915), 49; LBMH, Major Henry Albert Thorne, 'Monumental Inscriptions of Barbados', 223.

Significantly, he claimed membership by patrimony, the company's admissions register stating his father was one Peter Lascelles, gentleman, of Thoraby in Yorkshire.[26] In his youth, Peter Lascelles served an eight-year apprenticeship to a grocer, commencing in 1647. After release from his indentures, he may have set up in this trade, since the subsequent careers of Peter's sons reveal strong links between the sugar trade and the grocery business.[27] Participation in luxury groceries was also a characteristic shared by brother Philip, who is described as a tobacconist in court records of the mid-1680s. In one of these documents (dated 1684), an Edward Lascelles is referred to as 'his man', suggesting that Edward may have served as Philip's apprentice prior to his departure to Barbados, even though this is an unusual way of describing a brother.[28]

After 1701, Edward continued to retain a core interest in the sugar trade as both merchant and ship's owner. An indication of the scale of this branch of his business is provided by the London Port Book of 1719, which reveals that a minimum of 2,402 cwt of sugar was consigned to him from correspondents primarily based in Barbados, supplemented by a few clients in Antigua.[29] However, Edward had begun to diversify around his staple business. His name is listed among private traders participating in African trade. Between August 1703 and October 1709, for example, he exported six cargoes valued at £2,997.18s. to the Guinea coast. The proceeds of these shipments were probably used to purchase slaves or gold, since only £36.9s. of imports are recorded in the corresponding ledger of inward trade.[30] In addition, Edward also acted as a

---

[26] CLRO, ELJL/167/161, Admission of Edward Lascelles to the Grocers' Company, 17 July 1701. The author is grateful to Robert Barker for this reference.

[27] Edward's commission house (and later the firm of Lascelles & Maxwell) sold imported sugar to London's grocers, many of whom invested in the city's refineries.

[28] MCD 40, Deposition of Philip Lascelles of London, 24 December 1684.

[29] WRA, NH 2,440, London Port Book, 1719 (see below for details of the under-recording of sugar imports in this source). To put imports in context, 2,402 cwt was eight-and-a-half times the mean importation of sugar by Bristol firms in 1731 and represented a turnover greater than that of 90 per cent of Bristol importers operating in 1742, Jacob M. Price and Paul G. E. Clemens, 'A Revolution in Scale in Overseas Trade: British Firms in the Chesapeake Tobacco Trade, 1675–1775', *Journal of Economic History*, 47 (1987), 1–43. For further details of trading relations, see NA:PRO, C11/2012/47, *Richard Staple* vs *Edward Lascelles* (1725); I. K. Steele ed., *Atlantic Merchant-Apothecary: Letters of Joseph Cruttenden, 1710–1717* (Toronto, 1977), 59, 60, 61, 71, 88, 91, 107.

[30] NA:PRO, T70/1199, 'Sworn value of cargoes and amounts levied Outwards', 2 January 1701–4 July 1712 [n.p.]; 'Sworn value of cargoes and amounts levied Inwards' [n.p.]. Export goods consisted primarily of manufactures, supplemented with guns, gunpowder, tobacco, aqua vitae, and beans. Imports comprised elephants' teeth, beeswax, Guinea corn, redwood, and cow hides. The author is grateful to William Pettigrew for drawing attention to these ledgers. In addition to trading on his own account, Edward may have acted as an agent for the Royal African Company's

West Indian financier, granting loans to planters and acting as their executor and trustee.[31] His position as a creditor led him strenuously (and successfully) to oppose the Barbados land bank scheme of 1706, on the grounds that it would increase bad debts owed by planter correspondents.[32]

Politically, Edward can be linked to a London Whig club, though confirming his membership is complicated by the existence of a second Edward Lascelles in London, trading as a dry-salter.[33] Commercially, the two Edwards were linked in business: each was an associate of Samuel Vanderplank, while the doppelgänger also maintained an account with brother William, importing aloes and fustic from Barbados.[34] Regionally, there may also have been common ground, since the Whitby-based merchant Nathaniel Cholmley corresponded in 1686 with a 'Mr Edward Lascelles, Tobacconist, at ye Signe of the Golden boars head in Gracechurch Street', on the subject of dyestuffs.[35]

In terms of religion, Edward was a practising Anglican, but he also possessed some intriguing links with dissent. His wife, Mary, belonged to a family of former Quakers who retained links with New England nonconformists.[36] Aside from his implicit opposition to Dr Henry Sacheverell, direct knowledge of Edward Lascelles' religious affiliations is lacking. Two pieces of circumstantial evidence, however, further connect him with the community of Friends. Firstly, Richard Poor (a Quaker merchant of Barbados) despatched forty-four shipments of sugar to London between June 1718 and November 1720. Of these consignments,

Antiguan merchants, Elizabeth Donnan ed., *Documents Illustrative of the History of the Slave Trade to America* (4 vols., Washington D.C., 1930–5), vol. II, 295.

[31] BA, RB3/24/378–9; NA:PRO C11/2238/5; C11/2366/1 [Guy Ball]; CO28/9/67; CO29/10/134–40; BA, Hughes-Queree Collection, Abstract in Queree notebook, mortgage of £5,270 sterling granted to Joseph French[?], 1719.

[32] Curtis P. Nettels, *The Money Supply of the American Colonies Before 1720* (Madison, 1934), 269–70.

[33] H. Horwitz ed., 'Minutes of a Whig Club, 1714–1717', in *London Politics, 1713–1717*, London Record Society Publications, 17 (London, 1981), 37, 50. Edward Lascelles, dry-salter, is believed to be the individual listed in the 1695 listing of London's population, Glass ed., *London Inhabitants* 179. In some records he is also referred to as a grocer, NA:PRO, C11/1850/12, *Dowdell* vs *Lascelles* (1732).

[34] NA:PRO, C11/2042/10, *Sir Charles Crispe* vs *Edward Lascelles* (1731); MCD 40, Deposition of Edward Lascelles, 1686; WRA, NH 2,440. The latter source also records imports of logwood from Boston and pearl ashes from Hamburg. The dry-salter's son was also named Edward Lascelles; in 1730 (a year after his father's death) he declared himself bankrupt, NA:PRO C11/2042/10, *Crisp and Morrice* vs *Lascelles* (1731).

[35] North Yorkshire County Record Office, Northallerton, MIC 2554, Cholmley to Edward Lascelles, 26 February 1685[6], 27 May 1686. The date of the correspondence and a reference to alum both indicate that the doppelgänger was the recipient, since the other Edward by late May must have been on his way to Barbados.

[36] See Chapter Two.

thirty-one were carried by the Lascelles brothers' vessel, *Edward and Mary*.[37] Secondly, the Quaker merchant Lascelles Metcalfe was active in London from at least the early 1690s until his death in 1740[1]. The Lascelles and Metcalfes of Northallerton intermarried during the seventeenth and eighteenth centuries. Daniel Lascelles of Stank's first wife was Margaret Metcalfe, while Edward Lascelles' sole surviving Barbadian daughter, Mary, became his second.[38]

The material success of Edward Lascelles may be gauged by his ownership of English property. In addition to a London counting house (situated in Tokenhouse Yard at the time of Hugh Hall Jr's visit) and other property within the city, he acquired land at Stoke Newington.[39] By his death in 1727, Edward owned a smaller estate at Wellingborough; he also possessed land at Datchet and Upton Court in Buckinghamshire.[40] While it is not known how remunerative these investments were during his lifetime, in 1739 their combined rental amounted to £1,100.[41] The will refers to other assets (including shares in ships). In his final testament, Edward felt confident enough to leave his heirs legacies amounting to £8,670 and annuities of £610 per annum.[42]

Edward and Mary Lascelles' attempts at forming a family proved more successful at Stoke Newington than on Barbados and at the time of Edward's death, two sons and four daughters were still living.[43]

---

[37] HSP, Port of Philadelphia, Bills of Lading 1716–72. Richard Poor is currently the subject of a separate study by the author.

[38] S. D. Smith ed., *'An Exact and Industrious Tradesman': The Letter Book of Joseph Symson of Kendal*, British Academy Records of Social and Economic History, new series, 34 (Oxford University Press, 2002), 723; S. D. Smith, 'The Provenance of the Joseph Symson Letter Book', *Transactions of the Cumberland and Westmorland Antiquarian and Archaeological Society*, 3rd series, 3 (2002), 164. It may also be significant that Edward received goods from the mariner Richard Metcalfe in 1708–9, NA:PRO, T70/1198.

[39] This estate was probably purchased c. 1712 – the date he built a house here along the London road.

[40] Traces of the Lascelles can be found at Upton (now part of south-eastern Slough), though separating the imprint of the earlier Lascelles from later family members is problematic. 'Lascelles Road', 'Lascelles Playing Fields', and 'Lascelles Park', for example, all commemorate the 1922 royal marriage between Princess Mary and Viscount Lascelles. Upton Court, located near St Laurence's Church, was the residence of one William Lascelles Esq. of Middle Temple in 1806. There are claims Lascelles resided here as early as 1711, which if correct would suggest a possible link with the Barbadian branch of the family. Another property named Kent House, however, may mark the correct location of Edward Lascelles' estate, Morris, 'Transfer of Wealth', 98. Memorials to William Lascelles (d. 1808) and Frances Lascelles (d. 1818), eldest daughter of Edwin Lascelles, Baron Harewood, are preserved in St Laurence's Church, Slough.

[41] NA:PRO, PROB11/614 sig. 66; C11/837/11; C11/144/1.

[42] NA:PRO, PROB11/614 sig. 66.

[43] 'On the 27th of *February* died Mr *Edward Lascells*, an eminent Barbados Merchant of this City', *The Political State of Great Britain*, vol. XXXIII (1727), 220.

Matches of quality were made by at least three of the daughters. Mary, the only surviving child from Barbados, married Daniel Lascelles of Stank and MP for Northallerton in 1702. Their union thus established a direct link between the fraternal quartet and the future owners of Harewood House.[44] In 1716, the middle daughter, Sarah, married Joshua Ironmonger (or Iremonger). Her husband, a wealthy brewer, died barely two years afterwards, leaving an estate worth upwards of £20,000.[45] Interestingly, the Ironmongers were kinsmen and business partners of the Raymonds: a family whose business concerns included participation in the African slave trade to Barbados.[46] Sarah's second husband (whom she married in 1721) was Christopher Lethieullier. The Lethieulliers emigrated to England during the early seventeenth century as Protestant refugees from Valenciennes. Thanks to the business successes achieved by Sir John Lethieullier (1632/3–1719), by the early eighteenth century the family were well established among London's mercantile elite.[47] Finally, Edward Lascelles' youngest daughter, Mary, married William Ingram, a member of another respectable family of lawyers, military officers, and merchants.[48]

While the daughters made successful matches, Edward's sons failed the family dynasty. His youngest son, Thomas, died unmarried in 1733, followed in 1739 by the eldest son and heir, Edward Lascelles Jr, also without progeny.[49] The family's West India fortune, assembled over a lifetime in business, was then divided up between the Ingrams, Lethieulliers, and Lascelles in a series of legal disputes.

An estate inventory survives detailing the movable goods of 'Viol head' – the term Hugh Hall dismissively used to refer to Edward Jr. This

---

[44] Joseph Foster, *Pedigrees of the County Families of England: Yorkshire, West Riding* (3 vols., London, 1874), vol. II, 'Lascelles'.

[45] NA:PRO, C11/2366/1, *Joshua Ironmonger vs Sarah Ironmonger and Edward Lascelles* (1719[20]); C11/2443/16, *Lascelles Raymond Ironmonger vs John Raymond and Christopher Lethieullier* (1734[5]); C11/2446/23, Answer of Christopher Lethieullier (1734); Society of Genealogists, Boyd's Family Units, 'Ironmonger'; William Matthews ed., *The Diary of Dudley Ryder, 1715–1716* (London, 1939), 51, 310.

[46] Between 1712 and 1730, William Raymond was the owner or part-owner of slaver vessels that landed 4,815 Africans on Barbados between 1713 and 1724, NA:PRO, CO28/18/320–30; David Eltis, Stephen D. Behrendt, David Richardson, and Herbert S. Klein eds., *The Trans-Atlantic Slave Trade: A Database on CD-ROM* (Cambridge, 1999); Old Bailey Trials Online, Indictment of Amy Barns for stealing 2 gallons of beer from Joshua Ironmonger and Joseph Raymond, 5 December 1718; NA:PRO, PROB11/610, Will of William Raymond, proved 19 July 1726.

[47] H. G. Roseveare, 'Lethieullier, Sir John, 1632/3–1719', *ODNB*.

[48] NA:PRO, C11/837/11, *James Peters vs Edward Lascelles* (1745); WRA, Harewood Estates, Antiquarian, Extract of a letter from John Prettyjohn and Thomas Graeme (Barbados) to William Daling, 10 September 1790.

[49] NA:PRO, C11/2446/23, Answer of Chrisopher Lethieullier (1734).

document lists copious quantities of drinking vessels and alcoholic beverages. At Wellingborough, 2 punch bowls, 46 drinking glasses, and 6 gallons of 'Rack and Lanthorn' were found in the bedchamber. In the parlour, appraisers enumerated 1 punch bowl, 8 decanters, 45 drinking glasses, 21 bottles of rack, 140 bottles of rum and brandy, and 3 casks of ale. At a second location, a further 282 bottles 'of wine different sorts' were discovered, along with 144 additional containers with unspecified contents. Drinking facilities were also available at Stoke Newington, where the testator kept 2 hogsheads and 120 bottles of port.[50] Did alcoholism contribute to Edward Jr's early death? Perhaps; but it must be emphasised that wine and beer were consumed habitually by households during the eighteenth century as a healthier alternative to water. Moreover, Edward Jr's relations included brewers, while his father's business interests included trade in Madeira wine.[51]

At Edward Jr's death, a mortgage of £6,000 was owed by the estate to Henry son of Daniel Lascelles. Was this a debt born of profligacy or financial weakness? The existence of the loan itself is equivocal evidence. Even the wealthiest estate often lacked sufficient liquid resources to pay legacies' and executives' accounts indicate that Edward Jr's loan was employed for precisely this purpose.[52] Yet whatever the personal circumstances of Edward Jr at his decease, the Lascelles of Northallerton quickly gained the ascendancy in business over their kinsmen. By the time Edwin Lascelles was created Baron Harewood in 1790, memories of the achievements of the cadet branch had been all but effaced.

To assist the College of Arms' enquiry into his pedigree, Edwin Lascelles instructed his Barbadian agents to question some of the island's elderly inhabitants for information about the family's namesakes. 'There is an old lady, a Miss Thorpe', they replied, 'who says that she had heard that this E^d Lascelles [Edward Lascelles Sr.] was some relation of the two half brothers Henry & Edward Lascelles, who came to this island afterwards, but how nearly related she cannot tell.'[53] In addition to this letter, there is an intriguing entry in the diary of Joseph Farington (written in 1796), which claims that 'The grandfather of the present L^d [Edward] Harewood, though a distant relation, was a servant

---

[50] NA:PRO, C11/837/11, An Account of the Personal Estate of Edward Lascelles Esquire deceased (compiled 1739).
[51] BL, Add. MS 61,510, f. 136, 'Humble petition of diverse merchants trading to the island of Madeira', 18 January 1704[5]; CSPC (A&WI), vol. XIX (London, 1910), 162–3, 737.
[52] NA:PRO, C11/2446/23; C11/837/11.
[53] WRA, Harewood Estates: Antiquarian, Extract of a letter from John Prettyjohn and Thomas Graeme to Mr Daling, dated Barbados 10 September 1790.

at that time in the Lascelles family.'[54] Was this intended as a reference to Edward Lascelles Sr of Stoke Newington? If so, it is extraordinary to think that a man of such wealth and commercial connections could have been reduced so quickly in estimation to the menial position of a servant. The association of the Lascelles of Stoke Newington with servility could, however, reflect the ignominious fate of Edward Lascelles Jr, if indeed he died an alcoholic, heavily indebted to Henry Lascelles.

The Yorkshire Lascelles' engagement with the colonial trades stretched over a long period of time. No fewer than three attempts were made to build up a fortune from West India commerce. Yet only the last of these generated returns sufficient to lay the foundations of an aristocratic dynasty, with Harewood House as its seat. The ventures promoted by the two earlier sets of Lascelles were modest in comparison with what was to come. The wealth they accumulated was dissipated within a generation and did not prove self-sustaining.

[54] Kenneth Garlick and Angus Macintyre eds., *The Diary of Joseph Farington* (16 vols., New Haven, 1978–84), vol. II, 570.

4   Lascelles and Maxwell

I think the North of England has produced the best Governours for this Island

(John Frere to Robert Lowther, 1 September 1742).[1]

A Fraternal Trio

The extraordinary success achieved by Daniel Lascelles' sons in West India commerce owed as much to his family's own mercantile connections as it did to assistance from their new kinsmen. While the Stoke Newington Lascelles provided their Northallerton counterparts with useful connections, comparatively few cooperative ventures were pursued by the two families.[2] Within only a few years, Daniel's sons were following a different business trajectory to that of their predecessors and reaping rewards on a scale few other merchants of the age could rival.

Daniel Lascelles was son and heir of the Northallerton MP and dissenter Francis Lascelles Sr of Stank Hall. During the English Civil War, Francis served as Colonel in the Parliamentary army; he also numbered among the commissioners who tried Charles I for high treason. Significantly, the Northallerton Lascelles can be linked with the Thomson-Vassall circle of provincial, nonconformist merchants involved in colonial projects. In 1651, Lucy Lascelles (one of Francis' daughters)

---

[1] The Royal Bank of Scotland Group Archives, London, James Lowther Barbados Papers, GB 1502/CH/1/1.

[2] Edward Lascelles Sr acted as London attorney for Henry Lascelles, NA:PRO, C11/2285/ 18, *Henry Lascelles* vs *James Waldie* (1717). In April 1719, Henry received a letter 'from M^r: Edward Lascelles of Nuington' warning him that the Portuguese merchant Francis Lansa had been 'put on by [William] Gordon and William Sharpe [former President of Barbados] to Complaine Against Your Governour and You, for Receiving of Bribes as they Call it', CRO, D/Lons/L12/1/BM, Lonsdale Archive, Barbados Plantation Records, Box 1,032, Barbados Council Minute Book (1720), 195–6 (see below for more details of this case). On the marriage of Mary Lascelles (daughter of Edward Lascelles of Barbados and Stoke Newington) to Daniel Lascelles of Stank and Northallerton, see Joseph Foster, *Pedigrees of the County Families of England: Yorkshire, West Riding* (2 vols., London, 1874), vol. II, 'Lascelles'; LBMH, Eustace Shilstone Notebooks and Family Files, 'Lascelles'; NA:PRO C11/837/11.

married the Virginia merchant Cuthbert Witham, son of William Witham of Garforth in Yorkshire. The Withams were staunch Presbyterians, while George Witham (another of William's sons) was a business associate of both Maurice Thomson and Samuel Vassall.[3] Moreover, Francis Lascelles' eldest son and namesake was a nonconformist London merchant, also connected in trade with the Withams.[4]

The Vassalls and their circle participated in the Additional Sea Venture to Ireland of 1642, alongside other projects.[5] Oral histories and genealogical research reveal that the Northallerton Lascelles similarly involved themselves in Irish trade and investment during the Civil War and Commonwealth periods. Thomas Lascelles of Northallerton went out to Ireland and established himself as a merchant, first at Dromore and later at Lisburn. According to the family history of the Staveleys of Antrim and Cork, Francis Lascelles of Stank Hall likewise developed business concerns in Belfast during the later 1640s.[6]

Political factors help explain the apparent hiatus in the Lascelles' West India activity between 1661 and 1681. As a Regicide, Francis Lascelles occupied dangerous ground as the prospect of a Stuart restoration increased. He responded to the situation by negotiating with General Monk, brokering the return of the secluded members of the House of Commons in February 1660. Following the accession of Charles II, Lascelles' reward was inclusion in the Bill of Indemnity. In return for paying a fine equal to one year's rental, Francis kept his estates intact and escaped prosecution as one of the King's judges.[7] The Restoration, therefore, did not inflict serious damage on the Northallerton Lascelles, though the Royalist ascendancy in England and Barbados seems to have discouraged speculation in colonial trade.

---

[3] Robert Brenner, *Merchants and Revolution: Commercial Change, Political Conflict, and London's Overseas Traders, 1550–1653* (Cambridge, 1993), 482–3, 489, 492; NA:PRO, PROB11/251, Will of Cuthbert Witham (1655).

[4] Borthwick Institute for Archives, University of York, York Wills, vol. XLIX, 464b–466, Will of Francis Lascelles, dated 8 October 1668 and proved 14 January 1668[9].

[5] See Chapter Two for details of this scheme and links between Irish affairs and colonisation projects.

[6] PRONI, Ward Papers, D/2,499, 'Francis Lascelles of Killough, 1700–1743', 1–2 (typescript written in 1925 by Emily Ward, based on a manuscript account by Cornelius Lascelles, then in the possession of a Mrs Lascelles of Melbourne, Australia); copies of genealogical papers relating to the Lascelles of Killough, County Down, in the possession of Finbar McCormick of Queen's University, Belfast, and Killough. The Irish connection is strengthened by the fact that Thomas Lascelles' grandson Francis Lascelles acted as estate manager for the Wards at Killough during the early eighteenth century; his correspondence between 1723 and 1743 is preserved in the Ward Papers.

[7] C. H. Firth ed., *The Memoirs of Edmund Ludlow* (2 vols., Oxford, 1894), vol. II, 217, 285; Bodleian Library, Oxford, Carte Calendar, vol. XXX (1660), 613, 617, Francis Lascelles to the Marquess of Ormond, 4 May 1660.

Following the death of Charles II, interest in Barbados on the part of the Lascelles revived as opposition to James II intensified. As the previous chapter demonstrated, Edward Lascelles of Stoke Newington launched a series of West Indian ventures with his three brothers, beginning in 1680. The Northallerton Lascelles held back until after the flight of James II – an event they actively supported. Daniel joined Danby's Rising in December 1688, riding as Lieutenant in the Yorkshire Militia under Captain Charles Tancred.[8] At the same time, Thomas Lascelles of Lisburn rendered financial assistance to William of Orange's army.[9] These judicious manoeuvres left the Lascelles well placed to prosper from the change of regime. Political events were accompanied by commercial restructuring as merchants anticipated the demise of the Royal African Company. In 1687, no fewer than eighty 'New Commers Traders' are listed in the Bridgetown's annual levy, compared with an average of just twenty-four individuals (mostly ships' captains) for the years 1686, 1690–3, and 1695. Edward Lascelles' migration to Barbados, therefore, formed part of an influx of aspiring merchants eager to seize new opportunities for profit.[10]

Gaps in the historical record inhibit the drawing of definitive conclusions about the connectivity of the Lascelles' colonial projects during the later seventeenth and early eighteenth centuries. Nevertheless, the Yorkshire family origins of Edward Lascelles of Stoke Newington, coupled with his daughter's marriage to Daniel Lascelles and evidence of his own Whig political affiliations, surely indicate that they cannot be viewed in isolation.[11]

Colonial commerce was conceived as a family project by a majority of the merchants featuring in this book.[12] In the case of the Northallerton Lascelles, leadership roles in the West Indies trades were assumed by Daniel Lascelles' two eldest sons early in the eighteenth century

---

[8] BL, Egerton MS 3,344, f. 555.

[9] PRONI, Ward Papers, D/2,499, 'Francis Lascelles of Killough', 2–3.

[10] BA, St Michael's, Levy Books, vol. I (1686–1712). For growth in the number of private traders paying a 10 per cent levy for a licence to trade with Africa, see NA:PRO, T70/1199, 'Sworn value of cargoes and amounts levied Outwards', 2 January 1701 – 4 July 1712; T70/1198, 'Sworn value of cargoes and amounts levied Inwards'.

[11] Genealogical materials assembled by the Killough Lascelles and their descendants include the claim that Daniel Lascelles himself went out to Barbados after 1688, PRONI, Ward Papers, D/2,499, 'Francis Lascelles of Killough', 2. It has not proved possible to verify this claim; a rare reference to Daniel's direct involvement in West Indian trade occurs in 1720, when a slave consigned by his order was sold in Barbados, CRO, D/Lons/L12/1/BM, Lonsdale Archive, Barbados Plantation Records, Box 1,032, Barbados Council Minute Book (1720), 22–3.

[12] See Chapters Two, Three, and Seven for examples of younger sons working with elder brothers.

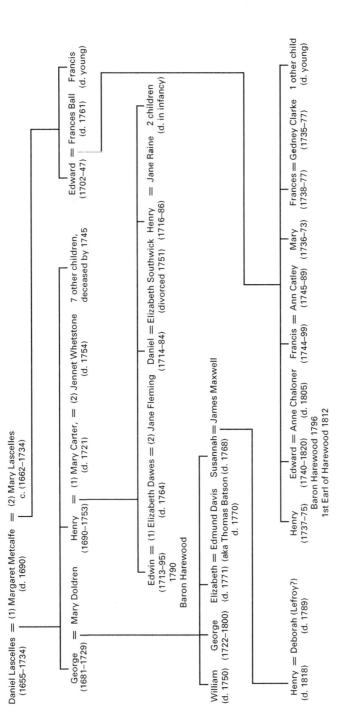

Figure 4.1. Simplified pedigree of the Lascelles family.

(fig. 4.1).[13] Twenty-five-year-old George Lascelles was on Barbados by 1706. During the succeeding six years, the rateable value of his Bridgetown business increased from 100 lb of sugar to 400 lb. Brother Henry, an aspiring merchant aged twenty-two, joined him in 1711 or 1712. Initially, the pair probably traded with their London-based kinsman Edward Lascelles. In 1715, however, a reorganisation of the family business occurred. George returned to England while his half-brother Edward (a youth of just thirteen) arrived on the island. Once established in London, George received sugar shipped from the West Indies, handling upwards of 1,004 cwt of sugar in 1719 alone (549 cwt of which originated from Barbados).[14]

By trading as sugar merchants, the brothers replicated a core feature of the quartet's earlier business model. In two important respects, however, the activities of the trio speedily diverged from the earlier set of brothers. Firstly, the Northallerton Lascelles demonstrated a greater commitment to the slave trade. Shortly after his arrival, Henry Lascelles married Mary, daughter of Edwin Carter, a Barbados merchant, slave trader, planter, and Deputy Collector of the Customs.[15] The scale of Carter's dealings in slaves is shown by his importation of 563 Africans between 1698 and 1703 valued at £7,594, and (with Joseph Marbin) a further 1,424 Africans between 1703 and 1707 worth £42,325.[16] Henry's own participation in the slave trade dates from 1713, when with two other merchants he despatched the *Carracoe Merchant* from Barbados laden with approximately one hundred slaves. The ship's intended destination was the French settlement of Petit Goaves on St Domingue, but bad weather forced the vessel to put into the Spanish port of St Domingo, where it was promptly impounded by customs authorities.[17] George and Henry fared better with other ventures, importing between them 1,101 slaves between December 1713 and December 1717. It is likely that Henry was directly involved in additional slaving investments

[13] George and Henry were children of Daniel Lascelles' first marriage to Margaret Metcalfe, member of a Northallerton gentry family, Foster, *Pedigrees*.
[14] BA, St Michael's, Levy Books, vol. I, ff. 306, 378, 391; vol. II, f. 54; David L. Kent, *Barbados and America* (Arlington, VA, 1980), 186. WRA, NH 2,400, London Port Book, 1719. In view of the fact that 137 days are missing in the port book, these figures should be regarded as an underestimate of the true total.
[15] Foster, *Pedigrees*; CRO, Barbados Plantation Records, Box 1,032, Barbados Council Minute Book (1720), 22–3; Bobby Morris, 'Transfer of Wealth from Barbados to England – From Lascelles Plantation, Barbados to Harewood House, Yorkshire', *JBMHS*, 50 (2004), 93.
[16] Elizabeth Donnan ed., *Documents Illustrative of the History of the Slave Trade to America* (4 vols., Washington, DC, 1930–5), vol. II, 25–7, 29–30.
[17] NA:PRO, C11/2069/31, *Henry Lascelles vs Neil Bothwell* (1737).

that have gone unrecorded, since he purchased fifty slaves from the Royal African Company in 1723.[18]

A second major difference lay in the Lascelles' exploitation of the fiscal apparatus of state for commercial advantage. In either 1714 or 1715, Henry was appointed Collector of Customs for the port of Bridgetown: one of the most valuable revenue posts in the British customs service.[19] Around 1730, he was succeeded in this post by brother Edward (though Henry continued to collect the $4\frac{1}{2}$ per cent export duty on the King's sugars until surrendering his bond and clearing his accounts in 1733).[20] The allegations levelled against each brother during their tenure as Collector reveal how the office generated a fruitful source of commercial capital.

Corruption and Faction

Henry was accused of improper conduct almost immediately he assumed the post of Collector. In the affair of the *St Louis* (a ship forced to dock in Barbados *en route* from Brazil to Lisbon in May 1715), the vessel's part-owner, Francis Lansa, accused both Governor Robert Lowther and Lascelles of extorting £2,000 from the ship's master, Jean de Morassin.[21] Complaints of more systematic frauds were soon afterwards submitted to the Lords Commissioners for Trade and Plantations in 1720 by Samuel Cox, a member of the Barbados Council. Lascelles was charged with pocketing the proceeds of slaves and vessels irregularly seized as prizes. Cox further alleged that Henry submitted fraudulent accounts for the collection of the King's $4\frac{1}{2}$ per cent duty on sugars shipped from the island. Neither the value nor quality of sugars received by the Collector, Cox argued, corresponded to the entries made in the customs house books. In support of these charges, a deposition from James Young (Collector of Customs at Holetown) was presented, testifying that in return for bribes, Henry gave the island's merchants blank documents (called cockets) to enable them to circumvent the

---

[18] NA:PRO, CO28/18/320–30; R. B. Sheridan, 'The Sugar Trade of the British West Indies, 1660–1756', unpub. Ph.D. thesis (University of London, 1951), Appendix, xxv.

[19] An appointment date of 1714 is cited in Pedro Welch, 'The Lascelles and their Contemporaries: Fraud in Little England, 1700–1820', *JBMHS*, 48 (2002), 93, and Morris, 'Transfer of Wealth', 93.

[20] Richard Pares, 'A London West-India Merchant House, 1740–1769', in Richard Pares and A. J. P. Taylor eds., *Essays Presented to Sir Lewis Namier* (London, 1956), 77; BL, Add. MS 33,028 f. 378, 'Minute for passing the accounts of Henry Lascelles, Collector of Customs in Barbados' (1733).

[21] [William Gordon], *A Representation of the Miserable State of Barbados* (London, 1719), 40–3.

Navigation Acts and pay lower rates of duty. These same documents, Young stated, were doctored to tally with the fraudulent entries in the customs accounts, to disguise the true value of commodities passing through the Collector's hands.[22]

Brother Edward was subject to similar allegations two decades later following the appearance in print of treatises on trade and revenue in the American colonies by John Ashley in 1740 and 1743. These tracts dealt extensively on the administration of the $4\frac{1}{2}$ per cents, alluding to corruption by the two Lascelles brothers, without actually naming them. Ashley's book raised a 'Clamour' and 'made so great a Noise' that Henry's tenure of office was re-examined for evidence of embezzlement at the same time that Edward was investigated.[23]

In 1720, Henry was summoned to London by the Commissioners for Trade and Plantations to answer Cox's first set of charges, but he escaped censure and remained in post.[24] Three years later, the Auditor General of Barbados submitted a report of revenue practices drawing attention to the same questionable procedures that Cox had complained of. It was not until 1734, however, that new instructions were issued to Collectors specifically designed to prevent frauds in the administration of the $4\frac{1}{2}$ per cents. In early 1743, Robert Dinwiddie (who a few years earlier had toured the sugar islands to review revenue procedures) was sent to Barbados with a special commission of Inspector General of Customs to enquire into the conduct of the Bridgetown Collector. In March 1744, Dinwiddie suspended Edward and the Comptroller, Arthur Upton, for not adhering to the 1734 instructions. Controversially, he also surcharged Henry for the large sum of £39,995.14s.4d (currency), notwithstanding the fact his accounts had been audited and cleared ten years previously.

The report Dinwiddie submitted to the Commissioners in February 1745 listed ten charges against Edward. The most serious of his accusations illustrate the methods employed to siphon capital from the revenue system to add to the Lascelles' own trading stock. According to Dinwiddie, when Edward received duty payments in cash, he entered the value in kind (chiefly sugar) in the customs books and charged

---

[22] *Journal of the Commissioners for Trade and Plantations*, vol. IV, 145; *CSPC(A&WI)*, vol. XXXI (London, 1933), 309, 356, 362. Welch, 'Lascelles and their Contemporaries', 93–5; Louis Knott Koontz, *Robert Dinwiddie: His Career in American Colonial Government and Westward Expansion* (Glendale, CA, 1941), 68–71.

[23] John Ashley, *Memoirs and Considerations Concerning the Trade and Revenues of the Colonies in America* (2 vols., London, 1740–3); *LMLB*, Lascelles & Maxwell to Arthur Upton (Barbados), 29 September 1743.

[24] Henry's wife Mary accompanied him; she died during the visit, on 17 May 1721, and was buried in Northallerton two days later, Foster, *Pedigrees*.

fictitious 'wastage' (an allowance for leakage and pilfering) of 3 per cent. Conversely, if planters paid duty in kind, Dinwiddie alleged that the Collector commuted the same for cash, by selling the sugars to business associates at rates below their true market value. It was claimed that perfectly good sugars worth 18s. to 20s. per cwt were sold as poor-quality produce for only 10s. to 13s. a cwt. According to Dinwiddie, capital was further leeched from the customs by Edward's permitting surpluses of cash and produce to accumulate on accounts submitted in arrears. The Collector, it was charged, even drew on this reserve to grant credit to planters for duty payments, charging them interest on the same.[25] The charges of embezzlement levelled at Edward resemble both Cox's earlier accusations against Henry, and the estimates of revenue fraud published by Ashley.[26]

At the subsequent hearings held in 1745–6, Edward was found to have 'essentially if not totally disregarded' the procedures introduced in 1734 to curb fraud. Therefore, the Collector and his deputy, the Comptroller Arthur Upton, were adjudged improper persons to continue as revenue officials. The Commissioners also requested that the Attorney General consider whether grounds existed for a formal prosecution and surcharge.[27]

Historians have taken a literal view of proceedings against the brothers, accepting that they were guilty of corruption yet able to evade punishment by virtue of their connections as leading West India merchants.[28] While correct, this interpretation is incomplete. Henry and Edward certainly lobbied strongly to protect their interests; they enlisted the support of the Barbados colonial agent John Sharpe, collected affidavits from friendly merchants and officials testifying to their good conduct, and drew on their patronage network to garner support.[29] At a critical time, the Lascelles' political stock of capital was bolstered

[25] William L. Clements Library, University of Michigan, Sydney Papers, Report Submitted by the London Customs House to the Lords Commissioners for Trade and Plantations on Robert Dinwiddie's Investigation [n.d., after 10 June 1745].

[26] Pares, 'West-India Merchant House', 77–8; NA:PRO, T1/320/22; Ashley, *Memoirs and Considerations*, 40–1, 47–8, 50–4.

[27] Clements Library, Sydney Papers, Report Submitted by the London Customs House to the Lords Commissioners for Trade and Plantations, c. 10 June 1745; NA:PRO, T1/320/21, Report of the Commissioners of Customs submitted to the Lords of Trade, 23 July 1746; Koontz, *Robert Dinwiddie*, 75–91.

[28] Welch, 'Lascelles and their Contemporaries', 95–6; Koontz, *Robert Dinwiddie*, 92–3; James Henretta, *'Salutary Neglect': Colonial Administration under the Duke of Newcastle* (Princeton, 1972), 228.

[29] BL, Add. MS 33,028 f. 378, 'Extract of papers referred to in the case of Henry Lascelles'; Add. MS 23,817, Henry Lascelles to Sir Thomas Robinson, 26 June 1744; University of Nottingham, Pelham-Newcastle Papers, Ne C182/1, Sir Thomas Robinson to Henry Pelham, 3 October 1744; Ne C182/2, Henry Lascelles to Sir

substantially. Henry and son Daniel were returned as MPs for North-allerton and Scarborough in 1745. Business partner George Maxwell commented that, in consequence, it was hoped 'they might have interest enough to bring these matters to a fair & impartial hearing & in a short time'. During the political crisis of the same year, son Edwin took up arms in repelling the Jacobite invasion, while Henry provided timely financial support for the Hanoverian regime, including underwriting £90,000 in loans to the Government. 'To be sure, all loyal people that have money will lend,' wrote Maxwell, 'for otherwise they would risque the loss of their whole property if the pretender was to get the better, which god forbid; for, it is said, he declares he will cancel all the publick Debts said to be near 60 millions.'[30]

Far more was involved in the attempted prosecutions of the Lascelles, however, than simple fraud investigations. The attacks on Henry and Edward must be understood in the context of warring factions in Britain and Barbados. In evaluating the brothers' reputations, it is also important to appreciate that contemporary accounts of events are generally written by authors opposed to the Lascelles and their associates, and who were usually themselves under investigation for corruption. Published histories of Barbados, for example, claim that Robert Lowther extorted £28,000 from the colony as Governor; that he was prosecuted by the Lords Justices in 1720; and that he was only reprieved by an act of grace following the accession of George II.[31] In addition to unlawful seizure of ships and prize cargoes, the Governor's critics accused him of manipulating the public debt in favour of cronies, who purchased credit notes at a heavy discount on advance information of their imminent redemption.[32]

Thomas Robinson, 10 August 1744; *LMLB*, Lascelles & Maxwell to Edward Lascelles (Barbados), 20 April 1744.

[30] *Gentleman's Magazine*, 14 (1744), 225; *LMLB*, Lascelles & Maxwell to Thomas Applethwaite, 15 January 1745[6]; Maxwell (London) to Nicholas Wilcox (Barbados), 22 November 1745; Maxwell (London) to Thomas Findlay (Barbados), 29 October 1745; Pares, 'West-India Merchant House', 78; Leo Francis Stock ed., *Proceedings and Debates of the British Parliaments Respecting North America* (5 vols., Washington DC, 1924–41), vol. V, 222.

[31] John Oldmixon [Herman Moll], *The British Empire in America* (2nd edn, 2 vols., London, 1741), vol. II, 68–70; John Poyer, *The History of Barbados* (London, 1808), 225–6. Oldmixon dedicated the 2nd edition to Jonathan Blenman(see below), while Poyer states his main source is derived from Oldmixon's book.

[32] [Gordon], *Miserable State*, 15–16. The scheme was put into effect by passing a law that reordered the priority in which debts would be paid by the Barbados treasury. It should be noted that insider trading was widely practised and poorly regulated at this time. The creation of the Bank of England (1697), the Sword Blade Company's Irish land speculation (1702), and the setting-up of the South Sea Company (1720) were all characterised by the promoters buying up heavily discounted assets in the certain

The most influential of Lowther's enemies was Jonathan Blenman: an attorney jailed by the Governor and tried at Grand Sessions in 1720, allegedly for tampering with evidence in the Lansa case.[33] Reaching an assessment of the Lascelles is complicated by Blenman's portrayal of himself as the defender of customary rights in opposition to Lowther's arbitrary and corrupt government. During the imperial crisis of the 1760s, the negative depiction of Lowther and his cronies was further reinforced in contemporary printed literature.[34] In consequence, nineteenth-century histories of Barbados dismiss Lowther as 'arrogant and tyrannical', while Jonathan Blenman is celebrated posthumously as 'one of the brightest ornaments of his country'.[35] Blenman might almost be said to have 'fixed' the history of Barbados, by influencing the content of two of the most frequently cited printed sources: *Caribbeana* and John Oldmixon's *The British Empire in America*. The dedication to the second, expanded edition of this latter work alludes to Blenman's imprint on contemporary accounts:

as you defended the Laws and Constitution of Barbados, you will protect its History, at least where the Merits of the Cause will warrant your Appearance in it.[36]

The attacks on Lowther and Lascelles on Barbados were orchestrated by Samuel Cox and the controversial cleric William Gordon. Cox, a disgruntled former Naval Officer, headed a faction opposed to the Governor; in Britain, he drew on the support of his brother, Sir Charles

---

knowledge that they would appreciate, John Carswell, *The South Sea Bubble* (Dover, 1993; originally published 1960), 25, 30, 46.

[33] CRO, Barbados Records, Box 1,033, Barbados Council Minute Book (1718–19), 364–7; Barbados Council Minute Book (1719–20), 90–103. Undoubtedly, Lowther profited handsomely from his years in Barbados; at his death, in 1745, he was worth £33,000. Much of his wealth, however, was acquired legitimately and represented the proceeds of Carleton Hall sugar estate (inherited by his wife Joanne Carleton, née Frere), in addition to his Governor's salary, John Vincent Beckett, 'Landownership in Cumbria, c. 1680–c. 1750', unpub. Ph.D. thesis (University of Lancaster, 1975), 253–4, 262–3, 267.

[34] Oldmixon, *British Empire*, vol. I, 66–73; [Samuel Keimer], Caribbeana (2 vols., London, 1741), vol. I, 213–19, 268–71; [Sir John Gay Alleyne], *Remarks Upon a Book, intitled, A Short History of Barbados* (Barbados, 1768), 14–15, 22–3, 41–3, 79–83; Andrew Jackson O'Shaughnessy, *An Empire Divided: The American Revolution and the British Caribbean* (Philadelphia, 2000), 86–7.

[35] Robert H. Schomburgk, *The History of Barbados* (London, 1971; Originally published 1848), 313; Poyer, *History of Barbados*, 257.

[36] Oldmixon, *British Empire*, vol. I, iv–v. John Oldmixon was a member of an ancient family established in Somerset since the fourteenth century which held the manor of Oldmixon. Blenman and Oldmixon thus shared a common regional affiliation.

Cox, a wealthy brewer, MP, and member of the Board of Trade.[37] The first clash between Henry and Cox took place in 1716, following the seizure of a cargo of indigo and annatto in a vessel owned by Cox, but shipped by Hezekiah Pacheco (a Jewish merchant), who failed to clear customs. Two years later, a similar case occurred when Lascelles seized another of Cox's ships, the *Dove*, for exporting sugar without certificates. On both occasions, the Collector's actions were upheld by the island's Admiralty Court; indeed, Cox stood accused of offering bribes to release the cargoes.[38] The various charges and counter-charges issued by both sides illustrate how appeals to the Board of Trade were inextricably tied to factional disputes on Barbados.

Opposition to Lowther during the Governor's second term coalesced around the Revd William Gordon: a conflict culminating in Gordon's indictment and imprisonment for sedition and corruption.[39] Ostensibly, differences over church policy divided the two sides. Gordon was an associate of Colonel Christopher Codrington, who in 1710 left a bequest intended to enable the Society for the Propagation of the Gospel to institute a religious order on Barbados.[40] In 1717, Gordon was appointed the colonial commissary of John Robinson, Bishop of London, and encouraged to develop the Codrington project.[41] Shortly

---

[37] *Journal of the Commissioners for Trade and Plantations*, vol. IV, 154–6; Eveline Cruickshanks, Stuart Handley, and D. W. Hayton eds., *The House of Commons, 1690–1715* (5 vols., Cambridge, 2002), vol. III, 771–4. Cox held the post of Naval Officer from 1698 until 1716, CRO, Barbados Plantation Records, Box 1,033, Barbados Council Minute Book (1718–19), 348, 358; Barbados Council Minute Book (1719–20), 236–7.

[38] CRO, Barbados Plantation Records, Box 1,034, Barbados Council Minute Book (1715–18), 340–53. Simultaneously, Cox was the subject of an ongoing investigation into alleged financial irregularities in the administration of customs bonds and public accounts during his time as Naval Officer, Box 1,033, Barbados Council Minute Book (1718–19), 1–25, Barbados Council Minute Book (1719–20), 236–47, 251–4.

[39] [Keimer], *Caribbeana*, vol. I, 269–70; CRO, Barbados Plantation Records, Box 1,033, Barbados Council Minute Book (1719–20), 103–14, 118–79. The *Barbados Gazette* portrays Gordon's imprisonment and release as a struggle between liberty and arbitrary authority; in contrast, the Council minutes emphasise factional politics.

[40] J. Harry Bennett, *Bondsmen and Bishops: Slavery and Apprenticeship on the Codrington Plantations of Barbados, 1710–1838* (Berkeley, 1958), 1–2; William Gordon, *A Sermon Preach'd at the Funeral of the Honourable Colonel Christopher Codrington* (London, 1710), 1. The title page of this tract states that Gordon held the degree of MA, but his alumnus records have not been traced.

[41] Gordon arrived in Barbados c. 1710–11, possibly after working for the SPG in North Carolina. Opponents later claimed he travelled as the indentured servant of Nathaniel Curtis and worked as a family tutor, before becoming a curate and running a church school. Gordon himself claimed to have arrived a cleric, who unexpectedly had to wait for a benefice to fall vacant on the island, Newberry Library, Chicago, Ayer MS 339, Office Book kept by Daniel Pulteney, a Commissioner of Trade and Plantations, 1717–21, Copy of a letter [from William Gordon] to Mr Secretary Addison upon the petition of the Agents of Barbados, 17 October 1717, 288; Copy of a letter from Governor Robert Lowther to the Bishop of London, 24 April 1717, 332–3; CRO, Barbados Plantation Records, Box 1,032,

afterwards, the Governor accused Gordon of seeking to introduce High Church Toryism into Barbados by means of an ecclesiastical court and a religious seminary.[42] According to Lowther, Gordon turned a sermon of thanksgiving held to celebrate the defeat of the 1715 Jacobite invasion of Britain, into 'a virulent Satyr against the King's best subjects and Friends', that labelled the Whigs as 'the Contrivers & formenters of the late Rebellion'.[43]

The Governor further sought to stymie ecclesiastical reform on the island by refusing to collate two of the Bishop's nominations to benefices. One was rejected on grounds of incompetence; the other, Dominick Langton, was alleged to have been a former friar, 'censured by the House of Commons in Ireland, for discountenancing & Obstructing the Conversion of several Papists to the Protestant Religion'.[44] Despite their undoubted convenience, the accusations of papism levelled against Langton may not simply have been inventions of Lowther. Following Langton's arrival, a trunk of books consigned to the cleric was found to contain 'several Popish books and other ill pamphlets'. The seizure included an answer to Charles Leslie's *The Case stated Between the Church of Rome and the Church of England* (London, 1713), along with eighteen sermons by Francis Atterbury and others.[45]

Distinguishing between religious differences and opportunistic rhetoric is a difficult task since the labelling of opponents formed part of the currency of political faction. Gordon and his supporters are described by their enemies as papists and Jacobite-sympathisers. Conversely, members of the SPG castigated obstructers of clerical reform and slave baptism as irreligious 'infidels' and fornicators.[46] Neither set of charges can be taken

Depositions (1719); Box 1,033, Barbados Council Minute Book (1718–19), Representation of William Gordon, 14 July 1715, 298–301. Some of this material is also preserved in the Colonial Office papers; e.g. NA:PRO, CO28/15, Papers relating to the attempt of Rev. William Gordon to set up an ecclesiastical court; CO28/17, Gordon to Addison, 17 October 1717.

[42] John Ellis Findling, 'Robert Lowther, Governor of Barbados, 1710–1720', unpub. MA thesis (University of Texas, 1965), 60, 66, 71, 73, 79–80.

[43] Ayer MS 339, Copy of a letter from Governor Robert Lowther to the Bishop of London, 26 April 1717, 332–3.

[44] Ibid., 327.

[45] CRO, Barbados Plantation Records, Box 1,034, Barbados Council Minute Book (1715–18), 322–5; Andrew M. Coleby, 'Compton, Henry (1631/2–1713)' and John B. Hattendorf, 'Robinson, John (1650–1723)', in *ODNB*. Langton's death occurred shortly after this discovery, precluding further investigation. It may be significant that John Robinson's first wife was Mary Langton of Yorkshire; while the shared surname could be a coincidence, nepotism cannot be ruled out as a factor responsible for Langton's appointment.

[46] John A. Schutz and Maud O'Neil, 'Arthur Holt, Reports on Barbados, 1725–33', *Journal of Negro History*, 31 (1946), Arthur Holt (Barbados) to the Bishop of London [Edmund Gibson], 30 April 1725, 448, 3 April 1732, 466–7.

at face value. Assuming that the book seizure was genuine, Langton may well have harboured Catholic sympathies. Nevertheless, opposition to Gordon centred less on his spiritual beliefs and more on his clerical reforms, particularly the attempt to diminish the influence of vestries over clergy by boosting parish stipends and his promotion of Codrington College.[47] Allegations of papism could reflect Gordon's friendly relations with Henry Compton (Robinson's predecessor as Bishop of London), who was a driving force behind the early work of the SPG and a supporter of Atterbury and Sacheverell.[48] However, the prospects for High Church Toryism (if such it was) almost certainly receded with the appointment of the more moderate John Robinson.

Gordon found himself arraigned at Grand Sessions in 1719 for publishing the libellous pamphlet *The Miserable State of Barbados*. Depositions from no fewer than thirty-five witnesses accompanied the indictment. These individuals were probably selected for their negative opinions of the clergyman since the testimonies consistently portray Gordon as a drunken, gambling, 'profligate, busey, Medling Immoral lying person', and 'a sower of Sedition and a factious party Man'. Allegations include complaints that Gordon attended mass on Martinique while trading in contraband French wine, brandy, and sugar.[49] Indeed, deponents claimed the cleric was commonly referred to as 'Le Marchand Spirituell' in French commercial circles, and 'the wandering Apostle' by Antiguan merchants.[50] Possible corroboration of claims that the cleric engaged in illegal commerce is provided by a report on the transatlantic slave trade written by a 'Reverend Gordon' in 1714. The author of this manuscript (who was almost certainly based on Barbados) possessed detailed knowledge of the intricacies of business, including the export of slaves to the French colonies.[51]

---

[47] Through the Bishop of London, Gordon lobbied for the passage of an Act of 1705 granting Barbados beneficed clergy a minimum annual income of £150 (currency), Nicholas Trott, *The Laws of the British Plantations in America, Relating to the Church and the Clergy, Religion and Learning* (London, 1721), 368–70; CRO, Barbados Plantation Records, Box 1,033, Barbados Council Minute Book (1718–19), 298–302.

[48] Compton appointed William Walker as his commissary on Barbados in 1690. According to Gordon, Walker established an ecclesiastical court and undertook visitations – actions that undoubtedly provoked resentment against interference by a central authority.

[49] CRO, Barbados Plantation Records, Box 1,032, Depositions taken on order of the Lords of the Committee for hearing complaints, particularly concerning the conduct of William Gordon, Clerk (1719).

[50] Ayer MS 339, 288; CRO, Barbados Plantation Records, Box 1,032, Depositions.

[51] Huntington Library, San Marino, California, Stowe MS ST9, 48–50, cited in James Pritchard, *In Search of Empire: The French in the Americas, 1670–1730* (Cambridge, 2004), 223. The author is grateful to David Eltis for supplying a transcript of this source, which

Early plans to develop Codrington College received warm encouragement from Bishop Compton.[52] News of the choice of Lowther as Governor in 1711 raised hopes that the initiative would soon make progress.[53] Once established on Barbados, however, Lowther aligned himself with Codrington's opponents and became embroiled in a controversy over the Society's two plantation accounts.[54] Bishop Robinson's submissions to the Board of Trade subsequently accused the Governor of a betrayal of trust.[55]

The timing of Cox's initial assault on Lowther and Henry coincided with shifts at the centre of British politics as well as island factional rivalries. In May 1714, Governor Lowther was recalled by Bolingbroke (the Secretary of State for the Southern Department). All of the members of the Board of Trade, however, were replaced in December 1714 as the Whigs swept into power.[56] Lowther's rapid restoration in 1715, following the death of Queen Anne and the fall of Bolingbroke, indicates the extent to which investigations of colonial officials were related to political circumstances. The rise of Sir Robert Walpole, and the formation of a new ascendant Whig governing coalition, proved highly beneficial to both Lascelles and Lowther. Henry was confirmed as Collector, while proceedings against the former Governor were stayed. In contrast, Cox (who had assumed the governance of Barbados as President of the Council), found himself ejected from political office and his own conduct investigated. Recognising defeat, he soon afterwards quit the island. On 21 July 1728, Gordon followed suit and boarded a ship bound to London with his family. Out in the Atlantic,

refers to the partnership of Betteris and Alleyne and also to the importation of slaves into Barbados by a young African trader. Betteris may be the same merchant whose account was handled by the Halls (see Chapter Two). Gordon's knowledge of the French Caribbean is also displayed in NA:PRO, CO29/17, Letter from William Gordon [n.d.] on the settlement of St Lucia.

52 Interestingly, the depositions against Gordon include the charge that he harboured slaves in his household, CRO, Barbados Plantation Records, Box 1,032, Deposition of Samuel Maynard.

53 MHS, Benjamin Colman Papers, 1641–1763, Dudley Woodbridge (Barbados) to Benjamin Colman, 10 July 1711.

54 A selection of extracts of documents relating to the Lowther-Gordon dispute have been printed. See e.g. *CSPC (A&WI)*, vol. XXXI, 54, 56–7, 188–205, 245–6, 353–4, 356, 363–4. (London, 1933), 203.

55 Ayer MS 339, Copy of a letter from the Bishop of London to Mr Lowther relating to the Commissaries at Barbados, 14 February 1717, 297–8; Copy of ye Lord Bishop of London's Reasons agtt the Board of Trade's Report of ye Pet^n of ye Agents at Barbados concerning an ecclesiastical Court [n.d., November 1717], 309–11.

56 Findling, 'Robert Lowther', 57–9; Schomburgk, *History of Barbados*, 314–15; I. K. Steele, *Politics of Colonial Policy: The Board of Trade in Colonial Administration, 1696–1720* (Oxford, 1968), 149.

their ship ran into a fierce storm and was last sighted in a state of distress by another vessel on 26 August.[57]

To understand the context of Dinwiddie's later attack on the Lascelles brothers it is necessary to go back to 1723. In this year, George Plaxton was created Treasurer of Barbados. Plaxton masterminded a scheme to issue £20,000 (currency) in bills to pay the large annual salary granted by the Assembly to Governor Worsley of £6,000. This debt issue was funded by a tax of 2s.6d. on every slave imported.[58] For reasons that are not clear, but are probably related to the deteriorating position of Governor Worsley, Plaxton was replaced as Treasurer in 1729 by Burch Hothersall. During Hothersall's tenure of office, payment of the Governor's salary fell into arrears. Whereas Plaxton's accounts balanced, a large discrepancy was discovered between the monies received and expended by Hothersall. By the time he was recalled to Britain, Worsley claimed no less than £16,000 (currency) was owing to him.

Hothersall and one of his sureties, Robert Warren, were debtors of the Lascelles; indeed, Henry held judgements against each of their estates.[59] In a bid to preserve his fortune and write off the deficit, Warren (with others) claimed that the original Act of Settlement had expired at the death of George I, freeing the colonists from their obligation of paying the levy on slaves. Jonathan Blenman (by now the island's Attorney General) rejected such arguments and ruled that Worsley was fully entitled to his remaining salary. In consequence, Blenman launched actions against Hothersall and Warren for the recovery of public monies, alleging they had embezzled funds to pay their creditors. The issue of the Governor's salary and a new excise tax to clear the public debt dominated the island's political agenda. In 1734, for example, Blenman reprieved Samuel Keimer (publisher of the *Barbados Gazette*) from imprisonment for libel, after he printed articles on the subject.[60]

Religious differences continued to feature in the island's factional policies, with the SPG remaining at the centre of events. Governor Worsley was considered sympathetic to the aspirations of Codrington

[57] [Keimer], *Caribbeana*, vol. I, 269, 342–4. Cox died in obscurity in New England.
[58] Hamilton College, New York Beinecke Collection, M43, George Plaxton (Barbados) to his brother William Plaxton, 5 January 1723, 26 November 1723; Barbados Public Library, Bridgetown, Lucas Manuscripts, 'Humble Petition of Jonathan Blenman Esq. His Majesty's Attorney General in this Island', ff. 278–81.
[59] See Chapters Six and Seven.
[60] Barbados Public Library, Lucas Manuscripts, 'Petition of Jonathan Blenman', ff. 282–4; Schomburgk, *History of Barbados*, 318–19; (Keimer), *Caribbeana*, vol. I, 40–6, 49–53, 96–9, 351. John Ashley (see fn. 23) was at this time a member of the Barbados Council and supported the prosecutions.

College's promoters, along with Blenman (a member of the Society). The subsequent triumph of Warren and other leading adversaries of the vanquished Governor left the SPG cleric Arthur Holt feeling utterly dejected.[61] The defeated parties, however, have left an imprint on Barbadian sources, demonstrating that history is not always a record of the victor's achievements. Holt's letters (never intended for publication, but preserved in the archives of Lambeth Palace) have coloured understanding of religious observance on the island.[62] The most significant contribution to the shaping of Barbadian history, however, emanates directly from Jonathan Blenman.

In 1739, a controversy erupted between Governor Robert Byng and Henry Peers, the Speaker of the Barbados Assembly. During this affair, Blenman was accused of leaking information to the press and writing speeches for members of the Assembly critical of the Government. In view of the political climate, Blenman judged it expedient to quit the island; accordingly, between 1739 and 1744 he resided in Britain.[63] During the five years spent away from the colony, the absentee Attorney General turned his hand to publishing. In 1740 and 1741, he very likely oversaw the printing of *Caribbeana* (a selection of articles from the largely lost original edition of the *Barbados Gazette*, with additional annotations).[64] This publication consistently reports the island's political controversies in ways favourable to Blenman and highlights a number of his legal judgements. One of the items selected for reprint, for example, was a poem (possibly written by Martha Fowke Sansom) commemorating Gordon and Blenman's victory over Lowther in 1720.[65]

Caribbeana was followed in 1742 by a book written by Blenman strongly critical of the 1732 Colonial Debts Act, arguing that it favoured London merchant creditors over indebted planters. This treatise also

---

[61] Schutz and O'Neil, 'Arthur Holt', Holt (Barbados) to the Bishop of London, 4 October 1731, 463–4.

[62] Ibid., 444–69.

[63] Cambridge University Library, Cambridge, Darnell Davis Collection, Box 3, No. 13. At the time of Blenman's ejection, Thomas Baxter was allied to him. Early in his exile, Blenman published *A Letter from a Gentleman at Barbados to his Friend now in London, Concerning the Administration of the late Governor B – g* (London, 1740), which purports to be a printed letter from Baxter to Blenman, dated 27 December 1740. After Blenman's return to the island, however, Baxter formed a faction hostile to his former friend (see Chapter Five). Governor Byng acted as godfather to one of the Lascelles' children, Morris, 'Transfer of Wealth', 93.

[64] Phyllis J. Gaskin, ' "Not Originally Intended for the Press": Martha Fowke Sansom's Poems in the *Barbados Gazette*', *Eighteenth-Century Studies*, 34 (2000), 64.

[65] [Keimer], *Caribbeana*, vol. I, 268–71, originally published in the *Barbados Gazette*, 9 February 1733 (no copy of the original newspaper is known to survive).

discussed abuses in the administration of the King's $4\frac{1}{2}$ per cents. By reprinting James Young's criticisms of the Bridgetown Collector, the tract as good as named Henry Lascelles as chief culprit. By this time, Blenman had been joined in London by John Ashley, who acted as Secretary of the Planters' Club. Ashley's two tracts, of 1740 and 1743, continued the thinly veiled attack on the Lascelles. Less than a year after the second volume's appearance, Blenman had returned to Barbados restored as Attorney General; at the same time, Dinwiddie set about his investigation of Edward and Henry.[66]

Dinwiddie's suspension and surcharging of the brothers occurred at a time of political uncertainty following the fall of Walpole. Henry viewed Dinwiddie's commission as manifesting 'the late torrent of power & success of his most inveterate Enemies'. 'This matter has been brewing ever since the fall of Orford,' Edward was warned, 'and your Brother became obnoxious to the New Ministry, I believe from some Publick Declarations in favour of the old to wch he was oblig'd.'[67]

As a result of the change in ministry, Henry's interest in the Board of Trade and Treasury was temporarily diminished. Mead (Commissioner of the Customs), Thomas Hill (Secretary of the Board of Trade), and Parson (Comptroller General) were all named as former members of the Opposition, who now exerted influence within the Government, much to Henry's detriment. The first of these was singled out as representing a particular problem: 'there is little good or relief to be expected', noted Maxwell, 'where Mead rules the roost'.[68] Yet the position of the Lascelles' enemies was not yet secure. 'The great jealousies amongst the Ministry composed of those of the old and new', meant that nothing could be taken for granted. Competition for the King's favour between Carteret's faction, and that of the Newcastle-Pelham group, was to prove an important factor in the outcome of Dinwiddie's investigation. Henry's natural allies (by virtue of his adherence to Walpole) were the Pelhams. After all, he had conspired on Barbados to remove Governor Worsley (a Carteret supporter) in 1731 during the political fallout over Hothersall's fraud.[69] The eventual triumph of the Pelhams, therefore, played greatly to Henry's advantage.

As before, the course of proceedings against the Lascelles mirrored political vicissitudes. In late December 1744, Barbados correspondents were informed of Carteret's removal from office, along with 'everyone

---

[66] University of London Library, MS 279, Memorandum of John Ashley (1745–7).

[67] *LMLB*, Lascelles & Maxwell to Arthur Upton, 29 September 1743; to Anthony Lynch, 15 November 1743; George Maxwell to Edward Lascelles, 4 July 1744.

[68] Ibid., Lascelles & Maxwell to Edward Lascelles, 20 April 1744.

[69] Henretta, '*Salutary Neglect*', 43–5.

besides that deserted the opposition upon L^{d}. Orford's fall'. By the following February, Edward was assured that neither Dinwiddie nor his supporters 'have any Interest now at the Treasury'.[70] This was perhaps an overstatement of the position, since in July 1746 the committee found against Edward and Upton. Nevertheless, the report contained encouraging signs. Dinwiddie was criticised for being overzealous and not all of his accusations were upheld. Conspicuously, there was no mention of Henry's surcharge, indicating that proceedings against him had been stayed. A minority of the committee also refused to put their names to the findings. By this stage, it must have been clear to all parties that there was no longer any realistic prospect of securing a dismissal. For Edward Lascelles and Upton, the verdict proved only a temporary inconvenience. In October 1746, both men were restored to their posts through the actions of Henry Grenville (the new Barbados Governor) and Lord Lyttelton at the Board of Trade. So complete was the turn-around that Edward was even elevated to the Barbados Council shortly before his death in 1747.[71]

Were Edward and Henry Lascelles corrupt? Undoubtedly, the brothers profited from their tenure of the Collectorship. At a time when standards of public accountability were still evolving, however, it is not clear that their conduct differed greatly from those of their contemporaries. It must also be acknowledged that nearly all of the charges levelled against them were partisan in nature; in consequence, the sources are not written from an objective perspective. The earliest corruption case, that of Francis Lansa, provides a good illustration of the difficulties in reaching a balanced judgement. Gordon's tract, *The Miserable State of Barbados*, reprints Lansa and de Morassin's depositions and presents details of the alleged extortion as fact.[72] A quite different perspective is obtained from the Barbados Council's Minute Books, which give the Governor's and the Collector's side of the story. In this document, one reads that de Morassin (far from putting into Carlisle Bay in distress) was a business associate of both Gordon and

---

[70] *LMLB*, Lascelles & Maxwell to John Pare, 31 December 1744; to John Brathwaite, 7 January 1744[5]; to Edward Lascelles, 28 February 1744[5].

[71] NA:PRO, T1/320/21, Report of the Commissioners of Customs submitted to the Lords of Trade, 23 July 1746; Koontz, *Robert Dinwiddie*, 75–91; *LMLB*, Pares Transcripts, H485, f. 78, Lascelles & Maxwell to Thomas Applethwaite (Barbados), 27 September 1746, 17 October 1746.

[72] Gordon, *Miserable State*, 40–3. CRO, Barbados Plantation Records, Box 1,033 contains a rare tract [Anon.], *An Answer to the Five Articles Exhibited against Four of the Suspended Counsellors* (Barbados, 1719) not listed in Jerome S. Handler, *A Guide to Source Materials for the Study of Barbados History, 1627–1834* (Carbondale, 1971) or his *Supplement to A Guide to Source Materials for the Study of Barbados History, 1627–1834* (Providence, RI, 1991).

Nicholas Hope, the private secretary of President William Sharpe. In one account sugar is appropriated by the Collector; in the other it is sold to island merchants for profit by de Morassin.[73]

Opposition to Henry and Edward emanated from two different sources: island factions and advocates of a centralising authority, such as Dinwiddie.[74] These opposing tendencies proved difficult to reconcile: a circumstance the brothers succeeded in exploiting. Sometimes, the Lascelles looked to the metropolitan authority for support in recalling a troublesome Governor, or obtaining a veto of colonial land bank schemes. At other times, they sided with localism by resisting central supervision of the customs, and coordinating opposition to increases in sugar duties.[75]

The League of Gentlemen

Henry remained a Barbados merchant until the death of his elder brother George in 1729. On receiving the news, Henry went to London, leaving half-brother Edward to deputise as Customs Collector and to assume direction of the Barbadian end of the family business.[76] Henry then returned to the island for what proved to be the last time, marrying his second wife, Jennet Whetstone, on Barbados in July 1731.[77] By late

---

[73] CRO, Barbados Plantation Records, Box 1,033, Barbados Council Minute Book (1718–19), 155–82.

[74] Koontz, *Robert Dinwiddie*, 68–71.

[75] For details of Lascelles & Maxwell's involvement in the defeat of the proposals to raise sugar import duties in 1744, see *LMLB*, Pares Transcripts, H574–5, H577–9. On 13 February 1744, the Pelham ministry was defeated by 176 votes to 168 on the Supply Bill, *LMLB*, Lascelles & Maxwell to George Hannay. Henry Lascelles' participation in the controversy complicated his efforts at staying Dinwiddie's proceedings against Edward and himself.

[76] An account at Drummond's Bank in Henry Lascelles' name details living expenses for a London residence between 1729 and 1731, The Royal Bank of Scotland Group Archives, London, Drummond's Bank, Customer Account Ledgers, GB 1502/DR/427/8, f. 290–DR/747/12, f. 187. Edward Lascelles remained on Barbados until his death; the only circumstantial evidence alluding to a possible visit is an undated portrait preserved at Harewood House attributed to 'circle of Enoch Seeman (1694–1744)'. It is not clear, however, whether Edward sat for this painting in London.

[77] Foster, *Pedigrees*, vol. II , 'Lascelles'. The Whetstones were a prominent West Indian family. Sir Thomas Whetstone became Speaker of Jamaica's Island Assembly in 1665; Admiral William Whetstone was the father-in-law of Woodes Rogers (Governor of the Bahamas between 1717 and 1721); John Whetstone (owner of three plantations on the island) held the posts of Receiver of the Casual Revenue and Deputy Colonial Secretary of Barbados, Stephen Saunders Webb, *The Governors-General: The English Army and the Definition of the Empire, 1569–1681* (Chapel Hill, 1979), 231, 449; Hamilton College, Beinecke Collection, M29, Edwin Stede Papers, John Whetstone to William Blathwayt, 13 August 1692; Stock ed., *Proceedings and Debates*, vol. IV, 160; Morris, 'Transfer of

March 1732, however, the newly wedded couple had moved to London, where Henry was soon arguing the merits of a significant piece of legislation: An Act for the more easy recovery of Debts in His Majesty's Plantations and Colonies in America. Henry's permanent return to Britain predated the decease of his father by two years. Old Daniel Lascelles' demise in 1734 left a minor, William Lascelles, heir to the family's ancestral property at Northallerton. Well before his nephew's early death in 1750, however, Henry had succeeded in gaining possession of these lands.[78] Without question, by the early 1730s, Henry Lascelles was established as a leading West Indian trader and the head of an ascendant gentry family. The ambitious commercial projects he now launched upon elevated himself into a super-merchant and set the Lascelles on the path to aristocratic eminence.

Henry's first project was to take over the commission house brother George had managed. Its core business consisted of the receipt and sale of cargoes of sugar and rum despatched by planters to London, the organisation of freight and insurance for these shipments, and the preparation of return cargoes of stores and goods for use on the plantations. The day-to-day activities of the commission house are recorded in wonderful detail by a surviving volume of correspondence spanning the years 1743 to 1746. Yet, in the wider scheme of things, the commission house was arguably the least original and significant aspect of Lascelles' business interests after 1734, though it provided a framework around which other activities were organised.

A second area of activity consisted of government contracts to supply armed forces with provisions and other stores.[79] Participation in the victuals trade commenced prior to Henry's departure from the island, but involvement in this branch of business increased substantially after his return.[80] In 1741, Henry commented that victualling was the branch of business 'which through good management (I reckon) I chiefly made

Wealth', 93; Christian Buchet, *Marine, Economie et Société: un exemple d'interaction: l'avitaillement de la Royal Navy durant la guerre de sept ans* (Paris, 1999).

[78] Henry's will recites that his nephew's land was acquired by purchase, BA, RB6/22/370–90. The power of attorney granted by Henry in 1734 probably relates to victualling rather than general business matters, since these duties were probably already assigned to Edward, BA, RB1/33/105, Power of Attorney, Henry Lascelles to Richard Morecroft (1734).

[79] Edward Lascelles of Stoke Newington earlier acted as victualler of naval vessels during his residence on Barbados, but on a lesser scale, Morris, 'Transfer of Wealth', 92.

[80] Buchet, *Marine, Economie et Société*, 195–7. The earliest reference to Henry Lascelles as 'victuallers agent' that has been found dates from 1730, BA, Hughes-Queree Collection, Abstract in Queree notebook, 'Grove'.

my fortune by'.[81] It is not clear to what extent this essentially off-hand remark can be taken at face value, but the scale of his investment in the contracting business was certainly considerable. Turnover in victuals between Henry and Samuel McCall of Philadelphia (just one of the North American merchants with whom he transacted) amounted to £24,000 (currency) during the seven years 1743 to 1749. If Lascelles had indeed made serious money from provisioning by 1741, profits generated during the Wars of Jenkins' Ear and the Austrian Succession (1739–48) surely boosted his fortunes further still.[82]

The third project of great note was the slave trade. Lascelles had invested in slaving while on Barbados with brother Edward.[83] Indeed, the merchant to whom he granted a power of attorney on his departure in 1734 was Richard Morecroft, a close business associate of the Lascelles. Morecroft was deputy agent victualler for Barbados and the Leeward Islands; between March 1731 and June 1737 he also imported 3,214 slaves into the island. At his death in 1742, Morecroft was a wealthy man, reputedly worth upwards of £40,000 (currency) and well known in Liverpool as a leading West Indian slave dealer.[84]

The new variation on the slave trade, devised by Henry in London, was the formation of a consortium of eight merchants, known collectively as the 'floating factory', between 1736 and 1744. This syndicate's business plan was to station vessels off the Guinea coast at Anomabu to receive slaves from forts or castles constructed at Cape Castle, including premises constructed by the syndicate with the agreement of local Fanti rulers. One of the agents wrote in 1739, for example, that: 'I have applied to ye King of ye Fantiens, who has allotted me a piece of Ground, Regularly settled att so much P. Annum to Build a Factory house and ware houses.'[85] A succession of ships were sent to rendezvous

---

[81] *LMLB*, Pares Transcripts, H356, Henry Lascelles to Edward Lascelles, 20 April 1741, cited in D. J. Hamilton, 'Private Enterprise and Public Service: Naval Contracting in the Caribbean, c. 1720–50', *Journal for Maritime Research* www.jmr.nmm.ac.uk (April 2004).

[82] HSP, Account Book of Samuel McCall Sr, 1743–9, 740.

[83] Clements Library, Shelburne Papers, vol. XLIV, #665, Edward Lascelles and Samuel Wadeson (Barbados) to Peter Burrell, 22 September 1736.

[84] Barbados Public Library, Lucas Manuscripts, Minutes of the Barbados Council, 26 November 1734, ff. 451–3; Donnan ed., *Documents*, vol. II, 427–31; HSP, Yeates Papers: John Yeates Correspondence, 1733–59, John Bayley (Barbados) to John Yeates (Philadelphia), 14 August 1742; *LMLB*, Pares Transcripts, H373, Lascelles & Lascelles to Richard Morecroft (Barbados), 17 March 1739[40], 28 March 1740, 22 May 1740, 28 June 1740, 13 September 1740, 6 December 1740, 20 April 1741, 27 October 1741, 29 December 1741, 16 February 1741[2].

[85] NA:PRO, C103/130, George Hamilton (Anomabu) to Thomas Hall (London), 2 December 1739.

with the 'floating factories', picking up slaves and delivering supplies. Upwards of twelve vessels are known to have engaged in this trade between 1736 and 1742.[86]

The initial capital subscribed in 1736 was £32,000 (sterling) for four years; in 1738–9 this sum was raised to £41,200 in order to extend the scheme for a further two years. Henry owned an eighth share and acted as treasurer; one of his sons also held an eighth part, while Morecroft and Edward Lascelles took a further eighth share between them. The syndicate was completed by the following London merchants: Thomas Hall (a wealthy merchant, specialised in slaving), Richard Pinnell, Edward Jasper, George Hamilton, and Robert Moore. Turnover greatly exceeded the amount of capital invested, as credit was raised on the reputation of the participants. In December 1739, for example, it was reported that upwards of £74,000 of assets were afloat in Africa.[87]

The coordination of an operation involving multiple shipping movements was an ambitious undertaking. A number of the personnel involved were connected with the victualling trades or were experienced commanders of naval vessels. The floating factory scheme can, therefore, be seen as an attempt to transfer logistical expertise accumulated in military operations to the arena of slave trading.[88] Complete accounts of the syndicate do not survive, but an indication of the scale of their trade is provided by the following statements. In December 1737, 368 slaves were sold in Barbados supplied by the floating factory for £8,391 (sterling). Insurance was made for 500 Africans due to be exported in November 1741, while a total of 914 slaves were despatched from Anomabu in September 1742, valued at £14,614.[89] In addition to trafficking in human beings, the investors traded in other merchandise. In 1736, a cargo of elephants' teeth, gold, gum, and malaguetta was

---

[86] Conrad Gill, *Merchants and Mariners of the Eighteenth Century* (London, 1961), 92–7; Joseph E. Inikori, *Africans and the Industrial Revolution in England: A Study in International Trade and Economic Development* (Cambridge, 2002), 293–5, 343–4, 419.

[87] NA:PRO, C103/130, Hamilton (Anomabu) to Richard Pinnell (London), 3 August 1738; Hamilton (Anomabu) to Pinnell (London), 2 January 1737[8]; Hamilton to Hall (London), 2 December 1739, 24 May 1739; C11/2189/18, *Lascelles et al.* vs *Hamilton and Moore* (1742).

[88] Henry, Edward, and Morecroft were all involved in victualling. In related slaving ventures, they drew on the services of Thomas Revell, 'of the victualling office'. The 'flagship' vessel stationed at Anomabu was the *Argyle*: a former man-of-war, captained by George Sclater. Francis Gashry, 'of the Admiralty office' was another associate connected with the investors, NA:PRO, C11/2551/33, *Neale et al.* vs *Sclater* (1737).

[89] NA:PRO, C103/130, Account of John Dunning's Commissions, settled with the owners of the *Mary*, 21 December 1737; Hamilton (Anomabu) to Hall (London), 8 November 1741; Hamilton (Anomabu) to Hall (London), 19 September 1742.

despatched worth £4,254; the following year £2,557 of elephants' teeth, guinea corn, and gold dust were shipped out.[90]

The risks inherent in a project of this magnitude, coupled with internal disputes among investors and with the consortium's agents, resulted in the winding up of the venture in 1744. That year a correspondent on Barbados was informed how 'the last floating Factory, had given him [Henry] in the course thereof a great deal of disquietude, and in the end did not turn out to any account, so he is resolved never again to be concern'd in any Trade there'.[91] An indication of the level of 'disquietude' is provided by the bitter recriminations of one of the associates:

The treatment you saw I sufered from Mr Lascelles last Evening, was so insulting, scurrilous, & un Gentlemanlike that I am obliged to ask your Pardon for the manner he obliged me to leave you; I am determined never more to meet him, unless in Westminster Hall.[92]

Even Henry's foes, however, were obliged to pay tribute to his business acumen and the influence his name commanded. 'He has those advantages that he will make mony lett what will happen,' complained Hamilton, 'itts plaine what ever step we take, he has an Interest therein.'[93] Henry's voice carried a long distance. His 'Daming, Villifying & abusing' of fellow syndics in London coffee houses was soon 'ye Public Taulk of ye Coast by all masters of ships out of London, Bristoll, or Leverpoole'.[94]

Lascelles' involvement in slaving did not end with the floating factory. In 1747, for example, he invested in shipments of slaves, gold, and elephants' teeth worth £14,678. By means that are not documented, Henry obtained contracts to maintain forts owned by the Royal African Company. In 1750, he lobbied (unsuccessfully) for the formation of a new joint-stock company to carry on trade. This defeat, however, was followed soon afterwards by his retirement from commercial concerns,

---

[90] NA:PRO, C12/2274/24, *Lascelles et al.* vs *Young* (1736); NA:PRO, C103/130, Account of John Dunning's Commissions, settled with the owners of the *Mary*, 21 December 1737.

[91] *LMLB*, Maxwell to Newton, 23 July 1744. Lascelles continued, however, to be involved in at least four slave ships up until his death (see next section) and he also provided finance for slavers through the house of Lascelles & Maxwell which acted as the financial guarantor for slavers who sold slaves on credit to planters, Donnan ed., *Documents*, vol. IV, 345–6; Jacob M. Price, 'Credit in the Slave Trade and Plantation Economies', in B.L. Solow ed., *Slavery and the rise of the Atlantic System* (Cambridge, 1991), in 312–13.

[92] NA:PRO, C103/130, John Dunning to [Thomas Hall], 10 July 1747.

[93] Ibid., Hamilton (Anomabu) to Pinnell (London), 3 August 1738.

[94] Ibid., Hamilton (Anomabu) to Hall (London), 19 April 1741.

to make way for his second son Daniel.[95] In consequence, while the Lascelles continued to concern themselves with the transatlantic slave trade after 1750, henceforth their role was confined to the provision of banking facilities, rather than the direct promotion of slaving projects.[96]

Henry's fourth business interest lay in owning ships, which complemented his involvement in the sugar, slave, and victualling trades. In addition to the dozen vessels involved in the floating factory, he held shares in at least six ships between 1713 and 1717.[97] At his death in 1753, Lascelles possessed shares in no fewer than twenty-one craft. In common with other merchants, Henry did not own any of these ships outright, but instead opted to spread his risks across a number of vessels. In total, he owned the equivalent of two whole ships, but did not hold more than a quarter share in any one vessel, and his interest in fifteen of the merchantmen was confined to shares of just one-sixteenth.[98]

By 1753, Lascelles had ceased to hold victualling contracts and he had also scaled back his involvement in slaving. Only four of the ships listed at this time are known to have engaged in the slave trade.[99] It is probable that most of the remaining vessels were engaged in the sugar trade, though a ship called the *Grantham* was employed in the East India trade. For this purpose it had been purchased around 1750 by a syndicate that included Henry, his youngest son (also named Henry Lascelles, who captained the vessel), and the Liverpool merchant and MP Charles Pole.[100]

[95] *LMLB*, Pares Transcripts, H375, Lascelles & Maxwell to Gedney Clarke, 6 May 1748; H377, George Maxwell to Walter Pringle, 29 September 1750.

[96] See Chapter Seven.

[97] Account Book of Henry Lascelles, 1753 (original source believed lost; photocopy of notes compiled by the late Richard B. Sheridan, in the possession of the author); NA:PRO, C103/130, CO28/28; David Eltis, Stephen D. Behrendt, David Richardson, and Herbert S. Klein eds., *The Trans-Atlantic Slave Trade: A Database on CD-ROM* (Cambridge, 1999).

[98] Total investment in shipping amounted to £15,750, Account Book of Henry Lascelles, 1753. Henry's brother Edward Lascelles was also involved in shipping; e.g. in 1742 he was the co-owner (with Samuel McCall) of the *Queen of Hungary*, HSP, 'Ships Registered at the Port of Philadelphia before 1776: A Computerized Listing' (printout deposited by John J. McCusker, 1970). Despite financing the building of ships for the West Indian trades, Lascelles avoided owning more than a quarter share in any vessel, *LMLB*, Pares Transcripts, H419, Lascelles & Maxwell to J. Fairchild, 16 August 1751, same to Samuel Husbands, 20 August 1751.

[99] Based on a search of the database compiled by Eltis, Behrendt, Richardson, and Klein eds., *Trans-Atlantic Slave Trade*.

[100] L. S. Sutherland, *A London Merchant, 1695–1774* (Oxford, 1933), 117, 119, 151–2. Henry Lascelles Sr owned 5/32 of the *Grantham*, Account Book of Henry Lascelles, 1753. See also BL, India Office Records, East India Company General Correspondence,

The fifth West India business activity pursued by Henry Lascelles after 1734 was money lending, primarily to Barbados planters. A database has been constructed that records seventy-eight loans he granted between 1723 and 1753 (the majority after 1734), amounting to £226,772. The principal features of Lascelles' financial relations with planters form the subject of a separate chapter that compares his West India lending with loans made to English debtors, investments in stock market securities, and holdings of land.[101] It can be noted here, however, that the London commission house served to support lending (by providing a means of receiving the remittances of indebted planters) rather than loans serving as bait with which to secure commission business. This contention is supported by the following calculation. At the end of his life, Henry had approximately £200,000 out on loan in the Caribbean yielding (at an average interest rate of 7 per cent) an annual gross income of £15,400. Standard commission rates in the sugar trade at this time were 2.5 per cent on produce, 0.5 per cent on insurance, and 0.5 per cent on receipts and payments. A good wholesale price for sugar in London was around 33.25s. per cwt. Even assuming, therefore, that the house was able to make 3.5 per cent in total on every cwt of sugar it handled, a turnover of 264,662 cwt of sugar a year would have been required to match the interest Lascelles received from his loans. Total imports into the whole of England and Wales averaged only 818,100 cwt per annum between 1740–9, and 991,600 cwt between 1749 and 1753. Since Lascelles' house was one of approximately ninety similar businesses trading in London, it was impossible for the firm's commission earnings to equal the interest earned on loans. In contrast, the volume of business implied by the interest payments remitted by planters (9,263 cwt per annum between 1749 and 1753), is consistent with estimates of total imports and the number of firms active in the London market.[102]

IOR/E/3/110, 269, Henry Lascelles to James Alison and John Hopkins (Governor and Warehousekeeper of Fort James on the Gambia), 31 May 1750.

[101] See Chapter Six.

[102] John J. McCusker, *Rum and the American Revolution: The Rum Trade and the Balance of Payments of the Thirteen Continental Colonies* (2 vols., New York, 1989), vol. II, 891ff., 1,144ff.; E. B. Schumpeter, *English Overseas Trade Statistics, 1697–1808* (Oxford, 1960), 61–2; Sheridan, 'Sugar Trade', 190–1; Richard B. Sheridan, *Sugar and Slavery: An Economic History of the British West Indies, 1625–1775* (London, 1974), 299–300. Sheridan suggests that only twenty-five of these London partnerships were major houses, but even so the conclusion that commission earnings cannot have matched interest payments remains valid.

George Maxwell of Haddington, Barbados, and London

A striking feature of Henry Lascelles' business activities after 1732 was his involvement with Scottish merchants. The floating factory venture, for example, included John Dunning and George Hamilton among its investors and key personnel. Both men originated from Edinburgh and were members of aspiring mercantile families.[103] From about the 1740s onwards, Scots factors formed highly effective commercial networks in transatlantic trade, particularly in the Chesapeake and Jamaican branches of commerce.[104] The Lascelles were quick to recognise the potential of working closely with such individuals. One of Henry's most important business associates was George Maxwell. After spending twenty years on Barbados, Maxwell returned to London in 1743, shortly after the departure of Daniel Lascelles (Henry's second son) for the East Indies.[105] On his arrival, a partnership agreement was drawn up and the commission house restyled 'Lascelles and Maxwell'.[106]

George Maxwell originated from the Royal Burgh of Haddington: a prosperous town situated on a bend in the River Tyne, located sixteen miles east of Edinburgh amidst the rich farmlands of East Lothian. George's father, David Maxwell, married firstly Helen Hunt (by whom he had six children), and secondly Helen Hepburn, mother of George. The Maxwells and Hepburns were members of the East Lothian gentry; during the seventeenth and eighteenth centuries these two families were linked through intermarriage.[107] It was probably through his regional

---

[103] NA:PRO, C103/130, John Dunning (Edinburgh) to Hall (London), 27 June 1744. Dunning's brother Alexander had a shop in Edinburgh; the Dunnings were also owners of a small estate situated nearby.

[104] J. H. Soltow, 'Scottish Traders in Virginia, 1750–1775', *Economic History Review*, 12 (1959), 83–98; Thomas M. Devine, *The Tobacco Lords: A study of the Tobacco Merchants of Glasgow and their Trading Activities, 1740–1790* (Edinburgh, 1975); Jacob M. Price, *Capital and Credit in British Overseas Trade: The View from the Chesapeake* (Cambridge, 1980); Alan L. Karras, *Sojourners in the Sun: Scottish Migrants in Jamaica and the Chesapeake, 1740–1800* (Ithaca, NY, 1992); Douglas Hamilton, *Scotland, the Caribbean and the Atlantic World, 1750–1820* (Manchester, 2005).

[105] See Chapter Seven, especially fn. 22, for the circumstances surrounding Daniel's departure.

[106] The initial articles of agreement were drawn up 10 August 1743, specifying a partnership of eleven years' duration, during which period the liabilities and profits would be shared equally by the partners, WRA, Harewood House, West India Papers, Accession 2,677, Bond of George Maxwell and Daniel Lascelles, 15 January 1754 (this document's recitals review earlier agreements, the originals of which have not survived).

[107] *LMLB*, George Maxwell to William Duke, September 1743; Maxwell to Edward Lascelles, 25 September 1745; Maxwell to John Fairchild, 5 October 1745; East Lothian Local Archive Office, Registry of Baptisms; IGI. George Maxwell was baptised 1 March 1699.

ties and family connections that George first came to Henry Lascelles'
attention as a prospective business partner. The Maxwell-Hepburns
produced a number of doctors and surgeons, including George
Hepburn (George's uncle), who was Sir Robert Walpole's physician and
also a correspondent of Henry Lascelles.[108] This connection undoubtedly explains Maxwell's familiarity with Houghton in Norfolk, which he
visited in 1722, prior to construction work starting on Walpole's great
house. On his return to England from Barbados in 1743, Maxwell was
welcomed again at Houghton Hall as the guest of Walpole, joining the
sixty-seventh birthday celebrations of the former first minister.[109] The
Walpole link may not have been the only point of contact between
Maxwell and Lascelles since Haddington connections were characteristics of other Barbadian associates, including William Patterson
(Surveyor General of the Leeward Islands).[110]

Two families called Maxwell were substantial plantation owners in
Barbados and Antigua. On Barbados, Thomas Maxwell is recorded in
the 1680 census as owning a sugar estate in Christ Church Parish that
became known as 'Maxwell's Plantation': a property which remained in
the family until 1762. On Antigua, the Maxwells (who originated from
Carriden in Linlithgow) were one of a cluster of families to settle on the
island during the eighteenth century and established a plantation of 460
acres and 300 slaves.[111] Maxwells originating from Scotland also became
landowners in Ireland during this period, and letters from family
members based in Dublin (including a George Maxwell) appear in the

[108] NA:PRO, PROB11/884, ig. 77, Will of George Maxwell; J. H. Plumb, *Sir Robert
Walpole*: vol. I, *The Making of a Statesman* (London, 1956), 205; Cambridge University
Library, Cholmondeley (Houghton) MS 2,163, Henry Lascelles to Dr George
Hepburn, 30 April 1734. There are also links between the Hepburn-Maxwells and
the Smart-Lethieulliers, NA:PRO, SP36/65/44, A. Hepburn to Mr Maxwell, 18 January
1744[5]. For evidence of Henry Lascelles' ability to secure favours from Walpole, see
LMLB, Pares Transcripts, H579a, Henry Lascelles & Son to Turner & Cowley
(Jamaica), 5 October 1740.

[109] *LMLB*, Maxwell to William Duke, September 1743. Duke published *Some Memoirs of
the First Settlement of the Island of Barbados and other the Carribee Islands* (Barbados,
1741).

[110] Nearby Long Yester formed part of the Yester estate, owned by the Hays of
Tweeddale. James Hay, 1st Earl of Carlisle, headed one of the principal syndicates
battling for proprietary control of Barbados during the colony's early history, Larry
Gragg, *Englishmen Transplanted: The English Colonisation of Barbados, 1627–1660*
(Oxford, 2003), 29–41. Subsequently, William Patterson was a correspondent of
John Hay, 4th Marquess of Tweeddale, under whom he had served in the Scottish
Department between 1742 and 1747, Handler, *Supplement to A Guide*, 61.

[111] BA, Hughes-Queree Collection Abstracts in Queree notebook; Vere Langford Oliver,
The History of Antigua (3 vols., London, 1896), vol. II, 260–1; R. B. Sheridan, 'The Rise
of a Colonial Gentry: A Case Study of Antigua, 1730–1775', *Economic History Review*,
13 (1961), 355–7.

correspondence of British politicians associated with the Lascelles.[112] Linking any of these families, however, with the George of Lascelles & Maxwell is problematic. The value of Maxwell to Henry Lascelles' operations appears to consist primarily in his East Lothian family ties, including medical practitioners associated with the Admiralty Sick and Hurt Board, rather than through links with these West Indian namesakes.

The letter book reveals that Maxwell was an educated and cultured man who had moved in prominent business and social circles in London prior to his departure for Barbados. 'I have been to the Lobby of the House of Commons', he wrote soon after his arrival in the capital, 'where I have often stood formerly, and could not remember the face of any one of the present Members, nor even tho' I heard some of them called by their names, and looked at them with great attention because they were my School fellows'.[113]

Maxwell's decision to go out to Barbados could have been the result of his meeting Henry Lascelles during the latter's visit to England in 1720.[114] There is, however, no proof of this; nor is there any conclusive evidence that he emigrated (as Pares suggested) as the result of financial losses incurred during the South Sea Bubble. In view of the fact that Maxwell held the post of Customs Searcher in Barbados, an equally plausible scenario is that he benefited from the patronage of Walpole, through his uncle George Hepburn, and recommended himself to Henry Lascelles as a business associate by virtue of his commercial abilities.[115]

Maxwell's fortune was tiny in comparison with Henry's, but he was not without independent means. It is true that Maxwell's will refers to 'my late dear friend and benefactor Henry Lascelles'; it is also true that in 1741 he took out a loan from his partner of £1,000, and still owed a

---

[112] See e.g. Cambridge University Library, Cholmondeley (Houghton) MS 2,163, Henry Maxwell to Walpole, (Dublin) 3 April 1716; Huntington Library, San Marino, California, HA 9,218, George Maxwell to Robert, Lord Ferras, 8 June 1703. There is also circumstantial evidence linking Arthur Upton (a subordinate of Henry Lascelles and George Maxwell in the Bridgetown customs, and a correspondent in the surviving letter book) with Ireland, see Edith Mary Johnson-Liik, *History of the Irish Parliament, 1692–1800* (6 vols., Belfast, 2002), vol. V, 223–4, 227; Francis Elrington Ball, *A History of County Dublin* (6 vols., Dublin, 1902–20), ch. 6.

[113] *LMLB*, Maxwell to William Duke, September 1743; Maxwell to Dr Joseph Gamble, 9 April 1744. For a possible identification of the school Maxwell refers to, see Chapter Seven.

[114] Lascelles was accompanied by his wife Mary, who died during the visit and was buried at Northallerton, Foster, *Pedigrees.*.

[115] *CSPC (A&WI)*, vol. XXXIII, 243; Wilkinson and Gaviller, Letter Book of Lascelles and Maxwell, Lascelles & Maxwell to Sir Thomas Robinson, 29 September 1743.

debt of £941.17s.8d. at the time of Henry's death.[116] The Lascelles were later to claim (in the course of litigation) that Maxwell owned little or no real estate during his lifetime, save 'one freehold house in the island of Barbados' worth £700, and two small English leaseholds worth £152 per annum.[117] This is contradicted, however, by Maxwell himself, who notes that on Barbados he had owned more than one hundred slaves, perhaps as a result of marriage on Barbados to the widow Dorothy Brodie in 1729. Dorothy was the widow of a medical doctor, James Brodie, whose family can also be linked through patronage circles with the Sick and Hurt Board.[118] Since Maxwell both baptised and sold slaves on the island, his claim to have been an owner, rather than just a renter of slaves, must be taken seriously.[119] In addition to a plantation, Maxwell also possessed property in Bridgetown. In 1749 (six years after quitting the island), he still owned two houses on Cheapside valued at rentals of £80 and £55, and a third house on Reeds Rent worth an additional £15.[120]

At his death in 1763, the residual value of George Maxwell's estate was not recorded. One indication of his wealth, however, is provided by the legacies listed in his will which amount to lump sums worth £1,050 and a further £518 per annum in annuities. Among the payments were £50 a year to his personal bookkeeper.[121] Another measure of George Maxwell's wealth is the half-share in the profits of Lascelles & Maxwell bequeathed to his nephew and heir, Henry Maxwell. In 1764, James Maxwell alleged that the value of the co-partnership, stock-in-trade, and securities owned by his younger half-brother exceeded £100,000. While

---

[116] NA:PRO, PROB11/884, sig. 77, Will of George Maxwell; Pares, 'West-India Merchant House', 79; Account Book of Henry Lascelles, 1753.

[117] NA:PRO, C12/1589/12, *Maxwell* vs *Lascelles* (1764).

[118] Joanne McRee Sanders ed., *Barbados Records: Baptisms, 1637–1800* (2 vols., Baltimore, 1984), vol. I, 113; BA, RB3/35/325–6. In the levy book for Bridgetown, 9 June 1729, George Maxwell was assessed as the owner of 30 acres of land in St Michael's Parish, BA, St Michael's Levy Books, C-shelf 1749069, 1729, f. 149.

[119] *LMLB*, Maxwell to John Braithwaite, November 1745; Lascelles & Maxwell to Miles James, 19 September 1743; Joanne McRee Sanders ed., *Barbados Records: Marriages, 1643–1800* (2 vols., Houston, 1982), vol. I, 149. It is conjectured that James Brodie's family were the Brodies of Lethens, near relations of the Campbells of Calder, and that this connection proved useful to the Lascelles during their involvement in the Nova Scotia settlement project of the mid-eighteenth century, BA, RB6/16/527–8, Will of James Brodie, entered 21 November 1729; National Maritime Museum, ADM/E/13, In Letters, Admiralty Orders, Leon Lockman (Halifax, Nova Scotia) to the Sick and Hurt Board, 26 November 1750.

[120] BA, St Michael's Levy Books, 1749, f. 50. Maxwell sold one of his Bridgetown houses to Gedney Clarke Sr, *LMLB*, Pares Transcripts, H471, Lascelles & Maxwell to Gedney Clarke (Barbados), 12 August 1758.

[121] NA:PRO, PROB11/884, sig. 77, Will of George Maxwell.

this appears an exaggeration (made for tactical reasons in a legal dispute), Henry Maxwell succeeded in negotiating a surrender of all claims on Lascelles & Maxwell's assets in return for an annuity of £1,200 per annum in 1796.[122]

Maxwell's half-brother, James Maxwell, was an army surgeon whose career benefited from the patronage of the Grenvilles.[123] In 1748 he married Susannah Lascelles, the daughter of Henry Lascelles' deceased elder brother George. This match further strengthened the links between the Lascelles and Maxwells. James' son Henry benefited from several inheritances from the Lascelles, as well as from his uncle George Maxwell. In 1753, Henry left him a legacy of £1,000; he also received his mother's one-third portion of her father's estate. Late in life, Henry Maxwell benefited further from a life interest in an estate of 530 acres in Wiltshire, which descended to him by virtue of the marriage of Elizabeth Lascelles (another of George Lascelles' daughters) to Edmund Davis of Hilldrop in Ramsey.[124] In consequence, Henry Maxwell grew wealthy enough to establish himself as a member of the landed gentry. In 1773, he purchased the manor of Ewshott-Itchell at Crondall in Hampshire for £15,000.[125] Here Henry fitted comfortably into his role as the Squire of Crondall. The grounds at Itchell were laid out by Capability Brown, while Maxwell exercised patronage by endowing an educational charity and restoring the parish church.[126]

Despite strong indications that George Maxwell was a man of resources and of good family, there is an additional piece of evidence of how Henry Lascelles regarded his business partner. As a result of dynastic misfortune, all three of Henry's sons died without leaving living heirs. By right of strict blood succession, therefore, the Harewood estate

---

[122] NA:PRO, C12/1589/12, *Maxwell* vs *Lascelles* (1764); WRA, Harewood House, Accession 2,677, Indenture between Edward Lascelles and Henry Maxwell, 17 February 1796.

[123] Foster, *Pedigrees*; Huntington Library, Stowe Collection, STG Box 18, No.7, James Maxwell, 'A Report of my Visitation of the several Hospitals and Sick Quarters for Sick and Wounded Men', Portsmouth, 15 February 1756; Buchet, *Marine, Economie et Société*, 82.

[124] BA, RB6/16/369–72, Will of George Lascelles; RB6/22/370–90 and NA:PRO, PROB11/804, Will of Henry Lascelles; Victoria County History, *History of Wiltshire*, vol. XII (London, 1983), 24; Foster, *Pedigrees*.

[125] Hampshire Record Office, Crondall Deeds, 55/M69/19–56, 60; 55/M69/21/2; Victoria County History, *History of Hampshire*, vol IV (London, 1911), 8; Francis Joseph Baigent, *A Collection of Records and Documents relating to the Hundred and Manor of Crondall in the County of Southampton* (London / Winchester, 1891), 468.

[126] R. P. Butterfield, *Monastery and Manor: The History of Crondall* (Farnham, 1948), 99; Hampshire Record Office, Odiham Grammar School Leases (1812), 21/M51/6; Victoria County History, *History of Hampshire*, 14.

should have passed in 1795 to the grandchildren of his elder brother, including Henry Maxwell.[127]

The terms of Henry Lascelles' will of 1753, however, ensured that Henry Maxwell would never inherit Harewood. As a younger son who had accumulated his own fortune, Henry was free to devise his estate in the manner of his choosing. And in the event of the failure of his own sons to produce male heirs, Lascelles determined that the estate would pass to the children of deceased younger half-brother Edward, rather than the heirs of elder brother George. In fact, Henry Lascelles' complex testamentary papers permitted his sons and executors to nominate a successor from among their eligible nephews. Following the deaths of his younger brothers, Edwin Lascelles was left with sole power to exercise discretion, and there is evidence that he negotiated with the two surviving candidates, Edward and Francis Lascelles, prior to his own death in 1795.[128] The diarist Joseph Farington comments that the elder nephew Edward was preferred 'on acct. of General Lascelles having married Miss Catley': a reference to Colonel Francis Lascelles' relationship with the celebrated singer and stage performer Ann Catley, who in her youth was embroiled in a sensational sexual scandal.[129]

When Henry Lascelles pondered the inheritance question in 1753, the possibility that the heir of his business partner might one day be elevated to the position of head of the family must have seemed remote. One reason why Henry Lascelles interrupted the natural order of succession lay in the personal deficiencies of his elder brother's surviving heir George Lascelles, who was condemned as 'a silly fellow'.[130] A desire to

---

[127] A similar dynastic fate was to befall the Maxwells. Henry Maxwell's wife Deborah perished in 1789 after reading a letter too close to the fire, while Maxwell himself died in 1818 and the couple's only daughter predeceased her father, Hampshire Record Office, Burial Registers, 9 April 1789, 29 July 1818; Butterfield, *Monastery and Manor*, 100.

[128] WRA, Harewood Title Deeds, 359. Edward Lascelles was required to assent to a modification of a trust prior to receiving £50,000 in advance of his inheritance.

[129] Kenneth Garlick and Angus Macintyre eds., *The Diary of Joseph Farington* (16 vols., New Haven, 1978–84), vol. II, 570. On Ann Catley and Francis Lascelles see Stanley Sadie ed., *The New Grove Dictionary of Music and Musicians* (20 vols., London, 1980), vol. IV, 12; Miss Ambross, *The Life and Times of the Late Miss Ann Catley, the Celebrated Actress* (London, 1789), 47–56; James Boaden, *The Life of Mrs Jordan* (2 vols., London, 1831), vol. I, 169–70; V. D. Broughton ed., *Court and Private Life in the Time of Queen Charlotte: Being the Journals of Mrs Papendiek* (2 vols., London, 1887), vol. II, 158–9. The sources suggest that Catley and Lascelles' relationship was affectionate and enduring, though it is unclear if they were legally married. Foster's pedigree (*Pedigress*) excludes the eight children of this union who all took the name Lascelles, including the author Rowley Lascelles.

[130] *LMLB*, George Maxwell to Edward Lascelles, 25 September 1745. At the time of Henry Lascelles' death, his nephew George appears to have been dependent on an annuity of £80 per annum granted by his uncle. In his will, Henry instructed his executors to cease payments if George made any attempt to break into the capital sum,

exclude the female line probably accounts for Henry's decision not to prefer the children of his niece Susannah. Other considerations may also have played their part. Lascelles could simply have felt a closer affinity with the family of his half-brother Edward, with whom he had spent many years on Barbados prior to his return to England, while also (consciously or subconsciously) regarding the Maxwells as inferiors.

George Maxwell exhibited signs of weariness resulting from the constant demands of trade and finance. 'My mind', he wrote, 'is in continual agitation about business'. After his return to Britain, Maxwell missed the company of his old Barbadian companions and experienced the added loneliness of separation from his wife Dorothy, who remained on the island until her death in 1757.[131] Theirs was also a childless union. As a Scot, Maxwell was deeply disturbed by the Jacobite rising of 1745 and this event seems to have increased his sense of unease. In the middle of such unrest, Maxwell dreamed of an escape to Bermuda in the company of friends and of 'retiring some where out of the busy world'. His ideal retreat was a colony lying between the Americas and Britain. On such an island might commerce, corruption, and slavery be forgotten; in such a land might a man who was a mixture of Scots, English, and Bajan find rest from his troubles.[132] Yet Maxwell was never to realise his dreams of escape. He was forced to content himself with the all-too-rare opportunities of riding out of the city (where few of his former friends remembered him) into the countryside.

The enslaved are largely 'invisible' in surviving correspondence of Lascelles & Maxwell. For the most part, slaves are mentioned in passing: as commodities to be bought and sold, or as the anonymous producers of the cargoes of sugar and rum that the partners sold on behalf of their planter correspondents. Yet, on rare occasions, a more human, personal element breaks through the documents that reminds the historian that the world that Lascelles and Maxwell inhabited did not consist solely of ledger entries and business affairs. In 1745, George Maxwell wrote an extraordinary letter to his friend John Braithwaite, a young man who had gone out to Barbados to run a plantation. Braithwaite's high

---

WRA, Harewood Accounts: Estate and General, vol. II, Accounts of T[homas] Crosfield with the executors of Henry Lascelles and Edwin Lascelles, 1753–6; BA, RB6/22/370–90 and NA:PRO, PROB11/804, Will of Henry Lascelles, 1753.

[131] BA, RB6/3/363–5, Will of Dorothy Maxwell, entered 21 October 1757. An indenture drawn up at the time of her marriage permitted Dorothy to bequeath £1,000 currency, should she predecease her husband.

[132] *LMLB*, Lascelles & Maxwell to Sir Thomas Robinson, 27 June 1744; Maxwell to John Fairchild, 5 October 1745; Lascelles & Maxwell to Thomas Findlay, 29 October 1745; Maxwell to John Braithwaite, November 1745.

expectations on leaving Britain had been disappointed. He was in financial difficulties and found the task of acting as a slave master unpleasant. Maxwell sympathised with his plight on both counts. 'The treatment of the negreos I might have forseen,' he wrote, 'had I considered, would ill suit the Gentleness of your nature, but that I happened to overlook having lived more years in that Island than you have done in the wourld'. Experience, Maxwell assured Braithwaite, would eventually inure him to the harsh realities of life on a sugar plantation:

It was become familiar to me by use. But I must declare that I was once owner of above 100 [slaves], and perhaps was one of the mildest masters. None clothed or fed better, yet they are by nature so stupid that I found none so ill served as I was; and therefore some correction is necessary. I used to pity their abject state at first, but afterwards found they were just as happy as their nature was capable of being.[133]

As the letter developed, Maxwell reflected on his own life and circumstances:

Did you truly know my Condition, you would not think it to be envied. My mind is in Continual agitation about business, and bating my being in good health which I own is a great blessing, I have as little enjoyment of Life as anyone. Most people here have real or imaginary Crosses, which are the same in effect.

Readers are invited to ponder the 'real or imaginary Crosses' that impelled George Maxwell to write these words.

The 'Tragical End' of Henry Lascelles

'DEATHS: Henry Lascelles, Esq; a very great Barbadoes merchant, and sometime member of parliament for Northallerton.'[134] Henry's obituary in the *London Magazine* emphasises the key achievements in the eyes of his peers: the extent of his business interests as a merchant, his immense wealth, his political standing as an MP, and his claim to gentility but lack of titled status.[135]

A guide to the extent of Henry's fortune is provided by his will and account book, both compiled in the year of his death. The will values his estate at £284,000 whereas the account book lists assets worth £392,704. While the difference between the two figures (£108,704) may

---

[133] Ibid., [Maxwell] to John Braithwaite, November 1745.
[134] *London Magazine*, 22 (1753), 485.   [135] 'Esquire' was still a privileged title.

indicate the gap between Lascelles' gross and net assets, it is certain that Henry's wealth greatly exceeded the figure recorded in his will because he made substantial gifts to his sons before his death.[136] By 1748, his eldest son, Edwin Lascelles, was installed as Lord of the Manor of Gawthorpe and Harewood: estates that Henry purchased in 1739 for £63,827. Second son, Daniel Lascelles, was similarly established as a partner in Lascelles & Maxwell before 1750.[137] Henry's account book lists only £85,154 of West India loans whereas other sources indicate that £193,890 was still outstanding in 1753.[138] Prior to Lascelles' death, therefore, approximately £108,846 of loans had been assigned to Daniel.[139] In consequence, the fortune Henry accumulated probably lies between £408,784 (net) and £565,251 (gross).[140] While his exact worth may never be known, indisputably Henry Lascelles died one of the richest men in Britain.

Independently of Henry's own wealth, half-brother Edward also accumulated a fortune of significance. In 1747, his son Edward Jr inherited an English estate at Kellington and Beale, £21,176 in securities, an annuity of £220, and Barbadian plantations worth at least £12,400.[141] With these resources behind him, he purchased an estate at Darrington, commissioning John Carr to build Stapleton Park.[142]

The polite death notice that appeared in the *London Magazine* left much unsaid about Henry, including the manner of his demise. Within a few weeks, however, the Yorkshire diarist Thomas Gyll reported that 'An account came from London of the death of old Mr. Lascells, who was reported to have cut his throat and arms and across his belly'. The

---

[136] NA:PRO, PROB11/804 and BA, RB6/22/370–90, Will of Henry Lascelles, proved 15 October 1753; Account Book of Henry Lascelles, 1753; Pares, 'West-India Merchant House', 106–7; Sheridan, 'Sugar Trade', 193.

[137] Mary Mauchline, *Harewood House: One of the Treasure Houses of Britain* (2nd edn., Derbyshire, 1992), 15; WRA, Harewood House, Accession 2,677, Indenture between Henry Maxwell and Edward Lascelles, 17 February 1796.

[138] See Chapter Six.

[139] Henry assigned over his share of debts due to Lascelles & Maxwell to Daniel in 1750, *LMLB*, Pares Transcripts, L & M 1750–2, W & G IV, Lascelles & Maxwell to Thomas Stevenson (Barbados), 20 November 1750.

[140] Assuming the ratio between the will total and the account book reflects the difference between net and gross worth.

[141] WRA, Harewood Title Deeds, 359, Volume of deeds relating to the estates of Henry Lascelles [n.d.]; BA, Hughes-Queree Collection, Abstract in Queree notebook, 'Guinea'. Guinea was valued at £12,804 (currency) in 1736 and £23,500 in 1758. The figure in the text is an interpolation converted to sterling.

[142] Edward Waterson and Peter Meadows, *Lost Houses of the West Riding* (York, 1998), 67. Stapleton House and estate were sold by Edward Lascelles in 1782 for £18,000, East Riding of Yorkshire Archives, Beverley, Constable Family Papers, DDCC/131, Deed of sale of Stapleton manor and lands from Edward Lascelles Esq. to Charles Philips, Lord Stourton, 1 July 1782.

identity of 'old Mr. Lascells' is confirmed in a letter sent by James Abercromby to old adversary Robert Dinwiddie, which sent news of 'the Tragical end of Harry Lasceles'.[143]

The motives for Lascelles' apparent suicide are unknown. Financially, Henry enjoyed immense wealth; politically, he appears to have put the troubles of the 1740s behind him.[144] By 1753, the investigation mounted by Dinwiddie had been dealt with; indeed, now it was Henry's turn to pose Dinwiddie awkward problems by allying himself with Peyton Randolph and Landon Carter in their attempts to undermine Dinwiddie's authority as Governor of Virginia.[145] Lascelles' chief political preoccupation immediately prior to his death was with the Pelham administration's Jewish Naturalization Bill. This Act was opposed by many London merchants and Lascelles' willingness to join the campaign for its repeal suggests that he was no longer dependent on government protection for his personal survival.[146] Of Henry Lascelles' physical and mental state, little can be said with certainty. In November 1747, he suffered from a double cataract in both eyes, which restricted him from coming into town from Richmond on business to just three days a week.[147] His complex business affairs must have exerted an immense strain on his mind and body over many years. In the end, perhaps

---

[143] 'The Diary of Thomas Gyll', 12 October 1753, *Publications of the Surtees Society*, 118 (1910), 195. John C. Can Horne and George Reese eds., *The Letter Book of James Abercromby, Colonial Agent, 1751–1773* (Richmond, VA, 1991), Abercromby to Dinwiddie, 25 October 1753, 95. Gyll indicates that Henry Lascelles died 6 October 1753.

[144] Romney Sedgwick cites Lord Egmont's electoral survey (c. 1749–51), which claimed 'Lascelles may be easily compelled by terror of an enquiry into his West Indian affairs'. Yet this statement was immediately qualified: 'But query whether for the sake of a great example, and in particular on account of one very obnoxious man who may be come at by such an enquiry, it may not be necessary to waive the advantage of his vote and influence', Romney Sedgwick ed., *The House of Commons, 1715–1754* (2 vols., London, 1970), vol. II, 199. Neither Pares' transcripts of the letters of Lascelles and Maxwell nor Henry's political actions (see below) indicate that he was 'running scared' during the early 1750s.

[145] John Richard Alden, *Robert Dinwiddie: Servant of the Crown* (Williamsburg, 1993), 12–13.

[146] Horne and Reese eds., *Letter Book James Abercromby*, 93–5, 98. The parliamentary campaign against the Jewish Naturalization Act was led by George, Lord Lyttelton, Rose Mary Davis, *The Good Lord Lyttelton: A Study in Eighteenth-Century Politics and Culture* (Bethlehem, PA, 1939), 207–10. Lyttelton's patronage of James Thomson (to whom the poem 'Rule, Britannia' is attributed, see Chapter Five, fn. 49) involved him in Barbadian affairs since he secured Thomson a sinecure in the customs service, but no other link to Lascelles has yet been found, Stowe Collection, STG Box 24, No. 6, Henry Grenville to George Grenville, 7 November 1747.

[147] *LMLB*, Pares Transcripts, H566, Lascelles & Maxwell to Mrs Millar, 20 November 1747. Cataracts might be cut out (without anaesthesia) using a pair of scissors, *Gentleman's Magazine*, 24 (1754), 325.

Lascelles paid the ultimate price for the great fortune he raised through his unrelenting drive and ambition.

The manner of Henry's death did not prevent a Christian burial taking place at All Saints, Northallerton. The funeral, moreover, was a public event and not a private affair conducted at night, out of sight of inquisitive eyes. Lascelles' executors recorded that the lavish sum of £250 was distributed to relatives for mourning, £100 to the town's poor people, and £3.5s. to thirteen of Lascelles' tenants who carried their landlord's coffin from the church gate to his grave.[148] There must, however, have been speculation and gossip as Henry's corpse arrived in Northallerton from London. After all, Gyll had already received news of the circumstances surrounding his death in Durham four days prior to the burial. Ominously, the executors' accounts noted that the business of the funeral was incomplete, and hinted that Henry Lascelles' remains might not remain undisturbed for long in consecrated ground. 'These are all the expenses here except the taking up and laying down the stones over the Grave', they wrote, 'which must not be laid yet.' Conspicuous by its absence in the nave of All Saints is any gravestone bearing the name of Henry Lascelles set into the floor beside those of his father, twin sister, and first wife.[149]

If the dark and imposing church at Northallerton received Henry's remains uneasily, the memory of 'old Mr Lascells' at the new family seat at Harewood was also uncomfortable. It is striking that there is no visible artefact at Harewood House commemorating the founder of the family fortune; not even a portrait to match that of his half-brother Edward, who stands proudly in front of his West India ship. If the owners of Harewood, through architecture and patronage of the arts, did seek to distance themselves from the origins of the wealth that had established their position as eminent Yorkshire aristocrats, they were to find this task difficult to accomplish. The family's political opponents capitalised on the Lascelles' recent enrichment through trade and their long association with slavery, most notably in the Yorkshire county election of 1807 fought by Henry Lascelles (1767–1841). The contest featured a lively debate over the abolition of the slave trade. Much of the anti-Lascelles electoral material dwelling on slavery concentrated on the wealth the Lords of Harewood would receive from a continuation of the trade. Attempts were also made, however, to associate the family more

---

[148] WRA, Harewood Accounts: Estate and General, vol. II, Accounts of T[homas] Crosfield with the executors of Henry Lascelles and Edwin Lascelles, 1753–6.
[149] For Lascelles' burial entry see North Yorkshire County Record Office, Northallerton, Draft Transcript Holy Trinity Parish Registers, 1753, 16/10.

generally with place, peculation, and corruption. In the following squib, for example, a shady past is alluded to:

Whence is LORD MILTON descended? (From a Family whose Patriotism & Virtues all the World knows.)
Whence is Lascelles descended? (From a Family Nobody knows.)[150]

Harry Lascelles' controversial career and his 'Tragical end' were not quickly forgotten. More than forty years after his death, the diarist Joseph Farington recalled how 'Mr Lascelles, the Father of the late Lord Harewood, of Daniel Lascelles, and of General Lascelles killed himself by opening the veins in his wrists', and how the same Henry Lascelles had been accused of extortion and corruption. Two decades later, in 1814, Henry's notoriety was similarly recalled when a small vault in the south transept of Northallerton church was opened, exposing his lead-lined coffin. On this occasion, Lascelles was remembered as 'one of those unprincipled men who were concerned in the shameful South Sea business, whereby he amassed great wealth to the ruin of many'.[151] A corpse cannot defend itself and no evidence has been found to substantiate a charge that the deceased never had to face in his lifetime. Nevertheless, the readiness of the annalist to speak ill of such a long-dead Northallerton MP provides a further indication of Henry's grim posthumous reputation.

---

[150] HH, Collection of assorted electoral materials, 'A Few Plain Questions ANSWERED' (Leeds, 1807). Milton was a member of the Rockingham family.
[151] Garlick and Macintyre eds., *Diary of Joseph Farington*, vol. II, 570.

5   The Gedney Clarkes

Esperez le mieux
(Clarke family motto)

'The greatest failure that ever happened here': thus did John Hawksworth describe the financial collapse of Gedney Clarke Jr in a letter of June 1774. For forty years, the Gedney Clarkes had occupied prominent positions among Barbados' merchant and planter elite (Fig. 5.1).[1] Now their reputations and their fortunes lay in ruins. 'I have heard', Hawksworth went on to inform Philadelphia merchant James Pemberton, 'that [Clarke Jr] will fall short from one hundred to one hundred & fifty thousand pounds short payments to his Creditors.'[2] The unnamed gossips who had spread news of Clarke's demise were not wide of the mark. In 1774, Clarke's gross liabilities hovered in the region of £229,806 sterling (Table 5.1), but his assets, at best, amounted to

---

[1] Gedney Clarke Sr (1711–64); Gedney Clarke Jr (1735–77).
[2] HSP, Pemberton Papers, 26/75, John Hawksworth to James Pemberton, 30th of 4 M° [Quaker calendar: 30 June, dated 30 May in HSP catalogue], 1774, cited in Richard Pares, *Yankees and Creoles: The Trade between North America and the West Indies before the American Revolution* (London, 1956), 83. See also Hawksworth to Pemberton, 10 October 1772, and Hawksworth to Pemberton, 6 April [2 M°; February in HSP catalogue] 1774, Pemberton Papers, 26/3 and 24/39. John Hawksworth was a member of a prosperous family of merchants based in Salem and Barbados, and his news of Gedney Clarke Jr's failure would certainly have been of interest to the Pembertons. Clarke Jr was a correspondent and debtor of James Pemberton, while George and Isaiah Pemberton owned land in Northern Neck, Virginia, close to tracts granted to Gedney Clarke Sr and his brother John Clarke Jr in the 1740s. Moreover, the merchant William Vans (a kinsman of both the Clarkes and the Pembertons) was the tenant of property owned by Gedney Clarke Sr and Jr in Salem, Clarke to Pemberton, 10 October 1772, Pemberton Papers, 24/39; Library of Virginia, Richmond, Land Office Patents and Grants, Northern Neck Grants G, ff. 445–6; PEM, Clarke Family Papers, Folder 1, John Clarke to Ann Clarke, 2 July 1769, 14 September 1769; Folder 4, Pedigree of the Clarke family; Harriet Silvester Tapley, *St Peter's Church in Salem Massachusetts before the Revolution* (Salem, 1944), 4–5.

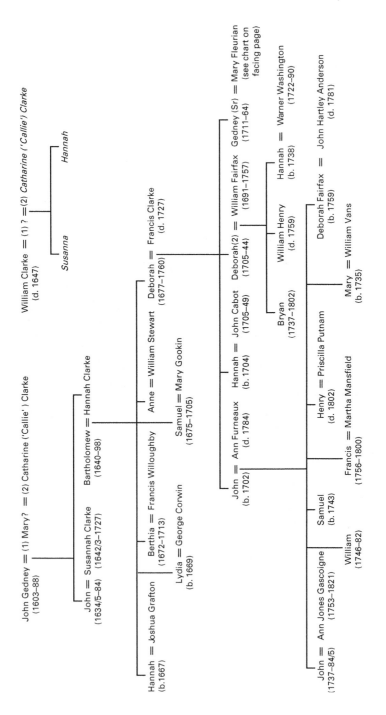

Figure 5.1. Simplified pedigree of the Clarke family

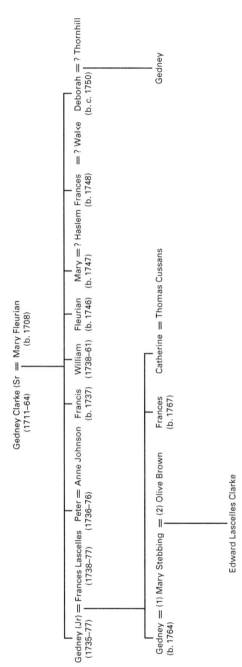

Figure 5.1. (cont.) Edward Lascelles Clarke

Table 5.1. *Debts owed by Gedney Clarke Sr (deceased) and Jr, c. 1774*

Debtor	Creditor	Dates recorded (dd/mm/yy)	Amount (£ stg)
GC(sr)	Edwin Lascelles and Daniel Lascelles (execs. of Henry Lascelles)	30.4.72	5,463
GC(sr)	Daniel Lascelles, surviving co-partner of George Maxwell (decd)	22.8.70; 30.4.72	9,541
	interest and charges on the above	1.1.75	264
GC(sr)	Daniel Lascelles and William Daling	4.7.70; 30.4.72	54,984
	interest and charges on the above	19.1.75	5,963
GC(sr)	Edwin Lascelles (exec. of Edward Lascelles)	30.4.72	5,584
GC(jr)	Daniel Lascelles and William Daling	17.4.72; 29.9.74	29,471
GC(jr)	Edwin Lascelles	17.4.72; 29.9.74	1,186
GC(jr)	Daniel Lascelles	17.4.72; 29.9.74	939
GC(jr)	Edwin Lascelles and Daniel Lascelles	17.4.72; 29.9.74	2,089
GC(jr)	Daniel Lascelles and William Daling	26.2.73; 29.9.74	15,000
Subtotal	*due to the Lascelles*		*130,484*
GC(sr) & GC(jr)	The Crown (4½ per cent arrears)	−.5.74	16,200
		−.9.76	4,081
GC(sr) & GC(jr)	Debts recorded on Barbados[a]	10.5.79	44,302
GC(sr) & GC(jr)	Judgements recorded on Tobago[b]	14.2.72–26.2.74	34,739
Subtotal	*due to other creditors*		*99,322*
Total			*229,806*

Notes:

[a] Excluding c. £99,993 debts claimed by the Lascelles and £4,438 debts claimed by the Crown duplicated in the table. The total has been multiplied by 0.80 (value of debts owed to the Lascelles c. 1775 relative to the value of the debts same owed 1779–80 with interest and charges for the intervening years).

[b] Excluding c. £63,686 of judgements recorded by the Lascelles, £16,200 recorded by the Crown, and £4,286 recorded by Peter Clarke, all duplicated in the table.

Source: HH:WIP (i) 'A list of papers belonging to Edward Lascelles Esq. as executor of the Rt. Honble Edwin Lord Harewood deced' [c. 1796], ff. 10, 11, 21; (ii) 'A statement of the debt of the Honourable Gedney Clarke esq. with Lascelles, Clarke, and Daling', 19 January 1775; (iii) 'A Statement of the Debt of the Estate of Gedney Clarke esq. decd to Lascelles, Clarke, & Daling', 19 January 1775; (iv) 'Statement of the Debt of Gedney Clarke esq. deceased with Daniel Lascelles surviving partner of George Maxwell deceased', 19 January 1775; (v) 'Indenture between James Workman, master of Barbados High Court of Chancery, and Daniel Lascelles and William Daling', September 1780; (vi) 'List of Judgements on Record in the Island of Tobago agst Gedney Clarke Esqr.' [n.d. c. 1774–5]; (vii) 'Copy of a case respecting G[edney] C[larke]', 29 September 1774; (viii) Correspondence, 'Legal opinion on whether John Prettyjohn is entitled to receive 2 judgements' [n.d., c. 1800].

between £149,000 and £154,000.[3] A balance sheet so heavily tipped to the negative is a powerful illustration of the vicissitudes of the eighteenth century's Atlantic economy. Unravelling the mysteries of the Clarkes' economic fates, then, can broaden understanding of the period, for though Barbados was a crucial hub of transatlantic trade and communication, its merchants have received far less scrutiny than their counterparts in Great Britain and North America.[4]

The port of Bridgetown housed 10,600 inhabitants in 1742 and so in population was the equal of Boston and New York. Indeed, in the whole of British Colonial America, only the city of Philadelphia exceeded Bridgetown in size (by 3,000 colonists).[5] Barbados' trading community has been neglected because, in part, of a bias in the historic record. It is exceptional for business archives of any description to survive, but it is rarer still for the papers of a resident West Indian merchant to be preserved. Survival mechanisms, such as well-endowed archives with a remit to purchase commercial papers, or aristocratic muniment rooms

[3] An estimate of Clarke Jr's insolvency is presented in Tables 5.1 and 5.3. Not all of Clarke's creditors had gained security for their loans by 1774. In 1802, Thomas Willison lobbied Edward, Lord Harewood for repayment of a debt of 7,290 livres tournois (c. £303 sterling) dating from 1773, HH: WIP, 'Memorial for Thomas Willison, surviving partner of Alexander McSween, formerly Tobago merchant, now residing in Dunkirk. Presented to Lord Harewood', 19 June 1802. Willison's claim, however, was small and no similar petitions are known to exist. Table 5.1, which excludes the double-counting of debts, can therefore be regarded as an accurate statement of the claims against Gedney Clarke Jr and his father's estate. For an assessment of the validity of the claims themselves, see below.

[4] For studies of North American merchants, see Virginia D. Harrington, *The New York Merchant on the Eve of the Revolution* (New York, 1935); W. T. Baxter, *The House of Hancock: Business in Boston, 1724–1775* (Cambridge, 1945); James B. Hedges, *The Browns of Providence Plantation* (Cambridge, MA, 1952); Bryon Fairchild, *Messrs William Pepperrell: Merchants at Piscataqua* (Ithaca, NY, 1954); Bernard Bailyn, *The New England Merchants in the Seventeenth Century* (Cambridge, MA, 1955); and Thomas M. Doerflinger, *A Vigorous Spirit of Enterprise: Merchants and Economic Development in Revolutionary Philadelphia* (Chapel Hill, 1986). Caribbean merchants best known to historians are those, such as Hugh Hall of Chapter Two and John Yeates of the present chapter, who moved their operations to Britain or North America at some point in their careers. See also John C. Jeaffreson ed., *A Young Squire of the Seventeenth Century* (2 vols., London, 1878); Richard Pares, *A West India Fortune* (London, 1950); David Hancock, '"A World of Business to Do": William Freeman and the Foundations of England's Commercial Empire, 1645–1707', *William and Mary Quarterly*, 57 (2000), 3–34. There are, however, examples of West Indian business papers describing the trade of merchants who did not so relocate. See, by way of illustration, J. H. Bennett Jr, 'Cary Helyar: Merchant and Planter of Seventeenth-Century Jamaica', *William and Mary Quarterly*, 21 (1964), 53–76; and P. F. Campbell, 'The Merchants and Traders of Barbados', parts 1 and 2, *JBMHS*, 34 (1974), 85–98, 166–86.

[5] NA:PRO, CO28/14, 29 and Jacob M. Price, 'Economic Function and the Growth of American Port Towns', *Perspectives in American History*, 8 (1974), 176, cited in Pedro Welch, *Slave Society in the City: Bridgetown, Barbados 1680–1834* (Kingston, Jamaica/Oxford, 2003), 53.

containing the papers of wealthy merchants marrying into the family, are typically less common in the New World than the Old. The Clarkes are a case in point: their business network can be reconstructed only by cross-referencing laboriously a variety of different sources and waging an archival assault on several fronts. Beyond the difficulties facing the researcher, however, is another, more systematic, reason why Caribbean merchants have not received all the attention they merit: the rise of the commission system during the early years of the eighteenth century. Under the commission system, planters established direct contact with merchant houses in London and the British outports, and they themselves assumed the risk of exporting cargoes of produce rather than selling their crops to merchants in the sugar islands.[6] It is clear that commission trading diverted business away from middlemen who had previously acted as the factors and correspondents of British firms, but its impact on merchants who could launch their own commercial initiatives is less clear. While some transatlantic merchants relocated to Britain, others did not. A number of those who elected to remain in the Caribbean, like the Clarkes, made large fortunes.[7] Historians would do well to examine their common assumptions about transatlantic colonial trade by paying heed to such individuals.[8]

Family Connections

The New England family into which Gedney Clarke Sr was born in 1711 had been involved in Atlantic commerce for three generations. In 1634, William Clarke migrated from London and by 1642 he had established

[6] K. G. Davies, 'The Origins of the Commission System in the West India Trade', *Transactions of the Royal Historical Society*, 2 (1952), 89–107; Richard Pares, *Merchants and Planters, Economic History Review*, Supplement 4 (Cambridge, 1960), 33–7; R. B. Sheridan, *Sugar and Slavery: An Economic History of the British West Indies* (London, 1974), 282–94. Pares argued that the commission system distinguished British from French colonial trade and was more prevalent in the sugar than the tobacco trade. It should be noted, however, that in neither the sugar nor the tobacco trade is the extent of commission trading precisely known (see Campbell, 'Merchants and Traders of Barbados', 169).

[7] For the inventoried wealth of West Indian merchants, see T. G. Burnard, ' "Prodigious Riches": The Wealth of Jamaica before the American Revolution', *Economic History Review*, 54 (2001), 514–16.

[8] The decline of 'indigenous' merchants in the Chesapeake and Carolinas has also been questioned, Charles G. Steffen, 'The Rise of the Independent Merchant in the Chesapeake: Baltimore County, Maryland, 1660–1769', *Journal of American History*, 76 (1989), 9–33; R. C. Nash, 'The Organisation of Trade and Finance in the Atlantic Economy: Britain and South Carolina, 1670–1775', in Jack P. Greene, Rosemary Brana-Shute, and Randy J. Sparks eds., *Money, Trade, and Power: The Evolution of Colonial South Carolina's Plantation Society* (Columbia, SC, 2001), 74–107.

'Clarke's Farm' on the border of the townships of Salem and Lynn.[9] Farming, however, was not Clarke's only business interest; he was the keeper of the Ship Tavern, at the head of Central Street, and an inventory of his estate lists ownership of three small vessels, 1,500 lb of tobacco, 40 lb of ginger, and 3 hhd of sugar.[10] Three years after arriving in Massachusetts, Clarke and his wife Callie attained full membership of the church, but in 1646 William found himself before the Salem court. The charges levelled against him included assaulting a constable and maintaining a 'shuffling board in his house, occasioning misspending of time'. Clarke's mercantile activities, however, and his support of a petition sent to Britain during the controversy over the Massachusetts charter, sparked by Robert Child's return to the colony the previous year, were likely the true sources of the elders' displeasure with him.[11]

In 1637, the Gedney Clarkes' other forefather, John Gedney, sailed from Yarmouth to New England on the *Mary Ann* with his wife, three children, and two servants.[12] The vessel's passenger list identifies Gedney as a Norwich weaver. Once in the colonies, however, it is unclear how he sustained himself until he assumed control of the Ship Tavern and Clarke's Farm following his second marriage to William Clarke's widow Callie, sometime after 1647.[13] Ties between the Gedneys and Clarkes were further strengthened when four of John Gedney's and Callie Clarke's children by their first marriages subsequently intermarried. In 1659, John Gedney Jr became the husband of Susannah Clarke, and in 1662 his brother Bartholomew Gedney married Susannah's sister Hannah.[14]

---

[9] James Savage, *A Genealogical Dictionary of the First Settlers of New England ...* (4 vols., Boston, 1860–2), vol. I, 40; 'Copy of the Original Book of Grants of Salem', *Essex Institute Historical Collections*, 5 (1863), 219. A land grant of 1642 awarded Clarke 60 acres 'in leiw of that Land wch hath lost by the laying out of Lyn bounds'. Upon his death in 1647, Clarke owned 200 acres of real estate. Readers are advised to consult the simplified Clarke pedigree (Fig. 5.1) in places where the text describes family relations.

[10] Francis Davis McTeer and Frederick C. Warner, 'The Children of William Clarke of Salem, Massachusetts', *American Genealogist*, 39 (1963); 'Abstract from Wills, Inventories, &c. on file in the office of Clerk of Courts, Salem, Mass.', *Essex Institute Historical Collections*, 1 (1859), 6. The value of Clarke's moveble goods was £587.3s.2d.

[11] 'Abstract from Clerk of Courts, Salem', 39; Richard S. Dunn, James Sharpe, and Laetitia Yeandle eds., *The Journal of John Winthrop, 1630–1649* (Cambridge, MA/ London, 1996), 679. Clarke died before he could be tried for conspiracy.

[12] Henry Fitzgilbert Waters, 'The Gedney and Clarke Families of Salem, Massachusetts', *Essex Institute Historical Collections*, 16 (1879), 242.

[13] Savage, *Genealogical Dictionary*, vol. II, 240–1; Peter Wilson Coldham, *The Complete Book of Emigrants, 1607–1660* (Baltimore, 1987), 187. The transfer of title to Clarke's Farm was recorded in 1649, suggesting that the marriage took place at about this time, 'Grants of Salem', 225.

[14] Waters, 'Gedney and Clarke Families', 32, 241–3.

In Salem, the Clarkes and Gedneys grew wealthy as they combined trade with public and military service, a career path followed by many of early New England's leading families.[15] The highly successful Bartholomew Gedney held a series of administrative and military appointments between 1676 and his death in 1698, including that of judge in the Court of Special Oyer and Terminer during the 1692 Salem witchcraft trials. In addition, Gedney possessed numerous business interests, including shipbuilding, landowning, and saw milling, near Clarke's Farm and in Casco Bay.[16] The Gedneys' social standing can be gauged from some superb matches: John Gedney Jr's daughter became the first wife of Captain George Corwin, a man whose family ranked among the most prominent landowners and office-holders of New England, and after she died, Corwin took Bartholomew Gedney's daughter as his second wife.[17]

During the eighteenth century, members of the Gedney and Clarke families – aided by the same combination of trade, matrimonial alliances, and public and military service that had served them well in Salem – dispersed along the eastern seaboard and overseas to the Caribbean. The children of Francis Clarke and Deborah Gedney achieved the families' greatest material triumph.[18] The couple's eldest surviving son, John, was a merchant as well as the commander of the Winter Island Fort in Salem.[19] While John remained in New England, his brother Gedney Clarke Sr relocated to Barbados in 1733, where he

---

[15] William Clarke held the office of Sheriff of the County while John Gedney was elected a Selectman in 1655, Waters, 'Gedney and Clarke Families', 255–9.

[16] A. C. Goodall, 'A Biographical Notice of the Officers of Probate for Essex County, from the Commencement of the Colony to the Present Time', *Essex Institute Historical Collections*, 2 (1860), 223–6; Waters, 'Gedney and Clarke Families', 249–50; Henry Wilder Foote, *Catalogue of Portraits in the Essex Institute Salem, Massachusetts* (Salem, MA, 1936), 29; James Duncan Phillips, *Salem in the Eighteenth Century* (Boston/ New York, 1937), 30; Benno M. Forman, 'Mill Sawing in Seventeenth-Century Massachusetts', *Old Time New England*, 60 (1970), 113; BPL, Arrest warrants for persons accused of witchcraft, signed by justices of the peace, MS Ch.K.1.40, v. 2, 12, 28, 50, 194, 208, 222, 248, 348, 350, 400; MS Ch.J.7.9; MS Ch.F.10.35.

[17] Waters, 'Gedney and Clarke Families', 260–1; Phyllis Whitman Hunter, *Purchasing Identity in the Atlantic World: Massachusetts Merchants, 1670–1780* (Ithaca/London, 2001), 41–3. The Corwins (or Curwens) were a branch of a Cumbrian gentry family. Whether the Christian name 'Bartholomew' reflected the intermarriage of the Gedney and Bartholomew families of Salem (the Bartholomews were also a mercantile family of East Anglian origin) is unclear.

[18] Waters, 'Gedney and Clarke Families', 32–3; M. Halsey Thomas ed., *The Diary of Samuel Sewall* (2 vols., New York, 1973), vol. II, 1,038. Francis Clarke represents an influx of fresh blood: he migrated from London in 1699, PEM, Clarke Family Papers, Box 1, Folder 1, John J. G. Clarke to Deborah Fairfax Anderson, 26 November 1819.

[19] John Clarke's eponymous son served as a Lieutenant under General Wolfe at the capture of Quebec in 1759, 'Unpublished Letters', David M. Randolph to Hon. Nathaniel Silsbee, 25 December 1817, *NEHGR*, 24 (1870), 293–5; Foote, *Catalogue of Portraits*, 30–1.

married and raised a family. A year later, Gedney's sister Deborah also moved away from Salem. Deborah had married Colonel William Fairfax, who, following a successful naval career and a term as Chief Justice of the Bahamas, was appointed to the post of Customs Collector for Salem and Marblehead in 1725.[20] Fairfax and his wife departed for Virginia to take up the opportunity of superintending the estates of his kinsman Lord Fairfax in Westmoreland County. Again with the assistance of family connections, he subsequently became president of the Virginia Council.[21]

Through the Fairfaxes, the Clarkes became aligned with a second noted Virginia family, the Washingtons. In 1743, William Fairfax's daughter Anne (by his first wife Sarah Walker) married Lawrence Washington, brother of the more famous George. Sometime after 1750, Fairfax's younger daughter Hannah (by his second wife, Deborah Clarke) married Warner Washington.[22] Gedney Clarke Sr was personally acquainted with both the Fairfaxes and the Washingtons. George Washington made his only visit outside North America in 1751 to Barbados, where he was the frequent guest of Clarke and his family. William Fairfax's son Bryan similarly enjoyed Clarke Sr's hospitality during his residence on the island between 1752 and 1754.[23]

Information about the Clarkes' and the Gedneys' family origins is not as complete as could be wished, but there are strong indications that they ranked among the more prosperous of the early migrants. Armorial designs used in a Gedney family tomb of 1762 are based on those of a line of Suffolk gentry, which seems to belie the 1637 identification of John Gedney as a Norwich weaver. The rapid ascent of the Clarkes is also consistent with affluent beginnings, and from at least 1731 family members in Boston and Salem attempted to draw up pedigrees that

[20] The Bahamas appointment was obtained through the influence of Colonel Martin Bladen, who had also married into the Fairfax family, Edward D. Neill, *The Fairfaxes of England and America in the Seventeenth and Eighteenth Centuries* (Albany, NY, 1868), 48.
[21] Ibid., 48–52. William Fairfax (1691–1757) was a nephew of the 5th Lord Fairfax and a cousin the 6th.
[22] Waters, 'Gedney and Clarke Families', 274; Neill, *Fairfaxes*, 49, 52; Caroline D. Dall, 'The Whittingham Genealogy and William Clarke's Statement', *NEHGR*, 34 (1880), 37.
[23] Donald Jackson and Dorothy Twohig eds., *The Diaries of George Washington*: vol. I, *1748–65* (Charlottesville, 1976), 27–8, 73; Gerry Webb, *Fairfax of York: The Life and History of a Noble Family* (York, 2001), 118–22; Waters, 'Gedney and Clarke Families', 274, 279. Bryan Fairfax (who succeeded in 1793 as 7th Baron Fairfax) was ordained in 1789 and became rector of Christ Church, Alexandria, in Virginia. Another Fairfax relation, Henry Fairfax, was also on Barbados at this time, Edward D. Neill, 'The Ancestry and Earlier Life of George Washington', *Pennsylvania Magazine of History and Biography*, 16 (1892), 274.

incorporated Yorkshire connections.[24] Such efforts, which illustrate the hold that English social norms retained among Massachusetts' commercial elite, probably include a significant element of wish-fulfilment.[25] Nevertheless, it is clear that through material success and advantageous marriages, the Clarkes had formed alliances with important families in New England, Virginia, and Yorkshire by the mid-eighteenth century.

Commercial Activities

The earliest known account of Gedney Clarke Sr's commercial activities appears in the ledger of the Salem merchant Timothy Orne, who between 1738 and 1745 recorded exchanges of fish and whale oil for sugar and rum. A similar trade is reported in the correspondence of Marblehead merchants Joseph Swett and Robert Hooper, a source documenting that Clarke's business interests had transcended simple commodity exchange by the early 1740s.[26] Swett and Hooper were involved in a network of merchant correspondents based in Europe, North America, and the Caribbean. While Clarke handled the firm's West Indian trade, a similar role was performed in London by

---

[24] Waters, 'Gedney and Clarke Families', 266, 268; Frederick Lewis Gay, 'William Clark's Genealogical Statement, 1731' and Isaac J. Greenwood, 'A Review of William Clarke's Genealogical Statement', *NEHGR*, 33 (1879), 226–9; Dall, 'Whittingham Genealogy', 34–7. See also Patrick Roach, 'A Genealogical Jigsaw Based on the Family of the Hon. Gedney Clarke', *JBMHS*, 40 (1992), 93–8. Vere Langford Oliver, *West India Bookplates* (London, 1914) contains details of the armorial adopted by Gedney Clarke Sr and the (ironically appropriate) family motto *Esperez le mieux*.

[25] William Clarke's 1768 letters to his sister Hannah, of Salem, illustrate the importance the Clarkes attached to polite, sociable behaviour. Hannah was urged, for example, to model her conduct on characters appearing in Samuel Richardson's *Clarissa* and *Sir Charles Grandison*, PEM, Clarke Family Papers, Box 1, Folder 1, William Clarke to Hannah Clarke, 1768. Similarly, the Hall family's gentry pretensions (including adopting a coat of arms) can be seen in both the intricate linguistic conventions and the polite behaviour recorded in Hugh Hall's letter book, Houghton Library, MS Am 1,042; Samuel E. Morison, 'The Letter-Book of Hugh Hall, Merchant of Barbados,1716–1720', *Transactions, Colonial Society of Massachusetts*, 32 (1937), 514–15.

[26] PEM, MS 41, Timothy Orne Ledger, 1738–53 (cited in Hunter, *Purchasing Identity*, 126); Letterbook of Joseph Swett Jr and Robert Hooper Jr, 1740–7. Clarke Sr's account with Orne was worth £161.10s.2¹/4d. For an account of the Newfoundland dried fish trade in the eighteenth century and its links with Europe and the West Indies, see Rosemary Ommer, 'The Cod Trade in the New World', in Alan G. Jamieson ed., *A People of the Sea: The Maritime History of the Channel Islands* (London, 1986), 245–68. The Clarkes' rise illustrates that Salem's fishing and shipping industries continued to produce merchants of high calibre during the eighteenth century. On Salem's prosperity, see James G. Lydon, 'Fish for Gold: The Massachusetts Fish Trade with Iberia, 1700–1773', *New England Quarterly*, 54 (1981), 539–82.

Samuel Storke, in Lisbon by Steers and Barrons, and in Bilbao by Joseph Gardoque y Mueta.[27] Clarke, Swett, and Hooper also invested in shipping and shipbuilding in association with other merchant syndicates; in addition, Clarke may well have supplied slaves to New England merchants after his arrival on Barbados.[28]

From Barbados, Gedney Clarke Sr controlled a multifaceted trading enterprise that dotted the North American seaboard. His 1764 will records that he owned a wharf and warehouses in Salem as well as at Goose Creek on the Potomac River in Virginia.[29] In both of these ventures, Clarke's brother John was initially a partner, but Gedney quickly gained the ascendancy over his elder sibling; between 1739 and 1747, John was obliged to transfer the Salem property to Gedney when he was unable to repay a loan secured by a mortgage.[30] During the early 1740s, Clarke conducted business on his own account with the Philadelphia provisions merchant John Yeates and the Charleston merchant and shipowner Robert Pringle. Ventures conducted with Pringle featured a triangular trade involving Barbados, South Carolina, and London. Cargoes of rice, naval stores, and lumber were exchanged

[27] Storke was one of London's leading colonial merchants during the first half of the eighteenth century and he was particularly well connected with New England where his kinsmen included the Sewall family of Boston, William I. Roberts III, 'Samuel Storke: An Eighteenth-Century London Merchant Trading to the American Colonies', *Business History Review*, 39 (1965), 147–70. For examples of business cooperation between Swett and Hooper, Clarke, and Storke, see PEM, Letterbook of Swett and Hooper, Hooper to Clarke, 5 November 1741; Swett and Hooper to Clarke, 2 March 1742; Swett and Hooper to Clarke, 7 December 1744; Hooper to Storke, 4 May 1747. Samuel Swett (or Sweet) was also a cousin of Samuel Sewall, ed., Halsey Thomas, *Diary of Samuel Sewall*, vol. I, 546.

[28] PEM, Letterbook of Swett and Hooper, Swett and Hooper to Clarke, 22 August 1741; Hooper to Clarke, 5 November 1741; Swett and Hooper to Clarke, (4 May 1742; Swett and Hooper to Clarke, 18 October 1743; Hooper to Clarke, 20 March 1743[4]. Gedney Clarke Sr is believed to be the "Mr Clarke" mentioned in a letter of instructions sent by Samuel Waldo of Boston to Samuel Rhodes, the captain of a slaving vessel, 12 March 1734, Elizabeth Donnan ed., *Documents Illustrative of the History of the Slave Trade to America* (4 vols., Washington, DC, 1930–5), vol. III, 45.

[29] BA, RB6/17/195–201, Will of Gedney Clarke, entered 4 September 1764 (a copy of Gedney Clarke's will is also preserved in PEM, Clarke Family Papers, Folder 3, and a precis of the will is printed in Tapley, *St Peter's Church*, 72–4); Waters, 'Gedney and Clarke Families', 276, 282; Eugene M. Scheel, *The Story of Purcellville, Londoun County, Virginia* (Purcellville, 1977), 3; information provided by Mary Lib Clark Joyce (pers. com.). Clarke conducted the Virginia part of his operations in association with Samuel Storke, Letterbook of Swett and Hooper, Hooper to Clarke, 5 November 1741.

[30] PEM, Clarke Family Papers, Box 1, Folder 1. Gedney was not the only relative whom John Clarke drew on for financial support. In 1735, he mortgaged his Salem property to indemnify Dr William Clarke of Boston, who had guaranteed a debt of 500 oz silver (c. £131 sterling) owed to James Bowdoin of Boston, MHS, Dolbear Family Papers, Box 1.

for sugar and rum, which were in turn remitted to London and the proceeds used to purchase manufactures or bills of exchange.[31]

By 1742, Gedney Clarke Sr had established himself as one of Barbados' leading merchants. 'We must be so free as to say we shod be Contented with Such a partner as you with us', Swett and Hooper deferentially replied when Clarke suggested taking shares in one of their ships, 'being well assured of your capacity of Life in Business Superior to Ours.'[32] The same year, Robert Pringle informed his brother Andrew to expect Clarke shortly in London. 'He has the Character of a very Honest Gentleman', wrote Pringle, '& Capt Gregory tells me that he Bears an Exceeding Good Character in Barbadoes.' Attractive trading opportunities could be expected, Robert went on, for Clarke was travelling to London because he had 'Great Interest there & in very good Bussiness'. 'He is from Boston in N. England & born there', Robert noted, '& hope you will make it your Bussiness & think it worth while to Corroborate our Acquaintance & Correspondence with him while in London.'[33] Such testimonials reveal that after having been involved in a successful trade between Barbados and the mainland colonies for nearly a decade, Gedney Clarke Sr was poised to embark on more ambitious commercial ventures with the support of sections of the metropolitan mercantile community.

Clarke's London visit was a turning point in his career. Thereafter, three trends came to characterise his business activities: 1) he invested heavily in new developing territories, particularly plantations in the Dutch Caribbean; 2) he integrated his trade in sugar and rum backwards into the supply of slaves and into plantation ownership; and 3) he extended the practice of fusing political and commercial connections, which had helped the Clarkes to prosper in Salem and Barbados, to London and the Dutch West Indies. A common feature of all three policies was a close involvement in business with Henry Lascelles. Clarke and Lascelles' collaboration intensified when the deaths of their partners – Samuel Storke of London in 1746 and Henry Lascelles' half-brother Edward in Barbados in 1747 – left each in need of a new

---

[31] HSP, Yeates Papers: John Yeates Correspondence, 1733–59, #740; Walter B. Edgar ed., *The Letterbook of Robert Pringle*: vol. I, *April 2, 1737–September 25, 1742;* vol. II, *October 9, 1742–April 29, 1745* (2 vols., Columbia, SC, 1972), vol. I, 335, 416; vol. II, 436, 439, 545, 551, 624, 627, 638, 666, 764, 784, 787.

[32] PEM, Letterbook of Swett and Hooper, Swett and Hooper to Clarke, 2 June 1742.

[33] Edgar ed., *Letterbook Robert Pringle*, vol. II, 439. Pringle confuses Salem (Clarke's birthplace) with Boston. Clarke's visit to London also attracted the notice of Swett and Hooper and John Yeates, PEM, Letterbook of Swett and Hooper, Swett and Hooper to Clarke, 13 May 1743; HSP, John Yeates Correspondence, Edward Polgreen (Barbados) to Yeates, 22 October 1742.

associate.[34] Their business relationship, however, probably stretched back much further. One clue is a voyage of the ship *Lascelles*, which delivered a cargo of Barbados molasses and rum to a Benjamin Clarke of New England in 1729–30. A second is Gedney's marriage to Mary Fleurian on Barbados in 1733, shortly after his move from Salem. The Fleurians connected Clarke Sr dynastically with Henry Lascelles, via the Carter family of slave traders.[35]

Gedney Clarke Sr acquired his first substantial real estate holding in 1740, when Lord Fairfax granted him 3,000 acres in north-western Virginia. The first investor to receive a portion of Northern Neck, Clarke held the property primarily in speculation, and his optimistically named 'Bonaventure' lands were never fully developed.[36] Clarke's most valuable real estate concerns (listed in Tables 5.2, 5.3) lay along the Demerara and Essequibo Rivers, which together with Berbice and Surinam comprised the eighteenth-century Dutch colonial settlements that today lie within the country of Guyana. From 1743, Gedney began trading with Surinam in an operation underwritten by a syndicate of ten merchants who had subscribed £1,500. The investors included Andrew Pringle, who had evidently followed his brother's advice to support Clarke's trade, and Henry Lascelles.[37] The trade included illicit rum imports, which Clarke Sr was tempted to smuggle

---

[34] Roberts, 'Samuel Storke', 169. Roberts notes that during the War of Jenkins' Ear and War of the Austrian Succession (1739–48) Storke did not speculate in wartime victualling contracts or privateering. Storke's conservative approach may have encouraged Gedney Clarke Sr to seek out more aggressive business partners. The successful outcome of the inquiry into Henry Lascelles' tenure as Bridgetown Customs Collector (leading to the restoration of Edward Lascelles as Collector shortly before his death) probably also strengthened the appeal of closer association with him.

[35] Maryanne Foussier married Samuel Pryor on Barbados in 1684. One of the couples' daughters, Margaret Pryor, married Peter Fleurian in 1699. A second daughter, Ann, became the second wife of Edwin Carter in 1711. Peter and Margaret Fleurian were the parents of Clarke Sr's wife; Edwin Carter was the father of Lascelles' spouse. The origins of the Fleurians are not clear (Peter Fleureo & Company are listed as trading on Bridgetown's Tuder Street in 1693), but they could be connected with a French slave trading family of this name at La Rochelle, Leo Francis Stock ed., *Proceedings and Debates of the British Parliament Respecting North America* (5 vols., Washington DC, 1924–41), vol. IV, 98; information provided by Lisa Jenkins (based on genealogical research), pers. com., 21 and 22 September 2004, 10 November 2004; BA, St Michael's Levy Books, vol. I, 1686–1712, f. 96; Virginia Tech, Digital Library and Archives, Special Collections, MS 74-001, records of the slave ship *Elizabeth* (1750).

[36] Clarke operated a wharf at Goose Creek, and in 1749 he was the owner of fourteen slaves in Fairfax County, Library of Congress, MMC-2488, Papers of Charles Green, 1745–9, 'List of Tithables in Fairfax County, 1749'. See also Handley Regional Library, Winchester, Virginia, James Wood Family Papers, 173 WFCHS (1735–1892), Colonel John Carlyle for Gedney Clarke, Suit to Frederick County Court, 1759.

[37] *LMLB*, Lascelles & Maxwell to Gedney Clarke, 23 December 1743, 4 April 1744, 14 July 1744.

Table 5.2. *Real estate holdings of Gedney Clarke Sr and Jr: listing of properties*

Location	Property name or description	Acres	Dates of ownership
London	Houses and wharf[a]	na	sold 1765
New England	House, wharf, and warehouses in Salem; possibly half of Clarke's Farm[b]	30	1739–69
	Sawmill, Casco Bay	na	na
Virginia	Northern Neck land grant	3,000–5,448	1740–c. 1777
	Wharf at Goose Creek	na	1740–c. 1777
Halifax, Nova Scotia	House and land	na	owned 1757 and 1764
Barbados	Belle★	484–537	1752–80
	Henley★	350	1777–83
Demerara-Essequibo	Nieuw Walcheren★	na	1746–c. 1769
	De Vrindschap★	2,500	c. 1752–c. 1772
	He't Loo★	2,000	c. 1752–c. 1772
	Blenheim★	2,000	c. 1752–c. 1769
	Golden Grove★	1,000	c. 1753–c. 1769
	York★	2,000	c. 1753–c. 1769
	Richmond★	2,000	c. 1753–c. 1769
	Hampton Court★	1,000	c. 1757–c. 1769
	The Beehive★	na	c. 1757–c. 1769
	Pyra★	na	1746–c. 1769
	Garden of Eden★	2,000	c. 1765–c. 1769
Tobago	Richmond★	600	c. 1765–c. 1774
	Bushy Park★	500	c. 1765–c. 1774
	Goodwood★	575	c. 1765–c. 1774
	Lancashire or Goldsboro★	576	c. 1770–c. 1774
Grenada	Clarke's Court★	800	c. 1763–73

Notes:
★denotes plantation.

[a] In 1765, Gedney Clarke Jr's houses and wharf in London were sold for £8,450, *LMLB*, Pares Transcripts, H676 IX 30.

[b] Full details of property ownership in New England and Nova Scotia are not available. Francis Clarke (Gedney Clarke Sr's father) owned what appears to be half of Clarke's Farm. His estate was declared insolvent in 1733. Francis' son and heir John Clarke Sr conveyed a warehouse and wharf to his brother Gedney in 1739 for £500 new tenor and a house and land (the 30 acres of Clarke's Farm?) followed in 1746[7]. Gedney Clarke Jr sold the same properties to John Clarke Jr in 1769 and signed a quitclaim in 1772, PEM, Clarke Family Papers, Box 1, Folders 1 and 3; Waters, 'Gedney and Clarke Families', 271, 276.

[c] Gedney Clarke was granted 3,000 acres in his own right in 1740. His brother John Clarke received grants of between 1,748 acres and 2,448 acres, also situated on the branches of Goose Creek, in the same year. The fate of these lands after John Clarke's financial difficulties is not known, but since the brothers acted in partnership and Salem property (above) passed to Gedney, it is possible that the Virginia lands were also transferred.

[d] 500 acres were added to the original 2,000 acres c. 1764, BA, RB6/17/195–201, Will of Gedney Clarke.

to Britain and North America as Barbadian produce.[38] Gedney's involvement was not confined to merchandise for long, however, and in 1746 he purchased the Nieuw Walcheren and Pyra plantations in Demerara for £3,074 and £3,000 (sterling) respectively.[39]

As sugar prices began recovering from the nadir to which they had plummeted in the late 1730s, Barbados' merchants and planters were attracted by the development potential of Demerara and Essequibo. The London commission house of Lascelles & Maxwell noted in 1743 that 'We conceive ... alurements of great proffits to be made at Isequibe have induced some people to purchase there.'[40] Barbadian activity in the region was boosted after 1746, when the Dutch West India Company opened the Demerara colony to foreign settlement. Gedney Clarke Sr was among the first Barbadian investors

Notes to Table 5.2 (*cont.*)
Sources: LMLB, H676 IX 30, IX f. 155, 5 June 1766; Waters, 'Gedney and Clarke Families', 270–1, 276; PEM, Clarke Family Papers, Box 1, Folder 3, Ann Jones Clarke to Deborah Fairfax Anderson, 31 March 1786; Phillips, *Salem*, 30; PEM, Essex County Court of Common Pleas, series 5, vol. XXXIV, v2 (1753–60), f. 447, *Gedney Clark vs John Clark*, Newbury Court, September 1757; Library of Virginia, Northern Neck Grants E, 1736–42, ff. 158, 178, 189; HSP, Yeates Papers #750, John Yeates Correspondence, Paul Bedford (Barbados) to Yeates, 26 April 1743; BA, St James, Barbados, recopied deeds, RB3/35/518–21; LBMH, Correspondence Files, List of plantation owners in Guiana compiled by Gosta Simmons based on 'Map of River Demerary and Esequibo' (1759) by Laurens Lodewyk van Bercheyck, copy preserved at the *Bodel Nijenhuis Museum* in Leiden; Harris and de Villiers ed., Gravesande vol. II, 399–400, 599; Rodway, *British Guiana* vol. I, 129; BA: (i) Hughes-Queree Collections Abstracts in Queree Notebook, [n.p.] 'Belle' and 'Henley'; (ii) RB6/17/195–201, Will of Gedney Clarke, entered 4 September 1764; HH:WIP (i) 'Indenture between James Workman, master of Barbados High Court of Chancery, and Daniel Lascelles and William Daling, September 1780'; (ii) 'Mortgage of Richmond, Goodwood, and Bushy Park Estates, Tobago', 1773; (iii) 'A Statement of the Debt of the Estate of Gedney Clarke esq. decd. to Lascelles, Clarke, & Daling', 19 January 1775; Pedro Welch, 'The Lascelles and their Contemporaries: Fraud in Little England, 1700–1820', *JBMHS*, 48 (2002), 99; information provided by Kristynn Monrose, of Clarke's Court rum distillery, based on materials in the National Museum of Grenada.

[38] On Gedney Clarke Sr's involvement in the rum trade during the early 1740s, *LMLB*, Pares Transcripts, W&G I, ff. 47, 68, 75, 308. In 1751, Clarke planned to consign rum from Demerara-Essequibo to the Isle of Man, W&G IV, f. 145, Lascelles & Maxwell to Gedney Clarke, 26 June 1751. Clarke also smuggled French rum under the guise of Barbados rum during the War of the Austrian Succession, PEM, Letter book of Swett and Hooper, Hooper to Clarke, 19 March 1746[7].

[39] BA, RB3/35/518–21; HSP, John Yeates Correspondence, Paul Bedford to John Yeates, 26 April 1743. Clarke bought out a syndicate of Barbados merchants who had purchased Pyra. The exchange rate conversion was carried out using data in John J. McCusker, *Money and Exchange in Europe and America, 1600–1775: A Handbook* (Chapel Hill, 1978), 44, 50, 59.

[40] *LMLB*, Lascelles & Maxwell to Conrad Adams, 16 September 1743.

Table 5.3. *Estimated gross asset value of real estate owned by Gedney Clarke Sr and Jr, c. 1755 and c. 1776 (£ sterling)*

Location	Value c. 1755	Value c. 1776
Virginia	1,344 [a]	1,851 [b]
Barbados	16,007 [c]	38,815 [d]
Essequibo-Demerara	80,000–100,000 [e]	8,308 [f]
Grenada	0	36,000–41,250 [g]
Tobago	0	63,700 [h]
Total	*97,351–117,351*	*148,674–153,924*

Notes:

[a] In 1796, part of the Clarkes' Northern Neck grant at Purcellville was sold to James McIlhaney for £2,700. The general price level and the value of land had risen between 1755 and 1796, but, at the time of the sale, rents due to the state were in arrears. The values for 1755 and 1776 are estimates calculated using the consumer price index in John J. McCusker, *How Much is That in Real Money? A Historical Price Index for Use as a Deflator of Money Values in the Economy of the United States* (Worcester, 2001), 52–3.

[b] According to family tradition, the property was confiscated by the State of Virginia in 1777 because the Clarkes were Loyalists. If this was the case, the gross asset value of the Purcellville estate would be zero in 1776, unless the Clarkes received compensation by the British Government for their loss. No record of any claim by the Clarkes, however, could be found in NA:PRO, AO12, which records summary details of Loyalist claims in fifty-six manuscript volumes. Doubt is also cast on the oral tradition of confiscation by PEM, Clarke Family Papers, Folder 1, John Clark to Frank Clarke, 30 June 1783.

[c] The figure is based on the value of Belle plantation plus an estimate of property owned at Bridgetown. The Clarkes owned Bridgetown property worth £1,850 in 1779, and the levy books record that the rental value of their holdings was £154 in 1753 and £107 between 1759 and 1765. The estimate of Bridgetown property for 1755, adjusting for changes in the price level, is (154/107) × £1,850 × (44.0/60.6) = £1,933.

[d] The figure is the inventoried value of Belle plantation and Bridgetown property only. Henley was acquired by Gedney Clarke Jr from the Society for the Propagation of the Gospel in 1777 for £11,011 currency, but no part of the purchase money was ever paid and in 1783 the property was returned to the SPG.

[e] An estimate based on Gedney Clarke Jr's 1762 report to Bentinck that in Demerary 'A Sugar Plantation must be reckoned at not less than £10,000 here and a Coffee Plantation about £8,000 here', BL, Egerton MS 1,720, f. 5. Pyra (containing 95–100 slaves) was purchased by a syndicate of Barbados merchants for £2,700 in 1743, and two years later the property was valued at c. £3,000. New Walcheren was purchased for 35,000 florins (£3,074 sterling) and Het Loo for £12,000, the differential indicating that the former price was paid for the land only but that the latter included slaves, HSP, John Yeates Correspondence, Bedford to Yeates, 26 April 1743; Rodway, *British Guiana*, vol. I, 129; Harris and DeVilliers ed., *Gravesande*, vol. II, 390.

[f] In 1766, Gedney Clarke Jr was debited for the interest of Samuel Carter's debt of £8,302 since he was in possession of Carter's Demerara property. Gedney Clarke Sr's will of 1764 notes that 500 acres adjoining 'Uriendschap' plantation in Demerara had been 'purchased lately' from Carter, *LMLB*, Pares Transcripts, H679 f. 155, Lascelles and Daling to Gedney Clarke, 5 June 1766; BA, RB6/17/195–201, Will of Gedney Clarke.

to purchase land in Demerara and Essequibo and he was considered by the Dutch governor of Demerara, Laurens Storm van's Gravesande, to be the most influential. His involvement also caught the eye of Barbados' Governor, Henry Grenville. 'Esequibe Estates are much in Fashion here', Grenville wrote in 1748, adding that '[Thomas] Baxter & Gedney Clarke are deeply concernd in them'.[41] During the 1750s and early 1760s, Clarke and his sons acquired nine further plantations, raising their combined holding to between 14,000 and 16,000 acres.

At the same time that he was buying up plantations, Gedney Clarke Sr also extended his involvement in slaving. From at least the mid-1740s, he served as middleman or broker for other colonial slave importers; thereafter, he participated directly in merchant syndicates based in Barbados, South Carolina, New York, and London.[42] Lascelles & Maxwell were Clarke Sr's London bankers as well as his partners in slaving ventures. The house received the proceeds from the sale of slaves and, under the system known to contemporaries as 'bills in the bottom', guaranteed bills of exchange drawn on merchants in Bristol and Liverpool in advance of remittance.[43]

Notes to Table 5.3 (cont.)

[g] The range of sums reflects the two offers made to purchase Clarke's Court in 1772 and 1774.

[h] This sum reflects the value of the mortgages charged on the Tobago properties to the Lascelles and the Crown.

Source: BA, St Michael' Levy Books, LBMH, Family Files, 'Gedney Clarke'; BL, Egerton MS 1,720, Bentinck Papers, 'Correspondence respecting the colony of Demerara, 1762–1766', f. 5; BA, Hughes-Queree Collection, Abstracts in Queree Notebook, [n.p.] 'Belle' and 'Henley'; HP:WIP: (i) 'An Inventory and Appraisement of the Belle Plantation', 26 May 1777; (ii) 'Mortgage of Richmond, Goodwood, and Bushy Park Estates, Tobago', 1773; (iii) 'John Piggott's offer for Clarke's Court Plantation, Grenada', 1772; (iv) 'Copy of an agreement for the sale of Clarke's Court estate, Grenada', 1774; (v) 'A list of papers belonging to Edward Lascelles Esq. as executor of the Right Honourable Edwin Lord Harewood deced' [n.d., c. 1796].

[41] James Rodway, *History of British Guiana* (3 vols., Georgetown, Demerara, 1891–4), vol. I, 129; C. A. Harris and J. A. J. de Villiers eds., *Storm Van's Gravesande: The Rise of British Guiana Compiled from his Despatches* (Hakluyt Society: 2nd series, vols. XXVI–XXVII, (2 vols., London, 1911), vol. I, 285, 295; CKS, Stanhope Collection, Grenville/Buckingham MS, U1590 S2/010, Copies of Letters to Secretary of State and Lords of Trade (2 vols., 1747–53), vol. I, Henry Grenville (Barbados) to John Sharpe (London), 20 June 1748.

[42] For examples of Clarke's middleman activities, see *LMLB*, Pares Transcripts, H375, f. 147, Lascelles & Maxwell to Capt. John Pickett, 28 May 1747, f. 271; Lascelles & Maxwell to Gedney Clarke, 6 May 1748.

[43] Donnan ed., *Documents*, vol. IV, 345–6. On bills in the bottom, see Jacob M. Price, 'Credit in the Slave Trade and Plantation Economies', in B. L. Solow ed., *Slavery and the Rise of the Atlantic System* (Cambridge, 1991), 312–13.

Clarke's most significant partner in the slave trade up until the mid-1750s was Samuel Carter, a Barbadian merchant and a nephew of Henry Lascelles. The scope of the trade conducted jointly by Clarke and Carter is glimpsed by the letters of Lascelles & Maxwell, which record that Clarke had guaranteed a debt of £20,000 due to the partners in 1756.[44] In 1744, after South Carolina lifted its prohibition on slave imports, imposed after the Stono slave uprising in 1739, Clarke shipped slaves first to Robert Pringle and subsequently to Henry Laurens in Charleston. A cargo of slaves consigned by 'Gidney Clarke of Barbados' valued at £3,150.15s., for example, was received by Laurens in 1756.[45] In New York, Gedney Clarke Sr's principal correspondent was John Watts, with whom he invested in a slaving vessel despatched to the Guinea coast in 1762.[46] Watt and Clarke also smuggled slaves into New York itself, making use of the coves and inlets of Long Island. The illicit trade was probably assisted by the Gedney family's ownership of a 200-acre plot close to Long Island Sound, bordered by the Mamaroneck River, which empties into a fine natural harbour. This smugglers' paradise is crowned by a vast rocky outcrop, providing a fine lookout post.[47] Laurens, Pringle, and Watts were North American merchants of the first order, but Clarke Sr's slaving interests were not confined to British colonies. In partnership with Carter, he engaged in both the legal activity of granting mortgage credit to Demerara planters wishing to import slaves, and the illicit practice of importing slaves directly into the colony in violation of the Dutch West India Company's monopoly.[48]

---

[44] *LMLB*, Pares Transcripts, H664 f. 17, Lascelles & Maxwell to Gedney Clarke, 4 September 1756. For further details of Carter's debt, see Chapter Seven. By 1768, Gedney Clarke Jr had taken possession of Carter's Demerara plantation, which Carter had acquired during the Barbadian investment boom in the Dutch colony during the early 1750s.

[45] Edger ed., *Letterbook Robert Pringle*, vol. II, 685, 715, 774; Philip M. Hamer and George C. Rogers eds., *The Papers of Henry Laurens*: vol. II, *November, 1, 1755–December 31, 1758* (Columbia, SC, 1970), 102–3, 140, 172, 207, 222, 254, 356–7.

[46] Dorothy C. Barck ed., *Letter Book of John Watts: Merchant and Councillor of New York, January 1, 1762–December 22, 1765* (Collections of the New York Historical Society, vol. LXI: New York, 1928), 32, 44, 56, 109–10, 159, 205, 232, 283, 359–60; Donnan ed., *Documents*, vol. III, 457–8.

[47] Edgar J. McManus, *A History of Negro Slavery in New York* (Syracuse, 1966), 38, citing Barck ed., *Letter Book John Watts*, 31–2. Eliezar Gidney Jr (sic) purchased 80 acres in Mamaroneck from Caleb Heathcote in 1716. Eliezar Jr was the son of Eliezar Gidney Sr, brother of Bartholomew and John Gedney of Salem, information provided by Eleanor Phillips Brackbill (the current owner of part of the Gedney property at Mamaroneck), pers. com., 11 February 2004.

[48] National Archives of Guyana, SB4/9B, Minutes of the Court of Justice of Essequibo, 1756–65, 144–5, 7 January 1760, Mortgage request of George Gascoigne; Algemeen Rijksarchief, The Hague, 1.05.01.02 inv.nr., 765, Secret Minutes of the Chamber of Zeeland of the Dutch West India Company, 1 June 1764, Minutes of discussion

Political and Military Patronage

Adhering to family precedents established in New England, the Clarkes combined commercial interests with military and public service on Barbados. In 1748, Gedney Clarke Sr succeeded Edward Lascelles as Customs Collector for Bridgetown. Clarke was nominated by Surveyor General William Patterson, member of a powerful political faction on the island centred on Thomas Baxter and British patron George, Lord Lyttelton.[49] By virtue of the Lyttelton connection, Clarke gained the favour, at least initially, of the new Governor of Barbados, Henry Grenville, who wrote to his brother George Grenville (then Lord Commissioner of the Treasury) to request that the Prime Minister, Henry Pelham, approve Clarke's tenure. In London, Henry Lascelles provided further support. Indeed, Gedney's appointment was informally confirmed at a dinner Lascelles attended with the Prime Minister's brother, the Duke of Newcastle.[50] The position of Customs Collector was to stay in the Clarke family for the next thirty years despite allegations of bribery, misconduct, and an attempt at usurping Gedney Clarke Sr.[51]

following the interception of a letter addressed to Samuel Carter in Demerara describing a planned illegal shipment of slaves from Guinea to the colony; NMM, Papers of Admiral Sir James Douglas, DOU/6 Letterbook, 1762–7, William Brisbane to Sir James Douglas, [n.d., July–August 1765] and 4 March 1766, Sir James Douglas to William Brisbane, 28 August 1766.

49 Huntington Library, San Marino, California, Stowe Collection, STG Box 24, No. 6, Grenville to George Grenville, 7 November 1747; No. 9, Grenville to George Grenville, 30 April 1748; No. 10, Grenville to George Grenville, 30 April 1748. Lyttelton was the patron of the Scottish poet James Thomson and obtained for him the sinecure of Surveyor General of Customs in Barbados for his support. 'Rule, Britannia' (1740) is conventionally attributed to Thomson. The irony of this famous work's references to naval power and slavery will not be lost to readers of the present study. Such links between colonial commerce and culture were by no means coincidental, as this chapter demonstrates. Governor Grenville was cruelly dismissive of Thomson: 'being fat, & gross of Constitution [he] cou'd not, or wou'd not Venture into this part of the World, & therefore recommends this Paterson to fill it in his room', STG Box 24, No. 9.

50 Formal notice was sent to Governor Grenville shortly after, Stowe Collection, STG Box 12, No. 24, Gedney Clarke II to Sir George Brydges Rodney, 12 October 1764; *LMLB*, Pares Transcripts, H567, f. 267, Henry Lascelles to Gedney Clarke, 26 March 1748; WRA, NH 2,833, Frederick Frankland to Sir Thomas Robinson, 2 February 1747[8], 11 February 1747[8], 23 February 1747[8], 27 March 1748, 5 April 1748; CKS, Grenville/Buckingham MS, U1590 S2/010, vol. I, Henry Grenville (Barbados) to Henry Pelham, 22 June 1748. In 1741, Lyttelton married Lucy Fortescue of Devonshire; it is not clear if this family are connected with the Barbados Fortescues, whose plantation later came into the possession of the Lascelles (see Chapter Seven). By 1763, Gedney Clarke Jr had a son-in-law called 'Mr Fortescue', *LMLB*, Pares Transcripts, H432, Lascelles, Clarke, & Daling to Gedney Clarke Sr, 5 March 1763.

51 Stowe Collection, STG Box 24, No. 16, ff. 119–23; Box 25, No. 1, ff. 211–12; Box 25, No. 12, f. 222; Box 25, No. 21, ff. 238–9. From 1714–15, when Henry Lascelles held the

In 1749, Clarke and Patterson were accused of appropriating revenue by failing to remit the net proceeds of seizures to the Casual Receiver or notify the Deputy Auditor. Attorney General Jonathan Blenman protested this matter to London, supported by Governor Grenville.[52] The case against Clarke Sr was strengthened by the evidence of Deputy Naval Officer William Moore, who accused Clarke and the Comptroller, Arthur Upton (Edward Lascelles' old accomplice), of 'Male practices ... Repugnant to the Acts of Trade, and Introducing ... frauds and abuses in his Majesty's Revenue'.[53]

The attempt to remove Clarke Sr formed a continuation of earlier attacks on the Lascelles. William Moore had acted as Bridgetown Collector during Edward Lascelles' suspension; in 1750 he made a direct bid to gain the office for himself.[54] As before, political factions and patronage networks influenced the investigation. Clarke and Baxter were members of an island faction, which Grenville termed the 'Baxterians', opposed to Blenman. Allegations against Clarke gained momentum after the sudden death (in 1749) of five of Barbados' 'most considerable inhabitants' in one stroke, including Baxter himself and two members of the Council.[55]

Governor Grenville's letters are scathing about all parties to these disputes.[56] Moore he regarded as a man of mean circumstances, who had been fortunate to marry well on the island. 'He is by Nature Excessive proud, pert & Insolent', Grenville commented, '& when the

---

position of Collector, this important customs post was effectively controlled by one family interest for sixty years, [William Gordon], *A Representation of the Miserable State of Barbados* (London, 1719), 40–3.

[52] CKS, Grenville/Buckingham MS, U1590, U1590 S2/010, vol. I, Grenville to Lords Commissioners of the Treasury, 5 April 1749; S2/012, Copies of Letters Wrote in Governor Grenville's Administration from 1747 to 1753, Grenville to Patterson, 25 April 1748; Grenville to Clarke, 26 April 1748, 20 December 1748, 23 December 1748.

[53] CKS, Grenville/Buckingham MS, S2/012, Grenville to Clarke and Upton, 6 February 1749[50], 20 February 1749[50]; Grenville to Moore, 12 February 1749[50]; Grenville to Blenman, 10 March 1749[50].

[54] Stowe Collection, STG Box 24, No. 16, Grenville to George Grenville, 15 March 1749[50].

[55] Ibid., No. 9, Henry Grenville (Barbados) to George Grenville, 30 April 1748; CKS, Grenville/Buckingham MS, U1590, vol. I, Grenville to John Sharpe (London), 20 June 1748; Grenville to George Grenville, 12 July 1749.

[56] Clarke and Upton submitted the counter-allegation that Blenman had given legal opinions (for fees) to merchants on both sides of disputes that he presided over as Judge of the Court of Vice Admiralty. Grenville does not appear to have taken their memorial seriously, though as his governorship proceeded he turned increasingly against Blenman, Stowe Collection, STG Box 25, No. 32, Memorial of Gedney Clarke and Arthur Upton [n.d., c. 1750–1]; Richard Pares, 'Barbados History from the Records of the Prize Court: IV. The Barbados Prize Court Under Judge Blenman', *JBMHS*, 6 (1939–40), 117.

Insolence of office is added to this, it is no difficult thing to conceive how insupportable such a man must be.' Patterson was dismissed as 'a poor Scotchman': a parasite who fed off Baxter's and Lyttelton's patronage. Baxter himself, Grenville sneered, had started life no more than 'a poor Irish Man', who arrived on the island, 'without a Coat, without a Penny, not knowing whether to turn Lawyer, Parson, Captain, or what Else'. It was Blenman who had taken Baxter into his household, 'cloath'd, fed, & supported' the wretch, instructed him in the law, and helped him marry a rich widow. Now Baxter bit the hand that had provided.[57] Yet despite his haughty contempt, Grenville's perspective on events is informative. He notes, for example, how the Scotch–Irish duo of Patterson and Baxter had allied themselves with his predecessor, Governor Thomas Robinson (a Yorkshireman), against Blenman, and also emphasises the support Clarke Sr derived from the Baxter–Lascelles–Lyttelton patronage circle.[58]

Gedney Clarke trounced his opponents in 1750. Not only was his own position safeguarded, but (much to Grenville's disgust) he also influenced the appointment of Upton's successor two years later.[59] When his father died in 1764, Clarke Jr's succession as Collector was secured by the patronage of Edwin Lascelles, despite strong representations to George Grenville from other quarters. At the same time, a cousin of the Clarkes, named Roberts, was appointed the new Comptroller.[60] Along with these two posts, the Clarkes controlled other colonial offices.

---

[57] Stowe Collection, STG Box 24, No. 6, Grenville to George Grenville, 7 November 1747; No. 9, Grenville to George Grenville, 30 April 1748. Grenville's criticism of Baxter's lack of independent means may be too harsh. In 1741, Baxter's status as a successful merchant is evidenced by his sale of Rock plantation to William Walker, who was granted a mortgage of £4,681, BA, Hughes-Queree Collection, Abstract in Queree notebook, 'Four Hills'. George Maxwell described Moore as 'a strutting insolent officer', LMLB, Maxwell (London) to William Rawlin (Barbados), 25 September 1745.

[58] Stowe Collection, STG Box 24, No. 9, Grenville to George Grenville, 30 April 1748.

[59] Clarke Sr lobbied for the appointment of Thomas Stevenson, a loan client of Henry Lascelles. Grenville regarded Stevenson as a corrupt retainer. 'I believe our Sharpe is the very Channel thro' which Stevenson ultimately hopes for success', he warned his brother, 'for I am told that old Mr Lascelles is to Patronize this Stevenson, & the Connexion between Mr Lascelles & Mr Sharpe I believe you very well know', Stowe Collection, STG Box 25, No. 21, Grenville to Henry Grenville, 7 November 1750. 'Sharpe' was probably John Sharpe (colonial agent for Barbados) rather than Joshua Sharpe (c. 1718–86), a solicitor of Lincoln's Inn, who appeared as legal counsel for several colonies before the Board of Trade and the Privy Council.

[60] CKS, Grenville/Buckingham MS, U1590 S2/011, vol. II, Grenville to John Sharpe, 20 October 1752; Stowe Collection, STG, Box 25, No. 62, Grenville to John Sharpe, 20 October 1752; ST7, vol. I, Grenville to Samuel Touchet, 17 October 1764; Grenville to John Dupre, 17 October 1764; Grenville to Lord Hyde, 20 October 1764; Grenville to Edwin Lascelles, 8 November 1764. BL, Add. MS 38,387, ff. 22–30, Essay written by Gedney Clarke to George Grenville, 27 November 1764.

Clarke Jr emulated his father by becoming a member of the Barbados Council in 1765(6).[61] From 1757, Clarke Sr was empowered to nominate whom he pleased as Clerk of Common Pleas in Barbados. On Tobago, his nephew, William Clarke, became Comptroller of Customs in 1771, where the family owned sugar estates.[62]

From at least 1742, Clarke Sr held the rank of Major; during the course of the Seven Years' War (1756–63), three of his sons were promoted to more senior military rank. Colonel Gedney Clarke Jr saw active service in the Martinique campaign that set out from Carlisle Bay in 1759. John Clarke was a Captain in the Forty-sixth Regiment of Foot, and Peter Clarke a naval commander.[63] Yet, though considerable, the influence the Clarkes exercised over colonial appointments was not unlimited. Blenman remained an obstacle, causing Clarke Sr more difficulties (and briefly imprisoning him) in a legal dispute over a prize ship that dragged on for four years between 1760 and 1764.[64]

Naval power was crucial for the security of the plantations and the defence of colonial trade. The Clarkes' influence in this area was, therefore, of paramount importance to the family's commercial

[61] Gedney Jr replaced John Frere, William L. Clements Library, Shelburne Papers, vol. LII, #477–80, Abstract of Despatches from Barbadoes, transmitted by the Board of Trade [n.d., 1766]. Note that the statement that the Clarkes sought appointment to the Council at the same time is incorrect, S. D. Smith, 'Gedney Clarke of Salem and Barbados: Transatlantic Super-merchant', *New England Quarterly*, 76 (2003), 515–16. It was the Freres who attempted this audacious manoeuvre (see Chapter Seven).

[62] Stowe Collection, STG, vol. I, Grenville to Lord Hyde, 20 October 1754; 'The Autobiographical Manuscript of William Senhouse', *JBMHS*, 2 (1934–5), 118; John Carter Brown Library, Providence, Rhode Island, ** MS Barb 1757, May 16/1–2; PEM, Clarke Family Papers, Box 1, Folder 3, 'Will of William Clarke, 1776'; Waters, 'Gedney and Clarke Families', 271–2. The office of Clerk of Common Pleas was controlled by the Lascelles and their associates since at least 1755, HH:WIP, Rental of James Butcher (200 pa) for the office of Clerk or Prothonatary of the several courts of Common Pleas in the island of Barbados, 25 February 1755.

[63] LBMH, Family Files, 'Gedney Clarke'; HH:WIP, Letter from Richard Husbands to Lascelles, Clarke, and Daling, 21 August 1764; Barck ed., *Letter Book John Watts*, 6, 17, 395; Letterbook of Swett and Hooper, Hooper to Clarke, 8 April 1746, 19 January 1746[7]; Jackson and Twohig eds., *Diaries of George Washington*, 73. Gedney Clarke Jr received a vote of thanks from the Barbados Assembly for his role in the Martinique expedition, *JBMHS*, 13 (1945–6), 205. In January 1763, John Clarke drew on Lascelles & Maxwell from Havana to purchase a Captain's commission, joining his Salem cousin who already held this rank in 1759, LMLB, Pares Transcripts, H674, f. 298. Peter Clarke was commander of the *Feret* in 1762 and the warship HMS *Kennington* in 1770. His wife, Anne (Johnson) Clarke, was the grandniece of Benjamin Franklin, Benjamin Franklin to Timothy Folger, 21 August 1770, *The Papers of Benjamin Franklin* (36 vols. to date, New Haven/London, 1959–), vol. XVII, 209–10.

[64] Pares, 'Barbados Prize Court', 127. Though Clarke Sr was defeated in this case, the dispute led ultimately to the ending of Blenman's long tenure as Attorney General and Judge of the Vice Admiralty Court, William Blenman, *The Case of Jonathan Blenman Esq. Attorney General of Barbados* (London, 1761).

interests, and they sought to shore it up by means of an elaborate hospitality. William Senhouse, the newly arrived Customs Inspector, was invited to stay at Gedney Clarke Jr's Belle plantation, where the principal inhabitants of the island had called to congratulate him.[65] In a memorandum of 1771, Senhouse recollected, 'Mr Clarke taking particular care to receive every one that came with the most cordial hospitality, and had on that account a different set of dining company every day.' As a member of an English gentry family that enjoyed the patronage of the Lowthers, Senhouse was accustomed to rituals of politeness, but he was nevertheless struck by Clarke's 'signal and obliging attention' to himself. Indeed, Senhouse recorded that it was 'his constant practice to entertain everyone that came and to keep a sort of open house for all Officers of the Navy, Army and strangers of every respectable denomination that eventually came to the island'.[66]

Hospitality was only one of the methods the Clarkes employed to influence military personnel, colonial officials, and merchants. Gedney Clarke Sr entered into partnerships with naval officers in order to prosecute the slave trade and to profit from victualling and privateering. The delivery of slaves to Henry Laurens, for example, was a venture Clarke conducted jointly with Admiral Thomas Frankland.[67]

---

[65] Gedney Clarke Sr received Washington and other visitors at his Bridgetown town house, situated at the foot of the West Bridge on the corner of Cheapside. This building (along with the family's warehouses) was destroyed in the two fires of 1766, necessitating a shift in the type of patronage offered by Clarke Jr, [Barbados], *The Public Acts in Force: Passed by the Legislature of Barbados, from May 11th 1762 to April 8th 1800, Carefully Compared and Examined* (London, 1801), 40–1; Martyn J. Bowden, 'The Three Centuries of Bridgetown: An Historical Geography', *JBMHS*, 49 (2003), 76, 82.

[66] 'Autobiographical Manuscript of William Senhouse', 115. Hospitality at the Belle plantation was extended to other visitors calling at Barbados, including Nathaniel Phillips, National Library of Wales, Aberystwyth, MS Slebech Papers 9402, Nathaniel Phillips, 'A Journey through the Caribbean in 1775', 29 October 1775. In appraising Clarke's conduct, however, it should be noted that in Britain, white West Indians enjoyed a reputation in Britain for warm hospitality, a virtual stereotype that prominent members of island society sought to cultivate. See Janet Schaw, *Journal of a Lady of Quality; Being the Narrative of a Journey from Scotland to the West Indies, North Carolina, and Portugal, in the Years 1774 to 1776*, eds. E. W. Andrews and C. M. Andrews (3rd edn, New Haven, 1939), 92–3. Senhouse's memorandum is also the retrospective work of an official who feared that he had been compromised by his association with the Clarkes (before leaving Britain he had been approached by Peter Clarke and Francis Holburne with an offer of free transportation to Barbados). As a younger son, Senhouse lacked financial security and he had struggled in the navy as a midshipman before gaining his appointment as Surveyor General through the patronage of Sir James Lowther, who had also lent him money to cover his living expenses. It is clear that Senhouse enjoyed the generosity of his host's hospitality (as he also was to do on Dominica as the guest of Sir William Young), and his comments on the lavishness of Gedney Clarke Jr's lifestyle provide insight into his own aspirations. (The author is grateful to Adrian Bodkin for sharing information on William Senhouse.)

[67] Hamer and Rogers eds., *Papers of Henry Laurens*, 254.

Clarke took prize cargoes in partnership with Edward Lascelles during the War of Jenkins' Ear (1739–42) and the War of the Austrian Succession (1742–8); he also acted in association with Admiral Sir Peter Warren.[68] During the next major conflict, the Seven Years' War, Gedney Clarke Sr, Samuel Carter, and their partner Andrew Hunter were the agents designated to dispose of prize goods taken by British warships in Barbados, again working closely with Admiral Frankland.[69]

Turnover from handling prizes was considerable, but the business involved considerable financial risk, on both land and sea. Lascelles, Clarke, & Daling received the proceeds of the *Santissima Trinidada*: a Spanish vessel captured in 1762 by the *Feret*, a ship under the command of Peter Clarke and part of the squadron commanded by Admiral George Brydges Rodney. The prize was valued at £30,000, when condemned in Barbados, yet Gedney's and his associates' net return fell far short of this figure.[70] Four prize ships captured in 1758, for example, had a gross value of £24,276 (sterling); the partners, however, only earned 6 per cent on net proceeds of £13,453. The British Treasury's refusal to allow the feeding of prisoners of war as an allowable expense further depressed returns. Added to this, political pressure was applied to Admiral Frankland at this stage of the war to advance more than £20,000 to the Prize Commissioners, draining the syndicate of capital.[71] Moreover, any gains from these five vessels were offset by a loss of at least £14,400 in compensation paid to the owners of the *Nuestra Senra*

---

[68] Letter book of Swett and Hooper, Hooper to Clarke, 13 August 1745; Julian Gwyn ed., *The Royal Navy and North America: The Warren Papers, 1736–1752* (Navy Records Society, vol. CXVIII: London, 1973), 143, 250–1, 294. The privateering operations with Warren were undertaken in association with Edward and Henry Lascelles. No precise estimate of the profits generated from prize cargoes is possible, but Gwyn has argued that the bulk of Warren's estate (valued at £159,000 in 1752) was generated from prizes and that he earned a minimum of £127,405 from this source between 1739 and 1747, Julian Gwyn, 'Money Lending in New England: The Case of Admiral Sir Peter Warren and his Heirs, 1739–1805', *New England Quarterly*, 44 (1971), 121; Julian Gwyn, *The Enterprising Admiral: The Personal Fortune of Admiral Sir Peter Warren* (Montreal, 1974), 18–20. See also D. J. Hamilton, 'Private Enterprise and Public Service: Naval Contracting in the Caribbean, c. 1720–50', *Journal for Maritime Research* www.jmr.nmm.ac.uk (April 2004).

[69] *LMLB*, Pares Transcripts, H581, f. 62, Lascelles & Maxwell to Gedney Clarke II, 10 February 1757; Clements Library, Miscellaneous Collection, Power of attorney from Sir Thomas Frankland to Gedney Clarke, Samuel Carter, and Andrew Hunter, dated 8 December 1756 and recorded in the Barbados Court of Vice Admiralty 22 January 1757.

[70] NA:PRO, C12/519/16.

[71] In consequence, Frankland urged Clarke Sr not to send further remittances to the Treasury but to keep the proceeds in his own hands, fearing the partners might be left with losses and uncancelled bonds by the end of the war, Hamilton College, Beinecke Collection, M134, Frankland to Clarke, Carter, and Hunter (Barbados), 23 October 1758.

de los Remedios, courtesy of a legal ruling delivered by Blenman at the end of a protracted court case.[72]

During the Seven Years' War, Clarke Sr expanded his participation in the victualling trade: a line of business that he had previously conducted with the Lascelles, who held the contracts for Barbados and the Leeward Islands from at least 1734.[73] By 1762, Clarke held victualling contracts in his own right, though the house of Lascelles & Maxwell continued to finance the operations.[74] In the case both of prize cargoes and of victualling, Admiral Francis Holburne (a relation of both the Lascelles and the Clarkes) provided another important conduit of patronage, practical expertise, and investment capital. Holburne was a versatile business associate. In 1745, he was captain of HMS *Argyle*, a vessel involved in Caribbean privateering. Two years later, Holburne was on Barbados managing Canewood plantation during a respite from naval command. Holburne enjoyed the political support of the Grenvilles and Archibald Campbell, Duke of Argyll; financially, he extended loans to Gedney Clarke Jr worth £5,000 in 1765 and £6,311 in 1773.[75]

Close relations between naval officers and colonial merchants were not uncommon. During wartime, the two professions naturally came together over victualling, privateering, prizes, and convoys.[76] In the slave trade, security considerations often dictated that captains of

---

[72] Pares, 'Barbados Prize Court', 124–8. It can also be noted that Admiral Rodney and Sir James Douglas appear to have made very little from prizes during the Seven Years' War, in contrast to Sir Peter Warren's successes during the Wars of Jenkins' Ear and the Austrian Succession, David Spinney, *Rodney* (London 1969), 209.

[73] Daniel A. Baugh, *British Naval Administration in the Age of Walpole* (Princeton, NJ, 1965), 401; Daniel A. Baugh, *Naval Administration, 1715–1750* (Navy Records Society, vol. CXX: London, 1977), 433–4; *LMLB*, Pares Transcripts, H567, Henry Lascelles to Gedney Clarke, 26 March 1748.

[74] *LMLB*, Pares Transcripts, H671, f. 237, Lascelles & Maxwell to Gedney Clarke I, 3 April 1762.

[75] N. A. M. Roger, *The Wooden World: An Anatomy of the Georgian Navy* (London, 1988), 273; Pares, 'Barbados Prize Court', 124; NA:PRO, C12/928/28, *Holburne* vs *Lascelles* (1779); HH:WIP, 'List of Judgements on Record inn the Island of Tobago agst Gedney Clarke Esqr.' [n.d.]. Francis Holburne became the second husband of Frances Lascelles (née Ball), widow of Edward Lascelles of Barbados and the mother of Frances Lascelles who married Gedney Clarke Jr in 1762. The marriage notice in *Gentleman's Magazine*, 32 (1762), 503 mistakenly identifies Frances as Holburne's niece. Holburne served as Commander-in-Chief of naval forces stationed in Barbados and the Leeward Islands during Henry Grenville's Governorship. Captain William Holburne (Francis' younger brother) was Sir Peter Warren's aide-de-camp in 1747. During the Seven Years' War, Francis was Admiral Rodney's lieutenant. It was through Rodney's patronage that he secured the promotion of relations, including the Clarkes, Spinney, *Rodney*, 210–11. For details of Holburne's involvement in slaving, see *LMLB*, Pares Transcripts, W&G III, Lascelles & Maxwell to Francis Holburne, 28 May 1748; H510, same to same, 29 November 1750.

[76] Gwyn, *Enterprising Admiral*, 7–26, 197–8.

warships and private merchant vessels forge agreements. Such relationships were neither exceptional nor illegal, though could easily involve participants in conflicts of interest. The influence wielded by the Clarkes, however, exceeded the norm and, on occasion, obliterated the distinction between public and private interest, as it did, for example, in the Dutch colonies of Demerara and Essequibo.

In 1763, enslaved Africans in Berbice launched an uprising that threatened to destroy the plantation system the Dutch had established in their Caribbean colonial settlements. Within two days of receiving news of the insurrection, Gedney Clarke Sr had despatched four armed vessels, closely followed by a fifth, to Demerara. The vessels carried fifty Barbados militiamen, whom Clarke victualled and maintained in the colony 'by Threats, Arguments & the force of money'. The militia was augmented by 100 marines and sailors aboard HMS *Pembroke*, lent to Clarke by Admiral Rodney and put into commission by Admiral Douglas. An assortment of sailors from the merchant marine and other personnel raised the total fighting force to 300 combatants.[77] In July 1763, then, a small, privately financed task force of armed men in public and private employ crossed national boundaries, without any official sanction, solely to protect the property of a leading Barbadian merchant.

When Admiral Rodney was recalled to England shortly afterwards, Gedney Jr reported that the officer 'much agst. his Inclination, sent for the 100 marines & seamen he had lent my Father'.[78] The Barbados militia, however, remained in Demerara and assisted in the defeat of a rebel stronghold at La Savonnette plantation. Ultimately, the Berbice uprising was suppressed not so much by Barbadians as by the native Indian inhabitants, whose support the Dutch and British planters had solicited.[79] Nevertheless, the appearance of Clarke's forces at the mouth of the Demerara River, and the fortification of his He't Loo plantation,

---

[77] BL, Egerton MS 1,720, Bentinck Papers, 'Correspondence respecting the colony of Demerara, 1762–1766', f. 9, Gedney Clarke Sr to Bentinck, 3 April 1763; f. 35, Gedney Clarke Jr to Bentinck, 8 July 1763; Harris and de Villiers eds., *Gravesande* 421, 444; Henry Bolingbroke, *A Voyage to the Demerary* (London, [1807]), 194; Sheridan, *Sugar and Slavery*, 443–4. Regarding relations between the Clarkes and Rodney, see also Stowe Collection, STG Box 12, No. 24, Gedney Clarke II to Sir George Brydges Rodney, 12 October 1764.

[78] BL, Egerton MS 1,720, f. 35. Rodney willingly returned to England at the end of the Seven Years' War hoping to reap the political rewards of his successful campaign to capture Martinique, Spinney, *Rodney*, 208–12.

[79] The present-day names of the native population groupings are the Guaharibo, Shiriana, Waica, and Warrau tribes. On the participation of the Guyanese Amerindians in suppressing the revolt (including the distribution of arms to them by Gedney Clarke Sr), see Harris and de Villiers ed., *Gravesande* 443, 449; BL, Egerton MS 1,720, ff. 47–8, 67.

discouraged the colony's enslaved from joining the revolt and its planters from taking flight.

Other noteworthy participants in Demerara and Essequibo were members of the Douglas family. Sir James Douglas, MP for the Orkney and Shetland Islands, owned Weilburg plantation in Demerara from about 1765. Clarke's relationship with the Douglas family paid a variety of dividends. Gedney Clarke Jr supplied Douglas' plantation with slaves and provisions, the gross value of his account being £5,588 during an eighteen-month period in 1766–7.[80] In addition to the command held by James Douglas, another member of the family, Robert Douglas, was in 1760 appointed Commander-in-Chief on the Leeward Island station, and two years later, he attained the rank of Rear Admiral. Beyond their financial and military heft, the Douglases were also politically useful by virtue of their connections in Scotland and Holland. Admiral James Douglas' patron (and probably kinsman) was James Douglas, 14th Earl of Morton, a leading member of the Scottish aristocracy. Through Robert Douglas, who had married into a prominent Dutch family, Gedney Clarke Sr and Jr gained an introduction to Count William Bentinck, the patron of Demerara at the Hague.[81] In due course, the Clarkes lobbied Bentinck, seeking to be compensated by the Estates General for their defence of the colony in the amount of 41,060 guilders 15 stuyvers.[82]

[80] NMM, Papers of Admiral Sir James Douglas, DOU/6 Letterbook, 1762–7. For references to Gedney Clarke Jr, see especially 25 February 1765, Lachlan McClean to Colonel Douglas; 28 August 1766, James Douglas to Willy [Douglas]; 26 July 1765, n.d. [c. July–August 1765], 4 March 1766, 20 March 1766, 14 April 1766, 3 October 1766, 3 January 1767, 8 March 1767, 24–26 March 1767, 18 June 1767, 21 July 1767 all William Brisbane to [Sir James Douglas?]; 1 July 1767, Robert Milne to Sir James Douglas; 8 July 1767, Robert Milne to Sir James Douglas. For details of accounts between Gedney Clarke Jr and the Douglases, see Papers of Admiral Sir James Douglas, DOU/14, Ledger 1766–70, February 1766–August 1767. See also John Carter Brown Library, Codex Eng 52, Accounts and Ledger of Weilburg plantation, Demerara, 1767–70, ff. 18, 20. For further details of the Douglas family's involvement in West Indies trade and in the navy see Philip C. Yorke ed., *The Diary of John Baker* (London, 1931), 78. During the Seven Years' War Commodore Sir James Douglas was Admiral Rodney's second in command, Spinney, *Rodney*, 199.

[81] Harris and de Villiers eds., *Gravesande* 379, 391. Robert Douglas was second in command of the expedition despatched from Holland against the slave revolt of 1763. He was also the recipient of promotions and honours in both Holland and Britain, including the rank of Vice Admiral 1770, Admiral 1778, and a Baronet in 1786. Douglas' involvement in slaving is alluded to in David Eltis, Stephen D. Behrendt, David Richardson, and Herbert S. Klein eds., *The Trans-Atlantic Slave Trade: A Database on CD-ROM* (Cambridge, 1999), voyage #77,596 (1751–2).

[82] Approximately £3,421.1s.3d. sterling: a sum less than half of the expedition's stated cost of £8,000, Rodway, *History of British Guiana*, vol. II, 219; Harris and de Villiers eds., *Gravesande*, vol. I, 43; vol. II, 483.

Consolidating Power and Influence

Notwithstanding the Navigation Acts, substantial quantities of merchandise and capital flowed between Dutch and British colonies during the eighteenth century.[83] Prior to the Colonial Debt Acts of 1773 and 1774, however, British officials took little notice of foreign investment in the colonies. Off the record, Barbadians who acquired property in Demerara and Essequibo were largely tolerated, but, as the correspondence of Lascelles & Maxwell reveals, they also ran the risk of falling foul of both the British and Dutch Governments. In 1743, for example, Lascelles & Maxwell warned Conrad Adams that 'the Dutch are always jealous of Strangers & may lay the Purchasers from Barbados under hard restrictions'. To avoid discrimination, Adams was advised, planters should not only 'go to Holland & become Dennizens of the Commonealth', but also 'reside in the Colony as Dutchmen, & give up, if there's anything in that, all pretensions of having been Englishmen'.[84] George Maxwell likewise cautioned Gedney Clarke Sr that, since he was Bridgetown Collector, owning a Dutch plantation would weaken his position if he were to find himself in dispute with Governor Grenville.[85]

To secure family investments, Gedney Jr was sent to Amsterdam in 1755, where he was to learn Dutch and become naturalised; at the same time, Clarke Sr transferred nominal ownership of several of his Demerara properties to his sons.[86] By living in Holland, Gedney Jr gained trading privileges that he was able to draw upon in 1766, in a shipping venture he launched jointly with Peter de Bruyn of Middleburg. 'Your Excellency will be pleased to observe that I am a Burgher of Middleburg as well as Demerara', Clarke wrote to Storm van's Gravesande, '& therefore I have as good a right to load my ship in Dimmerery as any man whatever'. Not only was Gravesande persuaded

[83] J. P. Van De Voort, 'Dutch Capital in the West Indies during the Eighteenth Century', *Low Countries History Yearbook: Acta Historiae Neerlandicae*, 14 (1981), 84–105; D. J. Ormrod, 'The Atlantic Economy and the "Protestant Capitalist International", 1651–1775', *Historical Research*, 66 (1993), 197–208. Demerara and Essequibo were originally settled by Barbadian colonists during the 1650s and 1660s, Vincent T. Harlow, *A History of Barbados, 1625–1685* (Oxford, 1926), 155–6, 183–7; Richard S. Dunn, *Sugar and Slaves: The Rise of the Planter Class in the English West Indies, 1624–1713* (Chapel Hill, 1972), 20. For an example of how easily merchants moved between the Dutch and British Caribbean territories, see Baker Business Library, Harvard, Lloyd Papers, MS 732, 1732–90, B747, vol. II (1767–80), 43.

[84] *LMLB*, Lascelles & Maxwell to Conrad Adams, 16 September 1743.

[85] *LMLB*, Pares Transcripts H352 (W&G VI), f. 161, George Maxwell to Gedney Clarke, 5 May 1755.

[86] Ibid.; Harris and de Villiers eds., *Gravesande*, 334.

on that matter, but in time he would also ask Clarke Jr to be the godfather of his children.[87]

Gedney Clarke Jr, the Creole son of a third-generation Yankee, had spent most of his twenties in Amsterdam, Zeeland, and Middleburg. He had lived on Barbados, one of the oldest settled colonies, and in the developing colonies of Demerara and Essequibo. He had also contemplated settling in New York.[88] Continuity was important, however, if the dispersed Clarke family was to sustain some form of collective identity within the Atlantic world, and in 1762 a measure of continuity was achieved. That year, the longstanding business relationship between the Clarkes and the Lascelles became a family affair when Gedney married Frances Lascelles, the daughter of Henry Lascelles' half-brother Edward, thereby cementing their kinship links.[89] Just as the name 'Gedney Clarke' reflected an earlier union of mutual advantage, so too did the Clarke–Lascelles match. The immediate benefits of the alliance were apparently more personal than financial, however. Frances, whom Gedney had known since childhood, had given him a compelling reason to suspend his relentless travels and to settle in London.[90] His timing was perfect. The next year George Maxwell's death created an opening within the firm, and in 1764 Clarke succeeded him as partner. Subsequently the commission house was 'new modell'd under the Stile of Lascelles, Clarke & Daling'.[91] To accommodate his new bride and to

---

[87] Harris and de Villiers eds., *Gravesande*, 391, 525–6; BL, Egerton MS 1,720, f. 1. An unnamed relative of Gedney Clarke Jr (his cousin? – see next note) also visited Demerara, Holland, and France in 1764, suggesting that Clarke Jr was not the only son to be exposed to European influences, Egerton MS 1,720, ff. 58, 60. It is worth noting that Sir Walter Farquhar's mother was Katherine Turing and her brother was consul at Middleburg. See Chapter Seven for dynastic links between the Scots and West Indian families of Stephenson, Harvie, Graeme, and Farquhar; see also J. F. Payne, revised Kaye Bagshaw, 'Sir Walter Farquhar, first baronet (1738–1819)', *ODNB*.

[88] John Watts wrote to Gedney Clarke Sr on 25 July 1763 that one of Clarke's sons, whom Watts congratulated for his recent success, had left for London the previous month. The departure was apparently regarded as permanent, for Watts had been instructed to sell the son's furniture, Barck ed., *Letter Book John Watts*, 159. Gedney Clarke Jr was replaced in New York in May 1764 by his cousin John Clarke, the son of John Clarke of Salem, Clarke Family Papers, Box 1, Folder 1, William Clarke to Ann Clarke, 1 May 1764.

[89] Joseph Foster, *Pedigrees of the County Families of England: Yorkshire, West Riding* (3 vols., London, 1874), vol. II, 'Lascelles'. The notice printed in *Gentleman's Magazine*, 32 (1762), 503, records the marriage on 15 October of 'Godney Clarke, jun. of Barbadoes, Esq; – to Miss Lascelles, niece to Adm. Holburne'. It is notable that, despite his wanderings, Clarke Jr was still identified with Barbados and that he was also accorded the title of esquire.

[90] In a letter of 7 June 1763 to Bentinck, Clarke Jr makes it clear that the death of Maxwell was an unexpected event that caused him to change his plans, BL, Egerton MS 1,720.

[91] William Daling joined Lascelles & Maxwell as a partner in 1753. Watts also reported that Gedney Clarke Jr had secured a 'handsome appointment': the post of Surveyor of

conduct business, Clarke purchased a house and other property in London.

Clarke Jr's decision to enter into partnership with Lascelles and Daling in 1764 is the first indication that the Clarkes may have thought of re-establishing themselves in Britain. In contrast to other West Indian merchants and planters, including Henry Lascelles, the Clarkes lacked an English country estate that could function as a dynastic centre. Though the family owned substantial amounts of landed property in the colonies (as Tables 5.2 and 5.3 record), no parcel seems to have been intended for a permanent home. The Atlantic was replete with opportunities for material advancement, the Clarkes recognised, provided family members were mobile enough to take advantage of them, and so they had not set a priority on creating a family seat. Dispersal was not, however, destructive of family bonds or identity. Kinship and acquaintances were maintained through mutual hospitality, active correspondence, and business association.

Gedney Clarke Sr's desire to maintain contact with communities he had left behind and to strengthen ties with ones being formed is a recurrent theme throughout his surviving records. Soon after arriving in Barbados in 1733, he paid £25 to rent pew number one in the newly constructed church of St Peter's, Salem's first Anglican church. Gedney's brother John was active in its establishment, and, listed among the contributors who offered donations during the ministry of Revd William McGilchrist, which commenced in 1747, is Clarke Sr's own name.[92] Additional acts of philanthropy strengthened Gedney Sr's New England bonds. In 1744, he made a gift of a peal of bells to the North Church in Boston. Two years later, with his business associates Sir Peter Warren and Robert Hooper, he helped to raise £2,000 for the relief of widows in Marblehead and other New England communities who had lost their husbands during the campaign to capture Louisbourg and Cape Breton from the French. To mark his appointment as Barbados Customs Collector in 1748, Clarke 'sent orders to his Brother John to give an entertainment to all the Merchants of Salem with whom he had done business'. When Salem's House of Refuge was established

---

Customs in the Leeward Islands, Brack ed., *Letter Book John Watts*, John Watts to Gedney Clarke I, 20 May 1763; *Gentleman's Magazine*, 33 (1963), 46.

[92] John Clarke contributed at least £354.11s.d. in 1743 to import an organ for the church. He also served as churchwarden 1738–9 and 1747–8, *NEHGR*, 24 (1870), 37, 93–5; Tapley, *St Peter's Church*, 10, 27–8, 36. However, for reasons that are not clear, neither Gedney's nor John Clarke's name appear in a 1731 list of subscribers 'towards the Erecting and Building of a Church of England' in Salem, PEM, MS E 51 C4 53 1731, reprinted in Tapley, *St Peter's Church*, 4–5.

in 1749, Clarke also despatched a gift of 500 bushels of corn from his Virginia property to relieve poverty in the town.[93]

The Barbadian Clarkes remained in close contact with their Salem kinsfolk and when John Clarke experienced financial difficulty, brother Gedney assisted that branch of the family. He took charge of his mother's funeral account in 1760, which included a £100 judgement against the estate, and he authorised the £88.6s.4d. in mourning expenses, among which there was a charge of £11.14s. for nine escutcheons. Clarke Sr's nephews John, William, and Samuel Clarke subsequently moved to Barbados, where Gedney Jr helped them in business, while the younger Francis Clarke was established in West Indian trade at Antigua. The brothers also received aid from the Clarkes' business associates, including John Watts of New York and Lascelles & Daling in London. Following a brilliant marriage in 1769 to the Barbadian heiress Ann Jones Gascoigne, 'a Lady from Twelve to Fifteen hundred pounds sterling P. Annum', John Clarke was able to regain title to his father's Salem property.[94]

Continuity also marks Gedney Clarke Sr's choice of business associates. Among merchants and naval officers, he gave preference to his kinsmen, and beyond that, he gravitated towards individuals who shared a common regional affiliation. The Lascelles, a long-established Yorkshire gentry family who had represented Northallerton in parliament for several generations, were his most important creditors. Through marriage, the Clarkes were related to another important Yorkshire family: the Fairfaxes of Denton and Oglethorpe, who held substantial interests in both New England and Virginia. The paths of

---

[93] *NEHGR*, 33 (1879), 294; Letter book of Swett and Hooper, Hooper to Clarke, 20 January 1745[6], 17 May 1746 (following the successful conclusion of the Cape Breton campaign Hooper sent Clarke 'Mr Princes's Thanksgiving sermon', Hooper to Clarke, 19 January 1746[7]; see also Gwyn, *Enterprising Admiral*, 24–5; *The Diary of William Bentley, DD Pastor of the East Church, Salem, Massachusetts* (4 vols., Salem, MA, 1914), vol. IV, 495; Joseph B. Felt, *Annals of Salem* (2 vols., Salem, MA, 1849), vol. II, 398; LMBH, Family Files, 'Gedney Clarke'; Donnan ed., *Documents*, 457.

[94] Clarke Family Papers, Box 1, Folder 1, 'Gedney Clarke Esq. Account of My Mothers Funeral Charges' (1760); William Clarke to Ann Clarke, 16 January 1764; John Clarke to Ann Clarke, 21 November 1765; Gedney Clarke II to Richard Darby, 11 November 1768; Samuel Clarke to Ann Clarke, 27 May 1769; John Clarke to Ann Clarke, 2 July 1769 and 15 October 1769. By his death in 1784/5, John Clarke had become a successful merchant and planter and owned Jones estate in St Philip's Parish, Barbados. Frank Clarke profited from mercantile activities during the War of Independence (1776–83) and established a dry-goods business with John Dalby. In contrast to his brothers, however, William Clarke suffered a reversal of fortune during the early 1770s related to his plantation investments on Tobago.

the Fairfaxes and Clarkes continued to cross in public and private affairs during the eighteenth century.[95]

Admiral Sir Thomas Frankland, Gedney Clarke Sr's partner in the South Carolina slave trade and in privateering during the Seven Years' War, married the daughter of wealthy Charleston merchant William Rhett. Moreover, Thomas' elder brother, Sir Charles Henry Frankland, held the post of Customs Collector in Boston between 1741 and 1757 and was a business associate of Admiral Sir Peter Warren.[96] Also an ancient Yorkshire family, the Franklands maintained their seat at Thirkleby. Successive generations of Franklands represented the town of Thirsk in parliament, the neighbouring constituency of the Lascelles at Northallerton, and held prominent naval appointments.[97] Local electoral accommodation between the Lascelles and the Franklands dated from at least the 1670s, and during the

---

[95] BL, Add. MS 30,305–6, Estate and Family Correspondence of the Fairfax Family, 1600–1827. The Fairfax's Yorkshire estates were sold after the death of Thomas, Lord Fairfax in 1710 to the Leeds merchant Sir Henry Ibbetson, who had married into the Fairfax family, Webb, *Fairfax of York*, 114. John Clarke and William Henry Fairfax both served on the same expedition to Quebec in 1759 (where the latter was killed). In 1774, another of Gedney Clarke Sr's nephews, William Clarke (by this time living in London in poor circumstances), was invited to stay with George Fairfax in Yorkshire soon after Fairfax left his post as Customs Collector in Virginia, Clarke Family Papers, Box 1, Folder 1, William Clarke to Ann Clarke, 4 May 1774; John Clark to Francis (Frank) Clarke, 30 June 1783. See also Waters, 'Gedney and Clarke Families', 274–5, 279–90.

[96] MHS, Payne-Gallwey Papers, 1910–11; BPL, MS Ch.M.1.10, 28: 'A List of Several Deeds & Specialties deposited in the hands of Sir Henry Frankland, Charles Anthony, & Thomas Hancock Esqrs as Attorneys to the Honble Peter Warren Esq.'; Gwyn, *Enterprising Admiral*, 109–10, 112–15. Elias Nason's *Sir Charles Henry Frankland, Baronet: or, Boston in the Colonial Times* (Albany, NY, 1965) is an inaccurate and sentimental account. Charles Henry and Thomas Frankland's brother William Frankland also held a customs post in North America. In 1764, bank stock valued at £27,700.12s.6d. was transferred to William by his brother Thomas as part of a joint business venture (Charles Henry thought William should have received £32,100 for his share), Stowe Collection, STG Box 22, No. 2, William Frankland to George Grenville, 19 June 1765; No. 3, William Frankland to George Grenville, 12 November 1764; MHS, Charles Henry Frankland, Diary 1755–67, entry n.d., Bath, 1764. Gedney Clarke was part-owner of the privateering vessel *Frankland* in 1757, Pares, 'Barbados Prize Court', 124.

[97] The Franklands have been largely absent from accounts of colonial history, but they were remarkably active in eighteenth-century commerce. By 1786, the family had probably been connected with Barbados for more than a century, BA, RB6/40/190–1, Will of William Frankland, dated 10 October 1684; David L. Kent, *Barbados and America* (Arlington, VA, 1980), 46, 185; BA, RB6/33/2–8, Will of Admiral Sir Thomas Frankland, dated 4 August 1785. In addition to the family's American connections, Henry Frankland (d. 1738) was appointed President of Calcutta (c. 1728), while the MP Frederick Frankland was a Comptroller of the Excise in 1763 and also a governor of the Bank of England, K. N. Chaudhuri, *The Trading World of Asia and the English East India Company, 1660–1760* (Cambridge, 1978), 99, 298, 311, 598; MHS, Payne-Gallwey Papers, 1910–11.

1750s both families supported the Pelham ministries.[98] The Douglases lacked Yorkshire roots, but their trade association with the Lascelles produced a dynastic attachment to that northern family. In 1734, for example, James Douglas and Henry Lascelles joined together in trade with Nova Colonia, and both were associates of the Antiguan merchant Thomas Kerby.[99] The diaries of William Hervey report close social relations between the two families, and in 1784 Edward Lascelles' daughter Frances married the Earl of Morton's second son John Douglas.[100]

The clutch of northern families in league with the Lascelles and the Clarkes shared common interests in the arts and sciences. Sir Thomas Frankland and James Douglas, 14th Earl of Morton were Fellows of the Royal Society and (along with Robert Douglas) correspondents of the explorer and naturalist Sir Joseph Banks.[101] It may be significant that James Douglas (1675–1742) was the author of several notable tracts on natural history (among them a history of coffee, which included an account of Barbados' early experiments in cultivating the plant), while another Douglas, John Douglas of Antigua (d. 1743), was likewise a FRS.[102] An

[98] Historical Manuscripts Commission, *Report on the Manuscripts of Mrs Frankland-Russell-Astley* (London, 1900), 38, 41; Romney Sedgwick, *The House of Commons, 1715–1754* (2 vols., London, 1970), vol. II, 50; R. G. Thorne, *The House of Commons, 1754–1790* (5 vols., London, 1986), vol. III, 830; Nikolaus Pevsner, *The Buildings of England: Yorkshire: The North Riding* (London, 1966), 364–5; Edward Waterson and Peter Meadows, *Lost Houses of York and the North Riding* (York, 1998), 58–9. In 1744, Henry Lascelles asked the Franklands for assistance when Robert Dinwiddie investigated accounts kept when he and his brother Edward held the post of Bridgetown Customs Collector, BL, Add. MS 23,817, f. 123. The Franklands had family links with the Smelts, who were also allies of the Lascelles in Yorkshire electoral politics, Thorne, *House of Commons*, vol. III, 830; James Henretta, 'Salutary Neglect': Colonial *Administration under the Duke of Newcastle* (Princeton, 1972), 228. The Franklands also married into the Payne family, another important West Indian dynasty with property on Antigua, Yorke ed., *Diary of John Baker*, 63; Yorkshire Archaeological Society, Leeds, MD 470, medical bills and accounts relating to the estate in Antigua of Sir Ralph Payne, and DD 94, Payne-Gallwey (Frankland) Estate Papers.

[99] NA:PRO, C12/300/20, *Neale vs Bank of England* (1741); Sheridan, *Sugar and Slavery*, 303. See also Norfolk Record Office, Douglas Family: Neville Diaries and Papers, MC 7/825–30, 396X1, Letters of William, Henry, and James Douglas from Antigua and Jamaica, 1731–42 (these include an unidentified Northallerton correspondent).

[100] *Journals of the Hon. William Hervey in North America and Europe from 1755 to 1814* (Bury St Edmunds, 1906), 363, 385; Foster, *Pedigrees*, vol. II. Frances Lascelles was the daughter of Edward Lascelles, the son of Henry Lascelles' half-brother Edward, who in 1795 inherited Edwin Lascelles' estate and the following year was dubbed Baron Harewood.

[101] The Franklands were kinsfolk of the Banks, who in turn were related to the Grenville family, Warren R. Dawson ed., *The Banks Letters: A Calendar of the Manuscript Correspondence of Joseph Banks* (London, 1958), 272, 343–5; Harold B. Carter, *Sir Joseph Banks, 1743–1820* (London, 1988), 3.

[102] A total of 379 mahogany trees were found in the garden of the Clarkes' former Belle estate on Barbados in 1798, some big enough to square the largest furniture, along with

interest in plant cultivation was shared by Henry Lascelles' half-brother Edward, who is credited with introducing the mango tree into Barbados. Gedney Clarke Jr conducted similar experiments in growing mahogany trees (solving the problem of seed germination outside a tropical rainforest environment); he also demonstrated a specialist interest in epidemiology.[103] Two of Henry Lascelles' Barbadian associates pursued research in applied botany and astronomy. Burch Hothersall corresponded with Philip Miller (keeper of the Apothecaries Garden in Chelsea) about improvements in coffee cultivation and experiments in fermenting wine from sugar cane. Thomas Stevenson (the Provost Marshall) received a patent for improving windmill design, published an almanac on the island, and maintained a ten-foot telescope and a pendulum clock in order to record astronomical observations.[104]

The Clarkes' British aristocratic associates were involved in major architectural projects of which Harewood House, built by Robert Adam and John Carr between 1759 and 1771, and landscaped by Capability Brown, is the best-known example. The Lascelles also built or

thirty-six fustic, nineteen lignum vitae, and eight bay or allspice trees, WRA, Harewood House, West India Papers, Letters and Papers on West India Estates and Affairs, 1795–1873, William Bishop (Barbados) to Elliot, Whalley, & Adams (London), 11 June 1798.

[103] C. H. Brock, 'James Douglas (1675–1742), Botanist', *Journal of the Society for the Bibliography of Natural History*, 9 (1979), 137–45; S. D. Smith, 'Sugar's Poor Relation: Coffee Planting in the British West Indies, 1720–1833', *Slavery and Abolition*, 19 (1998), 69, 85; Raymond Phineas Stearns, *Science in the British Colonies of America* (Chicago, 1970), 708. Letter from Joshua Steele of Barbados, 20 May 1785, *Transactions of the Society of Arts* (1786) cited in *JBMHS*, 20 (1953), 126–7; Griffin Hughes, *The Natural History of Barbados* (London, 1750), 177; LBMH, Family Files, envelope of materials including details of the cultivation of the mahogany tree by Gedney Clarke, derived from 'The Lucas Manuscript Volumes in the Barbados Public Library', *JBMHS*, 22 [1954–5], 177; William Sandiford, *An Account of a Late Epidemical Distemper, Extracted from a Letter Addressed to Gedney Clarke, Esq.* (London, 1771). In 1754 and again in 1766, Lascelles & Maxwell sent out a gardener to the Gedney Clarkes for terms of three and four years at £30 (sterling) per annum, *LMLB*, Pares Transcripts, H394, VI, Lascelles & Maxwell to Gedney Clarke Sr, 10 December 1754; H396 IX, Lascelles & Daling to Gedney Clarke Jr, 14 November 1766.

[104] Craig B. Waff and Stephen Skinner, 'Thomas Stevenson of Barbados and Comet Halley's 1759 Return', in Richard B. Goddard ed., *George Washington's Visit to Barbados, 1751* (Barbados, 1997), 201–9; Stearns, *Science in the British Colonies*, 361–3. Stearns' interpretation of scientific investigation on Barbados conceptualises science as experimental hypothesis testing, combined with the rigorous use of mathematics. Judged by these criteria, Barbados was deficient in scientists. However, if a broader concept of science is employed, to include practical experimentation by planters and merchants within restrictive fields (usually lying close to their commercial interests), then the island undertook more research than Stearns allows. For comparative descriptive material of scientific pursuits followed by 'Improving Gentlemen' in the first British empire, see Richard Drayton, *Nature's Government: Science, Imperial Britain, and the 'Improvement' of the World* (New Haven/London, 2000), 59–67.

remodelled houses at Darrington (Stapleton Park), Goldsborough, and Plompton, while the Franklands rebuilt Thirkleby Hall in 1780. The Douglas family carried out improvements as well, including creating gardens designed by John Abercrombie. The classics played a prominent part in the education of Gedney Clarke Jr, who completed a tour of Italy in 1755 before launching his business career.[105]

The Lascelles' interest in the Caribbean's natural history dates from the early 1680s. In addition to importing sugar and trading in tobacco, Philip Lascelles handled Barbadian plant and animal specimens. His clients included William Courten (a member of the Courteen family who sponsored the early settlement of the island) and his purchases are recorded in Sir Hans Sloane's collection.[106] It can further be noted that the original trustees of Sloane's collection, which was to form the core of the British Museum, included both the Lascelles' associate Sir George Lyttelton and their kinsman Smart Lethieullier.[107] Links between the Americas and the early history of the British Museum are further reinforced by the appearance in the list of trustees of John Fuller (kinsman of Rose Fuller, Jamaican planter), Sir James Lowther and Sir William Coddrington (Barbados planters), and General James Oglethorpe (a trustee of the colony of Georgia).[108]

---

[105] Mary Mauchline, *Harewood House: One of the Treasure Houses of Britain* (2nd edn, Derbyshire, 1992), 7–41; Helen Lazenby, *Plumpton Rocks, Knaresborough* (Yorkshire Gardens Trust: Leeds, 1997?), 3; Edward Waterson and Peter Meadows, *Lost Houses of the West Riding* (York, 1998), 67; Waterson and Meadows, *Lost Houses of York and the North Riding*, 58–9. John Abercrombie, the author of *Every Man his own Gardener* (London, 1767), was employed in the service of Sir James Douglas and married a relative of his employer. The Franklands would doubtless have upgraded the Elizabethan Thirkleby Hall before 1780 were it not for the life interest in the estate held by the widow of Henry Frankland (fraudulently in the view of her estranged sons) after 1738, MHS, Payne-Gallwey Papers, 1910–11. Sir Charles Henry Frankland donated books and scientific apparatus to Harvard College in 1743 and 1757, BPL, Winthrop Family Papers, vol. I, No. 22A; Nason, *Sir Charles Henry Frankland*, 26.

[106] BL, Sloane MS, 3,962, f. 54, Lord Coleraine to William Corten (alias Charleton), [n.d., 1688]; 3,961, f. 27, Papers of William Courten, 'Things bought in May, June, July and August 1689 ... of Mr Lassells' (the author is grateful to Dominik Collet for drawing attention to these references). Philip Lascelles is not identified by name by Courten, but see Chapter Three for evidence of the four brothers' movements during the 1680s. There is a good chance that Courten was referring to Philip since no other Barbados merchant by the name of Philip Lascelles is known to have traded in London at this time.

[107] *Gentleman's Magazine*, 23 (1753), 50. Sir George Lyttelton was among the MPs selected to draw up a bill in 1753 to establish a permanent home for Sloane's collection, [Great Britain], *Journal of the House of Commons* (London, 1803), vol. XXVI, 747–8. Smart Lethieullier subsequently donated antiquities and other artefacts to the British Museum, Geoffrey Treasure, 'Lethieullier, Smart (1701–1760)', *ODNB*.

[108] East Sussex Record Office, Lewes, Jamaica Correspondence of Rose Fuller, SAS-RF/21, Rose Herring (Jamaica) to Rose Fuller (London), 10 September 1758; RF/22, Lascelles & Maxwell (London) to Rose Fuller (London), 7 July 1758. On Sir Hans

Religion reinforced the bonds between Clarke and his associates. Colonel William Fairfax was 'one of the prime movers in the building of a church in Salem' and he served as treasurer of St Peter's during its construction; Sir Charles Henry Frankland subscribed to the organ fund in 1744. The Lascelles as well (albeit indirectly) were touched by the St Peter's project. Shortly after he returned to London from Massachusetts in 1734, George Plaxton signed a petition to the Bishop of London calling for a missionary for Salem.[109] In their own right, successive generations of Lascelles acted to defend the Protestant settlement. Henry Lascelles' grandfather Francis Lascelles, a Colonel in the Parliamentary army, numbered among the parliamentary commissioners who tried Charles I for treason. Henry's father, Daniel Lascelles, took part in Danby's Rising in 1688, and Henry's eldest son, Edwin Lascelles, was granted an honourable discharge for his part in defeating the 1745 Jacobite rising.[110] Henry Lascelles himself was among the London merchants opposed to the 1753 Jewish Naturalization Act, the modest provisions of which were magnified by its critics into an attack on the Anglican Church. In parliament, the campaign to repeal the bill was led by the same George, Lord Lyttelton who sponsored Gedney Clarke's successful bid to become Customs Collector.[111]

Religion factored into Clarke Sr's business dealings in both North America and the Caribbean. In Barbados, the vestry records of St Michael's are particularly revealing. In November 1743, Clarke Sr secured rights to Thomas Gordon's prominent pew, on which he was

Sloane's personal interest in Jamaica and the West Indies, see Stearns, *Science in the British Colonies*, 364–73.

[109] Tapley, *St Peter's Church*, 4, 6, 16–17, 28, 70–1. Plaxton was Treasurer of Barbados 1723–9 and had family connections in Marblehead as well as London. His brother William was a city lawyer; it is also believed that he was related to Revd George Plaxton, chaplain to Lord Gower in 1716. For evidence of business dealings between Plaxton and the Lascelles brothers, Henry and Edward, see BA, RB1/33/65, Powers of Attorney, Dorothy Prissick to Lascelles and Plaxton (1733) and William Eyles to Lascelles and Plaxton (1733). These associations suggest that Plaxton had shifted position since his connection with Worsley and Carteret during the 1720s. Indeed, on his departure from Barbados in 1734, Plaxton granted five powers of attorney to Arthur Upton, BA, RB1/33/

[110] C. H. Firth ed., *The Memoirs of Edmund Ludlow* (2 vols., Oxford, 1894), vol. II, 217, 285; History of Parliament, card index files of Professor Robert Walcott, 'Daniel Lascelles'; BL, Egerton MS 3,344, f. 55; *LMLB*, Lascelles & Maxwell to George Applethwaite, 15 January 1745[6]. Sir Peter Warren's conversion to Protestantism in order to further his naval career should also be noted, Gwyn, *Enterprising Admiral*, 7–8.

[111] John C. Van Horne and George Reese eds., *The Letter Book of James Abercromby, Colonial Agent, 1751–1773* (Richmond, VA, 1991), 93–5, 98; Rose Mary Davis, *The Good Lord Lyttelton: A Study in Eighteenth-Century Politics and Culture* (Bethlehem, PA, 1939), 207–10.

also permitted to place a lock. A decade later, Clarke Sr was negotiating means to protect the Lascelles' twin pews in St Michael's gallery. While the vestry refused Gedney permission to reserve the pews for the absentee Henry Lascelles and the deceased Edward Lascelles, it did agree to let him 'fix upon two familys to take those parts'. In September 1752, Clarke and his business associate Samuel Carter took over the Lascelles pews, while Robert Watts (a relation of the New York merchant John Watts) and another associate, John Gascoigne, were man-oeuvred into the Clarkes' vacated pews.[112]

At the Hague, Clarke Sr and Jr consistently called on the Zeeland Chamber of the Dutch West India Company to defend the infant colony of Demerara and to develop its infrastructure, specifically by constructing a town building, creating churches, and supporting ministers.[113] English-speaking settlers eventually built their church in 1760, and Gedney Clarke Sr played a major role in its founding.[114] As a partner of Lascelles & Daling, Gedney Clarke Jr participated in a scheme to settle German Protestants in Nova Scotia and other undeveloped regions of North America: a concern with which the Lascelles and other associates, including Sir Peter Warren, had been involved since the 1730s.[115]

Yorkshire affiliations intertwined with other strands of the Lascelles–Clarke business network. Gedney Clarke Sr's daughter Deborah was married into the Thornhill family of Barbados.[116] On Barbados, the Thornhills were among the loan clients of Henry Lascelles, while in England the family purchased a substantial Yorkshire property in

---

[112] 'Records of the Vestry of St Michael', *JBMHS*, 22 (1954–5), 204, and 24 (1956–7), 142. It can also be noted that in 1750, the Society for the Propagation of the Gospel in Foreign Parts granted Gedney Clarke joint power of attorney with Revd Thomas to conduct business on its behalf in Barbados, BA, RB1/8.

[113] BL, Egerton MS 1,720, ff. 4, 35.

[114] Storm van's Gravesande reported that Clarke had requested permission 'to have a church built at his own cost' and subscribed a further 400 guilders towards road building, Harris and de Villiers eds., *Gravesande*, vol. II, 378.

[115] The committee of which Clarke was a member was appointed to provide 'for the immediate support and maintenance of these poor emigrants ... and ... for their commodious transportation to Charles-Town South Carolina', New York Public Library, KF+ 1765, *Proceedings of the Committee Appointed for Relieving the Poor Germans who were Left Destitute in the Month of August 1764* (London, 1765), xii. For Henry Lascelles' involvement in similar schemes, see Board of Trade, *Journal of the Commissioners for Trade and Plantations* (London, 1938), vol. VI, 133; *CSPC (A&WI)*, vol. XXXVII, 232; Arthur Herbert Basye, *The Lords Commissioners of Trade and Plantations, Commonly Known as the Board of Trade, 1748–1782* (New Haven, 1925), 40–5. Palatine settlement was connected with land speculation, Gwyn, *Enterprising Admiral*, 76–7.

[116] Possibly kinsfolk of the Thornhills of Fixby in Yorkshire, though this connection cannot be verified.

Calverley in 1754 from Sir William Blackett (also known as Calverley), whose lands were heavily mortgaged to Henry Lascelles and his sons.[117]

The Gascoignes were yet another Yorkshire family linked to both the Lascelles and the Clarkes. For many centuries the Gascoignes were owners of the Manors of Gawthorpe and Harewood, but had lost possession of these estates in 1656. When he laid down £63,827 for both properties in 1739, Henry Lascelles acquired lands to which his family could claim ancestral ties through a shared lineage with the Gascoignes.[118] Lascelles' son Daniel purchased the neighbouring estate of Plompton in 1760 for £27,000, and Goldsborough two years later for £32,000, properties in which the Gascoignes held interests.[119] In the Americas, a branch of the Gascoignes established themselves in Virginia in 1619, and during the 1740s they bought up extensive tracts of land in Northern Neck at the same time as Gedney and John Clarke were doing likewise. Gascoignes also migrated to Barbados (Stephen Gascoigne was an agent for the Royal African Company in 1676), and, during the eighteenth century, the family invested in Demerara with the Clarkes. John Clarke's 1769 marriage to a wealthy Gascoigne heiress, therefore, was hardly an isolated bit of good fortune.[120]

[117] PEM, Clarke Family Papers, Box 1, Folder 3, 'Will of William Clarke, dated 1776' and Samuel Clarke to Ann Clarke, 27 May 1769; LBMH, Eustace Shilstone Notebooks, 20/133, notes on the will of Peter Clarke (1736–76); Yorkshire Archaeological Society, DD/12/I/5 and 6, Deeds of Calverley Manor; HH:WIP, bundle 8/2, Deborah Thornhill to Lord Harewood, 7 July 1795; BA, Hughes-Queree Collection, Abstracts in Queree notebooks, 'Mangrove Pond' plantation; Waters, 'Gedney and Clarke Families', 271–2; information provided by David Clarke and Mary Lib Clark Joyce (pers. com.); Vere Langford Oliver, *The Monumental Inscriptions in the Churches and Churchyards of the Island of Barbados, British West Indies* (London, 1915), 27, 124, 176; Robert H. Schomburgk, *The History of Barbados* (London, 1971; originally published 1848), 301–3; and see Chapter Six.

[118] Mauchline, *Harewood House*, 10 (n.8); A.W-C., 'The Gascoigne Family', *Leeds Art Calendar*, 64 (1969), 4–5; BL, Add. MS 33,919, f. 331.

[119] In addition to the Gascoignes, the Slingsbys of Scriven held an interest in the Goldsborough estate. The Slingsbys established a cadet branch of the family on Barbados with whom Henry Lascelles did business (Henry Slingsby married into the Hothersall family). During the seventeenth and eighteenth centuries, the English Slingsbys intermarried with the Bethells of Ellerton and Felthorp and produced several merchants named 'Slingsby Bethell', the best known of which was the Hamburg trader and author of *The Present Interest of England Stated* (1671). Another Slingsby Bethell, an eighteenth-century West Indian merchant, was a business associate of Henry Lascelles, and he also acted as a trustee in the Calverley-Blackett land transaction, NA:PRO, C54/5994; Yorkshire Archaeological Society, MS 1,036, f. 114 and DD/12/I/7; Sheridan, *Sugar and Slavery*, 59, 193, 303; LMLB, Letters to Henry Slingsby; see also Chapter Six.

[120] Edward Chase Earl Jr, '"A Gascony" and the Gaskins (Gascoigne) Family', *Northern Neck of Virginia Historical Magazine*, 4 (1954), 321; Nancy Gaskins Moncure, 'Genealogy Connected with the Gascoigne and Moncure Families', Virginia Historical Society, MS 6.1 M7448:1 (typescript compiled 1924); K. G. Davies, *The Royal African*

Additional Yorkshire connections can also be documented. Sir Thomas Robinson of Rokeby (Governor of Barbados between 1742 and 1747) was credited by Grenville for splitting Baxter from Blenman and aligning him with Clarke Sr by engineering a quarrel between Baxter and William Duke (another Blenman protégé).[121] Marriage into the same family as Baxter may have given Robinson additional leverage. The gossips commented that the free-spending Governor, who possessed ostentatious taste in architecture, had wasted no time in finding a perfect match in Sarah Salmon, whose recent legacy meant 'she now weighs £30,000 more than she did'.[122] Finally, but by no means least important, Henry Lascelles maintained an association with Martin Bladen, a Lord Commissioner for Trade and Plantations from 1717 and the dominant figure in the Board of Trade at this time. Bladen's family originated from Bolton Percy in Yorkshire and his mother was a member of the Fairfax dynasty.[123]

Company (London, 1957), 298; Donnan ed., *Documents*, vol. II, 199–209. George Gascoigne of Barbados invested in Demerara along with the Clarkes, and between 1753 and 1758, he acquired two properties covering 2,500 acres. In 1760, Gedney Clarke Sr provided Gascoigne with a mortgage. In 1730, a Mr (Henry?) Lascelles appeared before the Board of Trade 'in behalf of Mr Gascoyne' in connection with German Palatine settlement of Nova Scotia, National Archives of Guyana, SB4/9B, Minutes of the Court of Justice of Essequibo, 1756–65, 144–5, 7 January 1760, Mortgage request of George Gascoigne; Leiden, Bodel Nijenhuis Museum, *Caerte van de Rivier Demerary van ouds immenary gelegen op Suyd Americaes Noordkust op de Noorder Breedte van 6 gr: 40 min:* (1759) reproduction and typescript kept at LBMH; *Journal of the Commissioners*, vol. VI, 133.

[121] On the animosity between William Duke and Thomas Baxter, see *LMLB*, Pares Transcripts, H483, George Maxwell to William Duke, 17 January 1743[4]; Cambridge University Library, Cambridge, Darnell Davis Collection, Box 3, No. 13.

[122] Stowe Collection, STG Box 24, No. 6, Grenville to George Grenville, 7 November 1747; HSP, John Yeates Correspondence, John Bayley (Barbados) to Yeates (Philadelphia), 17 September 1742; Edward Polgreen (Barbados) to Yeates (Philadelphia), 24 September 1742; IGI, marriage of Sir Thomas Robinson to Sarah Salmon, 14 March 1743 (Robinson arrived on the island 8 October 1742). Sarah was the daughter of merchant Thomas Shaw and had married another prosperous merchant, Samuel Salmon, information provided by Ernest Wiltshire. Interestingly, Thomas Baxter married Sarah Salmon, 7 December 1728, IGI. In view of Blenman's patronage, she could be a relative of the 'Mr Salmon' who published *Acts of Assembly, Passed in the Island of Barbadoes, Part I from 1648 to 1718, Part II from 1717(18) to 1738* (2 vols., London, 1732, 1739). Robinson himself later fell victim to the island's factional politics, BL, Add. MS 33,029, ff. 12, 32; Add... MS 32,708, f. 135. Lascelles & Maxwell found employment in their house for Robinson's kinsman 'Mr Salmon', but sent him back to Barbados after he contracted 'a slight species of the French disease', *LMLB*, Lascelles & Maxwell to Thomas Stevenson, 2 March 1744. This individual could be Thomas Shawe Salmon, listed among the subscribers to Richard Hall, *Acts Passed in the Island of Barbados from 1643 to 1762* (London, 1764).

[123] Martin Bladen (1680–1746) acquired West India property by marriage; the Bladens also had real estate interests in Maryland, North Carolina, and Nova Scotia. A connection between Martin Bladen and Henry Lascelles can be traced from 1721 when Lascelles

Succession and Collapse

In August 1764, the firm of Lascelles, Clarke & Daling received news 'of the Extream Illness of Col°. Clarke (a Shock that cannot be Equall to anything but that of the General Concern we are under)'. Gedney Jr had joined the firm just the year before, and he and his wife were looking forward to establishing themselves among London's social set. Due to 'the severity of his Feaver and other disorders', however, Clarke Sr was unable to conduct business, his son was informed. In truth, matters were far worse than described. Not only was Gedney Clarke Sr dying, his business affairs were in turmoil. 'Thus am I placed in his shoes', wrote his son shortly afterwards.[124]

Between 1744 and 1753, Henry Lascelles had lent Gedney Clarke Sr a total of £12,286.[125] After Henry's death, his sons continued to offer financial assistance. By 1766, the next date for which a statement of indebtedness exists, Clarke's estate owed the Lascelles £46,336.[126] Roughly one-quarter of the debt related to slave trading during the 1750s, but Clarke Sr's involvement in the victualling trade during the later stages of the Seven Years' War had also generated sizable expenses. In early April 1762, Lascelles & Daling foresaw that Clarke would need significant cash to fulfil the government contracts he had been awarded, and, true to their prediction, between October 1762 and January 1763

appeared before the Board of Trade in connection with corruption charges mounted against Robert Lowther, the former Governor of Barbados. Lascelles had been an ally of Lowther and was also close to Edward Sutton, Speaker of the island's Assembly and part of the faction allied against Council President Samuel Cox. Sutton, like Bladen and Lascelles, hailed from Yorkshire and was a close correspondent of Bladen. Relations between Bladen and Lascelles continued up until Bladen's death (the two worked together in a successful attempt to quash an attempt by the Pelham ministry to raise additional sugar duties in 1744). Bladen was very close to Robert Walpole and he must be regarded as an important contact. As with other Yorkshire-born associates, Bladen had significant cultural interests: he was an author, dramatist, and translator of classical texts, Hamilton, 'Naval Contracting'; John Ellis Findling, 'Robert Lowther, Governor of Barbados, 1710–1720', unpub. MA thesis (University of Texas, 1965), 92–104; Sedgwick, *House of Commons*, vol. I, 465–6.

124 HH:WIP, Letter of Richard Husbands to Lascelles, Clarke, & Daling, 21 August 1764; BL, Egerton MS 1,720, f. 72, Gedney Clarke Jr to Bentinck, 17 September 1765. Gedney Clarke Sr's death was agonising (he suffered 'a violent Fever & Inflamation of ye Bowells', with three separate relapses). Clarke Jr initially attempted to install a compliant candidate in the post of Collector, but soon realised that he had no alternative but to assume the office himself, Stowe Collection, STG Box 12, No. 24, Gedney Clarke II to Sir George Brydges Rodney, 12 October 1764. Clarke Jr's house, warehouses, and wharf in London brought £8,450 when sold in 1765 (see Table 5.2).

125 See Chapter Six.

126 *LMLB*, Pares Transcripts, H679, f. 155, Lascelles & Daling to Gedney Clarke II, 5 June 1766.

alone, he drew on the house to the amount of £15,883.[127] Clarke Sr appears to have suffered losses on his contracts, however; losses compounded by speculation in navy and victualling bills. In 1763, the London money market took a sharp downturn, and those speculators who had expected the funds to rise were badly burned. Lascelles & Maxwell hinted darkly that Clarke Sr numbered among the financial casualties.[128]

The business empire Gedney Clarke Jr inherited from his father weakened, buckled, and finally collapsed in 1774, crushed by the credit crisis of 1772–3, a financial catastrophe that had been mounting since the conclusion of the Seven Years' War. During the 1740s, trade had steadily expanded as credit was extended to producers of staple commodities and consumers of manufactures. Speculations had outpaced reality, however, and in June 1772 the Scottish Ayr Bank and its London correspondent, the Fordyce Bank, both failed. The bankruptcies triggered a series of business collapses, and as creditor confidence evaporated, leading traders scrambled to liquefy their assets. Credit to the colonies was abruptly scaled back, and merchants unable to cover their liabilities were ruined.[129] The credit squeeze was particularly hard felt in the Dutch trade, which had been buoyed by expectations of high sugar and coffee prices. Between 1750 and 1770, long-term bonds termed *plantageleningen*, secured by plantation mortgages, had been issued, raising approximately 80 million guilders on the Amsterdam market for investment in Demerara and Essequibo. As capital poured into the region, valuations placed on real estate and slaves climbed, prompting

---

[127] Ibid. H672, f. 143, Lascelles & Maxwell to Gedney Clarke I, 6 March 1761; H675, f. 362, Lascelles & Daling to Gedney Clarke I, c. 18 July 1763; H671, f. 237; H673, f. 272; H674, f.298; H675, f. 362. At his death, Clarke Sr remained liable for Carter's slaving debt of £11,000. Clarke was involved in victualling before he received a formal contract. Admiral Rodney reported that Clarke had hired and outfitted several vessels to provision a combined naval and army operation against the French which Rodney and General Monckton launched from Barbados, NMM, ADM/D/34, Admiralty Board in-letters from Victualling Commissioners, Admiral George Rodney to the Victualling Commissioners, 24 September 1762.

[128] R. B. Sheridan, 'The British Credit Crisis of 1772 and the American Colonies', *Journal of Economic History*, 20 (1960), 162; *LMLB*, Pares Transcripts, H675, f. 362, Lascelles & Maxwell to Gedney Clarke I, 18 July 1763; T. S. Ashton, *Economic Fluctuations in England, 1700–1800* (Oxford, 1959), 124–7.

[129] Henry Hamilton, 'The Failure of the Ayr Bank, 1772', *Economic History Review*, 8 (1956), 405–17; Sheridan, 'Credit Crisis', 170–2; Jacob M. Price, *Capital and Credit in British Overseas Trade: The View from the Chesapeake, 1700–1776* (Cambridge, MA, 1980), 128–36. Bankruptcies increased from an average of 310 between 1763 and 1771 to 520 per annum between 1772 and 1773. Among mercantile firms, the failure rate rose even more sharply, Julian Hoppit, *Risk and Failure in English Business, 1700–1800* (Cambridge, 1987), 97–9.

investors to lend even larger sums since, on paper at least, debts were covered by mortgages.[130]

The profitability of working the exposed and difficult terrain of Demerara and Essequibo depended upon two factors: the stability of sugar and coffee prices in European markets and constancy in the cost of borrowing. Over time, external forces disrupted that fragile balance. The Berbice slave uprising of 1763, a devastating drought in 1769, and a drop in coffee prices in 1770 shook investors' confidence that the Dutch planters would be able to repay their loans. The 1772 credit crisis in Scotland and England, and the revolt of the Morranen 'Bosnegers' (bush slaves) in 1773, completed the devastation. As credit contracted and prices fell, the properties of marginal planters were repossessed. In consequence, the value of real estate in the colonies declined, and investor capital secured by colonial property was lost.[131]

Even though they repeatedly complained that the Dutch West India Company was mismanaging colonial trade, the Clarkes had remained committed to Demerara. In a display of confidence, Gedney Clarke Sr restocked three of his plantations with eighty female slaves in 1764, the year he died, and he had planned to import an equivalent number of males. Three years later, however, in August 1767, Gedney Jr arranged to sell all of the family's Demerara plantations, and he called in his outstanding debts.[132]

Clarke's decision to pull out was motivated primarily by the colony's factional politics, not his financial perspicacity. 'No doubt you have heard that Demereara is rent by division,' wrote Sir James Douglas' plantation manager William Brisbane, in April 1766, 'at the head of the first is Mr Clarke the other is headed by Mr [Lachlan] McClane', who, along with other settlers, resented his influence within the colony.[133] In 1764 the Clarkes had claimed £8,000 from the Dutch West India Company

---

[130] Jan de Vries and Ad van der Woude, *The First Modern Economy: Success, Failure, and Perseverance of the Dutch Economy, 1500–1815* (Cambridge, 1997), 472–3. Both the volume and value of Dutch colonial exports from this region doubled during the two decades after 1750. Peak output was attained during the decade 1764–74, when about 60,000 slaves worked 465 Surinam plantations, while in Essequibo, Demerara, and Berbice a further 22,000 slaves worked c. 240 plantations, Johannes Postma, 'The Fruits of Slave Labour: Tropical Commodities from Surinam to Holland, 1683–1794', in Maxine Berg ed., *Oceanic Trade, Colonial Wares, and Industrial Development 1600–1800*, Eleventh International Economic History Congress (mimeo.; Milan, 1994).

[131] de Vries and van der Woude, *First Modern Economy*, 473–4. Only about one-quarter of the loan capital extended to planters was recovered after the crisis of the early 1770s, Gert Oostindie, 'The Economics of Surinam Slavery', *Economic and Social History in the Netherlands*, 5 (1993), 8.

[132] BL, Egerton MS 1,720, f. 65; Harris and de Villiers eds., *Gravesande*, vol. II, 555, 582–3.

[133] NMM, Papers of Admiral Sir James Douglas, DOU/6 Letterbook, 1762–7, 14 April 1766, William Brisbane to [Sir James Douglas?].

to defray the cost of the expedition they had launched to suppress the slave revolt. Two years later, the directors responded by authorising a poll tax to meet half the claim, but many settlers refused to pay the new imposition. Opposition leader McClane was, Brisbane reported, 'full of himself & proud as he stiles himself of being his own master [and] houlds the other planters & managers in Deression'. Given this state of affairs, Gedney Clarke Sr's use of military force in 1763 takes on a new meaning. While the principal aim of his intervention was to suppress a slave uprising, the speed with which this wealthy and well-connected Barbadian mobilised an armed expeditionary force must also have conveyed a message to white colonists.[134]

Despite his timely exodus from Demerara and Essequibo, Gedney Clarke Jr simply exchanged one imminent disaster for another. With the proceeds from the sale of his Dutch property, he purchased four new plantations, plus a share in a fifth property, on the Ceded Islands of Grenada and Tobago (see Table 5.2).[135] The plunging commodity prices and contraction of credit that would hit the planters of Demerara and Essequibo would batter the Ceded Islands just as forcefully. As in the Dutch colonies, many estates in Grenada and Tobago had been purchased at inflated values using mortgages that could be financed only for as long as staple prices remained high and interest charges stayed low.[136] Adopting his father's strategy, Clarke Jr continued to invest heavily in developing regions where he was able to draw upon the political and military influence of his associates, whereas the more prudent course would have been to retrench and reduce his indebtedness.[137]

[134] Rodway, *History of British Guiana*, vol. II, 219; Harris and de Villiers eds., *Gravesande*, vol. I, 43; vol. II, 483; BL, Egerton MS 1,720, f. 53b. In Berbice itself, army deserters were among the instigators of the slave revolt.

[135] Exactly when Clarke Jr acquired plantations in Grenada and Tobago cannot be determined. The present proprietors of Clarke's Court, now a rum distillery, report that papers in the Grenada National Museum apparently indicate that Clarke took possession of the plantation at the end of the Seven Years' War, but it has not been possible to obtain copies of the relevant documents to substantiate that claim. Pedro Welch gives an approximate date of 1765 for Clarke's ownership of property in Tobago, but this too is unconfirmed, Pedro Welch, 'The Lascelles and their Contemporaries: Fraud in Little England, 1700–1820', *JBMHS*, 48 (2002), 99. Therefore, the contention that Clarke Jr liquidated his assets in Demerara and Essequibo in order to obtain plantations in Grenada and Tobago remains hypothetical.

[136] Hamilton College, Beinecke Collection, M237, 'Private Information of the Present State of the Island of Grenada' [n.d., c. 1770–9], submitted to the Commissioners of Trade and Plantations. See also Sheridan, 'Credit Crisis', 172–3; Smith, 'Sugar's Poor Relation', 76–84.

[137] HH:WIP, 'Copy of a Case from London respecting Mr Clarke's affairs' (n.d., c. 29 September 1774).

Assuming that sugar prices in Europe would remain high and that the system of transatlantic contacts that had functioned so well in the past would continue to produce dividends, Clarke Jr banked on the future earnings of his sugar estates to satisfy his creditors.[138] In the first year after claiming his new properties, however, earnings were disappointing. The Tobago plantations generated very little income in the 1768 season, while Belle plantation on Barbados produced only 106 casks of sugar and Clarke's Court on Grenada only another 120 casks. Income from the total yield barely covered Clarke Jr's current account with Lascelles & Daling, and so interest on his debts began to mount. Moreover, any surpluses that might accrue were earmarked for purchasing slaves and repairing the works on the Tobago estates.[139] To fund the cultivation of his new properties and to generate cash, Clarke resorted to embezzling customs revenue. His activities did not go unnoticed, and in 1771 a commission of inquiry was despatched to Barbados. The investigating officers discovered that Clarke Jr owed more than £15,400 (plus large balances in kind), but he lacked the effects to cover his obligations. Clarke and his subordinates were duly suspended from their posts.[140]

Despite the revelations of his fraudulent acts, Gedney Clarke Jr's supporters did not abandon him. On the contrary, in a few months, through the patronage of the Earl of Liverpool and the good offices of his wider circle of political friends, Clarke was restored to his position as Collector, just as his father and the Lascelles had survived similar crises.[141] He also managed to weather the immediate effects of the 1772 financial panic, but as the price of sugar and the value of plantations collapsed, so did the prospect that Clarke would ever be able to repay his and his father's debts. Since the plantations could be sold only at great loss, the Lascelles foreclosed on their loans and took possession of Gedney's properties.

In the aftermath of Gedney Clarke Jr's financial failure, the Lascelles, of all his creditors, were treated preferentially on both Barbados and

---

[138] Clarke was not alone in his optimism. See e.g. John Fowler, *A Summary Account of the Present Flourishing State of the Respectable Colony of Tobago* (London, 1774), which also lists Clarke Jr among the colony's planters (p. 43).

[139] *LMLB*, Pares Transcripts, H687, f. 23, Lascelles & Daling to Gedney Clarke Jr, 10 November 1768, IX f. 347, Lascelles & Daling to Gedney Clarke, 30 July 1768; BL, Add. MS 38,203, ff. 84–6, Gedney Clarke to Charles Jenkinson, 12 November 1768.

[140] 'Autobiographical Manuscript of William Senhouse', 126. Clarke had also raised cash by raising loans in Barbados and Tobago which were secured on property already fully mortgaged to the Lascelles, as Table 5.1 reveals.

[141] Clarke had been a correspondent of the Earl of Liverpool since at least 1764, BL, Add. MS 38,203, f. 324; 38,206, ff. 84–6.

Tobago.[142] Gedney's cousin John Clarke attributed the Lascelles' success in securing their debts to 'their very great influence in point of Fortune, for I conceive their accounts to be totally erroneous – made up of a Jumble of Family Debt, & Compound Interest and blended with Gedneys debt, to make my uncles the larger'.[143] Though John Clarke was not an unbiased observer (the Salem Clarkes had hoped to receive legacies when Clarke Sr died), the data in Tables 5.1 and 5.3 confirm his suspicions. Upon Clarke Sr's death, his plantations' assets exceeded his indebtedness, but Table 5.1 records that by 1774 his estate owed £81,799 to the Lascelles, while Clarke Jr owed an additional £48,685. The increase in the debt burden on Clarke Sr's estate – from £43,336 in 1766 to almost double that amount eight years later – cannot be accounted for solely by adding charges of simple interest. From the original documents, it is clear that the Lascelles grouped debts owed to Edwin and Daniel Lascelles as individuals with those owed to the partnership of Lascelles & Daling.[144] The more significant cause of the ballooning deficit, however, relates to the Lascelles' lending practices. For cases in which a debt was secured by a first mortgage, the lender could persuade the debtor to add his interest arrears to the principal.[145] The dates of the securities recorded in Table 5.1 indicate Gedney Clarke Jr was so persuaded, a decision that amplified his indebtedness and hastened the day when the Lascelles assumed ownership of his major assets.

Clarke Jr and his wife, Frances, did not have to bear reduced circumstances for long: in 1777, both died within a month of each other on Barbados from unknown causes. Despite the severity of his fall, Gedney Clarke Jr was buried with due solemnity, the minute guns of the garrison savannah pounding across Carlisle Bay at sunset.[146] Mary Clarke,

---

[142] For examples of complaints of creditors on Tobago over preferential treatment of the Lascelles by the liquidators of Clarke's property, see HH:WIP, Letter of John Prettyjohn to Lord Harewood, 18 July 1799; Legal opinion on whether John Prettyjohn be entitled to receive two judgements entered against Gedney Clarke [II] in Barbados, n.d. (c. 1799); Memorial of Thomas Willison presented to Lord Harewood, 19 June 1802.

[143] PEM, Clarke Family Papers, Box 1, Folder 1, John Clarke to Francis (Frank) Clarke, 30 June 1783.

[144] At a simple interest rate of 6 per cent, a debt of £43,336 in 1766 would have grown to £64,137 eight year later or, if interest were compounded, to £69,071.

[145] See Chapter Six.

[146] Foster, *Pedigrees*, vol. II [n.p.]; Board of Trade, *Journal of the Commissioners*, vol. LXXXV, 159, 188; James C. Brandow ed., 'Diary of Joseph Senhouse', *JBMHS*, 37 (1986), 402. Clarke Jr remained a member of the Barbados Council after his financial collapse, Board of Trade, *Journal of the Commissioners*, 188.

the widow of Gedney Clarke Sr, continued to live at the Belle on the proceeds of an annuity which her husband had wisely granted her in lieu of her dowry rights.[147] The Lascelles helped educate the orphaned Gedney Clarke III, found him employment as an attorney when he came of age, and permitted him to use Pot House – a small, 72-acre plantation in St Philips's Parish, Barbados – for a nominal rent payable to his near-destitute aunt Deborah Thornhill.[148] In fact, however, the Lascelles were less benevolent than such acts might suggest. Clarke Sr had not divulged his provision for his wife to his creditors, and when it came to light, the Lascelles briefly sought to overturn it before finally acquiescing. In 1799, when Clarke III attempted to purchase Pot House on credit but was rejected, he migrated to England with his wife and son against the wishes of Lord Harewood, who then refused to see him.[149] Moreover, the Lascelles did not extend their creditor privileges to all members of their circle; Peter Clarke's executors and Admiral Holburne were among those who never recovered the debts owed them.[150] In essence, however, the networks the Lascelles and Clarkes had constructed remained intact as the Clarkes' empire showed signs of strain, failed, and was finally dismantled. The Lascelles simply took over operations and restructured the firm.

[147] The agreement also granted Mary Clarke the use of seventeen slaves and ownership of their offspring. Belle plantation accounts record that these slaves were rented to the Lascelles for £100 per annum from 1805 until the abolition of slavery in 1834, HH:WIP, 'Case for the opinion of the Solicitor General: on Mrs Clarke's Rights', 12 December 1777; WRA, Harewood Accounts: West Indies, 'Abstract of the Produce of the Estates & other Property in the West Indies belonging to the Rt Hon.[ble] Lord Harewood Belonging to the late Partnership of Lascelles and Maxwell' (1805–39); BA, RB6/17/195–201, Will of Gedney Clarke. Mary Clarke's annuity was worth £500 currency a year.

[148] HH:WIP, 'A list of papers belonging to Edward Lascelles esq. as executor of the Rt Honble Edwin Lord Harewood deced' [c. 1796], f. 11, agreement dated 2 October 1790; Correspondence, Nelson Elliot to Lord Harewood, 22 October 1795; Deborah Thornhill to Lord Harewood, 7 July 1795. The Lascelles considered the 'rent' they charged on Pot House to be interest on the £900 they had laid out repairing the plantation after damage caused by the 1780 hurricane, which killed Mary Clarke and obliterated her will. Lord Harewood transferred the payment, with an additional £5, to Clarke III's aunt Deborah Thornhill, who had been abandoned by her husband and was living with her children in a state of near destitution.

[149] HH:WIP, Correspondence, Harewood to Gedney Clarke III, 25 May 1799. Genealogical information supplied by Timothy Anderson (pers. com.) reveals that Clarke III had married Mary Stebbing in London in 1788. After his first wife's death, he married Olive Brown in 1803, also in London.

[150] NA:PRO, C12/928/28, *Holburne vs Lascelles* (1779); PEM, Clarke Family Papers, Box I, Folder 1, John Clarke to Francis (Frank) Clarke, 30 June 1783.

Personal Fortune and Empire Building

In 1732, after having participated in the sugar and slave trades for nearly two decades, Henry Lascelles returned to London. Specialising as a financier in the metropolis, he invested large sums in the West Indies during his last ten years of life.[151] In 1733, Gedney Clarke Sr relocated from Salem to Barbados. After engaging in commodity trading and slaving, he expended the greater portion of his capital in plantations. Drawing on the web of patronage that characterised colonial administration under the Duke of Newcastle, exploiting to the full its system of appointments and contracts, taking great risks and by trusting in their own judgements, both Lascelles and Clarke managed to accumulate large fortunes in transatlantic business long after the sugar revolution had swept over the West Indies.[152]

The network the Lascelles and the Clarkes created was designed to exploit the advantages exposed by colonial maladministration. Gedney Clarke Sr did not hesitate, for example, to bribe Governor Grenville to secure the post of Customs Collector, an office from which the Lascelles brothers had earlier diverted revenue to subsidise their victualling contracts and other concerns, and which the Clarkes likewise manipulated for personal gain.[153] Governor Grenville regarded Gedney Clarke Sr's attempt to bribe him, first with presents and later with the offer of 'a golden Acknowledgement for my services', as brazen and offensive, but Grenville could not ignore Clarke's connections in Barbados and London.[154]

The physical size of the island of Barbados, which is a mere 21 miles long and 14 miles wide, belies its importance in the colonial Atlantic trade of the period, even if one adds to the equation Barbadian-owned plantations in other colonies. Merchants like the Clarkes were capable of raising and investing immense sums of capital, only a portion of which are recorded in conventional customs accounts, and of constructing networks that, like the filaments of a spider's web, criss-crossed the Atlantic. To prosecute trade on a large scale, metropolitan connections were essential. The model of dependency suggested by

---

[151] See Chapter Six.
[152] Philip S. Haffenden, 'Colonial Appointments and Patronage under the Duke of Newcastle, 1724–1739', *English Historical Review*, 78 (1963), 417–35; Henretta, *'Salutary Neglect'*.
[153] Stowe Collection, STG Box 24, No. 1, f. 86; STG Box 12, No. 24, Gedney Clarke to Sir George Brydges Rodney. Henry and Edward Lascelles were assisted by the complicity of their subordinates.
[154] Ibid., STG Box 23, No. 16. It should be noted that William Moore, Clarke's rival for the Collectorship in 1750, likewise offered bribes in such an overt manner as to provoke Grenville's disdain.

commission trading fails to define an arrangement such as that the Clarkes formed with the Lascelles, however, for relations between the two families were based on cooperation and complementarity, with many initiatives emanating from Barbados rather than London.[155] Henry Lascelles' ability to supply finance and patronage was not limited to the metropolis, and the connections that the Clarkes were able to exploit in their own right were not confined to the West Indies, but stretched into North America, Britain, and Holland.

'Gentry capitalism' is a phrase that more aptly describes the Clarkes' and the Lascelles' commercial relationship. Depending on the good offices of scores of individuals, the heads of the two families strengthened their ties through political patronage, dynastic alliance, religious affiliation, and shared artistic and scientific activities. Such people-based networks helped reduce risk, a vital consideration in granting short-term credit or, as with the Clarkes, substantial loans secured by bond or mortgage. Moreover, because they transcended national boundaries, networks built upon personal association helped merchants circumvent the Navigation Acts, as the Clarkes' involvement in Demerara and Essequibo demonstrates. Along the Atlantic seaboard, in the backcountry, on the sugar islands, and in regions of South America, similarly ambitious and well-connected merchants speculated in settling and developing land in colonies both native and foreign. While the boom lasted, individuals like Gedney Clarke Sr drove the engines of the Atlantic trade. In the 1760s and 1770s, however, markets fell on hard times. Given these new circumstances, gentry capitalism, the same system that had sustained the Atlantic economy, was perfectly positioned to destabilise Britain's first colonial empire in the Americas.

As the Gedney Clarkes watched their fortune slip away, the Lascelles deployed theirs to buy a status that transcended wealth. Henry Lascelles used his newfound riches to raise his Yorkshire family from respectable gentry to aristocratic eminence. His expanding influence enabled him to draw other Yorkshire families into his colonial projects, particularly those who had established cadet branches in the Americas, and such associations in turn helped him and his sons acquire landed estates that bestowed ancestral connections.

---

[155] See also David Hancock, *Citizens of the World: London Merchants and the Integration of the British Atlantic Community, 1735–1785* (New York, 1995), 48–59; and his '"A Revolution in the Trade": Wine Distribution and the Development of the Infrastructure of the Atlantic Market Economy' in in John J. McCusker and Kenneth Morgan eds., *The Early Modern Atlantic Economy* (Cambridge, 2000), 105–53. Hancock prefers the metaphor of 'spider's web' in preference to 'hub and spoke'.

6   Merchants and Planters

> The prosperity of the English sugar colonies has been, in a great
> measure, owing to the great riches of England, of which a part has
> overflowed, if one may say so, upon those colonies.[1]

In *Wealth of Nations*, Adam Smith marvelled at the speed with which the
English-speaking colonies in the Americas had developed since their first
settlement. Yet, he insisted, 'The progress of our North American and
West Indian colonies would have been much less rapid, had no capital
but what belonged to themselves been employed in exporting their
surplus produce.'[2] In Smith's eyes, the dependence of colonial expansion on capital exported from Britain was potentially dangerous. While
conceding that it might be advantageous for developing regions to
borrow from more advanced countries, he regarded it as unnatural for
colonies to be restricted, as they were under the navigation system, to a
single metropolitan creditor. Such a relationship, Smith concluded, had
distorted Britain's trade and manufacturing and left her vulnerable to
colonial trade boycotts. 'In her present condition', he warned, 'Great
Britain resembles one of those unwholesome bodies in which some of
the vital parts are overgrown, and which, upon that account, are liable to
many dangerous disorders scarce incident to those in which all the parts
are properly proportioned.'[3]

More than forty years ago, the question of capital and colonisation
was addressed by Richard Pares in his posthumously published
Merchants and Planters. In this study, Pares outlined an interpretation of
relations between debtors and creditors in the Caribbean sugar trade
that remains the starting point for any discussion of the subject. Pares
was sceptical of Adam Smith's view that the prosperity of the plantations
depended upon the overspilling of Britain's riches. Indeed, he questioned whether any significant long-term capital movements, from the

[1] Adam Smith, *An Inquiry into the Nature and Causes of the Wealth of Nations*, ed. E.
Cannan (2 vols., Chicago, 1976; originally published 1776), vol. II, 101.
[2] Ibid., vol. I, 405.   [3] Ibid., vol. II, 119, 127–30.

metropolis to the colonies, occurred prior to the disturbances to trade occasioned by the War of the American Revolution (1776–83).[4] Pares believed that, once the pioneering stage of sugar cultivation was over, capital imports diminished in importance and mostly took the form of short-term, commercial credit. West India fortunes such as that of the Pinneys of Bristol and St Kitts, he argued, were built up by ploughing back a plantation's profits. Though he conceded that successful planters exploited to the full the possibilities for expansion offered by short-term overdrafts, Pares argued that there was only one possible answer to the question 'Where did the money come from?' 'The money came', he responded, 'in the last resort, from the planters themselves.' Even during the later stages of West Indian enslavement, Pares insisted that, 'The profits of the plantations were the source which fed the indebtedness charged upon the plantations.'[5]

Despite disagreeing with Adam Smith over the importance of capital imports, Pares' interpretation of the process by which planters raised credit was, in important respects, similar to that of the author of *Wealth of Nations*. Smith had contended that the colonists contracted debt, 'not by borrowing upon the bond of the rich people of the mother country, though they sometimes do this too, but by running as much in arrear to their correspondents who supply them with goods from Europe, as those correspondents will allow them'.[6] Pares was of much the same opinion: he relegated the significance of borrowing on mortgage and emphasised the importance of short-term credit extension by merchants to planters on their current accounts. Pares held that, prior to the 1760s, mortgages were an uncommon source of security for a loan in the West Indies.[7] He also believed that the prosperity of sugar during its 'silver age' – a period spanning the Peace of Paris (1763) until the outbreak of the American Revolution (1776) – meant that neither planters nor merchants needed to make extensive use of mortgages prior to the last quarter of the eighteenth century.[8] Mortgages, Pares conceded, thereafter 'became commoner and commoner until, by 1800, almost every large plantation debt was a mortgage debt'. Pares argued, however, that even at this

---

[4] Richard Pares, *Merchants and Planters*, *Economic History Review*, Supplement 4 (Cambridge, 1960), 47.

[5] Ibid., 50.

[6] Smith, *Wealth of Nations*, vol. II, 116, cited in R. B. Sheridan, 'The British Credit Crisis of 1772 and the American Colonies', *Journal of Economic History*, 20 (1960), 162.

[7] Eighteenth-century mortgages, unlike the modern loan device bearing the same name, were 'perpetual'. That is to say, they did not contain any built-in provision for redemption of the debt, but simply specified the property used to secure the loan and the interest to be paid by the debtor.

[8] Pares, *Merchants and Planters*, 46, 90.

stage, mortgages had only limited independent significance and were characteristically expedients designed to buy time. A planter, he suggested, satisfied a creditor first by confessing a book debt and entering into a penal bond. If the debt remained unpaid it was further secured by a judgement, and, in due course, by a mortgage. 'Nearly every great debt', Pares conjectured, 'started as a debt on account-current and ended as a mortgage.'[9] Price has coined the useful phrase 'ontogeny of debt' to summarise what Pares described as the steady progression from bond, to judgement, and finally to mortgage, and this terminology will be employed in the remainder of the chapter.[10]

The business papers of the London firm of Lascelles & Maxwell were the most important source cited by Pares to support his interpretation. He contrasted the avoidance of mortgages by the partners during the period 1740 to 1769 with the reliance on mortgage loans by the Bristol commission house of the Pinneys between 1783 and 1850. In the case of the Lascelles, Pares argued that until the later 1760s, 'There was little talk of mortgages: it was generally believed that a planter's credit was blasted by a mortgage.'[11] Significance was attached to the fact that, prior to 1763, requests for mortgages were made infrequently to Lascelles & Maxwell. When the subject was raised at all in the correspondence of the firm, he was struck by 'the slight air of surprise, even squeamishness' on the part of the partners. Lascelles & Maxwell's reticence and sensitivity towards mortgages was taken as evidence that this form of security was rarely used except as a last resort, and that, during the 1740s and 1750s, a planter obliged to take out a mortgage was considered to be but a short step away from bankruptcy.[12] Moreover, Pares also believed that, prior to the mid-eighteenth century, local loans were at least as common in the West India colonies as sterling loans. In support of this contention he cited the example of Peter Beckford, a rich Jamaican planter, who owned no fewer than twenty-seven plantations and who was worth £300,000 currency (gross) when he died in 1739. Beckford's assets included £135,000 of debts owed by his fellow-planters. The inventories of other Jamaican planters, Pares noted, told a similar story, while the papers of the Lascelles family recorded debts owed by Barbadians to other Barbadians.[13]

---

[9] Ibid., 46, 48.

[10] Jacob M. Price, 'Credit in the Slave Trade and Plantation Economies', in B. L. Solow ed., *Slavery and the Rise of the Atlantic System* (Cambridge, 1991), 327.

[11] Richard Pares, 'A London West-India Merchant House, 1740–1769', in Richard Pares and A. J. P. Taylor eds., *Essays Presented to Sir Lewis Namier* (London, 1956), 99.

[12] Ibid., 101, and *Pares, Merchants and Planters*, 90.

[13] Pares, *Merchants and Planters*, 25, 47. For a qualified endorsement of Pares' thesis, see Price, 'Credit Plantation Economies', 324–8; R. B. Sheridan, *Sugar and Slavery: An*

In the absence of firm, quantitative evidence, it is not possible to reach an unequivocal verdict on the importance of either capital flows to the Caribbean or the nature of debtor–creditor relations. None the less, this chapter argues that the evidence that does exist provides more support for Adam Smith's interpretation of the role of capital imports in the expansion of the sugar colonies during the eighteenth century than for Pares' characterisation of relations between merchants and planters. It is contended, however, that the prominence that both Pares and Smith gave to current account deficits, at the expense of mortgage finance, was misguided. Contrary to the views of Pares and Adam Smith, it is argued that mortgages were being commonly demanded by planters in the 1740s, if not earlier, and that this type of credit instrument was no longer regarded in pejorative terms by the merchants and planters whom Pares studied. The ontogeny of debt thesis is also subject to challenge, particularly the argument that mortgages were characteristically taken out as a final expedient, and that large planter debts typically originated as account current deficits.

The nature of mortgage finance may at first sight appear an arcane subject of debate, but it is nothing of the kind. After 1750, the development of Jamaica accelerated dramatically and the growth of the sugar trade was boosted further by Britain's acquisition of the Ceded Islands of Dominica, Grenada, and St Vincent at the conclusion of the Seven Years' War (1756–63). These events had major economic, political, and social repercussions, not least for the enslaved Africans shipped across the Atlantic to work on the burgeoning sugar plantations. Pares' observation that 'there can be no colonization without capital' is beyond dispute.[14] The question is, was a fundamental change in the financial relationship between merchants and planters required to fund this expansion?

This chapter's principal source is a database of West Indian loans granted by Henry Lascelles between 1723 and his death in 1753, both on his own account and in partnership with George Maxwell and his son Daniel Lascelles.[15] The data consist of seventy-eight loans with a total value of £226,772 (sterling). Long-term lending is compared with short-term credit extension to planters on account current. In addition to investigating the ontogeny of debt hypothesis and the popularity of mortgages, the data will also be used to investigate other influences on overseas lending to the colonies. Chief among these is the interest rate

---

Economic History of the British West Indies (London, 1974), 295–8. In 1739, £1.4 Jamaican currency equalled £1.0 sterling, John J. McCusker, *Money and Exchange in Europe and America, 1600–1775: A Handbook* (Chapel Hill, 1978), 253.
[14] Pares, *Merchants and Planters*, 1.   [15] See the Appendix, Table 6.9 for details.

'gap' model deployed by both Pares and Sheridan, among others, to analyse the effect of warfare on credit extension.

A general thesis of West Indian finance cannot be constructed on a single example. Nevertheless, the finances of the Lascelles are worthy of serious consideration for two reasons. Firstly, the business records of this family were used by Pares as a core source for the thesis expounded in *Merchants and Planters*. Secondly, at the present time, there are no comparable studies of the loan portfolios of other London West India merchants. It is to be hoped that the results of this study will encourage historians to undertake similar projects, thereby rectifying a chronic shortage of evidence in a subject area of great importance.

The data detailing the West India loans of Henry Lascelles (presented in full in the Appendix, Table 6.9) are based on five sources. Firstly, Barbadian loans still outstanding at the time of Lascelles' death in 1753 were recorded in an account book that was begun by Henry and probably completed by his sons and executors, Edwin and Daniel Lascelles.[16] These debts were either owed to Henry's estate or assigned to Daniel. Secondly, a single volume of correspondence of the firm of Lascelles & Maxwell survives covering the period September 1743 until February 1746. This volume provides information about loans owed to both Henry Lascelles in his own right and to the partnership of Lascelles & Maxwell.[17] Thirdly, Pares' transcripts of documents that were destroyed during the Blitz provide further information. These notes and extracts were taken from ten volumes of the correspondence of Lascelles & Maxwell, spanning the years from 1739 until 1769 (of which the first six volumes are relevant to this study), plus one volume of Henry Lascelles' letters written between November 1731 and September 1753. Pares' transcripts, therefore, also provide information about loans made personally by Henry Lascelles and in partnership with George Maxwell. Fourthly, records of loans due to the estate of Henry Lascelles are included in the West India papers preserved at Harewood House, Yorkshire. Fifthly, additional information about lending is contained within the deeds series at the Barbados Archives (BA) and in the Hughes-Queree abstracts of Barbados deeds kept in the same

---

[16] Several entries in the account book are written in the first person suggesting that part of the document was compiled by Henry Lascelles just prior to his death.

[17] These two items survived the bombing raid of December 1940, which destroyed the London offices of Wilkinson and Gaviller, described by Pares in 'West-India Merchant House', 75. Judging from this article and the Pares' transcripts of the archive of Wilkinson and Gaviller at Rhodes House Library, Oxford, Pares did not view the account book when he worked on the records of Lascelles & Maxwell before the Second World War.

Table 6.1. *Chronological distribution of Henry Lascelles' lending (£ sterling)*

Years	All loans		Exclusive of mortgages		Inclusive of mortgages		Unspecified security or unsecured	
	No.	Value (£)	No.	Value (£)	No.	Value (£)	No.	Value (£)
1723–9	1	424	1	424	0	0	0	0
1730–4	13	28,523	11	23,746	2	4,777	0	0
1735–9	5	12,747	4	8,537	1	4,210	0	0
1740–4	14	26,987	5	4,280	2	6,873	7	15,834
1745–9	19	45,467	10	24,217	6	12,250	3	9,000
1750–3	26	112,624	10	34,369	12	48,761	4	29,494
Peace and war								
1723–38 (P)	18	37,484	16	32,707	2	4,777	0	0
1739–48 (W)	29	64,490	13	22,123	6	17,533	10	24,834
1749–53 (P)	31	124,798	12	40,743	15	54,561	4	29,494
Total	*78*	*226,772*	*41*	*95,573*	*23*	*76,871*	*14*	*54,328*

Sources: Appendix, Table 6.9.

repository.[18] The complementary nature of the five sources means that, at the very least, a large sample of the loans of Henry Lascelles exists for the period from about 1730 until 1753, and it is possible that the record is nearly complete.

In Table 6.1, a chronological account of lending is presented. Some important features of these data must be emphasised at the outset. Firstly, the data record, for the most part, the dates at which security for a loan was obtained by Henry Lascelles rather than the timing of the loan itself. Secondly, the table describes gross lending and does not, therefore, include details of loan terminations as a result of repayment, foreclosure, or the assignment of debts to other creditors.[19] Thanks to the Pares transcripts and the surviving volumes of letters and accounts, however, most of the loans appearing in Table 6.1 after 1739 can be dated. In instances where Henry Lascelles was approached directly by debtors for assistance, the date of the loan normally coincided closely

---

[18] For additional details of the sources see the Appendix, Table 6.9.

[19] Since the account book and the Harewood Papers are almost exclusively concerned with debts still current in 1753 or later, the debts most likely to have been repaid are those for which the Lascelles and Maxwell Letter Book (including the Pares transcripts) and/or the Barbados deeds are the only sources. Of the debts listed in the Appendix, £107,514 fall into this category, yet of the total only £32,772 were contracted before 1750 (including cases where the debtor is known to have offered security for later debts). This suggests that only c. 14.5 per cent of debts were retired or recycled.

with the date security was taken. The principal exceptions are the six loans Lascelles granted without security between 1740 and 1751, amounting to £15,270. In cases where Lascelles was assigned the loan by other creditors, the date of the original debt is generally not known, yet this omission is not an impediment to ascertaining the chronology of Lascelles' own lending, since the important date is that of the assignment, rather than the security or even of the debt itself, and this is the date recorded in the Appendix. The entries in Table 6.1 that must be viewed most critically are those for the earliest years. During the period 1723 until 1729, only the Barbados deeds series provides evidence of lending, and, in consequence, it is likely that not all loans are recorded. Moreover, the surge in lending between 1730 and 1734 probably reflects in part the decision by Henry Lascelles to obtain security for earlier debts, prior to his permanent departure from Barbados for London in 1732.[20]

If the interpretation of loans recorded for the years from 1730 to 1734 is correct, the data suggest that Henry Lascelles increased his gross lending to the West Indies during the two decades after his return to Britain. Growth in advances, however, was discontinuous. The amount and number of fresh loans increased sharply during the Wars of Jenkins' Ear and Austrian Succession (1739–48), particularly in the later stages of the conflict. With the return of peace, lending surged to an unprecedented level, and the average size of loans also rose from between £2,000 and £2,500, to around £4,300. The loans database also strongly suggests that, as lending increased, so too did the prominence of mortgages. Whereas mortgages were uncommon during the period 1723 to 1738, during the wars and afterwards this form of security first rivalled and then exceeded the alternatives.

The conclusion that mortgages grew in importance must be qualified to an extent because of the existence of loans for which security is unspecified or not known, though closer examination of these advances does not invalidate the hypothesis that mortgages were increasingly demanded of planters. The ten loans made between 1739 and 1748 (recorded in the lower half of Table 6.1), consist of five unsecured loans, worth £13,270, and five for which the security is not known, amounting to £11,564. Yet four of the unsecured loans, amounting to £13,000, were made to merchants rather than planters,[21] while of the unspecified loans, one of £2,564 was made to a merchant, and two loans of £2,000

---

[20] For details of Henry Lascelles' movements between Barbados and Britain, see Chapter Four.
[21] Gedney Clarke (two loans), George Maxwell, and William Harvie.

each were advanced to Lascelles' agents in Antigua and Barbados.[22] Moreover, three of the four loans falling into the unspecified category between 1749 and 1753 were all made in 1752 and amounted to £27,494. One of these loans, worth £10,124, was made to the Harvie brothers, who were merchants engaged in slaving, and their debt is known to have been secured later by a mortgage on Jamaican property.[23] Given the size of the other loans, it is likely that they too were secured by mortgage soon after Lascelles' death in 1753.

Mortgages were not, therefore, notable by their absence in Henry Lascelles' West Indian affairs. On the contrary, during the 1740s, if not before, the mortgage had become an integral part of his financial relations with debtors. Moreover, the Lascelles & Maxwell correspondence contains only one instance of a lending decision that could be regarded as evidence of 'squeamishness' about mortgages. In 1748, the firm agreed not to ask for a mortgage, in addition to a judgement, when lending £6,500 to John Braithwaite in case it damaged his credit.[24] Since Pares had sight of the original letter that is now destroyed, his interpretation of the document must be respected, but the response of Lascelles & Maxwell is surely indicative of the fact that by this date mortgages had become the norm when lending money to planters, such as Braithwaite, who wished to buy an estate or to obtain significant numbers of slaves.[25]

West Indian lending was not the only credit market in which Henry Lascelles was a participant. In addition to colonial loans, Lascelles also advanced money to individuals resident in England who provided domestic security. The available evidence of English loans is summarised in Table 6.2. Some caution should be attached to these data: the Account Book of 1753 is the sole source and, therefore, only loans still outstanding at the time of Lascelles' death are documented.[26] Lending

---

[22] Lessley, McCall, and Stevenson.   [23] See fn. 70.
[24] *LMLB*, Pares Transcripts, H599, Lascelles & Maxwell to John Braithwaite, 25 July 1747; H602, same to same, 9 June 1748.
[25] In the Braithwaite case, one factor in not insisting on a mortgage was that, 'you propose that the loans shall not make your debt to us exceed the value of what your Negroes, quick stock & utensils, separated from the lands, would amount to, or what your lands would be apprized at, detached from the Negroes, quick stock etc.', ibid., H613, Lascelles & Maxwell to John Braithwaite, 9 December 1752.
[26] Some of the loan details can be corroborated from other sources; e.g. the account book's record tallies exactly with Teesside Archives, Middlesborough, Pennyman Family of Ormesby Hall, U.PEN/1/188, Mortgage of Matthew Consett of Normaby to secure a loan of £3,050 from Henry Lascelles, 15 August 1746; U.PEN/1/191, Assignment of mortgage to William Maddeson of Stockton by Edwin Lascelles, Daniel Lascelles, and Joanna Consett (widow) of £2,800 (the sum remaining from the original mortgage). See also details of the Blackett loan below. The deficiencies with the account

Table 6.2. *Henry Lascelles' English loans by type of security*

Years	No.	Total value (£)	Inclusive of mortgages (£)	Exclusive of mortgages (£)	Security unknown and unsecured loans
1735–9	1	2,000	0	2,000	0
1740–4	4	79,089	78,500	589	0
1745–9	4	16,495	14,800	1,695	0
1750–3	13	76,351	43,000	33,100	251
Unspecified	6	9,212	2,643	0	6,569
Total	*28*	*183,147*	*138,943*	*37,384*	*6,820*

Source: Account Book of Henry Lascelles, 1753 (see Chapter Four, fn. 97).

to planters and lending at home differed in two important respects. Firstly, English loans were extended to fewer individuals, and one debtor, Sir Walter Blackett, accounted for no less than £113,000 of the total.[27] Secondly, English advances were made at lower rates of interest, at an average of 4.1 per cent, than in the case of West Indian loans, where an average of 6.98 per cent was charged. In the case of English loans, however, the proportion of debt secured by a mortgage was much greater. More than three-quarters of all English debt was backed by a mortgage, and this form of security was dominant throughout the years from 1737 until 1753. A comparison of Table 6.1 with Table 6.2 suggests, therefore, that, in terms of the security demanded, the market for loans in the West Indies had come to resemble more closely that of England.

book lie in loans cancelled before 1753, rather than the accuracy of the entries recorded at the end of Henry's life.

[27] The Blackett family's fortune was generated by developing the Newcastle coal trade. Sir Walter Blackett's loans were secured on his estates in Northumberland and Yorkshire. A kinship link existed between Blackett and Henry Lascelles: Blackett's wife, Elizabeth Ord[e], was the sister-in-law of Lascelles, J. Straker, *Memoirs of the Public Life of Sir Walter Blackett* (Newcastle, 1819), 26; Joseph Foster, *Pedigrees of the County Families of England: Yorkshire, West Riding* (3 vols., London, 1874), vol. II 'Lascelles'; Account Book of Henry Lascelles, 1753 (see Chapter Four, fn. 97). In addition, the Blacketts were connected with the Thornhill family who feature in both Henry Lascelles' Yorkshire land transactions and his Barbados loans, Yorkshire Archaeological Society, DD/12/I/6, Demise of Calverley Manor, 24 January 1750; DD/12/I/7, Deeds transferring Calverley from the Blackett to the Thornhill families, 24 January 1750, 12 February 1754, 26 December 1755, 2–3 July 1756; WRA, Stansfield Muniments, WYL500/741, Mortgage of Sir Walter Blackett and Launcelot Allgood to Henry Lascelles, secured on Calverley and Esholt, 24 June 1750; WYL500/742, Mortgage of £65,000 by the same to Edwin and Daniel Lascelles, executors of Henry Lascelles, of Calverley, Esholt, Yeadon, Guiseley, and Shipley lands, 12–13 February 1754. For more detail of the connection between the Blacketts and Lascelles' West Indian affairs, see Chapter Four.

If the ontogeny of debt thesis is correct, the fact that references to mortgages became more frequent need not mean that mortgages were of independent significance. But what evidence is there of ontogeny? The Appendix to this chapter records the details of twenty-one mortgages granted to eighteen creditors. The security for each is listed, but the interpretation of this information is problematic. For example, if ontogeny is defined as a clear progression from bond, to judgement, and finally to mortgage, five debts satisfy the criterion: the loans to Harper, Hothersall, Newton, Stevenson, and Walker. Yet if the additional criterion, that the debtor be insolvent and on the brink of bankruptcy, is included, then arguably only the debt of Burch Hothersall qualifies. This is because the loans to Robert Harper and Thomas Stevenson are intimately connected with that of Hothersall and arose out of the winding up of his estate, permitting these individuals to clear debts on property owned by Hothersall. The remaining two loans were not connected with insolvency.[28] William Walker borrowed money on the security of Four Hills and Rock plantations, probably to restock his estates with slaves. These two properties had been in the Walker family since at least 1674, and, since they were still held by the family in 1793, Walker can hardly have been a bankrupt.[29] Nicholas Newton's loan was similarly granted to stock his Jamaican sugar estate with slaves. Initially, Newton borrowed on the bond of two of the island's most respected planters. The upgrading of his debt to a mortgage did not coincide with a deterioration of his finances, but occurred after one of his two securities died in 1751.[30]

The remaining mortgages in the Appendix include three examples of creditors whose loans were secured by a mortgage alone. Yet of these debts, only that owed by Joseph Lynch is clearly *not* a case of ontogeny. Lynch purchased Pasfield's plantation in 1747 having formerly been a tenant of the property. Henry Lascelles not only granted Lynch a mortgage, but also involved himself in protracted negotiations with the owners of Pasfield's on behalf of Lynch to secure the sale.[31] The

---

[28] HH:WIP, papers relating to the debt of Burch Hothersall, 1697–1739; BA, Hughes–Queree Collection, Abstracts in Queree notebook; *LMLB*, George Maxwell to Thomas Findlay, 3 October 1743; Account Book of Henry Lascelles, 1753; *LMLB*, Pares Transcripts, H589, Henry Lascelles to Bruce Hothersall, 6 December 1740.

[29] BA, Hughes-Queree Collection, Abstracts in Queree notebook.

[30] *LMLB*, Pares Transcripts, H598, Lascelles & Maxwell to Nicholas Newton, 27 November 1745; H605, Lascelles & Maxwell to Nicholas Newton, 20 April 1751.

[31] *LMLB*, George Maxwell to Joseph Lynch, 17 January 1743 and 24 October 1744; BA, RB3/37/395–404. John Ashley was a former tenant of Pasfield's, but it is not known if his later hostility towards Henry was in any way aggravated by Lascelles' business links with the estate, BPL, MS U.1.21, Nos. 26–8, Indenture between Rebecca Dixon, Sarah Pollhill, John Ashley, and Mary Ashley, 20 April 1727; Inventory and Valuation of the

mortgage granted to Henry Slingsby is another loan which forms part of the liquidation of Hothersall's estate (Slingsby married Hothersall's daughter Ann and the loan cleared debts charged on two of Hothersall's former properties).[32] Joseph Ball's mortgage was granted to pay a £4,000 legacy charged on Chapman's estate which he had inherited from William Chapman. This plantation was later sold in 1762 for about £16,500 (currency) and the debt itself was settled in 1746, so there are grounds for viewing this as a sound loan backed by ample collateral. The Lascelles, however, had extensive dealings with the Ball family and it is unwise to view this debt in isolation, particularly given the fact that Henry Lascelles' half-brother Edward Lascelles obtained Guinea estate from Joseph Ball in 1736, followed by Canewood in 1747.[33]

Still more problematic are the eleven cases in the Appendix where a mortgage was coupled with another security within a short space of time to provide collateral. A loan secured by a mortgage was also typically secured by a bond. Even if it was not requested at the outset, a bond would probably be asked for if a planter restocked his plantation with slaves because the security provided by a mortgage was based on the land, buildings, slaves, and other movable goods detailed in the schedule. Moreover, though mortgages claimed the unborn offspring of the enslaved as well as the living, the dead gained final release. As the slaves died, the loan collateral diminished, so a penal bond was invariably also requested.[34] In consequence, where the stated security is a mortgage and bond, or a mortgage and a judgement, it is not possible to infer with certainty which form of security was entered into first.[35]

A direct examination of the securities fails to demonstrate strict progression to a mortgage, but in view of the difficulties in interpretation, it is prudent to assess the prevalence of ontogeny in other ways. Two pieces of evidence shed light on the issue. The first consists of the current account balances of Lascelles & Maxwell's correspondents, and the second is an analysis of arrears of interest owed by debtors. A comparison of the net balance on current account with the data of loan finance permits an assessment of the relative importance of short-term and long-term credit extended by Henry Lascelles. Table 6.3 presents

---

Negroes &c. on the Estate of Samuell Pasfield Esq. Deceased ... now in the Possession of John Ashley Esq., 20 April 1727.

[32] BA, Hughes-Queree Collection, Abstracts in Queree notebook; Account Book of Henry Lascelles, 1753; *LMLB*, George Maxwell to Thomas Findlay, 3 October 1743; *LMLB*, Pares Transcripts, H603, George Maxwell to Thomas Findlay, 9 July 1748.

[33] See Chapter Seven.

[34] *LMLB*, Pares Transcripts, H614, Lascelles & Maxwell to J. and A. Harvie (Jamaica), 3 March 1753.

[35] Ibid.

Table 6.3. *Short-term trade credit supplied by Lascelles & Maxwell on account current* (£ *sterling*)

	1744		1745		1748 (incomplete)		1751	
	No.	Value (£)	No.	Value (£)	No.	Value (£)	No.	Value (£)
Credit	24	9,953	39	22,338	18	8,535	25	14,123
Debit	34	14,023	28	9,981	8	5,105	13	4,106
Total and balance (credit or debit)	58	(DR) 4,070	67	(CR) 12,357	26	(CR) 3,430	38	(CR) 10,017

Sources: LMLB, Pares Transcripts, H601, H604; Sheridan, 'Sugar Trade, Appendix I, ii. For more details of the sources see the Appendix, Table 6.9.

the current account position of Lascelles & Maxwell for three complete years and one incomplete year. The data indicate that the net balance shifted from a deficit of £4,070 owed by the firm in 1744, to credits of £12,357 in 1745, and £10,017 in 1751. The ontogeny thesis argues that debt arose first on current account and was then secured successively by bond, judgement, and mortgage. Data in Table 6.1, however, suggest that gross lending rose from an average of £9,093 per year during the years 1745 to 1749, to £28,156 per annum between 1750 and 1753. This is clearly a much larger increase than the deterioration of the current account position of planters recorded in Table 6.3. Whereas the average account current debt owed to Lascelles & Maxwell lay in the region of £500, the typical loan granted between 1744 and 1751 was seven times this amount. It might be objected that Table 6.3 indicates net short-termcredit extension, whereas Table 6.1 records gross long-term lending. The sources, however, do not suggest that either foreclosure or assignment was common during the later period. Indeed, the number of loans recorded as outstanding at the death of Henry Lascelles indicates that gross lending was equivalent to net lending during the peak years of credit extension between 1750 and 1753.

A second test of ontogeny is the record of interest payments of debtors, which is known in twenty-three cases. The ontogeny thesis predicts that mortgages were used to buy debtors in financial difficulties extra time. One would expect, therefore, that the payment record of loans secured by a judgement was worse than debts secured only by bond, and that mortgage debts were worst of all. The sample sizes in Table 6.4 are small, but the findings are not consistent with ontogeny. Planters were generally in arrears on their interest accounts by more than one year, and, as might be expected, older debts were further in

Table 6.4. *Analysis of interest arrears on loans in 1753*

Classification	Sample size	Mean (days)	Standard deviation (days)
All cases	23 (22)	467.13 (427.27)	213.24 (104.87)
1732–43	12 (11)	531.08 (457.18)	255.02 (73.56)
1744–53	11	397.36	121.64
Bond only	5	421.20	81.85
Execution or judgement only	8	419.38	97.97
Exclusive of mortgage	15 (14)	489.13 (428.07)	245.62 (93.32)
Inclusive of mortgage	8	425.88	122.49

Source: Account Book of Henry Lascelles, 1753.
Notes: For the purposes of calculation it was assumed that the account book was compiled on 16 October 1753, the date of Henry Lascelles' burial. Figures in parentheses exclude one outlier case where arrears of 1,344 days were due on a loan granted in 1732.

arrears than more recent loans. The payment record of loans secured by mortgages, however, appears no worse than loans backed by other forms of security.

Ontogeny does not, therefore, provide a satisfactory explanation for the more frequent use of the mortgage by Henry Lascelles during the 1740s and early 1750s. The data suggest that not only did Lascelles greatly increase lending on security towards the end of his life, but that he also came to regard the mortgage as the most valuable credit instrument in his relations with debtors. Influences on the demand and supply of credit will now be examined in order to assess why the volume of lending and the use of mortgages both increased after 1740.

Planters sought credit for a variety of reasons, but their demand for loans can be grouped into two main categories. Productive loans arose from a need to purchase additional slaves, livestock, land, and mill equipment. High mortality rates among the enslaved, in particular, generated what Pares and others have seen as a persistent demand for credit.[36] Non-productive loans resulted from a need to finance consumption and to fund family inheritance under the system of primogeniture dominant in the English-speaking Caribbean, through the provision of legacies for younger children and marriage settlements. In the short term, a host of unexpected contingencies – particularly disease, crop failure, and warfare – might also influence demand for credit. Among these, warfare not only interrupted trade, but also could lead to the acquisition of new territories and a demand for capital to develop

[36] Pares, *Merchants and Planters*, 38–40.

them. Production and consumption were also strongly influenced by the price of sugar and the expected profitability of planting. High prices and optimism about the future generated demand for productive loans; low prices raised the burden of legacies charged on inherited estates and generated a need for bridging finance. It is likely that absenteeism and social stratification within the older settled colonies also increased demand for consumption loans.[37]

A feature of the literature on the supply of West Indian finance is the emphasis given to the operation of institutional constraints on the credit market. Particular significance has been attached to usury laws and legislation regulating the relationship between debtors and creditors. In Great Britain and its colonies legal ceilings constrained the rate of interest that could be charged. The legal maximum in Barbados declined from 15 per cent in 1661, to 10 per cent in 1688, to 8 per cent in 1729 (Jamaica followed suit in 1739), and to 6 per cent in 1752.[38] Both Pares and Sheridan emphasise the wedge between the rate of return on investing in the London money market and the colonial maximum interest rate in explaining the attractions of West Indian loans. Sheridan, for example, notes that London's insurance companies made short-term loans to West Indian merchants at rates of 3.5 to 4.0 per cent between 1736 and 1740, and between 1750 and 1755.[39] During wartime, however, the spread between British and colonial interest rates narrowed, at the same time as marine insurance rates rose and remittances became more difficult. It has been suggested, therefore, that lending to the colonies was encouraged by a peacetime interest rate gap, but that wars retarded the attractiveness of colonial loans. Pares and Sheridan both cite the correspondence of Lascelles & Maxwell as an illustration of the effects of the Wars of Jenkins' Ear and Austrian Succession on liquidity within the sugar trade.[40]

Henry Lascelles invested substantial sums in the stock market, in addition to lending money to individuals in England, at the same time as he extended loans to West Indian planters. A direct comparison is possible, therefore, between the rates of return earned from these activities. In addition, information is also available about Lascelles' investment in landed property in England. Tables 6.5, 6.6, and 6.7 present data of comparative rates of return and the value of fresh West

---

[37] Ibid., 42–4.

[38] Sheridan, *Sugar and Slavery*, 276–7; Pares, *Merchants and Planters*, 44.

[39] R. B. Sheridan, 'The Sugar Trade of the British West Indies, 1660–1756', unpub. Ph.D. thesis (University of London, 1951), 193.

[40] Ibid., 193–4; Richard Pares, 'The London Sugar Market, 1740–1769', *Economic History Review*, 9 (1956), 264–5.

Table 6.5. *Comparative rates of return earned by Henry Lascelles on loans and securities, 1732–53*

Type of investment	Weighted average annual rate of return (%)	Weighted average annual rate of return including capital gains/losses (%)
West Indian loans (1732–53)	6.98	not applicable
English loans (1737–53)	4.10	not applicable
Bank Stock (1735–53)	3.48	3.18
East India Stock (1735–53)	4.29	6.04
3% annuities (1737–53)	3.09	4.00
Navy 4% annuities (1749–53)	3.81	3.10

Notes: In the original published version of this chapter, an attempt was made to calculate the present value of flows of dividends and capital gains (or losses) earned from securities (S. D. Smith, 'Merchants and Planters Revisited', *Economic History Review*, 55 (2002), 446). The final version of the table expresses earnings as average annual percentage rates of return on investment (weighted by the size of the investment), simplifying analysis. It also incorporates additional information on the length of time stock was held.

The average annual rates of return for English and West Indian loans are the weighted average of interest rates on all loans granted during the specified time periods for which the interest rate is known. The weights used are based on the values of each loan. Calculating the average annual rate of return for Henry Lascelles' investments in securities is a more complicated task. The Bank of England and East India Company stock ledgers record the dates of purchase and sale of nominal stock. Market prices at the dates of purchase and sale are available in John Castaing's *The Course of Exchange* (for Bank Stock and East India Stock) and from *The Gentleman's Magazine* (for Navy annuities). Henry Lascelles was active in the market buying and selling securities during the years from 1735 until 1753 (between 1735 and 1743, Lascelles made a total of 143 trades in stock, an average of 7.94 trades per annum), but neither the Bank of England nor the East India stock ledgers enable the sale of a given amount of stock to be matched with its purchase. This information was only available for trades in annuities. It was assumed, therefore, that at each sale Lascelles acted rationally by disposing of the stock which either minimised his losses or maximised his gains. The criteria used for this purpose were the present value of dividends surrendered when the stock was sold (a discount rate of 4.5 per cent over a period of fifteen years was used to calculate this), and the capital gain (or loss) at the time of the sale.

Sources: (1) English loans: Account Book of Henry Lascelles, 1753.

(2) Stocks: ibid.; Bank of England, AC 27/131–3, 135, 137–40, 142, 145–6, 149–50, 153, 155, 159, 161–4, 431, 436, 439, 444, 448, 452–3, 456, 459–61, 463, 466–7, 5160–7; BL, East India Company, L/AG/14/5/7, 8, 9, 10, 11; John Castaing, *The Course of the Exchange* (London, 1735–53); *The Gentleman's Magazine* (1748–53); J. H. Clapham, *The Bank of England: A History* (Cambridge, 1945), vol. I, 292; K. N. Chaudhuri, *The Trading World of Asia and the English East India Company, 1660–1760* (Cambridge, 1978), 438, 451. Dividends for the East India Company are not available for the years 1746–50; the missing data were estimated from average rate of dividends paid 1735–45 and 1751–3. Prices of Bank Stock and Navy annuities were taken from the ESFDB database file compiled by Larry Neal from Castaing's *Course of Exchange* (http://www.le.ac.uk/hi/bon/ESFDB/NEAL/neal.html).

Table 6.6. *Summary of stock market positions taken by Henry Lascelles*

	Positions (N)	Average length of holding (days)	Average value of holding (£)
Bank Stock (1735–53)	19	3,562.2	1,367.4
East India Stock (1735–53)	24	2,775.1	791.7
3% annuities (1737–53)	16	1,507.9	1,730.7
4% annuities (1749–53)	29	433.3	4,777.5
All securities	*88*	*1,942.9*	*2,400.2*

Sources: As for Table 6.5.

Table 6.7. *New lending compared with holdings of securities and real estate, 1735–53 (£ Sterling)*

	West Indies loans: gross new lending	English loans: gross new lending[a]	Securities: market value of holdings (5 yearly average)[b]	English real estate: value of holdings (5 yearly average)
1735–9	12,747	2,000	19,434	13,660
1740–4	26,987	79,089	35,042	87,237
1745–9	45,467	16,495	59,768	115,643
1750–3	112,624	76,351	58,161	117,491

Notes:

[a] An additional £9,212 was lent to English creditors between 1735 and 1753, but the dates of the loans are not specified.

[b] Only Henry Lascelles' investments in securities are documented extensively. The only records that have been located describing his investments in private companies, other than the East India Company, are the sale of £1,221 London Assurance shares by his executors in 1754, an account at Drummond's Bank (the balance increased from £158 in 1728 to £1,029 in 1731, but in 1732 fell back to £53 and thereafter the account remained dormant), and an involvement in the River Dee navigation scheme, for which he acted as cashier, Account Book of Henry Lascelles 1753; The Royal Bank of Scotland Group Archives, Drummond's Bank, London, Customer Account Ledger, GB 1502/DR/427/8–21; NA:PRO, C11/2070/15; HH:WIP, 'The Account of the Right Honourable Edward Lord Harewood with the Estate of the Right Honourable Edwin Lord Harewood deceased, 1795').

Sources: West Indian loans: see Table 6.1. English loans, stocks, and securities: see Table 6.4. Land: BA, RB6/22/370–90, Will of Henry Lascelles (1753); WRA, Harewood Estate Records; NA:PRO, C54/5883/ entry 7, membrane 26; Mary Mauchline, *Harewood House* (2nd edn, Derbyshire, 1992), 10–11, 170.

Indian lending relative to his English lending, holdings of securities, and English real estate.

The interest rate charged by Lascelles is known for fifty-two of the seventy-eight West Indian loans and ranged from 5 to 10 per cent. Significantly, Lascelles never charged more than the legal maximum and his average rate of return, weighted by the amount of the loan, was

6.98 per cent between 1732 and 1753.[41] Peacetime interest rates in London during this period averaged between 3.5 and 4.0 per cent, rising in wartime to a maximum rate of 5.0 per cent per annum. A nominal interest rate gap, therefore, existed between London and Barbados of approximately 3.0 to 3.5 percentage points in peacetime.[42] Table 6.5 reveals that a comparable differential also existed between Henry Lascelles' West Indian lending and his earnings from English loans and securities, with the exception of East India Company stock which generated a return closest to the interest on Caribbean debts.

The exceptional performance of the East India securities included a significant capital gain. A study by Hancock of the investments of three London merchants in the funds records a similar result, one which Hancock suggests is 'indicative of what today we would call "insider trading"'.[43] By 1740, Henry Lascelles was one of the East India Company's twenty-four directors, and, like Hancock's merchants, as an insider he too would have enjoyed access to privileged information, including advance notice of the company's anticipated dividend, that conferred advantages in timing sales of stock.[44] In contrast to East India shares, Lascelles suffered small capital losses on Bank Stock and Three Per Cent Annuities, though these were offset by modest gains on Naval Four Per Cent Annuities.

---

[41] In 1752, a planter offered to give 8 per cent interest when the legal maximum was 6 per cent, but he was refused. Lascelles & Maxwell's policy was never to exceed the legal maximum and to vary the rate charged within the limit according to the goodness of the security offered, *LMLB*, Pares Transcripts, H613, Lascelles & Maxwell to Joseph Bruce, 9 December 1752. The data in the Appendix cast doubts on claims, voiced in the contemporary pamphlet literature and in parliamentary debates, that it was impossible to borrow in the islands for less than 8 per cent when the legal maximum was reduced to 6 per cent, see the citations in Price, 'Credit Plantation Economies', 328.

[42] Sheridan, 'Sugar Trade', 193.

[43] David Hancock, '"Domestic Bubbling": Eighteenth-Century London Merchants and Individual Investment in the Funds', *Economic History Review*, 57 (1994), 691. A correspondent was informed by Lascelles & Maxwell that 'when we have money to spare, we cannot make more than Interest of 3% by investing in India Bonds in the Funds', *LMLB*, Pares Transcripts, H609, Lascelles & Maxwell to Jeremiah Browne, 8 February 1752. In view of the data in Table 6.5, these comments appear somewhat disingenuous.

[44] *Kent's Directory, 1740* (London, 1740), 48; *Gentleman's Magazine*, 12 (1742), 215; 13 (1743), 215; 14 (1744), 225. Henry's capital gains were, however, accumulated steadily, rather than as a result of spectacular trades. It should also be noted that the annual dividends paid to East India holders of stock were usually greater than Bank Stock or annuity rates, yet that the dividend and price of East India Stock were subject to greater variation. The annual variance of Bank Stock and Bank dividends between 1735 and 1753 was 5.0% and 5.6% respectively, whereas for East India Stock and dividends the equivalent rates of variance were 6.9% and 7.3%. In consequence, holders of East India Stock may have received a higher return because they were exposed to greater risks.

A striking feature of the comparative data of assets in Table 6.6 is that there is no indication that Lascelles shifted resources from one form of investment to another in order to maximise returns. His behaviour in this respect differs from the combined portfolios of the three London colonial merchants studied by Hancock, which demonstrate an inverse relationship between investments in land and investments in the funds during the period 1740 until 1790.[45] Lascelles, in contrast, maintained a balanced portfolio until the last few years of his life when he increased his exposure to West India indebtedness. The loans he extended to planters, however, were not financed by any significant sales of securities or land; indeed, while extending credit to the West Indies, Lascelles was also able to finance increased lending at home.

It can only be conjectured how Lascelles was able to fund lending in the colonies and at home while maintaining a diverse asset base. If it is assumed that the £28,947 he laid out before 1735 came out of cash reserves, then ploughing back all of the accumulated interest could have financed a total of £136,635 of lending. Allowing for the recycling of debts, it is conceivable that up to £169,500 of West Indian loans were self-financing.[46] This leaves a shortfall of at least £57,272, which, coupled with the discontinuous chronology of lending, indicates that Lascelles must have had a substantial borrowing requirement. The fact that he maintained a large fortune in both securities and in real estate suggests that he represented a good credit risk and was in a position to raise funds from bankers at advantageous rates of interest. This hypothesis receives support from a comparison of the gross assets of £392,704 listed in his Account Book of 1753, and the valuation of £284,000 put on his estate in his will of the same year.[47] The differential of £108,704 provides an indication of the gap between Lascelles' gross and net assets.[48]

The correspondence of Lascelles & Maxwell makes explicit the fact that the partnership borrowed from London bankers, and that, at times, the firm's working capital was stretched. It was demonstrated in Table 6.3 that short-term credit could be volatile: in a single year the firm moved from a deficit of £4,070 to a surplus of more than £12,000. The commission house kept funds on deposit in the hands of bankers to meet

---

[45] Hancock, 'Domestic Bubbling', 697–8.   [46] See fn. 19.
[47] BA, RB6/22/370–90, Will of Henry Lascelles, 1753; Account Book of Henry Lascelles, 1753; Pares, 'West-India Merchant House', 107; Sheridan, *Sugar and Slavery*, 297.
[48] The Appendix reveals that Henry Lascelles extended loans on the account of Lascelles & Maxwell and also assigned some loans to his son Daniel Lascelles prior to his death. In consequence, the figure of £108,704 probably represents the lower limit of his borrowing.

normal contingencies, but heavy drawings by planters quickly exhausted this reserve. 'We have usually a large sum lying in the Bankers' hands to answer all occasions', one correspondent was informed in 1746, 'but in these calamitous times we were from hand to mouth, & obliged to read over every day the payments we were to make provision accordingly, so as not to overdraw on the Banker'. [49] To cover short-term requirements in 1751, for example, the partners raised between £5,000 and £10,000 by issuing promissory notes at 5 per cent interest, which were renewed monthly by the bankers. Borrowing on these terms, however, wiped out the return on lending in the colonies, and, if it continued for any length of time, Henry Lascelles stepped in to provide a cash injection. His account book records a loan to the house of £14,000 on bond in 1751 and he also authorised the sale of £12,535 of bank stock by Lascelles & Maxwell in September 1753, at a time when the city's bankers were refusing to accept promissory notes for periods longer than fourteen days. [50]

Reference to the sale of securities may provide a clue to a further significant source of credit. By entering into contracts to sell stock and buy it back at a future date, Henry could have raised short-term capital on his share holdings. During this period, options trading enabled investors of limited means to buy and sell shares in 'Exchange Alley', without formally owning or transferring securities. [51] Unfortunately, this hypothesis cannot be tested directly because such transactions do not appear in company registers. Nevertheless, the possibility provides an additional explanation for Lascelles' preference to hold shares and West Indian loans simultaneously, rather than selling one type of asset to invest in the other.

The Wars of Jenkins' Ear and Austrian Succession had the effects that Pares and Sheridan claim: the conflict narrowed interest rate differentials and raised the risk of investing in the Caribbean. In the Letter Book of Lascelles & Maxwell, the operation of these factors is vividly described. The Barbadian planter Michael Rice, for example, was informed in September 1744 that 'we have refused Sundry People of yr Island who

---

[49] *LMLB*, Pares Transcripts, H599, Lascelles & Maxwell to Benjamin Charnock, 3 November 1746. See also Pares, 'West-India Merchant House', 106–7; Sheridan, 'Sugar Trade', 193.

[50] *LMLB*, Pares Transcripts, H606, Lascelles & Maxwell to Gedney Clarke, 23 September 1751; H614, Lascelles & Maxwell to John Harrison, 8 November 1753; Account Book of Henry Lascelles, 1753. Stock was also sold in 1746 (at a 15 per cent discount) to cover obligations, Pares Transcripts, H598, Lascelles & Maxwell to Benjamin Charnock, 3 November 1746.

[51] Stuart Banner, *Anglo-American Securities Regulation, Cultural and Political Roots, 1690–1890* (Cambridge, 1998), 29–37.

have applied for loans as the French War does certainly render Security in the West Indies more precarious than it was in time of Peace'. In the February following, the Philadelphia merchant Samuel McCall was notified that government borrowing had lowered the stocks and raised the interest rates on private security, so that in consequence 'We are far from desiring to be in advance for our Employers for the advantage of 5 Pct. P. Annum Interest.'[52] The situation worsened with the Jacobite rising of 1745 at home and fears of a French attack in the colonies. Rumours that a naval force was arming itself in Martinique in readiness for an attack on Barbados created scenes of panic in London. George Maxwell described how 'the private Insurance Offices were seen crowded with planters endeavouring to Insure their plantations for 6 months, but some that had policies to insure £10,000 could not get above £800 underwrote at £10.10 p. Ct. Prmio'. A symptom of the slump in credit and confidence is the course of the exchange, which fell from an average of £133 currency per £100 sterling between 1740 and 1744 to £150 currency in 1745, and remained at this level for two years.[53]

The interest rate gap model thus contains elements of the truth, but closer inspection reveals its inadequacies. There is one fundamental problem with the model: if merchants like Henry Lascelles borrowed in the London market to lend in the colonies, why did not arbitrage equalise rates of return between the two markets? A peacetime gap of between 3.0 and 3.5 percentage points, though small, amounted to a large differential on rates charged to borrowers in Britain and Barbados.

Interest rate differentials far greater than those observed between Britain and Barbados are commonly recorded in the developing world between urban and rural credit markets. Two hypotheses seeking to explain such gaps have been developed and can help assist in understanding conditions in West Indian finance: these are the 'lender's risk' and 'segmented market' models. The lender's risk hypothesis argues that lenders in rural markets (or in the colonies in this case) face a higher risk of default than those in the metropolitan market. Stated formally, if a creditor discovers that on average a fraction q of loans are not repaid, then the expected return R on a loan of L, at an interest rate of i, is:

$$R = (1 + i)(1 - q)L - L$$

---

[52] *LMLB*, Lascelles & Maxwell to Michael Rice, 9 September 1744, and Samuel McCall, 28 February 1744[5]. George Maxwell reported that Henry Lascelles was unable to raise £3,000 in December except 'at an immense discount', Sheridan, 'Sugar Trade', 193.
[53] *LMLB*, George Maxwell to Michael Longbotham, 18 June 1745; McCusker, *Money and Exchange*, 243.

Dividing this expression by L gives the effective interest rate d, which can be expressed as:

$$d = i(1 - q) - q$$

It follows that if $q > o$, then $d < i$.[54] Under perfect competition, arbitrage should ensure that d, the rate of returns on colonial lending, is equal to i, the British interest rate for safe loans. Because of the possibility of default ($q > o$), however, the colonial interest rate must be set at a premium.[55]

English interest rates were earned on investments in government bonds secured by taxation, whereas the colonial rates of interest were paid by indebted planters who could go bankrupt. What is striking, therefore, about West Indian finance is the smallness of the interest rate gap between the two markets.[56] The default rate had to be kept low for any lending to be viable at these rates. Henry Lascelles' papers suggest that he accomplished this feat. To be sure, some of his clients suffered insolvency; Burch Hothersall is one example of this and Robert Warren possibly another. The breaking up of Hothersall's estate has already been described and in 1738 Warren was obliged to settle part of his debt by surrendering 150 acres of Holetown plantation to Lascelles.[57] Neither Hothersall nor Warren, therefore, evaded payment; indeed, very few debtors got away without paying anything. In 1743, the partnership of Lascelles & Maxwell was established and all the old balances of Henry Lascelles were carried forward into the new concern. It is striking that of these accounts, only two debts were described as being 'very bad'. These were unsecured deficits on current account granted to Thomas Waterman (an Assembly member) and Richard Austin, and they amounted to only a few hundred pounds. Similarly, Henry Lascelles' account book records very few desperate debts and none of the Barbados loans were classified as such.[58]

---

[54] The model is taken from Kaushik Basu, *Analytical Development Economics: The Less Developed Economy Revisited* (Massachusetts, 1997), 267–8. The model assumes that no interest is paid on the proportion of the loan defaulted.

[55] For example, if the British interest rate is 4% and the colonial yield on loans 8%, then the rate of default q which equalises rates of return is 4%.

[56] Indeed, Henry Lascelles invested in London securities on behalf of some clients precisely because metropolitan rates of return were more attractive than the local capital market. 'It is with much satisfaction I hear of your having placed the sum of money you mention in very secure hands,' he wrote to one planter, 'our Funds, as you observe, yield a very considerable Interest compared to what it brings in the West Indies', *LMLB*, Pares Transcripts, H589, Henry Lascelles to T. Needham, 30 May 1741.

[57] BA, Hughes-Queree collections, Abstract in Queree notebook; RB6/22/370–90, Will of Henry Lascelles. For more information about Hothersall and Warren, see Chapters Four and Seven.

[58] *LMLB*, Pares Transcripts, H593, George Maxwell to James Bruce, 4 October 1743; Henry Lascelles Account Book, 1753.

Lascelles could insure himself against opportunist behaviour on the part of debtors by spreading his loan capital among clients; the Appendix indicates the extent to which he did so. Yet since West Indian borrowers were linked, either directly or indirectly, with the state of the sugar market, Lascelles also faced a more systemic risk. Crop failure, hurricane, or a collapse in sugar prices were all capable of triggering a spate of defaults that hit planters indiscriminately. Insurance against general hazards such as these usually takes the form of a risk premium applied across a credit market. Usury laws, however, set an upper limit to the size of the premium that could be charged. An effective system of screening loan clients and recovering assets from debtors, therefore, was of particular importance.

In contrast to the small proportion of uncollectible debts, arrears of interest were common, as Table 6.4 records. The best payment record was arrears of 246 days and the worst 978 days. In some cases the unpaid interest was added to the principal and thereby compounded. This was, however, by no means universal practice. Henry Lascelles failed in an attempt to enforce compound interest on a recalcitrant debtor in 1741, and in 1745 the ability of lenders to charge more than simple interest received a setback in the Court of Chancery. In the case of *Brace* vs *Peers*, Lord Chief Justice Mills ruled that compound interest was not legitimised merely by a debtor's demurring to an adjusted current account, but that annual interest arrears could only be added to the principal if the debtor agreed to provide fresh security each year.[59] The difficulty of charging compound interest is of significance in appraising British and colonial interest rates, since London bonds typically paid interest quarterly or biannually, whereas planters, if Henry Lascelles' accounts are typical, were generally in arrears. A sum of £100 invested in bonds at 4 per cent paid quarterly yields £4.06, whereas the present value of £100 lent to planters at 8 per cent received in one year's time is £7.41, and in two years' time it is £6.86. The effect of simple interest and the allowance of arrears is to push the British and colonial rates closer together, thus making it even more important for lenders to avoid bad debts and recover assets efficiently in the West Indies.

The segmented markets hypothesis postulates that a personalised relationship exists between borrowers and lenders that grants creditors monopolistic control over a segment of the loans market. Monopoly power can arise either out of the lender's privileged knowledge of the debtor's circumstances, or because the borrower must agree to give their

business to the lender as a condition for receiving the loan.[60] Henry
Lascelles enjoyed both of these advantages in his dealings with debtors.
The office of Marshall in Barbados, charged with executing debt claims,
was under Lascelles' control. During the 1740s the post was occupied
by Thomas Stevenson: a loan client who paid one-quarter of the fees
generated by this post to Henry and his half-brother Edward Lascelles.
The patent right to the office of Marshall belonged to a Mr Reynolds, an
individual whom Henry Lascelles was able to influence. In 1745, for
example, Lascelles persuaded Reynolds to agree to better rental terms
despite interest in Stevenson's post from other quarters.[61]

In addition to having the Marshall moonlighting as his agent, Lascelles also granted loans to other prominent Barbadians and used his
political connections to obtain their appointment as members of the
Assembly and to colonial offices.[62] Henry's influence was strongest on
Barbados, where he made the bulk of his loans, where he had been a
merchant since 1712, and where his half-brother and friends could
watch over his interests. During the 1740s and early 1750s, however, he
expanded operations to other colonies where similar assurances could be
obtained. The Antiguan merchant and planter Andrew Lessley,
for example, was granted funds in 1747 to help him purchase property.
Lessley was involved with Lascelles in victualling contracts during the
Wars of Jenkins' Ear and Austrian Succession. George Maxwell
informed Lessley bluntly that Henry Lascelles expected this loan to yield
more than just interest. 'He thinks in return it demands your warmest
Endeavours and Attention to promote the Interest of our House', wrote
Maxwell, 'not only on Prize Goods taken by the Man of War, but also
with all the people of your island with whom you have any manner of

---

[60] For a brief discussion of credit islands and market fragmentation, see Basu, *Analytical Development Economics*, 274–8.

[61] *LMLB*, Maxwell to Thomas Stevenson, 2 March 1744[5]; *LMLB*, Pares Transcripts, H590, Henry Lascelles to Lascelles and Morecroft, 27 October 1741; W&G IV, Lascelles & Maxwell to Thomas Stevenson and Sons, 21 February and 23 February 1752. For more details of the relationship between Lascelles and Stevenson see Huntington Library, Stowe Collection, STG Box 25, No. 21, Henry Grenville to George Grenville, 7 November 1750. See also Chapters Four and Seven. It should be noted that Stevenson did not charge commission for collecting or remitting money on behalf of Lascelles, and that Henry Lascelles' Account Book reveals that Lascelles was still receiving one quarter of the profits of the Marshall's office (£2,457 currency or c. £1,820 sterling) in 1753.

[62] Pares, 'West-India Merchant House', 93; James Henretta, *'Salutary Neglect': Colonial Administration under the Duke of Newcastle* (Princeton, 1972), 228–31. The Barbados colonial agent, John Sharpe, assisted Lascelles to deputise friends and clients 'to most of the Patent Offices in the island of Barbados', *LMLB*, Pares Transcripts, H568, W&G V, Lascelles & Maxwell to R. Stirling (Jamaica), 25 September 1752.

influence.'[63] It is also clear that Henry Lascelles, in common with other London merchants, attempted to secure commission business from planters in return for granting loans. Pares has documented this aspect of trade in his study of the Bristol Pinneys, who, he suggests, employed the ratio of £2,000 to £3,000 of debt in return for handling 100 hogsheads of sugar per annum. Lascelles & Maxwell (reputably) reckoned on £5,000 of debt for 500 hogsheads of business.[64]

Henry Lascelles held important advantages over other potential entrants to the Barbadian loan market, but he was not a perfect monopolist since surviving correspondence reveals that borrowers compared rates between lenders and negotiated over terms. Among the constraints Lascelles faced were community conventions in Barbados, and, on occasion, he stepped outside the bounds of acceptable conduct. In 1741, for example, Lascelles was accused of 'inhumanity' when he took out an execution against Abel Alleyne's movable property. Alleyne received sympathy because he was the executor of a deceased planter named Foster who had owed the debt. Nevertheless, despite criticism, Lascelles ordered his agents to proceed, confident that observers would see the justice of his claim when they learned that he had not received payments for eleven years and was prepared to write off the interest due if he could recover the principal. It is significant, however, that Lascelles wanted his actions to be perceived of as reasonable, and he instructed his attorneys and friends to publicise his position in the Alleyne case.[65]

---

[63] *LMLB*, Pares Transcripts, H651, Lascelles & Maxwell to Andrew Lessley, 31 January 1747; George Maxwell to Andrew Lessley & Co., 25 July 1747. Lessley may be connected to the Scots Leslie family, whose head was Laird of Warthill in the Garioch district of west Aberdeenshire. Many branches of the Leslie family can be found in the region around Castle Leslie (see Chapter Seven). It can also be noted that Thomas Stevenson was a planter in Antigua prior to emigrating to Barbados between 1728 and 1730, Craig B. Waff and Stephen Skinner, 'Thomas Stevenson of Barbados and Comet Halley's 1759 Return', in Richard B. Goddard ed., *George Washington's Visit to Barbados, 1751* (Barbados, 1997), 202.

[64] Richard Pares, *A West-India Fortune* (London, 1950), 210, 253–6; *LMLB*, Pares Transcripts, H655, Lascelles & Maxwell to Gedney Clarke, 25 February 1754. The context of the letter to Clarke is that the house, because of financial pressures, did not wish to grant any more loans *even if* terms of £5,000 for 500 hhd of sugar were offered. Later, the ratio of £10,000 for 600 large hhd of sugar and 600 puncheons of rum is mentioned, Pares Transcripts, H624, Lascelles & Maxwell to Samuel Husbands, 5 February 1757. It is clear that Henry Lascelles could not have maintained such a ratio in practice. Assuming that 14.5 per cent of debts were retired (fn. 19), then total lending of £193,890 implies that 19,389 hhd of sugar per annum were handled by the firm if the lending formula was rigorously applied. Using a conversion rate of 1 hhd to 16 cwt, this results in a figure of 310,224 cwt. Since an average of only 818,100 cwt per annum were imported into all ports in England and Wales between 1740 and 1749, the figure of 310,224 cwt for a single firm is not feasible, E. B. Schumpeter, *English Overseas Trade Statistics 1697–1808*, (Oxford, 1960), 61–2.

[65] *LMLB*, Pares Transcripts, H590, Henry Lascelles to James Bruce, 29 December 1741.

In general, Henry Lascelles thought of himself as a man of forbearance, though his interpretation of forbearance was a trifle severe. 'I am not urgent to have the Money for Debt', he counselled Thomas Stevenson, 'I only want to have it ascertained & fixed beyond contradiction, to receive the interest of it annually but if this should not be instantly complied with, & secured to me, it is my positive order that the executions be forthwith levyed without any pretense or evasion whatsoever.'[66]

The system of tying sugars to commission houses also had limitations. It was not a legally enforceable contract and planters could, and on occasion did, switch their business to other merchants and shippers. Though Lascelles was furious with Henry Slingsby after he split his shipments of sugar jointly between himself and another merchant, the only remedy open to him was to threaten not to renew the loan after its term expired. If Slingsby had a good payment record, then Lascelles' loss was most likely another's gain. Moreover, it was common for both lender and borrower to be bound by defeasances not to demand or make repayment within a specified number of years. Devices such as this further tied the hands of lenders. A legal opinion taken out by Lascelles in 1751 confirmed that even produce in the hands of importers was subject to the orders of the consigner, while merchants in the colonies refused to defy trading conventions by overriding the instructions given to them by planters.[67]

The evidence reviewed above suggests that the following conclusions can be drawn about the Barbadian loan market. Though an interest rate gap existed between colonial and metropolitan markets, the differential was relatively small in comparison with modern experience in developing countries and it would have taken only a small proportion of bad loans to equalise rates of return. In consequence, British merchants could not turn an easy profit by raising money on the London market and lending it in Barbados. Loans to planters were forthcoming at the legal maximum, or under, from lenders who were confident that they could maintain a low default rate. Privileged information, personalised relationships, and an ability to bind a significant proportion of borrowers to their commission houses were key considerations. Yet though lending was restricted to merchants enjoying access to information and a command of the institutions of enforcement, the ability of creditors to extract monopoly profits was limited. Lascelles' attorneys were instructed to be

---

[66] Ibid., Henry Lascelles to Thomas Stevenson, 27 October 1741.
[67] Ibid., H597, George Maxwell to Harry Slingsby, 4 May 1745; H607, Lascelles & Maxwell to Jeremiah Brown, 31 October 1751; Sheridan, *Sugar and Slavery*, 290–1.

vigilant in preventing competitors from poaching his best clients. 'I dont know I should have my good Debts picked out', he warned, 'by People that wanted to lend out their money.'[68] Naturally, Lascelles was not adverse to cherry-picking himself when opportunity beckoned. And he and his half-brother Edward were in a good position to poach, since the pair were knowledgeable about the secondary debt market and either managed or wound up the affairs of many non-resident or deceased planters and merchants. The brothers were granted no fewer than nineteen powers of attorney between 1716 and 1736, several of which explicitly mention debt collection, while in London after 1732 Henry acted as attorney, executor, or trustee of the estates of a number of Barbadians.[69] In consequence, though Pares was correct to highlight the references in the Lascelles papers to Barbadians owing money to other Barbadians, the context appears to be that of rating the reputation and creditworthiness of debtors with a view to taking over their business.[70]

A final and fatal problem with the interest rate gap hypothesis is that during the Wars of Jenkins' Ear and Austrian Succession, when the differential was eroded and liquidity contracted, Henry Lascelles increased his lending in the West Indies. Planters were warned that money was tight and one was informed that 'None would wish to have money abroad in these unhappy times.' The fact remains, however, that Henry kept his head even if others panicked. 'I have talked with Mr Lascelles on this matter', Maxwell reassured another client, 'and I do not find he desires to call all his money home from Barbados.'[71] Nearly all of the applications for loans recorded in the Lascelles & Maxwell Letter Book were ultimately successful between 1743 and 1746. Table 6.1 records that, as a result, the amount of gross lending grew by £27,000 during the war. In fact, the only planter whose request for finance was rejected outright during the years covered by the letter book

---

[68] *LMLB*, Pares Transcripts, H610, Henry Lascelles to Gedney Clarke, 11 June 1752.

[69] See, e.g. BA, RB3/42/161–2, 164–5; NA:PRO, C11/873/1, C12/902/36, C12/785/16; Bristol Record Office, Ashton Court MS, AC/WO/9/83, 85, 93/a–b.

[70] Nor is the appearance of debts owing in the inventories of Jamaican planters, such as Peter Beckford, evidence, in itself, that local lending was more significant than overseas lending. This is because the inventories do not usually state the debts owed by the decedent. Alexander Harvie's inventory of 1765, for example, lists 85 debts owed to him amounting to £53,985 currency. The debts arose from the Harvie brothers' dry goods and slave trade businesses, which were financed by the Lascelles. Harvie's plantation, Williamsfield, was mortgaged to Lascelles & Maxwell for £57,349 sterling, and, in 1777, the loan was foreclosed and ownership of all of the Harvies' Jamaican properties passed to the Lascelles, JA, Inventories, IB/11/3/47; WRA, Harewood Accession 2,677, Indenture between Richard Lewing and Henry Lascelles, 1977; Pares, 'West-India Merchant House', 104–6.

[71] *LMLB*, George Maxwell to Henry Slingsby, 4 May 1745; Maxwell to John Braithwaite, November 1745.

was Alexander Crawford of Jamaica. His business would probably have been politely declined at the best of times. Crawford had previously been a client of Julius Beckford, who now refused to accept his bills, and the title to his plantation was not secure. Moreover, Crawford had not scrupled to approach other commission houses with the offer of his sugars behind Henry's back.[72]

The lending policy of Henry Lascelles and the firm of Lascelles & Maxwell during the 1740s and early 1750s combined various elements: developments specific to the firm, responses to institutional change, and a longer-term judgement about the future prosperity of the sugar colonies. The Lascelles and Maxwell Letter Book records that, after the return of George Maxwell to London from Barbados in 1743, Henry Lascelles spent an increasing amount of time with his family at Richmond away from the counting house. In August 1750, Henry installed his second son Daniel Lascelles in his place as partner with Maxwell.[73] Pares regarded Daniel as 'a colourless figure', and, though he conceded that 'he was not exactly a sleeping partner in the House', he added that 'he never wrote its letters and did not always see them before they were sent off'.[74] Given the destruction of all of the letter books after Daniel's succession, Pares' opinion must be respected. Nevertheless, it is significant that, immediately after his father's death, Daniel went to the West Indies and negotiated with Barbados merchants and planters over the continuation of credit. Moreover, during the 1760s the lending of the house became more extensive and riskier.[75] Though Henry Lascelles continued to scrutinise the activities of Lascelles & Maxwell, and was consulted about all lending decisions, the process of transition may have accelerated once Daniel was installed in 1750.

Henry Lascelles' pattern of lending strongly suggests that legal changes influenced the terms on which loans were granted, particularly with respect to the 1732 Colonial Debts Act, the 1745 case of *Brace* vs *Peers*, and the two reductions of colonial interest rates in 1729 and 1752. The Colonial Debts Act was of particular significance. The legal environment regulating debtor–creditor relations in colonial trade was subject to uncertainty during the decade following 1720 as falling

---

[72] *LMLB*, Pares Transcripts, H594, Lascelles & Maxwell to Alexander Crawford, 8 September 1744; H599, same to same, 7 April 1746; H595, Lascelles & Maxwell to F[lorentius] Vassall, 8 September 1744.

[73] *LMLB*, Lascelles & Maxwell to Sir Thomas Robinson, 27 June 1744; WRA, Harewood Accession 2,677, Deed of partnership between Daniel Lascelles and George Maxwell, 1750.

[74] Pares 'West-India Merchant House', 79.

[75] *LMLB*, Pares Transcripts, H618, George Maxwell to T[homas Stevenson], 11 July 1754; Pares, 'West-India Merchant House', 101–2.

commodity prices, particularly of sugar and tobacco, led to agitation in several colonial legislatures for debtor-friendly legislation and soft-credit measures such as land banks, paper currency, and cried-up exchange rates. After a struggle, these projects were mostly defeated and technical victory for creditor interests was secured by the passage of the 1732 Act. This piece of legislation introduced uniformity in the treatment of debtors throughout the British colonial empire. Specifically, the Act rendered land, houses, and slaves liable for the satisfaction of debts. As Sheridan observes, 'Slaves, which had previously been annexed to the soil in colonies dependent upon their labour, were now regarded as personal property when used as security for debts.'[76] In theory, there-fore, the new law rendered bonds, judgements, and mortgages more effective instruments for securing loans.

The Colonial Debts Act generated much controversy. Parliament and the Board of Trade were lobbied by the representatives of groups for and against the proposed new system. Henry himself gave evidence before a parliamentary inquiry in March 1732, arguing that creditor rights need-ed strengthening.[77] On Barbados, the colony's Assembly condemned the law as an unnecessary measure that 'will alter the Constitution of this Colony now so long established, & by long usage found equally beneficial to creditor and Debtor'. A memorial was prepared, reviewing the island's existing legislation, in an attempt to demonstrate that len-ders' rights were already safeguarded adequately. Among the objections was a complaint that the Act was originally designed to appease cred-itors lending to Chesapeake tobacco planters, and ought not to be applied indiscriminately within British Colonial America.[78]

The Barbados Assembly protested that the Colonial Debts Act 'will enable any one Crafty or Malicious Creditor not only to ruin his Debtor; but to Cheat all the other Creditors of the same Debtor of their just Debts'. In a book published in 1742, Jonathan Blenman argued that the law had operated just as the petitioners had anticipated. Blenman concentrated on the Act's replacement of a system of appraisal of mortgaged property by the forced sale of a defaulting debtor's assets 'at Outcry by the Marshall to the highest Bidder'. Appraisal's great merit, Blenman argued, was that it had enabled an estate's proceeds to be

---

[76] Sheridan, *Sugar and Slavery*, 289.

[77] Leo Francis Stock ed., *Proceedings and Debates of the British Parliaments Respecting North America* (5 vols., Washington DC, 1924–41), vol. IV, 160.

[78] PRO:NA, CO28/23, 'The humble Representation of the President, Councill and the Generall Assembly of the Island of Barbados', 18 January 1732[3]; Barbados Public Library, Lucas Manuscripts, Meeting of Council to Consider the Colonial Debts Act, 6 November 1734.

applied to creditors in order of seniority, determined by the date their judgements against a debtor were recorded in court. Under the system of outcry, the successful bidder was obliged to pay a 20 per cent penalty to the plaintiff (usually the holder of the first judgement against the estate), if payment was not made within five days. Blenman was convinced that this clause advantaged a major creditor over junior creditors (even if no collusion took place between the owner and purchaser), since the penalty weighed less heavy in proportion to the debt claimed.[79]

Historians are divided regarding the effectiveness of the Colonial Debts Act. Pares was sceptical about the enforcement of the legislation, whereas Price attaches more significance to the measure.[80] On the basis of Henry Lascelles' loans, the institutional changes, of which the 1732 law formed part, were indeed associated with changes in the pattern of lending in the West Indies. Financial theory predicts that the enforcement of a lower usury rate will encourage restructuring in the loans market, as lenders unable to allocate credit by means of a variable interest rate instead ration loans by concentrating funds in the hands of borrowers with superior collateral and credit worthiness.[81] The 1732 Act did not prove a dead letter because it conferred advantages not only to merchants looking to lend out their capital, but also to planters possessing good title to their estates. A mortgage, used in combination with a bond or execution, granted creditors improved collateral. At the same time, it became harder to break up estates to pay debts because a mortgage bound slaves and land together in the schedule. This circumstance privileged large lenders over smaller creditors.

Henry Lascelles' investment behaviour suggests that the potential offered by the mortgage remained unrealised in peacetime, and that the timing of credit innovation in the West Indian loan market was influenced by the uncertainties generated by the Wars of Jenkins' Ear and

---

[79] [Jonathan Blenman], *Remarks on Several Acts of Parliament Relating More Especially to the Colonies Abroad* (London, 1742), 2–3, 21–3, 25–32. Blenman is identified as the author of this tract in two copies of the text in the collections of the John Carter Brown Library and the Houghton Library, Jerome S. Handler, *A Guide to Source Materials for the Study of Barbados History, 1627–1834* (Carbondale, 1971), 31–2. Whereas the Barbados petitioners observed that the initiative for the 1732 act came from London merchants (a petition was presented to the Lords Commissioners 12 August 1731, Sheridan, *Sugar and Slavery*, 288), Blenman highlights the role of Bristol's mercantile community.

[80] Price, *Merchants and Planters*, 46; Price, 'Credit Plantation Economies', 307–10. See also Sheridan, 'British Credit Crisis', 164; Sheridan, *Sugar and Slavery*, 288–90.

[81] For application of economic theory to an historical example, see Peter Temin and Hans-Joachim Voth, 'Financial Repression in a Natural Experiment: Loan Allocation and the Change in the Usury Laws in 1714' [working paper], www.econ.upf.edu/~voth/usury.pdf.

Austrian Succession. These conflicts generated conditions whereby strong-nerved investors, seeking to advance their position in the West Indies loan market, adopted the mortgage as a method of responding to risk. At the end of the war, the outcome of *Brace* vs *Peers* in 1745 provided an additional incentive for lenders to seek the security of a mortgage, since, as George Maxwell noted, it was uncertain whether a fresh settlement of interest would be secured by an old judgement, whereas a mortgage was flexible enough to cover all future obligations or settlements.[82]

A further example of the effects of institutional change occurred in 1752 when the rate of interest in Antigua, Barbados, and Jamaica was reduced from 8 to 6 per cent. The initiative for the rate reduction came from the Jamaican planters and the concurrence of the Kingston merchants raised expectations that the measure would be adopted in Barbados and not overruled in Britain by the Lords Commissioners of Trade. Any remaining doubts were dispelled in early October 1752 when the Barbados colonial agent, John Sharpe, indicated that he would lobby for acceptance of the Act.[83] Henry naturally opposed the interest rate cut, just as he had sought to prevent an earlier Jamaican reduction in 1739.[84] At the same time as trying to block the measure, however, Lascelles rushed to extend credit in order to beat the imminent rate reduction. In May 1752, the following instructions were despatched to his agent Gedney Clarke in Barbados:

If the law does not take place to reduce interest to 6% before this reaches you, you may, if you can meet with undeniable security lend out for me to the amount of £10,000 sterling if you can get 8% interest, which you have the liberty to draw on me for, but under, I will not take, or if you buy up any old judgement upon estates that you know are undoubtedly good, & that are prior to estates it will do as well.[85]

Henry was joined in the scramble to lend by other merchants and the outflow of funds that resulted pushed up the rates charged by the

---

[82] *LMLB*, George Maxwell to Edward Lascelles, 28 February 1744[5].

[83] *LMLB*, Pares Transcripts, H612, Henry Lascelles to Gedney Clarke, 20 September 1752; Lascelles & Maxwell to Gedney Clarke, 5 October 1752. On the question of the interest rate cut, Sharpe sided with the planters, but the Lascelles & Maxwell Letter Book reveals that in other areas of business and politics (e.g. opposition to government proposals to raise sugar duties in 1743–4).

[84] Pares, 'West-India Merchant House', 94; Board of Trade, *Journal of the Commissioners for Trade and Plantations, 1704–1782* (14 vols., London, 1920), vol. VII, 292; *LMLB*, Pares Transcripts, H608, Henry Lascelles to Gedney Clarke, 5 November 1751.

[85] *LMLB*, Pares Transcripts, H610, Henry Lascelles to Gedney Clarke, 8 May 1752.

London bankers for short-term advances. By November 1753, money could be obtained only for fourteen-day periods at 5 per cent interest.[86]

The reduction in the legal maximum interest rate in 1752 undoubtedly dislocated the colonial loans market in the short term, but its principal effect was to accelerate longer-term developments. No lender is a supporter of usury and Henry voiced his opposition to the rate cut. He swiftly realised, however, that the reduction favoured an extension of lending on mortgage. Lascelles & Maxwell were also among the first merchants to appreciate that, despite the interruptions of war, prospects for sugar planting were extremely promising. Table 6.1 reveals that long before the peace of Aix-La-Chapelle (1748) or the rate cut, Henry had begun scooping up lending opportunities at a time when merchants with less confidence were withdrawing funds from the West Indies. The boom in sugar planting, and in colonial trade generally, is depicted in Table 6.8, which presents estimates of sugar prices and the real value of sugar exports from the British West Indies. These data are compared with movements in the prices of staples generally, and with the wider terms of trade between Great Britain (including Ireland) and British Colonial America. Table 6.8 indicates that staples cultivation, on trend, expanded at improving terms of trade between 1730 and 1770, shaking off several decades of sluggish growth or depression. Sugar led the way, and, in the Caribbean land used to cultivate cane appreciated in value. According to the evidence of probate inventories, Jamaican estates tripled in value during this period.[87] The price and terms of trade data in Table 6.8 detail the factors responsible for an appreciation in the value of real estate recorded in colonial probate inventories. It was this positive equity lying beneath the feet of the planters that mortgages were able to unlock.

Capital and credit have featured strongly in studies of eighteenth-century colonial trade during the past half-century.[88] More recently, credit networks have attracted the attention of historians investigating both the finance of transatlantic commerce and the cultural context

[86] Ibid., H615, Lascelles & Maxwell to Thomas Stevenson and Sons, 15 November 1753.
[87] Sheridan, *Sugar and Slavery*, 229; Sheridan reports that the median value of 502 sugar estates was £3,819 currency between 1741 and 1745 and £9,361 currency between 1771 and 1775. See also Alan L. Karras, *Sojourners in the Sun: Scottish Migrants in Jamaica and the Chesapeake, 1740–1800* (Ithaca, NY, 1992), 175.
[88] A. G. Checkland, 'Finance for the West Indies, 1780–1815', *Economic History Review*, 10 (1958), 461–9; K. G. Davies, 'The Origins of the Commission System in the West India Trade', *Transactions of the Royal Historical Society* 2 (1952), 89–107; Pares, *Merchants and Planters*, 38–50, 81–91; Jacob M. Price, *Capital and Credit in British Overseas Trade: The View from the Chesapeake* (Cambridge, 1980); Price, 'Credit Plantation Economies', 293–339, R. B. Sheridan, 'The Commercial and Financial Organization of the British Slave Trade, 1750–1807', *Economic History Review*, 11 (1958), 249–63.

Table 6.8. *Sugar exports and the colonial terms of trade, 1701–70 (Index Numbers, base 1701–10 and 1722–38)*

Years	Sugar PR[a]	Real sugar exports	Staples CPI[b]	Colonial ITT[c]
1701–10	100.0	100.0	100.0	100.0
1711–20	84.1	124.9	90.5	130.7
1721–30	59.5	110.3	67.4	141.9
1731–40	53.0	99.1	61.7	151.4
1741–50	78.2	171.0	72.4	177.1
1751–60	88.8	255.1	86.3	271.2
1761–70	85.7	282.7	91.7	468.8
War and peace				
1697–1701 (P)	154.1	99.8	na	na
1702–13 (W)	178.7	97.5	152.3	71.8
1714–17 (P)	149.4	144.2	146.5	100.9
1718–21 (W)	123.1	102.3	125.8	89.0
1722–38 (P)	100.0	100.0	100.0	100.0
1739–48 (W)	142.5	157.5	106.6	120.7
1749–55 (P)	142.7	163.5	126.7	177.7
1756–63 (W)	166.9	342.5	137.2	232.3
1763–74 (P)	154.6	309.6	146.5	319.6

Notes and Sources:
[a] Sugar price relative (PR) and real export earnings: John J. McCusker, *The Rum Trade and the Balance of Payments of the Thirteen Continental Colonies, 1650–1775* (2 vols., New York, 1989), vol. II, 891ff., 1,144ff. Sugar exports are English and Scottish and re-exports from all colonial producers inclusive of prize sugars.
[b] Staples commodity price index (CPI): (i) Sugar: Arthur H. Cole, *Wholesale Commodity Prices in the United States, 1700–1861* (2 vols., Cambridge, MA, 1938), vol. II, [n.p.]. (ii) Rum: John J. McCusker, 'How Much is that in Real Money? A Historical Price Index for Use as a Deflator of Money Values in the Economy of the United States', *Proceedings of the American Antiquarian Society*, 101 (1991), tables B-1, A-2. (iii) Rice: George Rogers Taylor, 'Wholesale Commodity Prices at Charleston, South Carolina, 1732–1791', *Journal of Business and Economic History*, 4 (1932); Peter A. Cochlanis, *The Shadow of a Dream: Economic Life and Death in the South Carolina Low Country, 1670–1920* (Oxford, 1989), table 3–29; US Bureau of the Census, *Historical Statistics of the United States: Colonial Times to 1970* (2 vols., Washington DC, 1975), series z, 558–77; (iv) *Historical Statistics*, series z, 578–82, 583–4. The weights for the staples CPI were obtained by calculating the value of staple exports using both constant prices of 1697–1704 and current prices. The final staples CPI is Fisher's ideal of the resulting Laspeyres and Paasche indexes. For further details, see S. D. Smith, 'British Exports to Colonial North America, 1697–1774', unpub. Ph.D. thesis (University of Cambridge, 1992), Appendix II.
[c] Colonial income terms of trade (I): this is defined as $P_x/P_m * Q_x$, where P_x is a price index of colonial exports, P_m a price index of colonial imports, and Q_x a quantity index of colonial exports. P_x is the staple CPI above. P_m is an import price index consisting of British and Irish goods and African slaves. Q_x is an index of staple exports. For details of the construction of P_x, P_m, and Q_x, see Smith, 'British Exports', 242–5, Appendices I and II.

within which early modern business was conducted.[89] As a result of this research, a great deal has been discovered about the organisation of the slave, sugar, and tobacco trades. Yet the central question posed by the *Wealth of Nations* remains unresolved. How dependent were the plantations, particularly the sugar colonies, on British capital? Despite its importance, this question remains unanswered because, in contrast to commodity trade and the shipment of enslaved Africans, little data have been assembled that quantify the amount of lending to planters. Invariably, in studies of capital in the colonial trades, the emphasis has been on trade credit granted for short-term periods of between nine and eighteen months. Paradoxically, therefore, though historians have long held the view that 'credit was the very life-blood' of the colonies, it also remains true to state that 'money lending in colonial America has not received the attention it deserves'.[90]

It is ironic that Adam Smith's principal contention about the function of capital in the development of the sugar colonies has not been fully researched because historians, from Pares onwards, have generally accepted what Smith had to say about the form metropolitan credit took in the plantation economies. One consequence of Smith and Pares' legacy is that Henry Lascelles' West Indian loan portfolio is the only one that has thus far been reconstructed. Since there is no other example against which to compare the findings of this chapter, judging the representativeness of Lascelles' lending is problematic. His activities as a money lender, however, did not occur in isolation and a brief consideration of the context in which he operated suggests areas in which further research may be fruitful.

Though much remains to be learned about plantation finance during Caribbean sugar's mid-seventeenth-century 'golden age', and during the years leading up to Emancipation in 1834, there are strong grounds for

---

[89] Recent examples of research into transatlantic credit networks during the seventeenth and eighteenth centuries are Nuala Zahedieh, 'Credit, Risk, and Reputation in Late Seventeenth-Century Colonial Trade', in O. U. Janzen ed., *Merchant Organisation and Maritime Trade in the North Atlantic, 1660–1815*, Research in Maritime History, 15 (St John's, NF, 1998), 53–74, and Kenneth Morgan, 'Business Networks in the British Export Trade to North America, 1750–1800', in Kenneth Morgan and John J. McCusker eds., *The Early Modern Atlantic Economy* (Cambridge, 2000), 52–5.

[90] Davies, 'Origins of the Commission System', 92; Julian Gwyn, 'Money Lending in New England: The Case of Admiral Sir Peter Warren and his Heirs, 1739–1805', *New England Quarterly*, 44 (1991), 117. Money lending on security in New England is currently the subject of research being conducted by Winifred B. Rothenberg, 'Mortgage Credit and the Origins of a Capital Market: Middlesex County, Massachusetts, 1642–1773', paper presented to a joint seminar of the McNeill Center for Early American Studies and the Programme in Early American Economy and Society, December 2000.

believing that indebtedness characterised financial relations between planters and merchants at the beginning and end of the system of plantation slavery.[91] It is the eighteenth century, the middle period of sugar and slavery in the West Indies, about which least is known. Sugar planting experienced strong growth during the decades following the Treaty of Utrecht (1713), Pares' 'silver age' of sugar, and the years immediately after the slave rebellion on St Domingue (1791). Checkland and Price have suggested that during these booms lending to planters by metropolitan creditors took place on a large scale, and that lending was also heavy after the end of the War of the American Revolution and the abolition of the slave trade (1807).[92] The evidence for investment surges consists mainly of contemporary correspondence, pamphlets, and reports. In testimonies before the House of Commons, for example, it was reported in 1775 that half of an estimated £60 million invested in the sugar colonies was 'the immediate property of, or was owing to persons resident in this country', While in 1790 George Hibbert, a leading London sugar merchant, gave evidence that £20 million of debts were due from the West Indies to British creditors.[93]

Analysis of Henry Lascelles' West Indian loans suggests that lending to planters also grew rapidly during the later stages of the War of the Austrian Succession. The increased lending undertaken by Lascelles was associated with financial innovation in the form of the more extensive use of mortgages. In theory, legal changes – particularly the 1732 Colonial Debts Act and the 1745 case of *Brace* vs *Peers* – increased the attractiveness of mortgages on plantations to creditors, but it is significant that the mortgage's potential was not grasped fully by

---

[91] Pares, *Merchants and Planters*, 5, 49; Pares, *a West India Fortune*, 316–17; Elizabeth Donnan ed., *Documents Illustrative of the History of the Slave Trade to America* (4 vols., Washington DC, 1930–5), vol. I, 125; Richard Ligon, *A True and Exact History of the Island of Barbados* (London, 1970; originally published 1657 and 1673), 109–16; R. B. Sheridan, 'The West India Sugar Crisis and British Slave Emancipation, 1830–1833', *Journal of Economic History*, 31 (1961), 555–61; Kathleen Mary Butler, *The Economics of Emancipation: Jamaica and Barbados, 1823–1843* (Chapel Hill/London, 1995), 16–18, 52–7.

[92] Pares, *Merchants and Planters*, 27, 40; Price, 'Credit Plantation Economies', 329–30; Checkland, 'Finance West Indies', 462.

[93] Sheridan, 'British Credit Crisis', 165–6. Some statistical corroboration of these statements is provided by synchronous movements in colonial and English price indexes. It is notable, for example, that fluctuation in colonial land prices mirrored movements in British commodity prices during periods of intensive investment in sugar. Yet in the absence of reliable quantitative estimates of capital exports to the Caribbean, the evidence is at best impressionistic, John J. McCusker and Russell R. Menard, *The Economy of British America, 1607–1789* (Chapel Hill, 1985), 60–4; Emily Mechner, 'Pirates and Planters: Trade and Development in the Caribbean, 1492–1680', unpub. Ph.D. dissertation (University of Harvard, 1999), 66a, 68.

Lascelles prior to the war years. He initially employed the mortgage as a means of reducing risk at a time of economic and political uncertainty. During the peace that followed, however, the position of the mortgage in Lascelles' West Indian loan portfolio was consolidated and his lending reached unprecedented levels.

Expansionary forces were felt in all parts of the Atlantic trading economy in the quarter century before the American Revolution. In addition to Henry Lascelles' loans, there is more general evidence that, as the sugar trade expanded from the middle of the eighteenth century, long-term lending on the security of mortgages also grew in importance. Records of Dutch overseas investment are superior to British sources and they reveal that substantial capital flows to Surinam, Demerara, and Essequibo occurred after 1750, concentrated in the period from 1765 until 1775. Planters in these regions were granted long-term credit financed by mortgages raised by merchants in Amsterdam and Rotterdam. Interestingly, Dutch lending to the British West Indies, though only around one-twentieth of the total invested in the Caribbean region, followed a similar trend.[94]

Neither the activities of Henry Lascelles, nor the record of Dutch investors, are unequivocal regarding the origin of the funds invested in colonial staples. Not all of the capital sunk into Demerara and Essequibo, for example, was provided by Dutch financiers; indeed, investors in this region included Barbadian planters and merchants.[95] Nevertheless, despite its limitations, the evidence presented in this chapter indicates that a rebalancing of probabilities, and perhaps also an adjustment in priorities, is in order. Lascelles' accounts suggest that Adam Smith's image of an overflowing of British riches into the Caribbean was closer to the truth than Pares' insistence on ploughed-back profits. The pattern of Henry's lending, however, also provides a strong challenge to the thesis of both Smith and Pares that short-term credit extension, rather than longer-term lending on mortgage, fuelled

---

[94] J. P. Van De Voort, 'Dutch Capital in the West Indies during the Eighteenth Century', *Low Countries History Yearbook: Acta Historiae Neerlandicae*, 14 (1981), 84–105; Price, 'Credit Plantation Economies', 329.

[95] See e.g. the list of the names of plantation owners on the Rivers Demerara and Essequibo in 1759, LBMH, Correspondence Files, List of plantation owners in Guiana compiled by Gosta Simmons. The primary source used by Simmons is 'Map of River Demerary and Esequibo' (1759) by Laurens Lodewyk van Bercheyck, copy preserved at the *Bodel Nijenhuis Museum* in Leiden. Barbadian and Antiguan merchants and planters invested in capital-intensive land-reclamation schemes from 1741 onwards, Mohammed Shahabuddeen, *From Plantocracy to Nationalisation: A Profile of Sugar in Guyana* (Georgetown, 1983), 13.

the boom in sugar planting that occurred during the third quarter of the eighteenth century.[96]

Appendix

Table 6.9. *Alphabetical listing of the West Indian loans of Henry Lascelles, 1723–53*

Name and colony[a]	Year	Amount (£ stg)[b]	Security[c]	Interest rate (%)	Sources[d]
ADAMS, Conrad & SHURLAND, John (B)	1732	2,167	Exec	8	H, J, P
ADAMS, Conrad Jr & Sr, & ADAMS, Joseph (B)	1732	1,383	Exec	8	H, J, P
ADAMS, Conrad (B)	1743	286	Bond[e]	8	J
ALLEYNE, Abel, John, & Reynold (B)	1735	402	Bond	5	J
ALLEYNE, Abel (B)	1735	6,991	Exec	na	H, J
ALLEYNE, John & Reynold (B)	1736	395	Bond	8	J, L&M
ALLIN, Jacob (J)	1745	1,200	Mort	na	P
AUSTIN, Richard (B)	1747	101	Bond & Exec	na	H, P
BALL, Joseph (B)	1732	3,077	Mort	na	Q
BARWICK, Samuel & SHURLAND, John (B)	1732	510	Bond & Exec	8	J, H
	1750	340	Judge	8	
BRAITHWAITE, John (B)	1747	6,500	Judge	na	H, L&M, P
BRUCE, James, and	1752	7,579	Judge	8	P, Q
BRUCE, Joseph (B)	1753	6,000	Mort	na	
BRYANT, William (B)	1752	10,370	na	na	P
CARMICHAEL, Archibald (B)	1748	740	Bond & Exec	na	H
CHARNOCK, Benjamin (B)	1752	7,000	Bond & Judge	5	P
CLARKE, Gedney (B)	1744	5,000	Unsec	5	L&M, P
	1748	3,000	Unsec	5	
	1753	4,286	Exec & Mort	8	
DOTIN, John (B)	1749	3,600	Exec & Mort	8	J
	1752	1,700	Exec	8	

[96] In the case of the Thirteen Continental Colonies, Smith's analysis also appears misleading, but for different reasons. The balance of payments for the Thirteen Continental Colonies between 1768 and 1772 recorded only small deficits, James F. Shepherd and Gary M. Walton, *Shipping, Maritime Trade, and the Economic Development of Colonial North America* (Cambridge, 1972), 137–55; and *The Economic Rise of Early America* (Cambridge, 1979), 96–112. It is possible that Smith was unduly influenced by the overseas sector, since data of debt claims lodged after the Revolution suggest indebtedness to British creditors mainly resulting from short-term credit extension, Sheridan, 'British Credit Crisis', 179–83; Price, *Capital and Credit*, 5–19; Price, 'Credit Plantation Economies', 326–7.

Table 6.9 *(cont.)*

Name and colony[a]	Year	Amount (£ stg)[b]	Security[c]	Interest rate (%)	Sources[d]
FENWICK, Thomas & HARRISON, John (B)	1752	1,000	Bond	na	H
FINDLAY, Thomas (B)	1746	1,500	Judge & Mort	6	L&M, P
FORBES, Thomas (B)	1751	2,800	Bond, Exec, & Mort	5	H, J
FOSTER, George (B)	1723	424	Bond & Judge	na	Q
FOSTER, John (B)	1735	749	Exec	na	H
FRERE, John & APPLETHWAITE, Thomas (B)	1734	10,408	Bond & Exec	8	H, J
FRERE, John (B)	1734	4,757	Exec	5	H, J
FRERE, Tobias (B)	1747	2,500	Exec[f]	5	J
GIBBES, William (B)	1752	7,000	na	na	H, P
GOLLOP, John (B)	1750	3,214[g]	Exec & Mort	8	J, Q
GRASSET, James (B)	1746	4,000	Judge[h]	na	H
HARPER, Robert (B, J)	1733	615	Exec	na	H, N
	1744	105	Bond	na	
	1750	200	Mort	na	
HARPER, Thomasine (B)	1752	10,407	Exec	8	J, L&M, P
HARVIE, John & HARVIE, Alexander (J)	1752	10,124	na	na	L&M, P
HARVIE, William (B)	1743	4,000	Unsec	na	P
HAWKE, Edward (B)	1740	270	Unsec	na	P
HOTHERSALL, Burch (B)	1732	858	Bond	6	H, J
	1741	460	Bond	6	
	1746	502	Exec	5	
	1749	800	Mort	5	
	1749	1,400	Mort	5	
	1750	356	Mort	5	
HOLDEN, William (B)	1749	6,004	Exec	8	J
HOWELLS, John (B)	1730	1,700	Judge & Mort	na	Q
JORDAN, Major (B)	1740	2,000	Judge	na	P
LAKE, Thomas (B)	1751	2,000	Unsec	5	P
LESSLEY, Andrew (A)	1747	2,000	na	5	P
LYNCH, Joseph (B)	1747	3,750	Mort	na	H, L&M, P, Q
MACFARLANE, Alexander (J)	1753	15,000	Bond & Mort	8	P
MCCALL, Samuel (B)	1744	2,564	na	na	P
MAXWELL, George (B)	1741	1,000	Unsec	8[i]	J, P
MAYNARD, William & BULLARD, Eliza (B)	1751	1,879	Exec	8	J

Table 6.9 *(cont.)*

Name and colony[a]	Year	Amount (£ stg)[b]	Security[c]	Interest rate (%)	Sources[d]
NEWTON, Nicholas (J)	1745	2,000	Bond	5	P
	1748	1,500	Bond	5	
	1752	800	Mort	5	
OSBORNE, Samuel (B) OSBORNE, Samuel & OSBORNE, James (B)	1750	6,000	Exec & Mort	8	J
	1751	5,525	Exec & Mort	8	J
PETRIE, George John & HUNTER, Andrew (B)	1751	714	Bond	8	H, J
	1752	750	Bond	8	
RICE, Michael (B)	1744	1,000	na	5	P
SLINGSBY, Henry (B)	1743	5,263	Mort	na	H, L &M, P, Q
STEVENSON, Thomas (B)	1740	2,000	na	na	H, J, P
	1749	370	Bond	8	
	1752	2,460	Bond (Mort)[j]	5	
THORNHILL, Henry & BONNET, Mary (B)	1752	3,000	Exec	8	J, P, Q
WALKER, Alexander (B)	1739	4,210	Exec & Mort	6	H, J, Q
WALKER, William (B)	1733	932	Exec	10	H, P
	1733	491	Exec	8	
	1733	935	Exec	8	
	1741	1,610	Judge, Exec, Mort	8	
WALTER, Abel (B)	1741	1,429	Exec[k]	8	H, J, Q
WEEKES, Ralph (B)	1731	690	Exec	na	H, L&M
WILCOX, Nicholas (B)	1745	4,000	na	5–6	L&M, P
YOUNG, William (A)	1750	2,120	Judge & Mort	5–6	P

Notes and Sources: [a] A: Antigua. B: Barbados. J: Jamaica.

[b] In cases where the original source gave the amount in colonial currency, the sum has been converted to the sterling equivalent using the exchange rates published in McCusker, *Money and Exchange*, 241–4.

[c] Bond: penal bond. Exec: execution. Judge: judgement. Mort: mortgage. Unsec: unsecured.

[d] H: HH:WIP. Account Book or Journal of J: Henry Lascelles, 1753, see Chapter Four, fn. 97. L&M: *LMLB*. N: National Institute of Jamaica. P: Pares Transcripts. Q: BA, Hughes-Queree Collection, Abstracts in Queree notebooks.

[e] Upgraded to Exec 1751.

[f] Execution dated 1743 but assigned to Henry Lascelles 1747.

[g] Journal gives £3,214 and Queree £3,462.

[h] Judgement dated 1744 but assigned to Henry Lascelles 1746.

[i] Interest rate reduced to 5 per cent by 1753.

[j] To obtain this loan Stevenson was obliged to assign a debt secured by a mortgage to Henry Lascelles.

[k] Execution dated 1738 but assigned to Henry Lascelles 1741.

7   A Labyrinth of Debt

> & of what avail is it, if a Man is possessed of 20 Plantations, if when he
> dies, they are all to be sold to pay his Debts?
>
> (Daniel Lascelles to Thomas Harvie, 25 May 1767)[1]

By the end of the eighteenth century, the Earls of Harewood controlled one of the greatest of all West Indian interests (Table 7.1). But the Lascelles were reluctant planters: the family had never aspired to become large-scale, absentee owners of sugar estates. Indeed, between the laying of Harewood House's foundation stone in 1759 to the time Robert Adam's and John Carr's masterpiece was ready for occupation in 1771, neither Edwin Lascelles nor his brother Daniel possessed a single slave or acre in the West Indies.

The family's lack of ownership of West Indian estates during the 1760s and early 1770s is extraordinary given the acquisition of plantations on Barbados by Edward Lascelles in 1648 and William Lascelles in 1684.[2] Barbadian merchants never divorced themselves from land completely despite a general retreat from plantation ownership during the later seventeenth century. Characteristically, the island's wealthiest traders combined commercial careers with ownership of at least a single property. Possession of a sugar estate complemented the activities of slave trading and sugar exporting, while landownership raised the prospect of nomination to the Barbados Council, election to the Assembly, or judicial appointment to one of the island's courts.[3] Estates came into the hands of merchants in a variety of ways: by

---

[1] LMLB, Pares Transcripts, H680, B, f. 24.
[2] See Chapter Three.
[3] [Barbados], *Acts of Assembly, 1717–1738* (2 vols., London, 1732, 1739), 'Act establishing the Courts of Common Pleas, 29 August 1661', 13–18; [Thomas Hodges], *Plantation Justice, Shewing the Constitution of their Courts, and What Sort of Judges They Have in Them* (London, 1701), 3–4, 9–10. Hodges' account is highly critical of Barbados' legal system, but stresses the role played by merchants and planters in the legal establishment.

Table 7.1. *Acquisition of West Indian estates, 1773–1818*

Year acquired (and debtor)	Name of estate (and colony)	Acreage	Slaves	Value (£)
1773 (Clarke)	Clarke's Court (G)	800	211	41,250 cy
1777 (Harvie)	Mammee Ridge (J)	1,000	98	20,356 cy
1777 (Harvie)	Nightingale (J)[a]	285	140	26,151 cy
1777 (Harvie)	Oldfield's Bog (J)[*a]	4,985	53	see Nightingale
1777 (Harvie)	Angel Pen (J)	70	0	420 cy
1777 (Harvie)	Williamsfield (J)[b]	1,440	272	40,671 cy
1777 (Harvie)	The Crawl (J)[+b]	1,250	0	see Williamsfield
1777 (Harvie)	Pedros Valley (J)[+]	11,400	0	see Williamsfield
1777 (Sober)	Castle (B)[*]	363	206	9,715 stg[e]
1777 (Alleyne)	Turner's Hall (B)[*]	187	180	10,514 stg[f]
1779 (Clarke)	Belle (B)	537	232	36,965 cy
1779 (Blenman)	Holetown (B)[c]	239	132	8,000 stg[h]
1781 (Clarke)	Richmond (T)[d]	648	163	16,843 stg[g]
1781 (Clarke)	Bushy Park (T)	500	30	4,969 stg[g]
1781 (Clarke)	Goodwood (T)	576	110	11,874 stg[g]
1784 (Blenman)	Cooper's Hill (B)[c]	301	101	12,469 cy
1784 (Blenman)	Mount (B)	292	120	13,191 cy
1784 (Blenman)	Kirtons (B)	181	79	9,434 cy
1785 (Blenman)	Mesopotamia (T)	500	120	16,752 cy
1787 (Frere)	Fortescue (B)[e]	169	132	14,543 cy
1787 (Frere)	Thicket (B)[e]	584	244	48,425 cy
1787 (Frere)	Pot House (B)[e]	72	14	3,476 cy
1787 (Frere)	Pilgrim (B)	226	93	19,412 cy
1788 (Beckles)	Maxwell's (B)[*]	450	217	26,457 cy
Total to 1788		*27,055*	*2,947*	*c. 293,166 stg*
1815	Sandy Gut (J)[b]	743	110	16,635 cy
1818	Glamorgan (T)[d]	575	>24	10,000 cy

Notes: B = Barbados, G = Grenada, J = Jamaica, T = Tobago.

[a,b,c,d]Related properties.

[e]Slaves only.

[f]Amount of security offered to Lascelles & Daling in 1770.

[g]Amount of security offered to Lascelles & Daling, 1772–3.

[h]1753 valuation.

[*]Estate managed by Lascelles' agents for a loan client.

[+]Undeveloped property or patented land. Exchange rate conversions: Barbados £1.39 = £1.00 sterling; Jamaica £1.40 currency = £1.00 sterling; Grenada £1.60 = £1.00 sterling; Tobago £1.65 = £1.00 sterling, John J. McCusker, *Money and Exchange in Europe and America, 1600–1775* (Cambridge, 1978), 244, 253, 272–4.

Source: BA, Hughes-Queree Collection, Abstract in Queree notebook, 'Belle', 'Castle', 'Cooper's Hill', 'Fortescue', 'Frere Pilgrim', 'Thicket'; RB3/146/349, An Inventory and Valuation of the Negroes on the Plantation of John Sober Esq. called the Castle,

purchase, by foreclosing on loans to planters, and by marriage or inheritance.

Edward Lascelles of Stoke Newington attempted to obtain Guinea estate in St John's, Barbados, in lieu of debt early in the eighteenth century (Map 2).[4] His nephew and namesake, Edward Lascelles (half-brother of Henry Lascelles), succeeded in obtaining this plantation in 1734, by prosecuting his wife Frances' claim against the estate and forcing her brother, Joseph Ball, to sell Guinea to him.[5] A year prior to

Note to Table 7.1 (*cont.*)

12 November 1777; RB3/193/204–15; RB3/193/185, Indenture between Applethwaite Frere and Edwin Lascelles, 22 October 1787, 'Pilgrim'; Indenture between Henry Frere and Edwin Lascelles, 'Fortescue', 'Thicket', 'Pot House'; HH:WIP, A list of papers belonging to Edward Lascelles Esq. as executor of the Right Honourable Edwin, Lord Harewood deceased [n.d., 1796], 9 'Maxwell's', 11 'Richmond', 'Greenwood', 'Bushy Park', 16 'Castle', 21 'Clarke's Court', 27 'Pilgrim', 'Fortescue', 'Thicket', 'Pot House', 28 'Mount'; Correspondence, John Cobham (Barbados) to John Wood Nelson (London), 13 October 1801; Statement of the indebtedness of Timothy Blenman deceased [n.d., c. 1785] 'Mesopotamia'; Sketch of Account from Nathaniel Elliot of William Blenman and Jonathan (Blenman) with Lord Harewood, [n.d., 1784], 'Cooper's Hill', 'Kirton's', 'Mount'; List of Judgements on Record in the Island of Tobago against Gedney Clarke Esq. (n.d., c. 1774); WRA, Letters and Papers on West India Estates and Affairs, 1795–1873, Valuation of Sandy Gut estate, 1815; Accession 2,677, Conveyance of Estates in Jamaica in consideration of debts owed by the late Thomas Harvie to Daniel Lascelles, 20 June 1777, 'Nightingale Grove'; Indenture between William Harvie *et al.*, Daniel Lascelles, Richard Lewing & Peter Ramsay, 31 November 1777, 'Williamsfield', 'Angel Pen', 'Nightingale Grove', 'Mammee Ridge', 'Oldfields Bog', 'The Crawl', 'Pedros Valley' Island Record Office, Spanish Town, Jamaica, Deeds 287/207, Indenture between William Harvie *et al.*, Richard Lewing & Peter Ramsay, 22 November 1777, same properties as preceding source; NA:PRO, C12/1388/34, *Elizabeth March* vs *Daniel Lascelles* (1773–4), 'Oldfields Bog'; Derbyshire Record Office, Buxton, Fitzherbert West India Papers, D239 M/E 20479–80, Lease and counterpart by William Fitzherbert Sr and Jr, 30 June 1770; Lieutenant Daniel Paterson, *A Topographical Description of the Island of Grenada; Surveyed by Monsieur Pinel in 1763* (London, 1780), 6, 'Clarke's Court'; Account Book of Henry Lascelles (1753), 'Holetown'; Institute of Commonwealth Studies, London, ICS 101, Wemyss Castle Estate Papers, Extract of deeds sent to Francis Graeme by Mr Millward, 26 March 1806, 'Oldfield's Bog', 'Williamsfield and the Crawl', 'Angel's Pen', 'Nightingale Grove', 'Mamme Ridge', 'Pedros Valley'.

---

[4] BA, RB3/24/378 and 380, Indentures between Guy Ball and Edward Lascelles (1701 and 1708); NA:PRO, C11/2238/5 (1715). In addition to Guinea, Edward Lascelles also held a mortgage lien over Netherlands plantation (St Philip's), Bobby Morris, 'Transfer of Wealth from Barbados to England – From Lascelles Plantation, Barbados to Harewood House, Yorkshire', *JBMHS*, 50 (2004), 92.
[5] BA, RB1/82/184; RB1/83/185; RB1/83/186; RB1/83/187, Indentures between Joseph Ball and Edward Lascelles, 1734.

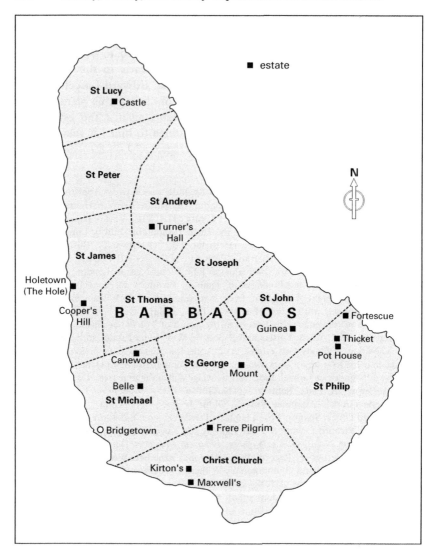

Map 2. Barbadian estates owned or managed by the Lascelles.

his death in 1747, Edward gained control of a second estate from the Balls called Canewood. This property, of 102 acres and sixty-seven slaves, was mortgaged to secure a debt of £3,000.[6] Henry Lascelles

---

[6] BA, RB3/38/50, Indenture between Joseph Young and Edward Lascelles (1746). After Edward's decease, Canewood and Guinea were managed by Francis Holburne, who

likewise acquired a limited amount of landed property on Barbados. In 1738, he obtained 155 acres of Holetown plantation from the estate of debtor Robert Warren (deceased).[7] The scale of operations at Holetown were expanded during the mid-1740s, when the nearby sugar estate of Cooper's Hill (also known as Walwyn's) was managed as a single unit alongside Lascelles' property.[8]

The loan client Robert Warren provided the Lascelles with more than just debt interest. After his death, *The Barbados Gazette* paid tribute to this artful island lawyer in a double-edged obituary:

He had practised as an Attorney-at-Law here, for nigh thirty Years, and was in very great Business almost the whole Time; so that 'tis supposed he must have acquired a vast Fortune, no body having better Opportunities in that Way, or knowing better how to improve them. As the Business and Affairs of most of the Gentlemen and Families in the Island have occasionally gone through his Hands, his Character cannot but be well known.[9]

During Robert Lowther's governorship, Warren was implicated in the Bernard Cook affair of 1719, along with Guy Ball.[10] Further evidence of an alignment with the Lascelles brothers is provided by his opposition to Governor Worsley and the SPG.[11] Warren was also a persistent adversary of Jonathan Blenman; the two men clashed repeatedly over the Burch Hothersall financial scandal, the recall of Governor Worsley, and the Act of Settlement and Excise controversies of the 1730s.[12] On the issue

---

married the widowed Frances Lascelles, CKS, Greenville-Buckingham MS, U1590, S2/07, Minutes of the Court of Exchequer in Barbados, 1747–53, *Stone* vs *Holburne*, 2 October 1751; LMLB, Pares Transcripts, W&G I, Henry Lascelles to Francis Holburne (Barbados), 16 November 1751, 21 November 1751.

[7] BA, Hughes-Queree Collection, Abstract in Queree notebook.

[8] Ibid. 'Holetown'; NA:PRO, PROB11/804, Will of Henry Lascelles (1753); *LMLB*, Pares Transcripts, W&G I, f. 112, Henry Lascelles & Son to Thomas Applethwaite (Barbados), October 1740, f. 161, 6 November 1740, f. 210, 20 February 1740(1). For more information about Cooper's Hill, see below. Henry Lascelles also purchased Pasfield's estate (St Philip's) in 1748 for £3,750. This property was immediately resold to Joseph Lynch on a mortgage, Hughes-Queree, 'Pasfields'; *LMLB*, Lascelles & Maxwell to Joseph Lynch, 20 September 1743; same to same, 17 January 1743(4).

[9] [Samuel Keimer], *Caribbeana* (2 vols., London, 1741), vol. II, 88.

[10] See below.

[11] Edward Lascelles provided Warren's security after his appointment as Registrar of the Court of Vice Admiralty in 1733, [Keimer], *Caribbeana*, vol.II, 88; Barbados Public Library, Bridgetown, Barbados, Lucas Manuscripts, Council Minutes, f. 360, Securities given for officials, 29 December 1733. See also Derbyshire Record Office, Buxton, Fitzherbert West India Papers, D239 M/E 20504, (William Henry) Warren to William Fitzherbert, 24 February 1750(1).

[12] Blenman accused Warren of alleged abuses of legal process to delay suits and obstruction of attempts to regulate fees charged by public officials, BA, Hughes-Queree Collection, Abstract in Queree notebook, 'Mangrove Pond'; John Poyer, *The History of*

of debtors and creditors, however, Warren demonstrated a notably
independent streak, joining the lobby against the 1732 Colonial Debts
Act, which Henry Lascelles strongly supported.[13] Whether this action
prompted the initiation of foreclosure proceedings against him is
unknown.

Despite acquiring Barbadian property during the course of business,
neither Henry nor Edward Lascelles pursued a sustained policy of
land purchases. The brothers preferred to invest in a range of interrelated
commercial and financial projects, rather than tie up resources in large
estate holdings. They declined to add to their portfolios even when
seemingly favourable opportunities arose to buy up property. In 1743, for
example, Henry eschewed purchasing Grove estate, when the island's
Provost Marshall sold off the property to satisfy claims against John
Howell.[14] From the 1730s onwards, rather than accumulating sugar
estates himself, Henry Lascelles began extending loans to planters
secured by mortgages. At his death in 1753, he had approximately
£194,000 (sterling) out on loan to clients in Barbados and Jamaica.
A significant and sustained extension of long-term credit, however,
was not accompanied by growth in Henry's personal ownership of
plantations.

After their deaths, the limited amount of real property accumulated
by the brothers was disposed of. Guinea, the most valuable estate, was
sold in 1758, just prior to the construction starting on Harewood
House.[15] The policy of West Indian lending without direct investment in

Barbados (London, 1808), 264, 280–1. Warren's associates included the lawyer
Gelasius MacMahon, who was tried controversially on Barbados for the murder of
Thomas Keeling in 1734, convicted of manslaughter and pardoned by President Joseph
Dotin, John Oldmixon, *The British Empire in America* (2nd edn, 2 vols., London, 1741),
vol. II, 90, 93–4; Poyer *History of Barbados*, 281–2, 289–90. Arthur Holt described
MacMahon as 'the lead man of the discontented party' against Worsley, John A. Schutz
and Maud O'Neil, 'Arthur Holt, Reports on Barbados, 1725–33', *Journal of Negro
History*, 31 (1946), Arthur Holt (Barbados) to the Bishop of London [Edmund Gibson],
4 October 1731, 463–4. Warren was linked to the Lascelles by kinship: he married
Mary Doldane, niece of George Lascelles (1681–1728/9)'s wife, Morris, 'Transfer of
Wealth', 94.

[13] Robert H. Schomburgk, *The History of Barbados* (London, 1971, 1999; originally
published 1848), 318; NA:PRO, CO28/23, Humble Representation of the President,
Councill and the Generall Assembly of the Island of Barbados to the Commisioners for
Trade and Plantations, 23 January 1732[3]; Leo Francis Stock ed., *Proceedings and
Debates of the British Parliaments Respecting North America* (5 vols., Washington DC,
1924–41), vol. IV, 160.

[14] BA, Hughes-Queree Collection, Abstract in Queree notebook, 'Grove'.

[15] Ibid. 'Guinea'. The plantation was sold to George Walker for £23,500 (currency), of
which £20,000 was a mortgage debt due to the estate of Edward Lascelles (deceased).
By 1769, the debt had been reduced to £7,000.

sugar estates was continued by Henry's son Daniel Lascelles, senior partner of Lascelles & Maxwell. In 1757, for example, Martin's Castle (mortgaged by the Atherley family of Barbados) was taken for debt; it was held by agent Thomas Stevenson for three years, then sold to the Revd Edward Brace.[16] Bagdale estate in Jamaica was likewise taken from Nicholas Newton in 1761 (after he was unable to keep up payments on a mortgage of £4,071), but then sold immediately to the London merchants Thomas Collet and John Powell. In both cases, the option of retaining ownership of the properties was rejected.[17]

While no systematic record exists of Daniel Lascelles' loan accounts, a consolidation of surviving sources indicates that by the mid-1770s he had advanced at least £360,000 (sterling) to borrowers in the West Indies (Table 7.2). The Appendix, Table 7.7, lists all known debtors and the value of their outstanding loans at benchmark dates. Adjusting for price changes, lending in real terms multiplied by more than one-and-a-half-times between 1753 and 1773. The Lascelles had become one of the greatest financiers of the West Indian plantocracy despite owning very few plantations themselves.

Then suddenly, between 1773 and 1787, more than 27,000 acres were added to the family's West Indian land portfolio. In just fourteen years, the Lascelles not only acquired property on Barbados, but also built up significant holdings in Jamaica and on the newly acquired British colonies of Grenada and Tobago.[18] For the remainder of the period of enslavement,

---

[16] HH:WIP, A list of papers belonging to Edwin Lascelles Esq. as executor of the Right Honourable Edwin Lord Harewood deceased [n.d., c. 1796] f. 6; *LMLB* Pares Transcripts, H624, f. 50, Lascelles & Maxwell to Thomas Stevenson (Barbados), 5 February 1757; H634, f. 103, same to same, 6 December 1760. Tobias Frere was owed £4,500 currency by John Atherley secured on the estate. Acceptance of Martin's Castle at its appraised value (£5,800 currency) helped Frere liquidate this debt, since he was himself a debtor of the Lascelles (see below). Brace could not keep up payments on Martin's Castle; in 1767 it was sold again to Thomas Payne, who owed £3,848 sterling in 1769, *LMLB*, Pares Transcripts, B, f. 29, Daniel Lascelles to Gedney Clarke (Barbados), 11 June 1767; HH:WIP, List of debts due Lascelles and Maxwell [n.d., c. 1769].

[17] National Library of Jamaica, Kingston, Jamaica, MS 1, 142, Indenture dated 24 July 1760 between (1) Daniel Lascelles and George Maxwell, (2) Nicholas Newton, (3) Thomas Collet and John Powell, and (4) Florentius Vassall.

[18] 'Lassel' plantation is depicted in Charles Bockhardt's 'A New and Exact Map of Jamaica' (1684). The property probably belonged to James Lascelles. In 1675, Lascelles was awarded a patent by the Jamaica Assembly for constructing a sugar mill with an extra set of rollers; in 1678, he was customs controller at Ferry Road, Carl Bridenbaugh and Roberta Bridenbaugh, *No Peace Beyond the Line: The English in the Caribbean, 1624–1690* (New York, 1972), 202–3, 293. No connection has been discovered between this individual and the Lascelles of Northallerton and Harewood. He may be connected

Table 7.2. *Capital out on loan in the West Indies, 1769–77 (£ sterling)*

Debtor	Locations of mortgaged property	Amount of indebtedness (principal plus interest)
Gedney Clarkes	Barbados, Grenada, Tobago	130,484
Harvies	Jamaica	64,694
Freres	Barbados	28,799
Blenmans	Barbados, Tobago	22,952
Sobers	Barbados	9,406
Stevensons	Barbados	8,960
Beckles	Barbados	7,258
Others (n = 24)	Mainly Barbados, some Jamaica and Grenada	82,984
Estimated under-recording[a]		13,203
Estimated total lending		*368,740*

Source: See Appendix, Table 7.7
Note: [a]There are twenty-two debts recorded in 1769 and twenty-six in 1777. Of the 1777 debts, thirteen do not appear in the 1769 list and only two give details of the amount of the loan (this excludes the debts of the Clarkes, Harvies, Freres, Blenmans, Sobers, Stevensons, and Beckles). To correct for under-recording, it was assumed that the average size of loans in 1777 was the same as 1769 (£3,300).

the Earls of Harewood remained large-scale planters, characteristically owning estates on more than one island.

Harewood House's association with slavery, therefore, arguably came about through historical accident. Following Henry Lascelles' death in 1753, the bulk of his estate was divided between his two eldest sons, Edwin and Daniel. Edwin Lascelles received a university education, toured Europe, and was elected MP for Scarborough. After a brief but distinguished military service (an honourable discharge was earned for his part in defeating the Jacobites in 1745), Edwin was installed as Lord of the Manors of Gawthorpe and Harewood a few years prior to his father's death.[19] Daniel's institution as the co-partner of George Maxwell came

with an independent line of Lascelles that is known to have resided on Jamaica during the eighteenth century; Charles Lascelles (1714–51), merchant of Kingston, and Anne Lassells (who c. 1743 married the novelist Tobias Smollett, probably on Jamaica) are among the representatives of this family, see *ODNB* and Lewis M. Knapp, 'Ann Smollett, wife of Tobias Smollett', *Pierpoint Morgan Library Annual Report*, 45 (1930), 1,035–49.

[19] John Venn and J. A. Venn, *Alumni Cantabrigienses* (2 parts in 10 vols., Cambridge, 1922–54), part 1, 48; Mary Mauchline, *Harewood House: One of the Treasure Houses of Britain* (2nd edn, Derbyshire, 1992), 15, 27. Edwin Lascelles was installed as Lord of the

about in August 1750, when Henry Lascelles nominally retired from business.[20] Almost certainly Henry had intended his younger son to play an active part in managing the family's West Indian concerns earlier than this. In either 1739 or 1740 (possibly coinciding with his arrival from Barbados), Daniel had joined the firm aged twenty-five or twenty-six.[21] The move to London proved disastrous: in September 1740, Daniel married Elizabeth Southwick clandestinely. On discovering the union, an enraged Henry cut his son out of the business. The marriage proved short-lived. By January 1741, Daniel had left his wife and sought a reconciliation with his father. To broaden his education and commercial experience (and also doubtless to remove him from temptation), Daniel was sent on a tour of Italy and France. Once this was completed, he left for the East Indies in 1742 and remained there until 1750.[22] Daniel was readmitted to the firm as partner only once his marriage was on the brink of dissolution.[23]

The death of Daniel Lascelles in 1784 (heirless), coupled with the death in 1786 of his younger brother Henry (also childless), brought about a forced reunification of a family fortune that had been split deliberately into separate English and West Indian components. Upon Edwin's own death in 1795, the Harewood estate passed to his cousin, Edward Lascelles, the Barbadian-born eldest son of old Henry's half-brother Edward. This line of succession resulted in the consolidation of all the West Indian interests

Manor by 1748, probably at the time his marriage settlement with Elizabeth Dawes was drawn up in January 1746, *Milner vs Lord Harewood*, 18 Vesey Junior 269, *English Law Reports*, vol. XXXIV (1789–1817).

[20] WRA, Harewood Accession 2,677, Deed of partnership between Daniel Lascelles and George Maxwell (1750).

[21] Richard Pares, 'A London West-India Merchant House, 1740–1769', in Richard Pares and A. J. P. Taylor eds., *Essays Presented to Sir Lewis Namier* (London, 1956), 75.

[22] Parliamentary Archives, HL/PO/PB/1/1751/25G2n79, 'An Act to dissolve the Marriage of Daniel Lascelles of London, Merchant, with Elizabeth Southwicke, his now Wife, and to enable him to marry again; and for other Purposes therein mentioned'. The author is grateful to Karen Lynch for providing this reference.

[23] The Act granting Daniel's divorce came into force in November 1751. According to the divorce petition, Elizabeth was guilty of adultery and 'had before the said Marriage entered into and lived in an unlawfull ffamiliarity with Henry Parminter of Lincolns Inn ffields Esquire', Ibid.; Parliamentary Archives, HL/PO/JO/3/245/39. It is impossible to be certain whether this allegation was true. In many divorce cases, women agreed (or were coerced, owing to lack of financial resources) into admitting adultery in return for a settlement. Elizabeth's subsequent fate makes for sad reading. She was repeatedly committed to the Fleet Prison for debt in 1760 and 1761. The schedule of her personal estate reveals that all of her possessions (including an annuity of £100 per annum, presumably part of the financial settlement) were either pawned or seized to pay landlords and other creditors. Elizabeth's portrait, 'set in Gold & a fine India white satin Counterpane', alluded to finer days; it was pledged for £6, CLRO, Insolvent Debtors' Schedules, DS 15/10 Fleet, Elizabeth Lascelles, divorcee of Stafford Row, 23 June 1761.

accumulated by the family from the early eighteenth century onwards into a single settlement trust. Thus was plantation aristocracy established at Harewood.

Dynastic accident alone, however, cannot account for the abrupt transformation that occurred in the family's ownership of sugar estates. In 1784, Edwin Lascelles assumed control of a Caribbean business interest that was in the process of being fundamentally reshaped. The credit crisis of 1772–3, followed swiftly by the American Revolutionary War (1776–83), confronted plantation agriculture with the challenge of altered commercial and political realities. In response to these stimuli, the Lascelles sought a realignment of their operations, rather than a withdrawal from West Indian concerns. Their new strategy comprised taking over the management of plantations formerly under the control of their business associates. The policy devised by Henry Lascelles, and continued by his son Daniel, of lending on perpetual mortgages was abandoned. Henceforth, credit was extended in the form of working capital, or assistance to purchasers to whom the Lascelles wished to sell estates. In the latter case, loans were made with fixed instalment terms; repayment mortgages replaced perpetual mortgages.

In 1787, the Lascelles' direct ownership of real estate in the West Indies reached its zenith. Four major blocks of creditors account for all of the property acquired between 1773 and this date. From the Gedney Clarkes, the family obtained five plantations, comprising 3,061 acres, split between Barbados, Grenada, and Tobago. In terms of land, the largest set of debtors were the Harvie brothers, who surrendered 20,430 acres of Jamaican property to the Lascelles (Maps 3 and 4). Most of their holdings, however, consisted of undeveloped land: measured by value, three estates of 2,795 acres formed the bulk of their assets. From the Blenman family, five properties containing a total of 1,513 acres were taken on Barbados and Tobago. Lastly, the Freres ceded four Barbadian estates occupying 1,051 acres.

In addition to lands seized outright, the Lascelles gained control of three further Barbadian estates from their debtors, as mortgagee in possession.[24] Castle (363 acres), Turner's Hall (upwards of 187 acres), and Maxwell's (449 acres) were by the 1770s heavily mortgaged

---

[24] For details of legal possession as an alternative to foreclosure, see Kathleen Mary Butler, *The Economics of Emancipation: Jamaica and Barbados, 1823–1843* (Chapel Hill/London, 1995), 45–6. Butler comments that during the 1820s, 'Problems involving legal title and the capital needed to put a run-down estate back in working order discouraged many creditors from taking possession of their debtors' property' (46). The Lascelles appear also to have regarded possession as an inferior option to foreclosure during the 1770s and 1780s.

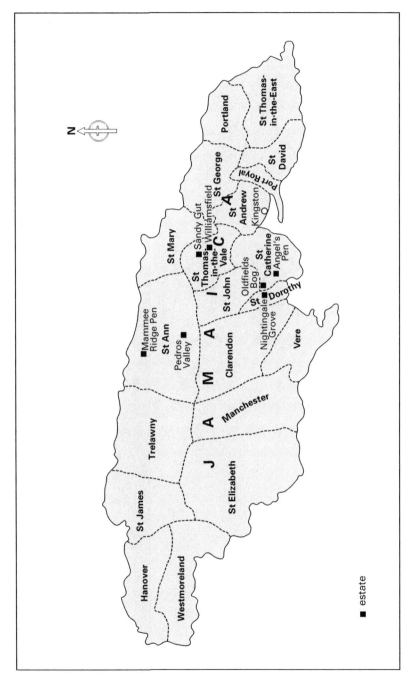

Map 3. Jamaican estates owned or managed by the Lascelles.

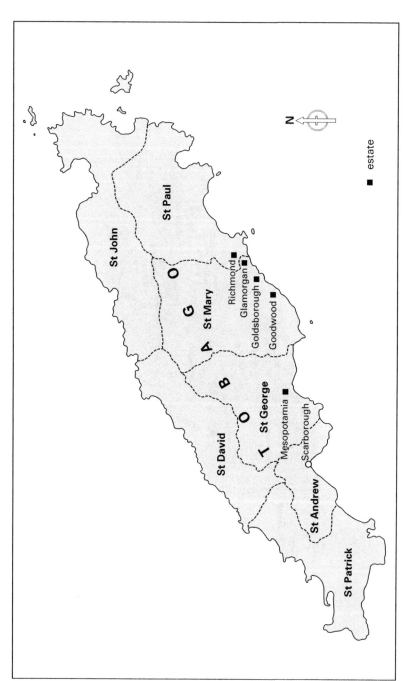

St John

St Paul

St David

T O B A G O

St Mary

Richmond
Glamorgan
Goldsborough
Goodwood

St George

Mesopotamia
Scarborough

St Andrew

St Patrick

N

■ estate

Map 4. Tobagonian estates owned or managed by the Lascelles.

to the Lascelles, for £9,406, £10,514, and £7,258 respectively.[25] Notionally these estates remained in the hands of the Sober, Alleyne/ Fitzherbert, and Beckles families, but decisions about the management of each plantation were taken by agents appointed by the Lascelles.[26] If these three estates are included, by 1787 a total of twenty-four Caribbean properties were directly owned or controlled by the Lascelles, covering 27,055 acres. Excluding patented land and undeveloped estates, twenty-two properties remain, worth approximately £293,000 (sterling) and comprising 14,405 acres and 2,947 slaves.

By no means all plantations secured by mortgages were taken into possession from debtors during the 1770s and 1780s. It is clear, however, that a far-reaching rescheduling of debts occurred between these decades. In cases where buyers and assignees could be found, heavily mortgaged estates were disposed of. The Walker-Walton families pledged Mount Wilton (Barbados) to secure loans; by the early nineteenth century, their debt had been assigned to the Daniels of Bristol and London.[27] In 1787, Evan Ballie (another Bristol merchant) assumed a debt owing from the estate of James Simmons (deceased), charged on his Grenada plantation.[28] To satisfy the debt owed by the Husbands family of Barbados, a portion of their Rendevous estate was sold, though most of the property was retained.[29] The Stevenson's Pool plantation also escaped

[25] Lascelles & Maxwell acted as the London agents for Turner's Hall from 1750, Derbyshire Record Office, Fitzherbert West India Papers, D239 M/E 20,504, Warren (Bath) to William Fitzherbert, 24 February 1750(1); D239 M/E 20,505, Lascelles & Maxwell to William Fitzherbert, 23 February 1750(1). The estate was mortgaged to secure a debt to Lascelles & Daling between 1770 and 1781, D239 M/E 20, 479, Lease and counterpart, 30 June 1770; E20,481, Lease and release, 10 December 1781. Castle was mortgaged by John Sober in 1777 to secure £9,406; by his death in 1784 the debt had grown to £13,805, BA, Hughes-Queree Collection, Abstract in Queree notebook, 'Ellis Castle (aka Sober Castle)'; HH:WIP, Correspondence, Sobers to Lord Harewood, 13 October 1800. Maxwell's was formed out of two properties; in 1789, a trust was created to manage the estate and to pay Edwin Lascelles interest on his debt and an allowance for managing the plantation, HH:WIP, List of debts due Edwin Lord Harewood; A list of papers belonging to Edward Lascelles Esq. as executor of the Right Honourable Edwin Lord Harewood deceased, f. 9.

[26] BA, Hughes-Queree Collection, Abstract in Queree notebook, 'Maxwell's'; HH:WIP, Correspondence, Elizabeth Beckles to Edward Lascelles, 30 May 1795; Acknowledgement of dismissal by John Prettyjohn, 17 July 1795; Nelson to Lord Harewood, 6 and 8 July 1799.

[27] BA, Hughes-Queree Collection, Abstract in Queree notebook, 'Mount Wilton'; HH:WIP, List of debts due the estate of henry Lascelles [n.d., c. 1769]; List of debts due to Lascelles & Maxwell [n.d., c. 1774]; List of specialities of Lascelles & Daling [n.d., c. 1784].

[28] WRA, Harewood Accession 2,677, Indenture between William Daling and Evan Ballie, 1 October 1787.

[29] BA, Hughes-Queree Collection, Abstract in Queree notebook, 'Husbands-Jordans'; HH:WIP, List of debts due to Lascelles & Maxwell [n.d., c. 1774]; List of specialities of

repossession; nevertheless, this Barbadian property, along with their Whim estate on Tobago, remained burdened with debt, and both were the subject of recovery suits in 1779 and 1789.[30] Sir Phillip Gibbes also struggled, but he managed to cling on to his Barbadian Springhead plantation. By 1820, Gibbes' account with the Lascelles was finally clear of debt and on his death in 1825 he was able to bequeath the estate to his grandson largely free of encumbrances.[31] The Greens were less fortunate. Land from Cotton Tree Hall in Barbados had to be sold in 1788 to satisfy their creditors.[32] On Jamaica, while James Prevost mortgaged his 190-acre pen called Stalford's to Daniel Lascelles in 1775, he avoided having to surrender the property.[33]

After 1773, relations between debtors and the Lascelles were reformulated as fresh lending ceased and pressure to repay loans intensified. Debtors were confronted by foreclosure proceedings and threatened with the loss of their mortgaged estates. The abrupt shift in the family's business strategy raises some crucial questions. Why did so many foreclosures take place during the 1770s, reversing a policy of credit extension that had begun in the 1730s? And why, in a majority of cases, did foreclosure result in the assumption of direct ownership of estates, rather than the resale or remortgaging of properties to new owners?

The literature on slavery discusses the financial health of planters during this period in the context of a decline paradigm. A school of interpretation, co-founded by Ragatz and Williams, regards the colonial wars and financial crises of the later eighteenth century as marking the beginning of the end of plantation agriculture. Scholars subscribing

---

Lascelles & Daling [n.d., c. 1784]; List of debts due Edwin Lord Harewood, 1796; large bundle of papers relating to the Husbands family and Rendevous estate, 1764–72.

[30] BA, Hughes-Queree Collection, Abstract in Queree notebook, 'Pool'; HH:WIP, A list of papers belonging to Edward Lascelles Esq. as executor of the Right Honourable Edwin Lord Harewood deceased [n.d., c. 1796], ff. 1, 2–3, 6. By c. 1800, Whim was owned by Charles and James Hamilton, HH: WIP, Correspondence, page layout for a plantation journal modelled on Whim plantation in Tobago [n.d., c. 1800]. See below for more details of financial relations between the Stevensons and Lascelles.

[31] BA, Hughes-Queree Collection, Abstract in Queree notebook, 'Springfield'; HH:WIP, List of debts due the estate of Henry Lascelles [n.d., c. 1769]; List of specialities of Lascelles & Daling [n.d., c. 1784]; List of debts due Edwin Lord Harewood, 1796; WRA, Letters and Papers on West India Estates and Affairs, 1795–1873, List of debts received since the death of Edwin Lord Harewood, 30 April 1820. On Phillip Gibbes, see J. Harry Bennett, *Bondsmen and Bishops: Slavery and Apprenticeship on the Codrington Plantations of Barbados, 1710–1838* (Berkeley, 1958).

[32] BA, Hughes-Queree Collection, Abstract in Queree notebook, 'Cotton Tree Hall'; HH:WIP, A list of papers belonging to Edward Lascelles Esq. as executor of the Right Honourable Edwin Lord Harewood deceased [n.d., c. 1796], f. 23.

[33] Island Record Office, Spanish Town, Jamaica, Deeds 274/35, Indenture between James Prevost and wife, and Daniel Lascelles, 5 September 1775.

to this view argue that Napoleon's Continental Blockade (1806–12), and the abolition of the slave trade in 1807, landed the final blows to an institution already on its knees, weakened by the Seven Years' War (1756–63) and the War of the American Revolution (1776–83).[34] Opposing the decline thesis are historians acknowledging that the years of war were difficult ones for planters, but who perceive the problem as one of short-term difficulties, resulting in successful restructuring and the continued viability of the plantation trades.[35] The financial health of planters remains a matter of debate. A study of a sample of properties, for example, suggests continuing profitability throughout the period of slavery; in contrast, an analysis of Jamaican sugar prices and slave valuations concludes that a marked deterioration in prospects occur- red.[36] Examination of the Lascelles' own relationships with indebted planters cannot in itself resolve this long-standing conundrum. Never- theless, the decline debate helps to inform analysis of debt and credit, while the Harewood case study provides a valuable, perhaps even unique, perspective on the condition of West Indian finance at a critical period in the history of Caribbean slavery. Two alternative interpreta- tions of events are possible. Firstly, the Lascelles may have been com- pelled, out of necessity, to foreclose on clients who were insolvent. In the absence of a viable alternative, the family assumed direct control of estates heavily encumbered with debt. This hypothesis is consistent with the Ragatz interpretation of decline. Yet a second explanation is also possible. Foreclosure and the assumption of managerial control could have formed part of a planned restructuring of the family's West Indian interest – a conclusion more consistent with the anti-Ragatz position.

This chapter investigates the relationship between the Lascelles and their four largest Caribbean debtors. In addition to the quartet of families whose mortgaged properties account for the bulk of the Lascelles'

---

[34] Lowell J. Ragatz, *The Fall of the Planter Class in the British Caribbean, 1763–1833: A Study in Social and Economic History* (New York, 1928); Eric Williams, *Capitalism and Slavery* (Chapel Hill, 1944). This thesis has been restated by Selwyn H. H. Carrington, *The Sugar Industry and the Abolition of the Slave Trade, 1775–1810* (Gainesville, 2002).

[35] Seymour Drescher, *Econocide: British Slavery in the Era of Abolition* (Pittsburgh, 1977); *Capitalism and Antislavery: British Mobilization in a Comparative Perspective* (Oxford, 1987); *The Mighty Experiment: Free Labor versus Slavery in the British Emancipation* (Oxford, 2002); John J. McCusker, 'The Economy of the British West Indies, 1763– 1790: Growth, Stagnation, or Decline?' in John J. McCusker, *Essays in the Economic History of the Atlantic World* (London, 1997).

[36] J. R. Ward, 'The Profitability of Sugar Planting in the British West Indies, 1650–1834', *Economic History Review*, 31 (1978), 197–213; 'The British West Indies in the Age of Abolition, 1748–1815', in P. J. Marshall ed., *The Oxford History of the British Empire: vol. ii, The Eighteenth Century* (Oxford, 2001) David Ryden, 'Does Decline Make Sense? The West Indian Economy and the Abolition of the British Slave Trade', *Journal of Interdisciplinary History*, 31 (2001), 347–74.

acquisition of real estate, reference will also be made to other loan clients listed in the Appendix, Table 7.7. Studies of British aristocrats have concluded that a high level of indebtedness was not necessarily a sign of imminent financial collapse. Many landed families were encumbered with debt, but few went bankrupt; on the contrary, longevity and survivorship were the dominant attributes of the British aristocracy.[37] The fact that West Indian estates also carried perpetual mortgages, therefore, may not be especially significant. During the later eighteenth and early nineteenth centuries, however, Caribbean landed families failed in large numbers; elites in the West Indies proved less adept at survivorship than their counterparts at home.

Two persistent themes feature in the debtor histories that follow. The first highlights the role of London merchant houses in financing the slave trade by providing credits to Caribbean merchants selling imported Africans to local planters. The second emphasises the importance of metropolitan credit in financing West Indian planters wishing to acquire estates in the Ceded Islands and to stock them with slaves. The ceded colonies consisted of territory taken from France and Spain during the Seven Years' War, control of which was disputed during subsequent international conflicts.

For simplicity, this chapter describes debts as being owed to the Lascelles of Harewood. In reality, the situation was more complex. Depending on the date at which they were first contracted, debts were owed either to the estate of Henry Lascelles, or to the successive partnerships of the commission house he founded: Lascelles & Maxwell; Lascelles, Clarke, & Maxwell; and Lascelles & Daling. Following Daniel Lascelles' death, however, his brother Edwin and cousin Edward Lascelles reached agreements with the heirs of Maxwell and Daling. In return for an annuity payment and a release from all liabilities, the debts and properties obtained from foreclosure were assigned to the owners of Harewood.[38] In consequence, it is sensible to group West Indian debts together, rather than to complicate matters needlessly

---

[37] David Cannadine, 'Aristocratic Indebtedness in the Nineteenth Century: The Case Re-Opened', *Economic History Review*, 30 (1977), 624–50; David Spring, 'Aristocratic Indebtedness in the Nineteenth Century: A Comment', *Economic History Review*, 33 (1980), 564–8; David Cannadine, 'Aristocratic Indebtedness in the Nineteenth Century: A Restatement', *Economic History Review*, 33 (1980), 569–73; Lawrence Stone and J. C. F. Stone, *An Open Elite? England 1540–1880* (abridged edn, Oxford, 1986).

[38] WRA, Harewood Accession 2,677, Indenture between William Daling and Edwin Lascelles, 29 June 1786; Agreement between Edwin Lascelles and Henry Maxwell, 15 February 1788; Indenture between Henry Maxwell and Edward Lascelles, 17 February 1796.

by referring in each case to the different partners who negotiated a specific transaction.

The term 'foreclosure' also requires comment. Foreclosure is a legal term that refers to the termination of the borrower's equitable right of redemption. Prior to this point, a debtor in default of a loan could 'redeem himself' (re-establish his standing with the lender), by paying back the amount owed (principal and interest), plus any penalties. William Blenman, for example, surrendered Mesopotamia estate in Tobago to Lascelles & Daling by a deed executed in February 1781. The equity of redemption, however, remained with Blenman until a further deed, drawn up in August 1784, was executed in September of the following year. In a strict legal sense, therefore, foreclosure did not occur until September 1785, but the Lascelles had already assumed possession of the estate several years prior to this.[39]

A long interval of time could separate the taking of a property for debt and extinguishing of a right of redemption. In the case of the Gedney Clarkes, the estates secured by mortgage passed into the hands of the Lascelles between 1773 and 1781, whereas the right of redemption was not finally surrendered until 1799.[40] In addition to its legal usage, however, foreclosure has the more practical meaning of the action of a lender in seeking to take possession of a property secured by mortgage by means of legal process. Recovery of the Blenmans' debt was initiated by obtaining a judgement against Timothy Blenman in 1774, followed by the mortgaging of the family's estates in 1776. The practical definition of foreclosure is the one that is employed in the rest of this chapter.

Gedney Clarke

The rise and fall of the great business empire created by the Gedney Clarkes has already been described in detail. A once-mighty family fortune was destroyed by miscalculations in slave trading, victualling and prize contracts, navy bills, and ill-timed speculation in the Ceded Islands. By 1774, Gedney Clarke Jr was insolvent and the black hole in his accounts public knowledge. While his debts to the Lascelles (£130, 484 sterling) were covered by plantation assets worth upwards of £148, 874, significant amounts were owed to others. Of Clarke's creditors, the most powerful

---

[39] HH:WIP, Indenture between William Blenman, Daniel Lascelles, and William Daling, 19–20 February 1781; Minutes of a deed of sale or surrender of the equity of redemption of Mesopotamia plantation by William Blenman to William Daling, 4 August 1785 (executed 28 September 1785).

[40] HH:WIP, Correspondence, John Prettyjohn to Lord Harewood, 18 July 1799.

was the Crown, which claimed £20,281. To recover this money, government officials began sequestrating his assets. On Barbados, William Moore (Attorney General) filed a writ in the Exchequer Court, obtaining a mortgage against Belle and Henley estates for £14,000. Management of Belle was placed in the hands of two customs officials: Inspector General George Mills and Surveyor General William Senhouse.[41] In response, the Lascelles were left with no option except to initiate foreclosure procedures to protect their interests. Simultaneously, they began negotiating with the Clarkes and the Crown to secure as many of the estates to themselves as possible.[42]

Despite the pressure of events, a clear alternative existed to the assumption of direct ownership in the case of at least one of the plantations. A bid for Clarke's Court (Grenada) was received in 1772 from John Pigott, who offered £36,000 (probably currency) for the property. The proposed payment scheme consisted of a deposit of £8,000, plus eight further annual instalments of £3,500, with interest on the outstanding balance at 5 per cent. The total amount of principal plus interest the Lascelles would receive over nine years was £44,100 (a net present value of £30,621).[43] A second bid for this estate was made in 1774 by Thomas Townsend and Thomas Wooldridge, who offered £51,613 (currency) in instalments over twelve years (net present value of £39,335), again with interest at 5 per cent.[44] To put these projected purchases into context, Clarke's Court was encumbered by a mortgage debt of £30,000 (sterling) at 5 per cent. At the point at which this property was taken into direct ownership, therefore, its market value exceeded the debt charged upon it. Sale of the property was a realistic

[41] HH:WIP, Judgements against the estate of Gedney Clarke, 1771–4; Copy of a Case from London respecting Mr Clarke's affairs [n.d., c. 1774]; Correspondence, Memorial for Thomas Willison presented to Lord Harewood, 19 June 1802; BA, Hughes-Queree Collection, Abstract in Queree notebook, 'Belle'; HH, List of papers belonging to Edward Lascelles Esq. as executor of the Right Honourable Edwin Lord Harewood deceased [n.d., 1796], 21; WRA, Harewood Accession 2,677, Indenture between James Workman, master of the Barbados High Court of Chancery, Daniel Lascelles and William Daling, September 1780. It is believed that William Moore is the same man who challenged Clarke Sr for the post of Bridgetown Collector in 1750; he subsequently served as estate manager for the Baron Harewood, see Chapters Four and Eight.

[42] In 1776, the Lascelles commenced an action in Chancery and sought a court ruling that their mortgage claim against Belle estate (Barbados) should take precedence over the Clarkes' debt to the Crown. The court decided, however, that public debts should be paid before private ones, BA, Hughes-Queree Collection, Abstract in Queree notebook, 'Belle'. On Tobago, the family were more successful in beating off rival claimants to secure estates: 'By some compromise, unknown to the Island Creditors,' Thomas Willison observed, 'Messrs Lascelles & Daling obtained the possession,' HH:WIP, Memorial for Thomas Willison, presented to Lord Harewood, 19 June 1802.

[43] HH:WIP, John Pigott's offer for Clarke's Court plantation, Grenada.

[44] HH:WIP, Copy of an agreement for the sale of Clarke's Court estate, Clarke's Court, Grenada.

possibility, though only over repayment periods of between eight and twelve years.

Clarke Jr's bankruptcy was a critical event in alerting the Lascelles to the altered realities of doing business in the West Indies. To protect the family's assets, and beat off the claims of rival creditors, his plantations were taken over. The block of five estates released by Clarke between 1773 and 1781 brought Belle (Barbados), Clarke's Court (Grenada), and Richmond, Bushy Park, and Goodwood (Tobago) into the hands of the Lascelles. The majority of these estates were undeveloped properties located on the Ceded Islands, and vulnerable to French occupation in the event of war being declared.

The Harvies

The Harvies were a family of Scots merchants who began trading in the West Indies at the beginning of the 1740s or shortly before. In an early reference to the family, John Harvie is described by George Maxwell as a private tutor, who had gone out to Barbados in 1740 to instruct the children of Nicholas Wilcox.[45] John did not remain a teacher for very long. In 1743, he was trading as a dry-goods importer, handling consignments of linen and calico worth £5,000.[46] Harvie was soon joined on Barbados by his brothers, William and Alexander. The trio were supplied with manufactured goods from Lascelles & Maxwell of London and merchants in Glasgow. In return, the brothers shipped cargoes of sugar and rum to their correspondents.[47]

For approximately a decade, the Harvies confined their energies to the import–export business. Yet from an early date they entertained ambitions of employing their commercial acumen in another direction. 'There is one trade by much the most beneficial of any carried on from Europe to the British West Indies which the people at Glasgow seem to take no notice of', Alexander Harvie wrote in 1746, 'and that is the trade

---

[45] *LMLB*, Pares Transcripts, H649, f. 33, Lascelles & Maxwell to Thomas Stevenson (Barbados), 27 September 1743. Lascelles & Maxwell sought out private tutors from Scotland themselves for some of their West Indian clients, see ibid., H390, II, Lascelles & Maxwell to John Frere (Barbados), 28 August 1747; H391, f. 193, same to same, 20 November 1747.

[46] Ibid., H649, f. 33, Lascelles & Maxwell to Thomas Stevenson (Barbados), 27 September 1743.

[47] In addition to bilateral trade with Britain, the Harvies developed an interest in trade with Virginia in North America, NAS, Boyd Alexander Papers, GD393/49, Alexander Harvie (Barbados) to Claude Alexander (Glasgow), 5 April 1746; same to James Crawford and Claude Alexander (Glasgow), 19 May 1746; James Crawford (Glasgow) to John Willougby (Norfolk, Virginia), 26 December 1746.

to the coast of Africa for slaves by which the people of Liverpool have enriched themselves.'[48] Their opportunity came in 1751 when John and Alexander Harvie relocated to Jamaica, leaving William to manage business affairs in Barbados. Three years later, the brothers had largely withdrawn from dealing in dry goods and henceforth specialised in the Jamaican slave import business.[49]

In order to break into the slave trade, the Harvies needed financial backing. In 1753, Lascelles & Maxwell gave John and Alexander a line of credit amounting to £20,000 (sterling) to start up operations. George Maxwell appears responsible for the decision to underwrite the Harvies' entry into the slave trade. He visited Liverpool to solicit business for the brothers and sent circular letters to the port's leading slave traders offering to guarantee the Harvies' remittances to the amount of the overdraft: 'so that you may go on in business with more ability than any other House in Jamaica was ever capable of doing'.[50] As a result of this initiative, eight shipments of slaves to Jamaica were consigned immediately from Liverpool.[51] More soon followed.

Lascelles & Maxwell's backing of the Harvies was a response to several interrelated factors. Firstly, sugar planting on Jamaica shared in a West Indian development boom that gathered momentum from the 1740s onwards. A recovery in sugar prices encouraged investors and gave rise to commercial optimism that Richard Pares christened the 'silver age' of sugar. Regions of Jamaica that had hitherto been sparsely populated were settled, primarily with African enslaved labour.[52] A second factor responsible for the growth of credit extension lay in the extension of the consignment trade. By the mid-eighteenth century, Jamaican planters shipped much of their crop direct to London commission houses offering attractive credit facilities, rather than selling

[48] Ibid., Alexander Harvie (Barbados) to Claude Alexander (Glasgow), 5 April 1746.
[49] Other members of the Harvie family remained in Britain. Lascelles & Maxwell arranged for Thomas Harvie to be fixed in partnership with a chemist in 1774, advancing £1,500 for this purpose, *LMLB*, Pares Transcripts, H655, Lascelles & Maxwell to Thomas Stevenson & Son (Barbados), 12 January 1754.
[50] Ibid., H662, Lascelles & Maxwell to J. & A. Harvie (Jamaica), 10 January 1756.
[51] Ibid., H653, f. 286, Lascelles & Maxwell to Robert Stirling (Jamaica), 10 April, 1751; W&G V, f. 85, Lascelles & Maxwell to William Harvie (Barbados), 10 January 1753; H380, f. 71, Lascelles & Maxwell to John and Alexander Harvie (Jamaica), 17 October 1754.
[52] Richard Pares, *Merchants and Planters, Economic History Review*, Supplement 4 (Cambridge, 1960), 46; S. D. Smith, '*Merchants and Planters* revisited', *Economic History Review*, 55(4) (2002), 457–8; Michael Craton, *Searching for the Invisible Man: Slaves and Plantation Life in Jamaica* (Cambridge, MA, 1978), 24; David Ryden, ' "One of the fertilest plesentest Spotts": An Analysis of the Slave Economy in Jamaica's St Andrew's Parish, 1753', *Slavery and Abolition*, 21 (2000), 32–55.

sugar and other produce to local merchants.[53] Thirdly, growth of business with the Harvies reflects the success with which Scottish merchants constructed transatlantic trade networks from the middle decades of the eighteenth century onwards, particularly in the Chesapeake and Jamaican branches of colonial commerce.[54]

As has been seen, the Lascelles were quick to recognise the potential of working closely with Scots associates.[55] George Maxwell's return to London in 1743 formed part of a strategy of harnessing talent from north of the border, by drawing on his Maxwell-Hepburn connections centred on East Lothian. In November 1745, Maxwell wrote to John Stevenson (Barbados) informing him that he had seen three of Stevenson's nieces at Haddington, one of whom had married the master of the town's grammar school, where the sons of some of the best East Lothian gentry families boarded. During his visit, Maxwell also describes meeting Alexander Stevenson in Glasgow, and comments that John's nephew had been given a good character by a 'Mr Harvie'.[56] By the 1760s, the Harvies and Stevensons were linked dynastically: Thomas Stevenson's daughter Anne married Alexander Harvie, while another of his daughters was the first wife of Thomas Harvie.[57]

Lascelles & Maxwell provided three types of financial service to their clients. Short-term, current account overdrafts were granted to

---

[53] K. G. Davies, 'The Origins of the Commission System in the West India Trade', *Transactions of the Royal Historical Society*, 5th series, 2 (1952), 89–107.

[54] J. H. Soltow, 'Scottish Traders in Virginia, 1750–1775', *Economic History Review*, 12 (1959), 83–98; Thomas M. Devine, *The Tobacco Lords: A study of the Tobacco Merchants of Glasgow and their Trading Activities, 1740–1790* (Edinburgh, 1975); Jacob M. Price, *Capital and Credit in British Overseas Trade: The View from the Chesapeake*, (Cambridge, 1980); Alan L. Karras, *Sojourners in the Sun: Scottish Migrants in Jamaica and the Chesapeake, 1740–1800* (Ithaca, NY, 1992).

[55] See Chapter Four.

[56] *LMLB*, Maxwell (London) to John Stevenson (Barbados), 18 November 1745. A complete list of masters at the school is not available. It can be noted, however, that in 1724 the master of the school was John Leslie (a family connected with the Farquhars – see below), while in 1750 Alexander Smart came to Haddington to teach English, information extracted from the Burgh Records and W. Forbes Gray, *A Short History of Haddington* (Edinburgh, 1944) by Sheilla Millar, Senior Librarian, East Lothian Local History Centre. Unfortunately, it has not proved possible to establish the family connections of Alexander Smart; nevertheless, the kinship links between the Smarts, Lethieulliers, Lascelles, Hepburns, and Maxwells should be noted, see Chapters Three and Four.

[57] *LMLB*, Pares Transcripts, H678, B, f. 19, Daniel Lascelles to Elizabeth Harvie, 18 January 1766; H680, B, f. 24, to Thomas Harvie (Jamaica), 25 May 1767; NA:PRO, PROB11/896, Will of Thomas Stevenson, proved 4 February 1764; Pedigree of the Farquhar, Stevenson, and Leslie families compiled by Dr Marion Diamond (University of Queensland), pers. com. 19 July 2005. The Stevensons' and Harvies' kinsfolk included the Graeme and Taylor families of Jamaica (Simon Taylor being the best-known representative of the latter, see below).

correspondents consigning sugars to them. Longer-term loans were made to planters able to provide collateral in the form of first-claim mortgages on plantations. The partners also undertook to guarantee the payments of slave importers on Barbados and Jamaica to their suppliers based in Bristol and Liverpool. None of these facilities were new, but commercial policy departed from practices in Henry Lascelles' time in two significant ways. Firstly, the amount of lending increased and was concentrated among a smaller number of debtors. Secondly, greater risks were taken. Henry's chief correspondent in the West Indies in the slaving business had been Richard Morecroft, with whom he also worked closely in the victualling trade. Morecroft, a well-capitalised merchant, invested in the Hall-Lascelles floating factory syndicate; prior to receiving underwriting for slaving ventures, he lodged a deposit in London with Henry.[58] Lascelles & Maxwell's relations with the Harvies were characterised by none of these safeguards.

George Maxwell exhorted the Harvies 'to give as short credits as you are able, & not to let money lye out in good hands for the benefit of a difference of interest'. His financial strategy depended on 'a great flow of business in the consignment of Guinea ships', and a corresponding flow of remittances. In short, a quick circulation of capital was the key to the system.[59] To Maxwell's initial disappointment and eventual despair, the Harvies did not deliver the desired rapid turnover. In consequence, their indebtedness rose persistently. By December 1754, the brothers' overall debt stood at £27,409. By September 1755 it had grown to £32,868, by August 1756 to £60,514, and by August 1758 to £79,705.[60] The rate with which the deficit climbed reflects the ability of the Harvies to secure business from Liverpool and Bristol

[58] Barbados Public Library, Bridgetown, Lucas Manuscripts, f. 451, Petition of Richard Morecroft, Deputy Agent Victualler, 26 November 1734; BA, RB1/33/105, Power of Attorney granted by Henry Lascelles to Richard Morecroft to exercise the office of Agent Victualler for Barbados and the Leeward Islands, 15 October 1734; NA:PRO, C103/130, Business Papers of Thomas Hall, George Hamilton (Anomabu) to Richard Pinnell (London), 3 August 1738; *LMLB*, Pares Transcripts, H656, Lascelles & Maxwell to Gedney Clarke, 29 March 1754; HSP, Yeates Papers, John Yeates Correspondence, 1733–59, #740, John Bayley (Barbados) to John Yeates (Philadelphia), 14 August 1742; NA:PRO, T1/320/21, Report of a committee of the Lords Commissioners for Trade and Plantations into the conduct of Edward Lascelles and Arthur Upton, 23 July 1746.

[59] *LMLB*, Pares Transcripts, H568, f. 71, Lascelles & Maxwell to J. and A. Harvie (Jamaica), 17 October 1752.

[60] Ibid., f. 107, Lascelles & Maxwell to J. and A. Harvie (Jamaica), 31 December 1754; H661, f. 232, Lascelles & Maxwell to J. and A. Harvie (Jamaica), 23 September 1755; W&G VII 1756–9, f. 7, Lascelles & Maxwell to J. and A. Harvie (Jamaica), 21 August 1756; H667, f. 214, Lascelles & Maxwell to Thomas Stevenson & sons (Barbados), 12 August 1758. These figures are all currency.

far in excess of the guarantees provided by the house.[61] Unable to
restrain the risk-taking of the Harvies within acceptable limits, the firm
faced a dilemma: if it failed to pay bills drawn on it, or attempted to talk
down the Harvies' credit, Lascelles & Maxwell's own standing in trade
would be damaged. The outbreak of the Seven Years' War added to the
strain, since the conflict raised the cost of borrowing in London. At
the beginning of the war, the Harvies further confounded Maxwell
by buying up real estate on Jamaica, including Williamsfield plantation.[62] 'You have brought us into a labyrinth of distress', Maxwell
lamented, 'and we cannot enjoy any quiet till we begin to see our way
out of it.'[63]

On paper, the Harvies' accounts remained approximately in balance.
In 1759, their assets consisted of around £50,000 (currency) in real
estate and slaves, £30,000 due to them from slave sales (of which
£20,000 was considered secure), plus working capital and other claims
on property. On the debit side, the brothers owed Lascelles & Maxwell
£64,460 sterling (approximately £90,244 currency).[64] The major
problem faced by the brothers was their lack of liquidity. Money owed to
the Harvies for slave purchases included dubious or bad debts (Tables
7.3, 7.4), while Williamsfield and the other properties could not be sold
readily to release collateral. The early years of the Seven Years' War
were difficult ones for West Indian merchants. Maxwell observed that in
London 'the produce of Jamaica is very low at our market, and the
planters of that island in the lowest credit here, & most of their bills are
returned protested'. The rate of exchange also tended to move against
the colonies during eighteenth-century wars, adding to the strain of
making remittances.[65]

---

[61] To break into the Bristol market (where the firm of Hibbert & Sprigge occupied a
    dominant position in the slave trade to Jamaica), the Harvies entered into an agreement
    with James Laroche and in early 1755 purchased a one-sixteenth share in a slaver named
    Black Prince (captain William Miller). This vessel delivered 627 slaves to Jamaica and
    500 to Virginia in three voyages completed between 1755 and 1760, David Eltis,
    Stephen D. Behrendt, David Richardson, and Herbert S. Klein eds., *The Trans Atlantic
    Slave Trade A Database on CD-ROM*, (Cambridge, 1999), #17,386, #17,432, #17,476.
[62] Williamsfield and The Crawl were purchased from William Nedham in 1756, who owed
    a debt to the Harvies, East Sussex Record Office, Lewes, Jamaica Correspondence of
    Rose Fuller, SAS-RF/21/9, William Nedham (Jamaica) to Rose Fuller, 1755; SAS-RF/
    21/54, same to same, 24 July 1756.
[63] *LMLB*, Pares Transcripts, H664, f. 17, Lascelles & Maxwell to J. and A. Harvie
    (Jamaica), 5 November 1756.
[64] Ibid., Pares Transcripts, H670, f. 362, Lascelles & Maxwell to Thomas Stevenson
    (Barbados), 3 November 1759.
[65] Ibid., Pares Transcripts, H664, f. 129, George Maxwell to Thomas Stevenson
    (Barbados), 13 October 1757.

Table 7.3. *West Indian assets and liabilities of the Harvies, 1765 and 1777 (£ currency)*

Assets: real estate

	1765	1777
Williamsfield (sugar estate)		
Slaves	15,801	19,190
Stock and sundries	3,607	6,980
Land	11,002	14,501
Total	*30,410*	*40,671*
Mammee Ridge (cattle pen)		
Slaves	1,340	6,775
Stock and sundries	178	3,670
Land	6,891	9,911
Total	*8,409*	*20,356*
Nightingale Grove (sugar estate)		**(Nightingale**
and Oldfield's Bog (cattle pen)		**Grove only)**
Slaves	11,346	10,182
Stock and sundries	9,780	952
Land	18,277	15,017
Total	*39,403*	*26,151*
Subtotal (real estate)	*78,222*	*87,598[a]*

Assets: debts owing to the Harvies

	1765	1777
All colonies	53,982	(48,082)[b]
Combined assets	*132,204*	*c. 136,040*

Liabilities

	c. 1765	c. 1777
Debts owing to the Lascelles	80,289	90,571
Other debts	11,900	6,000
Total liabilities	*92,189*	*96,571*

Note: All sums in £ currency; c. £1.40 Jamaica currency is equal to £1.00 sterling. Land values for c. 1765 are based on 1777 valuations, adjusted for changes in the general price level using John J. McCusker, 'Comparing the Purchasing Power of Money in the United States (or Colonies) from 1665 to 2003', Economic History Services (2004), : http://www.eh.net/hmit/ppowerusd/. The value of Oldfield's Bog c. 1765 is based on the estimated distribution of slaves between this property and Nightingale Grove (arrived at

Maxwell held the first of a series of crisis meetings with Daniel Lascelles in 1757. The firm depended on Daniel's reputation and fortune in order to secure its own short-term overdrafts from London bankers, enabling it to meet day-to-day obligations. Daniel was at first inclined not to take up any more of the Harvies' bills, but Maxwell steadied him and their line of credit was continued.[66] This decision was to involve financial sacrifice. In Yorkshire, John Carr's projected new house at Plompton was abandoned and Daniel consoled himself with more modest alterations of his Jacobean property at the nearby Goldsborough estate.[67] The early 1760s were very difficult years for the firm, but confidence in the house was maintained. London bankers continued to lend, and sufficient numbers of planters remitted interest payments for the partnership to survive.

The Harvies' debt position stabilised after 1759. Annual statements indicate that £49,670 sterling was owed in August 1760, and £48,813 in August 1761.[68] In the years that followed, however, little progress was made in reducing the deficit and a combination of interest arrears and new drawings had raised the debt again to £56,635 sterling (including interest) by April 1766.[69] During the 1760s, the original business

Notes to Table 7.3 (*cont.*)
by extrapolating backwards from the survivors on Nightingale in 1777 using plausible mortality rates) and the assumption that only about 150 acres of land were cleared and in use (derived from the estimate of slave numbers).
[a]The total includes Angel's Pen: a small property of 70 acres valued at £420 currency.
[b]An estimate. Since hardly any of the principal owing to the Lascelles was paid off between 1765 and 1777, it is assumed that the reduction in the Harvies' debts to other creditors (£5,900) reflected the amount collected from their own debtors.
Source: JA, IB/11/3/47, Inventory of Alexander Harvie, entered 17 December 1767; WRA, Harewood Accession 2,677: 1) Conveyance of estates in Jamaica in consideration of debts owed by the late Thomas Harvie to Daniel Lascelles, 20 June 1777; 2) Conveyance from Lewing and Ramsay to Lascelles & Maxwell, 21 November 1777; *LMLB*, Pares Transcripts, H680, B, f, 24. Daniel Lascelles to Thomas Harvie (Jamaica), 25 May 1767.

[66] Ibid., f 149, George Maxwell to Thomas Stevenson (Barbados), 5 November 1757. See also H660, f. 200, George Maxwell to J. and A. Harvie (Jamaica), 21 August 1755.
[67] Helen Lazenby, *Plumpton Rocks, Knaresborough* (Yorkshire Gardens Trust: Leeds, 1997?), 4. Daniel demolished the old house at Plompton in 1760, intending to rebuild; in 1763, however, he purchased the Goldsborough estate and moved into the existing house there, with only limited modifications by John Carr the following year.
[68] *LMLB*, Pares Transcripts, H671, f. 94, Lascelles & Maxwell to J. and A. Harvie (Jamaica), 2 August 1760; f 179, Lascelles & Maxwell to J. and A. Harvie (Jamaica), 7 August 1761. The Harvies did not, however, hit their target of reducing the debt to £30,000 by 1761, H669, f. 30, Lascelles & Maxwell to J. and A. Harvie (Jamaica), 20 November 1759.
[69] Ibid., H678, f. 29, Daniel Lascelles to William Harvie (Jamaica), 20 January 1766; Lascelles & Daling to Alexander Stevenson (Barbados), 12 July 1766.

Table 7.4. *Analysis of debts owed to Alexander Harvie (all colonies), 1765*

Size of debt (£ currency)	Number of debtors	Amount owed (£ currency)	Percentage of total debt
5,000–7,000	2	12,737.63	23.60
3,000–4,999	2	7,644.33	14.16
1,000–3,999	12	18,993.62	35.19
1–999	56	14,606.42	27.06
Total	72	53,982.00	100.01

Source: JA, IB/11/3/47, Inventory of Alexander Harvie, entered 17 December 1767.

associates began dying off: John Harvie died in 1761, George Maxwell in 1763, and Alexander Harvie in 1765.[70] Thomas and William Harvie replaced their deceased brothers on Jamaica and began negotiating with Daniel Lascelles for a new settlement. A mortgage of their Jamaican estates to secure a debt of £57,349 (sterling) was agreed in May 1767, at an interest rate of 5 per cent and with provision of annuities of £500 and £300 per annum to the widows of Alexander and John.[71] Remarkably, this measure was the first formal agreement drawn up between the parties since the letter granting an overdraft facility of £20,000 fourteen years earlier. Hitherto, as Daniel observed, 'no part of this Debt was upon loan, but arose in the course of Business'.[72]

Although formalisation of the debt situation did not occur until 1767, kinship connections provided the Lascelles with at least some reassurances prior to this event. In 1762, the Barbadian planter Thomas Stevenson (Henry Lascelles' former attorney and Provost Marshal of the colony), became Thomas Harvie's father-in-law.[73] Moreover, around the time the mortgage deeds were drawn up, Alexander Harvie

[70] Ibid., H671, f. 179, Lascelles & Maxwell to Thomas Stevenson & Sons (Barbados), 7 August 1761; IX, B, f. 16, Daniel Lascelles to Alexander Stevenson (Barbados), 5 November 1765, *London Magazine*, 32 (1763), 169.

[71] WRA, Harewood Accession 2,677, Conveyance from Lewis and Ramsay to Lascelles & Maxwell, 21 November 1777; Institute of Commonwealth Studies, London, ICS 101, Wemyss Castle Estate Papers, Extract of deeds sent by Mr Millward to Francis Graeme, 26 March 1806.

[72] *LMLB*, Pares Transcripts, H680, B, f. 24, Daniel Lascelles to Thomas Harvie (Jamaica), 25 May 1767. A mortgage was discussed in 1759, but the deed does not appear to have been drawn up and executed, H669, f. 360, Lascelles & Maxwell to J. and A. Harvie (Jamaica), 20 November 1759.

[73] NA:PRO, PROB11/896, Will of Thomas Stevenson, proved 4 February 1764.

married Elizabeth March, a teenage heiress under the guardianship of Lascelles & Maxwell. This match made excellent business sense. In 1756, Elizabeth's widowed mother, Maria March, had married William Beckford, head of one of Jamaica's richest absentee planter families. Alexander's bride had inherited a legacy of £1,200 per annum from her father, Francis March, secured on the proceeds of Oldfield's Bog, a Jamaican estate linked closely with Nightingale Grove.[74]

It would be wrong, therefore, to regard the Scottish Harvie brothers as brash upstarts, who thrust themselves as outsiders into the financial and social circles inhabited by the Lascelles and their associates. Indeed, the Harvies shared common ground with the Maxwells (including medical and military experience), Stevensons, and Graemes. Thomas Harvie trained as a physician and entered into partnership with a London chemist before going out to Jamaica.[75] In 1771, Thomas Harvie's widow Anne married Sir Walter Farquhar (1738–1819). Farquhar began his career as an army and naval surgeon, serving in Lord Howe's expedition against Belle Isle during the Seven Years' War. He later settled in London, where he practised as an apothecary and physician (his clients included William Pitt), and in 1801 he became physician to the future George IV.[76] Anne's daughter, Elizabeth Harvie, married Simon Halliday, partner in the banking house of Herries, Farquhar, Halliday, Davidson & Company.[77]

---

[74] NA:PRO, C12/788/10 (1758), C12/1338/34 (1773 and 1774), C12/905/19 (1775). Elizabeth's father, Francis March (the son of a London merchant of the same name with Jamaican interests), was a former Jamaican attorney of Lascelles & Maxwell, *LMLB*, Pares Transcripts, W&G IV, Lascelles & Maxwell to Florentius Vassall (Jamaica), 7 September 1750, NA:PRO, PROB11/679, Will of Francis March Sr, proved 22 October 1736. Francis March Jr managed Richard Oldfield's estate in Jamaica between 1736 and 1739. After this the property passed to Charles Bowles of New Windsor by inheritance, but the estate carried a mortgage and enentually passed into the possession of the Harvies via the March family, PROB11/695, Will of Richard Oldfield, proved 19 April 1739; PROB11/794, Will of Francis March Jr, proved 2 April 1752. In 1775, Elizabeth was living at the Beckford ancestral home of Fonthill Gifford, Wiltshire, *Memories of William Beckford* (London, 1859).

[75] Lascelles & Maxwell advanced £1,500 to establish Harvie in the chemist's trade, *LMLB*, Pares Transcripts, H655, Lascelles & Maxwell to Thomas Stevenson and Son, 12 January 1754.

[76] William Anderson, *The Scottish Nation; or the Surnames, Families, Literature, Honours and Biographical History of the People of Scotland* (3 vols., Edinburgh, 1866–77), vol. II, 'Farquhar'; J. F. Payne, revised Kaye Bagshaw, 'Sir Walter Farquhar, first baronet (1738–1819)', *ODNB*; NA:PRO, PROB11/1,617, Will of Sir Walter Farquhar, proved 30 June 1819. The Harvies' Farquhar connections may indicate links to the Harveys of Aberdeen and Grenada, VEre Langford Oliver, *The History of Antigua* (3 vols., London, 1894–99) vol. II, 24.

[77] The marriage took place in 1788, Ursula Halliday, 'The Slave Owner as Reformer: Theory and Practice at Castle Wemyss Estate, Jamaica, 1803–1823', *Journal of Caribbean History*, 30 (1996), 78. Sir Thomas Harvie Farquhar, 2nd Bt. (1775–1836), son and heir of Sir Walter Farquhar, later became principal of Herries, Farquhar, & Co, while one of Sir Walter's daughters married the Jamaican planter Gilbert Mathison.

By December 1767, Thomas Harvie had departed life and the headship of the family business devolved solely upon William. On receipt of this news, Lascelles & Maxwell sent a power of attorney to Jamaica to call in the Harvies' loans and sue persons still owing slaving debts to the brothers.[78] The threat to force a sale using an attorney, however, remained a negotiating tactic and foreclosure was not implemented immediately. William was invited to increase the amount of sugar he consigned from his Jamaican estates, to pursue his own creditors more vigorously for payment, and to dispose of some of his plantations voluntarily. In response, Harvie assigned a bond for £10,000 owing from Simon Taylor to the house.[79] Here matters stood until May 1770, when Daniel Lascelles exhibited a bill of complaint for non-payment in the Jamaican High Court of Chancery, and on 19 January 1773 received a judgement. The public sale of Harvie's properties was ordered on 6 November 1776, and an advertisement was placed in a tavern owned by Robert Pitcairn on 1 December that year. The highest bids for the Harvie estates amounted to £87,597 (currency). Dissatisfied with these offers, on 21 November 1777 the Lascelles assumed direct ownership of the plantations.[80]

Indebtedness arising from funding 'bills in the bottom' also affected the firm's balance sheet with other loan clients. The slaving accounts of the Gedney Clarkes, Samuel Carter, and Thomas Stevenson all tipped to the negative during the 1750s and 1760s. Samuel Carter was a kinsman of both the Lascelles and Clarkes, and this branch of business forms part of the Yorkshire gentry capitalist circle built up around Carter's uncle, Henry Lascelles.[81] In 1753, Carter was granted the same £20,000 sterling overdraft facility that the Harvies enjoyed, for which Gedney Clarke Sr stood surety. Carter's slave trade debts fluctuated between £10,000 and £15,000 until 1761, when he left off business in

---

[78] *LMLB*, Pares Transcripts, H683, f. B31, Daniel Lascelles to Gilbert Ford (Jamaica), 14 December 1767; IX, f. 36, Daniel Lascelles to William Harvie (Jamaica), 1 March 1768.

[79] Ibid., H685, f. 43, Daniel Lascelles to William Harvie (Jamaica), 2 August 1768; H688, B, f. 48, Daniel Lascelles to Scudamore Winde (Jamaica), 30 May 1769. Simon Taylor was a wealthy planter and member of the Jamaica Assembly, Richard B. Sheridan, 'Simon Taylor, Sugar Tycoon of Jamaica, 1740–1813', *Agricultural History*, 45 (1971), 285–96; Betty Wood ed., with T. R. Clayton and W. A. Speck, *The Letters of Simon Taylor of Jamaica to Chaloner Arcedekne, 1765–1775* (Cambridge, 2002).

[80] WRA, Harewood Accession 2,677, Conveyance from Lewis and Ramsay to Lascelles & Maxwell, 21 November 1777. The legal formalities were still not complete; see Island Record Office, Spanish Town, Earl Dalling MS 1171, Affidavit, 29 March 1779 confirming the transfer of properties from the Harvies to the Lascelles.

[81] As noted in Chapter Five, the Carter and Fleurian families intermarried on Barbados. Henry Lascelles' first wife was Mary, daughter of Edwin Carter, while Gedney Clarke Sr married Mary, daughter of Peter Fleurian.

Barbados as a slave trader and moved to Demerara. Clarke Sr took responsibility for Carter's final balance of £12,965, secured by a Demerara plantation. This obligation was subsumed into Clarke's own debts to Lascelles & Maxwell.[82]

Thomas Stevenson & Sons operated with the more modest overdraft facility of £6,000 sterling, raised to £8,000 in July 1756. Their arrears from dealing in slaves, however, were comparable to Carter's, and had already reached £12,000 by November 1758.[83] The following year, Stevenson extended the scope of operations by shipping 450 slaves in a Liverpool vessel to Guadeloupe, responding to the islands' capture by the British.[84] By 1760, therefore, Lascelles & Maxwell had extended credits of at least £75,000 (sterling) to finance bills in the bottom drawn by merchants importing slaves into Barbados and Jamaica. George Maxwell described the debts owed by planters to Stevenson as 'this labyrinth'.[85] Security for Stevenson's debt took the form of a £5,000 mortgage on a Barbados sugar estate called Pool: a property of 358 acres and seventy-eight slaves, acquired in 1756 for £14,000 (currency). In 1764, this estate (with an augmented labour force of 226 slaves) was valued at £21,531 (currency).[86]

Were the Harvies solvent when foreclosure occurred? Table 7.3 presents a statement of their indebtedness and the appraised value of their Jamaican assets at two benchmark dates: 1765 and 1777. The data reveal that assets were at least equal to liabilities. In 1765, at an interest rate of

---

[82] *LMLB*, Pares Transcripts, W&G V, f. 149, Lascelles & Maxwell to Gedney Clarke (Barbados), 10 May 1753; H672, f. 143, Lascelles & Maxwell to Gedney Clarke (Barbados), 6 March 1761.

[83] Ibid., H662, f. 357, Lascelles & Maxwell to Thomas Stevenson & Sons (Barbados), 3 July 1756; H667, f. 246, Lascelles & Maxwell, 4 November 1758.

[84] Ibid., H399, Lascelles & Maxwell to Thomas Stevenson & Sons, 2 November 1759; NA:PRO, PROB11/896, Will of Thomas Stevenson, proved 4 February 1764. Stevenson's Bridgetown store and warehouses undoubtedly occupied the same site as his son Alexander's, on a large plot between Bridge Street and Hardwood Alley. These premises burned down during the fires of 1766, Martyn J. Bowden, 'The Three Centuries of Bridgetown: An Historical Geography', *JBMHS*, 49 (2003), 76, 81.

[85] *LMLB*, Pares Transcripts, H671, f. 88, Lascelles & Maxwell to Thomas Stevenson & Sons (Barbados), 9 August 1760.

[86] WRA, Harewood Accession 2,677, Indenture 17 October 1755 between Jane Hallet, Daniel Lascelles, and George Maxwell; BA, Hughes-Queree Collection, Abstract in Queree notebook, 'Pool'; *LMLB*, Pares Transcripts, H622, f. 354, George Maxwell to Thomas Stevenson (Barbados), 3 July 1756; H621, f. 302, Lascelles & Maxwell to Thomas Stevenson & Sons (Barbados), 12 April 1756; H624, f. 50, Lascelles & Maxwell to Thomas Stevenson (Barbados), 5 February 1757. At the time of acquisition in 1756, Pool was an estate of 250 acres; 108 acres was simultaneously purchased from a planter named Atherley. Henry Lascelles' interest in Pool dates from 1752 when he was assigned a mortgage of £2,258 sterling by the London merchants John and Sir Joseph Eyles.

5 per cent, yearly remittances of £4,015 (currency) were required to
service the Lascelles' loan; by 1777 the annual payment required was
£4,529. Expressed in terms of a return on capital invested in plantations, debt service was between 5.1 and 5.2 per cent in both years.
According to a study of sugar's profitability published by Ward, a yield
of this level was well within the capacity of Jamaican producers; indeed,
Daniel Lascelles commented that he considered 6 per cent the minimum return expected of an estate.[87] While the amount owed (principal
plus interest) rose between 1765 and 1777, the increase was commen-
surate with the general price level. Since the debt burden hardly rose at
all during the twelve-year period under review, the Harvies' debt can be
regarded as sustainable. Their position was different to that of the
Gedney Clarkes, who ran out of money and were (in effect) bankrupted
by the Crown after assets were seized to cover customs arrears.

If the Harvies' finances were stable, why did foreclosure occur? Bargaining models suggest that the answer to this question lies in the value
placed by the mortgagor (borrower) and mortgagee (lender) on the
assets secured by a loan. If the Harvies considered their estates to
be worth less than the loan, it would have been rational to threaten
to default. Conversely, if gaining title and selling the properties involved
significant transaction costs, from the Lascelles' perspective it would be
rational to negotiate with the Harvies rather than to foreclose. Surviving
records provide an indication of the respective positions of both sides. In
1769, Daniel Lascelles threatened to foreclose, but gave William Harvie
the option of rescheduling the loan (then £57,349 sterling) over six years
(a net present value of −£8,836). Harvie responded by offering to pay
5 per cent interest plus £5,000 per annum to discharge his obligation
over twelve years (a net present value of −£14,444).

Although the brothers' payment record in serving the debt was
reasonable, their past efforts at reducing the principal had not been
effectual. Moreover, Daniel had no certain method of ascertaining what
proportion of monies owing to the Harvies (slave sales and other dealings from) consisted of good debts. If this source of remittances is
disregarded entirely, then Harvie would have to rely solely on the produce of the estates to discharge what he owed. At a 6 per cent return, the
debt would take seventeen years to repay (making no allowances for
poor harvests or interruptions to trade due to war). Lascelles contemplated a repayment interval of this length as a likely scenario,
commenting that he did not expect Harvie to pay back the loan in his

---

[87] Ward, 'Profitability of Sugar Planting', 207; *LMLB*, Pares Transcripts, H680, B, f. 24,
Daniel Lascelles to Thomas Harvie (Jamaica), 25 May 1767.

lifetime.[88] The net present value of such a stream of payments is −£19,311: much worse than Daniel's own repayment offer.

Foreclosure was not a costless option and the process took time to complete. The interval between issuing the first bill of complaint and conveyance of the Harvies' properties was 2,596 days. Even after a judgement was obtained, a total of 1,605 days elapsed until final conveyance. Once the properties were in Lascelles' hands, however, Daniel was still only halfway towards liquidating his assets, since a buyer would then have to be found for the estates. Cash buyers were a rarity for West Indian property; when the Lascelles sold estates, they nearly always granted mortgages and received payment in instalments over five or six years. Harvie's best offer (repayment over twelve years) lay close, therefore, to the likely timescale Lascelles faced if he selected the option of foreclosure and resale. Since Daniel did not regard this offer as credible, he set out on the long road to assuming ownership himself.

The Blenmans

The Blenman family name can be linked with Barbados from at least the early eighteenth century. In an early reference, George Blynman (formerly a Brisol linen draper) noted in his will of 1702 that he was 'now resident within the Isle of Barbadoes'.[89] It is likely he had precursors, since the Blynmans are known to have been active in colonial projects from the 1640s onwards. The Revd Blynman of Chepstow, for example, was leader of a group of colonists who arrived at Plymouth Colony around 1640. The family's involvement in Barbadian affairs, however, was not continuous. No one with the surname Blenman appears in the list of persons owning more than 10 acres in 1638, or among exporters from Barbados during the 1660s, or in the censuses of 1679–80 and 1715. Only a Thomas Blenman can be found among the 611 subscribers to William Mayo's 1722 map of the island.[90]

---

[88] *LMLB*, Pares Transcripts, H687, B, f. 45, Daniel Lascelles to Scudamore Winde (Jamaica), 13 February 1769.

[89] James C. Brandow ed., *Genealogies of Barbados Families: From Caribbeana and the Journal of the Barbados Museum and Historical Society* (Baltimore, 1983), 177–8.

[90] 'List of the Names of the Inhabitants of Barbados, in the year 1738, who then Possessed more than ten Acres of Land', printed in (William Duke), *Memoirs of the First Settlement of the Island of Barbados to the Year 1742* (London, 1743); Bodleian Library, Oxford, MS Eng. hist. b. 122, 'A Coppie Journall of Entries Made in the Custom House of Barbados Beginning August the 10th 1664 and ending August the 10th 1665' Hispanic Society of America, New York, M. 1480, 'A Coppie Journall Entries made in the Custom House of Barbados 1665–1667' (David Eltis kindly supplied a database of entries which was used to search for Blenman entries); William Mayo, *A New and Exact Map of the Island of Barbados in America* (London, 1722); John Camden Hotten ed., *The Original Lists of*

Jonathan Blenman's date of birth is unknown, but he entered Middle Temple as a young man in 1710 and proceeded to the Bar seven years later. In two early pamphlets (published in 1715 and 1717), the young Blenman defended dissenters living in the family parish of Croscombe (near Wells, Somerset) and described his role in founding a Whig political club.[91] This society, one of London's first mug houses, was 'set up with a design to encourage the dissenters and doing what we can for them'.[92] As a lawyer, Blenman remained an Anglican communicant; his religious views, however, were probably similar to those of the young Dudley Ryder, a fellow-associate in the mug-house project.[93]

By early May 1718, Blenman had moved to Barbados, where he acted as legal counsel for Samuel Cox. By aligning himself with Cox and William Gordon in the Francis Lansa case, Jonathan immediately fell foul of Governor Robert Lowther and Henry Lascelles, suffering arrest in consequence.[94] Following Lowther's recall in 1720, however, Blenman's career prospered. During Henry Worsley's governorship, he was appointed Attorney General in 1726 (possibly benefiting from Carteret's patronage); four years later, he became Judge of the island's Vice Admiralty Court.[95] Blenman was to prove a persistent adversary of the Lascelles and Clarkes. He lobbied against the 1732 Colonial Debts Act

Persons of Quality . . . and Others who Went from Great Britain to the American Plantations, 1600–1700 (New York, 1874).

[91] The Blenmans originated from the West Country regions of Monmouthshire, Gloucestershire, and Somerset.

[92] William Matthews ed., *The Diary of Dudley Ryder, 1715–1716* (London, 1939), 362; (Jonathan Blenman), *A Letter to the Reverend Mr Brydges, Rector of Croscombe in Somersetshire . . . being a Vindication of the Dissenters* (London, 1715) and *The Mug Vindicated* (London, 1717). For the attribution of authorship of these tracts, see Bill Overton ed., *A Letter to My Love: Love Poems by Women First Published in the Barbados Gazette, 1731–1737* (Newark, 2001), 23, 132.

[93] Matthews ed., *Diary of Dudley Ryder*, 362; Phyllis J. Guskin, "Not Originally Intended for the Press": Martha Fowke Sansom: Poems in the *Barbados Gazette'*, *Eighteenth-Century Studies*, 34 (2000), 75; Mary Sarah Bilder, *The Transatlantic Constitution: Colonial Legal Culture and the Empire* (Cambridge, MA, 2004), 123–4. Ryder later became Attorney General in England; he was much sought after as counsel in a number of colonial appeals to the Privy Council owing to his knowledge of transatlantic legal culture. In addition, Ryder's legal career drew him close to both Walpole and the Duke of Newcastle, rendering him a potentially useful source of support for Blenman.

[94] CRO, D/Lons/L12/1/BM, Lonsdale Archive: Barbados Plantation Records, Box 1,034, Barbados Council Minute Book (1715–18), 340–53; Box 1,033, Barbados Council Minute Book (1718–19), 298–301.

[95] [Samuel Keimer], *Caribbeana* (2 vols., London, 1741), vol. I, 268–71, 401–2; (Anon.), *The Barbadoes Packet* (London, 1720), 8–11, 14; William Blenman, *The Case of Jonathan Blenman, Esq. Attorney General of Barbados* (London, 1761); Overton ed., *A Letter to My Love*, 23. The Beinecke Collection, Hamilton College, has Blenman's copy of the *Acts of Assembly, Passed in the Island of Barbadoes* (London, 1732, 1739), complete with manuscript additions and annotations.

(taking a position diametrically opposed to that of Henry Lascelles) and joined battle with Gedney Clarke Sr over the administration of the Prize Court and alleged customs abuses.[96]

Despite a history of differences, references to Jonathan Blenman in the correspondence of Lascelles & Maxwell during the 1750s and 1760s are surprisingly amicable. In part, this reflects the fact that Blenman was a natural survivor, who succeeded in ingratiating himself with many of the island's governors. He remained particularly close to former Governor Worsley and also acted as advisor to Governor Grenville during his administration. Blenman also enjoyed a good working relationship with the Barbados agent, John Sharpe. As George Maxwell observed in 1753, 'Mr Blenman is not without friends in this country.'[97] The pragmatic decision to do business with the Attorney General reflects the fact that differences between Blenman and the Lascelles were largely factional and, therefore, time-limited. At root, both parties were supporters of the Hanoverian regime and strongly Protestant; both also wished to prosper from their affairs in the West Indies.

Blenman's will (written in 1763) exhibits the serenity of a man clear of debt and possessed of substantial landed property. In 1735, he had purchased Mount estate (St George's Parish) from William Rawlin Jr.[98] The will recounts how this property's mansion house had (at considerable expense) been renovated to provide 'a pleasurable residence', incorporating a well-laid-out garden. In Bridgetown, Blenman conducted private hearings in his town house and probably held meetings here to plan editions of the *Barbados Gazette* with Samuel Keimer. Pride of place among Blenman's possessions was his library, consisting primarily of law books and an extensive collection of tracts on divinity.[99] In

---

[96] *LMLB*, Pares Transcripts, H483, f. 104, George Maxwell to William Duke, 17 January 1743(4); CKS, Grenville-Buckingham MS, U1590, S2/012, Copies of Letters Wrote in Governor Grenville's Administration from 1747 to 1753, Grenville to Gedney Clarke, 20 December 1748, 6 February 1749(50) and 20 February 1749(50); Grenville to William Moore, 12 February 1749(50); Grenville to Jonathan Blenman, 10 March 1749(50); Richard Pares 'Barbados History from the Records of the Prize Courts: IV. The Barbados Prize Court Under Judge Blenman', *JBMHS*, 6 (1939–40).

[97] *LMLB*, Pares Transcripts, H485, f. 196, George Maxwell to Edward Lascelles, 20 November 1747; H486, W&G IV, 1750–2, f. 31, Lascelles & Maxwell to Gedney Clarke, 20 November 1750, 27 August 1751; W&G VI, 1754–6, f. 241, Lascelles & Maxwell to Gedney Clarke, 20 January 1752.

[98] Mount was one of the earliest large-scale plantations on Barbados, built up by land transfers between the Middleton and Drax families in 1647. William Rawlin Sr purchased Mount on mortgage from Benjamin Middleton in 1699, BA, Hughes-Queree Collection, Abstract in Queree notebook, 'Mount'.

[99] HH:WIP, Will of Jonathan Blenman, dated 3 July 1763. Blenman instructed his executors to divide the law books among his sons but to preserve the works of divinity at Mount estate, suitably protected against vermin. The long preamble to Blenman's will

addition to his Barbados property, he was also owner of an English estate at Croscombe.[100] Blenman's will granted generous legacies, including £3,000 (currency) each to his three younger children. His eldest son and heir, William Blenman (also a lawyer), was already a planter in his own right.[101] Marriage to Elizabeth Dottin in 1748/9, daughter and heiress of Joseph Dottin, had made William the master of Cooper's Hill (also known as Walwyn's) estate in St James.[102]

In 1766, an appreciably more anxious Blenman added a codicil to his will. In it, he lamented that the family were sufferers in the devastating Bridgetown fires of May and December 1766, which damaged or destroyed approximately two-thirds of the town, including Blenman's own residence.[103] Just prior to this disaster, Jonathan had bought Kirton's (alias Kent) plantation in Christ Church, intending it as 'a commodious addition' to his son William's estate of Cooper's Hill. To finance this purchase, the codicil notes he 'became considerably indebted who was before clear'. His creditors were the Lascelles.[104] Expansion was continued by William and Timothy Blenman after their father's death. Timothy was among the first British investors on Tobago and he assigned his promised legacy in order to buy an estate there called Mesopotamia. In 1768, additional funds were sought to clear 100 acres and purchase slaves to work the land.[105]

Daniel Lascelles acted as the major financier of both William and Timothy Blenman. A series of bonds, judgements, and executions were

provides further evidence of his scholarship of divinity. Cultural interests are further evidenced by a daughter's leaving her collection of music books to brother Timothy, HH:WIP, Will of Margaret Bevila Blenman dated 29 May 1772 (date of death, 18 February 1774).

[100] HH:WIP, Will of Jonathan Blenman. Blenman bought this estate from his brother Nehemiah. His will granted his three surviving brothers (Caleb, Benjamin, and Thomas) life interests in the property. Caleb and Benjamin held rent-free tenancies on the estate, while Thomas acted as Jonathan's British attorney.

[101] William Blenman entered Middle Temple in 1739. Blenman's second son Timothy likewise practised law; he was admitted to Gray's Inn in 1741 and renewed his chambers in 1748, Overton ed., *A Letter to My Love*, 27.

[102] BA, Hughes-Queree Collection, Abstract in Queree notebook, 'Cooper's Hill-Walwyn's'. Since there is evidence that Henry Lascelles had sought to merge this plantation with Holetown during the mid-1740s (see above), this transaction may represent something of a coup for Jonathan Blenman.

[103] HH:WIP, Codicil to the will of Jonathan Blenman, dated 26 December 1766; *Gentleman's Magazine*, 36 (1766), 425–6; *For the Unfortunate Inhabitants of Bridgetown, Barbados* (London, 1766); Martyn J. Bowden, 'The Three Centuries of Bridgetown: An Historical Geography', *JBMHS*, 49 (2003), 64.

[104] HH:WIP, Codicil to the will of Jonathan Blenman, dated 26 December 1766; *LMLB*, Pares Transcripts, H641, Lascelles & Daling to Gedney Clarke, 5 June 1766.

[105] NA:PRO, CO101/14(127), Present State of the Plantations now settling in Tobago; *LMLB*, Pares Transcripts, B, f. 343, Lascelles & Daling to Timothy Blenman, 4 August 1768; X, 1768–72, Lascelles & Daling to Timothy Blenman, 8 October 1768.

taken out against the brothers between 1772 and 1776, resulting in the mortgaging of their West Indian estates. The final reckoning came in 1784, when all of the Blenman properties were seized for debt. At the time of foreclosure, the West Indian account at first sight appears to have been in balance (Table 7.5). The legacies Jonathan Blenman granted in his will, however, ultimately broke the estate when the Lascelles elected to call in their loans.

In comparison with the Harvies and Clarkes, foreclosure seems a harsh decision. The Blenmans were, however, a family of lawyers and their head, William Blenman, resided in London: one of the world's major financial centres. If an escape route from their difficulties existed, it would surely have been taken. Yet there was no last-minute reprieve. The surviving documents do not reveal whether anything more than cold, financial calculation motivated Daniel and Edwin to humble the Blenmans. An element of hubris may well have been involved in pressing for foreclosure. Nevertheless, it must be emphasised that both Timothy and Jonathan Blenman Jr subsequently acted as two of the Lascelles' agents on Barbados.[106] The decision to place the children of a former enemy in positions of trust suggests that liquidation of the Blenman's assets was a mutually agreeable decision. The Lascelles' offer of support and employment was evidently not one that could be refused.

Ill-judged speculation in the Ceded Islands proved the undoing of other Barbadian loan clients. The Husbands family were advised by Lascelles & Maxwell in 1763 to sell their Rendevous estate on Barbados to clear debts, especially in view of impending payment of a legacy charged on the property. Samuel Husbands rejected this counsel, opting instead to purchase a Grenada plantation (borrowing a further £3,000 from the house in the process), with a view to living in Britain as an absentee owner in a 'rational scheme of pleasure'.[107] James Simmons part-financed his acquisition of Mount Bay estate in Grenada by borrowing £4,051 in 1766. This debt remained outstanding twenty years

---

[106] HH:WIP, A list of papers received from Timothy Blenman, 18 August 1770; Correspondence, Jonathan Blenman and Richard Cobham (Barbados) to John Wood Nelson (London), 27 September 1801; WRA, Letters and Papers on West India Estates and Affairs, 1795–1873, Nathaniel Eliot (London) to (Edward, Lord Harewood), 20 August 1796.

[107] LMLB, Pares Transcripts, H638, f. 307, Lascelles & Maxwell to Samuel Husbands (Barbados) 31 January 1763; H639, f. 383, Lascelles, Clarke, & Daling to Samuel Husbands (Barbados), 2 May 1763. Husbands was forced to sell this estate at a loss in 1766, IX, f. 124, Lascelles & Daling to Samuel Husbands (Barbados), 16 February 1766. Rendevous (c. 546 acres) was owned by Samuel's uncle, Richard Husbands, who owed £8,000 to the Lascelles in 1769. By 1800, the estate had been broken up and sold off in pieces for debt, BA, Hughes-Queree Collection, Abstract in Queree notebook, 'Rendevous'; letter from Ronnie Hughes, 22 October 1999 (pers. com.).

Table 7.5. *West Indian assets and liabilities of the Blenmans, c. 1784 (£ sterling)*

Barbados assets (Mount, Kirton, and Cooper's Hill estates)	25,067
Legacies charged on the Barbados estates	−7,857
Barbados debt owing to Lascelles (principal plus interest)	−17,285
Other Barbados debts	−5,563
Balance on Barbados account	−5,638
Tobago assets (Mesopotamia estate)	10,153
Tobago debts owing to Lascelles (principal plus interest)	−8,550
Other Tobago debts	−1,005
Balance on Tobago account	598
Overall balance on the Lascelles' account only	1,528
Overall balance on all accounts	−5,040

Note: Original statements in currency. Converted to sterling using the following exchange rates: £1.39 Barbados equals £1.00 sterling, £1.65 Tobago equals £1.00 sterling.
Source: HH:WIP, Account of William Blenman with Edwin Lord Harewood, 27 March 1784; Sketch of Account from Nathaniel Elliot of William Blenman and Jonathan (Blenman) with Lord Harewood (n.d., 1784); Account of Lord Harewood's demand on the estate of Timothy Blenman (deceased) (n.d., 1797).

later.[108] Richard Green similarly fell into debt after being tempted by a Dominica estate, which he wished to purchase before selling his Barbados property. Lascelles & Maxwell provided him with what was intended to be bridging finance, but it soon became an extended mortgage and Green was forced to put the property up for sale in 1769.[109] Unwise purchases on Tobago and Grenada likewise featured in the Gedney Clarkes' financial difficulties.

The scale of capital invested in the Ceded Islands is suggested by the following memorial presented to the Lords Commissioners for Trade and Plantations by a group of Grenada planters:

the British purchasers ... were induced to give very great prices for the Estates they Bought, from the easy terms of payment, as the French proprietors were content with one third or one Quarter in Money and the remainder to be paid by Instalments from one to ten Years, another inducement was the great facility with which they got Credit from the Merchants in Great Britain, who advanced to them large Sums, and became Security for considerable Loans procured from

---

[108] WRA, Harewood Accession 2,677, Indenture between William Daling and Evan Ballie, 1 October 1787.
[109] *LMLB*, Pares Transcripts, IX, f. 268, Lascelles & Daling to Richard Green (Barbados), 29 September 1767; X, 1768–72, f. 70, Lascelles & Daling to Gedney Clarke (Barbados), 16 June 1769.

Foreigners, and for Money raised by Annuitys; many of the French planters who could find Credit likewise became borrowers, the whole being to an incredible amount; Thus in a few Years near the whole property of the Island became British, either by purchase, Mortgage, or other Securitys.[110]

The effects of British investment can be seen in a shift on Grenada from coffee to the more capital-intensive sugar crop. Exports of sugar from Grenada increased from 9,000 hhd in 1762 to more than 51,000 hhd by 1772.[111] In comparison, coffee exports from the colony remained stagnant at around 6 million lb. London merchants (and their international associates) supplied the credit needed to import African slaves, without whose labour sugar cultivation on the island could not have been extended.[112]

The Freres

The Freres were descended from the gentry of Occold and Bressingham in Suffolk. By the early eighteenth century, a Somerset branch of the family had established itself at Nettlecombe, where some of the Barbadian Freres resided as absentee planters.[113] The Freres' early business strategy in the Caribbean featured two elements common to the Lascelles and their associates: connections with Puritan merchant syndicates and a policy of sending more than just the youngest sons out to the West Indies. Thomas Frere, a successful London merchant, joined with Maurice Thompson and William Pennoyer in financing the privateering activities of Captain William Jackson in the Spanish West Indies between 1638 and 1641.[114] Six of Thomas' sons subsequently

[110] Hamilton College, New York, Beinecke Collection, M237, Private information of the present State of the Island of Grenada [n.d., c. 1770–9].

[111] S.D. Smith, 'Accounting for Taste: British Coffee Consumption in Historical Perspective', *Journal of Interdisciplinary History*, 27 (1996), 204. The remaining coffee plantations must have increased in size, since the number of producers listed fell from 208 to 186 during this ten-year period.

[112] Beinecke Collection, M237. Peter Thellusson is an example of a London merchant with Swiss financial backing investing in Grenada, Suffolk Record Office, Thellusson Family: Financial Papers, Bacolet Estate, Grenada, 1812–60 (HB416/D1/1–3). See also the activities of the syndicate headed by Alexander Bartlet and George Campbell, The Royal Bank of Scotland Group Archives, London, GB 1502/WC/495 Papers re: trustees of the estate of Alexander Bartlet & Co.; Mark Quintanilla, 'The World of Alexander Campbell: An Eighteenth-Century Grenadian Planter', *Albion* 35 (2003), 1–29.

[113] John Bernad Burke, *Burke's Genealogical and Heraldic History of the Landed Gentry* (18th edn, 2 vols., London, 1965), vol. II, 225–30.

[114] Robert Brenner, *Merchants and Revolution: Commercial Change, Political Conflict, and London's Overseas Traders, 1550–1653* (Cambridge, 1993), 158. Thompson and Pennoyer were among the merchants whose investments generated the boom in the Barbados land market during the 1640s, John J. McCusker and Russel R. Menard, 'The Sugar

went out to Barbados and established themselves as merchants, attorneys, and planters during the three decades from 1640 to 1670. They were joined by three sisters, each of whom married successful merchant-planters, further extending the Freres' network of kinship and commerce.

Tobias (b. 1617) and John Frere Sr (b. 1626) proved the most successful of the brothers. The two men joined syndicates of merchant investors that speculated in more than 10,000 acres of land on Barbados during the 1640s and 1650s. In the 1679 census, John is listed as owning 180 acres and 80 slaves in Christ Church, while Tobias owned 395 acres and 150 slaves in the same parish, plus a further 209 acres and 82 slaves (jointly with Thomas Spire or Spiar) in St Philip's Parish.[115] In time, the colonial interests of the Freres came to be centred on Barbados, but they were not initially confined to the island. Tobias first concentrated his energies on the Chesapeake, moving there in 1635 aged eighteen. In Virginia, he formed a partnership with the merchant Robert Vause, trading in tobacco. As part of their business dealings, the two men purchased 400 acres in Yorke County in 1647, though it is not known if they developed this holding. After his move to Barbados (which occurred around 1650), Tobias continued to build up a portfolio of assets in the Atlantic world by investing in 3,000 acres of land in Surinam in association with two other Barbadians.[116]

The Freres' debts to the Lascelles consisted of dual strands advanced to two brothers and their heirs. The first recorded financial obligation dates from 1734, when John Frere III (a member of the Barbados Council) became indebted to Henry Lascelles for £10,407.13s.2d (sterling) at 8 per cent interest and £4,757.3s.10d. at 5 per cent. These loans were continued by Daniel Lascelles, who also granted Frere two powers of attorney in 1765 to conduct business on his behalf.[117] At the same time, Frere III acted as estate attorney for the Lowthers.[118] By 1775, John's debt to the Lascelles had swollen to

Industry in the Seventeenth Century: A New Perspective on the Barbadian "Sugar Revolution"', in Stuart B. Schwartz ed., *Tropical Babylons: Sugar and the Making of the Atlantic World, 1450–1680* (North Carolina, 2004), 295.
[115] Hotten ed., *Original Lists*, 329, 447. A third brother, William Frere, owned 120 acres and 40 slaves in Christ Church.
[116] Information provided by Opal Freer Spencer, based on genealogical research.
[117] BA, RB1/1/38, Powers of Attorney, Daniel Lascelles to Hon. John Frere.
[118] Royal Bank of Scotland Group Archives, James Lowther Barbados Papers, CH/1/1, John Frere to Robert Lowther, 1 September 1742; John Frere to Sir James Lowther, 10 May 1765.

£28,799.2s.2d. (sterling), which Daniel secured by obtaining a judgement against John III's son and heir, Henry Frere.[119]

A second line of credit consisted of advances to Tobias Frere Jr. In 1747, Tobias received a loan of £2,500 at 5 per cent, which was later increased to £3,500 (sterling). Tobias paid off this loan in 1755, piqued by George Maxwell's reluctance to extend his credit.[120] For a while he attempted to obtain finance by drawing on kinship resources in the West Country. In 1757, Tobias married Charlotte Trevelyan in Bath, Somerset.[121] Charlotte's sister was the wife of Sir William Yea of Pyrland (Taunton), who in 1763 granted a £10,000 (sterling) mortgage to Tobias secured on Pilgrim estate, giving Yea a first claim on this property. Despite this assistance, Tobias was ultimately obliged to return to Lascelles & Maxwell for funds. The same year as the Yea mortgage, he borrowed £1,300, and by 1770 his indebtedness to the firm had risen to £9,000 (sterling).[122]

Foreclosure proceedings against the Freres were completed by Edwin Lascelles in 1787. By this date, the first loan strand (owed by John and Henry Frere) amounted to £39,839.13s.9d. (sterling), secured on Thicket, Fortescue, and Pot House plantations. Technically, Freres' account remained in the black, since the three properties were collectively appraised at £49,218. Indeed, to gain possession, Edwin Lascelles was obliged to pay the balance of £8,778.7s.0d. to Henry Frere.[123] The second loan strand (owed by Tobias and Applethwaite Frere) by this

---

[119] BA, Hughes-Queree Collection, Abstract in Queree notebook, 'Fortescue'; Account Book of Henry Lascelles, 1753 (see Chapter Four, fn. 97); HH:WIP, Indenture between Henry Frere and Edwin Lascelles, 19 July 1787.

[120] LMLB, Pares Transcripts, H619, f. 206, Lascelles & Maxwell to Thomas Stevenson (Barbados), 17 July 1755.

[121] IGI, Family Search Database. Tobias Frere married firstly, in 1738, Arabella Peers, daughter of the Speaker of the Barbados Assembly, Henry Peers; secondly, in 1742, Amelia Burrell, BA, Queree-Hughes Collection, Abstract in Queree notebook, 'Searles'. Connections between the Freres and Trevelyan family may predate this union. The plantation that became known as Fortescue estate was bequeathed by Nathaniel Trevanion (Trevelyan?) in 1675 to his daughter and heiress Mary, who married William Fortescue. In 1734, Mary (by now widowed) willed the estate to her three daughters, Queree notebook, 'Fortescue'. The Freres may have gained possession of the property through marriage to one of the Fortescue heiresses. On dynastic connections between the Trevelyan and Fortescue families, see Alfred James Monday, *The History of the Family of Yea formerly of Pyrland in the Parish of Taunton St James, of Okehampton* (Taunton, 1885).

[122] HH:WIP, Correspondence, John W. Nelson to Lord Harewood, 5 August 1801; A list of papers belonging to Edward Lascelles Esq. as executor of the Right Honourable Edwin Lord Harewood deceased [n.d., c. 1796], f. 12.

[123] BA, RB3/193/194–6, Indenture between Henry Frere and Edwin Lascelles, 10 November 1787; HH:WIP, Indenture between Henry Frere and Edwin Lascelles, 19 July 1787; A list of papers belonging to Edward Lascelles Esq. as executor of the Right Honourable Edwin Lord Harewood deceased [n.d., c. 1796], f. 26–7.

time amounted to between £9,000 and £14,147 (sterling). The debt was secured by Pilgrim estate (appraised at £14,379), but since the Lascelles were only holders of the second mortgage charged on the property, its surrender did not cancel the amount owed.[124]

Ascertaining whether the Freres were solvent in 1787 is complicated by the fact that they owned at least four other estates on Barbados (Coverley, Searles, Moonshine, and Lower Estate). These plantations may also have been mortgaged for debt. John Frere III's Coverley estate had by 1824 passed out of the family to the Dottins (possibly by inheritance).[125] Tobias Frere Jr retained Searles during his lifetime, but financial problems resulted in his heirs having to sell off the property for £30,000 in 1801. Applethwaite Frere, however, remained owner of Lower Estate and Moonshine in 1810.[126]

The causes of the Freres' financial problems are less evident than in the cases of other debt clients of the Lascelles. Neither risky ventures in slave trading nor ill-considered speculation in the Ceded Islands appear to have marred their fortunes, in contrast to the Clarkes, Harvies, and Blenmans. Overdevelopment of the Freres' Barbadian holdings may, however, provide part of the answer. In 1766, Henry Frere inherited Thicket (already encumbered with debt) from John Frere III. Sometime before 1770 he had purchased the neighbouring Fortescue estate, and by 1787 New Netherlands had also been added to the property. The resulting amalgam of estates occupied 825 acres, making it one of the largest plantation complexes on the island. Thicket was intensively worked, with 439 acres devoted to cane and the remaining 145 acres allocated for cotton and corn. Cotton was grown on Fortescue, and Frere also experimented with indigo on the estate in an attempt to maximise revenue from his plantations.[127] The timing of this ambitious project proved unfortunate. It is possible that the Lascelles were

---

[124] BA, RB3/193/194–6, Indenture between Henry Frere and Edwin Lascelles, 10 November 1787; Hughes-Queree Collection Abstract in Queree notebook, 'Frere Pilgrim'; WRA, Harewood Accession 2,677, Agreement between Edwin Lascelles and Henry Maxwell, 15 February 1788. The debt stood at £9,000 in 1769 and £14,147 in 1796. Yea foreclosed on his loan at the same time as the Lascelles, NA:PRO, C12/489/27–8, Deposition and Interrogation in the case of *Sir William Yea* vs *Charlotte Frere* (1788). Negotiations between the Lascelles and Yea continued into 1801 (by which date the debt owed to him stood at £30,000), HH:WIP, Correspondence, John W. Nelson to Lord Harewood, 5 August 1801.

[125] BA, Hughes-Queree Collection, Abstracts in Queree notebook, 'Searles' and 'Coverley'.

[126] 'Letters of Yearwood Seale, 1796–1810', *JBMHS*, 16 (1948–9), 113–17.

[127] BA, Hughes-Queree Collection, Abstracts in Queree notebook, 'Fortescue' and 'Thicket'. The holdings included the small Pot House plantation.

tempted by the development potential of the site and were determined to acquire it.

As the Freres became more financially dependent on the Lascelles, the political value of the connections between them also evolved. Culturally, the two families continued to share religious, artistic, and intellectual interests. Henry Frere, for example, commissioned Benjamin West to paint *The Resurrection*, intending to install the work of art as a backdrop to the high altar in the parish church of St George's, where the Frere family vault is located.[128] Applethwaite Frere was a founder member of the Barbados Society for the Encouragement of Arts, Manufactures and Commerce, established by Joshua Steele in 1784.[129] Yet despite a long history of association and the existence of common ground, the Lascelles and Freres worked less closely together politically as the eighteenth century progressed than had been the case during the Lowther governorships.

In 1704, Robert Lowther became the fourth husband of Joan, daughter of John Frere Sr.[130] Joan Lowther's nephew, John Frere Jr, was subsequently implicated in two of the controversies surrounding Lowther's governorship. Prior to his final departure from the island in 1720, the Governor removed Samuel Cox and Timothy Salter from the Council in order to install Frere Jr as President.[131] Cox and Salter successfully petitioned for their restoration in 1720, only for the President to refuse to hand over the ensigns of office. For this act of insubordination, Frere was summoned to London, but he apparently died of smallpox before proceedings against him were completed.[132]

John Frere Jr was also embroiled in the Bernard Cook affair of 1719. Cook, a Bridgetown butcher, complained that Frere had wrongfully detained an estate belonging to him by blocking a legal suit. Following a

---

[128] *The Resurrection* was exhibited at the Royal Academy in 1786 before being shipped out to the colony. On arrival, however, it was relegated to Lower Estate until 1820, owing to a dispute between Henry Frere and the rector of St George's.

[129] John Newman, 'The Enigma of Joshua Steele', *JBMHS*, 19 (1951), 6–20.

[130] John Vincent Beckett, 'Landownership in Cumbria, c. 1680–c. 1750', unpub. Ph.D. thesis (University of Lancaster, 1975), 253–4. By virtue of this match, Robert Lowther gained control of a plantation in Christ Church.

[131] The senior member of the twelve-man Barbados Council assumed the role of President or interim Governor.

[132] Henry Frere's partisan account claims that his kinsman resigned office 'much against the inclination of the inhabitants of Barbados', and adds that 'he was given to understand, that his being sent for was to place him out of Cox's way, and to break the violence of party', (Henry Frere), *A Short History of Barbados* (London, 1768), 51–3; (Sir John Gay Alleyne), *Remarks Upon a Book, intitled, A Short History of Barbados* (Barbados, 1768), 10–13, 18, 82–3. For the attributions of authorship, see Jerome S. Handler, *A Guide to Source Materials for the Study of Barbados History, 1627–1834*, (Carbondale, 1971), 41, 103.

confrontation with Governor Lowther over the issue, Cook found himself the target of a lawsuit launched by Robert Warren and Samuel Adams, who accused him of slandering their wives. At a Court of Quarter Sessions, presided over by Guy Ball (a Lascelles kinsman), Cook was ordered to pay a fine of £100 to each of the plaintiffs. Refusal led to his being 'publickly whipt by the common Whipper of Slaves in an unhuman, cruel, and barbarous Manner'.[133] In subsequent hearings, Cook's adversaries sought to claim that the proceedings followed were common in slander cases. Court officials also deposed that there was no property dispute involving Frere directly and that the punishment administered was a general one, rather than an extension of the slavery code to a white colonist. This defence, however, was insufficient to prevent the Lords Commissioners for Trade and Plantations suspending Ball and Francis Bond (two of the Justices) from the Council.[134]

From the very first Barbados Council, established by Governor Bell in 1642, successive generations of Freres occupied prominent roles in the island's legislature. The continuing oligarchical ambitions of the Freres are revealed in 1753, when John Frere III attempted to secure the appointment of a son to the Barbados Council while still a councillor himself. This manoeuvre drew a rebuke from the colony's London agent, John Sharpe, who objected 'it was incompatible with the Publick Interest for a father & son to be at the same time Member of the same Board, by giving too great a weight to one family in the Administration of Equity'. Scarcely had Sharpe's reply been delivered, however, than Prest Weekes and Nathaniel Weekes accomplished precisely this feat, spurring the Freres to continuing trying (vainly) to realise their objective.[135]

Evidence of opposition to the Freres (based on more than just faction) developed during the 1760s. In 1768, Henry Frere published a history of Barbados in response to the Stamp Act controversy and Sir John Gay Alleyne's attempts at asserting the privileges of the Barbados Assembly. Frere's tract praised the system of Governor in Council, emphasising how 'Barbados hath always preserved a uniform and steady attachment to Great Britain and therefore is intitled to the affection and indulgence of the mother country.' Alleyne was infuriated by Frere's history,

---

[133] [Keimer], *Caribbeana*, vol. I, 343–4; Schomburgk, *History of Barbados*, 316; CRO, Barbados Plantation Records, Box 1,032, Barbados Council Minute Book (1720), 79–81.

[134] [Keimer], *Caribbeana*, vol. I, 344.

[135] *LMLB*, Pares Transcripts, H486, W&G IV, Lascelles & Maxwell to John Frere, 31 December 1753, 27 November 1754. The attempt at obtaining dual membership is wrongly attributed to the Clarkes in S. D. Smith, 'Gedney Clarke of Salem and Barbados: Transatlantic Super-merchant', *New England Quarterly*, 76 (2003), 515–16.

objecting strongly to its uncritical appraisal of past Governors and Presidents. His own published retort includes a review of Robert Lowther's administrations of the early eighteenth century, and John Frere's role in them.[136] Alleyne sent a copy of his counter-history to Lascelles & Daling in London. The house praised Alleyne's depiction of his actions defending parliamentary privileges in 1767 as the Assembly's Speaker. 'We would only add', commented the partners, 'that the confusions in America, & we may say at home, & the various other great affairs of the British Empire so take up People's minds & often agitate them, that we think that History has very little been noticed by the Publick'. [137]

Lascelles & Daling's reluctance to side with Frere in his dispute with Alleyne is striking. Taken alongside the willingness of the partners to do business with Jonathan Blenman (portrayed as the defender of liberty in disputes with Robert Lowther and Henry Lascelles), it suggests that the house shifted its position with respect to colonial politics. Alleyne was no radical. He accepted the authority of the British King in Parliament over the colonies and remained loyal to Britain during the American Revolutionary War. His political concerns lay in safeguarding the traditional privileges of the Barbadian merchants and planters making up the Assembly from any repetition of past abuses of power by Barbadian Governors.[138] By the 1760s, Lascelles & Daling had similarly accepted that the realities of doing business in the West Indies had changed since old Henry Lascelles' time.

Conclusions

The perpetual mortgages secured on West Indian property proved less sustainable than the debts charged on England's great estates. Caribbean property failed to provide a low-risk investment comparable to English acres, owing to the greater risks generated by colonial warfare and dependence on sugar. Usury laws prevented lenders from protecting

---

[136] [Frere], *Short History of Barbados*, vol. IV, 51–3; (Alleyne), *Remarks Upon a Book*, 14–15, 22–3, 41–3, 79–83. Alleyne accused Frere of plagiarism and praised his own defence of parliamentary privilege. The two men subsequently fought a duel over these allegations, Andrew Jackson O'Shaughnessy, *An Empire Divided: The American Revolution and the British Caribbean* (Philadelphia, 2000), 106, 121. See also Jack P. Greene, 'Changing Identity in the British Caribbean: Barbados as a Case Study', in Nicholas Canny and Anthony Pagden eds., *Colonial Identity in the Atlantic World, 1500–1800* (Princeton, 1987), 260–3.

[137] *LMLB*, Pares Transcripts, H487, X, Lascelles & Daling to J. G. Alleyne, 15 November 1768.

[138] O'Shaughnessy, *An Empire Divided*, 87, 131.

themselves in the West Indies by charging a risk premium. Up until the 1770s, gentry capitalism provided an alternative criterion by which to ration credit. The experiences of the Lascelles, however, reveal that the labyrinth of debt created by this system proved difficult to control.

Financial relations between merchants and planters were transformed during the final quarter of the eighteenth century. The credit crisis of 1772–3 exposed how estates in the Ceded Islands and Essequibo-Guyana had become leveraged to dangerous levels. When the inevitable market correction occurred, a substantial amount of investor capital was destroyed, leaving many purchasers with properties worth less than the mortgages charged on them. The War of American Independence subsequently raised freight and insurance costs, interrupted supplies, and threatened the West Indian islands with hostile attacks from French naval forces. For the Lascelles, Gedney Clarke Jr's bankruptcy was a shock that signalled the financial status of debtors had altered fundamentally.

The Lascelles were, by the standards of the day, large-scale financiers; however, the amount of credit the firm injected into Caribbean trade formed only a small portion of total capital invested in the West Indies. In this sense, the crisis of 1772–3 cannot be attributed to the actions of one set of partners. Yet it would be wrong to portray the financial collapse of the early 1770s as a wholly autonomous event. The business strategy adopted by Lascelles & Maxwell illustrates how instability was built into the expansion of the colonial trades during the third quarter of the eighteenth century. By granting slave traders overdrafts and planters mortgages, the house created assets in the form of ledger entries that could be drawn on to support more lending. The resulting debt pyramid can be seen most clearly in the relationship Lascelles & Maxwell developed with the Harvie brothers, whereby an initial credit of £20,000 quickly generated a debt superstructure four to six times as large.

When the specific histories of the Lascelles' loan clients are examined, it is not always apparent why estates carrying mortgages were repossessed in preference to a rescheduling of the loans or the sale of estates to new purchasers. The situation becomes clearer if the positions of the four principal debtors are consolidated (Table 7.6). Only in the case of the Clarkes was lending clearly unsustainable. All of the remaining loan clients were technically solvent: the value of their West Indian properties exceeded the mortgage debt charged on them, while debt service lay within reasonable estimates of plantation annual returns (6 per cent). The problem faced by the Lascelles lay in the scale of the Clarkes' indebtedness: the clients most closely associated with Demerara and the Ceded Islands. Their difficulties pushed debtors' overall balance sheet

Table 7.6. *Indebtedness of four major loan clients at foreclosure*

	Debt to Lascelles (£ stg)	Value of mortgaged estates (£ stg)	Other secured debts	Debt service (% of estate value)[a]	Assets > liabilities?	Offers for estates?	Best payment offers
Clarkes	130,484	148,674–153,924	99,332	7.5 – 7.7	No	Yes (one)	9–12 years
Harvies	64,694	62,570	Net-creditor	5.2	No (marginal)	Yes (all)	12 years
Blenmans	37,831	50,975	8,462	4.5	Yes	?	?
Freres	48,840–53,986	63,597	10,000	4.3 – 5.0	Yes (marginal)	?	?
Total	*281,849–286,995*	*325,816–331,066*	*117,794*	*6.0 – 6.2*	*No*	*–*	*–*

Note:
[a] Interest rate assumed to be 5 per cent.
Source: See text.

into the red and into a position whereby loans were no longer serviceable by annual remittances. By 1768, Lascelles & Daling could see no route out of Gedney Clarke Jr's difficulties: 'To tell you the truth the vast Debts your father's Estate & yourself owe, are too great burdens for us almost to assist any other ... those immense debts are enough to command a large business. They greatly restrain what we already have, & may prove the ruin of it.'[139] Once the Crown commenced sequestration proceedings, the Clarke bankruptcy compelled the Lascelles to create a management system capable of supervising operations on sugar estates situated an ocean apart.

By 1787, Edwin Lascelles had become the direct owner of a sprawling portfolio of West Indian real estate. Foreclosure generated an immense managerial challenge for the future Baron Harewood and his successors. The Lascelles had some prior experience of the difficulties of running complex colonial projects by remote control. Henry Lascelles had overcome logistical problems as a navy victualler and claimed to have grown wealthy as a result. His floating factory venture proved less remunerative, but it demonstrated the potential of organisations built around private associations of merchants. Financing planters, by granting loans on mortgage, was itself a far from passive operation. Henry and Daniel Lascelles employed agents to rate loan clients, collect

---

[139] *LMLB*, Pares Transcripts, H683, IX, Lascelles & Daling to Gedney Clarke (Barbados), 10 February 1768.

debts, initiate legal actions, and sell property. Within England, the Lascelles had also added substantially to their Harewood estate during the 1760s and 1770s and they recruited surveyors and overseers to administer these holdings. None of these managerial problems, however, compares in scale with the task of monitoring an amalgam of estates, scattered across three Caribbean islands, on which nearly three thousand slaves laboured daily.

On 10 October 1780, a mighty hurricane smote Barbados. The ferocious winds blasted Belle plantation, bringing the mansion house crashing down on the head of its hostess, widow Mary Clarke. In nearby Bridgetown, St Michael's Cathedral lay directly in the path of the storm's fury. Its proud spire (including the clock and peal of bells that Hugh Hall Sr had helped install) collapsed into the church, reducing Edward Lascelles' tomb to rubble.[140] Battered by financial crisis and shocked by the American Revolutionary War, the world of the Gedney Clarkes was swept away.

Appendix

Table 7.7. *Alphabetical listing of loan clients, 1777–1820 (with amounts owing in £ sterling where stated)*

1st Name	Surname	Interest rate	1769	c. 1777	1796	1799	1820	Security
John	Balfour				47			
	Barbados Planter (ship)				16			
Henry & Elizabeth	Beckles			7,258	9,165	9,793	0	M&J
	Bishop, Worrell & Cobham				800	974		
Mrs	Blenman					309		
Timothy	Blenman			y				J
William	Blenman			y	13,492			M & J
Edward	Brailsford				3,214		1,132	
Alexander	Bruce	5	936					J
James	Butcher			y				J

---

[140] 'The Autobiographical Manuscript of William Senhouse', *JBMHS*, 2 (1934–45), 200–8; HH:WIP, Correspondence, Deborah Thornhill (Barbados) to Lord Harewood, 21 December 1798; Joseph Foster, *Pedigrees of the County Families of England: Yorkshire, West Riding* (3 vols., London, 1874), vol. II, 'Lascelles'.

Table 7.7 *(cont.)*

1st Name	Surname	Interest rate	1769	c. 1777	1796	1799	1820	Security
Samuel	Carter	5	8,296					Land taken
James	Catlin	6	439					J
John	Charnock	5	4,925					
John	Clarke			y				J
Gedney	Clarke Jr		1,869					
Gedney	Clarke Jr dec'd			y	55,618	55,618		J&M
Gedney	Clarke Sr dec'd	5	4,702	y	14,226	14,226		B
Gedney	Clarke Sr dec'd			y				M&J
Gedney	Clarke Sr dec'd			y				J
Gedney	Clarke Jr				452			
Richard	Cobham			y				B&J
John	Collins dec'd			y				J
Isacc	Depiza			y				J
Anthony	Drake					365		
Grant	Elcock				863		o	
	Elliot, Walley & Adam				6,339			
	Elliot, Walley & Adam				9,722			
	Estate: Coopers				8,906		o	
	Estate: Holetown				9,256		4,665	
	Estate: Mammee Ridge				14,540		4,540	
	Estate: Pilgrim				14,379		o	
	Estate: Pot House				2,000		o	
Henry	Fisher		228	y				J
Thomas	Forbes	5	2,000					B
William	Forbes			y				B&J
Applethwaite	Frere			y				J
Henry	Frere			y				J
Henry	Frere			y				J

Table 7.7 *(cont.)*

1st Name	Surname	Interest rate	1769	c. 1777	1796	1799	1820	Security
John	Frere	5	4,757	y				J&E
John	Frere	6	10,408	y				J&E
Tobias	Frere	5	9,000	y	14,147	14,147	10,592	J&E
Phillip	Gibbes	6	10,000	y	8,500	8,000	o	J
Thomas	Graeme				3,200		o	
James	Grassett		2,697					J
James	Grassett	5	753					
Elizabeth	Green	5	700	y	524			J
Richard & Elizabeth	Green			y				M&J
William	Haggart			y				E
	House & Land Bridgetown				72	72		
Joseph Dottin	Husbands	5	1,278	y				J
Samuel	Husbands		1,736	y	1,000	1,000	o	J
Richard	Husbands dec'd		8,000	y				J&M; Sale of land
John	Kennion		9,279					
	Lady Harewood (ship)				620	125	o	
	Liberty (ship)					520		
Nathan	Lucas			3,110				J
Dominic	Lynch		1,564	y				B,J&M
Patrick	Lynch			y				J
Alexander	MacLeod				2,627			
Rebecca	Mapp			y	11	11		J
Benjamin	Mellowes				286		o	
Benjamin	Mellowes dec'd			y	373	373	o	Assignment
Thomas	Payne	6	3,848	y				J&E
Joseph	Price			y				Account proved
George	Shand				13,330	7,150	o	
James & Mary	Simmons	5	4,051	2,990				B&J
Martha Bersheba	Sober				474		o	
John	Sober dec'd		7,000	9,406	10,961	10,500	o	M&J
Alexander	Stevenson dec'd			y	6,500	3,800	o	J

Table 7.7 *(cont.)*

1st Name	Surname	Interest rate	1769	c. 1777	1796	1799	1820	Security
Thomas	Stevenson dec'd		5	2,460	y	2,800	o	B&M
	Sundry persons				445			
	Supply (ship)				6,672			
John	Thorne		180	y				Account proved
Joseph	Thorpe	5	4,667	y				J & Account proved
Abel	Walker	8	1,539					E
Abel	Walker	5	1,291	y				J
Alexander	Walker	6	4,210					E&M
Ralph	Weekes			y				E
Thomas	Workman			y				B
Thomas	Wynter dec'd				176		o	

B = bond; E = execution; J = judgement; M = mortgage; y = listed as a debtor but the sum owed not stated.

Sources: HH:WIP, 1) 'A list of debts due to the estate of Henry Lascelles Esq. Deceased, 21 December 1769'; 2) 'A list of debts due to Messrs Lascelles & Maxwell, with remarks, the securities being in the hands of Gedney Clarke esq.' [n.d., c. 1769]; 3) 'Specialties of Lascelles & Maxwell' [n.d., c. 1777]; 4) 'Specialtys of Lascelles & Daling' [n.d., c. 1777]; 5) 'List of debts due to and from the estate of Edwin Lord Harewood deceased and the books for West India affairs, 30 April 1796 & 28 February 1799'; 6) 'List of balances from the books of the Rt Honble Lord Harewood for Jamaica affairs, 31 August 1798'; WRA, West Indies Accounts, 1790–1848, 1) 'A list of debts received since the death of Edwin Lord Harewood' [n.d., c. 795]; 2) 'Sketches of the several accounts of Edward Lord Harewood with Adam & Adam, 30 April 1820'; NA:PRO, C12/550/29.

8   Managing a West India Interest

> Nothing I wish for more than to be Liberated from all Concerns in the Indies.
>
> (Edwin Lascelles, 1788)[1]

Absentee plantation ownership has been much criticised for its deleterious social effects and productive inefficiency.[2] The economic case against absenteeism was founded on arguments first advanced by Adam Smith. Slavery was one of the examples used by Smith to illustrate his theories of monitoring and incentives. A slave, he wrote, was a 'person who can acquire no property, can have no other interest but to eat as much and labour as little as possible'. While systems of coercion and control might succeed in preserving the profitability of enslavement, such an institution could never be efficient.[3]

Agency problems are created whenever a conflict of interest arises between an owner and the overseer of a business, and when the costs of monitoring the overseer's behaviour are high.[4] West Indian estates were located thousands of miles away from Britain and communications were very slow by modern standards (a letter sent out to the colonies might take up to two months to be delivered). White managers of absentee estates possessed powers of coercion over enslaved labourers; observing

---

[1] Edwin Lascelles (Harewood) to Nathaniel Elliot (London), 4 November 1788 (private collection of D. J. Almond, copy deposited in HH:WIP).

[2] Frank W. Pitman, 'The West Indian Absentee Planter as a British Colonial Type', *Proceedings of the Pacific Coast Branch of the American Historical Association* (1927), 113–27; Lowell J. Ragatz, 'Absentee Landlordism in the British Caribbean, 1750–1833', *Agricultural History*, 5 (1931), 7–26; Trevor Burnard, 'Passengers Only: The Extent and Significance of Absenteeism in Eighteenth-Century Jamaica', *Atlantic Studies*, 1 (2004), 178–80.

[3] Adam Smith, *An Inquiry into the Nature and Causes of the Wealth of Nations*, eds. R. H. Campbell and A. S. Skinner (Indianapolis, 1979; originally published 1776), 22–3.

[4] Kenneth Arrow, 'The Economics of Agency', in J. Pratt and R. Zeckhauser eds., *Principals and Agents: The Structure of Business* (Boston, 1985), 37–51; Joseph Stiglitz, 'Principal and Agent', in John Eatwell, Murray Milgate, and Peter Newman eds., *The New Palgrave: A Dictionary of Economics* (London, 1987).

the daily conduct of such overseers was well-nigh impossible. Smith's criticism of slavery argued that managerial failures compounded a slave's inherent lack of incentives. In consequence, agents were well placed to defraud distant grandee employers, more concerned with status-enhancing projects of conspicuous consumption than with scrutinising the cost schedules of their estates.[5]

Modern scholarship has attempted to reassess both the efficiency and social implications of absentee proprietorship. Revisionism has taken one of three main forms. The first counter-critique poses the question why absentee ownership persisted for so long if it was grossly inefficient? Non-residency's very survival provides a *prima facie* case that methods were found to overcome agency problems, for example through the preparation and scrutiny of detailed accounts and the choice of kinsmen or close associates as managers.[6] Adam Smith himself emphasised the profitability of sugar and the profit-maximising behaviour of planters; moreover, his dynamic analysis of the division of labour can be applied to the plantation system of colonial trades.[7] A second revisionist strand argues absenteeism was not a monolithic institution and that its importance in specific colonies has been exaggerated, with the result that claims of inefficiency are based on a limited number of case studies.[8] Finally, some scholars go further and argue (controversially) that non-residency can be seen as a dynamic, evolving system of management, which brought about 'amelioration' in the treatment of slaves during the later eighteenth and early nineteenth centuries.[9]

Conflict between principal and agent could, in theory, occur at three points within the system of absentee proprietorship. The vulnerable

---

[5] Seymour Drescher, *The Mighty Experiment: Free Labor Versus Slavery in British Emancipation* (Oxford, 2002), 23–4.

[6] Nuala Zahedieh, 'Making Mercantilism Work: London Merchants and Atlantic Trade in the Seventeenth Century', *Transactions of the Royal Historical Society*, 9 (1999), 152–8; David Hancock, '"A World of Business to Do": William Freeman and the Foundations of England's Commercial Empire, 1645–1707', *William and Mary Quarterly*, 57 (2000), 8–9; Peter Mathias, 'Risk, Credit, and Kinship in Early Modern Enterprise', in Kenneth Morgan and John J. McCusker eds., *The Early Modern Atlantic Economy* (Cambridge, 2000), 15–35. These approaches to plantation slavery form part of a more general re-examination of the constraints imposed by agency and the methods adopted to minimise the problem during the later seventeenth and eighteenth centuries; see Ann Carlos and Stephen Nicholas, 'Agency Problems in Early Chartered Companies: The Case of the Hudson's Bay Company', *Journal of Economic History*, 50 (1990), 853–75.

[7] Drescher, *The Mighty Experiment*, 23–33.

[8] Douglas Hall, 'Absentee-Proprietorship in the British West Indies to About 1850', *Jamaican Historical Review*, 4 (1964), 15–35; Burnard, 'Passengers Only', 178–95.

[9] J. R. Ward, *British West Indian Slavery, 1750–1834: The Process of Amelioration* (Oxford, 1988); W. A. Green, 'The Planter Class and British West Indian Sugar Production, Before and after Emancipation', *Economic History Review*, 26 (1973), 449–54.

relationships were: (1) between enslaved workers and white overseers or managers; (2) between colonial estate managers and British commission houses marketing West Indian produce; and (3) between commission houses and the owners themselves. As Adam Smith pointed out, since few natural incentives to work existed, monitoring costs were high. An enslaved individual's primary goal was self-preservation, rather than the maximisation of an absentee owner's profits. Overseers and managers in the Caribbean receiving fixed annual salaries unrelated to performance, likewise lacked incentives – particularly if they enjoyed no security of tenure beyond a yearly contract. The existence of natural hazards in the West Indies (disease and crop failure), coupled with the shortage of skilled white personnel, generated conditions in which shirking and negligence were not easily detectable and difficult to punish. The position of commission houses was less secure owing to the fact that alternative suppliers of commercial services existed in London and other British ports. Here too, however, the complexities of the sugar trade generated potential opportunities for malpractice.

The Lascelles were far from archetypal planters. Even in 1836 (after the family had divested itself of thousands of acres), the 2nd Earl of Harewood still ranked among the top 0.1 per cent of British West Indian slave owners.[10] Management practices employed to run a large-scale enterprise, therefore, may not be representative of the organisation of sugar estates in general. Nevertheless, the strategies adopted by the Lascelles can provide insights into the challenges confronting West Indian agriculture, and the ability of the plantation mode of cultivation to resolve them.

A Change of System

The early years of absentee ownership were disappointing ones for the family. In 1795, Edward Lascelles (later 1st Earl of Harewood) inherited West Indian estates from his cousin Edwin Lascelles (Baron Harewood) that were not generating an acceptable return. 'In the first two years, his Lordship experienced disappointment', observed Nelson and Adam (senior partners in the London commission house), '& on the third, investigated the causes.' In 1799, it was revealed that during the preceding seven years the Barbadian estates had struggled to break even. A failure to control costs was identified as a major factor responsible for their poor performance. Of particular concern were unrestrained drawings of bills of exchange to settle the 'island account' (the balance

---

[10] See below.

of local expenses and receipts).[11] Dissatisfaction was also expressed about the profitability of the Jamaican estates. Nelson and Adam complained to Lord Harewood's attorneys that a net return of 15s. per cwt of sugar constituted, 'a defalcation so glaring & so provoking, that the bare consideration of it excites disgust & anger & the idea of its longer continuance is absolutely intolerable'.[12]

The 1st Earl ordered a thorough review of his West Indian properties and held 'repeated conferences' with merchants and planters to gain answers to the following questions: 'What do other Proprietors gain annually by Property of the same kind & value; and in what proportion are they drained by bills & burdened by expenses?'[13] The outcome of the consultation exercise both displeased and troubled him. Harewood discovered that, 'some with single Estates live in splendour and affluence from the returns of their properties', whereas his own 'well stocked & most abundantly supplied' portfolio of thirteen properties, failed to yield, 'a sufficiency to defray their own current expenses, & much less to give their owner a surplus even of the smallest consideration'.[14]

An assessment of the revenue and performance of twelve of the Caribbean estates during the early 1790s is presented in Table 8.1.[15] Harewood's concern was amply justified. The ratio of net revenue to gross revenue was low and declining, while the profitability of the estates (measured in terms of net revenue as a percentage of their value) compared poorly with planting generally. Even excluding the Tobago

[11] HH:WIP, Correspondence, John Wood Nelson and John Adam (London) to William Bishop and John Cobham (Barbados), 20 August 1799.

[12] HH:WIP, John William Adam (London) to Lewis Cuthbert & Alexander MacLeod (Jamaica), 8 March 1798. The accounts for Williamsfield and Nightingale Grove during the years 1791 to 1796 give output of sugar in hhd and do not distinguish between revenue from sugar and rum production. Assuming that sugar's share of output was the same as during the years 1796–9 (when the two commodities are separated) and that the weight of the hhd reported between 1805 and 1818 can be applied to the earlier period, net revenue per cwt of sugar 1791–6 averaged 15.5 shillings. WRA, Abstract of accounts of Williamsfield and Nightingale Grove plantations, 1790–1835; Abstracts of produce of the estates and other property in the West Indies belonging to Lord Harewood, 1805–39.

[13] HH:WIP, Adam (London) to Cuthbert & MacLeod (Jamaica), 8 March 1798.

[14] WRA, Harewood House, Letters and Papers on West India Estates and Affairs, William Bishop (Barbados) to Nathaniel Elliot, Josiah Whalley, and John William Adams (London), 11 June 1798; HH:WIP, Adam (London) to Cuthbert & MacLeod (Jamaica), 8 March 1798.

[15] The thirteenth estate the Earl referred to was Maxwell's, a property administered separately by the Beckles Trust. In 1799, Maxwell's made about 2,903 pots of sugar (equivalent to 126 hhd), HH:WIP, Correspondence, Nelson (London) to Lord Harewood, 6 July 1799. The aim of the Beckles Trust, which operated under the direction of Lord Harewood's attorneys, was to assist Maxwell's to free itself from mortgage debt, Nelson to Harewood, 8 July 1799. While no additional information has come to light about this estate, its omission does not seriously distort the overview of cultivation presented by the data.

Table 8.1. *Revenue and performance of twelve estates, 1791–6*

Revenue	1791–3	1794–6	No. of estates	Value of estates (£ sterling)	Return on capital (%) 1791–3	1794–6
Barbados			8	122,842	5.4	2.4
gross (£)	12,217	8,538				
net (£)	6,585	2,918			Ward, 1792–8 6.1	
ratio	0.54	0.34				
Jamaica			2	47,730	20.5	6.6
gross (£)	32,172	11,009				
net (£)	9,772	3,167			Ward, 1792–8 13.9	
ratio	0.30	0.29				
Tobago			2	28,717	0.0^a	−3.4
gross (£)	0^a	4,061				
net (£)	0^a	−987			Ward, 1792–8 13.8	
ratio	0^a	—				
Total			*12*	*199,289*	*8.2*	*2.6*
gross (£)	44,389	23,608				
net (£)	16,357	5,098			Ward, 1792–8 12.6	
ratio	0.37	0.22				

Note: ^{a} A small amount of produce from the Tobago estates was consigned to France during the years of French occupation, 1781–93. Owing to the occupation, Timothy Blenman's estate remained the technical owners of the Tobago estates until 1794. The proceeds remitted to France are reported to be less than the interest owed on Blenman's debts and are not included in the Harewood accounts, HH:WIP, Account of Lord Harewood's demand on the estate of Timothy Blenman, deceased [n.d., 1797].
Sources: HH:WIP, Produce in Pocket of the Right Honourable Edward Lord Harewood from his Eight Estates in Barbados for 7 Years; Accounts of Richmond and Goodwood plantations, Tobago; WRA. Harewood West India Papers, Abstract of accounts of Williamsfield and Nightingale Grove plantations, 1790–1835; J. R. Ward, 'The Profitability of Sugar Planting in the British West Indies, 1650–1834', *Economic History Review*, 31 (1978), 207.

properties (which were in the process of reconstruction), the overall return was probably less than half the average received by West Indian proprietors. To outside observers, the Earl reaped a rich bounty from the Caribbean. For example, Edward Lascelles was thought by the contemporary diarist Joseph Farington to have come into a fortune of 'at least £25,000 a year in the West Indies'.[16] In reality, there was no such easy money to be made from absentee ownership.

[16] Kenneth Garlick and Angus Macintyre eds., *The Diary of Joseph Farington* (16 vols., New Haven, 1978–84), vol. II, 357.

Gaps in the surviving documents hinder a full assessment of West Indian management during Baron Harewood's tenure. Nevertheless, it is clear that planting was a difficult business for most of the twenty years between 1775 and 1795. The estates had been acquired from debtors in arrears; consequently, plantations suffered from inadequate capital investment. Scope for remedying neglect by ploughing back profits into the estates was undermined by the disruption during the War of the American Revolution (1776–83), and by post-war restrictions imposed on trade with North America. Imperial rivalry also cut off trade with the Tobago estates, which failed to generate any returns between 1781 and 1793. Richmond suffered damage and neglect during the periods of French occupation; Goodwood numbered among the plantations hit by a devastating insect infestation that blighted sugar cultivation on the island.[17] The parlous state of planting on these properties motivated Edwin Lascelles to declare in 1788 that, 'there is nothing I should more willingly give my Assent to than to the sale of my Estates in Tobago'.[18] Probably the only bright spot was a boom in sugar prices following the Haitian revolution of 1791. This dramatic event temporarily boosted the performance of the Jamaican estates and masked the extent to which conditions on Barbados had deteriorated.

The mention of only thirteen estates in accounts and correspondence during the early 1790s indicates that a number of plantations were either disposed of, or mothballed, or rented out soon after they were seized for debt. Clarke's Court on Grenada was sold to George Shand in 1791; in the same year negotiations took place for the rental of Mesopotamia on Tobago (though the French invasion swiftly rendered these academic).[19] Some of the capital released from sales may have been reinvested rather than being repatriated to Britain. A total of twenty-five slaves, for example, were purchased for Belle between April 1785 and May 1786.[20] Overall, however, several pieces of evidence suggest that comparatively little capital was sunk into the West Indies in Edwin Lascelles' time.

[17] WRA, Harewood MS, Letters and Papers, John Balfour (Tobago) to Edwin Lascelles, 27 May 1790.

[18] HH:WIP, Lascelles to Elliot, 4 November 1788 (private collection of D. J. Almond).

[19] HH:WIP, Correspondence, George Shand (London) to Lord Harewood, 4 November 1796. Shand (who bought the estate with a repayment mortgage of two-and-a-half years) may have been related to the Liverpool merchant William Shand of the firm Rodie & Shand, John Poyer, *The History of Barbados* (London, 1808), list of subscribers.

[20] HH:WIP, A List of papers belonging to Edward Lascelles Esq. as executor of the right Honourable Edwin Lord Harewood deceased [n.d., 1796], 24. The amount paid for the slaves was £1,163 currency (£831 sterling).

On Barbados, the number of enslaved living on Mount and Thicket had declined by Baron Harewood's death in 1795, as had Williamsfield's population on Jamaica. This finding, coupled with the low proportion of Africans listed on the Lascelles' estates in the first Slave Registration Return of 1817, suggests that relatively few purchases of new slaves were made. The reported condition of Belle on Barbados between 1795 and 1801 provides another indication of limited investment. In 1780, Belle was seriously damaged by one of the eighteenth century's most destructive hurricanes. The violent winds claimed the lives of five slaves, along with widow Mary Clarke. Damage to the mansion house was so extensive that Mary's will could not be found among the debris. It is significant that the building still lay in a state of disrepair two decades later.[21]

The performance of the Jamaican properties is the best documented of the West Indian estates prior to the 1790s. In addition to the two sugar estates (considered below), a pair of cattle pens were owned on the island: Angel Pen (St Catherine's) and Mammee Ridge (St Ann's Parish). Verene Shepherd has demonstrated how livestock keeping was potentially a dynamic sector, buttressing Jamaica's sugar estates by supplying them with animal power, fertiliser, transportation, jobbing labour, and provisions.[22] Dynamic is not the best adjective, however, to describe the level of activity on the Lascelles' cattle ranches.

Angel Pen, at just 70 acres, was too small to be an efficient unit; most livestock holdings on the island ranged from 350 to 750 acres during the period of slavery.[23] Receipts on Angel averaged just £983 (currency) between 1785 and 1788.[24] Mammee Ridge was, on paper, a better-looking proposition. The pen contained 1,000 acres and possessed a good working ratio of ninety-eight slaves and 481 head of stock in 1777.[25] Income from this property, however, was also disappointing: an annual average of only £1,738 (currency) was generated between 1780 and 1796. In comparison, gross revenue per slave on the sugar

---

[21] HH:WIP, Correspondence, [Nelson?] to John Blenman and Richard Cobham (Barbados), 4 December 1801; Deborah Thornhill (Barbados) to Lord Harewood, 7 July 1795.

[22] Verene A. Shepherd, 'Livestock and Sugar: Aspects of Jamaica's Agricultural Development from the Late Seventeenth to the Early Nineteenth Century', *Historical Journal*, 34 (1991), 627–43; 'Alternative Husbandry: Slaves and Free Labourers on Livestock Farms in Jamaica in the Eighteenth and Nineteenth Centuries', *Slavery and Abolition*, 14 (1993), 41–66.

[23] B. W. Higman, 'The Internal Economy of the Jamaican Pens, 1760–1890', *Social and Economic Studies*, 38 (1989), 73.

[24] JA, Accounts Produce, IB/11/4, vols. XII–XV.

[25] WRA, Harewood House, West India Papers, Accession. 2,677, Conveyance of Mammee Ridge Pen, 20 June 1777; Shepherd, 'Alternative Husbandry', 43.

estates was probably between two and three times higher than this. In 1797, Mammee Ridge was dismissed as a plantation 'which for the last twenty years has proved most unproductive', and sold to John Heath (described as a man of £50,000 property on Jamaica and no debt) for £10,000 (sterling), with a repayment mortgage of two-and-a-half years.[26]

A rationale for keeping the pens might have existed if it had proved possible to integrate livestock raising on pens effectively with sugar cultivation. Williamsfield and Nightingale Grove were located in parishes where cattle mills provided the chief energy source for sugar processing.[27] Indeed, these two estates' accounts for the years 1795 to 1815 record purchases of 156 steers, 117 mules, and an unspecified amount of cattle. Prior to its sale, a portion of livestock needs had been supplied from Mammee Ridge. Yet the transactions were small in scale, averaging no more than £235 (currency) per year for Nightingale, and £258 (currency) for Williamsfield.[28] Factoring these transactions into Table 8.1 raises the return from the Jamaican properties by just 0.8 per cent during the years 1794–6. Selling Mammee Ridge was, therefore, a sound decision. Purchases of livestock constituted too small a share of operating costs on the sugar estates to justify the retention of a cattle farm located on the other side of a mountain range with poor communications.

Even though the pens were sold, livestock keeping was not abandoned on Jamaica. On the contrary, the estate accounts record sales of cattle or livestock products on Nightingale Grove and Williamsfield in a majority of the years between 1791 and 1820. Moreover, in 1810 the 1st Earl subscribed £100 to the Committee of West India Merchants, 'towards a Fund for making Experiments on the use of Molasses in Fattening Cattle'.[29]

---

[26] HH:WIP, Correspondence, Lewis Cuthbert (Jamaica) to Lord Harewood, 5 March 1797. Angel Pen was sold at the same time.

[27] Williamsfield was situated in St Thomas-in-the-Vale; a map of 1804 indicates it had twenty-seven cattle, thirteen water, and four windmills in operation. Nightingale Grove was located in St Dorothy's Parish and had thirteen cattle and six watermills at the same date, Shepherd, 'Livestock and Sugar', 637.

[28] WRA, Harewood House, West India Papers, Abstract of accounts of Williamsfield and Nightingale Grove plantations, 1790–1835; JA, IB/11/4, vols. X, XIV, XV, XXIII. A sample of thirty-five properties also suggests that income from livestock and jobbing combined on 'Williamsfield Estate' (parish not stated) in 1820 was relatively small, Verene A. Shepherd, 'Trade and Exchange in Jamaica in the Period of Slavery', in Verene Shepherd and Hilary McD. Beckles eds., *Caribbean Slavery in the Atlantic World: A Student Reader* (Kingston, Jamaica, 2000), 361.

[29] WRA, Harewood House, West India Papers, Abstract of accounts of Williamsfield and Nightingale Grove plantations, 1790–1835; Abstract of the Produce of the Estates and other Property in the West Indies belonging to the Right Honourable Lord Harewood, 1805–39: Barbados Affairs.

Edward Lascelles concluded from his review of the West Indies that 'a total change of system' was required, 'both at home and abroad'.[30] At the heart of the new policy towards the West Indies lay a thorough overhaul of bookkeeping. Managers and attorneys were instructed to complete plantation journals and ledgers according to model examples, replacing the previous irregular and inconsistently maintained systems of accounting.[31] Annual returns of the enslaved populations were ordered, consisting of 'an accurate list of the Negroes on each Estate with a description of their age, sex, & condition as to health & capacity for service'. Biannual statements of slaves, livestock, and the state of the crop supplemented these reports.[32]

While Baron Harewood remained alive, the West Indian accounts lay up to two years in arrears.[33] The new regime recognised that systematic and up-to-date bookkeeping was crucial if decision-making was to be effective. Experienced accountants were regarded as key personnel and their salaries are enumerated separately in surviving accounts of properties.[34] At Belle, for example, the new bookkeeper was recruited from Messrs Thomas and John Daniel (leading West India merchants of Bristol and London).[35] The Lascelles were not alone in fashioning improved systems of bookkeeping, but they ranked among the most innovative planters in their flexible use of accountants, recognising the potential value of such individuals.[36] The importance of effective

[30] HH:WIP, Correspondence, Adam (London) to Cuthbert & MacLeod (Jamaica), 8 March 1798.

[31] Nine sets of Barbados journal and ledger books were received by John Cobham and subject to inspection, HH:WIP, 'A list of papers belonging to Edward Lascelles Esq. as executor of the Right Honourable Edwin Lord Lascelles deceased' [n.d., 1796].

[32] HH:WIP, Correspondence, Adam (London) to Cuthbert & MacLeod (Jamaica), 8 March 1798; [Nelson?] to Blenman and Cobham (Barbados), 4 December 1801; printed model example of a journal entry prepared for a Barbados plantation, based on Charles and James Hamilton's Whim plantation journal in Tobago [n.d., 1799]. Ragatz and Pares testify that the lost archive of Wilkinson and Gaviller contained a series of journals and ledgers for each estate, Lowell J. Ragatz, *A Guide for the Study of British Caribbean History, 1763–1834* (Washington DC, 1932), 35; Richard Pares, 'A London West-India Merchant House, 1740–1769', in Richard Pares and A. J. P. Taylor eds., *Essays Presented to Sir Lewis Namier* (London, 1956), 75–107.

[33] Lascelles to Elliot, 4 November 1788 (private collection of D. J. Almond).

[34] HH:WIP, Sketch of contingencies on Williamsfield and Nightingale Grove plantations partly paid or to be paid in the year 1798.

[35] WRA, Letters and Papers, Bishop (Barbados) to Elliott, Whalley, & Adams (London), 11 June 1798.

[36] Two recent studies emphasising the significance of accountancy in sustaining slavery and absenteeism are D. Oldroyd, R. K. Fleischman, and T. N. Tyson, 'The Culpability of Accounting in the Practice of Slavery in the British Empire', *British Accounting Association Northern Region* (Sheffield, 2004); 'Monetizing Human Life: Slave Valuations on US and British West Indian Plantations', *Accounting History*, 9 (2004), 35–62.

accountancy systems in plantation management is obscured by the
negative contemporary portrayal of bookkeepers as poor and resentful
individuals, inimical to change.[37]

On Jamaica, the roles of accountants were not confined to maintaining ledgers. 'Young men employed in the capacity of bookkeepers on
the estates, and receiving from the properties a small increase of salary',
are reported to have instructed slaves in the Christian religion, under the
supervision of Anglican clergymen. According to the Jamaican Diocesan
Committee, involvement of accountancy staff in catechetical missionary
work was particularly pronounced in the parish of St Thomas-in-the-
Vale. The committee claimed 'this mode of instruction has been
introduced on nearly all the larger properties', through the encouragement of the Revd William Burton.[38] The support given to Burton by
Harewood's attorney, George W. Hamilton, renders it probable that
Williamsfield numbered among these plantations.[39]

By the early nineteenth century, plantation managers were subjected
to closer scrutiny than before. Conditions had changed since William
Collier walked off a plantation belonging to a client of Lascelles &
Maxwell in 1743, complaining of 'the strange method . . . proposed of the
Book-Keeper being a cheque on the Overseer'.[40] More accurate record
keeping informed decisions to replace unsatisfactory managers, to sell
underperforming estates, and to merge plantations. Capital released
from estate sales (and from eliminating waste) was available for fresh
purchases of slaves, planting new varieties of sugar cane (particularly on
Tobago, in order to combat blast), and to fund the expansion of successful estates by acquiring neighbouring properties.

The personnel granted overall supervision of the Harewood West
Indian estates were far removed from the poor and disaffected drifters
who feature in criticisms of absenteeism. Jonathan Blenman Jr, William
Bishop, and the brothers John and Richard Cobham served as Barbados
attorneys from the mid-1790s. The Cobhams, like the Blenmans, ori-
ginated from the West Country and were originally Bristol merchants.
John Cobham was of sufficient standing to be appointed to the Barbados
Council.[41] William Bishop likewise possessed longstanding connections

---

[37] See Gilbert Mathison, *Notices Respecting Jamaica in 1808–1809–1810* (London, 1811),
45–7; James Stewart, *A View of the Past and Present State of the Island of Jamaica*
(London, 1823), 189.

[38] NA:PRO, CO141/27, *The Royal Gazette* (Kingston, Jamaica, 7–14 July, 183), 18.

[39] See Chapter Nine.

[40] *LMLB*, Pares Transcripts, H400, Lascelles & Maxwell to William Collier (Barbados),
16 March 1744[5].

[41] HH:WIP, Duke of Portland (Whitehall) to Lord Harewood, 3 December 1796; Lord
Harewood to Governor Rickett (Barbados), 30 December 1796; Governor Rickett

with Barbados and members of his family can be found among the earlier correspondents of Lascelles & Maxwell. In due course, William was also elevated to the Barbados Council and in 1800 he became President.[42] Following Richard Cobham's death in 1818, Foster Clarke was appointed attorney. The services of this highly regarded individual were retained for the remainder of the period of slavery.[43]

Beneath the attorneys, a manager was appointed with oversight of all the Barbadian estates.[44] Samuel Went first occupied this post, for which a salary of £180 was paid. Went was a partner in Stevenson & Went: merchants with a longstanding business association with the Lascelles.[45] Each estate also possessed its own individual manager or overseer. The terms offered to William and Samuel Wood provide an insight into hiring practices. Each received a three-year contract with graduated payments: £50 to £60 for the first year, £60 to £70 during the second, and £70 to £80 in the third (plus board and lodgings). The Woods were each required to enter into a bond of £300 for good performance.[46] A further indication that overseers were not rootless individuals with meagre resources is provided by the example of James Nurse, manager of Kirton's. Nurse was affluent enough to purchase this estate in December 1801, paying £5,000 down and the rest by a twelve-year repayment mortgage.[47] Under the terms of the agreement, he paid interest at 6 per cent and agreed to consign the annual crop to Lord Harewood's agents until the mortgage was redeemed.

(Barbados) to Lord Harewood, 27 March 1797; WRA, Letters and Papers, Thomas Graeme to Nathaniel Elliot, 18 December 1796.

[42] HH:WIP, Correspondence, Acknowledgement of dismissal by John Prettyjohn, 17 July 1795; Jonathan Blenman and Richard Cobham (Barbados) to Lord Harewood, 2 October 1801; John Cobham (Bristol) to Nelson (London), 1 July 1801; John Cobham (Bristol) to Lord Harewood, 1 January 1802; Wilkinson and Gaviller, Staplehurst, Kent, Lascelles and Maxwell Letter Book; Robert H. Schomburgk, *The History of Barbados* (London, 1971, 1999), 685. In return for their services, attorneys received a 5 per cent commission on remittances.

[43] WRA, Accounts of the Produce of the Estates and other Property in the West Indies, 1805–39: Barbados affairs; Kathleen Mary Butler, *The Economics of Emancipation: Jamaica and Barbados, 1823–1843* (Chapel Hill/London, 1995), 58–9.

[44] HH:WIP, Correspondence, Bishop, Worrell, & Cobham to Samuel Went, 20 July 1795; WRA, Letters and Papers, Edward Lascelles (Harewood) to Nathaniel Elliot (London), 24 September 1794; Elliot (London) to Lascelles, 29 September 1795.

[45] S. D. Smith, 'Reckoning with the Atlantic Economy', *Historical Journal*, 46 (2003), 1–2.

[46] HH:WIP, Indenture between William and Samuel Wood, John Wood Nelson, and Lord Harewood [n.d., 1796–9]. These two men may also have been kinsmen of Nelson, a partner in the London commission house.

[47] HH:WIP, Cobham (Barbados) to Nelson (London), 2 July 1799, Terms of sale of Kirton Plantation to James Nurse. Nurse may have been an inland merchant; his deposit was received in small amounts, probably from debts called in by him, HH:WIP, Bishp to Lord Harewood, 28 February 1801, Account of costs relating to the sale of Kirton plantation [n.d., 1801–2].

By reducing the number of their estates on Jamaica and Tobago, the Lascelles were able to dispense with one tier of management; on these colonies, attorneys supervised individual overseers. As on Barbados, the attorneys tended to operate on a large scale within the regions occupied by estates, making it less easy for the managers beneath them to move from post to post in the event of unsatisfactory performance. Jamaican attorneys were drawn primarily from the ranks of Scots gentry families. Francis Graeme was appointed in 1799 and remained in charge until his death in 1820.[48] Graeme, a planter in his own right and member of the island Assembly, was very active as an estate manager in St Catherine and St Thomas-in-the-Vale. In 1815, he testified that he represented 'forty-nine sugar estates, nineteen pens, and ten other plantations on which there are thirteen thousand Negroes'.[49] Graeme's eventual successor was George William Hamilton: another prominent island attorney, whose family can be linked to the Stevenson, Harvie, and Graeme circle.[50] Hamilton's mercantile interests included links with the firm of Bogles & Co.; he was also involved in parish administration and religious affairs in St Thomas-in-the-Vale.[51]

Oversight of the Tobago estates lay in the hands of Gilbert Francklyn during the 1780s. As attorney, Francklyn played an important role in

[48] HH:WIP, Cuthbert & MacLeod (Spanish Town) to Nelson (London), 29 April 1798. For details of Graeme's family background, see John Roby, *Monuments of the Cathedral Church and Parish of St Catherine: Being Part I of Church Notes and Monumental Inscriptions of Jamaica in the Year 1824* (Jamaica, 1831), 56. Graeme's monumental inscription notes that his father, Alexander Graeme of Drynie (Black Isle), was British consul at Fayal in the Azores. It appears probable that he belonged to the same family of Scots Graemes who were kinsmen of the Stevensons and Harvies, West Sussex Record Office, Chichester, Add. MS 39,743, Genealogical notes, family trees, and memoranda on the Turing, Davidson, Farquhar families.

[49] *Further Proceedings of the Honourable House of Assembly of Jamaica Relative to a Bill Introduced into the House of Commons, for Effectually Preventing the Unlawful Importation of Slaves and Holding Free Persons in Slavery in the British Colonies* (Jamaica, 1816), 55. Graeme was owner of Tulloch estate in St Thomas-in-the-Vale and co-owner of Farm Pen in St Catherine's. He was connected by kinship and business with the London partnership of Duncan Davidson and Charles Graeme (later Davidson, Barkly & Co.). Davidson originated from Tulloch Castle (the name given to Francis Graeme's Jamaican sugar estate) in Dingwall, Scotland (close to Black Isle), information provided by Mary Mill (pers. com.), 23 April 2005.

[50] Farquhar, Stevenson, Leslie Family Pedigree compiled by Professor Marion Diamond (University of Queensland), pers. com., 20 July 2005; West Sussex Record Office, Chichester, Add. MS 39,743, Genealogical notes, family trees, and memoranda on the Turing, Davidson, Farquhar families; Craig B. Waff and Stephen Skinner, 'Thomas Stevenson of Barbados and Comet Halley's 1759 Return', in Richard B. Goddard ed., *George Washington's Visit to Barbados, 1751* (Barbados, 1997), 203.

[51] NA:PRO, Slave Registration Returns for Jamaica, 1817–32, T71/13–18; T71/26–8, 30, 32; CO141/23, *The Royal Gazette* (Kingston, Jamaica, 24 June–1 July 1826), 25–6. Bogles & Co. of Kingston, Jamaica, failed in or before 1827, The Orkney Library and Archive, Kirkwall; DO33/1/22/18, Edward Clouston (Jamaica) to Peter Scollay (Orkney), 30 July 1827.

enabling the Lascelles to gain control of the Clarkes' estates, but his ability to manage the development of the plantations was handicapped by the subsequent French occupation. His successor (and kinsman) Charles Francklyn, proved to lack 'that knowledge of plantership that might be wished'. In 1798–9, he was replaced by Robert Mitchell.[52] A final change was made in 1802, when John Robley (one of the wealthiest planters on the island and later the purchaser of two of the Lascelles' estates), assumed the role of attorney.[53]

These staffing changes in themselves did not amount to an alteration of system since the replaced individuals were also, for the most part, men of distinction. Accountancy controls, rather than personnel, constituted the principal difference between estate administration under the 1st and 2nd Earls. On Barbados, the previous attorneys had been William Moore and John Prettyjohn. Moore was the colony's Attorney General; had he not elected to return to Britain, he may have continued in post. Originally from the West Country (his family estate lay in Bridport, Dorset), John Prettyjohn was a long-established merchant and planter of Barbados. In 1758, for example, Prettyjohn's partnership with William Collier was hailed by one London merchant as 'the most Flourishing house upon the Island'.[54] By the 1790s, Prettyjohn had accumulated twenty years' service with the Lascelles. His eventual dismissal came about through a combination of age, the unsatisfactory performance of the Barbados estates, and accusations that he treated the Beckles Trust as a sinecure.[55] On Jamaica, Edwin's attorneys had been Lewis Cuthbert and Alexander MacLeod. Cuthbert was a Scot, who originated from an ancient Inverness family of burgesses, and who held the patent office of Provost Marshal of the island. Cuthbert's deteriorating financial position (he had debts of £29,000 sterling at his death in 1802) may have been a

---

[52] WRA, Letters and Papers, John Balfour (Tobago) to Edwin Lascelles, 27 May 1790.

[53] Ibid., Lord Harewood to Francklyn (Tobago), October 1798; HH:WIP, Gilbert Petrie (Tobago) to Lord Harewood, 29 January 1799; James Gorden (Dunkirk) to Lord Harewood, 6 October 1802. See also Chapter Ten. Mitchell's uncle, Gilbert Petrie, took over as attorney briefly in 1799. It is believed that he was related to the Petrie of the firm of Petrie & Hunter, who did business with Henry Lascelles in slaving and victualling, HH:WIP, Bond of George John Petrie and Hunter to secure payment of £750 to Henry Lascelles, 8 January 1752. Francklyn later rented part of Mesopotamia between 1827 and 1839, WRA, Accounts of the Produce of the Estates and other Property in the West Indies, 1805–39: Tobago Affairs.

[54] Cambridge University Library, Add. MS 2,798, Robert Plumsted Letterbook, Robert Plumsted to John Prettyjohn Sr, 25 May 1758, Prettyjohn later numbered among the creditors of Gedney Clarke Jr.

[55] BA, Hughes-Queree Collection Abstract in Queree notebook, 'Charnock's; HH:WIP, Judgements against Gedney Clarke entered in Tobago [n.d., 1800]; Correspondence, Nelson to Lord Harewood, 8 July 1799. Following his dismissal, Prettyjohn claimed £3,585 from Clarke Jr's estate.

factor in the change of personnel, though Lewis Cuthbert's son George was later to work as an estate attorney alongside Francis Graeme and George William Hamilton between 1817 and 1832.[56]

Daniel Lascelles was the last member of the family to act as a partner in the London commission house. Exposure to risk after Daniel's death in 1784 was reduced by continuity of partners, repeat business, and the social characteristics of the firm's senior personnel. The partnerships of the house, during the century-and-a-half after Henry Lascelles' return to London in 1732, are listed in Table 8.2. William Daling (originally Henry's bookkeeper) remained at the helm until 1790.[57] Thereafter, Nathaniel Elliot and John Wood Nelson oversaw operations for the rest of the period of enslavement. Elliot combined a mercantile and legal career until 1799, at which point he retired to an estate at St Sidwells in Exeter. The Nelsons were similarly a professional family of repute, whose members included the architect Thomas Marsh Nelson.[58]

Once accountancy systems and staffing issues had been addressed, the estates themselves were subject to close scrutiny. After 1788, no significant net additions were made to the Lascelles' holdings of West Indian property. The process of rationalisation begun by Baron Harewood was continued by the 1st Earl (Table 8.3). Accounts of production on each estate, compiled by the separate bookkeepers, were analysed carefully. In ease case, a decision was reached whether to sell the plantation, merge it with another, rent out the property, or withdraw it from cultivation. On Jamaica, little attempt was made to develop the large tracts of land the Harvies had optimistically acquired. According to attorney Lewis Cuthbert, the undeveloped acres situated at Pedros Valley, The Crawl, and Oldfield's Bog carried arrears of quit rents amounting to more than their market value.[59] In effect, therefore, much

---

[56] NA:PRO, T71/13–18; T71/26–8, 30, 32. Lewis Cuthbert was a fund raiser for and subscriber to the Inverness Royal Academy, see Douglas Hamilton, *Scotland, the Caribbean, and the Atlantic World, 1750–1820* (Manchester, 2005), ch. ten.

[57] NA:PRO, PROB11/804, Will of Henry Lascelles, 15 October 1753.

[58] Information provided by Eleanor Gawne and John Meriton of the Victoria and Albert Museum. It is possible that further connections exist between families of architects and commission house partners via the kinsmen of Robert Adam and John Wood; additional research in this area is needed.

[59] Institute of Commonwealth Studies, London, ICS 101, Wemyss Castle Estate Papers, Lewis Cuthbert (Jamaica) to J. W. Nelson (London), 14 May 1802; Simon Halliday (London) to Gilbert Mathison (Jamaica), 27 April 1809. These assessments were disputed by Thomas Graeme, but only on the grounds that a James Syms of St Ann's Parish had acquired the reversionary rights; a few years later, a Mr Fraser expressed interest in the lands, Thomas Graeme (London) to Nelson, 16 October 1802; Francis Graeme (Jamaica) to Nelson, 27 March 1806. It seems most likely, therefore, that these holdings were either abandoned or sold for relatively small sums of money in an undeveloped state.

Table 8.2. *The evolution of 'Lascelles & Maxwell', 1732–1886*

Period	Trading name	Names of partners	Principal address
1732–43	Henry Lascelles	Henry Lascelles	Mincing Lane
1743–50	Lascelles & Maxwell	Henry Lascelles & George Maxwell	Mincing Lane
1750–3	Lascelles & Maxwell	Henry Lascelles, George Maxwell, & Daniel Lascelles	Mark Lane
1753–63	Lascelles, Maxwell, & Daling	George Maxwell, Daniel Lascelles, & William Daling	Mark Lane
1763–5	Lascelles, Daling, & Clarke	Daniel Lascelles, William Daling, & Gedney Clarke	Hylords Court, Crutched Friars
1765–84	Lascelles & Daling	Daniel Lascelles & William Daling	Hylords Court, Crutched Friars
1784–90	Daling & Elliot	William Daling & Nathaniel Elliot	Hylords Court, Crutched Friars
1790–8	Elliot, Whalley, & Adam	Nathaniel Elliot, Josiah Whalley, & John William Adam	Hylords Court, Crutched Friars
1798–1805	Adam, Whalley, & Nelson	John William Adam, Josiah Whalley, & John Wood Nelson	Hylords Court, Crutched Friars
1805–27	Nelson & Adam	J. W. Nelson & John Adam	Savage Gardens, Crutched Friars
1827–41	Nelson, Adam, & Nelson	J. W. Nelson, Benjamin Adam, John Henry Nelson	Savage Gardens, Crutched Friars
1841–51	Nelson & Adam	J. W. Nelson & William Adam	Savage Gardens, Crutched Friars
1851–4	William Adam	William Adam	Great Tower Street
1854–60	William Wilkinson	William Wilkinson	Great Tower Street
1860–86	Wilkinson & Gaviller	W. Wilkinson & A. Gaviller	Great Tower Street

Sources: HH:WIP, Correspondence; WRA, Harewood MSS, Letters and Papers on West India Estates, 1795–1873; Nathaniel Elliot Correspondence (private collection owned by Dr A. J. Almond, copies deposited at Harewood House); Records of Wilkinson and Gaviller, S. R. Evans, 'MEMO – on history of old Firm of WILKINSON & GAVILLER, 1734–1886' (1953) [n.p.]; *A Complete Guide to all Persons who have any Trade or Concern with the City of London* (London, 1740), 134; *A Complete Guide…London* (London, 1758), 135; *A Complete Guide…London* (London, 1763), 150; *The Universal Directory…by Mr Mortimer* (London, 1763), 43; *Baldwin's New Complete Guide* (London, 1768), 135; *The New Complete Guide* (London, 1772), 237; *The London Directory* (London, 1774), 101; *The New Complete Guide* (London, 1774), 245; *Kent's Directory* (London, 1774), 107.

of these lands were worthless. The two cattle pens were judged surplus to requirements, while slaves working the settled portion of Oldfield's Bog appear to have been either sold or absorbed into Nightingale Grove

Table 8.3. *Disinvestment of West Indian real estate, 1791–1975*

Year disposed of	Name and colony	Acreage	Year acquired	Ownership period (years)	Proceeds (£)
1791	Clarke's Court (G)	800	1773	18	21,570 stg
1796 (1809)[a]	Pot House	72	1787	9–22	2,000 stg
1797	Mammee Ridge (J)	1,000	1777	20	10,000 stg
1797	Angel's Pen	70	1777	20	300 stg
1800	Kirtons (B)*	181	1784	16	17,343 stg
1801	Pilgrim (B)*	226	1787	14	27,000 cy
1807 (1815)[b]	Cooper's Hill (B)*	301	1784	23	15,000 stg (1807) 26,279 cy (1815)
1807	Holetown (B)*	239	1784	23	10,000 stg
1809	Mesopotamia (T)	500	1785	6–24	rented out
1815	Maxwell's (B)[c]*	444	1773	42	33,507 cy
1820	Castle (B)[c]	363	1777	43	31,000 cy
1820	Richmond & Glamorgan (T)[d]*	648	1777	43	50,000 stg
1820	Goodwood (T)*	576	1777	43	8,000 stg
1825	Bushy Park (T)	500	1777	48	rented out for 50 stg (1847–8)
By 1836	Turner's Hall (B)[c]	187	1777	na	not available
1836	Nightingale (J)*	285	1777	59	10,947 stg
1836	Compensation payment for slaves on Belle, Mount, Thicket, Fortescue, Nightingale Grove, and Williamsfield				26,309 stg
1843	Williamsfield (J)[e]*	1,440	1777	66	rented out for 130 stg (1847–8)
Estimate of total amount of capital received 1791–1843					241,274 stg
1918	Fortescue (B)*	169	1787	131	see Thicket
1918	Thicket (B)*	439	1787	131	33,000 stg
1974	Mount (B)*	276	1780	194	$240,000
1975	Belle (B)*	637	1784	191	$501,560

Notes: *Mentioned in accounts of West Indian revenue between 1791 and 1799; [a]Conflicting dates, possibly reflecting sale on mortgage and repossession; [b]Sold on mortgage to Thomas Went; re-sold in 1815 to William Hinds Prescott, following the death of Went in 1813; [c]Indebted estate managed by the Lascelles' agents but not owned by the family; [d]Includes Glamorgan (added to the property in 1818); [e]Includes Sandy Gut (added to the property in 1815); 1836 valuation.

Sources: WRA, Letters and Papers on West India Estates and Affairs, 1795–1873, Nathaniel Elliot (London) to Edward Lascelles, 24 November 1796, 'Clarke's Court'; John Wood Nelson (London) to Lord Harewood, 22 October 1816, 'Castle' & 'Cooper's Hill'; Lord Harewood to James Swaby, 5 November 1836, 'Nightingale Grove'; West Indies Accounts, 1790–1848, 'Richmond', 'Glamorgan', 'Goodwood', 'Bushy Park', 'Clarke's Court', 'Pilgrim', 'Cooper's Hill', 'Holetown'; HH:WIP, Correspondence, John Wood Nelson to

and Williamsfield. On Tobago, a similar review was conducted, with the result that Bushy Park was taken out of production. The Barbadian estates of Kirton and Pilgrim were disposed of in 1800; around the same time, the possibility of combining Cooper's Hill and Holetown was explored, but rejected in favour of selling the properties in 1807. Cotton growing on Fortescue was abandoned and the estate merged with Thicket in 1815 to create a larger unit. In all, approximately 3,130 acres were sold off between 1797 and 1815, including two of the three Barbadian estates managed by the family on behalf of its debtors (Table 8.3). Proceeds from these sales funded two new acquisitions: Jamaica's Sandy Gut (1815) and Glamorgan on Tobago (1818).[60] These purchases enabled Williamsfield and Richmond to expand.

In addition to selling estates, capital was raised by recovering debts from loan clients. When Baron Harewood died in 1795, a total of £235,752 was owing from the West Indies.[61] This figure consisted of approximately £62,411 due from purchasers of estates who had taken out repayment mortgages, alongside £173,341 of older debts. By the time of the 1st Earl's death in 1820, 68 per cent of money (£42,615) owing on mortgage in the Caribbean had been repaid. Of the remaining debts, the old loans due from the Clarkes and Blenmans (amounting to £83,788) were written off, but £50,556 was recovered from other clients.[62]

Notes to Table 8.3 (cont.)
Lord Harewood, 5 August 1801, 'Pilgrim'; [Nelson & Adam] to William Bishop and John Cobham, 20 August 1799, 'Pilgrim'; Terms of sale of Kirton Plantation to James Nurse; John Cobham to John W. Nelson, 2 July 1799, 'Kirton's'; William Bishop to Lord Harewood, 23 November 1799, 'Pilgrim'; Lewis Cuthbert to Lord Harewood, 5 March 1797, 'Mammee Ridge'; George Shand to Lord Harewood, 4 November 1796, 'Clarke's Court'; List of balances from the books of the Right Honourable Lord Harewood for Jamaica Affairs, 1798, 'Angel's Pen'; BA, Hughes-Queree Collection, Abstract in Queree notebook, 'Castle', 'Cooper's Hill', 'Maxwell's', Estates Card Index, 'Thicket and Fortescue'; Bobby Morris, 'Transfer of Wealth from Barbados to England – From Lascelles Plantation, Barbados to Harewood House, Yorkshire', JBMHS, 50 (2004), 99, 'Pottery', 'Belle', 'Mount'.

[60] Castle and Cooper's Hill on Barbados were sold to fund the purchase of Glamorgan in Tobago, WRA, Letters and Papers, John Wood Nelson (London) to Lord Harewood, 22 October 1816.
[61] The net figure (allowing for debts owed by the estate on the West Indies account) was £224,815.
[62] HH:WIP, A List of Debts due to and from the Estate of Edwin Lord Harewood (deceased) in the Books for West India Affairs, 30 April 1796; WRA, Harewood MS, Letters and Papers on West India Affairs, 1795–1873, List of Debts Received since the death of Edwin Lord Harewood, 30 April 1820. The sum of £30,556 was received from loan clients who had owed £62,280 in 1796. The repayment record of the remaining debtors (owing £27,274 in 1796) is not known.

Table 8.4. *Revenue and performance of eight estates, 1805–20*

Revenue		No. of estates	Value of estates (£ sterling)*a*	Return on capital (%)
Barbados		4	97,776	6.9
gross (£)	10,187			
net (£)	6,743			Ward, 1799–1819
ratio	0.66			5.8
Jamaica		2	65,912	10.3
gross (£)	9,674			
net (£)	6,808			Ward, 1799–1819
ratio	0.70			9.6
Tobago		2	58,293	2.5
gross (£)	4,264			
net (£)	1,449			Ward, 1799–1819
ratio	0.34			10.0
Total		*8*	*221,981*	6.8
gross (£)	24,125			
net (£)	15,000			Ward, 1799–1819
ratio	0.62			9.6

Note: *a* Calculated using the method outlined by Ward and population estimates in Chapter Nine.

Sources: WRA, Harewood Accounts: West Indies, Abstract of accounts of Williamsfield and Nightingale Grove plantations, 1790–1835; Abstract of the Produce of the Estates and other Property in the West Indies belonging to the Right Honourable Lord Harewood, 1805–39; J. R. Ward, 'The Profitability of Sugar Planting in the British West Indies, 1650–1834', *Economic History Review*, 31 (1978), 207.

The effects of Edward Lascelles' 'total change of system' can be seen in Tables 8.4 and 8.5, which records production on seven estates between 1805 and 1820. For most of these years, war with France disrupted Atlantic trade routes. Moreover, in 1816, Thicket estate was damaged during Bussa's rebellion. Despite difficulties beyond the control of managers, these data show a clear improvement over the earlier period. Profits were higher and the operating ratio (net revenue relative to gross revenue) far more satisfactory. In consequence, the gap between returns on Harewood's estates and those achieved by planters more generally narrowed.

Production data for the estates can be looked at in a slightly different way using the technique of Data Enveloping Analysis (DEA) or frontier analysis. DEA generates measures of relative efficiency among what are termed decision-making units (DMUs) within an organisation.[63] In the

[63] A. Charnes, W. W. Cooper, and E. Rhodes, 'Measuring the Efficiency of Decision Making Units', *European Journal of Operational Research*, 2 (1978), 429–44.

Table 8.5. *Production data for eight estates, 1805–20*

	Opera- ting ratio	Sugar per slave (cwt)	Price per cwt sugar, f.o.b. (s.)	Variance hhd weight (%)	Variance output (%)	Variance price (%)
Belle (B)	.60	4.6	22.9	7.4	39.1	22.9
Fortescue & Thicket (B)	.70	9.4	17.9	10.1	23.3	17.9
Mount (B)	.67	6.8	28.0	5.1	39.1	28.0
Williamsfield (J)	.73	8.6	25.2	7.0	18.5	26.1
Nightingale (J)	.67	11.4	24.6	4.8	31.7	24.4
Goodwood (T)	.25	3.2	19.7	5.6	32.1	27.5
Richmond (T)	.39	9.8	20.0	6.8	31.0	25.5
Weighted mean[a]	.61	8.3	22.50	7.0	26.3	24.1

Comparative data: 1) Sugar per slave (cwt): Barbados 5.5, Jamaica 12.0, Ceded Islands 10.9,2) London price of Jamaica muscovados sugar (in bond), c.i.f., 1805–20: 44.8s. per cwt (variance 24.5%).
Note: [a] Weighted by average size of the sugar crop, 1805–20.
Sources: As for Tables 8.1 and 8.4; Arthur D. Gayer, W. W. Rostow, and Anna J. Schwartz, *The Growth and Fluctuation of the British Economy, 1790–1850* (2 vols., Oxford, 1953), Statistical Supplement, 729–30.

case of the Lascelles' West Indian property portfolio, the individual estates may be regarded as DMUs since they enjoyed flexibility with respect to some decision-making and turned inputs (land, enslaved labour, capital) into outputs (sugar, rum, and cotton). DEA rates a given DMU as fully efficient (100 per cent), if and only if the available evidence (the performances of the other DMUs) does not indicate that some of its inputs or outputs could be improved without worsening its other inputs or outputs. A hypothetical example (Fig. 8.1) illustrates the technique, with two inputs (land and slaves) and one output (sugar). Estates A and B are located on the envelope or efficiency frontier, whereas estate C lies within the envelope. The relative efficiency of estate C is found by drawing a line from the origin through the current position of C and calculating the ratio: 100 × (OC/OD).

For the Lascelles' estates, data are available for acreage (the size of the plantation), the enslaved population, expenses (freight, insurance, and the island account), and the gross value of the crop. There are, therefore, three available input measures (acreage, slaves, and expenses) and one output measure (value of the crop). A linear programme may be formulated to solve the DEA optimisation problem, assuming constant returns to scale across the relevant range.[64] The results are presented in

[64] Let K (k = 1 . . . K) denote the number of estates; let O_{ik} denote the ith output of estate k and M_{jk} the jth input of estate k. Let X_{ik} denote the weight of output i selected by estate

Sugar per acre

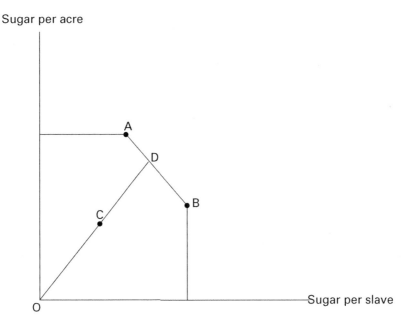

Figure 8.1. Data envelopment analysis: the efficiency frontier

Table 8.6.[65] Interpretation of these findings requires care and it is important to re-emphasise that the efficiencies are relative, not absolute. For example, it is not necessarily the case that Kirton was only a quarter as efficient as Belle during the 1790s; nevertheless, the data do suggest that Kirton (alongside other properties) was performing poorly, raising questions regarding the extent to which all of the estates were employing best practices.

k and Y_{jk} the weight of input j selected by estate k. The linear programme may be written as:

Maximise $\sum X_{ik} \star O_{ik}$ with respect to X_{ik} and Y_{jk}

Subject to $\sum Y_{jk} \star M_{jk} = 1$

$\sum X_{ik} \star O_{jl} <= \sum Y_j k \star M_j p$ for all p (where p denotes all estates other than k)

X,Y >0

Analysis was carried out with and without the subjective constraints that the weight for slaves exceeded land and expenses, and that land's weight also exceeded expenses. The rank order of estates was the same in both cases (Table 8.6 reports results with the subjective constraints). The solver function in Microsoft Excel was used to obtain the solutions.

[65] DEA allows each estate to select the input weights that maximise its efficiency relative to the others; these weights are then applied to the rest of the estates. The process is repeated k times with each estate gaining the opportunity to select its best weights. Efficiency scores reported in Table 8.6 are obtained by averaging the results.

Table 8.6. *Relative efficiency levels on twelve estates, 1791–1839*

Estate	1791–6	1805–19	1821–39
Belle	1.000	0.551	0.652
Holetown	0.594	sold	sold
Thicket	0.589	0.783	0.685
Fortescue	0.372	merged	merged
Pilgrim	0.421	sold	sold
Cooper's	0.531	sold	sold
Kirton's	0.242	sold	sold
Mount	0.543	0.762	1.000
Williamsfield	0.706	0.755	0.959
Nightingale Grove	0.829	1.000	0.801
Richmond	not in use	0.493	sold
Goodwood	not in use	0.306	sold

Sources: As for Tables 8.1 and 8.4.

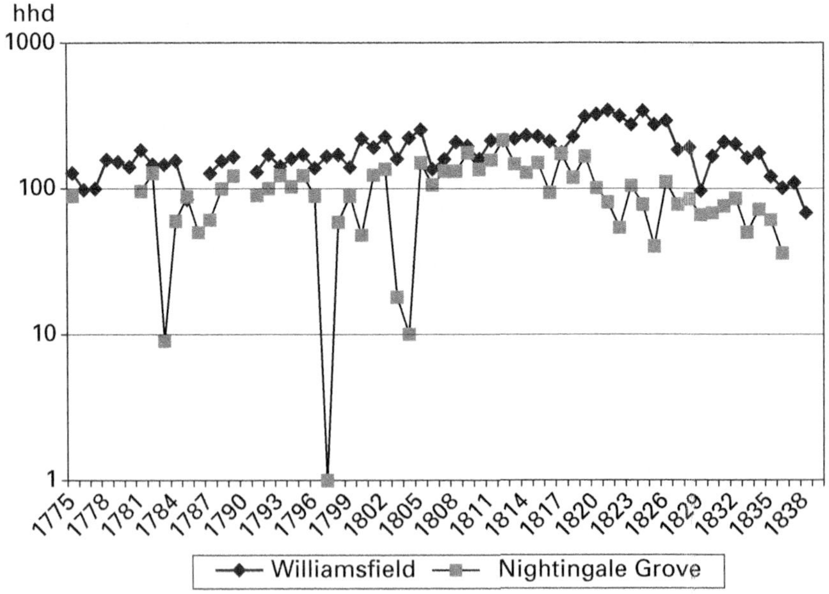

Figure 8.2. Sugar output on two Jamaican estates, 1775–1838 (semi-log scale)
Source: HH:WIP, Produce in Pocket of the Right Honourable Edward Lord Harewood from his Eight Estates in Barbados for 7 Years; Accounts of Richmond and Goodwood plantations, Tobago; WRA, Abstract of accounts of Williamsfield and Nightingale Grove plantations, 1790–1835; Abstract of the Produce of the Estates and other Property in the West Indies belonging to the Right Honourable Lord Harewood, 1805–39.

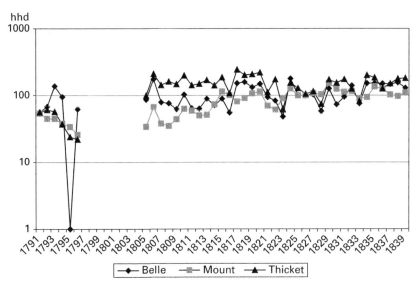

Figure 8.3. Sugar output on three Barbadian estates, 1791–1839 (semi-log scale)

While surviving sources do not provide a comprehensive account of how improvements in performance were achieved, a number of inferences can be drawn from the evidence. The physical quantities of sugar produced on plantations owned for the longest periods fluctuated around a nearly horizontal trend until the final years of slavery (Figs. 8.2, 8.3, and 8.4).[66] On Mount and Thicket, depressed output during the 1790s reflected a decrease in the numbers of the enslaved living on these properties that was subsequently reversed.[67]Aside from this factor, climatic effects (especially on Nightingale Grove, whose crop demonstrated the greatest tendency to fail) appear responsible for most of the variation in the annual produce. It is clear from the DEA analysis that the poorest performing units were sold or merged. On those estates which were retained, costs (particularly the island account) were brought under tighter budgetary control. The result was to push the efficiency levels of the properties closer towards the frontier during the period 1805 to 1819 (Table 8.6). Belle's performance constitutes the principal outlier. The relative deterioration in Belle's efficiency may

---

[66] Figures 8.2–4 present information for the estates with the longest series of production data.
[67] See Chapter Nine.

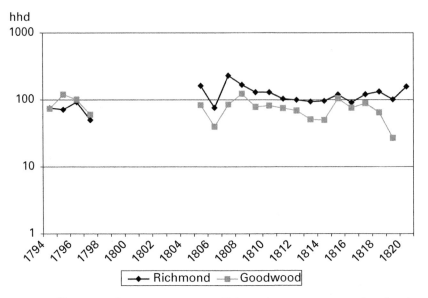

Figure 8.4. Sugar output on two Tobagonian estates, 1794–1820 (semi-log scale)

reflect a changing age-structure, generating more dependents within the population in comparison with the other estates.[68]

Despite the improvement in the management of the Lascelles' property empire, some problem areas remained, especially on Tobago. Performance here lagged behind the average recorded on the Ceded Islands, while output and crop quality (measured by the price received for sugar) were both disappointing on Goodwood and Richmond. In consequence, these estates were selected as the next to be disposed of and were duly sold between 1818 and 1820.

The 1st Earl turned a profit on plantation agriculture despite the inherent volatility of a sector dependent to a large extent on a single commodity. From year to year, the size of the crop and the price the Lascelles' sugar fetched in the market both fluctuated, on average by around 25 per cent. London's West India Committee (a trade association formed by leading planters) did not establish any system of production controls that might have helped stabilise prices. Possession of

[68] The worst survival (highest hazard of death) of the six estates examined between 1817 and 1834 was found on Belle (Chapter Nine, Table 9.8). This result reflects the age-structure of the estate's population (the likelihood of death was greatest at the youngest and oldest ages). Belle's dependency ratio in 1817 (45 per cent) also exceeded the Barbadian average (Chapter Nine, Table 9.5).

multiple properties, however, ensured that price variation experienced by the Lascelles was no worse than the sector as a whole.[69] The family's ownership of a portfolio of estates also provided a degree of insurance against output variability, since it was unlikely that simultaneous crop failure would occur (Table 8.5).

A notable feature of the crop accounts compiled for the London commission house between 1805 and 1820 is the inclusion of a statement of the weight of the hogsheads (hhd) received from the West Indies for a majority of these years. This statistic provides an illustration of one method of audit control employed to scrutinise the performance of plantation managers. Nominally, the hhd weighed 16 cwt, but it was common practice for estate managers to consign hhd weighing substantially less than this in order to disguise the true size of the crop.[70] In assessing production standards, allowance must be made for the fact that hogsheads and casks were hand-manufactured containers; some variability in capacity, therefore, was inevitable. In addition, sugar could gain weight during an Atlantic passage due to moisture seeping into casks (an allowance termed the 'tare').[71] Conversely, weight might be lost to leakage ('wastage') during the voyage home.[72] The average weight of hhd despatched from the Harewood estates between 1805 and 1818 was 13.29 cwt, with an annual variance of only 7 per cent. This figure lies comfortably within the margin allowed for tare or wastage, indicating consistency in standards.

An estimate of the contribution of earnings from the Caribbean to the Harewood estate is presented in Table 8.7. These data should be regarded as approximate and indicative only of the general situation. By the early nineteenth century, somewhere in the region of a quarter of the Lascelles' wealth was invested in slavery, and profits from the West Indies accounted for perhaps one-third of total revenue.[73] Whatever the exact situation, the trend at least is clear. When Henry Lascelles died in 1753,

---

[69] Based on a comparison of prices realised by estate sugars with the London price of Jamaican muscovados sugar, net of duty (Table 8.5).

[70] HH:WIP, Nelson to Edward Lord Harewood, 13 October 1800.

[71] London's grocers allowances for the tare in proportion to the weight of the hogshead or cask; in the case of containers weighing between 10 cwt and 16 cwt, tare lay between 8.3 and 9.1 per cent. Allowances were raised slightly in 1747, but for casks between 12 cwt and 16 cwt the range of the tare was little changed at 8.1 to 8.8 per cent, *LMLB*, Pares Transcripts, W&G II, Lascelles & Maxwell to Samuel Husbands, 19 September 1743; W&G V, same to same, 29 January 1754.

[72] Allowances for wastage were 56 lb per cask for first whites, 84 lb per cask for seconds, and 1 cwt per cask for coarse clays, ibid., W&G VI, Lascelles & Maxwell to Philip Gibbes (Barbados), 21 July 1755.

[73] This statement makes an allowance for the fact that not all debts were good ones and not all interest was received promptly.

Table 8.7. *Estimated value and income of the Harewood estate and Edward Lascelles' personal estate, c. 1799–1805 (£ sterling)*

	Value of investment	Annual return
English lands	568,974[a]	28,449
Stocks and securities	332,539[b]	11,639
Other	27,688[c]	831
Subtotal	*929,201*	*40,919*
West Indian estates	199,289–228,585[d]	5,098–15,108[d]
West Indian loans	111,946–162,186[e]	5,597–8,109[e]
Subtotal	*311,235–390,771*	*10,695–23,217*
Total	*1,240,436–1,319,972*	*51,614–64,136*
Ratio	.25 to .30	.21 to .36

Notes: [a]Capitalised at twenty years' purchase. [b]Assumed rate of return of 3.5%. [c] Assumed rate of return of 3.0%. [d] Estate valuations and returns from Tables 8.1 and 8.3. [e]Estimate based on debts owed in 1795–6 multiplied by the ratio of debts still outstanding in 1799 (where known), plus James Nurse's mortgage for Kirton's estate. The lower figure excludes mortgaged estates still owned in 1795; the higher figure includes mortgaged estates 1799–1801. Both estimates exclude bad debts (owed by the Clarkes and Blenmans) for which no interest was received and for which estates were taken. Note that c. £1,577 of annual West Indian revenue was paid to the Maxwell and Clarke families in annuities or rental for slaves.
Sources: WRA, Harewood Accounts: Estate and General, 1804–41; Table 8.3; Chapter Seven, Appendix.

dependence on the Caribbean had been significantly greater. Around 42 per cent of Henry's wealth was tied up in West Indian concerns (Table 8.8). By the 1800s, while still significant, sugar and slavery occupied a more subordinate role. In a letter to the Earl of Harewood, written in 1818, Nelson began by acknowledging, 'Your Lordship has always expressed yourself that no part of your Income arising from property here should be intruded upon for Foreign Concerns.' Yet, he continued, 'the converse, I think, has almost, if not quite as much sound policy'.[74] Nelson's plea was for capital released from the sale of Cooper's Hill and Holetown (on Barbados) to be reinvested in Jamaican and Tobago purchases, to permit operations on Williamsfield and Richmond to expand. His argument won the day, but the exchange illustrates how far attitudes towards the West Indies estates had shifted. Old Harry Lascelles had viewed slavery and sugar as the means to acquire wealth; the 1st Earl feared the West Indies might lose him money.

[74] WRA, Letters and Papers, Nelson (London) to Edward Earl of Harewood, 11 November 1816.

Table 8.8. *Comparative estimate of Henry and Edward Lascelles' gross wealth, c. 1753 (£ sterling)*

	Henry Lascelles (d. 1753)	Edward Lascelles (d. 1747)
English lands	117,491	c. 4,000
Stocks and securities	30,227	21,176
Loans	166,133	?
Miscellaneous	15,800	?
Subtotal	*329,651*	*25,176*
WI estates	8,000	12,400
WI loans	193,890	?
Trading capital	33,690	?
Subtotal	*235,580*	*12,400*
Total	*565,231*	*37,576*
English share	.58	.67
West Indian share	.42	.33

Note: The value of the English lands Edward Lascelles bequeathed to his heir in 1747 are not known. The figure of £4,000 is an annuity payment of £200 funded from the estate at twenty years' purchase.
Sources: NA:PRO, PROB11/804, Will of Henry Lascelles, 15 October 1753; WRA, Harewood Title Deeds 359, Volume of deeds relating to the estates of Henry Lascelles [n.d.]; BA, Hughes-Queree Collection, Abstract in Queree notebook, 'Guinea'; Account Book of Henry Lascelles (1753); R. B. Sheridan, *Sugar and Slavery: An Economic History of the British West Indies, 1623–1775* (London, 1974), 297; Mary Mauchline, *Harewood House* (2nd edn, Derbyshire, 1992), 10, 170; Chapter Six.

Apprenticeship and Emancipation

Henry Lascelles, the 2nd Earl of Harewood, presided over the last decades of chattel slavery in the British Caribbean. Although the West India lobby proved unable to defeat opponents of slavery, it won significant concessions in the debates leading up to emancipation. The British Parliament voted to pay £20 million compensation to former owners and established a commission to process claims from planters. In 1836, the 2nd Earl possessed six remaining properties on Barbados and Jamaica, on which 1,277 slaves worked approximately 3,264 acres. The parliamentary commissioners awarded a total of £26,309 in compensation for the freeing of his former slaves (Table 8.9).[75]

---

[75] This sum excludes indirect receipts from compensation awarded to remaining loan clients and passed on to the Lascelles as their creditors. By 1836, however, most accounts had been closed (a listing of 1820 records only £20,929 of debts – see Table 7.7).

Table 8.9. *Compensation payments to the Earl of Harewood, 1835–6 (£ sterling)*

Colony and parish	Estate	Acres	Slaves (no.)	Compensation for slaves (£)
Barbados, St Michael's Parish	Belle	537	292	6,486.08[a]
Barbados, St George's Parish	Mount	292	188	3,835.32[b]
Barbados, St Philip's Parish	Thicket	169	277	5,810.28[c]
Barbados, St Michael's Parish	Fortescue	541	176	3,291.57[d]
Jamaica, St Dorothy's Parish	Nightingale	1,440	112	2,599.02
Jamaica, St Thomas-in-the-Vale	Williamsfield	285	232	4,286.96
Total		3,264	1,277	26,309.23

Notes: [a]Harewood accounts give amount as £6,451.11; [b]Harewood accounts give amount as £3,812.01; [c]Harewood accounts give amount as £5,740.36; [d]Harewood accounts give amount as £3,274.09.
Sources: WRA, Harewood Papers, West Indies, Accounts 1790–1848, Inventory of Plantations; British Parliamentary Papers: Slave Trade 87, Sessions 1837–41: *Papers Relating to Negro Apprenticeship, Slavery, and the Abolition of the Slave Trade* (Shannon, 1969), 79, 82, 246, 261, 267.

The cash windfall provided by compensation enabled the Earl to liquefy some of the remaining capital invested in the West Indies. Abolition assisted in the rationalisation of the Lascelles' Caribbean interests, but emancipation marked neither the beginning of the Lascelles' disinvestment nor the end of absentee planter-ship. The four Barbadian sugar estates each survived as working units. On Jamaica, however, the situation was different; here, freedom proved incompatible with a continuation of the estate system. Nightingale Grove was disposed of in 1836, while Williamsfield was leased out from 1843 and sold in 1848, one year after the passage of the Sugar Duties Act, removing the imperial preference enjoyed by West India sugar.

On 1 August 1838, following pressure from abolitionists and resistance from the former slaves themselves, the transitional system of apprenticeship was abandoned on Jamaica and full emancipation granted. Just over three weeks later, the Earl of Harewood's attorney wrote describing the turmoil into which the plantation economy had been plunged. George Hamilton reported dolefully that 'the people have not yet turned out to work except in one solitary case or two, & even then it is altogether unsteady and uncertain'. In Hamilton's eyes, the black community 'seem to cling together', and he observed that the freed workers throughout the island showed 'no disposition to do any work, nor will they enter into any terms'.[76] The chaos

[76] WRA, Letters and Papers, G. H. Hamilton (Jamaica) to John Wood Nelson (London), 23 August 1838.

continued into September, when Hamilton alleged that even labourers paid high wages were proving difficult to control. Cattle minders, for example, were reportedly negligent and permitted livestock to stray into cane fields, causing destruction. In an attempt to remedy the situation, Governor Sir Lionel Smith visited St Thomas-in-the-Vale and addressed the free people. Hamilton was convinced that such a display would do nothing to alter conditions; it was with some relief that he noted that the Governor's 'eyes seem to be a little more open to who he has to deal', and that he 'does not now harangue them in the Mamby Pamby style he was wont to do'.[77]

Although the 2nd Earl accepted that emancipation ended the system of slavery, he envisaged a continuation of labour discipline by other means. Agents were instructed to adopt a policy of conciliation towards the estates' former slaves, and to offer high wages to entice labourers to remain on the estates, at least in the immediate aftermath of abolition. The Earl's managers were exhorted to treat emancipated workers 'in every respect in a manner conformable with their alter'd condition so as to establish their confidence'. Enforcing this strategy, however, proved difficult. Complaints reached Harewood that overseers on four estates (Williamsfield, Belle, Thicket, and Mount) harassed apprentices by instituting proceedings against them, exploiting the system of Special Magistrates established to implement the 1833 Emancipation Act. Some of the grievances were transmitted via the colonial authorities, but others took the form of anonymous letters, including one emanating from the free community on Barbados.[78]

In response, overseers and attorneys were ordered to prepare quarterly reports, detailing the work activities of apprentices and itemising all complaints submitted to the Special Magistrate. One of these quarterly submissions, for Belle (April–June 1836) has survived. On this estate, 238 apprentices (86 men, 112 women, and 40 children) were employed. Sixteen of the estate's workers were disciplined by the Special Magistrate, three-quarters of whom were accused of 'idleness'. Of Belle's 549 acres, the report notes that 438 were in cultivation, but only 80 acres were set aside as allotments for the labourers' use to grow food and keep livestock. Apprentices employed some of this land to grow cash crops; sugar, ginger, and arrowroot valued at £350 are mentioned in the

---

[77] Ibid., same to same, 7 September 1838.
[78] Ibid., Earl of Harewood to Lord Sligo (Governor of Jamaica), 22 September 1835; Foster Clarke (East Grinstead, Sussex) to Earl of Harewood, 11 August 1836 and 2 November 1836; Copy of a letter from Earl of Harewood to his agents in Barbados regarding the proposed emancipation of all slaves on 1 August 1838 (copy dated 20 November 1838); Statement of Special Magistrate William Hamilton that James King (overseer at Mount) has never presented unnecessary complaints against the apprentice labourers, 25 September 1836.

accounts.[79] Two abolitionists, who visited Belle in 1837, commented that workers on the estate 'cultivate a third of their half-acre allotments in cane on their own accounts'. It was reported that these apprentices, 'would plant the whole in cane if they were not discouraged by the planter', and that their proceeds during the current season amounted to $1,000.[80]

Comments written on the quarterly report, signed by the 2nd Earl, provide an insight into the paternalistic mode of thinking that informed his general response to emancipation. The Earl was concerned that allotments were being used to grow sugar at the expense of provisions and that apprentices were keeping horses and feeding them with plantation fodder. 'The cow is the proper stock for the labourer', he observed, 'if he can keep it honestly.' In his notes, the Earl revealed that the model guiding his thinking was the Labourers' Friend Society, which published extensively on the virtues of correctly managed allotment schemes during the middle decades of the nineteenth century, extolling the virtues of parish support of the respectable poor.[81] The report and comments reaffirm that apprenticeship was not perceived as an institution that might replace slavery by free wage labour, but rather as a means of substituting new labour controls in the room of the old system of coercion. The Earl of Harewood discouraged the abuse of the Special Magistrates by overseers, but he did not question the need for such an institution. Moreover, the amount of land redistribution he envisaged was limited to an adaptation of English parochial allotments, aimed at maintaining poor relief at a minimum level, rather than energising peasant producers.[82]

The problems experienced on the Lascelles' estates during the years from 1834 to 1838 were replicated more generally in the West Indies. Special Magistrates proved widely susceptible to the influence of planters

---

[79] WRA, Accounts of the Produce, Quarterly Report of the Belle plantation, by Thomas Marshall, ending 30 June 1836.

[80] James A. Thome and J. Horace Kimball, *Emancipation in the West Indies: A Six Months' Tour in Antigua, Barbadoes, and Jamaica, in the Year 1837* (New York, 1838), 63–4. Thome and Kimball present a very positive view of apprenticeship and advocated immediate emancipation; hence this account must be read with caution.

[81] WRA, Accounts of the Produce, Quarterly Report of the Belle plantation, by Thomas Marshall, ending 30 June 1836; John E. Archer, 'The Nineteenth-Century Allotment: Half an Acre and a Row', *Economic History Review*, 50 (1997), 21–36; Jeremy Burchardt, *The Allotment Movement in England, 1793–1873* (Suffolk, 2002). See also Thome and Kimball, *Emancipation in the West Indies*, 64.

[82] The 2nd Earl's views were shared by other planters. See e.g. Woodville Marshall, 'Henry James Ross: A Pioneer of Tenant Farming Systems', University of the West Indies, Grenada Country Conference, 2002, www.uwichill.edu.bb/bnccde/grenada/conference/papers/marshallwk.html.

and overseers (who made up most of their number), embittering relations between estate workers and managers prior to emancipation.[83] In strictly economic terms, the form freedom initially assumed in the Caribbean was circumscribed. Estate owners, who retained title to land and productive assets, sought to retain controls over labour by perpetuating plantation agriculture. In a majority of colonies, it proved difficult at first to maintain large-scale estates, due to a combination of worker resistance, depressed sugar prices, and the reduction and eventual removal of imperial preference. A new form of servitude, in the form of Asian immigrant indentured labour, was required to arrest the plantation's decline.[84]

On Barbados, however, large estates continued to operate relatively successfully, whereas Jamaican plantation sugar entered into a steep decline following emancipation.[85] The divergence in colonial experience can partly be explained by differences in population density.[86] Barbados possessed a limited land market, restricting the opportunities open to former slaves to leave the estates, occupy vacant plots of land, and grow provisions. On Jamaica, more alternatives to dependence on wage labour existed. A prolonged period of drought on the island, at a critical time, appears to have worsened the plight of marginal plantations.[87] Antigua's decision to abolish slavery in 1834 (without apprenticeship) may also have made the transition easier to accomplish, though it could be argued that on this colony economic and environmental factors rendered formal apprenticeship unnecessary in order to move from one system of labour control to another.

The different experiences of Barbados and Jamaica are reflected in the production histories of the Lascelles' own estates after 1834. On Jamaica, sugar production collapsed from 250 hhd per annum before emancipation to less than 50 hhd by the early 1840s. In contrast, output on Barbados held up well, in terms of both the physical quantities of sugar produced and the sterling value of the crop (Table 8.10). Belle, Mount, Thicket, and Fortescue occupied practically the same area in 1846, 1860, and 1870 as they had done at the time of their acquisition.[88]

---

[83] The journal of one Special Magistrate has been edited for publication: Roderick A. McDonald ed., *Between Slavery and Freedom: Special Magistrate John Anderson's Journal of St Vincent during the Apprenticeship* (Philadelphia, 2001).

[84] William A. Greene, *British Slave Emancipation: The Sugar Colonies and the Great Experiment, 1830–1865* (Oxford, 1976).

[85] B. W. Higman, *Montpelier Jamaica: A Plantation Community in Slavery and Freedom, 1739–1912* (Barbados/Jamaica/Trinidad and Tobago, 1998), 51–2.

[86] Greene, *British Slave Emancipation*, 192–3.

[87] Green, 'Planter Class', 454–5.

Table 8.10. *Annual output and gross revenue of six Barbadian and Jamaican estates, 1829–48*
a) Sugar production (hogsheads)

Estate	1829–33	1834–9	1843–7	1847–8
Belle	101.8	147.5	119.2	147.0
Thicket & Fortescue	141.4	169.7	198.6[b]	219.0
Mount	119.4	110.8	76.8[b]	90.0
Barbadian total	*362.6*	*428.0*	*394.6*	*456.0*
Williamsfield	174.6	123.2	45.7[a]	0.0
Nightingale	75.8	36.5	0.0	0.0
Jamaican total	*250.4*	*159.7*	*45.7*	*0.0*
Combined total	*613.0*	*587.7*	*440.3*	*456.0*

b) Gross output (£ sterling)

Estate	1829–33 Sugar	All output	1834–9 Sugar	All output	1843–7 Sugar	All output	1847–8 Sugar
Belle	1,475	1,475	2,901	2,901	2,243	2,244	2,786
Thicket & Fortescue	2,187	2,294	3,466	3,466	3,866[b]	3,867[b]	2,889
Mount	2,231	2,231	2,375	2,375	1,417[b]	1,420[b]	2,528
Barbadian total	*5,893*	*6,000*	*8,742*	*8,742*	*7,526*	*7,531*	*8,203*
Williamsfield	2,365	3,137	2,144	2,832	935[a]	977[a]	0
Nightingale	999	1,258	602	743	0	0	0
Jamaican total	*3,364*	*4,395*	*2,746*	*3,575*	*935*	*977*	*0*
Combined total	*9,257*	*10,395*	*11,488*	*12,317*	*8,461*	*8,508*	*8,203*

Note: [a]1834 only; [b]1844–7. Year ending 30 April in all cases.
Sources: WRA, Harewood House, West India Papers, Abstract of the Produce of the Estates and other Property in the West Indies belonging to the Right Honourable Lord Harewood, Belonging to the late Partnership of Lascelles & Maxwell, 1805–39; Summary of Accounts of the West India Estates of the Earl of Harewood to the 30th April each year by Nelson & Adam, 1843–7; Summary of Accounts of West India Estates, 30 April 1847 to 30 April 1848.

Harewood's response to complaints against the Special Magistrates may have helped to secure stability and continuity. Conciliation was accompanied by allowances of fish and pork to workers who continued working on the Barbadian estates (Fig. 8.5).

[88] BA, Estates Card Index (*Barbados Almanacs* for 1860 and 1870); WRA, Harewood House, West India Papers, Sir Robert Schomburgk, *Topographical Map Based on Mayo's Original 1721 Survey and Corrected to 1846*, annotated copy (it is not stated when the annotations, including details of acreage of the four estates, were made).

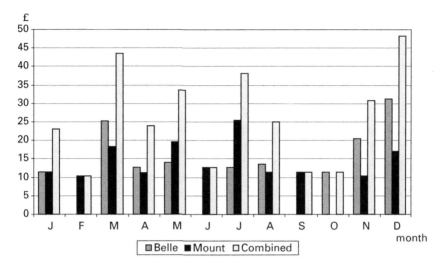

Figure 8.5. Monthly allowances of fish and pork on Belle and Mount estates, 1837 (£ sterling)
Source: WRA, Abstract of accounts of Williamsfield and Nightingale Grove plantations, 1790–1835; Abstract of the Produce of the Estates and other Property in the West Indies belonging to the Right Honourable Lord Harewood, 1805–39.

The 2nd Earl escaped any significant financial losses as a result of emancipation. For several decades prior to abolition, the Lascelles had steadily reduced their exposure to risk in the West Indies. While the termination of apprenticeship brought production to an end on Jamaica, upwards of £14,029 (sterling) was realised from the sale of Nightingale Grove and in compensation money. Additional funds may have been generated from the sale of Williamsfield, since this property was leased out for an annual rent of £130.4s.11d. in 1846 and 1847, indicating that it still possessed a positive value. Taking into account the length of time the Lascelles owned the two Jamaican estates (and their earnings record prior to 1834), it is evident that the Harvies' original debts were recovered (with interest) long before the slaves were liberated.

Conclusions

Slavery was abolished in the British West Indies sixty-one years after the Lascelles started to assemble their portfolio of estates in 1773. Though a number of properties were disposed of within a decade of their acquisition, the average length of time estates were retained is equal to two-thirds of the remaining period of enslavement. As late as 1838, five estates remained in the Earl of Harewood's possession (Table 8.3) and members of the family continued to occupy the position of absentee owners for a further 132 years. The persistence of estate ownership over such an extended period provides a strong indication that the Lascelles found means to mitigate the principal-agent problems associated with non-residency.

A large, well-capitalised West Indian interest possessed advantages beyond the reach of lesser planters. During years of warfare, freight and insurance rates rose as convoy duty and higher insurance premiums reflected increased risks. The 1st Earl was part-owner of at least eight ships between 1796 and 1819, enabling him to recoup some of the higher operating costs.[89] The status and reputation of the Lascelles within the West Indian trading community also ensured that they transacted business (and mixed socially) with an emerging financial and mercantile elite. Club membership, subscription dinners, and similar functions created bonds of trust and ideals of gentlemanly conduct during the later eighteenth and early nineteenth centuries.[90] By appointing as attorneys and managers individuals connected with this circle, the Lascelles reduced moral hazard on the part of their associates and employees.

While the 1st Earl succeeded in boosting the profitability of his West Indies estates, his system of management is scarcely an endorsement of the plantation system's efficiency. The Earls of Harewood were not reactionary or unimaginative in their approach to estate management and plantation agriculture. They embraced new varieties of sugar cane and attempted a degree of crop diversification. When opportunities offered, they sold their least productive plantations and were alert to the potential of merging estates, combining workforces, and reallocating labour among properties to boost productivity. A system of accountancy was established to reduce the scope for fraud and to detect poor performance by attorneys and managers. The combined effect of these

---

[89] WRA, Accounts of the Produce of the Estates and other Property in the West Indies, 1805–39: Barbados affairs; HH:WIP, An Account of the Right Honourable Edward Lord Harewood with the Right Honourable Edwin Lord Harewood deceased [n.d., 1796].

[90] Sample entries from the accounts include: 'Subscription for plate to be given Capt. Edgecombe £10/10/0', 'Subscription for dinner given to R[ight] H[onourable] Duke of Clarence £3/13/6' (both 1806), 'Subscription dinner to Lord Combermere' (1817), 'Subscription to the Dinner given to Sir Jas. Lyon' (1829), 'Proportion of expence dinner given Marquis of Chandos' (1830), WRA, Accounts of the Produce of the Estates and other Property in the West Indies, 1805–39: Barbados affairs.

strategies raised net revenue, enabling the owners to benefit from the recovery in sugar prices that occurred after the Napoleonic Wars.

Nevertheless, the achievement was limited. Consolidation and retrenchment, leading to the repatriation of capital, formed the basis of the Lascelles' West India policy from the later eighteenth century onwards. Underperforming estates were sold rather than being turned around, and few new investment opportunities were identified. There is little evidence that output levels were boosted in sustained fashion on any of the estates, in contrast to improvements in cost controls. Organisation of production remained dominated by the concept of regulation and labour control: a tendency reinforced by the accountancy systems. The Earls of Harewood were reluctant planters who succeeded in making plantation slavery pay during difficult trading conditions. By virtue of careful monitoring and well-timed sales of estates, they escaped the worst effects of both absentee ownership and emancipation.

This chapter has demonstrated that, from the Earls of Harewood's perspective as plantation owners, slavery remained a viable system in the sense that their estates generated an acceptable rate of return. Neither the Lascelles' own accounts nor the profit estimates presented in this chapter, however, take into consideration physical and mental suffering as a cost of production. The next chapter analyses the basic demography underlying plantation agriculture in the West Indies, revealing the extent to which slavery was accompanied by a terrible waste of human life.

9   The Enslaved Population

Humanity and benevolence must be the characteristics of every man in my service.[1]

(the names need not be enumerated only numbers).[2]

The Second Great Fire of London

German bombs falling on London's financial district the night of 29 December 1940 obliterated all of the plantation journals painstakingly prepared by the Lascelles' estate attorneys and managers.[3] Alas, only one scholar was able to spend any significant time working at the offices of Wilkinson and Gaviller before catastrophe struck. Richard Pares was that solitary researcher. In years to come, Pares greatly regretted his decision to examine only the firm's commercial correspondence at 34 Great Tower Street in the single summer of research he completed.[4]

Stray references in Harewood House's West India papers confirm the richness of the incinerated archive. Shortly after Baron Harewood's death in 1795, a list of papers relating to West Indian affairs was drawn up for the benefit of his heir and executors. The items included a series of journals and ledgers maintained for eight Barbadian plantations during the preceding sixteen years.[5] The 1st Earl of Harewood's later

---

[1] (Edwin Lascelles *et al.*), *Instructions for the Management of a Plantation in Barbadoes and for the Treatment of Negroes* (London, 1786), 22.

[2] HH:WIP, Nelson & Adam (London) to Blenman and Cobham (Barbados).

[3] Ragatz's great pre-war compendium of source material for Caribbean history reveals how a nearly intact series of account books and ledgers awaited researchers at Wilkinson and Gaviller's city premises, Lowell J. Ragatz, *A Guide for the Study of British Caribbean History, 1763–1834* (Washington DC, 1932), 35, 548.

[4] Richard Pares, 'A London West-India Merchant House, 1740–1769', in Richard Pares and A. J. P. Taylor eds., *Essays Presented to Sir Lewis Namier* (London, 1956), 75–7. Such self-recrimination, however, scarcely detracts from his prodigious feat of making detailed notes of no fewer than eleven large manuscript volumes of letters, spanning thirty years of business (1739–69).

[5] HH:WIP, 'A list of papers belonging to Edward Lascelles Esq. as executor of the Rt Honble Edwin Lord Harewood deced' (c. 1795–6), f. 35.

overhaul of estate bookkeeping resulted in the creation of additional volumes, containing an even greater amount of detail. John Wood Nelson, for example, reminded newly appointed Barbados attorneys that an annual enumeration of all the slaves for each property was expected; these returns were supplemented by biannual statements describing the sugar crop, the condition of the enslaved, the number of livestock, 'and attendant occurences' on each estate.[6] Not a trace remains of any of these materials; everything, it seems, perished in the flames of the Blitz.

What can the historian do in the face of such a disaster? While it has not been possible to repair the destruction wrought in 1940, a partial reconstruction of the lost material has been attempted, by collating in a single database information scattered in different archives.[7] The dataset primarily consists of entries for ten estates (Table 9.1) and 3,734 individuals. Six of these plantations (containing information for about 3,107 persons) can be analysed in detail owing to the fact that they remained in the Lascelles' possession for sufficient time to generate significant documentary traces.[8]

Not for nothing have the enslaved been described as 'invisible' in plantation records.[9] Even if the ledgers at Wilkinson and Gaviller had escaped the conflagration of war, there are limits to what can be learned about the working lives of slaves from sources written by white managers for the benefit of non-resident owners. Despite these caveats, however, the material in the database provides a rare opportunity to study a group of estates on three contrasting islands under the ownership of a single proprietor.

This chapter opens with a brief review of the population history of the ten estates owned continuously by the Lascelles for the longest periods. A middle section discusses qualitative material illustrating aspects of the treatment of slaves, including the involvement of the Earls of Harewood in the abolition and amelioration campaigns. The concluding part is quantitative in nature; it applies the techniques of historical demography to the study of six enslaved communities. An appendix to the chapter

---

[6] HH:WIP, (John W. Nelson) to John Blenman and Richard Cobham, 4 December 1801.
[7] This database has been given the name 'Enslaved Database' and is constructed from sources listed in Table 9.2.
[8] A total of 4,602 enslaved persons are contained in the whole database.
[9] For studies of individual plantations and an insight into the limitations and pitfalls of estate journals and ledgers, see Michael Craton, *Searching for the Invisible Man: Slaves and Plantation Life in Jamaica* (Cambridge, MA, 1978); B. W. Higman, *Montpelier Jamaica: A Plantation Community in Slavery and Freedom, 1739–1912* (Kingston, Jamaica, 1998).

Table 9.1 *Characteristics of ten estates included in the Enslaved Database*

Property name	Colony and parish location	Dates of ownership	Acreage	Principal activity
Belle	St Michael (B)	1780–1975	537 (1780)	sugar estate
Mount	St George (B)	1784–1974	292 (1795)	sugar estate
Fortescue	St Philip (B)	1787–1918	241 (1787)[a]	cotton plantation
Thicket	St Philip (B)	1787–1918	584 (1787)[b]	sugar estate
Mammee Ridge	St Ann (J)	1777–1797	1,000 (1777)	cattle pen
Nightingale Grove	St Dorothy (J)	1777–1836	285 (1777)	sugar estate
Williamsfield	St Thomas-in-the-Vale (J)	1777–1848	1,440 (1777)	sugar estate
Richmond	St Paul (T)	1777–1820	600 (1770)	sugar estate
Glamorgan	St Mary (T)	1777–1820	575 (1770)	sugar estate
Goldsborough & Goodwood	St Mary (T)	1781–1818	1,151 (1770)	sugar estate

Note: [a] includes 72 acres of Pot House plantation;
[b] includes land known as the Netherlands. B = Barbados, J = Jamaica, T = Tobago.

considers the accuracy of the statistical sources used to estimate mortality and fertility on Barbados and Jamaica.

Overview of the Estates' Populations

Summary population totals for the ten estates between 1767 and 1835 are presented in Table 9.2. Although a crude measure of change, the numbers tell distinct stories. On Barbados, the labour force stagnated for approximately two decades after the Lascelles' assumption of ownership. Following the abolition of the slave trade in 1807, the decline was reversed (Fig. 9.1). The demographic experience of the enslaved living in Jamaica was the inverse of their Barbadian counterparts. Numbers on Williamsfield and Nightingale Grove increased between 1767 and 1796; in contrast, the last decades of slavery were characterised by population losses, particularly on Williamsfield (Fig. 9.2). Only two benchmark counts have been found for the Tobago properties. These reveal a significant increase in numbers occurred, but the pattern of growth cannot be established on the basis of just a couple of data points.

Belle was acquired by Daniel Lascelles in 1780 as part of the settlement of the Gedney Clarkes' debts.[10] An early increase in numbers was

[10] BA, Hughes-Queree Collection, Abstracts in Queree notebook, 'The Belle', 1780/150/340.

Table 9.2 *Population totals on ten estates, 1767–1835*

	BARBADOS				JAMAICA			TOBAGO		
Year	Belle	Mount	Fort.	Thicket	Night.	Will.	Mammee	Rich.	Glam.	Gold.
1767					110	240	26			
1770								135	24	173
1772	231									
1776	236									
1777	237				140	272	98			
1780	232									
1787			132	244						
1788		125								
1795		101	121	221	154	258				
1801		80								
1817	295	133	136	247	108	326				
1818					108	330				
1819					108	321				
1820	290	145	137	254	114	322		157	153	312
1821					117	317				
1823	291	144	147	254	110	303				
1826	282	176	153	253	107	293				
1829	294	170	169	265	109	275				
1832	299	177	174	266	111	243				
1834	291	188	183	231	112	231				
1835	292	188	176	277	112	232				

Key: Fort. = Fortescue; Night. = Nightingale; Will. = Williamsfield; Rich. = Richmond; Glam. = Glamorgan; Gold. = Goldsborough

Source: HH:WIP 1) A list of papers belonging to Edward Lascelles Esq. as executor of the Rt Honble Edwin Lord Harewood deced [1795–6], f. 10; 2) Indenture 17 September 1776 between Gedney Clarke, Mary Clarke, and the Crown; 3) Indenture between Henry Frere and Edwin Lascelles, 19 July 1787; 4) Inventory and Appraisement of the Belle Plantation, 26 May 1777; 5) Correspondence, John Cobham to John W. Nelson, 13 October 1801 (includes an appraisal of Mount dated 10 August 1795). WRA, Harewood MSS, 1) Acc. 2,677, Conveyance of estates in Jamaica by Thomas Harvie to Daniel Lascelles, 20 June 1777; Conveyance from Lewing and Ramsay to Lascelles & Maxwell, 21 November 1777; 2) Crop Accounts for Nightingale Grove and Williamsfield; 3) Letters and Papers on West India Estates and Affairs, 1795–1873, correspondence between Lord Harewood and James Swaby regarding possible sale of Jamaican estates, 5 November 1836. NA:PRO, T71/13–18, 25–8, 30, 32, 520–1, 524–5, 527, 534–6, 540, 544, 547, 549–50, 553, 556–7, 268–9; CO28/62/251; CO101/14(127). BA, 1) Hughes-Queree Collection, Abstracts in Queree notebook, 'The Belle' (St Michael), 'The Mount' (St George); 2) Recopied Deed Books, RB3/193/194–6, Indenture between Henry Frere and Edwin Lascelles, 29 September 1787 1780/150/340. JA, IB/11/3/47, Inventory of Alexander Harvie, 17 December 1767; Inventory of Edwin, Lord Harewood, 27 October 1796, IB/11/3/85. *Jamaica Almanac* 1818, 1821, 1822. British Parliamentary Papers, Slave Trade 87, Sessions 1837–41, *Papers Relating to Negro Apprenticeship Slavery and the Abolition of the Slave Trade* (Shannon, 1969), 79.

Figure 9.1 Population totals on four Barbadian estates, 1772–1835 (semi-log scale)
Source: As for Table 9.2.

achieved in part by introducing new slaves on to the property. In 1785, for example, twenty-five slaves were purchased for Belle – probably from within the island, since only half a dozen Africans are listed in the 1817 registration return (five of whom were reportedly older than seventy years).[11] Along with its Creole majority, the enslaved community on this estate possessed two further striking features. Firstly, Belle possessed a female majority; secondly, the population was predominantly youthful, with 35 per cent of all slaves aged under fifteen years (Table 9.3).

Mount was acquired from the Blenman family in lieu of debts in 1784 when it was home to 125 enslaved workers.[12] Initially, the plantation was not regarded highly. In 1795, island attorney John Cobham commented that he had, 'always considered it the worse that his Lordship possesses in Barbados'. A report of 1801 noted, 'the labourers on the Mount have been oppressed to keep the land in tolerable order, in consequence of which their Number have, within these two or three last years *greatly decreased*'.[13] Mount's population had by this point fallen to just eighty slaves. Reasons for the drop in population are not known; it could reflect

[11] HH:WIP, A list of papers belonging to Edward Lascelles esq. as executor of the Rt Honble Edwin Lord Harewood deced (1795–6), f. 24.
[12] HH:WIP, Account of William Blenman with Edwin Lord Harewood, 27 March 1784.
[13] HH:WIP, John Cobham to John W. Nelson, 13 October 1801.

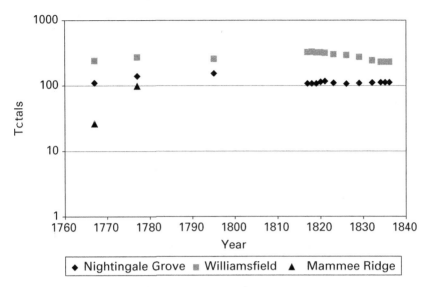

Figure 9.2 Population totals on three Jamaican estates, 1767–1836 (semi-log scale)
Source: As for Table 9.2

either natural decrease (a surplus of deaths over births), or the removal of workers from a property that was perceived to be less profitable than others owned by the Lascelles.

Mount's decline was arrested and reversed by the relocation of upwards of thirty-two slaves to the plantation from other estates between 1817 and 1826. Twelve slaves were removed from both Belle and Fortescue, and eight from Thicket.[14] In view of the growth in population implied in Figure 9.1, it is possible that additional workers were also transferred to Mount between 1801 and 1816. Qualitative and quantitative evidence, however, suggests that only limited recourse was made to the slave trade prior to abolition. 'I would as soon advise (Lord Harewood) to throw his money into the sea', wrote John Cobham in 1801, 'as to advise his purchasing Africans.'[15] Cobham's comments are consistent with the listing of only four Africans in the 1817 and 1820 registration returns. Mount shared some of Belle's social characteristics. The estate was home to a predominantly young Creolised community, with 43 per cent of the enslaved aged under fifteen in 1817. Females were also in a majority on this plantation (Table 9.3).

[14] Ten of those enslaved were redeployed between 1817 and 1820; a further twenty were moved between 1823 and 1826.
[15] HH:WIP, Cobham to Nelson, 13 October 1801.

Table 9.3 *Gender and origin of the populations of four Barbadian estates*

Estate	Gender	1787 (1776 Belle)	1817	1820	Whole database
Belle	females	123	166	169	356
	males	111	129	129	309
	Africans	–	6	4	6
	Creoles	–	289	294	385
Mount	females	–	75	77	122
	males	–	56	56	108
	Africans	–	3	3	4
	Creoles	–	128	130	226
Fortescue	females	77	76	78	137
	males	54	60	59	110
	Africans	1	0	0	1
	Creoles	130	156	137	246
Thicket	females	134	141	144	356
	males	110	106	111	334
	Africans	42	10	9	47
	Creoles	202	237	246	641
Total	*females*	*334*	*458*	*468*	*971*
	males	*275*	*351*	*355*	*861*
	Africans	*43*	*19*	*16*	*58*
	Creoles	*332*	*810*	*807*	*1,498*

Note: African and Creole totals exclude unknowns (listed before 1817).
Source: As for Table 9.2.

Thicket and Fortescue's histories are intertwined. Sometime before 1770, the smaller property of Fortescue was sold by the Beckles family to Henry Frere. Thicket was the name given to an amalgam of plantations owned by the Spiar and Frere families consolidated into one estate by inheritance. At the time of transfer to the Lascelles family (in 1787), Thicket included a recently acquired plot of land in St Philip (known as the Netherlands), suggesting the property was in the process of expansion.[16]

Production on the two estates was organised separately between 1787 and 1820; in consequence, the enslaved populations formed distinct groups. On Fortescue, Henry Frere experimented unsuccessfully with indigo before switching to a combination of cotton and guinea corn. In contrast, slaves on Thicket were employed as sugar workers.[17] The

[16] BA, Hughes-Queree Collection, Abstracts in Queree notebook, 'Fortescue' and 'Thicket'.
[17] HH:WIP, 'A list of papers belonging to Edward Lascelles Esq. as executor of the Rt Honble Edwin Lord Harewood deced' [c. 1795–6], f. 11, rental agreement for Pot House dated 1790; 'The Lucas Manuscripts', *JBMHS*, 22 (1954–5), 118.

resulting division of labour is reflected in Fortescue's and Thicket's crop accounts from 1805 to 1815 and also the slave registration returns of 1817 and 1820, which list men, women, and children in separate group sequences. After 1815, cultivation of cotton was abandoned on Fortescue in favour of sugar; from 1823 the two enslaved populations are listed jointly in the returns.[18] These two changes suggest that the estates were managed in tandem during the last decade of slavery.

Fortescue and Thicket are the only estates owned by the Lascelles for which four complete listings of the population by age are available. Each of the counts emphasises the population's youthful age structure. The percentages of slaves less than fifteen years old was 34.5 in 1787, 50.5 in 1817, 42.0 in 1820, and 39.0 in 1834. As in the case of Mount and Belle, the enslaved communities were also characterised by a female surplus (Table 9.3). The properties differed, however, in their degree of Creolisation. Only one African appears in Fortescue's 1787 enumeration and none in the 1817 registration return; in contrast, Thicket was home to forty-three Africans in 1787, and eleven in 1817 (including six survivors from the earlier listing).

The Lascelles acquired all of their Jamaican estates from the Harvie brothers.[19] Given the Harvies' extensive investments in the transatlantic slave trade, it can be considered a certainty that Africans were brought on to these Jamaican properties in substantial numbers early in their development, boosting their populations. Williamsfield and The Crawl were acquired in 1756 by purchase from William Nedham, who owed a debt to the brothers.[20] James Hakewill visited Williamsfield during his tour of Jamaica (1820–1) and published a brief account of the estate's history, based on oral testimonies gathered from among enslaved persons living on the property:

Williamsfield Estate ... according to what can be gathered from the old Negroes (there being no early records) was first settled, nearly eighty years ago, by Mr Needham, who was at that time a large proprietor on the island; but while in its infancy (within three or four years after it was commenced), it was purchased by a Mr Harvey, who came from Barbadoes, and was a merchant in Kingston.[21]

---

[18] WRA Harewood House, West India Papers, Abstract of the Produce of the Estates and other Property in the West Indies belonging to the Right Honourable Lord Harewood, 1805–39; NA:PRO, T71/521, T71/525.

[19] See Chapter Seven.

[20] East Sussex Record Office, Lewes, Jamaica Correspondence of Rose Fuller, SAS-RF/ 21/54, William Nedham (Jamaica) to Rose Fuller, 24 July 1756.

[21] James Hakewill, *A Picturesque Tour of Jamaica, from Drawings Made in the Years 1820 and 1821* (London, 1825) cited in Barry W. Higman, *Jamaica Surveyed: Plantation Maps and Plans of the Eighteenth and Nineteenth Centuries* (Kingston, Jamaica, 1988), 111. The information supplied by the enslaved corroborates written evidence, indicating either that some of the Africans introduced on to the estate were still living during the early

Only two population counts survive for the cattle pen, Mammee Ridge; these reveal that population more than tripled between 1767 and 1777.[22] Mammee's initial workforce of twenty-six was very small (given the 1,000 acres occupied by the pen), implying that it had not long been settled. The property was first intended as a sugar estate; indeed, William Harvie's 1767 inventory lists a boiling and still house, indicating that some cane was grown on the plantation. Cattle farming, however, constituted the property's dominant economic activity; livestock numbers increased from just seven animals in 1767 to 481 by 1777. As the pen grew in size, its population developed a small male surplus (Table 9.4). This finding is consistent with the thesis that freshly imported slaves were responsible for increased numbers, since males were shipped disproportionately from Africa.

Nightingale Grove's early population history is complicated by its relationship with the neighbouring property of Oldfield's Bog.[23] The 1767 count cited in Table 9.2 is an estimate; the original source gives only a combined total of 193 for Nightingale and Oldfield's slaves.[24] If the suggested revised figure of 110 is accurate, Nightingale Grove increased in size between 1767 and 1796. Any gains, however, were then reversed; by 1817, numbers had declined by up to one-third and no discernible recovery took place for the remainder of the period of slavery. Surviving crop accounts for Nightingale Grove include details of the purchase of fifty-three slaves during the 1790s. Eight slaves are also known to have been purchased between 1827 and 1829 from within Jamaica. In comparison with the Barbadian estates, the enslaved population on Nightingale Grove was slightly older, with 28 per cent aged under fifteen years. The estate's slaves also included a significant African component; in 1817, for example, this group made up 29 per cent of the community. Notwithstanding the apparent influence of slave imports, Nightingale Grove possessed a female majority by the time registration commenced (Table 9.4).

Williamsfield's declining population attracted the attention of the contemporary observer R. G. Amyot, who drew attention to the estate's high mortality levels in a parliamentary report compiled during the

1820s, or that an oral tradition existed preserving memories of the former owner of the property.

[22] JA, Inventory of Alexander Harvie, 17 December 1767; WRA, Harewood Accession 2,677, Conveyance of Mammee Ridge Pen, 20 June 1777.

[23] See Chapter Seven for the administration of this property by Lascelles & Maxwell prior to the Harvies gaining control.

[24] The 1777 Nightingale listing includes 87 of the 193 slaves listed in 1767. The estimated population of Nightingale for 1767, excluding Oldfield's Bog slaves, is $(53 + 87)/(53 + 87 + 105) \times 193 = 110$.

Table 9.4. *Gender and origin of the populations of three Jamaican estates*

Estate	Gender	1767	1777	1817	Whole database
Mammee	females	10	43	–	42
	males	10	55	–	56
	na	1	3	–	4
	Africans	–	–	–	–
	Creoles	–	–	–	–
Nightingale	females	91	82	57	226
	males	83	51	44	188
	na	19	8	0	34
	Africans	–	–	29	37
	Creoles	–	–	101	136
Williamsfield	females	99	139	174	380
	males	102	119	152	383
	na	36	8	0	69
	Africans	–	–	103	103
	Creoles	–	–	223	314
Total	*females*	*200*	*264*	*231*	*648*
	males	*195*	*225*	*196*	*627*
	na	*56*	*19*	*0*	*107*
	Africans	–	–	*132*	*140*
	Creoles	–	–	*324*	*450*

Source: As for Table 9.2.

political debate over emancipation.[25] By 1832, Williamsfield's population was smaller than it had been in 1796, even though 214 slaves are known to have been brought on to the estate between 1792 and 1815. The majority of these new arrivals arrived after the abolition of the slave trade. In 1810, thirty-one slaves were purchased from the estate of

[25] *Parliamentary Papers, House of Lords Sessional Papers, 1831–2* vol. II, 449–55 cited in Michael Craton, 'Jamaican Slave Mortality: Fresh Light from Worthy Park, Longville, and the Tharp Estate', *Journal of Caribbean History*, 3 (1971), 13. A modern study confirms that the crude death rate (per 1,000) on Williamsfield exceeded the parish average in St Thomas-in-the-Vale:

	1817–20	1820–3	1823–6	1826–9	1829–32
Whole parish	22.9	25.0	25.9	23.2	30.4
Williamsfield	20.6	36.3	34.7	35.2	57.5

B. W. Higman, *Slave Population and Economy in Jamaica, 1807–1834* (Cambridge, 1976), 106. Since neither Higman's nor Amyot's data are age-specific, however, it is difficult to make a meaningful comparison between Williamsfield and other estates on the basis of the crude rates alone.

Michael McDonald (deceased); this was followed, in 1815, by the acquisition of 110 slaves, from the adjacent plantation of Sandy Gut, along with 255 acres of land.[26]

The registration return for 1817 reveals that 31.6 per cent of Williamsfield's population was African – a finding signifying that slave imports (prior to 1807) influenced the demographic history of the estate.[27] As was the case on Nightingale Grove, the proportion of population listed aged under fifteen years was 28 per cent (less than on the Barbadian estates). As the property grew in size, the female majority was replaced by a more balanced sex ratio (Table 9.4). Purchases of new slaves from within the island (particularly from the merger with Sandy Gut), assisted in equalising the numbers of males and females. Of the 141 enslaved brought on to the estate between 1810 and 1815, 57 per cent were male.

Knowledge of the demographic history of the Tobago properties is more limited than in the case of Barbados and Jamaica because these estates were sold by the Lascelles around the time the first registration returns were compiled. Richmond, Glamorgan (itself a recent acquisition), and Goodwood/Goldsborough were purchased by John Robley between 1818 and 1820. Robley was one of Tobago's wealthiest planters and the owner of six other plantations on the island. The Lascelles' loss of control over the estates means that it is problematic to investigate their population histories any later than the 1819 returns.[28]

The only statement of numbers for Tobago that has been found prior to registration is for the year 1770. At this time, the estates were at an early stage of cultivation. Richmond and Goldsborough (another of Gedney Clarke Jr's properties) had erected sugar works and were already producing sugar, but more than two-thirds of their available land remained in woodland. Only a fifth of Goodwood's acreage was cleared, and this estate did not enter into production until the following year.[29] Planting on Tobago was badly affected by the Wars of the French Revolution and Napoleonic Wars. French troops occupied the island during the years from 1781 to 1793, and again from 1802 until 1803.

By 1819, the estates were more developed and the enslaved population living on them had nearly doubled in size. The registration returns reveal that 35 per cent of the inhabitants living on the properties had

[26] WRA, Harewood Accession 2,677, 1) List and valuation of slaves belonging to the estate of Michael McDonald Esq. deceased purchased for the Williamsfield estate, 3 December 1810; 2) conveyance by George Kinghorn, Joseph Timperon, and John Thanet to Edward Lord Harewood, 3 July 1815.

[27] There were 3.3 Creoles per African in Sandy Gut listed in 1817 and 2.84 Creoles per African in the rest of Williamsfield's population.

[28] See Chapter Ten.

[29] NA:PRO, CO191/14(127).

been born in Africa, indicating that purchases of imported slaves up until 1807 were substantial. Twenty-seven slaves are known to have been bought for Goodwood in 1799, but details of other purchases are not available.[30] On the three Tobago properties combined, 30.2 per cent of the slaves in 1819 were aged less than fifteen, while women made up 53.1 per cent of the enslaved communities.

It was usual for the enumerators of an estate's population to record the occupations of the slaves living on a plantation.[31] In Table 9.5, the job classifications of 2,194 members of the enslaved communities on nine plantations on Barbados, Jamaica, and Tobago are summarised. The estimates of participation rates are approximate owing to the fact that some occupations (for example 'watchman'), could describe persons who were in reality superannuated. Numbers of invalid or infirm slaves are also not recorded consistently in all listings. It is still significant, however, that the participation rates on these nine estates are higher than predicted by the dependency ratio, emphasising the work contributions of children and older members of the community. The data also illustrate the importance of female labour for the cultivation of tropical staples. In common with plantation agriculture across British Colonial America, women comprised a majority of field workers, while a majority of the field gangs were female.[32]

Emancipation and 'Amelioration'

The campaign to abolish the Atlantic slave trade provoked a fierce contemporary debate over whether or not the importation of Africans reduced incentives for planters to treat their slaves humanely. Opponents of abolition claimed slavery contained progressive elements, arguing that owners (through a combination of benevolence and profit) were concerned for the welfare of the enslaved. Following the passage of

---

[30] HH:WIP, Correspondence, Memorandum: Mr Mitchell's notes on the crop in Tobago, 30 March 1799. There is no detailed study of the demographic history of Tobago. Analysis of the neighbouring island of Trinidad found that the enslaved population was unable to reproduce itself due to heavy mortality and that in 1813 on plantations Africans comprised 35% of the males and 21% of females, A. Meredith John, *The Plantation Slaves of Trinidad, 1783–1816: A Mathematical and Demographic Enquiry* (Cambridge, 1988), 51, 159.

[31] This information, however, is missing for the Jamaican estates in the registration returns compiled in 1817 and after.

[32] Marietta Morrissey *Slave Women in the New World: Gender Stratification in the Caribbean* (Lawrence, 1989), 7, 9, 37, 65–75; Lucille Mathurin Mair, 'Women Field Workers in Jamaica During Slavery', 1986 Elsa Goveia Lecture, University of the West Indies, Mona Campus, reprinted in Verene Shepherd and Hilary McD. Beckles eds., *Caribbean Slavery in the Atlantic World: A Student Reader* (Kingston, Jamaica, 2000), 390–7.

Table 9.5. *Summary occupational classifications for nine estates*

	Jamaica (2 estates) 1777	Fortescue & Thicket 1787	Barbados (4 estates) 1817	Tobago (3 estates) 1819	Combined (9 estates) 1777–1819
Males					
Field gangs	0.19	0.38	0.50	0.50	0.42
Other outdoor employments	0.26	0.10	0.08	0.09	0.12
Skilled workers	0.31	0.21	0.11	0.17	0.18
Head people	0.06	0.04	0.03	0.03	0.04
Domestics	0.02	0.05	0.03	0.02	0.03
Infirm/superannuated	0.03	0.02	0.03	0.04	0.03
Young, not employed	0.13	0.20	0.21	0.15	0.18
Others	0.01	0.00	0.01	0.00	0.00
	1.00	1.00	1.00	1.00	1.00
Number	*171*	*164*	*351*	*290*	*976*
Females					
Field gangs	0.74	0.66	0.60	0.60	0.64
Other outdoor employments	0.00	0.06	0.05	0.04	0.04
Head people	0.00	0.01	0.02	0.00	0.01
Domestics	0.09	0.04	0.09	0.09	0.08
Infirm/superannuated	0.01	0.04	0.05	0.10	0.06
Young, not employed	0.15	0.19	0.19	0.16	0.18
Others	0.00	0.00	0.00	0.00	0.00
	1.00	1.00	1.00	1.00	1.00
Number	*221*	*211*	*458*	*328*	*1,218*
Both sexes					
Field gangs	0.50	0.55	0.55	0.58	0.55
Other outdoor employments	0.11	0.08	0.06	0.07	0.08
Skilled workers	0.14	0.09	0.05	0.04	0.07
Head people	0.03	0.02	0.02	0.02	0.02
Domestics	0.06	0.04	0.07	0.06	0.06
Infirm/superannuated	0.02	0.03	0.04	0.08	0.05
Young, not employed	0.14	0.19	0.20	0.16	0.18
Others	0.00	0.00	0.00	0.00	0.00
	1.00	1.00	1.00	1.00	1.00
Number	*392*	*375*	*809*	*618*	*2194*
participation ratio	0.84	0.77	0.75	0.76	0.77
dependency ratio	na	0.39	0.41	0.35	0.41

Note: Dependency ratio: ratio of slaves aged fifteen years and under and sixty-five and over to total population (not available for Nightingale Grove and Williamsfield).
Source: As for Table 9.2.

a Commons motion in 1823 advocating the gradual emancipation of slaves, the issue of humane treatment revived as leaders of the West Indian interest began articulating the doctrine of amelioration. Planter spokesmen such as Stephen Fuller, Charles Ellis, and Sir William Young argued that persuading masters to adopt good practices, rather than abruptly freeing their slaves, was the best way of reforming the institution of chattel slavery. Advocates of amelioration claimed that improvements in the moral, spiritual, and physical welfare of the enslaved were underway in the Caribbean, preparing the groundwork for freedom.[33]

Members of the Lascelles family joined in both of these debates. Edwin Lascelles was among a group of nine Barbadian planters responsible for publishing a treatise on the treatment of slaves in 1786.[34] This tract was ostensibly written as an advice manual for plantation managers, but it also provided a riposte to critics pressing for the immediate abolition of the transatlantic slave trade.[35] The co-authors argued that planters were concerned to protect the welfare of their estate labourers for moral reasons, as well as a desire to boost efficiency.[36]

Instructions for the Management of a Plantation begins by observing that, 'If negroes are fed plentifully, worked moderately, and treated kindly, they will encrease in most places.'[37] The authors propose that natural

---

[33] Robert E. Luster *The Amelioration of the Slaves in the British Empire, 1790–1833* (New York, 1995), 1–10; Gordon K. Lewis, *Main Currents in Caribbean Thought: The Historical Evolution of Caribbean Society in its Ideological Aspects, 1492–1900* (Baltimore, 1983), 106–13. For details of amelioration legislation enacted on Barbados between 1823 and 1826, see Claude Levy, 'Slavery and the Emancipation Movement on Barbados, 1650–1833', *Journal of Negro History*, 55 (1970), 10.

[34] Printed on the title page of the *Instructions* are the names of Edwin Lascelles, James Colleton, Edward Drax, Francis Ford, John Brathwaite, John Walter, William Thorpe, Holder James Holder, and Philip Gibbes. The name of John Barney is also inscribed in the copy of the treatise preserved at the LBMH.

[35] In 1788, 'Dolben's Act' regulated the shipment of slaves on British vessels for the first time. Four years later, a motion to gradually abolish the slave trade was passed in the House of Commons, though full abolition of the trade was not achieved until 1807.

[36] Edwin's cousin and heir Edward Lascelles (later Earl of Harewood) subsequently voted against the abolition of the slave trade in a House of Commons vote in March 1796. Edward 'Beau' Lascelles (son of Edward, Earl of Harewood) likewise voted against abolition in February 1807, R. G. Thorne ed., *The House of Commons, 1790–1820* (5 vols., London, 1986), vol. IV, 376.

[37] The best-known example of an advice manual is William Belgrove, *A Treatise Upon Husbandry or Planting* (Boston, 1755). The author of this tract styled himself as 'A regular bred, and long experienc'd Planter of the Island of Barbados'. Belgrove's tract is bound with *Instructions for the Management of Drax-Hall and the Irish-hope Plantations: To Archibald Johnson by Henry Drax, Esq.* Edwin Lascelles' *Instructions* concludes (pp. 53–64) with a reprint of *Instructions for the Management of Drax Hall*. This treatise was at least a century old. Drax (d. 1682) was a Barbados planter; an early version of the text exists in manuscript form: 'Instructions which I would have observed by Mr Richard

increase, 'is the only test of the care with which they are treated'.[38] A ten-page section headed, 'Instructions for the Treatment of Negroes', explores welfare issues more deeply. Strong emphasis is placed on the treatment of mothers and young children. The authors condone the active employment of pregnant women, provided they are prevented from carrying heavy loads. They suggest, however, that women suckling babies, 'should not be required to appear in the field till seven o'clock', and on rainy days they should be assigned an indoor work schedule.[39] It is also recommended that managers ensure baskets, 'or proper trays with a cover to the heads', are available to shelter babies taken into the fields by their mothers. In the event of rain, the authors further advise that 'light portable sheds' be erected to protect infants from the elements.[40]

Once weaned, *Instructions* directs that infants be placed under the care of, 'some careful, good humoured woman', enabling their mothers to return to field labour. It is recommended these children receive two daily meals. The tract cautions that infants ought not to be put to labour in the children's gang too early, though a minimum age is left to managers' discretion.[41] In the case of older children, overseers are exhorted to maintain 'A watchful eye' on their health. Dietary supplements are advised, 'if any child should seem to decline, though not absolutely ill'. In all cases, the authors urge that breakfast and dinner be prepared for young children by a specially appointed 'good-humoured woman', and that these meals be taken before the manager to provide him with an opportunity to check young gang members' health, and to monitor the quality of food served to them and the cleanliness of eating utensils.[42]

A concern for maintaining family structures on plantations is a further feature of the *Instructions*.[43] The authors recommend that the enslaved live in houses headed by a husband and his wife, and that provision

---

Harwood in the management of my plantation', Bodleian Library, Oxford, Rawlinson MS A. 348 (n.d., c. 1670–9?). For further discussion of the Drax–Belgrove tract see Jerome S. Handler, *Supplement to A Guide to Source Materials for the Study of Barbados History 1627–1834* (Providence, RI 1991), 56–7.

[38] (Lascelles *et al.*), *Instructions*, 2.

[39] Ibid., 24–5.   [40] Ibid., 30.   [41] Ibid., 28–9.

[42] Ibid., 26–7. Dinner was a lunchtime meal served at noon, John Dovaston, 'Agricultura Americana or Improvements in West India Husbandry Considered' (2 manuscript volumes, 1774), John Carter Brown Library, Providence, Rhode Island, Codex Eng 60, vol. II, 269. Similar advice to overseers is given in Gilbert Mathison, *Notices Respecting Jamaica in 1808–1809–1810* (London, 1811), 108–9.

[43] A body of contemporary opinion argued that African men and women were disinclined by nature to form stable, monogamous relationships. See e.g. Bryan Edwards, *The History, Civil and Commercial, of the British West Indies* (5th edn, 5 vols., London, 1819), vol. II, 97–8. Consequently, these passages of *Instructions* can be interpreted as a form of racially preconceived social engineering.

grounds be tended through the use of family labour.[44] Managers are instructed to assist in the construction of such slave dwellings by providing rafters and a ridge pole, and to take care that such buildings were spaced evenly apart. The inhabitants of these quarters are divided into 'the leading people' of the plantation, whose houses should measure 12 x 9ft, and the so-called inferior slaves, who are allocated housing measuring 10 x $7\frac{1}{2}$ ft. Young couples lacking parents should receive support in the form of accommodation built at the owners' expense; a 'dowry' is also advised, taking the form of a water jar, an iron pot, a corn store, a sow, and a goat.[45]

In comparison with other works written prior to the abolition of the slave trade, Instructions places unusual emphasis on the care of mothers and children. For example, John Dovaston's manuscript treatise of 1774, 'Agricultura Americana', treats these subjects only lightly. The author's major preoccupation lies with the moral and religious welfare of the enslaved on Jamaica, rather than improving their material condition.[46] Edward Long's better-known three-volume history of Jamaica, published the same year, likewise devotes just a few pages to this subject. In contrast to Instructions, however, Long argues that black children ought to be cared for by their mothers, rather than a nurse, and advocates a light work regime (or better still exemption from labour) for mothers.[47] William Beckford's account of Jamaica's slaves (published in 1788), similarly gives a fairly cursory account of maternity and child-raising.[48]

An insight into child-raising practices on the Jamaican estates is provided by evidence submitted by Francis Graeme (or Graham), the Earl of Harewood's island attorney. In 1815, Graeme testified before the

---

[44] This passage suggests that some slaves secured labour services from others (either by exchange or through a form of payment) in order to assist in the cultivation of provisions.

[45] (Lascelles et al.), Instructions, 25, 29–30.

[46] Dovaston, 'Agricultura Americana', vol. II, 245–83.

[47] Edward Long The History of Jamaica: Reflections on Its Situation, Settlements, Inhabitants, Climate, Products, Commerce, Laws, and Government (3 vols., London, 1774), vol. II, 436–7.

[48] William Beckford, Remarks Upon the Situation of Negroes in Jamaica (London, 1788). Beckford notes that blacks are naturally benevolent towards their children; he concludes from this that, 'if they were encouraged as nurses I am apt to believe that so many would not be lost within so short a period as nine days after their birth' (23–4). Later in the tract Beckford recommends that young children be assigned 'a proper woman to attend them' and further advises that 'they should not be made to depend upon their mothers for food; but should be daily supplied from the overseers house; and he should direct them to be fed three times a day either under his own eye or that of a book-keeper' (36). A disproportionate amount of space is devoted to defending the slave trade and the prospects for the moral improvement of the enslaved.

Jamaica Assembly that he had consulted with all the proprietors of estates under his direction and followed what he described as a scheme of 'uncommon indulgence' in encouraging maternity. Expectant mothers were excused from work until their babies reached the weaning stages (at twelve to fifteen months), thereby avoiding the exposure of young children to strong heat or rain. During this period, mothers and babies also received food supplements from overseers.[49] The procedures described by Graeme appear to combine elements of *Instructions* with the advice along the lines of Long's *History*.

What ideological influences informed the approach taken by Edwin Lascelles and his co-authors to slave welfare? An important clue lies in the fact that Sir Philip Gibbes (a Barbados planter and a loan client of the Lascelles) is listed among the authors of *Instructions*. In 1786, Gibbes published (anonymously) a treatise of his own, entitled *Instructions for the Treatment of Negroes*; an enlarged second edition followed a decade later in 1797. There are close similarities between Gibbes' work and the section entitled 'Instructions for the Treatment of Negroes' contained within the *Instructions*.[50] An appreciation of Gibbes' tract, therefore, helps to interpret the intellectual context of the recommendations set out in the text.

In 1797, Nathaniel Elliot (senior partner of the London commission house) wrote to the 1st Earl as follows. 'I have read Sir Philip's pamphlet with pleasure', Elliot began, 'particularly with regard to the care & management of the Negroes.' Elliot proposed, 'to send a few of them to your att[orne]ys to give one to each of your Managers with orders to attend to the instructions therein given as far as circumstances will allow'.[51] Additional insights are provided by a letter of 1798, in which attorney William Bishop identified Gibbes as the author of 'a little book ... part of which I remember fell from his pen some years past, and part taken from the benevolent principles of Count Rumford'. Bishop added that, 'If Lord Harewood's and all the Negroes under my care as well as my own were not dealt as humanely as his to the full, I should be afraid upon being called out of the World to knock at the Gates of my Saviour least they should not be opened.'[52]

---

[49] *Further Proceedings of the Honourable House of Assembly of Jamaica Relative to a Bill Introduced into the House of Commons, for Effectually Preventing the Unlawful Importation of Slaves and Holding Free Persons in Slavery in the British Colonies* (Jamaica, 1816), 55–8.

[50] For a discussion of the two pamphlets, see Jerome S. Handler, *A Guide to Source Materials for the Study of Barbados History, 1627–1834* (Carbondale, 1971), 48–50.

[51] That Elliot thought it necessary to send a copy of this treatise questions the extent to which the recommendations of the *Instructions* was implemented on the estates during Baron Harewood's lifetime.

[52] WRA, Letters and Papers on West India Estates and Affairs, 1795–1873, William Bishop (Barbados) to Elliot, Whalley, & Adams (London), 11 June 1798.

Benjamin Thompson (Count Rumford) – a former spy for the British in North America – was employed by the Bavarian Government from 1784 onwards to improve army discipline and also to devise policies that would reduce the numbers of mendicants on the streets of Munich.[53] Thompson's solutions to the problem of begging included a garden allotment scheme and establishing workhouses; the latter institutions made use of soup kitchens and child labour. Rumford was credited with successful reforms in both areas of public policy. In 1795, he was motivated to publish a series of pamphlets outlining his approach to tackling urban poverty at a time when the issue of poor law reform in Britain was the subject of vigorous debate.[54]

The Count mixed coercion (Munich's poor were rounded up from the streets, institutionalised, and denied food if they failed to work) with incentives. Inducements to work included the offer of shelter, meals, and payment on a piecework basis. Great emphasis was placed on the moral virtue of labour and the advantages of introducing young children (from the age of five upwards) to the experience of work. An efficiency diet formed the final element of Rumford's system. By drawing on an eccentric water-based theory of nutrition and his practical experience of troop provisioning, the Count concluded that garden allotments, supplemented by soup kitchens, generated sufficient sustenance for labour. A single hot meal a day of soup, he argued, delivered the maximum amount of food to a large body of labourers at least cost.[55]

The treatment of the enslaved advocated by Gibbes, Lascelles, and their associates was informed by the European experience of poor law administration during the 1780s and 1790s. While the collaborators were not alone in comparing plantation slavery with European poor relief, the analysis they presented in the *Instructions* was more sophisticated than that of most other commentators.[56] The authors conceived of the enslaved as naturally indolent beings, similar to paupers; yet at the same time, the humanity of slaves was also recognised in the sense that they

---

[53] HSP, Gratz Collection, Case 7, Box 24, Benjamin Thompson to Dr Samuel Williams, Manheim, 24 June 1785.

[54] Sanborn C. Brown ed., *Collected Works of Count Rumford* (5 vols., Cambridge, MA, 1970), vol. V, 1–99; Handler, *Guide to Source Materials*, 57.

[55] Sanborn C. Brown, *Benjamin Thompson, Count Rumford* (Cambridge, MA, 1979), 126–7, 159–61. Rumford published three essays on his theory of poor relief between 1796 and 1797.

[56] Beckford, *Remarks Upon the Situation*, 55–6. Beckford argued that slavery (properly managed) extolled the virtue of work, asserting that slaves enjoyed better conditions than European paupers or convicts. Perhaps his most famous observation consists of this anecdote: 'At the time that the trial of Somerset was determined at Westminster hall, a negro very shrewdly remarked that Lord Mansfield had told them they were free, but did not tell them where to get food' (96).

were considered amenable to moral improvement through a carefully designed work regime. However, pragmatism, rather than morality, is the dominant theme within the *Instructions*. The authors outline those material incentives judged most likely to induce the enslaved to adapt their behaviour in ways considered conducive to the creation of a stable and prosperous plantation society.

It is tempting to condemn the *Instructions* for sacrificing humanitarian principles for profit and to ridicule many of its practical proposals. Neither response, however, is historically justified. While shocking to a modern audience, the proposals for plantation management articulated concepts similar in nature to poor law reform within Europe. Indeed, the recommendations of Edwin Lascelles and his fellow authors were no less bizarre than Rumford's own system, which drew praise from some quarters.

Evidence documenting the Lascelles' later support of amelioration is scanty, partly owing to the destruction wrought by the 1940 bombing raid. Nevertheless, the scraps of information that remain indicate strong sympathy for the campaign's aims, particularly the religious conversion of slaves. Material is most detailed for Jamaica; however, since similar initiatives also took place on Barbados, it is likely that missionary work was also supported by the Earl of Harewood's attorneys on this colony.[57] Taken collectively, the evidence suggests a shift away from the essentially pragmatic approach to slave well-being taken by the *Instructions* and a move towards a more moralistic position, whereby Christianisation is viewed as a central component of welfare policy.[58]

Following the successful 1823 emancipation motion in the House of Commons, religious activity on Jamaica intensified. In 1825, Jamaica's own Assembly passed the Clergy Bill, establishing the right of Anglican, Moravian, or Presbyterian ministers to convert slaves. In the same year, the island's first Bishop also arrived to begin his ministry. Francis Graeme testified in 1815 that, 'for some years past he has observed that the slaves have shewn a contented and quiet disposition, and a very considerable number of those under his care have at their own request been made

---

[57] Luster, *Amelioration of the Slaves*, 64–5, 71; Mary Turner, *Slaves and Missionaries: The Disintegration of Jamaican Slave Society, 1787–1834* (Chicago, 1982), 1–37.

[58] The Lascelles archive can in this respect be compared with Jamaican estate attorney Simon Taylor's correspondence with absentee proprietor Chaloner Arcedeckne. Taylor resisted the Christian instruction of slaves while remaining committed to a model of management based on the use of material incentives (as a supplement to physical coercion), Betty Wood and Roy Clayton, 'Jamaica's Struggle for a Self-Perpetuating Slave Population: Demographic, Social, and Religious Changes on Golden Grove Plantation, 1812–1832', *Journal of Caribbean Studies*, 6 (1988), 287–8, 290–1.

Christians; that in every application of the kind, he has forwarded their wishes'.[59] This statement implies that missionary work on the Lascelles' estates predated centralised initiatives; nevertheless, from the 1820s onwards, commitment to religious policies seems to have increased. George William Hamilton (another of the Earl's island attorneys and vestry officer for St Thomas-in-the-Vale) raised funds in 1826 to present a gift of plate to the rector, William G. Burton. The silver cup presented was engraved with the inscription: 'for the religious and moral improvement of the Negroes under his charge'.[60] In the same year, the 2nd Earl of Harewood was encouraged to erect a chapel on land donated from Williamsfield estate.

Harewood Chapel is described in a contemporary report as 'a solid substantial building, and very neatly fitted up, and will contain about four hundred persons'.[61] A contemporary report of its consecration highlights the attendance of slaves from all the neighbouring parishes, 'who were allowed a holiday on the occasion, and who were all decked out in their best attire'. The published account of proceedings highlights the propaganda value of events such as this for the amelioration campaign:

The Slaves appeared to view the whole with much interest and respect, and, notwithstanding the general anxiety, evident among them, to see as much as they could, such was their decorum and good behaviour that not the slightest inconvenience or interruption took place, although the number that attended was very great. Neither civil nor military authority was thought necessary to preserve order, and the confidence of the Gentlemen who managed on the occasion, that neither were wanting to ensure their good behaviour, was well repaid by the gratifying spectacle of so many thousands of well dressed Slaves, conducting themselves with as much propriety and decency as ever were witnessed in the Mother-Country.[62]

Four years later, it was reported that catechisms were daily occurrences on Williamsfield, taking place at noon for three-quarters of an hour. By this date, it seems probable (though it is not stated) that a catechetical

[59] *Further Proceedings of the Honourable House of Assembly of Jamaica*, testimony of Francis Graeme, 15 November 1815.

[60] NA:PRO, CO141/23, *The Royal Gazette* (Kingston, Jamaica, 24 June–1 July 1826), 26. Burton was appointed in 1816, BL, *The Royal Gazette* (Kingston, 21–28 September 1816), 23. In addition, Hamilton subscribed £16 to a Presbyterian Institute in 1822 and £21.6s.8d. to a Kirk in 1832 (the largest and second-largest contributions at each date), NA:PRO, CO141/19, *The Royal Gazette* (Kingston, 28 September–5 October 1822), 18; CO141/27, *The Royal Gazette* (Kingston, 15–22 December 1832), 19.

[61] WRA, Abstract of the Produce of the Estates and other Property in the West Indies belonging to the Right Honourable Lord Harewood, 1805–39: Jamaica Affairs; NA:PRO, CO141/23, *The Royal Gazette* (Kingston, 8–15 July 1826), 5.

[62] NA:PRO, CO141/23, *The Royal Gazette* (Kingston, 8–15 July 1826), 5.

Table 9.6 *Name changing among mothers listed on Nightingale Grove and Williamsfield estates, 1817–32*

	1817–20	1820–3	1823–6	1826–9	1829–32
Mothers with new children	27	26	26	18	23
Surnames	12	22	24	17	23
	.44	.85	.92	.94	1.00
Baptism or alias [a]	9	15	14	11	15
	.33	.58	.54	.61	.65

Note: [a] The compilers of the 1832 return substituted the term 'alias' for baptism. A total of 69 mothers are recorded between 1817 and 1832. Of these women, 32 had changed name; 26 are listed with a given and surname without reference to name change; and 11 are listed with a given name only.
Source: NA:PRO, T71/13–18, 25–8, 30, 32.

school was established on the estate to provide enslaved children with a basic religious education.[63]

An indication of the spread of Christianity among the Jamaican enslaved is provided by the proportion of mothers on Nightingale Grove and Williamsfield possessing a second name (Table 9.6). Baptism was not the only means of acquiring a second name; some of the mothers in the database may have inherited names used by their own parents, while others gave second names to the offspring of interracial unions. The table differentiates, therefore, between mothers who are listed using a first or given name only, mothers with given names and surnames, and mothers who are explicitly recorded as having changed their name through baptism or the adoption of an alias. On the basis of these data, it appears that while the consecration of Harewood Chapel helped to sustain the number of baptisms, significant missionary activity predated the Jamaican Clergy Bill of 1825. Francis Graeme's comments on the prevalence of baptism in 1815 are thus corroborated by the finding that in 1817 between 33 and 44 per cent of slave mothers had either changed their names or were using surnames.

The leading role of the 2nd Earl in the amelioration campaign is revealed by his chairmanship of a 'General Meeting of Proprietors, Merchants, Bankers, Ship Owners, Manufacturers, Traders, and Others interested in the Preservation of the West India Colonies', convened in London on 5 April 1832. The contemporary report of the Earl's opening speech is reproduced in full in Appendix II at the end of this chapter. Two

[63] NA:PRO, CO141/26, *The Royal Gazette* (Kingston, 14–22 January 1831), folded sheet at the end of the edition. According to this source, twenty-eight Church of England catechetical schools were established on estates in St Thomas-in-the-Vale in 1830.

features of his opening address are particularly notable. Firstly, the Earl likened slave proprietorship to the paternal support of the poor, portraying it as a social duty and a private burden shouldered for the public benefit:

A West India proprietor is not at liberty to cast upon the public every bad or inefficient servant he may have, for if he does so he may injure, a whole community. A West India proprietor cannot, the moment he becomes a loser, dismiss his slaves, but he is obliged, from a regard to the peace and security of the Colony and of his property, to maintain the unproductive labourer.

Secondly, Harewood contended that the material condition of the enslaved was steadily improving, notwithstanding the charges of ill-treatment critics of slavery levelled against the institution:

It is important to us to see what has occurred with respect to this subject. Some Resolutions have been lately come to, which are calculated to produce an impression on the public mind, that nothing has been done, and that all is yet to do, regarding the amelioration of the condition of the slaves. But it was not fair to the West India body to keep out of sight any amelioration that had been made in the condition of the slaves. I ask what has occurred since 1823?[64]

The next section attempts to answer the Earl's question by analysing survivorship on his Barbadian and Jamaican properties.

Survivorship and Reproduction

Qualitative accounts of living conditions under slavery on the Lascelles' estates are fragmentary and highly impressionistic. In the great majority of cases, very few facts survive to document the lives of individual slaves. While quantitative analysis also suffers from defects, it provides an opportunity to reconstruct the profile of the enslaved population, despite limited archival resources. It is important to emphasise that the form in which data survives inevitably equates a slave community with the plantation. Although Africans and Creoles occupied the geographical space delimited by a specific estate, it is clear that smaller family units were created within the plantation. The enslaved might also form relationships with persons living outside the boundaries of a given property. These aspects of slave life are largely hidden from view in estate records. Nevertheless, since all vital events (births and deaths) took place in the context of the plantation, the application of demographic techniques to estate accounts can generate valuable information. Quantitative study of the unfree population is also

---

[64] *Proceedings at a Public Meeting of Persons Interested in the Preservation of the British West India Colonies Held at the City of London Tavern the 5th April 1832*, BL, Tracts relating to the West Indies: Tract 4 (London, 1832), 8.

important because it leads to a deeper appreciation of the human suffering associated with plantation regimes in the Caribbean.

What were the life-chances of those enslaved living on the Lascelles' Barbadian and Jamaican plantations? Was Amyot correct, for example, in stating that Williamsfield suffered from an abnormally high death rate? In the absence of emancipation, could slavery on the estates have remained viable demographically? An opportunity to answer these questions is provided by the Slave Registry Bill of 1816. This legislation was followed in 1817 by a census of most of the slave population of the British West Indies; thereafter, triennial returns of births and deaths were submitted by plantation owners or their agents.[65]

During the period of registration (1817–34), the Lascelles owned six estates continuously on Barbados and Jamaica. Complete returns survive for five of these properties: the Barbadian estates of Belle, Thicket, and Fortescue; and the Jamaican plantations, Nightingale Grove and Williamsfield. A sixth property, Mount (Barbados), is missing a return for 1829, but is otherwise complete.[66]

To maximise the amount of information available from the registration returns, the technique of left and right censoring (LRC) was adapted to the study of the enslaved populations.[67] Four requirements (all of which are satisfied by registration) are necessary for LRC: 1) the date a person first appears in a census (which need not be the date of birth); 2) the date the same individual is last listed (which need not be the date of death); 3) the individual's age at first censoring; and 4) the reason enumeration ceases. For each enslaved person, the total number of years spent on a Lascelles' estate between 1817 and 1834 was calculated, from birth to age eighty, at five-yearly intervals. An example illustrates the procedure adopted. Ayer, an enslaved woman, is first censored in a listing for 1817, aged twenty; she is last mentioned in the registration return for 1832. Her final entry states that Ayer had died at some point since the last triennial return was submitted in 1829.[68]

---

[65] For a description of these records and a guide to their use in demographic analysis, see Higman, *Slave Population and Economy in Jamaica*; B. W. Higman, *Slave Populations of the British Caribbean, 1807–1834* (Baltimore/London, 1984); Meredith John, *Plantation Slaves of Trinidad*.

[66] The analysis that follows incorporates the Mount data since excluding this estate made little difference to the results obtained.

[67] The spreadsheet and array formulae used to generate the left and right censored life table were produced in association with Roger Avery during a visiting fellowship held at The John Carter Brown Library in February–March 2005.

[68] Where the age at death is not stated, it was assumed that the individual died at the midpoint of the triennial period.

Ayer's LRC profile, therefore, may be set out as follows:

Name	Date 1st census	Date last census	Age 1st census	Exit reason	Years spent on the estate in each 5-year age interval[69]								
					0–4	5–9	10–14	15–19	20–4	25–9	30–4	+35 ... 80	
Ayer	1817	1830.5	20	death	0	0	0	0	5	5	3.5	0	

Table 9.7 *LRC generated life table for six estates, 1817–34*

Age group	Deaths (number)	q_x	l_x	L_x	T_x	e_x
0–1	30	0.1895	100000.0	90522.5	2520062.7	25.2
1–2	74	0.1991	81045.0	72975.7	2429540.2	30.0
2–4	96	0.1979	64906.3	175451.4	2356564.5	36.3
5–9	38	0.0924	52061.3	248276.3	2181113.2	41.9
10–14	13	0.0332	47249.2	232323.5	1932836.9	40.9
15–19	14	0.0349	45680.2	224411.7	1700513.4	37.2
20–24	21	0.0609	44084.5	213710.2	1476101.7	33.5
25–29	21	0.0682	41399.6	199943.9	1262391.5	30.5
30–34	25	0.0862	38578.0	184575.1	1062447.6	27.5
35–39	28	0.1098	35252.1	166585.5	877872.5	24.9
40–44	24	0.0967	31382.2	149321.3	711287.0	22.7
45–49	26	0.1175	28346.3	133404.4	561965.7	19.8
50–54	35	0.1717	25015.4	114338.2	428561.4	17.1
55–59	35	0.2404	20719.9	91145.0	314223.1	15.2
60–64	20	0.1969	15738.1	70941.6	223078.1	14.2
65–69	14	0.1811	12638.5	57471.9	152136.5	12.0
70–74	18	0.2792	10350.2	44526.8	94664.6	9.1
75–79	18	0.4771	7460.5	28403.7	50137.8	6.7
80+	21	1.0000	3901.0	21734.1	21734.1	5.6

Note: Six estates: Belle, Mount, Thicket, Fortescue, Nightingale Grove, Williamsfield.
Key: q_x – probability of dying during the five-year age interval for a person alive at the beginning of each age interval.
l_x – the inverse of q_x (a survivorship index, based on an initial cohort of 100,000 people). The figure 100,000 (termed the radix of the life table) is a convenient constant chosen to illustrate the survivorship index.
L_x – total number of person years lived in each age group (a measure of the population's age structure).
T_x – total number of person years remaining to be lived by persons alive at the beginning of each age interval.
e_x – life expectancy (in years) for a person alive at the beginning of each age interval.
Source: NA:PRO, T71/13–18, 25–8, 30, 32, 520–1, 524–5, 527, 534–6, 540, 544, 547, 549–50, 553, 556–7.

[69] These entries did not need to be inputted but are given for the purposes of illustration. A spreadsheet template was created which automatically calculated the entries for each age group using the information entered about age and census dates.

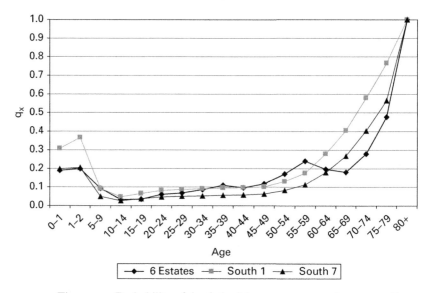

Figure 9.3. Probability of death (q_x) by age group on six estates, 1817–34 and two model life tables
Source: NA:PRO, T71/13–18, 25–8, 30, 32, 520–1, 524–5, 527, 534–6, 540, 544, 547, 549–50, 553, 556–7; Coale and Demeny, *Regional Model Life Tables*, 384–5.

The following additional information about Ayer is also recorded in the registration returns: gender (female), origin (Creole), colony location (Barbados), and estate (Belle).

A life table was constructed by summing the total number of years lived by each of the 1,815 slaves on the six Lascelles estates in each age interval. These person years of life form the numerators of the LRC life table; the corresponding denominators are the number of deaths occurring in each age interval during the period surveyed. The advantage of an LRC generated life table is the amount of information it utilises. By adopting this method, a total of 572 deaths and 18,783.5 person years could be examined.

Mortality and Survival

The aggregate life table generated by the LRC technique is presented in Table 9.7 and the associated probability of death at different ages (q_x) is depicted in Figure 9.3. It is clear that life expectancy was dismal for babies born on the Lascelles' estates, but improved during the earliest years of life. The sharp drop in mortality between birth and age four implies that infant mortality (death during the first months of life) is understated in the returns: a finding confirmed by other studies of slave demography.[70] The first month of life for all newborns is a hazardous time. While rates of neonatal mortality are not known with certainty, in a society possessing only rudimentary healthcare (with limited knowledge of basic hygiene), the death rate was probably comparable to the highest levels experienced in the contemporary developing world. Contemporaries comment, for example, on the frequency of deaths arising from tetanus or lockjaw following the cutting of the umbilical cord.[71] The weaning and crawling stages constituted two further phases of childhood carrying a high risk of infection. Babies born in the Caribbean were vulnerable all-year-round to parasitic diseases, since the climate lacked a winter season. Like nearly all recorders of the enslaved, the compilers of the registration returns omitted to record the fate of the youngest members of the population, many of whose brief lives spanned less time than a butterfly's.[72] Private listings were usually submitted to absentee owners wishing to inform themselves of the extent of their slaveholdings, or for the benefit of lenders holding a lien on slaves. The compilers of such records lacked an incentive to take notice of the deaths of babies and young children occurring just prior to the survey. Official population counts (including the registration returns themselves) similarly neglect to record details of all infants dying within a few days or weeks.

In consequence, the aggregate life table is inaccurate at the youngest ages. An indication of the margin of error is provided by Fig. 9.3, which compares the q_x curve with two Coale-Demeny model life tables for populations experiencing high mortality (South Levels 1 and 7).[73] The LRC q_x curve follows the life table data closely; in particular, it possesses the expected points of inflection: (1) a peak at the first years of life; (2) declining mortality in childhood until ages ten to fourteen; (3) slow acceleration to approximately age forty-five to forty-nine; and (4) an increasing probability of dying thereafter. The close correspondence of the curves suggests, therefore, that the corrected life expectancy for

---

[70] Higman, *Slave Populations of the British Caribbean*, 26–35; Meredith John, *Plantation Slaves of Trinidad*, 82–92.

[71] Mathison, *Notices Respecting Jamaica*, 28–9.

[72] Higman, *Slave Populations of the British Caribbean*, 26–35.

[73] Ansley J. Coale and Paul Demeny, *Regional Model Life Tables and Stable Populations* (2nd edn, London, 1983), 384–5. These life tables are used for the purpose of illustration; similar comparisons could be made with West 1 and 7.

persons born into slavery on the Lascelles' plantations probably lies between twenty and twenty-two years at birth.

Babies born into slavery remained at high risk until well after the toddler stage. Knowledge of child deaths is weakest for ages below one because of under-registration. The life table records survivorship more accurately between ages one through four, though this measure still understates deaths owing to the failure of enumerators to record all deaths of babies born during the triennial. Nevertheless, the fact that *at least* 36 per cent of children aged one in the LRC life table had died by their fourth birthday reiterates just how low the rate of survivorship was at the youngest ages on the six estates. Adjusting for under-registration by recourse to the model life tables, implies that approximately 56 per cent of all newborns died before reaching the age of five.

Five was a significant age for an enslaved child, since it marked the point at which the new generation began entering the plantation labour force. Data for participation rates confirm that on the Lascelles' plantations, as in the West Indies generally, children began work grass-gathering at these ages (see below). One of the most striking findings of the LRC life table is that the annual probability of death between the ages of five and nine was 9.2 per cent. Such a death rate ranks among the highest recorded in documented human populations. A notable feature of the *Instructions* is that it prioritised the care of this age group, recognising the risks to which they were exposed. Yet instead of adopting Edward Long's advice, that children should be kept with their mothers and not placed in gangs under the supervision of a field nurse, the tract articulates Rumford's contrary philosophy of exposing the very young to work experience.[74] Deaths among five to nine year olds were probably the most easily preventable on the West Indian estates; the failure to reduce mortality in this age group emphasises how limited the achievements of amelioration were in practice.

Slavery was an extremely unpleasant experience for the human beings unfortunate enough to have been its victims. Paleo-demographic studies, though few in number, have reached consistent findings about the low quality of life endured by populations living under slavery. To date, the only excavation of a slave burial ground located in the Caribbean is that of Newton plantation on Barbados. Analysis of skeletal remains discovered at this site revealed that the enslaved suffered from periods of chronic malnutrition and disease, combined with degenerative joint ailments. These findings are consistent with a physically exacting work regime and

[74] Long, *History of Jamaica*, vol. II, 437.

inadequate nutritional provision.[75] Visually, those enslaved individuals 'in the prime of life' would have looked much older than their years.

Direct evidence for material conditions on the Lascelles' estates is lacking. It is clear from surviving correspondence, however, that plantations belonging to the Earls of Harewood were run along similar lines to other West India properties. The q_x curve provides some evidence of morbidity: the lingering effects of disease at young ages on mortality at higher ages. In comparison with model life table South Level 1 (and high mortality tables inspected from other regions), q_x accelerated from ages forty-five through fifty-nine. A remorseless work regime, coupled with sickness earlier in life, is consistent with these data and with the archaeology and paleo-demography of the Newton site.

In consequence, the finding that e_5 was approximately forty-two years in no sense detracts from the unhealthiness of the work environment confronting the enslaved on the Lascelles' plantations. The life expectancy estimate does, however, help explain why slavery endured as a viable system of labour exploitation. The ability to keep slaves alive and productive for an average of more than four decades after age five was a key element in the estates' continued profitability. These returns were attained, however, only at the cost of years of suffering by workers condemned to forced labour and, in a majority of cases, an early grave.

A minority of slaves defied the odds and died of natural causes at advanced ages. These individuals constituted what plantation accounts typically refer to as the 'superannuated'. Older slaves were given light duties or were exempted from labour for their owner (but not necessarily from provision ground cultivation for their own subsistence). The LRC life table's q_x curve (Fig. 9.3) is located further to the right than the model life tables South Levels 1 and 7 (and other Coale-Demeny life tables). It is a natural response to dismiss the slave registration returns as inaccurate at older ages, but this may well not be the case. Age misreporting at advanced ages is a serious problem in most modern census returns, including those for Britain and the United States. Indeed, inadequate data have been a factor in the failure to predict the extent of mortality decline among the oldest age groups, with dire consequences

---

[75] Robert S. Corruccini, Jerome S. Handler, and Frederick W. Lange, 'Osteology of a Slave Burial Population from Barbados, West Indies', *American Journal of Physical Anthropology*, 59 (1982), 443–59; Robert S. Corruccini, Keith P. Jacobi, Jerome S. Handler, and Arthur C. Aufderheide, 'Implications of Tooth Root Hypercementosis in a Barbados Slave Skeletal Collection', *American Journal of Physical Anthropology*, 74 (1987), 179–84.

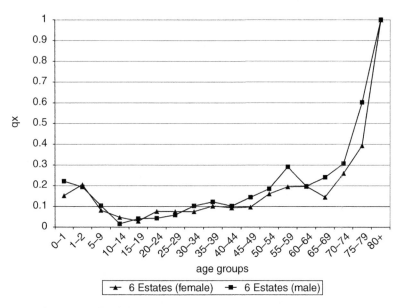

Figure 9.4 Probability of death (q_x) by age group: males and females on six estates, 1817–34
Source: As for Table 9.7.

for social welfare budgets and pension provision.[76] It is by no means clear that an enslaved population, fixed in one place and enumerated triennially, generates data that are worthless in comparison with a mobile population counted decennially. West Indian slave populations ought, therefore, to be studied more closely. In addition to providing perspectives on the conditions of plantation life, the data are invaluable for potential insights into morbidity and survivorship outside the range of existing model life tables.

Women formed a majority (52 per cent) of the estate populations on Barbados and Jamaica. The q_x curves for men and women reveal why this is the case (Fig. 9.4). The female surplus recorded in the slave listings arises primarily because of higher male infant mortality. While the actual rates of death are understated for both boy and girl babies, the male q_x curve lies above the female equivalent. Model life tables similarly record higher rates of male infant mortality, reflecting the fact

[76] For a review of the problem and an investigation of whether age misreporting suffers from upwards or downwards bias at older ages, see Samuel H. Preston, Irma T. Elo, and Quincy Stewart, 'Effects of Misreporting on Mortality Estimates at Older Ages', Population Aging Research Center, University of Pennsylvania, working paper series, 98–01.

that, biologically, boys are more vulnerable than girls during the first weeks of life. Nature compensates by supplying a higher male birth rate (approximately 104 males are born per 100 females). Such a rate of compensation, however, proved insufficient to combat the hostile tropical environment and rigours of plantation life into which slave children were born. A tendency for females to outlive males at older ages (again for biological reasons) provides a secondary reason for the surplus of women, which is also reflected in these data.[77]

The influence of different factors on survival can be examined by applying time to event analysis to the study of plantation mortality.[78] The explanatory variables available for analysis are of two types depending on the scale of measurement employed. Four characteristics (containing fourteen separate groups) are measured using a categorical scale: origin (African or Creole born), location (by colony and estate), colour (blacks and persons of colour), and gender (male or female). Age of the enslaved constitutes the exception, since this is measured on a continuous scale.[79]

The effect of each attribute upon survival time was examined in a two-stage process using the technique of non-parametric Cox regression.[80] Firstly, the individual effect of each variable upon survival was examined separately (univariate analysis). Subsequently, the joint effect of the explanatory variables upon survival was determined (multivariate analysis), in order to isolate the underlying effect of each characteristic upon survival by adjusting for the effects of the others. A backwards selection procedure was used to choose the most suitable regression model.[81]

---

[77] Two unusual features of the Lascelles' estates are the low rates of male child deaths at ages ten to fourteen and, conversely, the high rate of male deaths at ages fifty-five to fifty-nine. Age heaping may be responsible for generating these outliers (see Appendix I).

[78] For an overview of this subject, see Paul Allison, *Event History Analysis: Regression for Longitudinal Event Data* (Beverly Hills, CA, 1984). The outcome measure in the study is the length of time from the first census to the time of death. For those enslaved who did not die during the observation period, the length of time from their first census to the last census is recorded. These subjects are treated as 'censored' (that is to say, it is known that they survived for at least as long as the times between censuses).

[79] An additional categorical variable, occupation, was not included in the analysis because this information is unavailable for the Jamaican estates.

[80] Survival Analysis using censored data violates the assumption in ordinary least squares regression that the residuals are distributed normally. For a discussion of Cox regression using the STATA statistical program, see Mario Cleves, William W. Gould, and Roberto Gutierrez, *An Introduction to Survival Analysis Using Stata* (rev. edn, College Station, TX, 2004; originally published 2002).

[81] Initially all explanatory variables are included in the analysis and the regression model fitted. If one or more variables is found not to be statistically significant, the least significant variable is removed and the model refitted. This procedure is repeated until all remaining variables are statistically significant, resulting in the final model.

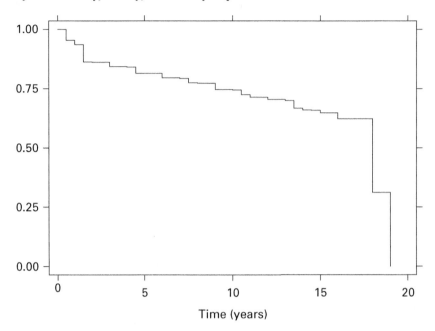

Figure 9.5. Kaplan-Meier cumulative survival plot for six estates,
1817–34
Source: As for Table 9.7.

Figure 9.5 presents a Kaplan-Meier cumulative survival plot for the
enslaved individuals on the six estates during the seventeen years
spanned by the data.[82] The individual effects of each variable on length
of survival are reported in Table 9.8. In time to event analysis, the
impact each characteristic has on survival can be demonstrated by calculating hazard ratios. These ratios indicate the hazard (or likelihood) of
death at any time for a particular subject compared to the hazard of
death for another subject. A hazard ratio greater than one implies that
the risk of death is higher in the selected group than a baseline group;
conversely, a hazard ratio of less than one implies that the risk of death
at any time is lower than that of the baseline. Univariate analysis reveals
that estate location, age, and origin each exerted a statistically significant
effect on survival times. The worst survival (highest hazard of death) was
found on the Belle, Thicket, and Williamsfield estates, while Fortescue

[82] Figure 9.5 plots $S(t_i)$, the proportion of the enslaved surviving to the start of each year of
observation. $S(t_i) = (r_i - d_i / r_i) \star S (t - i)$, where r_i denotes the number of slaves alive at
time i and d_i the number of deaths occurring at time i.

Table 9.8. *Hazard ratios for six estates (univariate analysis)*

Variable	Group/term	Hazard ratio (95% confidence interval)	P-value
Colony	Barbados	1.00	
	Jamaica	1.04 (0.87, 1.24)	0.66
Estate	Belle	1.00	
	Mount	0.72 (0.50, 1.04)	
	Thicket	0.90 (0.72, 1.13)	
	Fortescue	0.61 (0.43, 0.85)	
	Nightingale	0.71 (0.50, 1.00)	
	Williamsfield	0.98 (0.78, 1.22)	0.02
Gender	Female	1.00	
	Male	1.14 (0.97, 1.35)	0.11
Age	Linear	0.63 (0.56, 0.70)	<0.001
	Quadratic	1.09 (1.07, 1.10)	
Age (grouped)	<5	1.00	
	5–15	0.24 (0.17, 0.33)	
	15–30	0.37 (0.28, 0.48)	
	30–50	0.62 (0.50, 0.78)	
	>50	1.26 (1.00, 1.58)	<0.001
Origin	African	1.00	
	Creole	0.58 (0.46, 0.74)	<0.001
Colour	Blacks	1.00	
	Persons of Colour	0.78 (0.55, 1.13)	0.20

Note: [a] The significance of the result of each statistical test can be measured by the size of the p-value (a test of the null-hypothesis that the parameter is not significantly different to the baseline). A p-value of less than 0.05 is usually regarded as evidence of a statistically significant result; a result of 0.01 (or less) can be viewed as highly significant.
[b] In the case of age (the variable measured on a continuous scale), the hazard ratios are reported for a ten-year increase in age.
Source: As for Table 9.7.

was characterised by the best survival. At any given time, Creole slaves faced a hazard of death almost half that of Africans. No evidence was found, however, that colony location, gender, or colour exerted any significant effect upon survival.

The analytical problems associated with age were tackled by measuring this variable on both a continuous scale and a categorical scale. In the former case, the relationship between age and survival was found to be non-linear, complicating the interpretation of the hazard ratios. The quadratic term for age, however, exceeds one, suggesting that an approximate 'U' shape relationship best describes the data, with a higher hazard of death occurring at either end of the age scale. This hypothesis

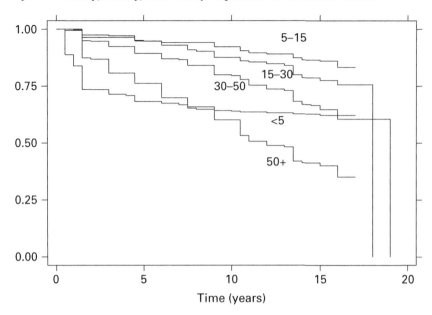

Figure 9.6. Kaplan-Meier cumulative survival curves by age group, 1817–34
Source: As for Table 9.7.

was confirmed when age was examined using a categorical scale. While the selection of the age groups is constricted by the sample size, this approach has the advantage of generating results that are easier to interpret. The greatest likelihood of death was faced by those enslaved aged over fifty, with the under-five age group possessing the second highest hazard of death. The lowest hazard of death was found to lie in the five-to-fifteen age range, who at any time faced only a quarter of the hazard for the under-fives (Fig. 9.6).[83]

The populations of the six estates each contained different mixes of age groups, Africans, and Creoles. To ascertain whether age and origin (rather than location) determined length of survival, the joint effect of the explanatory variables listed in Table 9.8 was estimated. A backwards selection procedure was used to retain only the statistically significant variables affecting survival. This procedure was performed twice: firstly with age measured on a continuous scale, and secondly with age on a

---

[83] These results make no allowance for the under-reporting of infant births and deaths during the first year of life.

Table 9.9a. *Hazard ratios for six estates (multivariate analysis): age measured on a continuous scale*

Variable	Group/term	Hazard ratio (95% confidence interval)	P-value
Age[a]	Linear	0.95 (0.94, 0.96)	<0.001
	Quadratic	1.0008 (1.0007, 1.0009)	
Origin	African	1.00	
	Creole	0.68 (0.51, 0.90)	0.008

Note: [a] Hazard ratios reported for a ten-year increase in age.

Table 9.9b. *Hazard ratios for six estates (multivariate analysis): age measured on a categorical scale*

Variable	Group/term	Hazard ratio (95% confidence interval)	P-value
Age (grouped)	<5	1.00	
	5–15	0.24 (0.17, 0.33)	
	15–30	0.36 (0.27, 0.47)	
	30–50	0.53 (0.42, 0.68)	
	>50	1.08 (0.84, 1.39)	<0.001
Origin	African	1.00	
	Creole	0.63 (0.48, 0.82)	<0.001

Source: As for Table 9.7.

categorical scale. The results and the final model are summarised in Tables 9.9a and 9.9b.

Multivariate analysis reveals that only age and race exerted a significant effect upon the length of survival. After adjusting for the effects of these two variables, there was no evidence that estate location exercised an independent influence. This finding suggests that differences in survival between the estates can be explained primarily by the different mix of ages and the proportion of Africans contained within their separate populations. A similar relationship between age and survival was observed in both multivariate and univariate analyses (the hazard ratios are almost identical), regardless of whether age was measured using a continuous or categorical scale. Creole subjects were again found to have better survival than Africans, but the size of the differential was reduced slightly after allowing for the effect of age differences.

An earlier analysis of a period life table calculated for Trinidad during the years 1813 to 1816 found that Africans and Creoles experienced

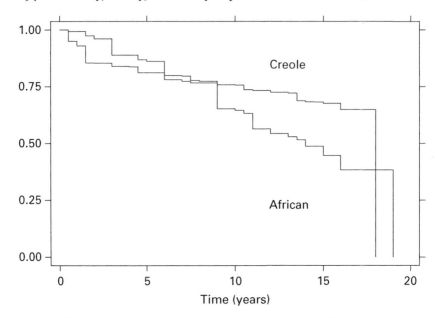

Figure 9.7. Kaplan-Meier cumulative survival plots by origin, 1817–34
Source: As for Table 9.7.

Table 9.10. *Hazard ratios for children aged three and under*

Variable	Year	Hazard ratio (95% confidence interval)	P-value
Year first censored	1817	1.00	
	1820	2.10 (1.27, 3.49)	
	1823	2.31 (1.38, 3.84)	
	1826	2.42 (1.46, 4.00)	
	1829	2.68 (1.62, 4.45)	
	1832	3.22 (1.94, 5.39)	<0.001

Source: As for Table 9.7.

similar mortality across all age groups surveyed.[84] In contrast, on the Lascelles' estates those Africans surviving the seasoning process faced a greater likelihood of death at older ages than Creoles (Fig. 9.7).[85] The

[84] Meredith John, *Plantation Slaves of Trinidad*, 115–16.
[85] In the case of the more recently settled colony of Trinidad, relatively few Creoles had lived long enough to survive to older age groups by 1816, preventing a differential of this kind from emerging in the data.

LRC data imply that the effects of adjustment to the colonial environment were not confined to the period immediately following arrival; morbidity appears to have afflicted the survivors of the heavy mortality associated with seasoning.

An additional analysis examined if there was a difference in survival for those enslaved aged three and under (the length of the triennial), depending on the year in which they were first censored. It can be seen in Table 9.10 that for these young enslaved children there was a significant overall difference in the hazard rate. The later the date of first census, the greater the likelihood of death (and therefore the shorter the survival times) on the estates. Such a finding casts further doubt on the hypothesis that amelioration improved life expectancy during the decades immediately prior to emancipation.

Fertility and Reproduction

While primarily designed to measure mortality, the LRC life table can also be used to ascertain whether the enslaved populations on the six estates were able to sustain themselves. By taking into account the number of live births registered, the probability an enslaved girl would survive to adulthood and give birth to a female child can be estimated. The measure required is the net-reproduction rate (NRR), or replacement rate (R_o), of a population. NRR calculates fecundity: the average number of girls (m_x) born to a woman surviving to the age of reproduction. A critical value for R_o is one; a figure less than this reveals that a population is failing to maintain itself, whereas values greater than one indicate growth is occurring. The following equation is used to estimate R_o:

$$NRR = (B^f/P^f_{15-44}) \times 30 \times 1 - (l_{30}/l_o)$$

The first term of this expression adds up the total number of female births during the period under observation (284), divides it by the person years lived by women between the ages of fifteen and forty-four (5,013), and multiplies it by the thirty years observed.[86] The second term states the probability of a woman surviving to age thirty (the midpoint of the years of reproduction). From the female equivalent LRC life table, this is l_{30}/l_o, or 60.2 per cent.

The value of R_o obtained for the six estates was 1.02 for the period 1817 to 1834. Given the very high levels of infant mortality, the ability of

---

[86] A total of 573 births were recorded on the six estates during the years covered by the LRC life table.

the slave population to maintain itself is remarkable. From an owner's perspective, this finding provides further evidence that, prior to emancipation, the Lascelles' estates were viable plantations, capable of maintaining their workforces during the decades following the abolition of the slave trade. Yet, just as e_5 describes upwards of forty years of unremitting toil, the true meaning of R_o lies in the extraordinary waste of human life associated with the plantation system. By encouraging slaves to give birth to large numbers of children, and working the survivors hard, West Indian planters sought to operate sustainable business enterprises.

Unfortunately, it is not possible to investigate fertility in much greater detail. The reason for this lies in the failure of the registration returns to record the ages of mothers, preventing the calculation of age-specific fertility rates. Historical demographers have attempted to overcome this deficiency by using the 'own-child' method (OCM) to generate age-specific birth rates for women of child-rearing age. This technique seeks to match children with their living mothers at a given census date. OCM stands or falls by the three key assumptions it makes. Firstly, estimation assumes that the distribution of unmatched children is the same as that of matched children. Secondly, OCM assumes that the pattern of mortality remains constant during the ten to fifteen years prior to the census.[87] Thirdly (and perhaps most critically in the case of slave populations), OCM assumes that reported matches are true matches of mothers and their children. In practice, it is not always clear whether a woman caring for a child is the mother, sister, relative, or kinswoman of that child. Even in studies of the contemporary developing world, where it is possible to conduct field interviews, assumptions about childcare arrangements can distort research findings.[88]

In the case of the Lascelles' estates, only the slave registration returns for Nightingale Grove and Williamsfield provide information about the mothers of children. Ironically, the strikingly high proportion of matched children on these estates (Fig. 9.8) means that OCM emphatically *cannot* be used. Childbirth in a tropical climate, with only the most basic of medical facilities, was a hazardous time for mothers; yet, according to

---

[87] For example, children aged fifteen appearing in the enumeration are the survivors of a cohort of infants born fourteen years previously; similarly, mothers aged forty-nine are the survivors of a larger group of women alive at the birth of the oldest children being matched. The own-child technique employs a life table to reconstruct past populations, replacing children and mothers who have died prior to the census.

[88] For further details of the own-child technique, see J-L. Cho, R. D. Retherford, and M. K. Choe, *The Own-Children Method of Fertility Estimation* (Honalulu, 1986).

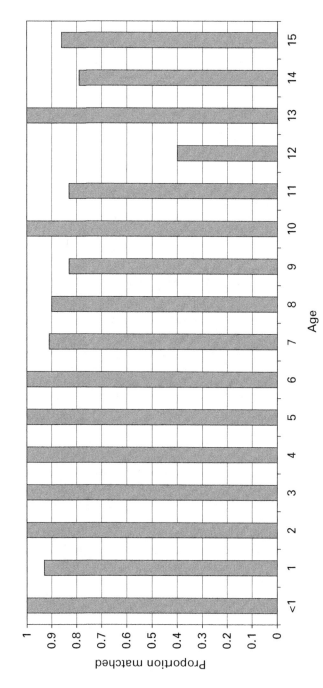

Figure 9.8. Proportion of children on Williamsfield and Nightingale Grove matched with 'mothers', 1817
Source: NA:PRO, T71/13–18, 25–8, 30, 32.

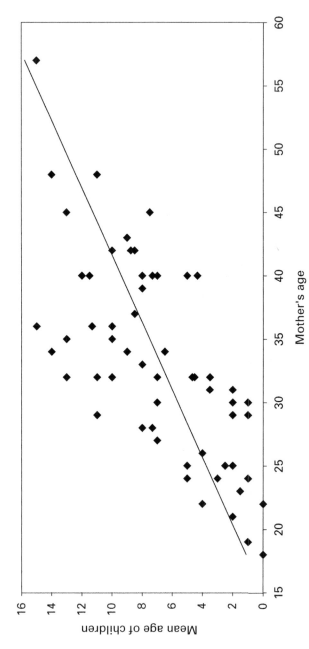

Figure 9.9. Cross-plot of 'mother's' age and matched child's mean age on Williamsfield and Nightingale Grove, 1817
Source: As for Figure 9.8.

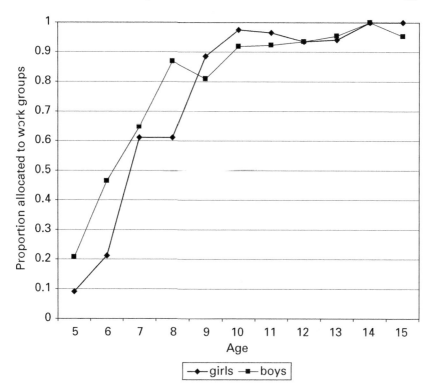

Figure 9.10. Child participation rates on ten estates, 1787–1834
Source: As for Table 9.2.

the 1817 registration returns, these two communities contained hardly any orphans!

Although not valid for the purposes of estimating fertility, the data are still useful in other respects. A simple cross-plot of child's age and mother's age group (Fig. 9.9) reveals that older children were matched by the census takers with older women on the two estates. This is an interesting finding; so too is the failure of matches to tail off towards the end of childhood (Fig. 9.8). Children were put to work on the Lascelles' estates (as in West Indies generally during the period of enslavement) from the age of five upwards (Fig. 9.10). The earliest tasks assigned to children were 'meat picking', or grass (fodder) gathering for cattle feed. A special gang, called the grass gang, was organised for this purpose.[89]

---

[89] Figure 9.10 implies that boys were recruited at slightly younger ages than girls, but this difference is not statistically significant.

Table 9.11. *Family groupings recorded on Nightingale Grove estate, 1777*

Family type	Families (number)	Slaves (number)
M + F	2	4
M + F + C	4	17
m + C	1	3
C + C	4	9
F + C	16	43
Total	27	76[a]

Key: M = male, husband; m = male, non-husband; F = female; C = child.
Note: A total of 71 slaves were grouped in families, but a small number are double-counted.
Source: WRA, Harewood Accession 2,677, Conveyance of Estates in Jamaica in Consideration of Debts Owed by the Late Thomas Harvie to Daniel Lascelles, 20 June 1777.

Between the years of ten to twelve, young slaves were transferred to the 'children's gang' and set to work weeding the cane pieces. The proportion of 'mother–child' matches on the Jamaican estates at higher ages implies that children remained under the care of a female (either their mothers or possibly another kinswoman) for some years after they entered the labour force.

An earlier listing for Nightingale Grove contains additional information about family groupings. In 1777, a total of 71 of Nightingale Grove's 140 enslaved population were described as living in families, including 25 of the 27 children under sixteen whose age is stated (Table 9.11). Unfortunately, few additional references to families occur in surviving records. During apprenticeship, however, Belle estate was reported to possess forty-two families, containing a total of 125 individuals aged six and over (no mention was made of younger children). The same report commented that fifty-four couples lived on the plantation (of whom eighteen were married), while there were also '118 young men & girls that have not coupled themselves'.[90]

The Lascelles' estates were characterised by high infant mortality but even higher fertility. In consequence, their populations increased in number, despite the fact that approximately half of all babies born on these estates died before reaching their fifth birthdays.[91] A major difference, however, existed between the two colonies. While the

---

[90] WRA, Letters and Papers on West India Estates and Affairs, 1795–1873, Memorandum for Mr Foster Clarke, June 1835; Quarterly Report of the Belle plantation, by Thomas Marrshall, ending 30 June 1836.

[91] To set this result in context, Higman reports that Barbados was the only West Indian slave colony to have achieved population growth through natural increase by 1817, Higman, *Slave Populations of the British Caribbean*, 308.

Table 9.12. *Net-reproduction rates on six estates, 1817–34*

Estate and colony	Bf	Pf_{15-44}	GFR	$Bf/Pf_{15-44}{}^\star\,30$	$1-(lf_{30}/lf_0)$	R_0
Belle	87	1,316	60.4	1.98	0.68	1.35
Mount	33	320	93.9	3.09	0.51	1.58
Fortescue & Thicket	110	1,718	57.4	1.92	0.60	1.15ᶜ
Barbados	*230*	*3,354*	*62.0*	*2.06*	*0.60*	*1.24*
Nightingale Grove	22	417	47.2	1.58	0.39	0.62
Williamsfield	32	1,244	22.5	.77	0.60	0.46
Jamaica	*54*	*1,661*	*28.6*	*.98*	*0.52*	*0.51*
Six estates	*284*	*5,015*	*50.7*	*1.70*	*0.60*	*1.02*

Key:

Bf	Live female births. An understatement of the true number of births owing to defective registration; however, since unregistered infant deaths are balanced by unregistered births, this deficiency leaves the estimate of R_0 unaffected.
Pf_{15-44}	Person years lived by women between the ages of fifteen and forty-four in the enslaved database.
GFR	Gross fertility rate (per 1,000).
$Bf/Pf_{15-44}{}^\star30$	Average number of girls born to women surviving to the ages of reproduction.
$1-(lf_{30}/lf_0)$	Average proportion of the female population still living at age thirty (the mid-point of the age band fifteen to forty-four).
R_0	Replacement ratio: $Bf/Pf_{15-44}{}^\star30^\star1-(lf_{30}/lf_0)$.

Source: As for Table 9.7.

Barbadian estates were all sustainable demographically by natural increase, on Nightingale Grove and Williamsfield the replacement ratios were too low to prevent population losses (Table 9.12). While Amyot correctly observed that Williamsfield possessed a high death rate, low fertility (rather than exceptional mortality) was the primary cause of decreasing numbers on the estate. Reproductive failure meant that the Jamaican slave populations were not sustainable without introducing slaves from other properties. Recognising this fact, the Lascelles elected to purchase enslaved people from two neighbouring estates in order to combat population decline.

Lack of information about age-specific rates restricts investigation of the determinants of fertility. It is instructive, nevertheless, to compare the child–woman ratio (CWR) on the individual estates, along with the ratio of males to females of reproductive age (FMR).[92] These measures are easily calculated from census data. Table 9.13 provides confirmation

---

[92] CWR = children aged 0–4/women aged 15–44. MFR = all males aged 15 and over/females aged 15–44.

Table 9.13. *CWR and FMR on six estates, 1787–1834*

	1787		1817		1820		1834	
	CWR	FMR	CWR	FMR	CWR	FMR	CWR	FMR
Belle			0.57	0.89	0.52	1.04		
Mount			0.42	0.97	0.47	1.06		
Fortescue	0.44	1.00	0.61	1.07	0.60	0.94		
Thicket	0.39	1.00	0.52	0.99	0.57	0.96	0.66	1.04
Barbados			*0.54*	*0.96*				
Nightingale			0.38	0.67				
Williamsfield			0.29	1.02				
Jamaica			*0.31*	*0.92*				

Notes: Fortescue was joined to Thicket after 1820. CWR = children aged 0–4/women aged 15–44; FMR = females aged 15–44/males aged 15+.
Source: As for Table 9.7.

that fertility levels were higher on the Barbadian estates (CWR on all four properties exceeded those on Jamaica). Moreover, Fortescue and Thicket's CWR rose on trend as these estates' populations grew. In comparison, the FMR was similar on all properties, with the exception of Nightingale Grove, where a scarcity of female partners may have contributed to lower fertility.

The Lascelles' estates form an interesting case study since the plantations were under common ownership and the primary output of the plantations on both Barbados and Jamaica was sugar.[93] A higher proportion of Africans lived on the Jamaican properties, where fertility rates were lower (Tables 9.3 and 9.4). It can also be noted that Thicket's CWR was lower than Fortescue's in 1787, but that the CWR rates on the two closely related properties subsequently converged as Thicket's population became more Creolised. In the absence of additional information, the reasons for higher fertility on Barbados must remain conjectural. Nevertheless, disparities in the rates of Creolisation on the estates lend some support to explanations of fertility differentials based on differences between African and Creole enslaved communities, including lactation practices and associated child-spacing.[94] It is not

[93] Some historians have attempted to argue that sugar cultivation reduced fertility rates on plantations, but Barbados poses a problem for this explanation, Michael Tadman, 'The Demographic Cost of Sugar: Debates on Slave Societies and Natural Increase in the Americas', *American Historical Review*, 105 (2000), 1,534–75.
[94] H. S. Klein and Stanley L. Engerman, 'Fertility Differentials Between Slaves in the United States and the British West Indies', *William and Mary Quarterly*, 35 (1978),

possible to test this hypothesis directly in the case of the Lascelles dataset, but the passages in *Instructions* advising managers on child-raising practices on Barbados are consistent with a truncated period of weaning by mothers, whereas on Jamaica (if Graeme's evidence is accurate), mothers may have been excused field work and enabled to suckle their children for longer periods.

Conclusions

Previous investigations of slave survivorship in the West Indies have tended to concentrate either on individual plantations, such as Worthy Park on Jamaica or Newton's estate on Barbados, or else have surveyed a colony's enslaved population between two registration dates.[95] Ana-lysis of a single estate permits a cohort life table to be constructed, providing a complete demographic history of each individual from birth (or arrival on the property) until death or exodus from the population. The disadvantage of the single-estate approach lies in the relatively small number of person years included in a single cohort life table, the length of time required to generate age-specific death rates, and the impact of local events on a given property's population history. Aggregate surveys possess the advantage of utilising more data, but typically they analyse deaths occurring during a short interval of time, applying the results to a hypothetical cohort of individuals in what is termed a period life table. The most detailed study of this kind observed 25,717 slaves on Trinidad between the years 1813 and 1816 in order to calculate $_nS_x^{2.75}$ (the probability of survival for individuals grouped by age for Trinidad over an interval of 2.75 years). While this approach harnessed a great deal of information (in terms of person years), the results are sensitive to exceptional events occurring during the short census period; moreover, 'unless mortality remains unchanged for several decades, no real birth cohort will experience the mortality embedded in a period life table'.[96]

The LRC life table calculated in this chapter occupies a middle-ground position. It utilises evidence from six estates (lessening the distortions of local factors), and is based on an observation period (measured by number of person years) not greatly inferior to the

358–9, 362, 368, 370, 373. Klein and Engerman argue that lactation practices among Africans resulted in longer child-spacing, thereby reducing fertility.

[95] Michael Craton and James Walvin, *A Jamaican Plantation: A History of Worthy Park, 1670–1970* (London, 1976); Craton, *Invisible Man*, Jerome S. Handler and Frederick W. Lange, *Plantation Slavery in Barbados: An Archaeological and Historical Investigation* (Cambridge, MA, 1978).

[96] Meredith John, *Plantation Slaves of Trinidad*, 82.

Trinidadian data. The construction of the life table possesses the further advantage of bringing few outside assumptions to bear on the data, while the results obtained embody the experiences of actual individuals living and working in the Caribbean between 1817 and 1834. There is no reason why the LRC technique could not be extended to all of the registration returns and private listings of enslaved communities in the British West Indies specifying the age of slaves. Collection of the data would require time and resources, but the resulting perspectives on the demographic conditions of the enslaved would considerably enrich understanding of human demography and would also augment the existing Coale-Demeny model life tables.

Reviewing the evidence of survivorship, it is clear that the *Instructions'* aim of lowering infant mortality was not achieved, though on Barbados it is conceivable that the manual's guidelines contributed to raising fertility. Reading over the *Instructions*, however, one is struck most forcibly by what the treatise's authors omit to mention. The advice given to planters regarding welfare of the enslaved fails to refer to one of the central elements of estate management practised by the Lascelles. Mergers, sales, and amalgamations of property formed a major part of the reorganisation of the 2nd Earl of Harewood's West Indian portfolio after 1795. These activities inevitably disrupted communities, provoking anxiety and resentment among the enslaved. Higher fertility levels on Barbados may, in consequence, have occurred in spite of managerial intervention.

The review of the estates conducted during the later 1790s identified Kirton's, Mount, and Pilgrim as underperforming properties. The sale of all three of these plantations was envisaged, with an associated redeployment of labour to strengthen short-handed estates.[97] In the event, Kirton's and Pilgrim were duly sold, but Mount was retained and its numbers boosted by slaves removed from other properties. Early in the nineteenth century, Cooper's Hill and Holetown were similarly subject to merger plans, with the objective of expanding cotton growing on the former property and cane cultivation on the latter. 'I should be happy to lose the name of Cooper Hill entirely', the 1st Earl informed his agents, 'to unite the gangs make one set of works, & one managers establishment, as I have always been informed the expenses of produce of two small estates are by no means in proportion to one of the cojoint strengths.'[98] After consultation, however, it was decided to keep the workforces apart and only to combine the management. 'The negroes should be kept separate & worked on separate gangs', the Earl was

---

[97] HH:WIP, Correspondence, Nelson & Adam (London) to Lord Harewood, 20 August 1799.
[98] Ibid., [Nelson?] to Blenman & Cobham (Barbados), 4 December 1801.

advised. 'The distance of the negro houses from one plantation to another would make it inconvenient in a degree almost impracticable to work them together, or to form them into one gang.'[99] Thicket and Fortescue also experienced reorganisation between 1815 and the early 1820s, resulting in the joint management of these two estates and probably greater coordination of the two workforces.

Rationalisation of the enslaved workers on Oldfield's Bog and Nightingale Grove occurred on Jamaica after the acquisition of these properties from the Harvies in 1777. In addition, 141 slaves were attached to the Williamsfield estate as a result of mergers between 1810 and 1815. Slaves from Goodwood were added to the Richmond estate on Tobago during the early 1790s, following the estate's replanting with 'Bourbon cane' (a variety more resistant to insect infestation). Lastly, the acquisition of Glamorgan in 1818 led to its amalgamation with Richmond; the joining together of these two plantations formed a prelude to the sale of all of the Earl of Harewood's estates on this island in 1820.[100]

There is strong evidence, therefore, that the Lascelles reorganised their slave populations between 1795 and 1820 on Barbados, Jamaica, and Tobago through a combination of sales, mergers, and amalgamations. The joining together of slave communities was no easy undertaking.[101] Francis Graeme noted in 1815 that special care was required when moving the enslaved from one estate to another. Ideally, Graeme testified, new arrivals ought to be placed on, 'good established grounds and houses' some distance from the existing estate community. Where this was impractical, Graeme preferred to contract with the vendor to provision the population on the seller's estate for up to twelve months, rather than introducing the new slaves immediately.[102]

Some of the difficulties involved in relocating settled communities are described in the correspondence of the Antiguan agent John Johnson, who supervised the movement of Lavington estate's population to Sanderson's on the island in 1824. While these properties were not owned by the Lascelles, the issues that arose during the merger reinforce the comments made by Graeme. Johnson observed that, 'Negroes are very tenacious of any interference in their domestic arrangements or comforts, unless it is solicited by them.'[103] On Antigua, the merger was complicated by a history

[99] Ibid., undated fragment [c. 1801].
[100] WRA, Letters and Papers on West India Estates and Affairs, 1795–1873, John Balfour (Tobago) to Edwin Lascelles, 27 May 1790.
[101] Long, *History of Jamaica*, 502.
[102] *Further Proceedings of the Honourable House of Assembly of Jamaica*, 55–8.
[103] Hamilton College, Beinecke Collection, M526, 'Reports Relating to Mr Gordon's Estates in the West Indies, 1824', part II, 9.

of antipathy between the two neighbouring enslaved communities involved. Resentments were aggravated by the manager at Sanderson's, who treated the slaves unequally (granting, for example, a holiday to Sanderson's gangs, while continuing to work the Lavington slaves).

A total of 82 slaves were moved in 1824, raising Sanderson's population to 317 and reducing Lavington's to 151. Johnson wrote that, 'I found much difficulty in making the selection in Families, with a due regard to having sufficient strength at Lavingtons.' An attempt at pacification was made by offering personal reassurances to the individuals selected for removal and by distributing a shilling to all of the slaves on the estate. In addition to this palliative measure, Johnson sought to defuse tensions by rehousing the former Lavington slaves in a new village located away from the existing slave community at Sanderson's. It is not known how smoothly the merger proceeded; Johnson's report merely comments that the majority of the affected slaves, 'betrayed no particular surprise or regret' on receiving news of the decision.[104]

In the case of the Lascelles' properties, the disposal of properties and rumours of further sales or mergers generated apprehension.[105] Eight field slaves ran away, for example, after a report began circulating that Belle, Thicket, Holetown, and Cooper's Hill were about to be sold. Proposals to join the workforces of Cooper's and Holetown had the same effect; indeed, opposition on these properties may have contributed to the decision to drop amalgamation plans.[106] Slaves living on two estates directly affected by reorganisation plans joined in the 1816 insurrection on Barbados.[107]

Advocates of amelioration argued that their policies constituted a viable alternative to immediate emancipation. Francis Graeme, for example, reflected in 1815 that the condition of the enslaved had improved since he first arrived on Jamaica in 1797:

he thinks that the situation of the slaves in every way has been made more comfortable than in former times; that the amelioration has been regular and progressive, and he attributes the same to the overseers and white people of the present day being a better informed race of men in general, of humane dispositions, and attending to the instructions given them by their employers, as to the comfort of the slaves, more strictly than was done in former days.[108]

---

[104] Ibid., 14–15.
[105] HH:WIP, Correspondence, (Nelson?) to John Blenman and Richard Cobham (Barbados), 4 December 1801.
[106] Ibid., Jonathan Blenman & Richard Cobham (Barbados) to John Wood Nelson (London), 27 September 1801.
[107] See Chapter Ten.
[108] *Further Proceedings of the Honourable House of Assembly of Jamaica* 55–8.

Table 9.14. *Consistency of age reporting: Thicket and Fortescue estates, 1787–1834*

	Census comparisons					
	1817 & 1787	1820 & 1787	1823 & 1787	1820 & 1817	1834 & 1817	1834 & 1820
Interval (years)	30	33	47	3	17	14
Mean difference (years)	30.33	33.32	47.42	2.99	17.10	14.09
Standard deviation	1.56	1.63	1.83	0.29	0.29	0.82
Number of observations	117	104	62	349	255	278

The 2nd Earl of Harewood's oration at the 1832 meeting of the West India interest similarly emphasised the achievements of voluntary reform:

I ask what has occurred since 1823? Has there been a stoppage of improvement in the slave population? Has there been any turning back from the course of amelioration? No; a progressive state of improvement has gone on.[109]

While it may be true, as Graeme contended, that slave owners sent out revised instructions to managers of their estates, on the bases of the data examined above the success of these measures in improving survivorship appears limited. At the time the 2nd Earl rose to his feet to call for the continuation of slavery, the mortality rates on his West Indian estates still ranked among the highest of any recorded human population.[110]

Appendix I: The Accuracy of the Demographic Data: Some Tests

It is rare to encounter complete age listings of populations in pre-modern history. The question that must be asked of the registration returns is whether reliable conclusions can be based on materials that were compiled primarily to enforce a prohibition on slave importations, rather than to provide historical demographers with data.

In the case of Fortescue and Thicket, four complete listings of the enslaved by age survive for the years 1787, 1817, 1820, and 1834. These records permit an assessment to be made of the accuracy with which slave ages are recorded and also the degree of under-registration of post-infant deaths. Table 9.14 compares the mean differences in reported

---

[109] *Proceedings at a Public Meeting of Persons*, 7.
[110] Excluding the effects of warfare, plague, or famine.

ages between two censuses with the length of the census interval. It can be seen that the internal consistency of the dataset is very good. The primary reason for this, however, may reflect the enumerators' practice in simply adding three to the 1817 listings in order to calculate slave ages in subsequent returns. For similar reasons, the close correspondence of the 1817 return with the 1787 schedule could arise from the use of this document to compile the first registration return.

Age heaping is a feature of many pre-census age listings. Enumerators, lacking a precise date of birth, characteristically grouped subjects disproportionately into ages ending in zero or five. Whipple's index, designed to test age heaping, ranges from 100 (no age reporting ending in five or zero) to 500 (all ages ending in zero or five).[111] In the case of the 1817 registration return, the index measures 242 suggesting moderate clustering around these ages. While subsequent listings possess lower index readings, this may reflect the contemporary practice of adding three to previously recorded ages, since Whipple's index can detect heaping only in ages ending in zero or five. The 1787 schedules for Fortescue and Thicket also possess low index scores. While this result may reflect the source's greater accuracy, it could equally reflect the influence of lost earlier enumerations that feature age heaping on the compilation of the listing.[112]

Age clusters is one of the factors that generates a q_x curve for the six estates lacking in smoothness. An additional source of distortions consists of the impact of local factors on the demographic histories of the individual estates. Past outbreaks of disease impact disproportionately on different age cohorts. In September 1816, for instance, news reached London that 'the Williamsfield negroes have been troubled with fevers & Bowel complaints but are now recovering tho not without the loss of a child'. In contrast it was reported that, 'the [Nightingale) Groves negroes are very healthy'.[113] The data presented in this chapter are not smoothed by model life tables in an effort to combat these effects. The reason for this is that smoothing detracts from the unique features of the data, conveying an impression of demography that does not accord with actual experience. Survival analysis, however, was used to identify cohort effects and the results are reported above.

---

[111] The Whipple index is obtained by summing the age returns between twenty-three and sixty-two years (inclusive) and calculating the percentage accounted for by the sum of the returns ending in zero or five to one-fifth of the total sum.

[112] When graphed, all of the frequency counts exhibited signs of clustering at certain ages.

[113] WRA, Letters and Papers on West India Estates and Affairs, Francis Graeme (Jamaica) to Nelson (London), 6 September 1816.

Table 9.15. *Survivorship on Thicket and Fortescue estates, 1787–1817*

Age group	Alive 1787	Alive 1817	LRC prediction
0–4	44	22	19
5–9	60	27	24
10–14	30	11	11
15–19	32	16	10
20–24	27	8	8
25–29	21	1	6
30–34	32	7	7
35–39	56	10	10
40–44	29	8	5
45–49	10	0	1
50–54	19	0	1
55–59	5	0	0
60–64	8	0	0
65–69	0	0	0
70–74	1	0	0
75–79	1	0	0
80+	0	0	0
Total	*375*	*110*	*102*

Under-registration of infant mortality is discussed in the text. An estimate of the under-recording of non-infant deaths on Thicket and Fortescue was obtained by counting the number of slaves failing to appear in the final 1834 enumeration whose deaths are also not reported in earlier returns.[114] Just 4 per cent of slaves on Thicket and Fortescue fell into this category, indicating that most adult deaths are recorded.

The existence of the earlier 1787 listings of slaves by age for Thicket and Fortescue permits a test to be made of the accuracy of the LRC life-table data. Actual survivorship over forty years can be compared with predictions of $_nS_x^{40}$. The results are presented below. It can be seen that the life table performs well in predicting survivorship since the differences are not significant statistically (Table 9.15).[115]

The conclusion of this survey is that the data are of relatively good quality and the evidence can bear the weight of the interpretations it supports. Nevertheless, the limitations must be borne in mind when using the evidence to make general observations about the material

---

[114] The last census date at which these twenty-four slaves were recorded as living was entered into the database and a separate coding (unknown reasons) was used to record their exit from the study.

[115] Z-test of differences: $z = -1.067$ ($p = 0.286$: not significant at 80 per cent confidence).

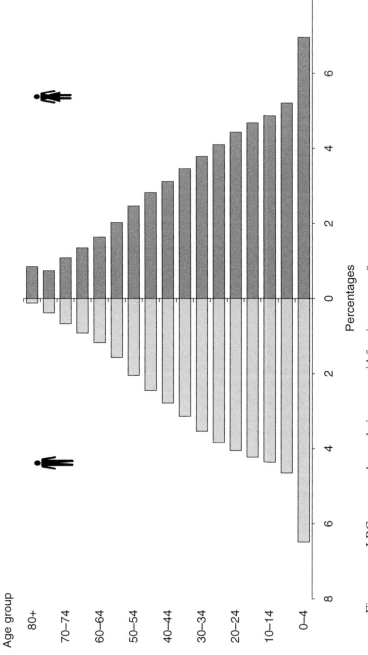

Age group

80+

70–74

60–64

50–54

40–44

30–34

20–24

10–14

0–4

8   6   4   2   0   2   4   6   8

Percentages

Figure 9.11. LRC generated population pyramid for six estates, 1817–34.

conditions of the enslaved. A population pyramid (generated from the male and female L_x schedules of the LRC life table) provides a final overview of those enslaved population living and working on the Lascelles' estates in Barbados and Jamaica during the last decades of chattel slavery in the West Indies (Fig. 9.11).

Appendix II

Report of a speech advocating the continuation of slavery delivered by Henry Lascelles, 2nd Earl of Harewood, at a public meeting held 5 April 1832.[116]

At a
GENERAL MEETING of PROPRIETORS, MERCHANTS, BANKERS, SHIP OWNERS, MANUFACTURERS, TRADERS, and Others interested in the Preservation of the West India Colonies, convened by public Advertisement, and held at the City of London Tavern, on Thursday, the 5th April, 1832:
Present,
THE RIGHT HON. THE EARL OF HAREWOOD,
IN THE CHAIR;

The Marquis of Sligo.	Admiral Adam. M.P.
The Earl of Selkirk.	Admiral Douglas.
The Lord Viscount St. Vincent.	Admiral Lambert.
The Viscount Stormont, M.P.	Sir John Lilley.
The Lord Saltoun.	Sir Wm. Myers.
The Lord Reay.	Sir Ralph Rice.
The Lord Rivers.	Mr. Alderman Atkins, M.P.
The Rt. Hon. Sir E.H. East, Bt.	Mr. Alderman Thompson, M.P.
The Hon. Col. Sir Ed. Cust, M.P.	Mr. Alderman Copeland, M.P.
The Hon. W.S. Lascelles, M.P.	Mr. Alderman Lucas.
The Hon. W. Best, M.P.	Col. Marcus Bereford, M.P.
The Hon. Col. Ellis.	Col. Hugh Baillie.
The Hon. Wm. Fraser.	Col. Wallace, R.A.
Sir W.H. Cooper, Bart.	Col. Mayne.
Sir M. Shaw Stewart, Bart. M.P.	Capt. Ffarington, R.N.
Sir Alexander Cray Grant, Bart.	Capt. Hardy, R.N.
Sir C. Bethel Codrington, Bart.	James Evan Baille, Esq., M.P.
Sir W. Windham Dalling, Bart.	J. Barham, Esq., M.P.
Sir H.W. Martin, Bart.	Ralph Bernal, Esq., M.P.
Sir Wm Young, Bart.	Wm. Burge. Esq., M.P.,
Sir Thomas Neave, Bart.	Agent for Jamaica.
Sir John Rae Reid, Bart.	John Capel, Esq., M.P.

[116] *Proceedings at a Public Meeting of Persons.*

Duncan Davidson Esq., M.P.
W.R. Keith Douglas, Esq., M.P.
R.A. Dundas, Esq., M.P.
J.W. Freshfield, Esq., M.P.
H. Houldsworth, Esq., M.P.
John Irving , Esq., M.P.
B.L. Lester, Esq., M.P.
James Mackillop, Esq., M.P.
J.A. Stewart M'Kenzie, Esq., M.P.
Joseph Marryat, Esq., M.P.,
Agent for Grenada.
A.W. Robarts, Esq., M.P.
G.R. Robinson, Esq., M.P.
Charles Ross, Esq., M.P.
George Sinclair, Esq., M.P.
–Smith, Esq., M.P.
–Smith, Esq., M.P.
P.M. Stewart, Esq., M.P.
G. Watson Taylor, Esq., M.P.
John Young; Esq., M.P.
J.P. Mayers, Esq., Agent for Barbados.
A. Browne, Esq., Agent for Antigua
and Montserrat.
J. Colquhoun, Esq., Agent for
St. Vincents, Dominica Kitt's, Nevis,
and the Virgin Islands.
T.A. Curtis, Esq.

David Bevan, Esq.
Charles Mills, Esq.
B. Barnard, Esq.
S. Hibbert. Esq.
John Fairlie, Esq.
John Dent, Esq.
Russell Ellice, Esq.
Wm. Ward, Esq.
Jeremiah Harman, Esq,
George Palmer, Esq.
Nathaniel Gould, Esq.
George Frederick Young, Esq.
Jacob Montefiore, Esq.
Melvill Wilson, Esq.
George Arbuthnot, Esq.
Jonathan Chapman, Esq.
John Bainbridge, Esq.
Jeremiah Olive, Esq.
Frederick Mangles, Esq.
George Hibbert, Esq.
A. Colvile Esq.
A. Arcedeckne, Esq.
W. Dickenson, Esq.
David Baillie, Esq.
Henry Bright, Esq.
&c. &c. &c.

and upwards of Six Thousand other persons of great
respectability and influence in the City of London:
The Noble CHAIRMAN proceeded to address the Meeting to the following effect:

Gentlemen, – Before I proceed to the business of the day, I must beg, in the first place, to mention that a noble Lord, (the Marquis of Chandos), who has been in the habit of representing the interests of the West India body, is unavoidably prevented from attending to-day, which alone is the cause of my having the honour of being appointed to the Chair. That noble lord has been unremittingly attentive to the interests of the West India planters, and I would much rather have seen him in the Chair upon this occasion than myself. I therefore beg leave to offer on his behalf his apology for not attending, being prevented by unavoidable Parliamentary duty. I feel that, standing before so numerous and respectable a body as that now present, a most arduous and melancholy duty is imposed upon me; in endeavouring to draw your attention, which I shall do, not by anything from myself, but trusting all to the cause, to the situation in which the West India proprietors are involved. I do not desire to attribute the distress they labour under to any particular circumstances connected with party or political persons, but I desire that that distress may be considered as it operates not only on individuals, but on the national interests of this country. I am more particularly desirous of delivering my sentiments on this occasion, and in the heart of this metropolis, because I feel that aspersions have gone forth against the great body of West India proprietors, which deserve to be met fairly and honestly, and refuted, as we can refute them, before our country. (*Cheers.*) I, among others, am a sufferer; but I am not a sufferer equal to those who may have nothing but their West India property to depend upon. (*Hear, hear.*) It is on their behalf that I am anxious to plead the cause, if I can – indifferent, I may say, as to the fate of my own interests. (*Hear, hear.*) There have been strong feelings of prejudice created in this country against all proprietors of West India property, as possessors of a slave population. Not only has that been a topic of charge against US, but it has been urged, as if we were wickedly and improperly deriving profit from the labour of those Individuals. That is not the fact. I will speak not only for myself, but I will speak for the whole of the proprietors of West India property, and I will assert that we should be most anxious to do without that description of labour if we could. (*Cheers.*) But we say that, being proprietors, we are not fairly or justly dealt with. I am not appealing merely to West India proprietors; I am appealing to many who have no direct or immediate interest in the subject, except as members of the general community, and I am appealing against a portion of my countrymen who are endeavouring to sink the West India interest into utter ruin; a party who, by misrepresentation and falsehood, are seeking to accomplish their object, and who knew at the time when those misrepresentations were concocted that they were false, or that they gave a colour to proceedings and circumstances, which in honesty and justice they ought not to be made to bear. (*Loud cheers.*) Why, is it to be said, because in a slave population some acts will be done which, for the honour of human nature, we must always deplore, but which, from the wickedness of human nature, are inevitable, that therefore the whole of the West India proprietors are to be held up to odium, and their property, from an isolated or a few cases of cruelty or of vice, to be reduced in public estimation, and rendered worse than worth nothing? (*Hear, hear.*) How does the matter stand? The West India proprietors are most unfortunately circumstanced. If our returns are bad, if they amount even to nothing, or are worse than nothing, (*Cheers*) what course are we compelled to adopt? Why, to hold on and support those persons from whose labour we derive nothing. (*Hear, hear.*) Is that the case with any other description of property? If persons engaged in manufactures or in commerce employ labourers, or if labourers are employed in public works, the moment the occupation of the labourer ceases to be beneficial to the employer, the employer can put an end to his responsibility by dismissing the labourer. But can we do that? – No. (*Cheers.*) Why do I mention this? It is to show that we, the West India proprietors, do not wish to hold a population in that state of existence if we could do otherwise. We are in the difficulty; it is not of our making; and it is the duty of those who are so loud in their complaints respecting it, to show us our way out. A West India proprietor is not at liberty to cast upon the public every bad or inefficient servant he may have, for if he does so he may injure, a whole community. A West India proprietor cannot, the moment he becomes a loser, dismiss his slaves, but he is obliged, from a regard to the peace and security of the Colony and of his property, to maintain the unproductive labourer. It will not do, therefore, to say that if a West India proprietor is a loser he can liberate, and so get rid of his labourers, for, in their present state of mind, to set them free would be to endanger the Colonies. (*Hear, hear.*) It is in that state of society that we are now living. I mention these things to remove that unwarrantable blame which has been cast upon us as persons who are wilfully and willingly resisting all attempts at emancipation. That charge is not true. (*Loud cheers.*) But let it not be supposed that I attribute all our distresses to the interference with the slave population. Upon a close consideration of the subject, I am bound to say, as I am here to speak the truth, that there are other circumstances operating injuriously on the property in the old Colonies. The ceded Colonies produce a large quantity of sugar, which depreciates the price of that of the old English Colonies. That and other circumstances have an effect; but is it, therefore, the policy of this country to leave its old possessions, founded and carried on by British enterprize and capital, to utter ruin? Never, until late years, was such the policy of this country; and since that crooked policy has crept in, this distressed state of circumstances has occurred. I would wish to mention a subject which I know to be of rather a delicate nature; and as I am disposed at this Meeting, both with regard to the respectable parties assembled, and from my own feelings, to exclude anything bearing a complexion of political or party views, before I mention that subject, I again disclaim all such feeling. I would not appear here today in the situation I now hold, if I were required to entertain the subject in that point of view. But having thus guarded myself against misconception, I cannot help adverting to the Order in Council of the 2nd Nov. last. In adverting to that Order in Council, I am led to notice the Resolutions come to by Parliament in 1823, and I must say that those who were parties to those Resolutions ought not to have been parties to the Order in Council. (*Loud cheering.*) We are living in times of great colonial distress – we are living in times when great Colonial agitation is on foot, and it would have been but wise and politic to conciliate rather than inflame. But what has been the effect of the Order in Council of 1831? It bears on the face of it irritation to the Colonies, and injustice to the proprietors. (*Cheers.*) As long as you permit those Colonies to have Local Legislatures, and to have the right of deciding questions relating to the several Colonies, it is unjust and illegal – (*Cheers*) to interfere in the manner proposed in this Order in Council. But from whom did the Order in Council come? The dictation to the Colonial Legislatures did not proceed from Parliament, (*Hear, hear.*) – but from the Privy Council, and really to me the whole matter, to say the least of it, appears extraordinary. By the framers of this Order in Council it is said – 'We have certain benefits to confer on this Colony, and if you, the Colonial Legislature, do not agree precisely to what we dictate, you, even in your present depressed and sinking condition, shall not receive those benefits'. But what must be the effect of this upon the Mother Country herself? On the one hand, you attempt to coerce the Colonies, and upon the other, if the Colonies do not give way, you punish the Mother Country for the disobedience of the Colonies. It is idle to suppose that the Colonies can be ruined or injured without the Mother Country suffering also. (*Hear, hear.*)

There is neither sense nor justice in such a proceeding. And look at the statistics of the case. The duties alone upon the produce of the Colonies amount annually to 7,000,000 *l.*, and the amount of British exports to those Colonies is annually 5,000,000 *l.*; is that great revenue to be sacrificed because an Order in Council is not obeyed? (*Hear, hear.*) And under what circumstances is it that the duties upon our West India produce amount to 7,000,000 *l.*? Any person would naturally suppose that the property upon which so large a sum was levied gave an immense return to the proprietors. Is the fact so? So far from it, the duties levied on West India property are in reality, in some cases, the confiscation of that property. (*Hear, hear.*) Can a country go on in such a state of things? Does it prove, or does it not, that justice is not consulted, but that some popular feeling merely is leant to? It is important to us to see what has occurred with respect to this subject. Some Resolutions have been lately come to, which are calculated to produce an impression on the public mind, that nothing has been done, and that all is yet to do, regarding the amelioration of the condition of the slaves. But it was not fair to the West India body to keep out of sight any amelioration that had been made in the condition of the slaves. I ask what has occurred since 1823? Has there been a stoppage of improvement in the slave population? Has there been any turning back from the course of amelioration? No; a progressive state of improvement has gone on. Then where under such circumstances, is the wisdom or the propriety of issuing such Orders in Council, which appeared to indicate that an utter disregard had been manifested by the West India proprietors towards the state of the Slave population? It is unfair, it is strengthening the prejudice against the proprietors, it is lowering an interest, already sunk so low, and it is not just towards the efforts already cheerfully exerted. (*Cheers.*) I beg to say again, that in any observations I make upon the Order in Council, I am actuated by no political feelings. I remark on those Orders as in my conscience I believe they will work, that is, injuriously to the peace of the Colonies. But as to the distresses. There is an accumulation of hardships, particularly as regarding two of the Colonies; one of which, Barbados, has suffered from the visitation of God, which we can only lament, not complain of; and the other has suffered from another cause, which has not only sacrificed the interests of the proprietors, many of whose property is destroyed, but also thrown back the course of civilization. (*Cheers.*) Those anxious to promote the welfare of that population are doing unwisely towards these people and the proprietors to allow any irritation or false conceptions to go forth to those Colonies, as they can, only be injurious to the master, and throw back the civilization, of the slave. (*Hear, hear.*) We are in such a situation that we are complainants on the one hand, and beggars on the other. (*Hear, hear.*) I therefore wish to deal as leniently as I can, and come in *forma pauperis* before those who can give us relief. I shall therefore say no more as to the mismanagement of colonial affairs; but I could not resist stating what I have stated respecting the Order in council. I will therefore conclude by saying we are all thankful for any assistance we may obtain in support of ourselves and property under the misfortunes at Barbados and Jamaica; I say we are not only thankful for what has been done, but we shall be thankful for what we have a right to expect to be done – a right which, as British subjects, we state strongly, and we claim at the hands of Parliament that protection which is due to every British subject who lives under its dominion, and to such especially as employ their capital and their industry for the benefit and advantage of the country. (The Noble Earl resumed his seat amidst loud applause.)

***

On the motion of W. BURGE, Esq. MP, seconded by HENRY BRIGHT, Esq.,

Unanimously Resolved,

That this Meeting are anxious to offer to the Right Hon. the Earl of Harewood their most cordial thanks for his Lordship's condescension in taking the Chair, and for the eminent ability, urbanity, and zeal with which he has discharged the duties of the day.

On the 17th of April, the EARL OF HAREWOOD presented to the House of Lords the Petition adopted, and most numerously and respectably signed, on this occasion; and their Lordships, then, on the motion of the Noble Earl, agreed to the appointment of a Select Committee,

'To enquire into the laws and usages of the several West India Colonies in relation to the Slave population; the actual condition and treatment of the Slaves, their habits and dispositions; the means which are adopted in the several Colonies for their progressive improvement and civilization, and the degree of improvement and civilization which they have at present attained; and also to enquire into the distressed condition of those Colonies.'

The following were named for this Committee:

Archbishop of Canterbury.
The Lord President.
Duke of Richmond.
Duke of Wellington.
Duke of Buckingham.
Earl of Selkirk.
Earl Bathurst.
Earl of Clarendon.
Earl of Rosslyn.
Earl of Harewood.
Earl of Munster.
Viscount St. Vincent.

Viscount Combermere.
Viscount Goderich.
Bishop of London.
Bishop of Lichfield and Coventry.
Lord Howard de Walden.
Lord Napier.
Lord Holland.
Lord Suffield.
Lord Auckland.
Lord Redesdale.
Lord Ellenborough.
Lord Monteagle.

10   Between Black and White

The Braffo, Head Caboceiro, or Negroe Chief, values himself upon his
English Name, which is John Corrente.[1]

Intercultural relations and the identities they fashioned profoundly
influenced the development of Creole society in the West Indies.[2] In the
case of the Lascelles archive, however, few documents survive describing
interracial relationships in detail. The sources that remain are dominated by two types of interaction: instances of resistance by the enslaved
and sexual relationships between slave women and white attorneys or
overseers. Despite the undoubted importance of these two themes, it is
evident that the social life of the plantation consisted of far more than
resistance and interracial sex. Very little information, for example, exists
describing such basic activities as the pattern of daily work allocations
on the Lascelles' estates, or the methods used to discipline plantation
labourers. Insights into slave culture (such as songs, dances, and
courtship rituals) are similarly almost entirely absent from the historical
record. In consequence of these and other omissions, the scope of the
conclusions that can be drawn in this chapter are limited. Nevertheless,
despite its limitations, the material is of considerable interest.

Resistance and Cooperation

Resistance by the enslaved probably formed an endemic feature
of chattel slavery during the two centuries the institution endured in
the British West Indies.[3] Rebellion, running away, and acts of passive

---

[1] [Anon.], *The Royal African: or, Memoirs of the Young Prince of Annamaboe* (London, [n.d.,
1750?]), 25.
[2] An influential early study in this field was Edward [Kaumu] Brathwaite, *The Development
of Creole Society in Jamaica: 1770–1820* (Oxford, 1971).
[3] Hilary Beckles,'The 200 Years War: Slave Resistance in the British West Indies, an
Overview of the Historiography', *Jamaican Historical Review*, 13 (1982), 1–10.

disobedience were three ways in which the enslaved challenged their condition; each type of resistance occurred on estates owned by the Lascelles or their associates.

A latent fear of the consequences of rebellions existed in all colonies where slavery existed. In 1745, news reached London of an uprising among the Jamaican Maroons. 'We wish for its suppression', responded George Maxwell, 'as we do for that of the unnatural Rebellion in this Country.'[4] Maxwell's anxious comment on what was a comparatively minor incident emphasises how much material has been lost to historians. If events in 1745 caused Lascelles & Maxwell disquiet, one can only imagine how the partners responded to Tackey's rebellion in 1760, or the Baptist War of 1831.

During the eighteenth century, two major slave insurrections threatened to destroy plantations owned by the Lascelles' associates. In 1763, Gedney Clarke Sr rushed to defend his Demerara estates after the Berbice rebellion broke out; his prompt response illustrates the seriousness with which slave revolts were viewed.[5] Three decades later, the Grenada insurrection of 1795–6 rocked George Shand, who had purchased a plantation on the island from Edwin Lascelles in 1791. 'Clarkes Court and a neighbouring Estate', Shand wrote, 'were the Barriers of the Insurrection for above a year.'[6] During the two seasons the rebellion lasted, the estate was able to produce only half a crop, impairing Shand's ability to keep up his mortgage repayments.

The Lascelles' own properties were not directly affected by slave rebellions prior to 1816. In 1802, however, a suspected planned rebellion was foiled on Tobago. The 1st Earl's deep concern at events is revealed by his correspondence with island attorney John Robley, and the survival among the Harewood papers of printed copies of the examination of those enslaved accused of participating in the conspiracy.[7] The Tobago scare was followed in 1816 by 'Bussa's revolt' on Barbados: a colony hitherto considered to be one of the most secure slave societies. This insurrection is of particular significance because slaves living on Mount and Thicket participated in the uprising. Arson was committed on both estates, while Thicket suffered further damage during fighting

---

[4] *LMLB*, George Maxwell (London) to Jacob Alleyne (Barbados), 27 November 1745.
[5] See Chapter Five.
[6] HH:WIP, Correspondence, George Shand (Grenada) to Lord Harewood, 4 November 1796.
[7] Ibid., John Robley (Tobago) to Lord Harewood, 10 April 1802; Examination of slaves involved in the insurrection and printed report of the insurrection in a speech to the Tobago Assembly [n.d., 1802].

between the rebels and the militia.[8] Approximately £5,150.10s. of damage was sustained on Mount, whereas the Earl of Harewood was informed that in the case of Thicket, 'the injury done to your Estates by the deluded negroes' amounted to £3,989.[9]

Bussa's rebellion also badly affected Kirton's estate on Barbados, purchased from the Lascelles by Joshua Nurse in 1801. Sixteen acres of cane fields were burnt on this plantation, along with several buildings and the crop store. Nurse's losses (estimated at £10,000) caused his remaining mortgage repayments to fall into arrears.[10] The timing of the rising, which broke out on Sunday 14 April during the Easter post-harvest period, magnified the impact of arson attacks with the result that approximately one-fifth of the island's sugar crop was destroyed during the insurrection.

On both Mount and Thicket, property belonging to white estate workers was targeted by the rebels. Gratuities of £111.2s.3d. to each of Harewood's managers were authorised in 1816, compensating them for losses. The enslaved's own living quarters also suffered damage, though it is unclear whether this resulted from deliberate acts of vandalism or the effects of military occupation. Island attorney Richard Cobham provides the following brief description of the aftermath of the uprising:

It was the general opinion here that the negroes should not immediately enjoy their accustomed comforts, after their atrocious misdeeds against their owners. They have been, however, sheltered in the buildings they thought proper to spare. As soon as the boiling & distil Houses at the Mount are completed I will have the negroes houses rebuilt. They remain tranquil. Seven of the prisoners belonging to his Lordship have been released & six remain to be tried. – The conflagration was too intensely promoted by rum & sugar to spare as much of the lumber, with which the boiling & distil Houses at the Mount were constructed.[11]

---

[8] Major Oxley testified during an official inquiry held after the rebellion that 'a body of the rebels were said to have made a stand' at Thicket, Hilary McD. Beckles, 'Bussa: the 1816 Revolution in Barbados', *Rewriting History*, No. 2 (Barbados, 1998), 63.

[9] Beckles, 'Bussa', 85; WRA, Letters and Papers on West India Estates and Affairs, Nelson (London) to Lord Harewood, 22 October 1816.

[10] WRA, Letters and Papers, Joshua Nurse (Barbados) to Nelson & Adam (London), 18 May 1816; Abstract of the Produce of the Estates and other Property in the West Indies belonging to the Right Honourable Lord Harewood, 1805–39: Barbados Affairs. Joshua Nurse acted on behalf of his brother James, who in 1816 was reportedly about to take holy orders. A statement of Nurse's damages does not appear in the listing of 'The Particular and Amount of Property Destroyed by the Insurrection of the Slaves' sworn before the Barbados Assembly. Joshua B. Nurse, however, swore that damages of £5,849.15s.6d. were sustained, but on an estate named Horn's not Kirton's, Beckles, 'Bussa', 86.

[11] WRA, Letters and Papers on West India Estates and Affairs, 1795–1873, Richard Cobham (Barbados) to John Wood Nelson (London), 1 September 1816.

The fate of the prisoners Cobham refers to is not known. No slaves belonging to the 1st Earl appear in the list of ringleaders of the rebellion, but in the absence of population listings for the years prior to 1817 it is impossible to be certain whether any of the six accused were executed or transported for their parts in the insurrection.[12] One of Harewood's slaves, however, was manumitted as a reward for loyalty during the crisis and received a pension of £10 per annum.[13]

The colonial militia succeeded in confining the main part of the uprising to St Philip's where limited numbers and inadequate arms ultimately condemned the rebellion to failure.[14] The major insurrection was put down within four days, though skirmishes continued to break out for several months across the island. To honour Colonel Edward Codd's role in defeating Bussa, the 1st Earl subscribed £200 towards a dinner held in his honour in 1819.[15] Yet despite the favourable outcome, the uprising caused the authorities great anxiety and strengthened calls for emancipation.[16] To contemporary observers, there appeared little to suggest that the rebellion had been triggered by material deprivation, specific grievances, or religious extremism. During a subsequent inquiry, confessions obtained from several slaves stated that the pending Slave Registry Bill was to blame for the insurrection. Under cross-examination, it emerged that false reports circulated that the Act was intended to bring about manumission, but that the planters planned to deny freedom to their slaves.[17]

While the Registry Bill contributed to the uprising, there are problems in taking confessional evidence at face value. The antipathy of Barbadian whites to the legislation is well attested and slave witnesses may, therefore, have testified under duress. On the Earl of Harewood's estates, local discontents need also to be taken into consideration. Prior to the uprising, plans were drawn up to merge Fortescue and Thicket; indeed, some slaves living on these properties had already been moved to Mount. The resulting dislocation of the enslaved communities (coupled with the links that population movements established between these estates), may help explain why slaves on Mount and Thicket

---

[12] Beckles, 'Bussa', 28.
[13] BL, *The Royal Gazette* (Kingston, Jamaica, 8–15 February 1817), 17.
[14] Hilary Beckles, *Black Rebellion in Barbados: The Struggle against Slavery, 1627–1838* (Bridgetown, Barbados, 1987), 86–110.
[15] WRA, Abstract of the Produce of the Estates and other Property in the West Indies belonging to the Right Honourable Lord Harewood, 1805–39: Barbados Affairs.
[16] For a discussion of pro- and anti-slavery narratives of the revolt, see David Lambert, 'Producing/Contesting Whiteness: Rebellion, Slavery and Enslavement in Barbados, 1816', *Geoforum*, 36 (2005), 29–43.
[17] Beckles, *Black Rebellion in Barbados*, 109–10; Beckles, 'Bussa', 54–6, 57–9, 64–5, 66–8.

rebelled, whereas Belle plantation was less obviously affected by the uprising.[18]

Although a powerful symptom of resistance, insurrection was far less common than more petty acts of disobedience, such as verbal abuse, sluggish performance, pilfering, sabotage (on a minor scale), and refusals to work through feigning injury and other deceptions.[19] Running away was one of the most visible signs of dissent. Surviving series of newspapers, published on Barbados and Jamaica, carry advertisements seeking the return of runaways and report the detention of recaptured slaves in public 'workhouses' (institutions designed to exact punishment as well as holding areas).[20]

Studies of runaways on the colonial mainland (based on more continuous series of newspaper advertisements) suggest that absconders formed a minority of the slave population and that they tended to be males in their twenties and thirties fleeing to join family and kin, or to escape cruelty and punishment.[21] In the case of slaves on the Harewood estates, running away was also employed as a method of protest and occurred in response to uncertainty over the future ownership of plantations. Eight unnamed slaves ran away together in 1801, for example, after rumours circulated that the 1st Earl intended to sell all his properties.[22] Runaways who returned voluntarily, or who were captured,

---

[18] It has been suggested that the opposition of Henry Lascelles (the future 2nd Earl) to the abolition of the transatlantic slave trade ten years earlier contributed to a sense of grievance against the Lascelles, Bobby Morris, 'Transfer of Wealth from Barbados to England – From Lascelles Plantation, Barbados to Harewood House, Yorkshire', *JBMHS*, *50* (2004), 100. There is no clear method of verifying this interesting possibility; the failure of Belle's enslaved to participate in the uprising, however, implies that specific resentments were of more significance, though slaves were also moved from this property to Mount (see Chapter Nine).

[19] James C. Scott, *Weapons of the Weak: Everyday Forms of Peasant Resistance* (New Haven, 1985), xv–xvii.

[20] John Carter Brown Library, Accession 76–104, Extracts From The Royal Gazette, Jamaica, 30 September–7 October 1826; Beckles, 'Bussa', 11.

[21] Jerome S. Handler, 'Escaping Slavery in a Caribbean Plantation Society: Marronage in Barbados, 1650s–1830s', *Nieuwe West-Indische Gids*, 71 (1997), 184–91; Marvin L. Michael Kay and Lorin Lee Cary, 'Slave Runaways in Colonial North Carolina', *Slavery and Servitude*, 63 (1986), 1–39; Lathan A. Windley, 'Profile of Runaway Slaves in Virginia and South Carolina from 1730 through 1787', unpub. Ph.D. thesis (University of Iowa, 1974), 79–86; Michael Johnson, 'Runaway Slaves and the Slave Communities in South Carolina, 1799–1830', *William and Mary Quarterly*, 38 (1981), 418–41. The broad profile of Virginia runaways were similar; advertisements from the *Virginia Gazette* are available online as part of Tom Costa's project 'The Geography of Slavery in Virginia', hosted by the University of Virginia, www.vcdh.virginia.edu/gos/ (last checked 23 September 2005).

[22] HH:WIP, Correspondence, Jonathan Blenman & Richard Cobham (Barbados) to John Wood Nelson (London), 27 September 1801; [Nelson?] to John Blenman and Richard Cobham (Barbados), 4 December 1801.

usually suffered punishment by whipping. Persistent offenders might incur more serious penalties, including branding or removal from the colony to another island. It is not known what actions (punitive or otherwise) were employed in an attempt to reduce the number of fugitives by managers of the Lascelles' plantations. An entry in Nightingale Grove's estate accounts for 1813 reads: 'value of a Negro sentenced to be shipped off the Island'. Although neither the identity of the slave nor the nature of the offence are stated, this could refer to the punishment of a repeated absconder.[23]

Obstruction, insubordination, theft, and sabotage were among the methods employed by slaves seeking to express their opposition to forced labour.[24] While detailed evidence is lacking, the comments of the Lascelles' associates indicate that such behaviour was widely encountered. George Maxwell, for example, recalled that his own slaves on Barbados had been, 'by nature so stupid that I found none so ill served as I was'. Behaviour that Maxwell deemed 'stupid' can be interpreted as a form of calculated resistance to his authority. Island attorney Francis Graeme complained of 'unthinking negroes that will make use of provisions before they are ripe'.[25] Naval commander Thomas Frankland similarly chastised the work of 'inept' black mechanics while stationed at English Harbour in Antigua.[26] Comments such as these provide insights into a culture of lethargy and indifference, developed by the enslaved community in order to provide an outlet for their frustrations.[27]

Although resistance may have been endemic within slave societies, a simple model of coercion and opposition provides an inadequate practical explanation of the day-to-day workings of plantations. Hierarchical models of repression based on a strict master–slave dichotomy have also been criticised on theoretical grounds (most notably by adherents of Foucault) for failing to recognise the significance of decentralised, overlapping power relationships within slave society.[28] Some degree of accommodation and cooperation was essential for slavery to remain a

---

[23] WRA, Abstract of accounts of Williamsfield and Nightingale Grove plantations, 1790–1835.

[24] M. Schuler, 'Day-to-Day Resistance to Slavery in the Caribbean During the Eighteenth Century', *African Studies Association of the West Indies*, Bulletin No. 6 (1973), 57–77.

[25] *LMLB*, Maxwell (London) to John Braithwaite (Barbados), [n.d.] November 1745; WRA, Letters and Papers, Francis Graeme (Jamaica) to Nelson (London), 16 August 1816.

[26] Cited in David Barry Gaspar, *Bondmen and Rebels: A Study of Master–Slave Relations in Antigua, with Implications for Colonial British America* (Baltimore, 1985), 117.

[27] James C. Scott, *Domination and the Arts of Resistance: Hidden Transcripts* (New Haven, 1990), 2–5.

[28] See e.g. Robert J. C. Young, 'Foucault on Race and Colonialism', *New Formations*, 25 (1995), 57–65.

viable system of production. In consequence, slave opposition can be interpreted as part of a bargaining process, aimed at improving living conditions and reaching accommodations with estate managers.[29] Negotiable aspects of slavery included ownership of provision grounds, compensation for Sunday labour, and the terms of access to slave villages. The evolving concepts of 'master's time' and 'free time' may similarly be regarded as the outcome of an ongoing bargaining process relating to specific aspects of slavery.[30]

In the case of the Lascelles' estates, most evidence documenting cooperative relations is confined to references to privileged slaves holding positions of responsibility. *Instructions for the Management of a Plantation* (1786) recognised that, 'Upon every plantation there are leading people with capacity to distinguish,' and stressed it was indispensable for managers 'to adopt such a conduct towards them, as will engage the affections and good opinion of the principal people'.[31] Head slaves were almost exclusively male and accounted for just 2 per cent of individuals living on the Lascelles' plantations.[32] Such individuals occupied the roles of superintendents, leading gangs in the field or heading teams of craftsmen. The *Instructions* indicate they could expect to receive superior accommodation and extra allowances of food and clothing, in recognition of their responsibilities.[33]

Household slaves, a majority of whom were female, accounted for a further 6 per cent of the enslaved living on the Lascelles' properties. Domestic servants could occupy positions of trust.[34] Direct evidence is lacking for the presence of black or coloured servants in the Lascelles' own household, but the responsibilities of Lascelles & Maxwell included looking after the slaves of West Indian clients of the firm sent over to England. An enslaved man named Sampson, for example, arrived in London from St Kitts in June 1752 suffering from an enlarged growth.

---

[29] Sidney Mintz and Richard Price, *An Anthropological Approach to the Afro-American Past: A Caribbean Perspective* (Philadelphia, 1976), 20–35; Hilary Beckles and Karl Watson, 'Social Protest and Labour Bargaining: The Changing Nature of Slaves' Responses to Plantation Life in Eighteenth Century Barbados', *Slavery and Abolition*, 8 (1987), 2,722–93.

[30] James Walvin, 'Slaves, Free Time and the Question of Leisure', *Slavery and Abolition*, 16 (1995), 1–13.

[31] [Edwin Lascelles *et al.*], *Instructions for the Management of a Plantation in Barbadoes and for the Treatment of Negroes* (London, 1786), 22.

[32] See Table 9.5 for data of the occupations of slaves working on the Lascelles' plantations.

[33] (Lascelles *et al.*), *Instructions*, 30.

[34] By way of illustration, Betty and Nanney spent many years working as the nurses of the children of Hugh Hall Sr. Their loyalty was remembered in Hall's will, which granted the women small legacies of 7s.6d., 'besides their usual allowance', BA, RB6/1/1–4, Will of Hugh Hall, dated 1 September 1698.

Sampson was placed in the care of the surgeon Samuel Sharpe at Guy's Hospital and admitted to the Foul Ward. George Maxwell wrote to Sampson's owner, Jeremiah Brown, reassuring him that he had visited the patient several times, in order to 'keep him in good spirits, as Negroes are like Children, to be humoured, as well as from a principle of Humanity, as in regard to yourself to whom we are much obliged'.[35] In addition to attempting to maintain Sampson's morale, Maxwell provided money for the washing of his clothes and the purchase of fresh supplies. When it became clear that his condition was not improving, the patient was transferred from Guy's into the care of Dr James Maxwell: the medical younger half-brother of George, who had married into the Lascelles family.[36]

Glimpses of other African-Caribbean visitors to Britain are sighted in the Lascelles & Maxwell archive. Planters' wives crossing the Atlantic often travelled with their black ladies' maids. One such case involved an unnamed young slave girl, who accompanied Barbara Husbands (the wife of Richard Husbands of Barbados, a planter and loan client). In January 1755, the firm arranged for the maidservant's passage back to the West Indies, paying 10 guineas to secure her a cabin with two other maids. As in the case of Sampson, a mixture of humanitarian concern and financial prudence motivated their actions. Lascelles & Maxwell paid a premium to secure the girl private accommodation, partly to prevent her from being harassed by the ship's crew, and partly 'to prevent any danger of her being corrupted here and made free'.[37]

A more intriguing reference occurs in 1765, when the partners notified Richard Watson of Barbados that they had 'paid your Black, James Alexander, £6 for a years allowance from you due last midsummer'. Despite receiving payments from Watson, it does not appear that Alexander was in London doing his master's bidding, since the two men had evidently not been in regular communication for some time; indeed, the firm felt it necessary to inform Watson that Alexander

[35] *LMLB*, Pares Transcripts, H371, f. 338, Lascelles & Maxwell to Jeremiah Browne (St Kitts), 29 June 1752. Jeremiah Browne's will (dated 10 July 1754) refers to property in Nevis, St Kitts, and an English estate called Apps Court in Surrey, Vere Langford Oliver ed., *Caribbeana* (4 vols., London, 1910–16), vol. I, 36. The Sampson case is the subject of research by J. E. Bowden-Dan, 'Looking Back Briefly: Mr Guy's Hospital and the Caribees', paper presented to Centre of Caribbean Medicine Conference, St Thomas' Hospital, London, 6–7 July 2000.

[36] *LMLB*, Pares Transcripts, W&G f. 13, unidentified letter [Lascelles & Maxwell to Jeremiah Browne (Jamaica), c. 1752–5?].

[37] Ibid., W&G V, f. 126, Lascelles & Maxwell to Richard Husbands (Barbados), 6 January 1755.

'still lives'.[38] The letters of Lascelles & Maxwell also refer to John Nooker, the slave of an unnamed planter, who served on HMS *Buckingham* during the Seven Years' War (1756–63) and earned wages of £40 (money that his owner attempted to claim).[39]

Surviving plantation records documenting the management of the Lascelles' estates make only sparse reference to free persons of colour or privileged coloured slaves. Yet in view of the fact that only a fraction of the original accounts and correspondence has survived, these fragments are probably representative of a more numerous set of relationships. On Barbados, Lord Harewood's agents rented out property in Bridgetown to three free coloureds named Christian Addison, Rachel LeGay, and Elizabeth Smith. A black slave named Hamilton also occupied a tenancy on the same site and a manumitted shoemaker named Kitt (a free man of colour?) stood security for him. 'Thos Hall Free Negro' was likewise a tenant of property leased out by the Lascelles on Barbados during the mid-1780s. In 1824, slaves were also sold to James Edward Spencer, 'a free man of colour'.[40] On Jamaica, two persons of colour, named Isabella Cole and William Duncan, were in 1813 included among the guardians of the minor Samuel Smith. In order to purchase Sandy Gut plantation in 1815, it was first necessary for the Earl of Harewood's representatives to negotiate with these individuals.[41] Though limited in number, these examples reveal that transacting with free persons of colour was regarded as a normal business activity by the Lascelles and their associates.

Cooperative relations were also formed with Africans participating in the transatlantic slave trade. A notable example of interracial association is provided by the English residence (c. 1748–50) of the African William Ansah (Prince William Ansa Sasraku). Ansah was an adopted son of caboceer John Currantee (Eno Baisie Kurentsi). In 1744, en route to England, he was reportedly betrayed by the ship's captain transporting him and sold as a slave on Barbados.[42] By drawing on his commercial connections, Currantee secured his son's release,

---

[38] Ibid., W&G IX, f. 47, Lascelles & Maxwell to Richard Watson (Barbados), 2 April 1765.

[39] Ibid., W&G VIII, Lascelles & Maxwell to ?, n.d., c. 1759–63.

[40] HH:WIP, A list of papers belonging to Edward Lascelles Esq. as executor of the Rt Honble Edwin Lord Harewood deced [1795–6], ff. 24–5; Lease of land to Thos Hall Free Negro, found among a list of specialities of Lascelles & Daling [n.d., c. 1784]; Indenture between Henry Earl Harewood, Foster Clarke, and James Edward Spencer (1824); agreement with William Earl, 'free man of colour' [n.d., Barbados c. 1817–20].

[41] WRA, Harewood Accession, 2,677, Conveyance from George Kinghorn, Joseph Timperon, John Hurst, and Edward Lord Harewood, 3 July 1815.

[42] For an account of the incident, see Wylie Sypher, 'The African Prince in London', *Journal of the History of Ideas*, 2 (1941), 237–47.

whereupon he proceeded on his journey to London.[43] On arrival, William Ansah received 'generous & polite treatment' from members of the Company of Merchants Trading to Africa. He was placed in the care of Lord Halifax (a leading Commissioner for Trade and Plantations), and introduced to George II. The contemporary observer Horace Walpole observed how the African prince was 'in fashion at all assemblies'.[44]

John Currantee was an important business associate during the period when Henry Lascelles was directly concerned in the slave trade and held contracts to maintain forts belonging to the former Royal African Company.[45] Caboceers were the representatives of African leading families, appointed to deal with European merchants and naval commanders engaged in slaving and other forms of trade. Rituals of gift-giving were a feature of commercial relations, reflecting both the elite status of the caboceers and their diplomatic functions. In 1750, Captain John Roberts wrote to Henry Lascelles, for example, informing him that on his arrival at Anomabu he had presented Currantee with, 'a Hat & Feather Scarlet Cloaths and a Considerable Quantity of Liquor'.[46] The caboceers were frequently connected by blood or marriage with African dynasties or head families. Cudjoe Caboceer, one of the most influential intermediaries operating in the Cape Castle region, was brother of King Amroe Coffee. John Currantee himself took as his wife Ekua, daughter of Nana Ansa Sasraku, King of Akramu.[47]

William Ansah's visit was one of a series of African encounters with London society that took place during the mid-eighteenth century.[48] Following his arrival, Ansah's portrait (by Gabriel Mathias) was painted

---

[43] Elizabeth Donnan ed., *Documents Illustrative of the History of the Slave Trade to America* (4 vols., Washington DC, 1930–5), vol. II, 490–1; Ruth A. Fisher, 'Extracts from the Records of the African Companies [Part 3]', *Journal of Negro History*, 13 (1928), 347–9.

[44] Margaret Priestley, *West African Trade and Coast Society: A Family Study* (London, 1969), 20; Donnan, *Documents*, vol. II, 490–1.

[45] *Journals of the House of Commons* (London, 1756; reprinted 1803), vol. XXVII, 414–15, 'Petition of J. Robert, late governor, treasurer, and chief agent of the late Royal African Company'; Board of Trade, *Journal of the Commissioners for Trade and Plantations* (14 vols., London, 1920), vol. X, 19, 14 March 1754. Lascelles' contract was worth £10,000 in 1749.

[46] NA:PRO, T70/1476, John Roberts to Henry Lasselles [sic] of London, 23 March [1750], cited in Fisher, 'Extracts'.

[47] Priestley, *West African Trade*, 19–20; Ty M. Reece, 'An Economic Middle Ground? Anglo-African Interaction, Cooperation and Competition in the Late Eighteenth-Century Atlantic World', *American Historical Association Conference Proceedings, Interactions: Regional Studies, Global Processes, and Historical Analysis: Networks and Connections Beyond the Nation State* (Library of Congress: Washington DC, 2001), www.historycooperative.org/proceedings/interactions/reese.html.

[48] Donnan ed., *Documents*, vol. II, 490–1; Priestley, *West African Trade*, 20–3. The timing was related to the competition for business and influence between French and British

in the style of a gentleman wearing fashionable apparel, and reproduced (by John Faber) as a mezzotint print. Images also appeared in the *Gentleman's Magazine*, juxtaposing William Ansah in European dress with an earlier African visitor to London, the Muslim Ayuba b. Sulyman.[49] A book with the title *The Royal Prince* appeared at the same time, recounting the story of Ansah's voyage and acknowledging his royal status:

> A Person who has the supreme Authority in any District, let it be of a larger or lesser Extent, is, in the common Acceptation of Speech, a Prince; and if from his Influence our Trade may be either advanced or hindered, he deserves a proportionable Respect from us, tho' he would be certainly entitled to strict Justice, whether he had that Influence or not.[50]

Undoubtedly, the trading privileges wielded by African head families and the caboceers weighed heavily with the Court and the Commissioners for Trade and Plantations in their decision to award Ansah privileged diplomatic status. Indeed, a contemporary account indicates that the initiative for the visit may have emanated from London's mercantile community, anxious to counter French influence in the Cape Castle region.[51] Despite the undoubted significance of such pragmatic considerations, the public reception given to William Ansah, Philip Quaque, and other visitors reveals that African origin was not automatically equated with inferiority or servitude.[52] At the upper echelon of the social hierarchy at least, a middle ground (or 'valuable communicating link') existed. While the capture and temporary enslavement of Ansah illustrates that the meeting ground could be precarious terrain, perhaps the most interesting aspect of this incident is the speed with which the prince's status was restored once John Currantee called on his merchant associates for assistance. The incident further served to

merchants. John Currantee is reported to have sent two sons to Europe: one to France and the other to England, (Anon.), *The Royal African*, 28.

[49] John Faber, *William Ansa Sasraku* (London, 1749), mezzotint after a painting by Gabriel Mathias (National Portrait Gallery); *Gentleman's Magazine*, 20 (1750), 273; *JBMHS*, 27 (1959–60), 1–2. Ayuba b. Sulyman (known also to Europeans as Job Ben Solomon) was enslaved in 1730 and taken to Maryland in 1733. According to contemporary published accounts, an officer of the Royal African Company freed him in 1733 and took him back to Africa via London, Michael Gomez, 'Muslims in Early America', *Journal of Southern History*, 60 (1994), 690; Philip Curtin 'Ayuba Suleiman Diallo of Bondu', in Philip Curtin ed., *Africa Remembered: Narratives by West Africans from the Era of the Slave Trade* (Madison, 1967).

[50] (Anon.), *The Royal African*, vii. Two fictitious love poems by William Dodd, 'The African Prince to Zara' and 'Zara to the African Prince', also appeared in 1749, reinforcing Ansah's association with gentility and polite conduct, *Gentleman's Magazine*, 19, 323–5, 372–3.

[51] (Anon.), *The Royal African*, vii.

[52] See Margaret Priestley, 'Philip Quaque', in Curtin ed., *Africa Remembered*.

underline the respectability of slave traders such as Henry Lascelles, who conducted legitimate commerce with African elites, by contrasting their organised commercial ventures with the predatory and opportunistic behaviour of interlopers and unscrupulous ships' captains.

The family history of Richard Brew, the Governor of Anomabu and builder of Brew Castle, provides a further example of a relationship between whites and elite blacks of the Gold Coast that defies simple racial classifications. Brew aligned himself with John Currantee by forming a relationship with his sister, Effua Ansah (sister of William Ansah). A second connection was made with the Quaque family (relations of Cudjo Caboceer) through Brew's coloured son Harry. These interracial alliances persisted over time, generating a sequence of cross-cultural links that cascaded down through several generations, connecting the Fanti Brews with English society.[53] An alliance formed originally to further Richard Brew's commercial and political ambitions developed into a long-term dynastic union.

Intercultural Relations

West Indian planters were in theory the white, absentee masters of black slaves. In practical terms however, the system of chattel slavery that developed in the Caribbean contained many contradictions and much ambivalence. Colonial societies were modelled on the rigid dichotomies of enslaved–enslaver and black–white, but these fundamental concepts were modified in order to accommodate privileged blacks and coloureds, who occupied distinct social and economic niches.[54] The existence of such groups constituted an anomaly in a plantation system constructed on the basis of race. Studies of slavery's ultimate collapse in the Caribbean have paid special attention to the growth of the coloured segment of society and its relationship with both the white governing minority and enslaved black majority. The attitude of the 'gens de couleurs', for example, are considered pivotal to the success of the slave revolution that broke out on St Domingue in 1791. A hardening of attitudes towards miscegenation in Jamaica, following the realisation that the island would never become the hoped-for white settler society, has also been identified as a critical theme in the development of Britain's largest Caribbean colony, especially after Tackey's rebellion of 1760.[55]

---

[53] Priestley, *West African Trade*, 106–9, 117–28.
[54] Gad J. Heuman, *Between Black and White: Race, Politics, and the Free Coloreds in Jamaica, 1792–1865* (Westport, CT, 1981), 3–10.
[55] David Geggus, 'The Haitian Revolution', in Franklin Knight and Colin Palmer eds., *The Modern Caribbean* (Chapel Hill, 1989); Trevor Burnard, 'Not a Place for Whites: Demographic Failure and Settlement in Comparative Context: Jamaica, 1655-1780', in

Coloured slaves occupied an ambivalent position within the social hierarchies of West Indian island communities. Outside the plantation, persons of colour might suffer legal and social discrimination that emphasised their non-whiteness. On Jamaica, laws were passed in 1761 (promoted by Tackey's revolt) with the aim of bolstering white privileged status. These measures included imposing a threshold on the value of property owned by coloureds in order to maintain racial divisions.[56] The Barbadian legal system, from 1721 onwards, placed a bar on coloureds testifying against whites in court that served a similar purpose.[57] Social institutions regulated race relations in ways that reinforced the notion of a white governing elite. On Barbados, seating in the island's churches was racially segregated and there is evidence that the system of parish vestry relief was employed to discourage interracial relationships forming between poor white women and men of colour. Access to clubs and dining rooms by coloureds on the islands was also restricted.[58] In addition to prescriptions emanating from within the Barbadian white community, European visitors often commented negatively on cohabitation between the races, reinforcing the sense of subjugation experienced by persons of mixed race.[59]

Coloured slaves remaining on a sugar estate were more likely to occupy higher positions within the plantation hierarchy than other

---

Kathleen Montieth and Glen Richards eds., *Jamaica in Slavery and Freedom* (Kingston, Jamaica, 2002).

[56] Gad Heuman, 'White Over Brown Over Black: The Free Coloureds in Jamaican Society During Slavery and After Emancipation', *Journal of Caribbean History*, 14 (1981), 46–9. Persons of colour also suffered discrimination as a result of the so-called deficiency legislation, introduced in 1715, which prescribed a minimum number of white personnel on plantation holdings. For more detailed discussion of the treatment of coloureds and the maintaining of white privilege during the later years of slavery on Jamaica, see Heuman, *Between Black and White*, 44–58.

[57] J. S. Handler, *The Unappropriated People: Freedmen in the Slave Society of Barbados* (Baltimore, 1974), 66–81. The legal presumption behind the Act of 1721 is that no person of African descent could attain the status enjoyed by whites.

[58] Handler, *Unappropriated People*, 190–201; Cecily Jones, 'Mapping Racial Boundaries: Gender, Race, and Poor Relief in Barbadian Plantation Society', *Journal of Women's History*, 10 (1998), 195–232. Jones' research juxtaposes contemporary fears that liaisons between poor white women and black males would bring about 'degeneration' of the white race with the complex 'taxonomies of whiteness' that characterised Barbadian society, Cecily Forde-Jones, 'Contesting the Boundaries of Gender, Race, and Sexuality in Barbadian Plantation Society', *Journal of Women's History*, 12 (2003), 9–31.

[59] See e.g. Janet Schaw, *Journal of a Lady of Quality; Being the Narrative of a Journey from Scotland to the West Indies, North Carolina, and Portugal, in the Years 1774 to 1776*, eds. E. W. Andrews and C. M. Andrews (3rd edn, New Haven, 1939; originally published 1921), 112; John Augustine Waller, *A Voyage in the West Indies* (London, 1820), 93–6. For similar comments relating to Jamaica, see James Hakewill, *A Picturesque Tour in the Island of Jamaica, from Drawings Made in the Years 1820 and 1821* (London, 1825), 6–8.

members of the enslaved population. Males were disproportionately skilled or employed as house servants; in some instances, female 'coloured favourites' were able to secure privileged status for themselves and their children.[60] A striking example of the degree of autonomy attainable under enslavement is provided by the estates of absentee owner James Brebner Gordon on Antigua and St Vincent. Although the Gordon plantations are not linked directly with the Lascelles, they provide useful contextual material. In 1824, these estates were visited by attorney John Johnson, who submitted a detailed report of conditions on the properties for the benefit of their owner.[61]

On Antigua, Gordon possessed two plantations: Sanderson's and Lavington's. Johnson reported that on Sanderson's approximately 11 per cent of the slaves were coloured. The absentee proprietor, however, was the owner of a number of absentee slaves, since the majority of the women of colour lived off the property with white partners. 'It would be beneficial to the Estate', Johnson concluded, 'if all of the coloured women were disposed of', even at rates below their nominal market value. In practice, he reported, such slaves performed little work and were contemptuous of authority. 'Several of the Ladies in question', Johnson wrote, 'positively refused receiving their allowance, unless they were permitted to *send* for it, or unless it were *sent* to them.'[62] Johnson ordered the women back on to Sanderson's, in the hope that offers might be made for their freedom. He achieved a measure of success. One woman was manumitted immediately, while three others began negotiating terms for their emancipation. Yet the policy was not implemented without friction. A woman of colour, named Eliza Bishop,

---

[60] Barbara Bush, 'White "Ladies," Coloured "Favourites" and Black "Wenches": Some Considerations on Sex, Race and Class Factors in Social Relations in White Creole Society in the British Caribbean', *Slavery and Abolition*, 2 (1981), 245–62. Note, however, that while skin colour influenced the type of work an individual carried out on a plantation, it did not confer a significant survivorship advantage, see Chapter Nine.

[61] Hamilton College, Beinecke Collection, M526, 'Reports Relating to Mr Gordon's Estates in the West Indies, 1824'. The Gordon and Brebner (pronounced Bremner) families originated from Aberdeen and by the 1730s had become plantation owners on St Kitts, extending their interests to Antigua and St Vincent during the course of the eighteenth century. In addition to Caribbean property, the Gordons acquired land in the English counties of Hertfordshire and Somerset. There is no direct connection between the Gordon-Brebners and the Lascelles, the material being cited for purposes of illustration only. The Gordon's eighteenth-century patron, however, was the Duke of Argyll, who was connected with the Lascelles via the Douglases. James Gordon's business associates also included kinsmen (the Ball family) of the Lascelles, NA:PRO, C11/1145/17 (1733). J. Johnson was the author of two books on the Caribbean, both illustrated with detailed prints: *Views in the West Indies* (London, 1827) and *An Historical and Descriptive Account of Antigua* (London, 1830). The Gordon reports also include watercolours and estate surveys executed to a high standard.

[62] 'Reports Relating to Mr Gordon's Estates', Part II, 12.

was singled out as a particular troublemaker. Johnson complained that, 'she treated every rule or regulation of the Estate with the same contempt as she did my positive orders relating more particularly to herself'.[63] After allegedly threatening to cut Johnson's throat before the assembled slaves, Eliza was confined on the plantation until an offer of £95 (currency) was received for her freedom.

On Lavington's, the percentage of coloured persons was reported to be about 5 per cent greater than on Sanderson's. Most slaves of colour living on Lavington's were the Mustee offspring of a mulatto woman named Polly Johnson, who lived with her white partner off the estate. Johnson faced fewer difficulties on this property, due in part to the opportune death of Polly, which assisted him in arranging either for the sale (manumission) or return of her children.[64]

Gordon's sugar estate on St Vincent was an amalgam of two properties called Fairhall and Brebner. Johnson reported difficulties with those enslaved of colour on this plantation as well, though here female coloured autonomy expressed itself in a different form. Richard Robertson, the estate's manager, had formed a relationship with a Mulatto woman named Eliza. In consequence, Eliza had assumed a position of authority over other slaves, causing her to become a hated figure within the enslaved community. According to Johnson, Eliza 'undertook the office of inflicting ie ordering punishment occasionally herself'. Moreover, when Robertson was absent from the property, it was reported that he permitted 'the Management of the Estate to devolve on her'. At other times, Eliza was allowed 'to Keep the keys of the Stores and distribute the supplies'.[65] In an extraordinary examination of twenty-four slaves, Johnson heard various allegations of ill-treatment and malpractice by Robertson and his mistress, including the claim that Eliza misappropriated plantation stores for sale at her own private business premises.[66] A feature of the slave testimonies recorded by Johnson is that they do not include allegations of sexual assault. Instead, the complaints levelled against Robertson emphasised the tensions generated by the favouritism the white manager bestowed on his coloured partner.

Despite the destruction of much archival material, it is possible to draw some broad conclusions regarding the size and profile of the coloured population living on the Lascelles' West Indian estates. The enslaved database identifies 254 persons of colour inhabiting nine

---

[63] Ibid., 13.   [64] Ibid., 24.   [65] Ibid., Part III, 12.   [66] Ibid., 16–19.

plantations located on Barbados, Jamaica, and Tobago.[67] On first inspection, gender appears to be the most striking characteristic of the sample, with women making up 58.7 per cent of the total: a higher proportion than in the case of either blacks or Creoles.

The female majority is all the more striking because there is no evidence that women of colour were brought on to the properties in greater numbers than men; on the contrary, the database reveals that the thirty coloured slaves associated with second properties were divided fairly evenly between men (fourteen) and women (sixteen).[68] Data deficiencies are the most likely cause of the observed gender imbalance. Significantly, under-reporting of male slaves of colour is a phenomenon confined to the Barbadian and Jamaican estates where 61.5 per cent of persons of colour were reportedly female. In contrast, the 1819 Tobago returns list forty-one males and forty-seven females of colour living on the Lascelles' estates: approximately the same sex ratio as for the population as a whole.

A population pyramid for the seventy-two male and female slaves of colour appearing in the 1817 registration returns for Barbados and Jamaica is presented in Figure 10.1. The percentage distribution of population by age group reveals that the female surplus is concentrated from birth to fourteen years and in the age range from twenty to thirty-four years. This finding suggests that the compilers of the listings were more likely to record accurately the colour of women of child-rearing age and their female offspring than males of similar ages.

Legal status in the British West Indies was determined by maternal descent. The child of a union taking place between a black woman and a white man was, therefore, deemed by law to be a chattel slave. This practice ran counter to the usual principle of primogeniture employed in Britain and in the English-speaking Caribbean colonies, whereby male heirs enjoyed superior rights to property by inheritance.[69] On Jamaica, the terms Mulatto, Quadroon, Sambo, and Mustee were routinely applied to slaves to denote their degree of whiteness or blackness.[70]

---

[67] The estates are: Belle (B), Fortescue (B), Glamorgan (T), Goldsborough/Goodwood (T), Mount (B), Nightingale (J), Richmond (T), and Williamsfield (J). Minimum qualification for inclusion was five slaves (a total of 192 coloured slaves are contained in the database as a whole) described as either Mulatto, Sambo, Mustee, or Quadroon in the original manuscripts.

[68] A total of 320 boys and 347 girls were born on these estates between 1817 and 1834: an insignificant differential. Runaway and manumission rates were both too low to affect the population totals.

[69] Primogeniture operated, however, only in the case of legitimate offspring. The de facto prohibition on interracial marriages denied legal rights to mixed-race children of either sex.

[70] B. W. Higman, *Slave Population and Economy in Jamaica, 1807–1834* (Cambridge, 1976), 139.

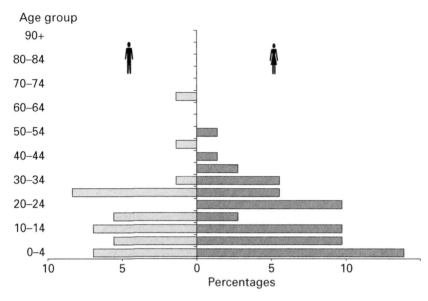

Figure 10.1 Population pyramid for slaves of colour on six estates, 1817
Source: NA:PRO, T71/13–18, 25–8, 30, 32, 520–1, 524–5, 527, 534–6, 540, 544, 547, 549–50, 553, 556–7.

In contrast, on Barbados these phenotypes were not recognised, thereby preventing a person of African descent from ever attaining white status.[71] Nevertheless, despite this important legal distinction, on both colonies an incentive existed to record an individual's racial status. Initially, it appears that greater emphasis was placed on matrilineal descent, resulting in the more consistent recording of the colour of females. As the number of free coloureds on Barbados and Jamaica increased, however, the status of males was also subject to closer scrutiny.

The triennial registration returns of births and deaths provide further evidence that the observed female majority of the coloured population does not accurately reflect gender divisions. Table 10.1 presents the raw data and Chi-square analysis of disparities between the male and female entries for Barbados and Jamaica.[72] The data suggest the compilers of the Lascelles' registration returns recorded the colour of the enslaved

---

[71] Handler, *Unappropriated People*, 68–9.
[72] The Lascelles' Tobago estates had by this time been sold and so are excluded from the analysis.

Table 10.1. *Chi-square analysis of births and deaths of coloured slaves for six Barbadian and Jamaican estates, 1817–32*

	1817–26	1827–32
Observed female births	31	10
Expected female births	23	7
Observed male births	15	14
Expected female births	23	7
Chi-square test and probability	2.869 (p = .090)	0.248 (p = .618)
Observed female deaths	14	6
Expected female deaths	9	8
Observed male deaths	4	10
Expected male deaths	9	8
Chi-square test and probability	3.010 (p = .083)	0.508 (p = .475)

Source: As for Figure 10.1.

more accurately in the later returns than the early ones. By the later 1820s, male slaves of colour were identified more consistently in the records, whereas initially attention had concentrated on females. In view of these findings, the number of slaves of colour on the Lascelles' estates on Barbados and Jamaica was probably around two-and-a-half times greater than the registration returns imply.[73]

The reported incidence of coloured slaves varied considerably between properties, ranging from just 3.5 per cent of births in the case of Belle to 40 per cent on Mount (Table 10.2). These data are not out of line with other studies, which have unearthed rates varying from 2 to 50 per cent.[74] The sex ratio of the enslaved and the proportion of whites to blacks are both thought to have influenced the incidence of coloured births on individual plantations.[75] On the Lascelles' estates, persons of colour were most prevalent on the smallest estates (Mount and Nightingale) possessing a surplus of females within the age range fifteen to forty-four years. These properties probably possessed a higher ratio of whites to blacks, owing to the need for a minimum number of white managers regardless of scale. Yet even allowing for the influence of these factors, the wide disparity in reported rates among the estates indicates significant misreporting.

---

[73] The reported share of coloureds on the six Barbadian and Jamaican estates in 1817 is just 5.7 per cent. In contrast, 14 per cent of female births occurring on the plantations between 1817 and 1834 consisted of babies of colour. On the three Tobago estates, 14.3 per cent of the population likewise comprised persons of colour.

[74] Higman, *Slave Population and Economy in Jamaica*, 140–1.   [75] Ibid., 148.

Table 10.2. *Female births on six Barbadian and Jamaican properties, distinguishing coloured children, 1817–32*

Property	All female births (number)	Female births of colour (number)	Percentage coloured
Belle	87	3	3.5
Mount	32	13	40.6
Thicket/Fortescue	89	10	11.2
Barbados total	*208*	*26*	*12.5*
Williamsfield	31	5	16.1
Nightingale Grove	24	7	29.2
Jamaica total	*55*	*12*	*21.8*

Note: Data for Mount excludes the years 1827–9.
Source: As for Figure 10.1.

The low number of mixed-race children born on Belle is consistent with the finding that only 4.2 per cent of the female population was coloured in 1817. Qualitative evidence, however, cautions that under-recording may still have occurred on this property. Free coloureds holding tenancies in Bridgetown in 1795, for example, rented housing that formerly belonged to Belle. In 1799, a free woman, identified only as West, wrote to Lord Harewood seeking to purchase a girl on Belle. William Bishop (Harewood's agent) described West as, 'a black woman ... who keeps a little Huxter's shop in Bridge Town'. Bishop cautioned that West intended the girl, 'even for a worse purpose than assist her in Huxtering'. Two interesting features of this episode are, firstly, that West was seemingly literate; secondly, that Bishop regarded the girl concerned as, 'one of a family of seventeen of the best People upon the Belle estate'.[76] The letter can be interpreted as evidence of

[76] HH:WIP, Correspondence, William Bishop to John Wood Nelson, 20 April 1799. This is one of the few references in the surviving Lascelles papers alluding to the participation by those enslaved in commodity production and distribution outside the plantation, see Hiliary McD. Beckles, 'An Economic Life of Their Own: Slaves as Commodity Producers and Distributors in Barbados', in Ira Berlin and Philip D. Morgan eds., *The Slaves' Economy: Independent Production by Slaves in the Americas* (London, 1991), 31–47. A plausible interpretation of this reference is that West was involved in brothel-keeping in addition to huxtering; see Hilary McD. Beckles, 'Property Rights in Pleasure: The Marketing of Enslaved Women's Sexuality', in Roderick McDonald ed., *West Indies Accounts: Essays on the History of the British Caribbean and the Atlantic* (Kingston, Jamaica, 1996), 169–88, reprinted in Verene Shepherd and Hilary McD. Beckles eds., *Caribbean Slavery in the Atlantic World: A Student Reader* (Kingston, Jamaica, 2000), 695–7.

links between the enslaved community on Belle and free coloureds living in nearby Bridgetown.

Statistical information about the coloured population can be supplemented by qualitative accounts drawn from family histories. While this type of material is not without problems of interpretation, it does provide an invaluable additional perspective, while also suggesting an agenda for future research. The remainder of this chapter will consider three case studies of interracial relationships on Barbados, Jamaica, and Tobago.

In the case of Barbados, a tradition exists that a female member of the Lascelles family was coloured. The person concerned is Frances Ball, daughter of the planter and member of the Barbados Council, Guy Ball. In 1732, Frances married Edward Lascelles (Henry's half-brother).[77] Following Edward's death in 1747, Frances married Admiral Francis Holburne and relocated to Britain.[78] Monuments to the couple survive in the church of St Mary Magdalene (Richmond, Surrey). Frances' memorial commemorates her virtue as follows:

> In the feverall characters
> Of a Wife, a Mother, a Friend
> And Miftress of a Family
> none excell'd her
> To perpetuate as long as Marble can
> The Memory of so good a Woman

Sentiments such as these often appear in eighteenth-century funerary art; in this case, however, they have acquired an additional meaning. While the marble succeeds in perpetuating the memory of Frances, doubt exists over the identity of the woman being remembered.

The family files of the library of the Barbados Museum in Bridgetown include a number of letters written at intervals during the twentieth century identifying Frances as a descendant of mixed race. The tradition that Frances was coloured seems to originate from a junior branch of the Lascelles family. By 1937, however, the 6th Earl of Harewood was corresponding with E. M. Shilstone (the archivist and librarian of the Barbados Museum) on the subject of Frances' paternity. One of the issues that perplexed Shilstone and the Earl was the failure of Frances' name to appear in the will of her father. Remarkably, their

---

[77] Joseph Foster, *Pedigrees of the County Families of England: Yorkshire, West Riding* (3 vols., London, 1874), vol. II, 'Lascelles'.
[78] For details of Holburne's career and notice of his marriage, see K. Laughton, 'Holburne, Francis (1704–1771)', rev. Ruddock Mackay, *ODNB*.

correspondence fails to mention colour specifically, but it had evidently occurred to Shilstone that Frances' omission might be owing to her race.[79]

In 1953, Shilstone received an enquiry from a Mr John Hill of Berkshire regarding the existence of 'a black woman' in the Lascelles pedigree. Hill's first letter claimed that he had met a number of descendants of General Francis Lascelles and the opera singer Ann Catley, and had heard persistent 'rumours of a "black woman" either as mother, grandmother or great-gd-mother of Gen[l] Lascelles'. His second letter was more forthcoming. Hill named Frances Ball as the black ancestor and speculated that her birth 'was a throw back, who surprized (and shocked) her Hon[ble] Guy Ball father by showing her dusty parentage'.[80] Shilstone replied to Hill as follows:

I never heard the tale of a black woman in the Lascelles family. The Sixth Earl was very frank about his Barbados ancestry and yet he never mentioned the rumour to me. He was also puzzled about Frances, daughter of Guy Ball, and wondered why she did not figure in her father's will and other documents.[81]

Shilstone chose his words carefully. He may never have heard the rumour that Frances was black expressed explicitly, but he was certainly aware of the ambiguities regarding Frances' parentage. Indeed, he was particularly interested in her mother, Catherine Dubois, whose ancestry the 6th Earl was himself anxious to establish. Moreover, Shilstone had previously written to an Annabel St Hill regarding Frances' family. If this correspondent was related to John Hill, then Shilstone must also already have been aware of the Lascelles–Hill connection.[82]

The persistent John Hill wrote again in 1960. This time he presented new information obtained from one Ian Rankin, a man claiming descent from Edward Lascelles. Rankin had told Hill that, 'in his family it is generally called "the mistake in the sugar plantation"'. For good measure, Hill added that, 'several times ... from various descendants of General (Francis) Lascelles, I have heard tell of this "black woman"'.[83] In response, Shilstone recited the details of various wills and deeds of the Ball and Dubois families, before cautioning Hill against submitting

---

[79] LBMH, Family Files ('Lascelles'), Earl of Harewood to E. M. Shilstone, 29 January and 25 April 1937; Shilstone to Earl of Harewood, 23 February and 10 March 1937.
[80] LBMH, John Hill to Shilstone, 29 May and 8 July 1953.
[81] LBMH, Shilstone to Hill, 6 July 1953.
[82] LBMH, Shilstone to Annabel St Hill, 2 October 1937.
[83] LBMH, Family Files ('Ball'), John Hill to Shilstone, 12 March and 19 April 1960.

material on the subject to the *Journal of the Barbados Museum and Historical Society*:

> I cannot throw any light on the subject of the 'Black woman' in the family of both branches. I do not think it should be mentioned in anything published in the *Journal*. Gerald Lascelles [younger son of Lord Harewood and owner of Thicket and Fortescue plantations] is a life member of our Society and a benefactor. His father never referred to this legend in correspondence or verbally.[84]

Undoubtedly, Shilstone regarded the question of Frances' colour as an extremely sensitive matter. In addition to the Earl of Harewood's own royal connections, he was acutely aware that Anthony Armstrong-Jones was descended from Catharine Holburne (the daughter of Frances and Francis Holburne), who had married Thomas Cussans of Jamaica.[85]

The controversy regarding Frances Ball is interesting primarily for what it reveals about family traditions and attitudes to miscegenation. While it is not possible to be certain, on the balance of probability Frances was almost certainly white. Shilstone was misled into giving credence to the tradition of the 'black woman' (despite his written statements to the contrary) by the omission of Frances' name from her father's will. The manuscript he examined, however, was a recopied will and not the original document, which is lost. Copied manuscripts can be problematic and this example contains an inconsistency. Whereas the will grants legacies to two sons and two daughters before naming a third son as the residual legatee, the document includes a provision that, 'if any of my said three sons *or three daughters* dye before their respective legacy or legacies' become due, then such legacies shall be sunk in the residue of the estate.[86] The inference is that the copyist omitted the details of Frances' legacy by accident. That Frances was entitled to a legacy is proved beyond doubt by the actions of her first husband, Edward Lascelles, who sued successfully for his wife's inheritance portion.[87] Furthermore, if Frances was coloured, no mention of the fact is recorded in contemporary diaries or correspondence despite her

---

[84] LBMH, Shilstone to John Hill, undated [April 1960].

[85] Frances' great-granddaughter Anne Cussans married Ludwig Messel of Nymans, and his granddaughter Anne (Messel) was the mother of Anthony Armstrong-Jones, 1st Earl of Snowdon, who married Princess Margaret in May 1960, LBMH, Family Files ('Ball'). For information about Thomas Cussans, see Betty Wood and Martin Lynn eds., 'The Letters of Simon Taylor of Jamaica to Chaloner Arcedekne, 1765–1775', in *Travel, Trade and Power in the Atlantic, 1765–1884*, Camden Miscellany, vol. XXXV, Camden Fifth series, No. 19 (2003).

[86] BA, RB6/6/423–4, Will of Guy Ball, dated 20 November 1719 and entered 30 April 1722 (italics added).

[87] BA, RB1/83/187–9 and RB1/87/149–51, deeds of sale of Guinea plantation by Joseph Ball to Edward Lascelles, entered 1 November 1734 and 30 August 1739.

marriage to Admiral Holburne and her presence in England. Nor is there any suggestion of mixed race in Frances' surviving portrait (by John Theodore Heins) preserved at Harewood House.

The evidence strongly suggests that Frances Lascelles was not a woman of colour. But the notion of her partial African ancestry was never erased from the Lascelles' family history and it is still significant that branches of the family *remembered* her as being 'a black woman', and selected her as the most likely candidate for what John Hill and Ian Rankin both referred to as 'the mistake in the sugar plantation'. The incident also raises issues surrounding genealogy and a family's collective memory: who begat whom in the family tree and what principles of selectivity operate in the compilation of pedigrees.

In the second illustration, the family history is that of the Cloustons, who originated from the Scottish isles of Orkney.[88] During the eighteenth and early nineteenth centuries, a number of Cloustons participated in Atlantic trade. Members of the family established themselves as merchants in Sierra Leone, Massachusetts, and Hudson's Bay.[89] This diffusion from a seemingly remote point of origin is less remarkable than first appears. Successive generations of Cloustons earned their livelihood as mariners and merchants, while the Hudson's Bay Company recruited actively from the Orkney isles, valuing the skills and loyalty of the inhabitants of a close-knit community used to working in harsh conditions. In 1799, for example, no fewer than three-quarters of personnel employed by the Company in North America were Orkadians.[90]

Among those electing to try their fortunes in the Americas was Edward Clouston (1787–1866), who in 1811 is described as a Jamaican planter. In addition to being the master of a small number of slaves in his own right, Clouston acted as island attorney for absentee owners of sugar estates and cattle pens in the parishes of St Catherine and St Thomas-in-the-Vale.[91] Although never an attorney of the Earl of

---

[88] Research into the Clouston family was greatly assisted by Mary Mill, who generously shared information on which the following paragraphs are largely based. The author accepts sole responsibility, however, for the accuracy and interpretation of this evidence.

[89] J. Storer Clouston, *The Family of Clouston* (privately printed, Kirkwall, 1948), 116, 120–1; The Orkney Library and Archive, Kirkwall, Sheriff Court Wills, SC1/1/51/3, Will of Revd William Clouston, dated 31 October 1826; *The Royal Gazette, and Sierra Leone Advertiser* (Freetown), 27 September 1823, 156, 3 January 1824, 264, 10 June 1826, 715.

[90] Ann Carlos and Stephen Nicholas, 'Agency Problems in Chartered Companies: The Case of the Hudson's Bay Company', *Journal of Economic History*, 50 (1990), 853–75; Stephen J. Hornsby, *British Atlantic, American Frontier: Spaces of Power in Early Modern British America* (Hanover/London, 2005), 66, 221.

[91] BL, *The Royal Gazette* (Kingston, Jamaica, 14–21 September 1811); NA:PRO, T71/159–60, 28–32, 5, 9, 11. See also The Orkney Library and Archive, Gray of Roeberry Papers,

Harewood, Clouston's name appears in connection with Williamsfield in 1818, when he was present on this estate in order to receive debt owing to the estate of one James Fraser (deceased).[92]

In 1815, Harewood purchased Sandy Gut, a neighbouring property to Williamsfield. The listing of the enslaved on Sandy Gut includes a Mulatto woman named Eliza (b. c. 1793).[93] At an unknown date (but probably after this transaction was completed), Clouston formed a relationship with Eliza, fathering two Quadroon children by her: Edward Clouston (b. c. 1819) and Little Henry or Henry Clouston (c. 1822–98). Prior to this, Eliza gave birth to two Quadroon sons (presumably fathered by a different white man), named William Burrows (b. c. 1811) and Lewis Burrows (c. 1813–20).[94] In 1828, Eliza was manumitted, along with Henry (her surviving son by Edward Clouston), in return for a payment of £120.[95] It appears that just before obtaining her freedom, Eliza also gave birth to a Quadroon daughter named Isabella Clouston.[96] After obtaining their freedom, Eliza, Henry, and Isabella resided on a small property named Scholars Cot in St Thomas-in-the-Vale.[97] William Burrows may also have lived with his mother, though legally he remained a slave of Lord Harewood until Eliza purchased him sometime between 28 June 1832 and 1 August 1834.[98]

D33/1/22/18, Edward Clouston to Peter Scallay, St Thomas-in-the-Vale, Jamaica, 30 July 1827. Clouston owned a property called 'Orkneys' during the early 1820s, situated in the Blue Mountain Division of St Thomas' in the East (information extracted from the *Jamaica Almanacs*). This is possibly the small property named 'Orkney', which in 1825 comprised 20 acres and twelve slaves, NA:PRO, CO141/22, *The Royal Gazette* (Kingston, 23–30 April 1825).

[92] BL, *The Royal Gazette* (Kingston, 5–12 September 1818), 19.

[93] WRA, Harewood Accession 2,677, Deed of Conveyance of Sandy Gut plantation from George Kinghorn and Joseph Timperson to Edward Lord Harewood, 3 July 1815. The schedule of slaves includes Dolly, Mulatto Eliza, Mulatto Ann, Matilla (Myrtilla), Lawrence, and Jammie [Jamaica].

[94] These two boys are assumed to be Qua'n William and Qua'n Lewis, both of whom are listed in the 1815 deed of conveyance of Sandy Gut to the Earl of Harewood at Sheepscar.

[95] NA:PRO, CO137/184, A Return of all Manumissions granted in Jamaica (1817–30), 112. Eliza was by this date described as 'Eliza Fox'.

[96] Isabella's name does not appear in the slave registration returns among the listings of births. This could be because the manumission of Eliza and Henry was agreed prior to the birth of Isabella, but the execution of the deed did not take place until after she was born.

[97] It is likely that, prior to her manumission, Eliza and her children lived with Edward Clouston as his housekeeper, or mistress.

[98] Following emancipation, Eliza (along with all slave holders) claimed compensation for William Burrow's freedom, NA:PRO, T71/950, claim no. 25. By this date Edward Clouston was the owner of twenty-one slaves at Scholars Cot for which he also claimed compensation, T71/951, no. 298. See also House of Commons Sessional Papers, vol. XLVIII (1837), 'Sums of money awarded for slavery compensation on uncontested claims (Jamaica)', 8–9.

Eliza and Edward Clouston were separated on 15 May 1833 when Edward sailed from Jamaica to New York, probably en route to Scotland.[99] Clouston's departure signifies the end of their relationship since it is clear that he intended to quit the island for an extended period.[100] There is no indication that Clouston ever returned to Jamaica, or that he saw Eliza again prior to her death in February 1836.[101] Whether Clouston sailed with his children or sent for them later is ambiguous; it is clear, however, that he did not abandon his son and daughter and cared for both children once they were brought to Britain. By 1838, Henry was in London where he was indentured by his father to the mariner George Traill. Although George Traill cannot be conclusively connected with the family of Orkney Traills, the existence of a kinship link seems likely.[102] A decade later, Isabella Clouston (by now a resident of South Leith) married the Liverpool merchant Robert Thin, brother of Edward Clouston's new wife Julia Gordon Thin. The couple's son, Edward Clouston Thin (1852–1927), followed the trade of his father as a Liverpool merchant and also became a shipowner.[103]

Whereas Isabella remained in Britain, Henry Clouston spent most of his life living and working overseas. Following his apprenticeship, Henry appears to have found employment as a sea captain working initially for George Traill. His seaman's register ticket records a date of birth that is reasonably accurate (1822), but intriguingly the document states that Henry was born in Aberdeen, rather than Jamaica, while stating

[99] Guildhall Library, London, MS 8,616, Davidson Newman & Company Papers, Henry Lowndes to Davison Newman & Co, 8 June 1833; NA:PRO, CO141/28, *The Royal Gazette* (Kingston, 11–18 May 1833), 16. Clouston had settled in Edinburgh, according to a deposition signed by him dated 2 March 1834, The Orkney Library and Archive, P.R. 37, 255.

[100] Clouston gave advanced notice of his departure to enable creditors and debtors to come forward and settle their accounts, NA:PRO, CO141/28, *The Royal Gazette* (Kingston, 23 February–3 March 1833), 21.

[101] IGI, Film No. 1291731, Burials [Anglican] in the Parish of St Thomas-in-the-Vale, County of Middlesex, Jamaica, 129.

[102] Indenture dated 8 November 1838 in the possession of a Clouston family descendant. The Revd William Clouston (father of Edward Clouston) married Isabella, daughter of Thomas Traill, Laird of Holland, Storer Clouston, *Family of Clouston*, 105–6. Interestingly, the Traills also possessed colonial connections. James Traill of Jamaica was a debtor of Thomas Harvie in 1765, while David Traill married Deborah Pitman on Barbados in 1741, JA, IB/11/3/47, Inventory of Thomas Harvie (d. 1765) entered 17 December 1767; IGI. It may also be significant that the engineer John Trail published a survey of Barbados' forts and batteries in 1746 (the first map known to be published on the island), Jerome S. Handler, *A Guide to Source Materials for the Study of Barbados History, 1627–1834* (Carbondale, 1971), 32–3.

[103] Edward Clouston married Julia Gordon Thin in Edinburgh, 30 April 1838. Julia was the daughter of Edinburgh architect and builder John Thin.

his complexion was that of a 'Man of Colour'.[104] Henry joined the nineteenth-century flow of emigrants to British colonial territories, settling in New Zealand between 1849 and 1851. For a number of years he worked as a mariner, operating ships between the ports of Nelson, Port Cooper, and Sydney. Henry finally quit the sea in 1868 and then entered into public service. He was at various times the governor of a gaol, an inspector of weights and measures, and a meteorologist. By the end of his life, he enjoyed propertied status as the owner of 75 acres in the Maitai.[105]

During his time spent in New Zealand, Henry created multiple persona. He was a seafaring captain, an early New Zealand colonist, an elder of the Presbyterian Church, a government official, and a landowner. Photographs of Clouston in later life survive, one of which was published in a late-nineteenth-century history of the Presbyterian Church in New Zealand.[106] What is lacking from Clouston's personal history is any suggestion that he was a Jamaican Creole or a former slave; his ethnicity as a person of colour is also not readily apparent from these sources. In consequence, the slavery connection was lost from the Clouston family's history for a long period until it was rediscovered by descendants researching their genealogy.

The third example of an interracial union concerns John Robley of Tobago. The Robleys were one of the wealthiest and most distinguished West Indian families of the later eighteenth and early nineteenth centuries. John Robley (a member of the Tobago Assembly) was the nephew of Joseph Robley, former governor of the colony. From his father and uncle, John Robley inherited three estates: Golden Grove, Friendship, and Studley Park. Within two years of arriving on Tobago in 1808, he had purchased a fourth estate called Betsey Hope, and a two-thirds interest in two plantations on St Vincent. By 1819, the Tobago estates of Cove and Goldsborough (the latter formerly owned by the Gedney Clarkes) had also been acquired.[107] Robley's Tobago portfolio was completed by the purchase of Richmond, Goodwood, and

---

[104] NA:PRO, BT113/3, Seamen's Register Tickets, no. 246, 39 for Henry Clouston, London, 8 May 1845. The ticket states Clouston was born in Aberdeen. Similarly, the 1881 census states that the birthplace of Isabella Thin (née Clouston) was Great Britain (Birkenhead), rather than Jamaica.

[105] Mervyn H. Clouston, 'The Family of Captain Henry Clouston' (1997), privately circulated but ISBN 0-473-01028-3, copy held at the The Orkney Library and Archive, Kirkwall.

[106] John Dickson, *History of the Presbyterian Church of New Zealand* (Dunedin, 1899), 126–7; Nelson Provincial Museum, New Zealand, Tyree Studio Collection, 2 29628/3, photograph of Captain Clouston [n.d.].

[107] NA:PRO, T71/462, ff. 37–48. In January 1819, Robley's six Tobago estates (Golden Grove, Friendship, Cove, Studley Park, Goldsborough and Goodwood, and Betsey

Glamorgan from the 1st Earl of Harewood between 1818 and 1820.[108] In addition to his West Indian lands, Robley was also owner of substantial English property, including a Buckinghamshire estate and London houses in Russell Square and Bloomsbury.[109]

While his wife and four children remained in England, Robley formed two additional families on Tobago. His most important interracial relationship was with Eliza McKenzie. In 1812, Robley described Eliza as 'a free Mulatto woman residing with me as my housekeeper' on Golden Grove. Eliza was the mother of at least six of John's children, each of whom is acknowledged in his will. These testamentary papers refer to an additional natural daughter named Jane, whom Robley fathered by Ann Allison (possibly also a woman of colour). A third child of mixed race, called John, is mentioned in this document, though it is not clear what relationship the child was to the deceased. John was the son of a Mulatto woman named Betsey Robley and was born on Golden Grove estate in 1804.[110]

Bequests of land, slaves, and money were made to Robley's children of colour in his will. Of the legacies, the most substantial were made to Eliza McKenzie's three surviving daughters, Phillis Aida, Sibyl, and Clara, who were each left £5,000 (sterling). Alongside financial support, Robley recognised his Tobago offspring by applying his surname to all of the mixed-race children. By 1819, Eliza herself had likewise taken the name Eliza McKenzie Robley and she is referred to thus in the last codicil to Robley's will.[111] The nomination of white kinsmen as the

Hope) contained 1,587 slaves. The soon-to-be acquired properties of Richmond and Glamorgan were the homes of a further 310 enslaved persons.

[108] WRA, Letters and Papers on West India Estates and Affairs, 1795–1873, Proposals for the sale of Goodwood estate to Mr Robley, 1, 2, 9 November 1816; William Blake's statement of the estate of John Robley (deceased), 18 August 1824; Accounts, 1790–1848, List of debts received since the death of Edwin Lord Harewood, 30 April 1820.

[109] NA:PRO, PROB11/1671, Will of John Robley of Bloomsbury and Tobago, proved 7 May 1823.

[110] Neither Betsey nor John Robley are listed among the enslaved on Golden Grove in the slave registration return dated 30 January 1819. A Mustee boy named John aged fourteen years four months, however, is listed as a 'Slave not in the Possession of the Honorable John Robley at the time of making this Return; and is supposed to have been clandestinely and fraudulently sent off the Island'. NA:PRO, T71/462, 1–14.

[111] NA:PRO, T71/461, f. 244; PROB11/1671, Will of John Robley. In the 1819 slave registration return, Eliza was the owner of three female slaves: a black domestic named Sarah (aged forty-six), a Mulatto infant named Mary (aged seven and likely to be a daughter of Eliza), and a black sempstress named Mopsey (aged twenty-five). The same source lists Elizabeth Robley, 'free woman of colour', as the owner of twenty-seven slaves, and a 'free black woman' named Peggy Robley as owner of five slaves. The relationships between Elizabeth and Peggy to John Robley's family are not known but are evidence of further miscegenation, possibly involving Robley's father or brother.

trustees and guardians of the coloured children is a further signal of their acceptance.

Robley's will was the subject of litigation after his death. The disputes arose owing to the length of time it took to wind up the complex affairs of a large man of property and over the size of the legacies due to Eliza's children.[112] Legal cases of this nature, stretching over many years, were frequent occurrences following the deaths of wealthy individuals. At no stage was the paternity of Robley's mixedrace offspring challenged; on the contrary, their right of inheritance was accepted by all parties.[113] Robley made frequent additions to his will between 1812 and 1821, each time amending the clauses that affected his partners and their offspring. The fact he involved relatives as executors implies that little attempt was made to hide the children of mixed race from his English family.[114]

Conclusions

The portrayal of interracial relationships in terms of a simple dichotomy results in the creation of unsatisfactory historical categorisations. In this chapter, examples of slave resistance have been juxtaposed against evidence of closer relationships formed by the Lascelles and their associates with Africans and persons of colour. Attempts at reconciling these opposing perspectives tend to result in the problematic characterisation of Africans as either rebels or victims. It might be argued, for example, that the caboceers who cooperated with Europeans were coerced into supplying slaves.[115] Similarly, it is possible to interpret interracial sex as either the outcome of forced unions or the exercise by

---

[112] WRA, Letters and Papers on West India Affairs, 1795–1873, Bundle of fifty-nine letters on the subject of John Robley (deceased)'s Tobago estates, 1829–33. The daughters submitted claims in excess of £5,000 bequeathed to them.

[113] NA:PRO, PROB37/472, *Smith and Blake vs Cunningham, Testator John Robley of Russell Square and Tobago Esq.* (1822–3); TS 11/908, *John Horatio Robley vs Phillisaide [Phillis Aida] Robley*, Chancery, 8 April 1837.

[114] On the six properties on Tobago owned by Robley in January 1819, just 2.3 per cent of the enslaved are described as coloured, NA:PRO, T71/462, 1–61.

[115] The gun-slave and horse-slave hypotheses are two versions of the argument that states African rulers were compelled to participate in transatlantic slavery because they otherwise faced the prospect of invasion by rival tribes supplied by guns and horses by Europeans. For an exposition and critique of these hypotheses, see Walter Hawthorne, *Planting Rice and Harvesting Slaves: Transformation Along the Guinea-Bissau Coast, 1400–1900* (Portsmouth, NH, 2003). See also Walter Rodney, 'African Slavery and Other Forms of Social Oppression on the Upper Guinea Coast in the Context of the Atlantic Slave Trade', *Journal of African History*, 7 (1966), 431–44; J. D. Fage, 'Slavery and the Slave Trade in the Context of West African History', *Journal of African History*, 10 (1969), 393–404; Paul Lovejoy, 'The Impact of the Slave Trade on Africa: A Review of the Literature', *Journal of African History*, 30 (1989), 365–94; Martin A. Klein, 'The Impact of the Atlantic Slave Trade on the Societies of the Western Sudan', in Joseph

female slaves of one of the few viable options available to improve conditions for themselves and their children. While some members of the enslaved community can be categorised as resistors or cooperators (willing or otherwise), in the majority of cases it is not clear which classification to apply. This uncertainty arises partly owing to a fundamental lack of evidence. However, the master–slave paradigm itself requires modification, since the records that do survive are not always compatible with a hierarchically constructed set of resisters and oppressors. It is too constricting to be forced to choose to cast Africans either in the passive role of an exploited people or as active resisters. In theory, chattel slavery was predicated on the racially determined division of black slaves and white masters. In practice, not all participants within the system can be fitted easily into this schema.

Reaching an objective assessment of intercultural relations is made difficult by the influence of negative depictions of privileged whites in abolitionist literature, reinforced by sources that have become familiar by citation. The Jamaican overseer Thomas Thistlewood is a prime example. Thistlewood is unusual since he maintained a diary, providing a unique source of information.[116] In addition to being a harsh and unpredictable disciplinarian, this source records his having sexual intercourse with 138 different women during the thirty-seven years spanned by his journals.[117] Coercion, sexual opportunism, enforced prostitution, and predation characterised many of these encounters. Remarkably, a stable relationship coexisted alongside this catalogue of abuses. For thirty-three years, Thistlewood's principal sexual partner was Phibbah: mistress of his household and a privileged slave with an influence over plantation management and discipline perhaps comparable to Eliza's on Fairfield estate.[118] The difficulty in interpreting Thistlewood is not just assessing the extent to which this unusually well-documented case is representative, but also how to reconcile conflicting elements within the text itself.

Although Barbados' historiography lacks a Thistlewood persona, depictions of planters as faithless or rapacious predators are often encountered. Perhaps the best-known depiction of an interracial sexual liaison is a graphic image, published in L'Abbé Raynal's *Histoire des*

Inikori and Stanley L. Engerman eds., *The Atlantic Slave Trade: Effects on Economies, Societies, and Peoples in Africa, the Americas, and Europe* (Durham, 1992), 25–47.

[116] Trevor Burnard, *Mastery, Tyranny, and Desire: Thomas Thistlewood and his Slaves in the Anglo-Jamaican World* (North Carolina, 2004), 149–50, 155–62, 163–7. A small selection of material from the diaries is available in Douglas Hall, *In Miserable Slavery: Thomas Thistlewood in Jamaica, 1750–1786* (London, 1989).

[117] Burnard, *Mastery, Tyranny, and Desire*, 156.   [118] Ibid., 210–40.

Figure 10.2. *Un Anglais de la Barbade vend sa maîtresse* (1770)
Source: Guillaume [Abbé] Raynal, *Histoire Philosophique et Politique des Europeens dans les Deux Indes* (7 vols., Geneva, 1780; originally published in 4 vols., Amsterdam, 1770), vol. VII, 377.

Indes, capturing the moment in which a Barbadian merchant sells his African mistress to a sea captain (Fig. 10.2). This illustration is carefully constructed to enhance its dramatic power. The enslaved woman (bare-breasted and chained, to emphasise her physical beauty and vulner-ability), turns away in anguish unable to look at the faces of either her treacherous lover or her swarthy new owner. The transaction is wit-nessed by several nearby crewmen, whose open-mouthed expressions suggest a degree of shock as a bag of money is thrust forward crudely to seal the bargain. In the background, goods are routinely loaded and unloaded from the vessel by slaves: despite the drama, business goes on as usual – the majority of bystanders are either oblivious or unconcerned at the turn of events.

Histoire des Indes contains only scant details of Barbados' history, trade, and social structure. Given the author's superficial knowledge of the colony, why was this print included in the text? Handler has sug-gested the image carries with it literary references to the story of Yarico: a native Amerindian woman, betrayed and sold into slavery on Barba-dos. Yarico's tale was first published by Richard Ligon in 1657, only to be reissued in a much embellished form by Richard Steele in 1711, who added the character of Thomas Inkle, a London merchant. The account of Yarico's betrayal was retold at intervals during the eighteenth century in a variety of literary genres, including poems and stage plays.[119] As has been seen, the theme of a European duping an African and selling the victim into slavery on Barbados also reappears in the narrative of William Ansah. In both cases, participants in the colony's slave market were associated with ruthless commercial opportunism.

Relations between white males and enslaved females contain many unknowns and uncertainties. The prevalence of interracial sex, the extent of female subordination to white male dominance, the likelihood of manumission, and the long-term prospects for slave mistresses and their coloured children in white colonial society are all less clear than was once thought.[120] The examples considered above suggest that much untapped information about slavery lies buried within family histories that might shed further light on this subject. Academic researchers could profitably liaise with amateur genealogists and family historians to uncover more of these valuable studies, since it is probable that similar

---

[119] Handler, *Guide to Source Materials*, 21, 29, 32, 39, 43, 51.
[120] Michael Craton, *Searching for the Invisible Man: Slaves and Plantation Life in Jamaica* (Cambridge, MA, 1978), 166, 242; Hilary Beckles, *Natural Rebels: A Social History of Enslaved Black Women in Barbados* (London, 1989), 135–6; Marietta Morrissey, *Slave Women in the New World: Gender Stratification in the Caribbean* (Lawrence, 1989), 147–9.

stories lie buried in the pedigrees and oral traditions maintained by present-day descendants of persons involved in plantation agriculture and Caribbean trade. The issue of unknown or unacknowledged black ancestors has caused controversy in the United States, where it is estimated that about one-fifth of all whites have at least one black ancestor within four generations.[121] It is likely that the family histories of a significant number of Britons with past colonial connections similarly include ancestors who experienced enslavement in the Caribbean.[122]

Edward Clouston took his two children by Eliza to Britain where they were cared for. Francis Graeme (one of the Earl of Harewood's Jamaican attorneys) similarly fathered a coloured daughter named Nancy in 1805. She too was sent to Scotland, married a kinsman of the Graemes, and was left a legacy of £5,000 by her father.[123] Johnson's report on Gordon's estates provides some encouragement to look for further examples in family histories since his report implies that comparable behaviour can be found on Antigua and St Vincent. Hugh Perry Keane's relationship with a Mulatto slave on St Vincent, named Betty Keane, provides further evidence of the existence of affective relationships within the British West Indies.[124]

---

[121] F. James Davis, *Who Is Black? One Nation's Definition* (2nd edn, Philadelphia, 2001; originally published 1991).

[122] The pioneering study in this field is Robert S. Stuckert, 'The African Ancestry of the White American Population', *Ohio Journal of Science*, 55 (1958), 155–60. Stuckert predicted (on the basis of statistical genealogy) that 21 per cent of whites living in the United States possessed black ancestors within four generations. The problem with Stuckert's methodology is that his model was very simple; adjusting assumptions about gross net reproduction rates, age-specific fertility, and the geographical mobility of the population, generate formidable data-collection problems. Detection of racial admixture, by means of the analysis of allele frequencies in living world populations, provides one method of overcoming data deficiencies in the historical record of interracial unions. Remarkably, genetic studies have largely replicated Stuckert's estimate, Esteban J. Parra *et al.*, 'Estimating African American Admixture Proportions by Use of Population-Specific Alleles', *American Journal of Human Genetics*, 63 (1998), 1,839–51; E. J. Parra *et al.*, 'Ancestral Proportions and Admixture Dynamics in Geographically Defined African Americans Living in South Carolina', *American Journal of Physical Anthropology*, 114 (2001), 18–29.

[123] NA:PRO, PROB11/1808, Will of Sir Michael Benignus [Benjamin] Clare, 27 December 1,832. Nancy Graeme or Graham was the ward of Sir Michael Benignus Clare.

[124] Mark Quintanilla, 'The Domestic World of a Vincentian Planter and His "Sable Venus"', paper presented at St Vincent and the Grenadines Country Conference, 22–24 May 2003, www.uwichill.edu.bb/bnccde/svg/conference/papers/quintanilla.html. Quintanilla qualifies his findings by suggesting that affection was more likely to be displayed in private than in public, and also that interracial sexual unions on newly settled islands were possibly more complex than on older colonies. For a contrary view, arguing that white, coloured, and black women were valued differently by white males in terms of domesticity and sexual companionship/adventurism, see Beckles, 'Property Rights in Pleasure', 698.

In the absence of more detailed research, it is difficult to be certain how representative Edward Clouston or Francis Graeme were of the white men who formed intercultural relationships in Jamaican society during the early nineteenth century. Jacob Graham and Simon Taylor provide two more equivocal examples of planters fathering coloured children by enslaved women. Although these individuals named mixed-race offspring in their wills, it is clear that limits were placed on the assimilation of such children into each of the men's families.[125]

The will of Thomas Stevenson (a Barbadian debtor and island attorney of the Lascelles) provides an illustration of some of the difficulties of interpretation confronting historians. At his death, Stevenson left £10 (currency) to each of his white servants at Pool plantation; in contrast, the 226 slaves living on the estate shared £20 and 400 cwt of salted fish between them. Stevenson's will singles out an enslaved woman named Rose, whom he instructed was to 'be kindly used and treated... Indulged and employed only in easy Service'. It is not made clear whether Rose was Stevenson's mistress, but he specified that her son, Alexander, should receive a legacy of £100.[126] Stevenson treated even those enslaved who were close to him differently from whites; nevertheless, his will exhibits a sense of paternal responsibility towards slaves living on Pool.

An insight into developing social mores on Jamaica is provided by a contemporary author, who condemned the failure of fathers of mixed-race children to provide safeguards against sale in the event of their own death or bankruptcy. This anonymous writer contrasted such negligence with the actions of fathers sending their coloured children to Britain, where mixed-race ancestry was considered less of a hardship.[127] Viewed from this perspective, Clouston's and Graeme's care of their children seems less exceptional. It must be emphasised, however, that the failure of private documents (such as diaries) to survive limit understanding of these and other affective relationships.

Much remains to be discovered about slaves of colour and the niches they occupied within British and colonial society. If the Lascelles' properties are typical, the size of the coloured population is understated in the registration returns and their distribution among properties uneven. The dominance of coloured births on Mount suggests that

---

[125] Christer Petley, 'Boundaries of Rule, Ties of Dependency: Jamaican Planters, Local Society and the Metropole, 1800–1834', unpub. Ph.D. thesis (University of Warwick, 2003), 228–32, 234–6 (citations by kind permission of the author). Petley reports that Graham's bequests to his coloured children included their still enslaved half-brothers and sisters, while Taylor did not acknowledge all of his coloured children.
[126] NA:PRO, PROB11/896, Will of Thomas Stevenson, proved 12 January 1764.
[127] [Anon.], *Marly; or a Planter's Life in Jamaica* (Glasgow/London, 1828), 180–1, 186.

women of colour on this property could have attained a status similar to that reported by Johnson on the Gordon estates, but in the absence of written records it is impossible to confirm this. Johnson's report cautions that official rates of manumission (which were low for all slaves in the British West Indies) may provide misleading information about freedom levels if women of colour were able to occupy positions of privilege, on or off the estates, while nominally remaining enslaved.[128]

To obtain slaves for his syndicates' clients, Henry Lascelles transacted with caboceers in Africa such as John Currantee. The claims of Currantee and his sons to elite status were recognised; they were treated deferentially by Lascelles' mercantile associates, by factors sent out to trade along the Guinea coast, and by sections of polite society in mid-eighteenth-century London. Planter correspondents in the Caribbean sent favoured slaves to London, where Lascelles & Maxwell were expected to exercise a duty of care over their welfare. The Earl of Harewood's West India attorneys acknowledged the property rights of former slaves with whom they routinely transacted within the Caribbean. On Tobago, a small part of the West Indian property empire accumulated by the Lascelles eventually passed into the possession of coloured favourites and their offspring.

---

[128] Handler, *Unappropriated People*, 51–2.

11 Epilogue

The Act of Emancipation brings this book to a close, yet the Lascelles' association with the Caribbean extended far beyond 1833. Indeed, the history of this Yorkshire family's connection with the West Indies is still developing, as the revival of interest in slavery at Harewood House demonstrates. A hiatus in the surviving records hinders detailed discussion of the Barbadian estates during the second half of the nineteenth century and afterwards. The following notes, however, illustrate some of the many changes that occurred in the later operation of the plantations.

The adoption of steam power suggests that the Lascelles continued to maintain and invest in their remaining sugar estates. By 1887, a 16 hp steam engine operated on Belle and a second engine of unknown generating capacity supplemented wind power on Thicket and Fortescue. For the time being, Mount's sole energy source remained a horizontal windmill; by 1913, however, it too employed a steam manager.[1]

As late as the First World War (1914–18), the Earls of Harewood retained ownership of the four Barbadian estates.[2] At the conclusion of the war, however, the 5th Earl sold Thicket and Fortescue. The reasons for the sale are not recorded, but wartime disruption to trade and pessimism about future returns were most likely responsible for the decision. At the same time, Belle and Mount were devised to the Earl's younger son, Major Edward Lascelles, and his heirs for life.[3] This action finally secured the permanent separation of the West Indian properties

---

[1] BA, Estates Card Index; original sources *Barbados Business and General Directory* (1887) and *Sinckler's Handbook* (1913).

[2] E. M. Shilstone, 'The Earl of Harewood KG, and the Relationship of the Lascelles Family with Barbados', *JBMHS*, 2 (1937), 83–4.

[3] BA, Estates Card Index. The original trust was modified in 1882 by an indenture that granted Henry Ulrich Lascelles (then Viscount Lascelles) a life interest in Thicket and Fortescue, LBMH, Eustace Shilstone Notebook: Records of Jews in Barbados and other Family Records – C – indexed, 270–1. The following year, however, the Lascelles' estate attorney, Sir George Clarke Pile, received instructions to seek buyers for the estates. Depressed land values reportedly led to the abandonment of this attempt at divestment, Bobby Morris, 'Transfer of Wealth from Barbados to England – From Lascelles Plantation, Barbados to Harewood House, Yorkshire', *JBMHS*, 50 (2004), 101.

from the main Harewood estate, which Henry Lascelles had envisaged as long ago as 1753. Following the death of Major Lascelles in 1935, his son, the Honourable Gerald Lascelles (younger brother of the 6th Earl), duly inherited a life interest in the two remaining plantations.

The Lascelles' economic interest in the West Indies lasted for one further decade. During the early 1960s, the prospect of Barbados gaining independence raised speculation about the possible nationalisation of sugar plantations. Gerald Lascelles visited Barbados in 1963 to inspect Belle and Mount, perhaps with a view to selling the estates. Three years later, in a move that coincided with independence, the two properties were placed in a freshly devised trust that permitted their disposal.[4] Between 1974 and 1975, Mount and Belle were duly sold, bringing to an end 194 years of continuous ownership of plantations on Barbados by members of the Lascelles family. The reasons for the sale are again not clear. Uncertainties about the implications of Britain's entry into the Common Market (which occurred in 1974) may have played a part, even though the quota principles enshrined in the 1951 Commonwealth Sugar Agreement were subsequently incorporated into the 1975 Sugar Protocol.

Very little quantitative evidence has survived documenting the performance of the Barbadian sugar estates during the twentieth century. Production accounts have, however, been found for the years 1937–8 and 1952. Partial summaries of costs and revenue are also available for the years 1940–2 and 1951. The years spanned by these accounts coincide with a final growth spurt in the history of sugar on Barbados. Sugar production on Barbados increased from an average of 50,444 tons per annum during the 1930s, to reach 74,593 tons in the 1940s, and 191,000 tons (an all-time peak) by the 1950s.[5] In 1936, Lord Harewood and the Princess Royal visited the island. The following year saw the family inject capital into its Barbadian investments. Operations on Belle were expanded by the purchase of the adjoining Waterford plantation and £7,060 expended in improvements to the estate's factory.[6]

The surviving accounts contain evidence of modernisation and organisational innovation. It is less clear, however, whether the changes resulted in significant improvements in either productivity or profits. A new power source is mentioned in the accounts for 1937, when £27.17s.2d. was expended in maintaining the 'electric system' at Belle's

[4] BA, Estates Card Index; pers. com. from Lord Harewood, 24 January 2001.
[5] Ian McDonald, 'The Sugar Industry of the Caribbean Community (CARICOM): An Overview', Report published by the Sugar Association of the Caribbean (n.d. [Barbados, 2004?]), 1.
[6] Morris, 'Transfer of Wealth', 102.

processing plant. By 1951, the estates maintained 'Motor Lorries' in addition to the carts and harnesses of earlier records. Spending on livestock on Belle plantation, in consequence, fell in real terms from £964 in 1937–8 to £622 in 1951–2. Payments for freight transport by all properties similarly declined from £2,265 to just £430 per year.[7] Responsibility for repairing the roads appears also to have shifted from the plantation to municipal authorities, since by the early 1950s this charge disappears from the cost schedules.[8]

New technologies were accompanied by organisational change. By the later 1930s, the management systems in place at Belle and Mount had diverged. Mount continued the pre-emancipation plantation model by integrating cane cultivation and processing on a single agricultural unit. The estate's chief output (accounting for 58 per cent of gross revenue) was the traditional one of sugar, consigned for sale to Wilkinson and Gaviller in London. In addition, Mount generated earnings from producing syrup (18 per cent of revenue), molasses (9.2 per cent), quarrying (5.4 per cent), and miscellaneous sales. On Belle, in contrast, the planting and processing functions were divided. The plantation specialised in growing cane, which was then sold to Belle Factory for manufacture into syrup. Despite the fact that Belle supplied the factory with more than 80 per cent of its primary input, the accounts of the two enterprises were kept separately.

By the early 1950s, Belle Factory's capacity had increased. The concern manufactured syrup using cane purchased primarily from large estates, supplemented by small producers. Belle plantation supplied the factory with approximately half of its sugar requirements, with Mount contributing a further 27 per cent. Expansion of the factory ended cane processing on Mount and the shift from sugar exports to syrup production probably explains Gerald Lascelles' decision to dispense with the services of Wilkinson and Gaviller in 1954. This act terminated a business connection that had lasted more than two hundred years and an involvement in the consignment trade by the Lascelles that can be dated back to 1680.[9]

The limited available information about the performance of the Barbados properties is collated in Table 11.1. In real terms, gross revenue

---

[7] The accounts are recorded in dollars and pounds sterling. The deflator employed is the United Kingdom retail price index, maintained on-line by EH.Net at www.eh.net/hmit/ppowerbp/ (checked 25 September 2005).

[8] HH:WIP, Trustees of the Honourable G. D. Lascelles: Estates in Barbados, 1937–8; Wilkinson and Gaviller, Staplehurst, Kent, Trustees of the Honourable G. D. Lascelles: Estates in Barbados, 1952.

[9] Wilkinson and Gaviller, Staplehurst, Kent, Letter from Wilkinson and Gaviller to Messrs Nicholl, Manisty, Few & Co., 7 April 1954.

Table 11.1. *Performance of Barbadian properties, 1937–8 and 1951–2*

a) Gross annual revenue of Barbados properties (£ sterling)

	Belle plantation	Mount	Belle Factory	Total
1937–8	6,956 (906)	5,529 (5,529)	12,924	25,409 (19,359)
1952	40,872 (15,331)	17,529 (3,609)	77,611	136,012 (117,072)
1952 deflated	10,117 (3,795)	3,563 (734)	22,302	35,982 (26,831)

Notes: Figures in parentheses deduct sale of cane to Belle Factory. See section c) for deflators.

b) Net annual revenue of Barbados properties (£ sterling)

	Belle plantation	Mount	Belle Factory	Total
1937–8	293	1,058	9[b]	1,351
1952	12,256	3,640	605	16,501
1952 deflated	3,034	740	174	3,948

Notes: See section c) for deflators. [b]Additions to the capital stock are excluded from operating revenue.

c) Prices and partial productivity data

	Belle Factory	Belle Factory	Belle Factory	Belle plantation	Belle plantation
	Syrup price: (cents per gallon)	Gallons of syrup per ton of cane	Total costs per gallon of syrup (old pence)	Cane price: $ per ton	Total costs per ton of cane (£ sterling)
1937–8	17.25	34.08	7.44	3.55	0.792
1951–2	60.00	35.13	27.12	14.33	2.219
1937–8 index	100.0	100.0	100.0	100.0	100.0
1951–2 index	347.8	103.1	364.5	403.7	280.2

Sources: HH:WIP, Trustees of the Honourable G. D. Lascelles: Estates in Barbados, 1937–8; Wilkinson and Gaviller, Staplehurst, Kent, Trustees of the Honourable G. D. Lascelles: Estates in Barbados, 1952.

grew by a factor of 1.4 between 1937–8 and 1951–2, while net revenue multiplied by a factor of 2.9.[10] Cane yields per acre on the estates are not known, but summary data of land use are available. Belle cultivated 381 acres of arable land in 1951–2 (of which between 335 and 362 acres were

[10] Cane production on Belle plantation grew by a factor of 1.5 and Belle Factory's output of syrup by a factor of 2.1.

under cane); in contrast, a total of 473 acres (out of 631 acres) had been under arable in 1935.[11] These figures suggest that farming on the estate became more intensive in the post-war years, as other productive factors were substituted for land. Total costs per ton of cane increased on Belle, but the estate managed to keep cost inflation below the increase in product prices, with the result that net revenue remained healthy.

Trading conditions at the factory appear less promising than on the estates. The partial productivity index (measuring gallons of syrup extracted per ton of cane sugar) hardly improved at all, while total costs per gallon of output rose faster than syrup prices. In consequence, it is unclear whether the investment in Belle made in 1937–8 generated a positive return. Growth in net revenue was achieved by virtue of the high post-war sugar price, coupled with the achievement of higher yields on Belle plantation.

Hardly any information is available detailing the size and composition of the labour force employed at the factory and two plantations during the twentieth century. The accounts of the 1950s nevertheless make some discreet allusions to social changes in the workplace during the early post-war period. Listed among the factory's general expenses is a charge for 'Workmen's Comprehensive Insurance'. In 1952, Belle plantation gave paid holidays to its workers employed in cultivating and reaping cane. Salaried staff also received pensions and a small amount of sick relief. Holiday pay is not listed in the Mount accounts, but salaried employees enjoyed the same benefits as those on Belle.

On Barbados, only a few physical signs of the Lascelles' long period of contact with the island remain. Belle plantation is now the home of several businesses premises working in the construction industry. A tile and cement company is located in the plantation yard, while the factory works is the site of Accord Industry Ltd, manufactures of windows for residential and office buildings. Mount plantation's surviving windmill is creeper covered, suggesting the site has been abandoned for some time. Thicket plantation house is currently occupied by Barbados' Youth With a Mission (YWAM): an organisation that trains ministers of religion.

At Bridgetown, the Barbados Museum of History's collections include portraits of the 1st and 2nd Earls.[12] At the time of writing, both

---

[11] On Mount, in contrast, the amount of acres under arable remained constant at 173 acres, with 122–30 acres in cane in 1951–2. The 1935 data are from BA, Estates Card Index (the original source is the 1935 *Barbados Yearbook*).

[12] The painting of Edward, 1st Earl of Harewood was sent out to Barbados in 1819 for reasons that are not known, WRA, Abstract of the Produce of the Estates and other Property in the West Indies belonging to the Right Honourable Lord Harewood, 1805–39: Barbados Affairs. Commission and charges of £35.13s.4d. were paid in 1819 'on a Portrait of Lord Harewood sent to Barbados'.

portraits had been taken down from the West Wing of the Parliament building and placed into storage. As one Barbadian commentator observes, these artefacts pose: 'a serious challenge to our country in terms of what can be done with these symbols of colonialism, defenders of slavery, and a progenitor of a family now related to the current head of the House of Windsor'.[13] The dilemma possesses similarities to the ongoing debate on Barbados regarding the current location of Nelson's statue in Heroes' Square, Bridgetown, while that of Bussa (leader of the 1816 rebellion) stands in the middle of a road traffic roundabout.

Until recently, 'Lascelles House' at Holetown functioned as a luxury holiday home. Publicity material prepared for tourists in the 1990s stated that the building formed part of 'a seventeenth-century estate called Lascelles plantation'. The nomenclature is interesting since the Harewood papers always refer to the estate as Cooper's Hill or Holetown, suggesting a divergence between written record and public memory. In April 2004, the site changed hands; shortly afterwards, a reception was held at the house for the Barbados and England cricket teams during the Third Test at Bridgetown.

The new owner has sensitively restored the original coral and wooden structure of the building. Local investigators believe that the house occupies the site of the Indian Bridge plantation: one of the first estates on the island to be established, c. 1627. Archaeological analysis of samples of coral taken from the building itself and also a perimeter wall are consistent with this chronology. Lascelles' house lies a short distance from an elevated position known as Lascelles Hill, the administrative centre of the colony prior to Governor Hawley's removal of his Courts of Law to the Indian Bridge (Bridgetown) in 1630–1. There are plans to turn the building and a neighbouring mill (which originally formed part of the plantation's works) into a heritage centre. Negotiations are also taking place with the Barbados Museum of History to place the portraits of the 1st and 2nd Earls of Harewood on public display at the restored property.[14]

It is not clear how much physical evidence of the Lascelles' influence survives on other former colonial territories. Parts of Harewood Chapel in Jamaica may still exist. The church is now part of St Catherine's Parish and Professor James Walvin visited the site in July 2000. He reports finding a burnt-out vicarage and a near-derelict timber-clad building with a zinc-red roof. The church, renamed All Saviours, ministers to the small local community of Harewood. Professor Walvin

---

[13] Morris, 'Transfer of Wealth', 103.
[14] Information provided by Robert Griffiths (pers. com., 25 April 2005).

describes the village as: 'a classic poor Jamaican rural settlement; small-holdings and precarious cabins clinging to the sides of the hills'.[15] It is not known whether the local inhabitants identify the chapel and the name of the community with Yorkshire aristocrats. Fieldwork would probably yield further valuable information regarding these points.

Clarke's Court estate on Grenada has lent its name to 'Clarke's Court Rum', which has been produced on the site since 1937 by the Grenada Sugar Factory Ltd. The distillery is located a short distance from the site of the original plantation. Its pure white rum is considered the brand leader on Grenada and forms one of the island's leading export commodities. Hurricane Ivan's passage in 2004 caused widespread devastation on Grenada, badly damaging the works. Happily, the company remains in operation and at the time of writing is rebuilding. Grenada Sugar Factory maintains a history section on its website, including information about Gedney Clarke.[16]

The question of what role the Lascelles should occupy in post-colonial histories of the Caribbean is an open one. By presenting members of the family and their associates as gentry capitalists, this study highlights the ambiguities and complexities inherent in reaching an assessment of their activities. Individuals such as Henry Lascelles, George Maxwell, and Gedney Clarke were gifted, intelligent, and ambitious. Their circle included men who were cultured and well-educated, and who exhibited interests across a wide range of artistic and scientific fields. Corruption, patronage, and influence all feature strongly in the Lascelles' transatlantic network. While they were not necessarily any more corrupt than other contemporary businessmen, the associates' attempts at personal aggrandisement cautions against viewing the Lascelles in progressive terms as integrators of an Atlantic economy. Rather, Henry Lascelles' accumulation of great wealth emphasises how poorly integrated and regulated the Atlantic world remained during the first half of the eighteenth century. Yet, in the absence of such networks, it is doubtful whether the flow of capital to the West Indies would have been as great, given the risks inherent in Caribbean investment and the institutional constraints facing investors. In consequence, gentry capitalism helped boost the number of Africans shipped across the Atlantic, with dismal consequences for the individuals affected and their immediate descendants in terms of lost liberty and lost years of life and health.

---

[15] University of York, memo written by Jim Walvin, 11 July 2000 (author's copy).
[16] Material supplied by the author has been added to these web pages, but an awareness of the association predates this contribution.

The contents of this book summarise what has been learned from a damaged and incomplete record of events. Phoenix-like, the contents of archives either burnt to cinders by German bombers or neglected for centuries in the confines of a country house have been reconstituted. The significance of the Lascelles' story, along with other notable British participants in enslavement, lies in the present as well as the past. Their history helps explain the formation and expansion of the transatlantic slave economy; it also illuminates the subtle connections linking the histories of peoples living in specific regions of Britain, Africa, and the Americas. At Harewood House and many other heritage sites, conversations are beginning to take place about slavery; scenes from history, long obscured, are at last becoming visible.

Archival Sources

LONDON

BANK OF ENGLAND

AC 27

BRITISH LIBRARY (BL)

Add. MSS 23,817, 30,305, 30,306, 32,708, 33,028, 33,029, 33,919, 38,203, 38,206, 38,387, 61,510, 62,898
Egerton MSS 1,720, 3,344
India Office Records, East India Company General Correspondence and Stock Ledgers
Sloane MSS 2,302, 3,961, 3,962

CORPORATION OF LONDON RECORDS OFFICE (CLRO)

Admissions to the Grocers' Company
Insolvent Debtors' Schedules
Mayor's Court Depositions (MCD)

GUILDHALL LIBRARY

Add. MS 754
Davidson Newman & Company Papers

INSTITUTE OF COMMONWEALTH STUDIES

ICS 101, Wemyss Castle Estate Papers

LIBRARY OF THE SOCIETY OF FRIENDS, FRIENDS HOUSE

Minutes of the London Yearly Meeting, Vol. II (1694–1701)

MIDDLESEX UNIVERSITY

Bernie Grant Archive

NATIONAL ARCHIVES: PUBLIC RECORD OFFICE (NA:PRO)

Audit Office: AO 12

Seamen's Register Certificates: BT 113

Chancery Papers: C 11, C 12 (Bills and Answers), C 54 (Close Rolls), C 103 (Chancery Master's Exhibits)

Colonial Office (Barbados): CO 28, CO 29

Naval Officers' Lists (Barbados): CO 33

Present State of the Plantations now settling in Tobago: CO 101

Manumission Returns (Jamaica): CO 137

Royal Gazette of Jamaica: CO 141

Register of the High Court of Delegates Processes: DEL

Wills: PROB 11

State Papers Domestic: SP

Slave Registration Returns: T 71

Treasury Papers: T 1

Royal African Company: T 70

NATIONAL MARITIME MUSEUM (NMM), GREENWICH

ADM/D, Victualling Board Letters, 1703–1822

In Letters, Admiralty Orders

Papers of Admiral Sir James Douglas

PARLIAMENTARY ARCHIVES

Private Acts

THE ROYAL BANK OF SCOTLAND GROUP ARCHIVES

Drummond's Bank, Customer Account Ledgers

James Lowther Barbados Papers

Papers re: trustees of the estate of Alexander Bartlet & Co.

UNIVERSITY OF LONDON LIBRARY

MS 279

ENGLISH PROVINCES

BODLEIAN LIBRARY, OXFORD

Carte Calendar, vol. XXX

MS Eng. hist. b. 122

Rhodes House Collection, Rawlinson MS A. 348 Pares Transcripts

BORTHWICK INSTITUTE FOR ARCHIVES, UNIVERSITY OF YORK

York Wills, vol. XLIX

BRISTOL RECORD OFFICE

Ashton Court MSS

CAMBRIDGE UNIVERSITY LIBRARY, CAMBRIDGE

Add. MS 2,798, Robert Plumsted Letterbook
Cholmondeley (Houghton) MS 2,163
Darnell Davis Collection

CARLISLE RECORD OFFICE (CRO)

Lonsdale Archive: Barbados Plantation Records (copyright resides
with the Lowther Family Trustees)

CENTRE FOR KENTISH STUDIES (CKS), MAIDSTONE

Grenville-Buckingham MS

DERBYSHIRE RECORD OFFICE, BUXTON

Fitzherbert West India Papers

EAST RIDING OF YORKSHIRE ARCHIVES, BEVERLEY

Constable Family Papers

EAST SUSSEX RECORD OFFICE, LEWES

Jamaica Correspondence of Rose Fuller

HAMPSHIRE RECORD OFFICE

Burial Registers
Crondall Deeds, 55/M69
Odiham Grammar School Leases, 21/M51

HAREWOOD HOUSE(HH), WEST YORKSHIRE

West India Papers (WIP), Accounts and Correspondence

JOHN RYLANDS UNIVERSITY LIBRARY, MANCHESTER

Eng. MS 900, Minutes of the Barbados Council, 1703–4

NORFOLK RECORD OFFICE, NORWICH

Douglas Family: Neville Diaries and Papers

NORTH YORKSHIRE COUNTY RECORD OFFICE,
NORTHALLERTON

Draft Transcript Holy Trinity Parish Registers
MIC 2554, Account Book and Letter Book of Nathaniel Cholmley

SUFFOLK RECORD OFFICE, IPSWICH SUFFOLK

Thellusson Family: Financial Papers, Ipswich HB 416/D1/1–3

TEESSIDE ARCHIVES, MIDDLESBOROUGH

Pennyman Family of Ormesby Hall Estate Papers

UNIVERSITY OF NOTTINGHAM

Pelham-Newcastle Papers

WEST RIDING OF YORKSHIRE ARCHIVES (WRA), SHEEPSCAR BRANCH, LEEDS

Harewood Accounts: Estate and General
Harewood Accounts: West Indies
Harewood Estates: Antiquarian
Harewood House, West India Papers, Accession 2,677
Harewood Title Deeds
Letters and Papers on West India Estates and Affairs, 1795–1873
Newby Hall Papers: NH 2,440, 2,833
Stansfield Muniments
West Indies Accounts, 1790–1848

WEST SUSSEX RECORD OFFICE, CHICHESTER

Genealogical notes, family trees, and memoranda on the Turing, Davidson, Farquhar families

WILKINSON AND GAVILLER, STAPLEHURST, KENT

Letter Book of Lascelles and Maxwell, 1743–6
Memos on the history of Wilkinson and Gaviller
Trustees of the Honourable G. D. Lascelles: Estates in Barbados

YORKSHIRE ARCHAEOLOGICAL SOCIETY, LEEDS

DD 94, Payne-Gallwey (Frankland) Estate Papers
DD/12/I/5–7, Deeds of Calverley Manor
MD 470, medical bills and accounts relating to the estate in Antigua of Sir Ralph Payne
MS 1,036

SCOTLAND

EAST LOTHIAN LOCAL ARCHIVE OFFICE

Registry of Baptisms

NATIONAL ARCHIVES OF SCOTLAND (NAS), EDINBURGH

Boyd Alexander Papers

THE ORKNEY LIBRARY AND ARCHIVE, KIRKWALL

Gray of Roeberry Papers
Sheriff Court Wills

WALES

NATIONAL LIBRARY OF WALES, ABERYSTWYTH

Slebech Papers

NORTHERN IRELAND

PUBLIC RECORD OFFICE OF NORTHERN IRELAND (PRONI),
BELFAST

Ward Papers

BARBADOS

BARBADOS ARCHIVES (BA), BLACK ROCK

RB1 (Powers of Attorney)
RB3 (Deeds)
RB6 (Wills)
Estates Card Index
Hughes-Queree Collection
St Michael's Levy Books

BARBADOS PUBLIC LIBRARY, BRIDGETOWN

Lucas Manuscripts

LIBRARY OF THE BARBADOS MUSEUM & HISTORICAL SOCIETY
(LBMH), BRIDGETOWN

Correspondence Files
Eustace Shilstone Notebooks
Family Files
Letter Book of Lascelles and Maxwell, 2 vol. transcript, 1743–5(6).
Major Henry Albert Thorne, 'Monumental Inscriptions of Barbados',
    bound MS, Volume, n.d.
Quaker Files

JAMAICA

ISLAND RECORD OFFICE, SPANISH TOWN

Deeds

JAMAICA ARCHIVES (JA), SPANISH TOWN

Accounts Produce
Inventories

NATIONAL LIBRARY OF JAMAICA, KINGSTON

MS 1,142

NORTH AMERICA

BAKER BUSINESS LIBRARY, HARVARD, MASSACHUSETTS

Lloyd Papers

BOSTON PUBLIC LIBRARY (BPL)

Arrest warrants for persons accused of witchcraft
MS Ch.M.1.10, 28
MS 4.1.21
Winthrop Family Papers

HAMILTON COLLEGE, NEW YORK, BEINECKE COLLECTION

M29, M43, M134, M173, M176, M185b, M206, M212, M217, M237, M526

HANDLEY REGIONAL LIBRARY, WINCHESTER, VIRGINIA

James Wood Family Papers

HISPANIC SOCIETY OF AMERICA, NEW YORK

M. 1480

HISTORICAL SOCIETY OF PENNSYLVANIA (HSP), PHILADELPHIA

Account Book of Samuel McCall Sr, 1743–9
Etting Papers, vol. XXXVII
Gratz Collection, Case 7, Box 24
Logan Papers, vol. XVII
Pemberton Papers
Port of Philadelphia, Bills of Lading 1716–72
Ships Registered at the Port of Philadelphia before 1776: A
    Computerized Listing (compiled and submitted by John J. McCusker)
Yeates Papers: John Yeates Correspondence, 1733–59

HOUGHTON LIBRARY, HARVARD, MASSACHUSETTS

MS Am 1,042, Hugh Hall Letterbook

HUNTINGTON LIBRARY, SAN MARINO, CALIFORNIA

HA 9,218
Stowe Collection

JOHN CARTER BROWN LIBRARY, PROVIDENCE, RHODE ISLAND

Codex=Eng 9
Codex Eng 52
Codex Eng 60
** MS Barb 1757

LIBRARY OF CONGRESS, WASHINGTON DC

MMC-2488, Papers of Charles Green, 1745–9

LIBRARY OF VIRGINIA, RICHMOND, VIRGINIA

Deeds and Wills
Land Office Patents and Grants, Northern Neck Grants
Prince George County Court, Wills

MASSACHUSETTS HISTORICAL SOCIETY (MHS), BOSTON

Account Book of Hugh Hall, 1728–33
Benjamin Colman Papers, 1641–1763
Charles Henry Frankland, Diary 1755–67
Dolbear Family Papers
Hugh Hall Papers, 1709–73
Payne-Gallwey Papers

NEWBERRY LIBRARY, CHICAGO

Ayer MS 339

NEW ENGLAND HISTORIC GENEALOGICAL SOCIETY, BOSTON

MS C1093, Hugh Hall Diary (Almanac), 1723

NEW YORK PUBLIC LIBRARY

NYPW03-A201, Weather Almanac of Hugh Hall Jr, 1714–17

PEABODY ESSEX MUSEUM (PEM), SALEM, MASSACHUSETTS

Clarke Family Papers
Essex County Court of Common Pleas, series 5, vol. XXXIV
Letterbook of Joseph Swett Jr and Robert Hooper Jr, 1740–7
Timothy Orne Ledger

VIRGINIA HISTORICAL SOCIETY, RICHMOND, VIRGINIA

MS 6.1 M7448:1

VIRGINIA TECH, BLACKSBURG, VIRGINIA, DIGITAL LIBRARY
AND ARCHIVES, SPECIAL COLLECTIONS

MS 74-001

WILLIAM L. CLEMENTS LIBRARY, UNIVERSITY OF MICHIGAN

Miscellaneous Collection
Shelburne Papers
Sydney Papers

OTHER ARCHIVES

ALGEMEEN RIJKSARCHIEF, THE HAGUE

Secret Minutes of the Chamber of Zeeland of the Dutch West India
Company

NATIONAL ARCHIVES OF GUYANA

Minutes of the Court of Justice of Essequibo, 1756–65

NELSON PROVINCIAL MUSEUM, NEW ZEALAND

Tyree Studio Collection

Index

Abercrombie, John, 125
Abercromby, James, 88
Adam, John, 228–9
Adam, Robert, 124, 177
Adams, Conrad, 20, 118
Adams, Samuel, 218
Addison, Christian, 325
Admiralty Sick and Hurt Board, 81, 82
African Diaspora, remembering, 3–5
Africa Reparations Movement, 4
Aix-la-Chapelle, Peace of (1748), 169
Alexander, James, 324
Allen, William, 12–14
Alleyne, Abel, 162–3
Alleyne family, 189
Alleyne, Sir John Gay, 218–19
Allison, Ann, 343
American Revolution, 140, 172, 186, 191, 220, 231
Amyot, R. G., 268, 282, 301
Anne, Queen, 67
Ansah, Effua, 328
Ansah, William, 325–8, 347
Anti-Nazi League, 3
Antigua
    interest rate reduction, 168–9
    Maxwell properties, 80
    relocation of slaves, 305–6
archives
    18th-century Barbadian wills, 19
    1940 London destructions, 260–1
    Barbados, 143
    Harewood House, 5, 143
    Lascelles-Maxwell business papers, 141
    Lascelles-Maxwell correspondence, 143
Argyll, Archibald Campbell, Duke of, 115
aristocracy, indebtedness, 192
Armada, 24, 25
armed forces, victualling, 73–4, 115–16, 130, 161
arms, Gedney family, 99

Armstrong-Jones, Anthony, Earl of Snowdon, 338
arts and sciences, 123–5
Ashley, John, 60–61, 70
Atherley family, 183
Atlantic trade, networks, 7–9
Atterbury, Francis, 65
Austin, Ann, 26
Austin, Richard, 159
Ayer, slave woman, 282–4
Ayr Bank, 131
Ayuba b. Sulyman, 327

Ball, Frances, 179, 336–9
Ball, Guy, 181, 218, 336, 337, 338
Ball, Joseph, 149, 179
Ballie, Evan, 189
Banks, Sir Joseph, 123
Barbados
    17th century, 11, 14–15, 33–42
    20th-century sugar trade, 352–5
    1780 hurricane, 222, 232
    abolition of slavery, 1834, 255
    archives, 143
    and Atlantic trade, 137
    Barbados Council, 218–19, 235–6
    Bridgetown, 18, 95
    Bridgetown fires 1766, 210
    Bridgetown place names, 19
    Bussa's rebellion 1816, 243, 318–321
    Clarke power, 109
    corruption and factions, 59–72, 137
    credit policy, 166–7
    early pro-business legislation, 37
    empire building families, 137–8
    historiography, 62–3, 345–7
    Holetown, 356
    independence, 352
    interest rate reduction, 168–9
    interracial sex, 336
    Lascelles legacy, 355–6

Barbados (*cont.*)
  Lascelles original plantation, 10
  Lascelles plantation management,
    228–59
  Lascelles rise, 43–53
  map, 180
  Marshall Office, 161
  Maxwell property, 80, 82
  merchants, 95–6
  merchants and planters, 177–9
  Newton slave burial ground, 286–7, 303
  Quakers, 26–30, 34–5, 38
  race laws, 329, 333
  St Michael, 23, 43, 126–7, 222
  slave demography, 262–4
  slave trade with New England, 18–26
  sugar production, 44, 247
Barbados Gazette, 35–6, 68–9, 209
Barbados Museum & Historical Society, 7,
    355–6
Batson family, 26
Bavaria, 277
Baxter, Richard, 27
Baxter, Thomas, 107, 109–11, 129
BBC, 6
Beale, 87
Beckford family, 203
Beckford, Julius, 165
Beckford, Peter, 141
Beckford, William, 275
Beckles family, 189, 266
Beckles Trust, 238
Bell, Governor of Barbados, 218
Bentinck, Count William, 117
Berbice
  Clarke property, 103
  slave uprising, 116–17, 132, 318
Berlin, Ira, 5
Bermuda, 85
Betteress, Samuel, 12–14
bills of exchange, 228
Binning, John, 14
Bishop, Eliza, 330–1
Bishop, William, 235–6, 276, 335–6
Blackett, Sir William, 128, 147
Bladen, Martin, 129
Blenman family
  assets and liabilities, 212
  debts written off, 242
  insolvency, 186, 193, 207–13
Blenman, George, 207
Blenman, Jonathan, 63, 68–70, 110,
    110–12, 115, 129, 166–7, 181,
    208–10, 219
Blenman, Jonathan Jr, 235

Blenman of Chepstow, Revd, 207
Blenman, Thomas, 207
Blenman, Timothy, 193, 210–11
Blenman, William, 193, 210–11
Blight, Robert, 12–13
Bogles & Co., 237
Bolingbroke, 1st Viscount, 67
Bolton Percy, 129
Bond, Francis, 218
bookkeeping, 234–5, 261
Boston
  18th-century slave imports, 14–18, 20
  Gedneys, 99
  North Church, 120
Bowdoin family, 41–2
Brace, Revd Edward, 183
Brace vs *Peers*, 160, 165, 168, 172
Braithwaite, John, 85–6, 146
Bressingham, 213
Brew, Harry, 328
Brew, Richard, 328
Brisbane, William, 132–3
Bristol, 140, 162, 189, 234–5
British Museum, 125
British National Party, 3
Brixton riots, 3
Broadwater Farm riots, 3
Brodie, Dorothy, 82, 85
Brodie, James, 82
Brown, Dr James, 36
Brown, Lancelot (Capability Brown), 83,
    124
Browne, Jeremiah, 324
Buckinghamshire, 50
Buckworth, Mary, 30, 32
Burrows, Lewis, 340
Burrows, William, 340
Burton, Revd William, 235, 279
business associations, 1
Byng, Robert, 69

caboceers, 326, 344
Calendar, Revd Elisha, 33
Calverley, 127
Campbell, P. F., 34
candle trade, 17
Cape Breton, 120
capital
  See also credit
  colonial trade, 137–74, 171
  Dutch colonies, 173
  Henry Lascelles slave trade, 75
  Lascelles-Maxwell partnership, 141,
    156–7
Caribbeana, 63, 69

Caribbean
    commission system. *See* commission
        system
    control, 1–2
    failures of landed families, 192
    Lascelles association with, 10, 351–8
    Lascelles legacy, 357
    Lascelles-Maxwell loan database, 78,
        142–3
    slave trade with New England, 18–26
    sugar trade financing, 139–74
Carolinas, 21
Carr, John, 87, 124, 177, 201
Carracoe Merchant, 58
Carriden, 80
Carter, Edwin, 58
Carter family, 103
Carter, Landon, 88
Carter, Mary (†1721), 58
Carter, Samuel, 108, 114, 127, 204–5
Carteret, John, 1st Earl of Granville, 70–1,
    208
Catley, Ann, 84, 337
Ceded Islands, 192, 220
Chandos, Marquis of, 312
Chapman, William, 149
Charles I, 54, 126
Charles II, 55
Charleston merchants, 101
Checkland, A. G., 172
Chesapeake, 12, 19, 22, 79, 214
Child, Robert, 97
Cholmley, Nathanial, 49
Clarke, Benjamin, 103
Clarke, Callie, 97
Clarke, Deborah (1705–44), 99, 127
Clarke family
    consolidation of power, 118–129
    debts written off, 242
    empire building, 137–8
    genealogy, 92–3, 180–92
    gentry capitalism, 138
    Grenadian legacy, 357
    insolvency, 220, 222
    Lascelles alliance, 118–29, 136
    Lascelles loans, 134–5, 186, 193–5, 220,
        242
    origins, 96–100
    political and military patronage, 109
    religion, 126–7
    slaving accounts, 204
Clarke, Foster, 236
Clarke, Francis (†1727), 98–9
Clarke, Francis (1756–1800), 121, 124
Clarke, Gedney (1711–64)

American connections, 99
Atlantic trade, 20, 21
background, 25–6, 96–100
Berbice uprising, 318
botanical interests, 124
bribery, 137
career, 7–8
commercial activities, 100–8
consolidation of power, 118–29
death, 130, 135
debts, 94
financial losses, 130
Henry Lascelles, business with, 102–3
hospitality, 113
maladministration, 209
plantation slaves, 132
political and military patronage, 109
property holdings, 104
settlement on Barbados, 98, 137
slave trade, 107–8, 113–14
Clarke, Gedney (1735–77)
    death, 135
    early career, 118–20
    education, 125
    embezzlement, 134
    financial failure, 91–5
        Lascelles mortgages, 186, 193–5, 220,
            242
    Lascelles marriage, 119–20
    Martinique campaign 112
    member of Barbados Council, 112
    Nova Scotia settlement, 127
    property holdings, 104
    Tobago plantations, 263–70
Clarke, Gedney III, 136
Clarke, Hannah, 97
Clarke, John (b. 1702), 98, 101–2, 120, 121
Clarke, John (1737–84/5), 121, 128, 135
Clarke, John (s. of Gedney Clarke II), 112
Clarke, Peter, 112, 114, 136
Clarke, Samuel (b. 1743), 121
Clarke, Susannah, 97
Clarke, William (†1647), 96
Clarke, William (1746–82), 112, 121
Clouston, Edward (1787–1866), 339–41,
    348–9
Clouston, Edward (b.1819), 340
Clouston family, 339
Clouston, Henry (c.1822–98), 340–2
Clouston, Isabella, 340–1
Cobham, John, 235, 264–5
Cobham, Richard, 235, 319
Codd, Colonel Edward, 320
Codrington, Christopher, 39, 64, 67
Codrington, Sir William, 125

Coffee, Amroe, King, 326
coffee, prices, 132
Cole, Isabella, 325
Collet, Thomas, 183
Collier, William, 235, 238
Colonial Debts Act 1732, 54, 165, 167, 172,
    182, 208
Colonial Williamsburg Foundation, 7
Commission for Racial Equality, 3
commission system
    18th-century Caribbean, 96, 137
    Henry Lascelles money lending, 78
    Jamaican sugar, 196
    and plantation management, 228
    tied contracts, 163
Compton, Henry, Bishop of London, 66,
    67
Cook, Bernard, 181, 217–18
Cordwent, Edward, 39
Corwin, Captain George, 98
cotton, 266–7
Courten, William, 125
Cox regression, 289
Cox, Samuel, 59–61, 63–4, 67–8, 208, 217
Cox, Sir Charles, 63
Crawford, Alexander, 165
credit
    1772–3 crisis, 131–2, 186, 220
    assignment of debts, 150
    Brace vs Peers, 160, 165, 168, 172
    Caribbean sugar trade, 139–74
    Colonial Debts Act 1732, 54, 165, 167,
        172, 182, 208
    colonial dependency on British capital,
        139, 171, 192
    Edward Lascelles' activities, 49
    effect of wars, 152, 157, 164, 199
    enforcement measures, 162–3
    foreclosure, 150, 193, 207
    institutional constraints, 152, 167
    interest arrears, 150–1, 160
        compound interest, 160
    interest rates, 38, 152–5, 153–74
        differentials, 158–9, 163–4
        reduction, 168–9
    Lascelles late-18th-century policy
        abrupt shift, 186, 190
        acquired properties, 178–9
        Blenman family, 186, 193, 207–13, 242
        foreclosure, 191
        Freres, 186, 213–19
        Gedney Clarkes, 134–5, 186, 193–5,
            242
        generally, 186–222
        Harvie brothers, 186, 195–207, 220

    loan clients, 222–5
Lascelles-Maxwell loans
    chronological account, 144–5
    database, 78, 142–3
    domestic loans, 146–7
    Henry Lascelles' activities, 78
    interest arrears, 151
    loan clients, 174–6
    mortgage increase, 145–51, 172–3
    returns, 153–74
    securities, 147
    short-term credit, 150
    types of loans, 197–8
legal changes, 165–9, 172
monopoly powers, 160–4
mortgages. See mortgages
networks
    control, 1
    Halls' slave trade in 18th century,
        16–17
    historiography, 169
    ontogeny of debt, 140–2, 148–51
    purchase of slaves, 151
    purposes, 151–2
    slaves as securities, 149, 166
    sugar market risks, 160
    usury laws, 160, 168–9, 219
Crondall (Hampshire), 83
Cudjoe Caboceer, 326
Cunningham, Nathaniel, 15
Currantee, John, 325–8, 350
Curwen, Alice, 27
Cussans, Thomas, 338
Cuthbert, George, 239
Cuthbert, Lewis, 238–9

Daling, William, 239
Danby's Rising, 56, 126
Daniel family, 189
Daniel, John, 234
Daniel, Thomas, 234
Darrington, 87, 125
Data Envelopment Analysis, 243–8
Davis, Edmund, of Hilldrop, 83
Demerara
    Berbice uprising, 116–17, 132, 318
    capital flows, 173
    Clarke involvement with, 138
    Gedney Clarke crisis, 131–3
    Gedney Clarkes in, 105–7, 116–17, 119,
        127
    slave trade, 108
demography, slaves. See slaves
Dinwiddie, Robert, 60–1, 68, 70–2, 88
Dominica, sugar trade, 142

Dottin, Elizabeth, 210
Dottin family, 216
Dottin, Joseph, 210
Douglas family, 117, 123, 125
Douglas, James, 123, 132
Douglas, James (1675-1742), 123
Douglas, Sir James, MP, 117
Douglas, John, 123
Douglas, John, of Antigua (†1743), 123
Douglas, Rear Admiral Robert, 117
Dovaston, John, 275
The Dove, 64
Downing, George, 18
Dubois, Catherine, 337
DuBois database, 23
Duke, William, 129
Duncan, William, 325
Dunning, John, 79
Dutch West India Company, 105, 108, 127, 132

East India Company, 155
East Lothian, 79, 81, 197
Edmonson, John, 26
Edmundsen, William, 27
Edward and Mary, 50
elephants' teeth, 75-6
Eliza, Mulatto woman, 331, 340-1
Elizabeth I, 24
Elliot, Nathaniel, 239, 276
Ellis, Charles, 273
empire, ideology, 9
English provincial networks, 8-9
Enslaved Database, 261-2, 317
Essequibo, 105-7, 116-17, 119, 131-3, 138, 173
European Union, Sugar Protocol, 352
Ewshott-Itchell manor, 83

Faber, John, 327
Fairfax, Anne, 99
Fairfax, Bryan, 99
Fairfax family, 129-30
Fairfax, Hannah, 99
Fairfax, Lord, 99, 103
Fairfax of Denton and Oglethorphe, 121
Fairfax, William (1691-1757), 99, 126
Farington, Joseph, 52, 84, 90, 230
Farquhar, Sir Walter, 203
fish, 17
Fisher, Mary, 26
Fitzherbert family, 189
Fleurian family, 103
Fleurian, Mary, 103, 135, 222, 232
Fonthill Gifford, 203

foodstuffs, 17
Fordyce Bank, 131
Foucault, Michel, 322
Fox, George, 27
Frames, 43-53
France
    colonial rivalries, 327
    effect of war on Atlantic trade, 191, 243
    occupation of Tobago, 238, 270
Francklyn, Charles, 238
Francklyn, Gilbert, 237-8
Frankland, Sir Charles Henry, 122, 126
Frankland family, 122-3, 125
Frankland, Admiral Thomas, 113-14, 123, 322
Franklin, Benjamin, 35
Fraser, James, 340
free blacks, 325
Frere, Applethwaite, 215-17
Frere family, 186, 213-19
Frere, Henry, 215, 216-17, 218-19, 266
Frere, Joan, 217
Frere, John (b. 1626), 214
Frere, John III, 214-16, 217-18, 219
Frere, John Jr, 217
Frere, Thomas, 213
Frere, Tobias (b.1617), 214
Frere, Tobias, Jr, 215-16
Fuller, John, 125
Fuller, Rose, 125
Fuller, Stephen, 273

Gardoque y Mueta, Joseph, 101
Gascoigne, Ann Jones (1753-1821), 121
Gascoigne family, 128
Gascoigne, John, 127
Gascoigne, Stephen, 128
Gawthorpe, 6, 87, 128, 184
Gedney, Bartholomew (1640-98), 97-8
Gedney Clarkes. *See* Clarke family
Gedney, Deborah (1677-1760), 98-9
Gedney family, origins, 98-100
Gedney, John (1603-88), 97-9
Gedney, John (1634/5-84), 97
Gedney, Lydia, 98
genealogy, 339, 347-8
gentlemanly capitalism, 9
gentry capitalism, 9-8, 138, 357
George I, 68
George II, 62, 326
George IV, 203
Germany, linens exports, 17
Gibbes, Sir Phillip, 190, 273, 276
Gilchrist, Revd William, 120
gold, 75-6

Goldsborough, 128, 201
Goose Creek, 101
Gordon, Captain John, 36
Gordon, James Brebner, 330, 348, 350
Gordon, Revd William, 63, 64–6, 67, 69,
    71, 208
Gordon, Thomas, 126
Gosse, Daniel, 15
Graeme, Francis, 237, 239, 275–6, 280,
    303, 305, 307, 322, 348–9
Gragg, Larry, 34
Graham, Jacob, 349
Grant, Bernie, MP, 4
The Grantham, 77
Green family, 190
Green, Richard, 212
Greene, Jack P., 34
Grenada
    and Gedney Clarke, 211–13
    Lascelles legacy, 357
    Lascelles plantations, 231
    shift from coffee to sugar, 213
    slave insurrection 1795–6, 318
    sugar trade, 142
Grenville faction, 83, 115
Grenville, George, 71, 109, 111
Grenville, Henry, 107, 109, 110–11, 118,
    209
Grocers' Company, 47
Grove, John, 27, 29
Grove, Joseph, 29
Guinea coast, 74
guinea corn, 266
gum, 75
Guyana, 103
Gyll, Thomas, 87, 89

Haddington, 79, 80
Haiti, revolution, 231
Hakewill, James, 267
Halifax, Lord, 326
Hall, Charles, 11, 30, 41
Hall family, 13–18, 42
Hall, Gyles (c.1603–87), 32–3
Hall, Hugh the Elder, 26–30
Hall, Hugh Sr, 30–2, 39, 222
Hall, Hugh Jr, 11–8, 32–42, 50
Hall, Mary, 11, 31, 47, 49
Hall, Richard, 39–40
Hall, Richard Jr, 40
Hall, Sarah, 41
Hall, Thomas, 75
Hall, Wentworth, 41
Halliday, Simon, 203
Hamilton, George, 75–6, 79

Hamilton, George W., 235, 237, 239,
    252–3, 279
Hancock, David, 155–6
Harewood, 1st Earl (Edward Lascelles,
    1740–1820)
    1747 inheritance, 87
    1795 inheritance, 84, 185
    agreement with Maxwells and Dalings,
        192
    portrait, 355–6
    reorganisation of plantations, 228–50,
        304–5
    shipping interests, 258
    and slave revolts, 320
    Tobago estates, 343
Harewood, 2nd Earl (Henry Lascelles.
    1767–1841)
    1832 slave condition speech, 280–1, 306,
        311–16
    election 1807, 89
    and emancipation of slaves, 251–7
    Harewood Chapel, 279, 356–7
    portrait, 355–6
    reorganisation of plantations, 304
    slave compensation payments, 251–2
    slave ownership, 228, 251
Harewood, 5th Earl, 351
Harewood, 6th Earl, 6, 336–7, 352
Harewood Chapel, 279, 356–7
Harewood estate
    1753 inheritance, 87
    1760s/1770s additions, 222
    1795 inheritance, 83–5
    Caribbean earnings, 249–50
    Caribbean plantations, 184
    plantation management, 258–9
    revenues 1799–805, 250
Harewood House
    archives, 5, 143
    BBC programme, 6
    construction, 124, 177
    funding, 53
    and Henry Lascelles, 89
    Harewood House Trust, 2–3, 6
    Harewood manor, 128, 184
Harper, Robert, 148
Harrison, Henry, 12, 14
Harrison, Nathaniel, 12, 14
Harte, William, 46
Harvie, Alexander, 195–97, 202
Harvie brothers
    assets and liabilities, 200–1
    insolvency, 186, 195–207, 220
    Jamaican plantations, 267
    Lascelles loans, 146

Harvie, Elizabeth, 203
Harvie, John, 195, 202
Harvie, Thomas, 177, 197, 202
Harvie, William, 196, 202, 204, 268
Hawksworth, John, 91
Hawley, Governor, 356
Heath, John, 233
Heins, John Theodore, 339
Hepburn family, 79–80, 197
Hepburn, George, 80–1
Hepburn, Helen, 79
Hervey, William, 123
Hibbert, George, 172
Hill, John, 337–9
Hill, Thomas, 70
HMS Argyle, 115
Hoare's Bank, 38
Holburne, Catherine, 338
Holburne, Francis, 115, 136, 336, 338
Holetown, 356
Holt, Arthur, 69
Hooper, Robert, 100–2, 120
Hope, Nicholas, 71
Hothersall, Ann, 149
Hothersall, Burch, 68, 70, 124, 148–9, 159, 181
Houghton, 80
Howe, Lord, 203
Howell, John, 182
Hudson's Bay Company, 339
Hughes, Griffin, 36
Hunt, Helen, 79
Hunter, Andrew, 114
Husbands, Barbara, 324
Husbands family, 189, 211
Husbands, Richard, 324
Husbands, Samuel, 211

Ilfracombe, 4
indigo, 266
Ingram, William, 51
insider trading, 155
institutional racism, 4
intercultural relations, 328–50
Interculture Organisation, 6
interracial associations, 322–8
Ireland
    1641 rebellion, 23
    1642 Additional Sea Venture, 23, 55
Ironmonger family, 51
Ironmonger, Joshua, 51

Jackson, William, 213
Jacobite Rising, 1715, 65
Jacobite Rising 1715, 56, 62, 85, 126, 158, 184

Jacobs, Susannah, 16
Jamaica
    18th-century plantations, 24
    Christianisation of slaves, 278–80
    English capture from Spanish, 24
    Harewood Chapel, 279, 356–7
    interest rates, 152, 168–9
    Lascelles legacy, 356–7
    Lascelles plantations, 229, 231–3, 237–42, 305
    map, 187
    Maroon uprising, 318
    plantation finance, 141, 148
    post-1750 growth, 142
    post-emancipation plantations, 252–3, 255–7
    race laws, 329
    race terminology, 332
    St Thomas-in-the-Vale, 235, 253, 279
    Scottish merchants, 79
    Seven Years' War, effect, 199
    slave account, 275
    slave demography, 262, 267–70
    sugar production, 191, 196, 246
James II, 56
Jasper, Edward, 75
Jenkins, Henry, 12
Jewish Naturalization Bill, 88, 126
Johnson, John, 305–6, 348, 350
Johnson, Polly, 331
Jones, James, 13

Keane, Betty, 348
Keane, Hugh Perry, 348
Keimer, Samuel, 35, 68, 209
Kellington, 87
Kerby, Thomas, 123
kinship, uses, 9

land. See plantations
Langton, Dominick, 65
Lansa, Francis, 59, 71, 208
Lascelles (ship), 103
Lascelles, Clarke, & Daling, 119
Lascelles, Daniel (1655–1734), 50–2, 54–9, 73, 126
Lascelles, Daniel (1714–84)
    and Blenmans, 210
    career, 184–5
    death, 192
    on debt, 177
    departure for West Indies, 79
    father's succession on Barbados, 165
    and Harvie brothers, 202, 204, 206–7

Lascelles, Daniel (*cont.*)
  inheritance, 87
  landed property, 177, 183
  loans, 142–3, 190, 201, 206
  marriage, 185
  MP for Northallerton 56, 62
  Yorkshire property, 128
Lascelles, Edward (dry-salter in London),
  49
Lascelles, Edward
  Barbadian acquisitions, 177
  Barbadian career, 43–4
Lascelles, Edward, of Stoke Newington
  Barbadian career, 31, 56
  Barbados tax assessments, 46–7
  career, 11–13, 46–53
  genealogy, 52
  Guinea estate, 179
Lascelles, Edward Jr (†1739), 12, 51, 53
Lascelles, Edward (1702–1747)
  Barbados corruption, 60–4, 68–72
  Barbados trade, 58
  Bridgetown Collector of Customs, 59, 72
  death, 102
  heirs, 84
  introduction of mango tree to Barbados,
    124
  landed estates, 179–80, 182–3
  money lending, 164
  portrait, 89
  prize cargoes, 114
  slave trade, 75
  tomb, 222
  wealth, 87, 149, 251
  wife's inheritance, 338
  wife's race, 336–9
Lascelles, Edward (1740–1820).
  See Harewood, 1st Earl
Lascelles, Major Edward (†1935), 351
Lascelles, Edwin, 1st Baron Harewood
  (1713–95)
  agreement with Maxwells and Dalings,
    192
  Caribbean interests, 186, 226
  Caribbean landed property, 177, 221
  created baron 1790, 52
  death 1795, 84
  early career, 184
  and Freres, 215–16
  *Instructions for the Management of a
    Plantation*, 273–5, 277–8, 286, 304, 323
  Jacobite supporter, 62, 126
  patronage, 111
  plantation management, 231–5
  on treatment of slaves, 273–6

Yorkshire estates, 87
Lascelles, Elizabeth (†1771), 26, 83
Lascelles family
  anti-competitive influence, 9
  Barbados legacy, 355–6
  business network, 7
  Caribbean legacy, 357
  Caribbean real estate, 183–92, 241–2
  Caribbean, association, 10, 351–8
  corruption, 137
  emergence, 43–53
  empire building, 137–8
  Gedney Clarke alliance, 118–29, 136
  genealogy, 57
  gentry capitalism, 138
  Grenadian legacy, 357
  historical significance, 1–2, 5–7
  Jamaican legacy, 356–7
  money lending. *See* credit
  plantation management. *See* plantation
    management
  royal connections, 3–6, 338
  slave trade. *See* slave trade
  Yorkshire, 50, 127
Lascelles, Frances (m. Gedney Clarke Jr),
  119–20, 135
Lascelles, Frances (m. John Douglas), 123
Lascelles, Francis Sr of Stank Hall, 54–5,
  126
Lascelles, Francis Jr, 55
Lascelles, Francis (1744–99), 84, 337
Lascelles Frigate, 46
Lascelles, George (1681–1729), 58–9, 72–3,
  83
Lascelles, George (1722–1800), 84
Lascelles, Gerald, 338, 352–3
Lascelles, Henry (1690–1753)
  Barbados trade, 58–9
  Bridgetown Collector of Customs, 59, 67
  burial, 89
  business partners, 25, 123
  corruption, 59–64, 68–72, 88, 90, 110,
    208
  death, 7, 86–90
  documentary drama, 7
  fortune, 86–7, 137, 221, 251, 357
  Gedney Clarke Sr, business with, 102–3
  Hanoverian supporter, 62
  insider trading, 155
  landed estates, 152, 180–3
  loans
    bad debts, 159
    chronological account, 144–5
    clients, 174–6
    domestic loans, 146–7

Edward Lascelles Jr, 52–3
enforcement methods, 162–3
features, 78
generally, 143–74
lending policy, 165–6
loan database, 78, 142–3
monopoly powers, 160–4
parliamentary evidence, 166
securities, 147
territorial scope, 138
London business career, 72–8, 145
marriages, 58, 72
MP for Northallerton, 62, 86
options trading, 157
partnership with Maxwell, 79–86
political power, 109, 161–2
and Scottish merchants, 79
slave trade, 74–7, 326, 350
stock market investments, 152, 154–74
super-merchant type, 1–9
use of slavery, 250
will, 84–5
Yorkshire property, 128
Lascelles, Henry (1716–86), 77, 185
Lascelles, Henry (1767–1841),
    See Harewood, 2nd Earl
Lascelles, Lucy, 54
Lascelles, Mary I (1662–1734), 47, 50–1
Lascelles, Mary II, 51
Lascelles-Maxwell partnership
    See also Lascelles, Henry; Maxwell,
    George
    correspondence, 143
    evolution 1732–1884, 240
    loan database, 78, 142–3
    money lending, 143–74
    working capital, 156–7
Lascelles, Peter, 48
Lascelles, Philip (†1713), 44–5, 47–8, 125
Lascelles, Robert, 45–6
Lascelles, Sarah, 51
Lascelles, Susannah, 85
Lascelles, Susannah (†1768), 83
Lascelles, Thomas (†1733), 51
Lascelles, Thomas of Lisburn, 55–6
Lascelles, William (†c.1686), 44–5, 49, 177
Lascelles, William (†1750), 73
Laurens, Henry, 108, 113
Lawrence, Stephen, 4
Leeward Islands, 74, 80, 115
LeGay, Rachel, 325
lending. See credit
Leslie, Charles, 65
Lessley, Andrew, 161–2
Lethieullier, Christopher, 51

Lethieullier family, 51
Lethieullier, Sir John (1632–1719), 51
Lethieullier, Smart, 125
Leverett, John, 33
Ligon, Richard, 347
Liverpool, Earl of, 134
loans. See credit
London
    1940 archival destructions, 260 n
    colonial merchants, 155–6, 234
    commission houses. See commission
    system
    financing of slave trade, 192
The London, 4
Long, Edward, 275, 286
Longworth, Roger, 26
Louisburg, 120
Lowther family, 214
Lowther, Sir James, 125
Lowther, Robert, 59, 62–5, 67, 69, 208,
    217, 219
Lynn, 97
Lyttelton, Sir George, Lord, 71, 109, 111,
    125–6

McCall, Samuel, 74, 158
McClane, Lachlan, 132–3
McDonald, Michael, 269
McKenzie, Eliza, 343–4
Mackey, Benjamin, 43
MacLeod, Alexander, 238
Macpherson inquiry, 4
malaguetta, 75
mango trees, 124
Marbin, Joseph, 58
Marblehead, 99–100
March, Elizabeth, 203
March, Francis, 203
Marshall office, 161
Martinique, 66, 112
Mary Ann, 97
Mary, Princess Royal, 6, 352
Massachusetts Bay Company, 22
Mathias, Gabriel, 326
Maxwell, David, 79
Maxwell family, 79–80
Maxwell, George (1699–1763)
    Barbados factions, 62, 70
    Batson inheritance, 26
    on Blenman, 209
    business career, 79–86
    death, 119
    and Dutch colonies, 118
    and Freres, 215
    and Harvie brothers, 195–6, 198–202

Maxwell, George (*cont.*)
  on Jacobite rising, 62, 158
  loans, 142–3, 164, 168
  political power, 161
  and Scottish merchants, 197
  on slaves, 318, 322, 324
  on Stevenson, 205
Maxwell, Henry (†1818), 82–5
Maxwell, James, 82–3, 324
Mayo, William, 207
Mead, Commissioner of Barbados
    Customs, 70
Metcalfe family, 50
Metcalfe, Lascelles, 50
Metcalfe, Margaret (†1690), 50
Miller, Philip, 124
Mills, George, 194
Millwall, 3
miscegenation, 338
Mitchell, Robert, 238
Moe, Christopher, 36
Monk, General George, 55
Monticello House, 7
Moore, Robert, 75
Moore, William, 110–11, 194, 238
Morassin, Jean de, 59, 71–2
Morecroft, Richard, 74–5, 198
Morranen slave revolt 58, 132
mortgages
  chronological increase, 145–51
  debate, 140–2
  Lascelles late – 18th-century policy
    acquired properties, 178–9
    Blenman family, 186, 207–13
    Freres, 186, 213–19
    Gedney Clarkes, 186, 193, 193–5, 220,
      242
    generally, 186–91
    Harvie brothers, 186, 195–207, 220
  Lascelles-Maxwell partnership, 172–3
  perpetual mortgages, 219–20
  and slaves, 167–8
  sugar trade financing, 140–2
Morton, James Douglas, 14th Earl of
    Morton, 117, 123

Napoleonic Wars, 191, 270
naval warfare
  prize ships, 113–16
  victualling, 73–4, 115–16, 130, 161
Navigation Acts, 59, 118, 138
Nedham, William, 267
Nelson, John Wood, 228–9, 239, 250, 261
Nelson, Thomas Marsh, 239
Netherlands

Caribbean trade crisis, 131
colonial funding, 173
linens exports, 17
West Indian business, 118–19
Nettlecombe, 213
New England
  18th-century slave imports, 14–26
  historiography, 19
  impact of slavery, 21–2
  Vassall family, 22–5
New York, slave smuggling, 108
Newcastle, Duke of, 109, 137
Newton, Nicholas, 148, 183
Newton slave burial ground, 286–7, 303
Nisbett, Philip, 14, 17
Nooker, John, 325
Northallerton, 51, 54–9
Northern Neck, 128
Nova Scotia, 127
Nurse, James, 236, 319

Occold, 213
Oglethorpe, General James, 125
Oldmixon, John, 34, 63
ontogeny of debt, 140–2, 148–51
options trading, 157
Orkney, 339
Orne, Timothy, 100
Oswicke, Robert, 43

Pacheco, Hezekiah, 64
Pares, Richard, 81, 139–46, 151–2, 157, 162,
    164–5, 167, 171–3, 196, 260
Patterson, William, 80, 109–11
Peace of Paris (1763), 140
Peers, Henry, 69
Pelham faction, 70, 88, 123
Pelham, Henry, 109
Pemberton, James, 91
Pennoyer, Wiliam, 213
Petiver, James, 34
Pevsner, Nikolaus, 6
Philadelphia merchants, 101–2
Pigott, John, 194
Pinnell, Richard, 75
Pinney family, 140, 162
Pitcairn, Robert, 204
Pitt, William, 203
Pitts, Elizabeth, 16
Pitts family, 41–2
Pitts, James (1710–76), 41–2
Pitts, John, 16
plantation management
  absentee ownership, 226–8, 235
  agents and principals, 226

Baron Harewood's tenure, 231–5
bookkeeping, 234–6, 238–9
crop diversification, 258
Data Envelopment Analysis, 243–8
Earl of Harewood's change of system,
    228–50, 304–5
emancipation period, 251–7
*Instructions for the Management of a
    Plantation*, 273–5, 277–8, 286, 304, 323
Lascelles family, 228–59
moral hazard, 258
revisionist accounts, 227
slaves. *See* slaves
and Special Magistrates, 253–6
plantations
    efficiency levels 1791–1839, 246–4
    failures of landed families, 192
    historiography, 190–1
    Lascelles disinvestment 1791–1975, 241–2
    Lascelles in early 18th century, 177
        acquisition list, 178–9
    Lascelles in late 18th century, 183–92
    Lascelles revenues 1791–6, 230
    Lascelles revenues 1805–20, 243
    Lascelles sugar production 1829–47, 256
    Lascelles sugar revenues 1829–47, 256
    metropolitan credit, 192
    production data 1805–20, 244
    returns, 152
    secured by mortgages, 186–91
Plaxton, George, 20, 68, 126
Plompton, 125, 128, 201
Pole, Charles, MP, 77
Poor Law, 277–8
Poor, Richard, 49
Powell, John, 183
powers of attorney, 164
Prettyjohn, John, 238
Price, Jacob M., 141, 167, 172
primogeniture, 151, 332
Pringle, Andrew, 103
Pringle, Robert, 101, 108
privateering, 113–16
prize ships, 113–16
provincial networks, 8–9
Provost, James, 190
Puritans, 213
Pym, John, 24

Quakers, Barbados, 26–30, 34–5, 38
Quaque family, 328
Quaque, Philip, 327

race
    Barbados race laws, 329, 333

contemporary race relations, 3–5
cooperation, 322–8
institutional racism, 4
Jamaican race laws, 329
legal status, 332–3
sexual relations, 328–50
terminology, 332
Ragatz, Lowell, 190–1
Randolph, Peyton, 88
Rankin, Ian, 337, 339
Rawlin, William, 36
Rawlin, William Jr, 209
Raymond family, 51
Raynal, Abbé Guillaume, 345–7
real estate. *See* plantations
religion
    and Gedney Clarkes, 126–7
    Harewood Chapel, 279, 356–7
    Puritans, 213
    Quakers. *See* Quakers
    Salem Anglican Church, 120, 126
Reynolds, Mr, 161
Rhett, William, 122
Rice, Michael, 157
Richmond, Surrey, 336
Roberts, Captain John, 326
Robertson, Richard, 331
Robinson, John, Bishop of London, 64,
    66–7
Robinson of Rokeby, Sir Thomas, 129
Robinson, Thomas, 111
Robley, Betsey, 343
Robley, Clara, 343
Robley family, 342
Robley, John, 238, 270–305,
    318, 342–4
Robley, Joseph, 342
Robley, Phillis Aida, 343
Robley, Sibyl, 343
Rodney, Admiral Sir George Brydges, 114,
    116
Rose, slave woman, 349
Rous family, 27
Royal African Company, 56, 59, 76, 128,
    326
Royal Society, 123
Royall, Jacob, 15
rum, 103
Rumford, Benjamin Thompson, Count,
    276–8, 286
runaways, 321–2
Ryder, Dudley, 208

St Domingo, 58
St Domingue, 58

St Domingue slave rebellion 59–60, 172, 328
St Hill, Annabel, 337
St Kitts, 140
St Louis, 59
St Vincent, sugar trade, 142
Salem, 20, 97–9, 120, 126
Salem witchcraft trials, 98
Salmon, Sarah, 129
Salter, Timothy, 217
Sampson, slave, 323–4
Sansom, Martha Fowke, 69
Sasraku, Nana Ansa, 326
sciences, 123–5
Scottish merchants, 79, 197
Searle, Daniel, 26
Senhouse, William, 113, 194
Seven Years' War
    Ceded Islands, 142
    effect on Caribbean trade, 199
    effect on plantations, 191
    financial crisis, 131, 199
    Gedney Clarkes, 112
    prize goods, 114
    victualling, 115, 130
sexual relations, interracial, 328–50
Shaftesbury, Lord, 32
Shand, George, 231, 318
Sharpe, John, 61, 168, 209, 218
Sharpe, Samuel, 324
Sharpe, William, 72
Sheridan, Richard B., 143, 152, 157, 166
Shilstone, E. M., 336–8
Simmons, James, 189, 211
slander, 217–18
slave revolts
    Baptist War 1831, 318
    Berbice uprising 1763, 116–17, 132, 318
    Bussa's rebellion 1816, 243, 318–21
    Jamaican Maroons 1745, 318
    Lascelles estates, 317–22
    Morranen revolt 58, 132
    St Domingue 1791, 172, 328
    Tackey's rebellion 1760, 318, 328–9
    Tobago 1802, 318
slave trade
    18th-century Atlantic trade, 13–14, 26
    abolition 1807, 172, 191, 262
    abolition debate, 269–81
    cooperating Africans, 322–8, 325–8
    DuBois database, 23
    financing, 146, 192
    Gedney Clarke Sr, 107–8, 113–14
    guarantees, 198
    Henry Lascelles, 74–7

Lascelles of Northallerton, 58–9, 89–90
    and naval warfare, 115
slaves
    17/18th-century Barbados, 38–9
    Adam Smith on, 226–8
    amelioration debate, 269–81, 306–7
    as securities, 149, 166
    children, 273–86, 294, 297, 299–300
    Christianisation, 235, 278–80
    cooperation, 322–8
    credit for purchase, 151
    demography
        accuracy tests, 307–11
        age reporting, 307–8
        data, 281–4
        Enslaved Database, 261–2, 317
        family groups, 300
        fertility, 295–303
        gender, 266–9, 288–9
        generated life table, 283
        hazard ratios, 291, 293–4
        Lascelles plantation returns, 234, 261
        Lascelles plantations, 262–4
        left and right censoring (LRC), 282–4, 303–4, 309–11
        methodologies, 303–4
        mortality rates, 284–95
        occupations, 272
        origins, 266–9
        'own-child' method, 296–9
        population totals 1767–1836, 263
    Earl of Harewood's speech 1832, 280–1, 306, 311–16
    emancipation, 251–7, 278
    family structures, 274–5
    freed slaves, 325
    household slaves, 323–4
    How to Make a Million from Slavery, 7
    infants, 274, 276, 284–6, 304
    Instructions for the Management of a Plantation, 273–5, 277–8, 286, 304
    interracial sexual relations, 328–50
    invisibility, 261, 358
    Lascelles-Maxwell partnership, 85–6
    memory, 3–5
    mixed-race slaves, 329–37
    mothers' names, 280
    Newton slave burial ground, 286–7, 303
    old slaves, 287–8
    pregnant women, 274, 276
    privileged slaves, 323
    Quaker opposition to slavery, 27
    relocation, 305–6, 320–1
    remembering slavery, 3–5
    resistance, 317–22

runaways, 321–2
Slave Registration Return 1817, 232,
265–7, 282–2
Slave Registry Bill 1816, 265–7, 282–2,
320
women, 332
Slingsby, Henry, 148, 163
Sloane, Sir Hans, 125
Smith, Adam, 139, 140, 142, 171, 173,
226–8
Smith, Elizabeth, 325
Smith, Lionel, 253
Smith, Samuel, 325
Smollett, Tobias, 184
Sober family, 189
South Sea Bubble, 81, 90
Southwick, Elizabeth, 185
Special Magistrates, 253–6
Spencer, James Edward, 325
Spiar family, 266
Stapleton Park, 87, 125
Staveley family, 55
steam power, 351
Steele, Richard, 347
Steers and Barrons, 101
Stevenson, Alexander, 197
Stevenson, Anne, 197, 203
Stevenson family, 189
Stevenson, Thomas, 148, 161, 163, 183,
197, 202, 204–5, 349
Stockdale, David, 6
Stoke Newington, 12, 50, 52–4
Storke, Samuel, 100, 102
Storm van 's Gravesande, Laurens, 107, 118
Straw, Jack, MP 4
sugar trade
18th century, 172
20th-century Barbados, 352–5
1975 EC Sugar Protocol, 352
Barbadian production, 247
boom, 169, 196, 231
colonial terms of trade, 170
Commonwealth Sugar Agreement, 352
financing of Caribbean trade, 139–74
golden age, 171
Jamaican production, 246
Lascelles production 1829–47, 256
Lascelles revenues 1829–47, 256
prices, 166, 191, 231
profitability, 227
risks, 160
Tobagonian production, 248
types of sugar cane, 235, 258
Surinam, 103, 173
Swan, Anne, 31

Swett, Joseph, 100–2

Tackey's rebellion 318, 328–9
Taylor, Simon, 349
tetanus, 285
Thin, Edward Clouston, 341
Thin, Julia Gordon, 341
Thin, Robert, 341
Thirkleby, 122
Thirkleby Hall, 125
Thirsk, 122
Thistlewood, Thomas, 345
Thomas, Dalby, 34
Thompson, Benjamin, See Rumford,
Count
Thompson, Maurice, 213
Thomson family, 54
Thomson, James, poet, 88
Thomson, Maurice, 26, 55
Thornhill, Deborah, 136
Thornhill family, 127–8
Thorpe, Miss, 52
tobacco, 22, 166
Tobago
1802 slave rebellion, 318
colonial rivalries, 231
female slaves, 332
French invasion, 231, 238
and Gedney Clarkes, 112
Lascelles plantations, 231, 237–8, 242,
248
reorganisation, 305
map, 188
mixed-race property owners, 350
slave demography, 262, 270–61
sugar production, 248
types of sugar cane, 235, 258
Townsend, Thomas, 194
Traill, George, 341–2
Trent, Andrew, 20
Trent, John, 20
Trevelyan, Charlotte, 215
Trinidad, slave mortality, 293, 303
turpentine, 17

United States
See also specific places, 18
mixed-race population, 348
remembering slavery, 5
Revolution, 140, 172, 186, 191,
220, 231
Upton, Arthur, 60–1, 71, 110
usury laws, 160, 168, 219
Utrecht, Treaty of (1713), 172

Vanderplank, Samuel, 49
Vassall family, 22–5, 42, 54
Vassall, Florentius (1689–1778), 24–5
Vassall, Henry, 22, 32, 42
Vassall, John (1544–1625), 24–5
Vassall, John (1625–88), 22, 24
Vassall, Leonard (1678–1737), 24–5
Vassall, Samuel (1586–1667), 22–5, 55
Vassall, William (1593–c.1655–7), 22–4, 32
Vassall, William (1715–1800), 25
Vause, Robert, 214
victualling trade, 73–4, 115–16, 130, 161
Virginia
    Atlantic trade, 17, 21
    Gedney Clarke property, 103
    Virginia Council, 99

Walduck, Thomas, 34
Walker family, 189
Walker, William, 148
Walpole, Horace, 326
Walpole, Sir Robert, 67, 70–1, 80–1
Walton family, 189
Walvin, James, 356–7
War of Austrian Sucession, 114, 145, 152, 157, 161, 164, 172
War of Jenkins' Ear, 114, 145, 152, 157, 161, 164
War of Spanish Succession, 35, 38
Warren, Admiral Sir Peter, 114, 120, 122, 127
Warren, Robert, 68–9, 159, 181–2, 218
Washington family, 99
Washington, George, 99
Washington, Lawrence, 99
Washington, Warner (1722–90), 99

Waterman, Thomas, 159
Watson, Richard, 324
Watts, John, 108, 121
Watts, Robert, 127
Weekes, Nathaniel, 218
Weekes, Prest, 218
Wellingborough, 50, 52
Went, Samuel, 236
Wentworth family, 41
Wentworth, Hugh Hall, 41
West, Benjamin, 217
West, free woman of Bridgetown, 335–6
Whetstone, Jennet (†1754), 72
Wilcox, Nicholas, 195
Wilkinson and Gaviller, 6, 260, 353
William III, 56
Williams, Eric, 190
Winthrop, John Jr, 18, 21
Witham, Cuthbert, 55
Witham family, 55
Witham, George, 55
Witham, William of Garforth, 55
Wood, Samuel, 236
Wood, William, 236
Woodbridge, Dudley, 20
Wooldridge, Thomas, 194
Worsley, Henry, 68–70, 181, 208–9

Yarico, Amerindian woman, 347
Yea of Pyrland, Sir William, 215
Yeates, John, 101
Yorkshire
    1807 county election, 89
    Lascelles-Clarke connections, 127
Yorkshire Country House Partnership, 2
Young, James, 59–60, 70
Young, Sir William, 273